INTERMEDIATE PUBLIC ECONOMICS

INTERMEDIATE PUBLIC ECONOMICS

Jean Hindriks and Gareth D. Myles

The MIT Press
Cambridge, Massachusetts
London, England

MIT Press books may be purchased at special quantity discounts for business or sales promotional use. For information, please email special_sales@mitpress.mit.edu or write to Special Sales Department, The MIT Press, 55 Hayward Street, Cambridge, MA 02142.

This book was set in Times Roman on 3B2 by Asco Typesetters, Hong Kong and was printed and bound in the United States of America.

Library of Congress Cataloging-in-Publication Data

Hindriks, Jean.
Intermediate public economics / Jean Hindriks and Gareth D. Myles.
    p.   cm.
Includes bibliographical references and index.
ISBN 0-262-08344-2 (alk. paper)
1. Welfare economics. 2. Finance, Public. 3. Economic policy. I. Myles, Gareth D. II. Title.
HB846.5.H56   2006
336′.001—dc22   2005051702

10 9 8 7 6 5 4 3 2 1

à Nathalie pour son amour et à mes adorables enfants Mattéo, Moïra, et Salomé (JH)

to Tracy, to Harriet, and to Georgina—it began before you could walk but was finished through your help with the typing (GDM)

Contents

Preface

This book has been prepared as the basis for a final-year undergraduate or first-year graduate course in Public Economics. It is based on lectures given by the authors at several institutions over many years. It covers the traditional topics of efficiency and equity but also emphasizes more recent developments in information, games, and, especially, political economy.

The book should be accessible to anyone with a background of intermediate microeconomics and macroeconomics. We have deliberately kept the quantity of math as low as we could without sacrificing intellectual rigor. Even so, the book remains analytical rather than discursive.

To support the content, further reading is given for each chapter. This reading is intended to offer a range of material from the classic papers in each area through recent contributions to surveys and critiques. Exercises are included for each chapter. Most of the exercises should be possible for a good undergraduate but some may prove challenging.

There are many people who have contributed directly or indirectly to the preparation of this book. Nigar Hashimzade is entitled to special thanks for making incisive comments on the entire text and for assisting with the analyses in chapters 10 and 21. Thanks are also due to Jean Marie Baland, Paul Belleflamme, Tim Besley, Chuck Blackorby, Christopher Bliss, Craig Brett, John Conley, Richard Cornes, Philippe De Donder, Sanjit Dhami, Peter Diamond, Jean Gabszewicz, Peter Hammond, Arye Hillman, Norman Ireland, Michael Keen, François Maniquet, Jack Mintz, James Mirrlees, Frank Page Jr., Susana Peralta, Pierre Pestieau, Pierre M. Picard, Ian Preston, Maria Racionero, Antonio Rangel, Les Reinhorn, Elena del Rey, Todd Sandler, Kim Scharf, Hyun Shin, Michael Smart, Stephen Smith, Klaas Staal, Jacques Thisse, Harrie Verbon, John Weymark, David Wildasin, and Myrna Wooders. Jean also wishes to thank Fabienne Henry for her secretarial services.

Public Economics is about the government and the economic effects of its policies. This book offers an insight into what Public Economics says and what it can do. We hope that you enjoy it.

Jean Hindriks
Louvain La Neuve

Gareth Myles
Exeter
February 2005

I PUBLIC ECONOMICS AND ECONOMIC EFFICIENCY

1 An Introduction to Public Economics

1.1 Public Economics

The study of public economics has a long tradition. It developed out of the original political economy of John Stuart Mill and David Ricardo, through the public finance tradition of tax analysis into public economics, and has now returned to its roots with the development of the new political economy. From the inception of economics as a scientific discipline, public economics has always been one of its core branches. The explanation for why it has always been so central is the foundation that it provides for practical policy analysis. This has always been the motivation of public economists, even if the issues studied and the analytical methods employed have evolved over time. We intend the theory described in this book to provide an organized and coherent structure for addressing economic policy.

In the broadest interpretation, public economics is the study of economic efficiency, distribution, and government economic policy. The subject encompasses topics as diverse as responses to market failure due to the existence of externalities, the motives for tax evasion, and the explanation of bureaucratic decision-making. In order to reach into all of these areas, public economics has developed from its initial narrow focus upon the collection and spending of government revenues, to its present concern with every aspect of government interaction with the economy. Public economics attempts to understand both *how* the government makes decisions and *what* decisions it should make.

To understand how the government makes decisions, it is necessary to investigate the motives of the decision-makers within government, how the decision-makers are chosen, and how they are influenced by outside parties. Determining what decisions should be made involves studying the effects of the alternative policies that are available and evaluating the outcomes to which they lead. These aspects are interwoven throughout the text. By pulling them together, this book provides an accessible introduction to both these aspects of public economics.

1.2 Methods

The feature that most characterizes modern public economics is the use made of *economic models*. These models are employed as a tool to ensure that arguments are conducted coherently with a rigorous logical basis. Models are used for analysis because the possibilities for experimentation are limited and past experience cannot always be relied on to provide a guide to the consequences of new policies. Each model is intended to be a simplified description of the part of the economy that is relevant for the analysis. What distinguishes economic models from those in the natural sciences is the incorporation of independent decision-making by the firms, consumers, and politicians that populate the economy. These actors in the economy do not respond mechanically but are motivated by personal objectives and are strategic in their behavior. Capturing the implications of this complex behavior in a convincing manner is one of the key skills of a successful economic modeler.

Once a model has been chosen, its implications have to be derived. These implications are obtained by applying logical arguments that proceed from the assumptions of the model to a set of formally correct conclusions. Those conclusions then need to be given an interpretation in terms that can be related to the original question of interest. Policy recommendations can then be derived but always with a recognition of the limitations of the model.

The institutional setting for the study of public economics is invariably the mixed economy where individual decisions are respected but the government attempts to affect these through the policies it implements. Within this environment many alternative objectives can be assigned to the government. For instance, the government can be assumed to care about the aggregate level of welfare in the economy and to act selflessly in attempting to increase this. Such a viewpoint is the foundation of optimal policy analysis that inquires how the government should behave. But there can be no presumption that actual governments act in this way. An alternative, and sometimes more compelling view, is that the government is composed of a set of individuals, each of whom is pursuing their own selfish agenda. Such a view provides a very different interpretation of the actions of the government and often provides a foundation for understanding how governments actually choose their policies. This perspective will also be considered in this book.

The focus on the mixed economy makes the analysis applicable to most developed and developing economies. It also permits the study of how the government behaves and how it should behave. To provide a benchmark from which to judge the outcome of the economy under alternative policies, the command economy with an omniscient planner is often employed. This, of course, is just an analytical abstraction.

1.3   Analyzing Policy

The method of policy analysis in public economics is to build a model of the economy and to find its equilibrium. Policy analysis is undertaken by determining the effect of a policy by tracing through the ways in which it changes the equilibrium of the economy relative to some *status quo*. Alternative policies are contrasted by comparing the equilibria to which they lead.

In conducting the assessment of policy, it is often helpful to emphasize the distinction between *positive* and *normative* analysis. The positive analysis of government investigates topics such as why there is a public sector, where government objectives emerge, and how government policies are chosen. It is also about understanding what effects policies have upon the economy. In contrast, normative analysis investigates what the best policies are, and aims to provide a guide to good government. These are not entirely disjoint activities. To proceed with a normative analysis, it is first necessary to conduct the positive analysis: it is not possible to say what is the best policy without knowing the effects of alternative policies upon the economy. It could also be argued that a positive analysis is of no value until used as a guide to policy.

Normative analysis is conducted under the assumption that the government has a specified set of objectives and its action are chosen in the way that best achieves these. Alternative policies (including the policy of *laissez faire* or, literally "leave to do") are compared by using the results of the positive analysis. The optimal policy is that which best meets the government's objective. Hence the equilibria for different policies are determined and the government's objective is evaluated for each equilibrium.

In every case restrictions are placed on the set of policies from which the government may choose. These restrictions are usually intended to capture limits on the information that the government has available. The information the government can obtain on the consumers and firms in the economy restricts the degree of sophistication that policy can have. For example, the extent to which taxes can be differentiated among different taxpayers depends on the information the government can acquire about each individual. Administrative and compliance costs are also relevant in generating restrictions on possible policies.

When the government's objective is taken to be some aggregate level of social welfare in the economy, important questions are raised as to how welfare can be measured. This issue is discussed in some detail in a later chapter, but it can be noted here that the answer involves invoking some degree of comparability between the welfare levels of different individuals. It has been the willingness to proceed on the basis that such comparisons can be made that has allowed the development of public economics. While differences of opinion exist on the extent to which these comparisons are valid, it is still scientifically justifiable to investigate what they would imply if they could be made. Furthermore general principles can be established that apply to any degree of comparability.

1.4   Preview

Part I of the book, consisting of this chapter and chapter 2, introduces public economics and reviews the efficiency of the competitive equilibrium. The discussion of the methodology of public economics has shown that a necessary starting point for the development of the theory of policy analysis is an introduction to economic modeling. This represents the content of chapter 2 in which the basic model of a competitive economy is introduced. The chapter describes the agents involved in the economy and characterizes economic equilibrium. An emphasis is placed upon the assumptions on which the analysis is based since much of the subject matter of public economics follows from looking at how the government should respond if these are not satisfied. Having established the basic model, the chapter then investigates the efficiency of the competitive equilibrium. This leads into some fundamental results in welfare economics.

The analysis of government begins in part II. Chapter 3 provides an overview of the public sector. It first charts the historical growth of public sector expenditure over the previous century and then reviews statistics on the present size of the public sector in several of the major developed economies. The division of expenditure and the composition of income are then considered. Finally, issues involved in measuring the size of the public sector are addressed. The issues raised by the statistics of chapter 3 are addressed by the discussion of theories of the public sector in chapter 4. Reasons for the existence of the public sector are considered, as are theories that attempt to explain its growth. A positive analysis of how the government may have its objectives and actions determined is undertaken. An emphasis is given to arguments for why the observed size of government may be excessive.

The focus of part III is on the consequences of market failure. Chapter 5 introduces public goods into the economy and contrasts the allocation that is achieved when these are privately provided with the optimal allocation. Mechanisms for improving the allocation are considered and methods of preference revelation are also addressed. This is followed by an analysis of clubs and local public goods, which are special cases of public goods in general, in chapter 6. The focus in this chapter returns to an assessment of the success of market provision. The treatment of externalities in chapter 7 relaxes another of the assumptions. It is shown why market failure occurs when externalities are present and reviews alternative policy schemes designed to improve efficiency. Imperfect competition and its consequences for taxation is the subject of chapter 8. The measurement of welfare loss is discussed and emphasis is given to the incidence of taxation. A distinction is also drawn between the effects of specific and ad valorem taxes. A symmetry of information between trading parties is required to sustain efficiency. When it is absent, inefficiency can arise. The implications of informational asymmetries and potential policy responses are considered in chapter 9.

Part IV provides an analysis of the public sector and its decision-making processes. This can be seen as a dose of healthy scepticism before proceeding into the body of normative analysis. An important practical method for making decisions and choosing governments is voting. Chapter 10 analyzes the success of voting as a decision mechanism and the tactical and strategic issues it involves. The main results that emerge are the Median Voter Theorem and the shortcomings of majority voting. The consequences of rent-seeking are then analyzed in chapter 11. The theory of rent-seeking provides an alternative perspective upon the policy-making process that is highly critical of the actions of government.

Part III focuses on economic efficiency. Part V complements this by considering issues of equity. Chapter 12 analyzes the policy implications of equity considerations and addresses the important restrictions placed on government actions by limited information. Several other fundamental results in welfare economics are also developed including the implications of alternative degrees of interpersonal comparability. Chapter 13 considers the measurement of economic inequality and poverty. The economics of these measures ultimately re-emphasizes the fundamental importance of utility theory.

Part VI is concerned with taxation. It analyzes the basic tax instruments and the economics of tax evasion. Chapters 14 and 15 consider commodity taxation and income taxation, which are the two main taxes levied on consumers. In both of these chapters the economic effects of the instruments are considered and rules for setting the taxes optimally are derived. The results illustrate the resolution of the equity/efficiency trade-off in the design of policy and the consequences of the limited information available to the government. In addition to the theoretical analysis, the results of application of the methods to data are considered. The numerical results are useful, since the theoretical analysis leads only to characterizations of optimal taxes rather than explicit solutions. These chapters all assume that the taxes that are levied are paid honestly and in full. This empirically doubtful assumption is corrected in chapter 16, which looks at the extent of the hidden economy and analyzes the motives for tax evasion and its consequences.

Part VII studies public economics when there is more than one decision-making body. Chapter 17 on fiscal federalism addresses why there should be multiple levels of government and discusses the optimal division of responsibilities between different levels. The concept of tax competition is studied in chapter 18. It is shown how tax competition can limit the success of delegating tax-setting powers to independent jurisdictions.

Part VIII concentrates upon intertemporal issues in public economics. Chapter 19 describes the overlapping generations economy that is the main analytical tool of this part. The concept of the Golden Rule is introduced for economies with production and capital accumulation, and the potential for economic inefficiency is discussed. Chapter 20 analyses social security policy and relates this to the potential inefficiency of the competitive equilibrium. Both the motivation for the existence of social security programs and the determination of the level of benefits are addressed. Ricardian equivalence is linked to the existence of gifts and bequests. Finally, the book is completed by chapter 21, which considers the effects of taxation and public expenditure upon economic growth. Alternative models of economic growth are introduced and the evidence linking government policy to the level of growth is discussed.

1.5   Scope

This book is essentially an introduction to the theory of public economics. It presents a unified view of this theory and introduces the most significant results of the analysis. As such, it provides a broad review of what constitutes the present state of public economics.

What will not be found in the book are many details of actual institutions for the collection of taxes or discussion of existing tax codes and other economic policies, although relevant data are used to illuminate argument. There are several reasons for this. This book is much broader than a text focusing on taxation, and to extend the coverage in this way, something else has to be lost. Primarily, however, the book is about understanding the effects of public policy and how economists think about the analysis of policy. This should give an understanding of the consequences of existing policies, but to benefit from the discussion does not require detailed institutional knowledge.

Furthermore tax codes and tax law are country-specific, and pages spent discussing in detail the rules of one particular country will have little value for those resident elsewhere. In contrast, the method of reasoning and the analytical results described here have value independent of country-specific detail. Finally there are many texts available that describe tax law and tax codes in detail. These are written for accountants and lawyers and have a focus rather distinct from that adopted by economists.

Further Reading

The history of political economy is described in the classic volume:

Blaug, M. 1996. *Economic Theory in Retrospect*. Cambridge: Cambridge University Press.

Two classic references on economic modeling are:

Friedman, M. 1953. *Essays on Positive Economics*. Chicago: University of Chicago Press.

Koopmans, T. C. 1957. *Three Essays on the State of Economic Science*. New York: McGraw-Hill.

The issues involved in comparing individual welfare levels are explored in:

Robbins, L. 1935. *An Essay on the Nature and Significance of Economic Science*. London: Macmillan.

Exercises

1.1.   Should an economic model be judged on the basis of its assumptions or its conclusions?

1.2.   Explain the economic implications of the imposition of quality standards for drinking water.

1.3.   Can economics contribute to an understanding of how government decisions are made?

1.4.   What should guide the choice of economic policy?

1.5.   Are bureaucrats motivated by different factors than entrepreneurs?

1.6.   What restricts the policies that a government can choose? Are there any arguments for imposing additional restrictions?

1.7.   "Physics is a simpler discipline than economics. This is because the objects of its study are bound by physical laws." Do you agree?

1.8.   If individual welfare levels cannot be compared, how can it be possible to make social judgments?

1.9.   "Poverty should be reduced to lessen the extent of malnutrition and raise economic growth." Distinguish the positive and normative components of this statement.

1.10.   "It is economically efficient to maintain a pool of unemployed labor." Is this claim based on positive or normative reasoning?

1.11.   "High income earners should pay a high rate of tax because their labor supply is inelastic and the revenue raised can be used to assist those on low incomes." Distinguish between the positive and normative components of this statement.

1.12.   Consider two methods of dividing a cake between two people. Method 1 is to throw some of the cake away, and share what is left equally. Method 2 is to give one person 75 percent of the cake and the other 25 percent. Which method do you prefer, and why?

1.13.   A cake has to be apportioned between two people. One is well-nourished, and the other is not. If the well-nourished person receives a share x, $0 \leq x \leq 1$, a share $y = [1 - x]^2$ is left for the other person (some is lost when the cake is divided). Plot the possible shares that the two people can have. What allocation of shares would you choose? How would your answer change if $y = [1 - x]^4$?

1.14.   Can an economic model be acceptable if it assumes that consumers solve computationally complex maximization problems? Does your answer imply that Tiger Woods can derive the law of motion for a golf ball?

1.15.   To analyze the effect of a subsidy to rice production, would you employ a partial equilibrium or a general equilibrium model?

1.16.   If the European Union considered replacing the income tax with an increase in VAT, would you model this using partial equilibrium?

1.17.   What proportion of the world's economies (by number, population, and wealth) can be described as "mixed"?

1.18.   What problems may arise in setting economic policy if consumers know the economic model?

1.19.   Should firms maximize profit?

1.20.   To what extent is it possible to view the government as having a single objective?

1.21.   Are you happier than your neighbor? How many times happier or less happy?

1.22.   Assume that consumers are randomly allocated to either earn income M_ℓ or income M_h, where $M_h > M_\ell$. The probability of being allocated to M_ℓ is π. Prior to being allocated to an income level, consumers wish to maximize their expected income level. If it is possible to redistribute income costlessly, show that prior to allocation to income levels, no consumer would object to a transfer scheme. Now assume there is a cost Δ for each consumer of income M_h from whom income is taken. Find the maximum value of π for which there is still unanimous agreement that transfers should take place.

2.1   Introduction

The link between competition and efficiency can be traced back, at least, to Adam Smith's eighteenth-century description of the working of the invisible hand. Smith's description of individually motivated decisions being coordinated to produce a socially efficient outcome is a powerful one that has found resonance in policy circles ever since. The expression of the efficiency argument in the language of formal economics, and the deeper understanding that comes with it, is a more recent innovation.

The focus of this chapter is to review what is meant by competition and to describe equilibrium in a competitive economy. The model of competition combines independent decision-making of consumers and firms into a complete model of the economy. Equilibrium is shown to be achieved in the economy by prices adjusting to equate demand and supply. Most important, the chapter employs the competitive model to demonstrate the efficiency theorems.

Surprisingly, equilibrium prices can always be found that simultaneously equate demand and supply for all goods. What is even more remarkable is that the equilibrium so obtained also has properties of efficiency. Why this is remarkable is that individual households and firms pursue their independent objectives with no concern other than their own welfare. Even so, the final state that emerges achieves efficiency solely through the coordinating role played by prices.

2.2   Economic Models

Prior to starting the analysis it is worth reflecting on why economists employ models to make predictions about the effects of economic policies. Models are used essentially because of problems of conducting experiments on economic systems and because the system is too large and complex to analyze in its entirety. Moreover formal modeling ensures that arguments are logically consistent with all the underlying assumptions exposed.

The models used, while inevitably being simplifications of the real economy, are designed to capture the essential aspects of the problem under study. Although many different models will be studied in this book, there are important common features that apply to all. Most models in public economics specify the objectives of the individual agents in the economy (e.g., firms and consumers), and the constraints they face, and then aggregate individual decisions to arrive at market demand and supply. The equilibrium of the economy is then determined, and in a policy analysis the effects of government choice variables on this are calculated. This is done with various degrees of detail. Sometimes only a single market is studied—this is the case of *partial equilibrium* analysis. At other times *general equilibrium* analysis is used with many markets analyzed simultaneously. Similarly the number of firms and consumers varies from one or two to very many.

An essential consideration in the choice of the level of detail for a model is that its equilibrium must demonstrate a dependence on policy that gives insight into the functioning of the actual economy. If the model is too highly specified, it may not be capable of capturing important forms of response. On the other hand, if it is too general, it may not be able to provide any clear prediction. The theory described in this book will show how this trade-off can be successfully resolved. Achieving a successful compromise between these competing objectives is the "art" of economic modeling.

2.3   Competitive Economies

The essential feature of competition is that the consumers and firms in the economy do not consider their actions to have any effect on prices. Consequently, in making decisions, they treat the prices they observe in the market place as fixed (or *parametric*). This assumption can be justified when all consumers and firms are truly negligible in size relative to the market. In such a case the quantity traded by an individual consumer or firm is not sufficient to change the market price. But the assumption that the agents view prices as parametric can also be imposed as a modeling tool even in an economy with a single consumer and a single firm.

This defining characteristic of competition places a focus on the role of prices, as is maintained throughout the chapter. Prices measure values and are the signals that guide the decisions of firms and consumers. It was the exploration of what determined the relative values of different goods and services that led to the formulation of the competitive model. The adjustment of prices equates supply and demand to ensure that equilibrium is achieved. The role of prices in coordinating the decisions of independent economic agents is also crucial for the attainment of economic efficiency.

The secondary feature of the economies in this chapter is that all agents have access to the *same* information or—in formal terminology—that information is *symmetric*. This does not imply that there cannot be uncertainty but only that when there is uncertainty all agents are equally uninformed. Put differently, no agent is permitted to have an informational advantage. For example, by this assumption, the future profit levels of firms are allowed to be uncertain and shares in the firms to be traded on the basis of individual assessments of future profits. What the assumption does not allow is for the directors of the firms to be better informed than other shareholders about future prospects and to trade profitably on the basis of this information advantage.

Two forms of the competitive model are introduced in this chapter. The first form is an exchange economy in which there is no production. Initial stocks of goods are held by consumers and economic activity occurs through the trade of these stocks to mutual advantage. The second form of competitive economy introduces production. This is undertaken by firms with given production technologies who use inputs to produce outputs and distribute their profits as dividends to consumers.

2.3.1   The Exchange Economy

The exchange economy models the simplest form of economic activity: the trade of commodities between two parties in order to obtain mutual advantage. Despite the simplicity of this model it is a surprisingly instructive tool for obtaining fundamental insights about taxation and tax policy. This will become evident as we proceed. This section presents a description of a two-consumer, two-good exchange economy. The restriction on the number of goods and consumers does not alter any of the conclusions that will be derived—they will all extend to larger numbers. What restricting the numbers does is allow the economy to be displayed and analyzed in a simple diagram.

Each of the two consumers has an initial stock, or *endowment*, of the economy's two goods. The endowments can be interpreted literally as stocks of goods, or less literally as human capital, and are the quantities that are available for trade. Given the absence of production, these quantities remains constant. The consumers exchange quantities of the two commodities in order to achieve consumption plans that are preferred to their initial endowments. The rate at which one commodity can be exchanged for the other is given by the market prices. Both consumers believe that their behavior cannot affect these prices. This is the fundamental assumption of competitive price-taking behavior. More will be said about the validity and interpretation of this in section 2.6.

A consumer is described by their endowments and their preferences. The endowment of consumer h is denoted by $\omega^h = (\omega_1^h, \omega_2^h)$, where $\omega_i^h \geq 0$ is h's initial stock of good i. When prices are p_1 and p_2, a consumption plan for consumer h, $x^h = (x_1^h, x_2^h)$, is affordable if it satisfies the budget constraint

$$p_1 x_1^h + p_2 x_2^h = p_1 \omega_1^h + p_2 \omega_2^h. \tag{2.1}$$

The preferences of each consumer are described by their utility function. This function should be seen as a representation of the consumer's indifference curves and does not imply any comparability of utility levels between consumers—the issue of comparability is taken up in chapter 12. The utility function for consumer h is denoted by

$$U^h = U^h(x_1^h, x_2^h). \tag{2.2}$$

It is assumed that the consumers enjoy the goods (so the marginal utility of consumption is positive for both goods) and that the indifference curves have the standard convex shape.

This economy can be pictured in a simple diagram that allows the role of prices in achieving equilibrium to be explored. The diagram is constructed by noting that the total consumption of the two consumers must equal the available stock of the goods, where the stock is determined by the endowments. Any pair of consumption plans that satisfies this requirement is called a *feasible plan* for the economy. A plan for the economy is feasible if the consumption levels can be met from the endowments, so

$$x_i^1 + x_i^2 = \omega_i^1 + \omega_i^2, \qquad i = 1, 2. \tag{2.3}$$

The consumption plans satisfying (2.3) can be represented as points in a rectangle with sides of length $\omega_1^1 + \omega_1^2$ and $\omega_2^1 + \omega_2^2$. In this rectangle the southwest corner can be treated as the zero consumption point for consumer 1 and the northeast corner as the zero consumption point for consumer 2. The consumption of good 1 for consumer 1 is then measured horizontally from the southwest corner and for consumer 2 horizontally from the northeast corner. Measurements for good 2 are made vertically.

The diagram constructed in this way is called an *Edgeworth box* and a typical box is shown in figure 2.1. It should be noted that the method of construction results in the endowment point, marked ω, being the initial endowment point for both consumers.

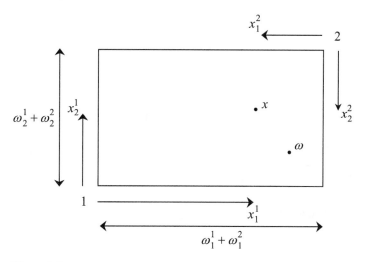

Figure 2.1
Edgeworth Box

The Edgeworth box is completed by adding the preferences and budget constraints of the consumers. The indifference curves of consumer 1 are drawn relative to the southwest corner and those of consumer 2 relative to the northeast corner. From (2.1) it can be seen that the budget constraint for both consumers must pass through the endowment point, since consumers can always afford their endowment. The endowment point is common to both consumers, so a single budget line through the endowment point with gradient $-\frac{p_1}{p_2}$ captures the market opportunities of the two consumers. Thus, viewed from the southwest, it is the budget line of consumer 1, and viewed from the northeast, the budget line of consumer 2. Given the budget line determined by the prices p_1 and p_2, the utility-maximizing choices for the two consumers are characterized by the standard tangency condition between the highest attainable indifference curve and the budget line. This is illustrated in figure 2.2, where x^1 denotes the choice of consumer 1 and x^2 that of 2.

In an *equilibrium* of the economy, supply is equal to demand. This is assumed to be achieved via the adjustment of prices. The prices at which supply is equal to demand are called *equilibrium prices*. How such prices are arrived at will be discussed later. For the present the focus will be placed on the nature of equilibrium and its properties. The consumer choices shown in figure 2.2 do not constitute an equilibrium for the economy. This can be seen by summing the demands and comparing these to the level of the endowments. Doing this shows that the demand for

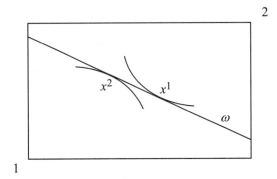

Figure 2.2
Preferences and demand

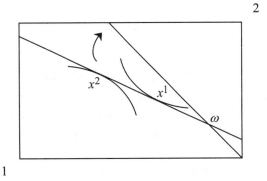

Figure 2.3
Relative price change

good 1 exceeds the endowment but the demand for good 2 falls short. To achieve an equilibrium position, the relative prices of the goods must change. An increase in the relative price of good 1 raises the absolute value of the gradient $-\frac{p_1}{p_2}$ of the budget line, making the budget line steeper. It becomes flatter if the relative price of good 1 falls. At all prices it continues to pass through the endowment point so a change in relative prices sees the budget line pivot about the endowment point.

The effect of a relative price change on the budget constraint is shown in figure 2.3. In the figure the price of good 1 has increased relative to the price of good 2. This causes the budget constraint to pivot upward around the endowment point. As a consequence of this change the consumers will now select consumption plans on this new budget constraint.

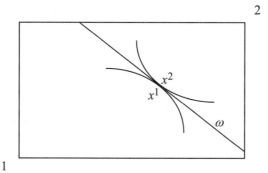

Figure 2.4
Equilibrium

The dependence of the consumption levels on prices is summarized in the consumers' demand functions. Taking the prices as given, the consumers choose their consumption plans to reach the highest attainable utility level subject to their budget constraints. The level of demand for good i from consumer h is $x_i^h = x_i^h(p_1, p_2)$. Using the demand functions, we see that demand is equal to supply for the economy when the prices are such that

$$x_i^1(p_1, p_2) + x_i^2(p_1, p_2) = \omega_i^1 + \omega_i^2, \qquad i = 1, 2. \tag{2.4}$$

Study of the Edgeworth box shows that such an equilibrium is achieved when the prices lead to a budget line on which the indifference curves of the consumers have a point of common tangency. Such an equilibrium is shown in figure 2.4. Having illustrated an equilibrium, we raise the question of whether an equilibrium is guaranteed to exist. As it happens, under reasonable assumptions, it will always do so. More important for public economics is the issue of whether the equilibrium has any desirable features from a welfare perspective. This is discussed in depth in section 2.4 where the Edgeworth box is put to substantial use.

Two further points now need to be made that are important for understanding the functioning of the model. These concern the number of prices that can be determined and the number of independent equilibrium equations. In the equilibrium conditions (2.4) there are two equations to be satisfied by the two equilibrium prices. It is now argued that the model can determine only the ratio of prices and not the actual prices. Accepting this, it would seem that there is one price ratio attempting to solve two equations. If this were the case, a solution would be unlikely, and we would be in the position of having a model that generally did not have an equilibrium. This situation is resolved by noting that there is a relationship between the two equilibrium conditions that ensures that there is only one independent equation. The single price ratio then has to solve a single equation, making it possible for there to be always a solution.

The first point is developed by observing that the budget constraint always passes through the endowment point and its gradient is determined by the price ratio. The consequence of this is that only the value of p_1 relative to p_2 matters in determining demands and supplies rather than the absolute values. The economic explanation for this fact is that consumers are only concerned with the real purchasing power embodied in their endowment, and not with the level of prices. Since their nominal income is equal to the value of the endowment, any change in the level of prices raises nominal income just as much as it raises the cost of purchases. This leaves real incomes unchanged.

The fact that only relative prices matter is also reflected in the demand functions. If $x_i^h(p_1, p_2)$ is the level of demand at prices p_1 and p_2, then it must be the case that $x_i^h(p_1, p_2) = x_i^h(\lambda p_1, \lambda p_2)$ for $\lambda > 0$. A demand function having this property is said to be *homogeneous of degree* 0. In terms of what can be learned from the model, the homogeneity shows that only relative prices can be determined at equilibrium and not the level of prices. So, given a set of equilibrium prices, any scaling up or down of these will also be equilibrium prices because the change will not alter the level of demand. This is as it should be, since all that matters for the consumers is the rate at which they can exchange one commodity for another, and this is measured by the relative prices. This can be seen in the Edgeworth box. The budget constraint always goes through the endowment point so only its gradient can change, and this is determined by the relative prices.

In order to analyze the model, the indeterminacy of the level of prices needs to be removed. This is achieved by adopting a *price normalization*, which is simply a method of fixing a scale for prices. There are numerous ways to do this. The simplest way is to select a commodity as *numéraire*, which means that its price is fixed at one, and measure all other prices relative to this. The numéraire chosen in this way can be thought of as the *unit of account* for the economy. This is the role usually played by money, but formally, there is no money in this economy.

The second point is to demonstrate the dependence between the two equilibrium equations. It can be seen that at the disequilibrium position shown in figure 2.2 the demand for good 1 exceeds its supply, whereas the supply of good 2 exceeds demand. Considering other budget lines and indifference curves in the Edgeworth box will show that whenever there is an excess of demand for one good there is a corresponding deficit of demand for the other. There is actually a very precise relationship between the excess and the deficit that can be captured in the following way: The level of *excess demand* for good i is the difference between demand and supply and is defined by $Z_i = x_i^1 + x_i^2 - \omega_i^1 - \omega_i^2$. Using this definition the value of excess demand can be calculated as

$$p_1 Z_1 + p_2 Z_2 = \sum_{i=1}^{2} p_i [x_i^1 + x_i^2 - \omega_i^1 - \omega_i^2]$$

$$= \sum_{h=1}^{2} [p_1 x_1^h + p_2 x_2^h - p_1 \omega_1^h - p_2 \omega_2^h]$$

$$= 0, \tag{2.5}$$

where the second equality is a consequence of the budget constraints in (2.1). The relationship in (2.5) is known as *Walras's law* and states that the value of excess demand is zero. This must hold for any set of prices, so it provides a connection between the extent of disequilibrium and prices. In essence, Walras's law is simply an aggregate budget constraint for the economy. Since all consumers are equating their expenditure to their income, so must the economy as a whole.

Walras's law implies that the equilibrium equations are interdependent. Since $p_1 Z_1 + p_2 Z_2 = 0$, if $Z_1 = 0$ then $Z_2 = 0$ (and vice versa). That is, if demand is equal to supply for good 1, then demand must also equal supply for good 2. Equilibrium in one market necessarily implies equilibrium in the other. This observation allows the construction of a simple diagram to illustrate equilibrium. Choose good 1 as the numéraire (so $p_1 = 1$) and plot the excess demand for good 2 as a function of p_2. The equilibrium for the economy is then found where the graph of excess demand crosses the horizontal axis. At this point excess demand for good 2 is zero, so by Walras's law, it must also be zero for good 1. An excess demand function is illustrated in figure 2.5 for an economy that has three equilibria. This excess demand function demonstrates why at least one equilibrium will exist. As p_2 falls toward zero then demand will exceed supply (good 2 becomes increasingly attractive to purchase), making excess demand positive. Conversely, as the price of good 2 rises, it will become increasingly attractive to sell, resulting in a negative value of excess demand for high values of p_2. Since excess demand is positive for small values of p_2 and negative for high values, there must be at least one point in between where it is zero.

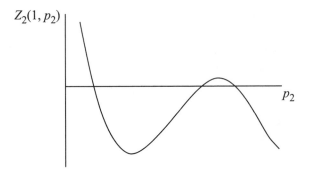

Figure 2.5
Equilibrium and excess demand

Finally, it should be noted that the arguments made above can be extended to include additional consumers and additional goods. Income, in terms of an endowment of many goods, and expenditure, defined in the same way, must remain equal for each consumer. The demand functions that result from the maximization of utility are homogeneous of degree zero in prices. Walras's law continues to hold so the value of excess demand remains zero. The number of price ratios and the number of independent equilibrium conditions are always one less than the number of goods.

2.3.2   Production and Exchange

The addition of production to the exchange economy provides a complete model of economic activity. Such an economy allows a wealth of detail to be included. Some goods can be present as initial endowments (e.g., labor), others can be consumption goods produced from the initial endowments, while some goods, intermediates, can be produced by one productive process and used as inputs into another. The fully developed model of competition is called the *Arrow-Debreu economy* in honor of its original constructors.

An economy with production consists of consumers (or households) and producers (or firms). The firms use inputs to produce outputs with the intention of maximizing their profits. Each firm has available a production technology that describes the ways in which it can use inputs to produce outputs. The consumers have preferences and initial endowments as they did in the exchange economy, but they now also hold shares in the firms. The firms' profits are distributed as dividends in proportion to the shareholdings. The consumers receive income from

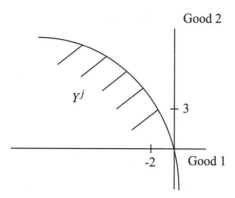

Figure 2.6
Typical production set

the sale of their initial endowments (e.g., their labor time) and from the dividend payments.

Each firm is characterized by its production set, which summarizes the production technology it has available. A production technology can be thought of as a complete list of ways that the firm can turn inputs into outputs. In other words, it catalogs all the production methods of which the firm has knowledge. For firm j operating in an economy with two goods a typical production set, denoted Y^j, is illustrated in figure 2.6. This figure employs the standard convention of measuring inputs as negative numbers and outputs as positive. The reason for adopting this convention is that the use of a unit of a good as an input represents a subtraction from the stock of that good available for consumption

Consider the firm shown in figure 2.6 choosing the production plan $y_1^j = -2$, $y_2^j = 3$. When faced with prices $p_1 = 2$, $p_2 = 2$, the firm's profit is

$$\pi^j = p_1 y_1^j + p_2 y_2^j = 2 \times [-2] + 2 \times 3 = 2. \tag{2.6}$$

The positive part of this sum can be given the interpretation of sales revenue, and the negative part that of production costs. This is equivalent to writing profit as the difference between revenue and cost. Written in this way, (2.6) gives a simple expression of the relation between prices and production choices.

The process of profit maximization is illustrated in figure 2.7. Under the competitive assumption the firm takes the prices p_1 and p_2 as given. These prices are used to construct *isoprofit curves*, which show all production plans that give a specific level of profit. For example, all the production plans on the isoprofit curve labeled $\pi = 0$ will lead to a profit level of 0. Production plans on higher isoprofit

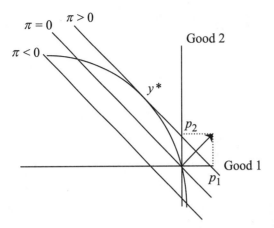

Figure 2.7
Profit maximization

curves lead to progressively larger profits, and those on lower curves to negative profits. Since doing nothing (which means choosing $y_1^j = y_2^j = 0$) earns zero profit, the $\pi = 0$ isoprofit curve always passes through the origin.

The profit-maximizing firm will choose a production plan that places it upon the highest attainable isoprofit curve. What restricts the choice is the technology that is available as described by the production set. In figure 2.7 the production plan that maximizes profit is shown by y^*, which is located at a point of tangency between the highest attainable isoprofit curve and the production set. There is no other technologically feasible plan that can attain higher profit.

It should be noted how the isoprofit curves are determined by the prices. The geometry in fact is that the isoprofit curves are at right angles to the price vector. The angle of the price vector is determined by the price ratio, $\frac{p_2}{p_1}$, so that a change in relative prices will alter the gradient of the isoprofit curves. The figure can be used to predict the effect of relative price changes. For instance, if p_1 increases relative to p_2, which can be interpreted as the price of the input (good 1) rising in comparison to the price of the output (good 2), the price vector become flatter. This makes the isoprofit curves steeper, so the optimal choice must move round the boundary of the production set toward the origin. The use of the input and the production of the output both fall.

Now consider an economy with n goods. The price of good i is denoted p_i. Production is carried out by m firms. Each firm uses inputs to produce outputs and maximizes profits given the market prices. Demand comes from the H consumers in the economy. They aim to maximize their utility. The total supply of each good is the sum of the production of it by firms and the initial endowment of it held by the consumers.

Each firm chooses a production plan $y^j = (y_1^j, \ldots, y_n^j)$. This production plan is chosen to maximize profits subject to the constraint that the chosen plan must be in the production set. From this maximization can be determined firm j's supply function for good i as $y_i^j = y_i^j(p)$, where $p = (p_1, \ldots, p_n)$. The level of profit is $\pi^j = \sum_{i=1}^n p_i y_i^j(p) = \pi^j(p)$, which also depends on prices.

Aggregate supply from the production sector of the economy is obtained from the supply decisions of the individual firms by summing across the firms. This gives the aggregate supply of good i as

$$Y_i(p) = \sum_{j=1}^m y_i^j(p). \tag{2.7}$$

Since some goods must be inputs, and others outputs, aggregate supply can be positive (the total activity of the firms adds to the stock of the good) or negative (the total activity of the firms subtracts from the stock).

Each consumer has an initial endowment of commodities and also a set of shareholdings in firms. The latter assumption makes this a *private ownership economy* in which the means of production are ultimately owned by individuals. In the present version of the model, these shareholdings are exogenously given and remain fixed. A more developed version would introduce a stock market and allow them to be traded. For consumer h the initial endowment is denoted ω^h and the shareholding in firm j is θ_j^h. The firms must be fully owned by the consumers, so $\sum_{h=1}^H \theta_j^h = 1$. That is, the shares in the firms must sum to one. Consumer h chooses a consumption plan x^h to maximize utility subject to the budget constraint

$$\sum_{i=1}^n p_i x_i^h = \sum_{i=1}^n p_i \omega_i^h + \sum_{j=1}^m \theta_j^h \pi^j. \tag{2.8}$$

This budget constraint requires that the value of expenditure be not more than the value of the endowment plus income received as dividends from firms. Since firms always have the option of going out of business (and hence earning zero profit), dividend income must be nonnegative. The profit level of each firm is dependent on prices. A change in prices therefore affects a consumer's budget constraint through a change in the value of their endowment and through a change in dividend income. The maximization of utility by the consumer results in demand for good i from consumer h of the form $x_i^h = x_i^h(p)$. The level of aggregate demand is found by summing the individual demands of the consumers to give

$$X_i(p) = \sum_{h=1}^{H} x_i^h(p). \tag{2.9}$$

The same notion of equilibrium that was used for the exchange economy can be applied in this economy with production. That is, equilibrium occurs when supply is equal to demand. The distinction between the two is that supply, which was fixed in the exchange economy, is now variable and dependent on the production decisions of firms. Although this adds a further dimension to the question of the existence of equilibrium, the basic argument why such an equilibrium always exists is essentially the same as that for the exchange economy.

As already noted, the equilibrium of the economy occurs when demand is equal to supply or, equivalently, when excess demand is zero. Excess demand for good i, $Z_i(p)$, can be defined by

$$Z_i(p) = X_i(p) - Y_i(p) - \sum_{h=1}^{H} \omega_i^h. \tag{2.10}$$

Here excess demand is the difference between demand and the sum of initial endowment and firms' supply. The equilibrium occurs when $Z_i(p) = 0$ for all of the goods $i = 1, \ldots, n$. There are standard theorems that prove such an equilibrium must exist under fairly weak conditions.

The properties established for the exchange economy also apply to this economy with production. Demand is determined only by relative prices (so it is homogeneous of degree zero). Supply is also determined by relative prices. Together, these imply that excess demand is homogeneous of degree zero. To determine the equilibrium prices that equate supply to demand, a normalization must again be used. Typically one of the goods will be chosen as numéraire, and its price set to one. Equilibrium prices are then those that equate excess demand to zero.

2.4   Efficiency of Competition

Economics is often defined as the study of scarcity. This viewpoint is reflected in the concern with the efficient use of resources that runs throughout the core of the subject. Efficiency would seem to be a simple concept to characterize: if more cannot be achieved, then the outcome is efficient. This is certainly the case when an individual decision-maker is considered. The individual will employ their resources to maximize utility subject to the constraints they face. When utility is maximized, the efficient outcome has been achieved.

Problems arise when there is more than one decision-maker. To be unambiguous about efficiency, it is necessary to resolve the potentially competing needs of different decision-makers. This requires efficiency to be defined with respect to a set of aggregate preferences. Methods of progressing from individual to aggregate preferences will be discussed in chapters 10 and 12. The conclusions obtained there are that the determination of aggregate preferences is not a simple task. There are two routes we can use to navigate around this difficulty. The first is to look at a single-consumer economy so that there is no conflict between competing preferences. But with more than one consumer some creativity has to be used to describe efficiency. The second route is met in section 2.4.2 where the concept of Pareto-efficiency is introduced. The trouble with such creativity is that it leaves the definition of efficiency open to debate. We will postpone further discussion of this until chapter 12.

Before proceeding some definitions are needed. A *first-best* outcome is achieved when only the production technology and the limited endowments restrict the choice of the decision-maker. The first-best is essentially what would be chosen by an omniscient planner with complete command over resources. A *second-best* outcome arises whenever constraints other than technology and resources are placed on what the planner can do. Such constraints could be limits on income redistribution, an inability to remove monopoly power, or a lack of information.

2.4.1   Single Consumer

With a single consumer there is no doubt as to what is good and bad from a social perspective: the single individual's preferences can be taken as the social preferences. To do otherwise would be to deny the validity of the consumer's judgments. Hence, if the individual prefers one outcome to another, then so must society. The unambiguous nature of preferences provides significant simplification of the discussion of efficiency in the single-consumer economy. In this case the "best" outcome must be first-best because no constraints on policy choices have been invoked nor is there an issue of income distribution to consider.

If there is a single firm and a single consumer, the economy with production can be illustrated in a helpful diagram. This is constructed by superimposing the

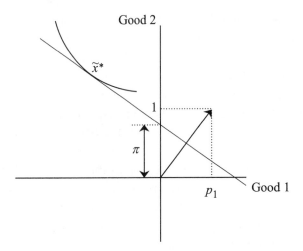

Figure 2.8
Utility maximization

profit-maximization diagram for the firm over the choice diagram for the consumer. Such a model is often called the *Robinson Crusoe economy*. The interpretation is that Robinson acts as a firm carrying out production and as a consumer of the product of the firm. It is then possible to think of Robinson as a social planner who can coordinate the activities of the firm and producer. It is also possible (though in this case less compelling!) to think of Robinson as having a split personality and acting as a profit-maximizing firm on one side of the market and as a utility-maximizing consumer on the other. In the latter interpretation the two sides of Robinson's personality are reconciled through the prices on the competitive markets. The important fact is that these two interpretations lead to exactly the same levels of production and consumption.

   The budget constraint of the consumer needs to include the dividend received from the firm. With two goods, the budget constraint is

$$p_1[x_1 - \omega_1] + p_2[x_2 - \omega_2] = \pi, \tag{2.11}$$

or

$$p_1\tilde{x}_1 + p_2\tilde{x}_2 = \pi, \tag{2.12}$$

where $\tilde{x}_i$, the change from the endowment point, is the *net consumption* of good i. This is illustrated in figure 2.8 with good 2 chosen as numéraire. The budget constraint (2.12) is always at a right angle to the price vector and is displaced

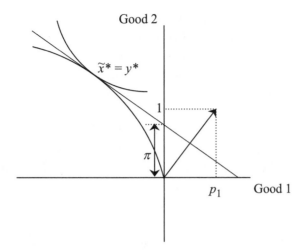

Figure 2.9
Efficient equilibrium

above the origin by the value of profit. Utility maximization occurs where the highest indifference curve is reached given the budget constraint. This results in net consumption plan $\tilde{x}^*$.

The equilibrium for the economy is shown in figure 2.9, which superimposes figure 2.7 onto 2.8. At the equilibrium the net consumption plan from the consumer must match the supply from the firm. The feature that makes this diagram work is the fact that the consumer receives the entire profit of the firm so the budget constraint and the isoprofit curve are one and the same. The height above the origin of both is the level of profit earned by the firm and received by the consumer. Equilibrium can only arise when the point on the economy's production set that equates to profit maximization is the same as that of utility maximization. This is point $\tilde{x}^* = y^*$ in figure 2.9.

It should be noted that the equilibrium is on the boundary of the production set so that it is efficient: it is not possible for a better outcome to be found in which more is produced with the same level of input. This captures the efficiency of production at the competitive equilibrium, about which much more is said soon. The equilibrium is also the first-best outcome for the single-consumer economy, since it achieves the highest indifference curve possible subject to the restriction that it is feasible under the technology. This is illustrated in figure 2.9 where $\tilde{x}^*$ is the net level of consumption relative to the endowment point in the first-best and at the competitive equilibrium.

A simple characterization of this first-best allocation can be given by using the fact that it is at a tangency point between two curves. The gradient of the indifference curve is equal to the ratio of the marginal utilities of the two goods and is called the *marginal rate of substitution*. This measures the rate at which good 1 can be traded for good 2 while maintaining constant utility. The marginal rate of substitution is given by $MRS_{1,2} = \frac{U_1}{U_2}$, with subscripts used to denote the marginal utilities of the two goods. Similarly the gradient of the production possibility set is termed the marginal rate of transformation and denoted $MRT_{1,2}$. The $MRT_{1,2}$ measures the rate at which good 1 has to be given up to allow an increase in production of good 2. At the tangency point the two gradients are equal, so

$$MRS_{1,2} = MRT_{1,2}. \tag{2.13}$$

The reason why this equality characterizes the first-best equilibrium can be explained as follows: The MRS captures the marginal value of good 1 to the consumer relative to the marginal value of good 2, while the MRT measures the marginal cost of good 1 relative to the marginal cost of good 2. The first-best is achieved when the marginal value is equal to the marginal cost.

The market achieves efficiency through the coordinating role of prices. The consumer maximizes utility subject to their budget constraint. The optimal choice occurs when the budget constraint is tangential to highest attainable indifference curve. The condition describing this is that ratio of marginal utilities is equal to the ratio of prices. Expressed in terms of the MRS, this is

$$MRS_{1,2} = \frac{p_1}{p_2}. \tag{2.14}$$

Similarly profit maximization by the firm occurs when the production possibility set is tangential to the highest isoprofit curve. Using the MRT, we write the profit-maximization condition as

$$MRT_{1,2} = \frac{p_1}{p_2}. \tag{2.15}$$

Combining these conditions, we find that the competitive equilibrium satisfies

$$MRS_{1,2} = \frac{p_1}{p_2} = MRT_{1,2}. \tag{2.16}$$

The condition in (2.16) demonstrates that the competitive equilibrium satisfies the same condition as the first-best and reveals the essential role of prices. Under the competitive assumption, both the consumer and the producer are guided in their

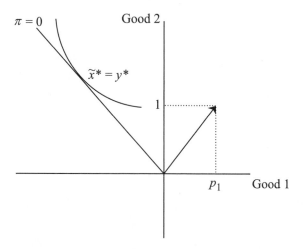

Figure 2.10
Constant returns to scale

decisions by the same price ratio. Each optimizes relative to the price ratio; hence their decisions are mutually efficient.

There is one special case that is worth noting before moving on. When the firm has constant returns to scale the efficient production frontier is a straight line through the origin. The only equilibrium can be when the firm makes zero profits. If profit was positive at some output level, then the constant returns to scale allows the firm to double profit by doubling output. Since this argument can be repeated, there is no limit to the profit that the firm can make. Hence we have the claim that equilibrium profit must be zero. Now the isoprofit curve at zero profit is also a straight line through the origin. The zero-profit equilibrium can only arise when this is coincident with the efficient production frontier. At this equilibrium the price vector is at right angles to both the isoprofit curve and the production frontier. This is illustrated in figure 2.10.

There are two further implications of constant returns. First, the equilibrium price ratio is determined by the zero-profit condition alone and is independent of demand. Second, the profit income of the consumer is zero, so the consumer's budget constraint also passes through the origin. As this is determined by the same prices as the isoprofit curve, the budget constraint must be coincident with the production frontier.

In this single-consumer context the equilibrium reached by the market simply cannot be bettered. Such a strong statement cannot be made when further consumers are introduced because issues of distribution between consumers then arise. However, what will remain is the finding that the competitive market ensures that firms produce at an efficient point on the frontier of the production set and that the chosen production plan is what is demanded at the equilibrium prices by the consumer. The key to this coordination are the prices that provide the signals guiding choices.

2.4.2   Pareto-Efficiency

When there is more than one consumer, the simple analysis of the Robinson Crusoe economy does not apply. Since consumers can have differing views about the success of an allocation, there is no single, simple measure of efficiency. The essence of the problem is that of judging among allocations with different distributional properties. What is needed is some process that can take account of the potentially diverse views of the consumers and separate efficiency from distribution.

To achieve this, economists employ the concept of *Pareto-efficiency*. The philosophy behind this concept is to interpret efficiency as meaning that there must be no unexploited economic gains. Testing the efficiency of an allocation then involves checking whether there are any such gains available. More specifically, Pareto-efficiency judges an allocation by considering whether it is possible to undertake a reallocation of resources that can benefit at least one consumer without harming any other. If it were possible to do so, then there would exist unexploited gains. When no improving reallocation can be found, then the initial position is deemed to be Pareto-efficient. An allocation that satisfies this test can be viewed as having achieved an efficient distribution of resources. For the present chapter this concept will be used uncritically. The interpretations and limitations of this form of efficiency will be discussed in chapter 12.

To provide a precise statement of Pareto-efficiency that applies in a competitive economy, it is first necessary to extend the idea of feasible allocations of resources that was used in (2.3) to define the Edgeworth box. When production is included, an allocation of consumption is feasible if it can be produced given the economy's initial endowments and production technology. Given the initial endowment, ω, the consumption allocation x is feasible if there is production plan y such that

$$x = y + \omega. \tag{2.17}$$

Pareto-efficiency is then tested using the feasible allocations. A precise definition follows.

Definition 1   A feasible consumption allocation $\hat{x}$ is Pareto-efficient if there does not exist an alternative feasible allocation $\bar{x}$ such that:

i. Allocation $\bar{x}$ gives all consumers at least as much utility as $\hat{x}$;
ii. Allocation $\bar{x}$ gives at least one consumer more utility than $\hat{x}$.

These two conditions can be summarized as saying that allocation $\hat{x}$ is Pareto-efficient if there is no alternative allocation (a move from $\hat{x}$ to $\bar{x}$) that can make someone better off without making anyone worse off. It is this idea of being able to make someone better off without making someone else worse off that represents the unexploited economic gains in an inefficient position.

It should be noted even at this stage how Pareto-efficiency is defined by the negative property of being unable to find anything better than the allocation. This is somewhat different from a definition of efficiency that looks for some positive property of the allocation. Pareto-efficiency also sidesteps issues of distribution rather than confronting them. This is why it works with many consumers. More will be said about this in chapter 12 when the construction of social welfare indicators is discussed.

2.4.3   Efficiency in an Exchange Economy

The welfare properties of the economy, which are commonly known as the *Two Theorems of Welfare Economics*, are the basis for claims concerning the desirability of the competitive outcome. In brief, the First Theorem states that a competitive equilibrium is Pareto-efficient and the Second Theorem that any Pareto-efficient allocation can be decentralized as a competitive equilibrium. Taken together, they have significant implications for policy and, at face value, seem to make a compelling case for the encouragement of competition.

The Two Theorems are easily demonstrated for a two-consumer exchange economy by using the Edgeworth box diagram. The first step is to isolate the Pareto-efficient allocations. Consider figure 2.11 and the allocation at point a. To show that a is not a Pareto-efficient allocation, it is necessary to find an alternative allocation that gives at least one of the consumers a higher utility level and neither consumer a lower level. In this case, moving to the allocation at point b raises the utility of both consumers when compared to a—we say in such a case that b is *Pareto-preferred* to a. This establishes that a is not Pareto-efficient. Although b improves on a, it is not Pareto-efficient either: the allocation at c provides higher utility for both consumers than b.

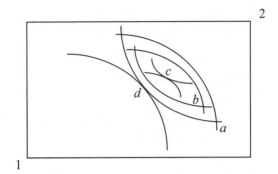

Figure 2.11
Pareto-efficiency

The allocation at c is Pareto-efficient. Beginning at c, any change in the allocation must lower the utility of at least one of the consumers. The special property of point c is that it lies at a point of tangency between the indifference curves of the two consumers. As it is a point of tangency, moving away from it must lead to a lower indifference curve for one of the consumers if not both. Since the indifference curves are tangential, their gradients are equal, so

$$MRS^1_{1,2} = MRS^2_{1,2}. \tag{2.18}$$

This equality ensures that the rate at which consumer 1 will want to exchange good 1 for good 2 is equal to the rate at which consumer 2 will want to exchange the two goods. It is this equality of the marginal valuations of the two consumers at the tangency point that results in there being no further unexploited gains and so makes c Pareto-efficient.

The Pareto-efficient allocation at c is not unique. There are in fact many points of tangency between the two consumers' indifference curves. A second Pareto-efficient allocation is at point d in figure 2.11. Taken together, all the Pareto-efficient allocations form a locus in the Edgeworth box that is called the *contract curve*. This is illustrated in figure 2.12. With this construction it is now possible to demonstrate the First Theorem.

A competitive equilibrium is given by a price line through the initial endowment point, ω, that is tangential to both indifference curves at the same point. The common point of tangency results in consumer choices that lead to the equilibrium levels of demand. Such an equilibrium is indicated by point e in figure 2.12. As the equilibrium is a point of tangency of indifference curves, it must also be Pareto-efficient. For the Edgeworth box, this completes the demonstration that a competitive equilibrium is Pareto-efficient.

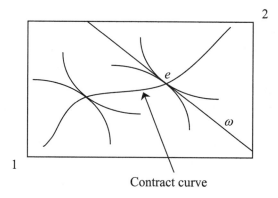

Figure 2.12
First Theorem

The alternative way of seeing this result is to recall that each consumer maximizes utility at the point where their budget constraint is tangential to the highest indifference curve. Using the *MRS*, we can write this condition for consumer *h* as $MRS_{1,2}^h = \frac{p_1}{p_2}$. The competitive assumption is that both consumers react to the same set of prices, so it follows that

$$MRS_{1,2}^1 = \frac{p_1}{p_2} = MRS_{1,2}^2. \tag{2.19}$$

Comparing this condition with (2.18) provides an alternative demonstration that the competitive equilibrium is Pareto-efficient. It also shows again the role of prices in coordinating the independent decisions of different economic agents to ensure efficiency.

This discussion can be summarized in the precise statement of the theorem.

Theorem 1 (First Theorem of Welfare Economics)   The allocation of commodities at a competitive equilibrium is Pareto-efficient.

This theorem can be formally proved by assuming that the competitive equilibrium is not Pareto-efficient and deriving a contradiction. Assuming the competitive equilibrium is not Pareto-efficient implies there is a feasible alternative that is at least as good for all consumers and strictly better for at least one. Now take the consumer who is made strictly better off. Why did they not choose the alternative consumption plan at the competitive equilibrium? The answer has to be because it was more expensive than their choice at the competitive equilibrium and not affordable with their budget. Similarly for all other consumers the new allocation has to be at least as expensive as their choice at the competitive equilibrium. (If it were cheaper, they could afford an even better consumption plan that made them strictly better off than at the competitive equilibrium.) Summing across the consumers, the alternative allocation has to be strictly more expensive than the competitive allocation. But the value of consumption at the competitive equilibrium must equal the value of the endowment. Therefore the new allocation must have greater value than the endowment, which implies it cannot be feasible. This contradiction establishes that the competitive equilibrium must be Pareto-efficient.

The theorem demonstrates that the competitive equilibrium is Pareto-efficient, but it is not the only Pareto-efficient allocation. Referring back to figure 2.12, we have that any point on the contract curve is also Pareto-efficient because all are defined by a tangency between indifference curves. The only special feature of e is that it is the allocation reached through competitive trading from the initial endowment point ω. If ω were different, then another Pareto-efficient allocation would be achieved. There is in fact an infinity of Pareto-efficient allocations. Observing these points motivates the Second Theorem of Welfare Economics.

The Second Theorem is concerned with whether any chosen Pareto-efficient allocation can be made into a competitive equilibrium by choosing a suitable location for the initial endowment. Expressed differently, can a competitive economy be constructed that has a selected Pareto-efficient allocation as its competitive equilibrium? In the Edgeworth box this involves being able to choose any point on the contract curve and turning it into a competitive equilibrium.

From the Edgeworth box diagram it can be seen that this is possible in the exchange economy if the households' indifference curves are convex. The common tangent to the indifference curves at the Pareto-efficient allocation provides the budget constraint that each consumer must face if they are to afford the chosen point. The convexity ensures that given this budget line, the Pareto-efficient point will also be the optimal choice of the consumers. The construction is completed by choosing a point on this budget line as the initial endowment point. This process of constructing a competitive economy to obtain a selected Pareto-efficient allocation is termed *decentralization*.

This process is illustrated in figure 2.13 where the Pareto-efficient allocation e' is made a competitive equilibrium by selecting ω' as the endowment point. Starting from ω', trading by consumers will take the economy to its equilibrium allocation e'. This is the Pareto-efficient allocation that was intended to be reached. Note that if the endowments of the households are initially given by ω and the equilib-

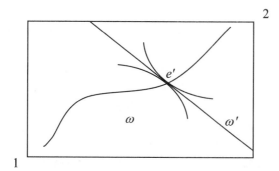

Figure 2.13
Second Theorem

rium at e' is to be decentralized, it is necessary to redistribute the initial endowments of the consumers in order to begin from ω'.

The construction described above can be given a formal statement as the Second Theorem of Welfare Economics.

Theorem 2 (Second Theorem of Welfare Economics)   With convex preferences, any Pareto-efficient allocation can be made a competitive equilibrium.

The statement of the Second Theorem provides a conclusion but does not describe the mechanism involved in the decentralization. The important step in decentralizing a chosen Pareto-efficient allocation is placing the economy at the correct starting point. For now it is sufficient to observe that behind the Second Theorem lies a process of redistribution of initial wealth. How this can be achieved is discussed later. Furthermore the Second Theorem determines a set of prices that make the chosen allocation an equilibrium. These prices may well be very different from those that would have been obtained in the absence of the wealth redistribution.

2.4.4   Extension to Production

The extension of the Two Theorems to an economy with production is straightforward. The major effect of production is to make supply variable: it is now the sum of the initial endowment plus the net outputs of the firms. In addition a consumer's income includes the profit derived from their shareholdings in firms.

Section 2.4.1 has already demonstrated efficiency for the Robinson Crusoe economy that included production. It was shown that the competitive equilibrium achieved the highest attainable indifference curve given the production possibilities of the economy. Since the single consumer cannot be made better off by any change, the equilibrium is Pareto-efficient and the First Theorem applies. The Second Theorem is of limited interest with a single consumer because there is only one Pareto-efficient allocation, and this is attained by the competitive economy.

When there is more than one consumer, the proof of the First Theorem follows the same lines as for the exchange economy. Given the equilibrium prices, each consumer is maximizing utility, so their marginal rate of substitution is equated to the price ratio. This is true for all consumers and all goods, yielding

$$MRS_{i,j}^h = \frac{p_i}{p_j} = MRS_{i,j}^{h'} \qquad (2.20)$$

for any pair of consumers h and h' and any pair of goods i and j. This is termed *efficiency in consumption*. In an economy with production this condition alone is not sufficient to guarantee efficiency; it is also necessary to consider production. The profit-maximization decision of each firm ensures that it equates its marginal rate of transformation between any two goods to the ratio of prices. For any two firms m and m' this gives

$$MRT_{i,j}^m = \frac{p_i}{p_j} = MRT_{i,j}^{m'} \qquad (2.21)$$

a condition that characterizes *efficiency in production*. The price ratio also coordinates consumers and firms, giving

$$MRS_{i,j}^h = MRT_{i,j}^m \qquad (2.22)$$

for any consumer and any firm for all pairs of goods. As for the Robinson Crusoe economy, the interpretation of this condition is that it equates the relative marginal values to the relative marginal costs. Since (2.20) through (2.22) are the conditions required for efficiency, this shows that the First Theorem extends to the economy with production.

The formal proof of this claim mirrors that for the exchange economy, except for the fact that the value of production must also be taken into account. Given this fact, the basis of the argument remains that since the consumers chose the competitive equilibrium quantities, anything that is preferred must be more expensive and hence can be shown not to be feasible.

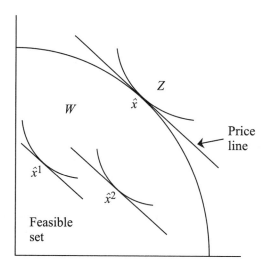

Figure 2.14
Proof of the Second Theorem

The extension of the Second Theorem to include production is illustrated in figure 2.14. The set W describes the feasible output plans for the economy, with each point in W being the sum of a production plan and the initial endowment; hence $w = y + \omega$. Set Z describes the quantities of the two goods that would allow a Pareto-improvement (a re-allocation that makes neither consumer worse off and makes one strictly better off) over the allocation $\hat{x}^1$ to consumer 1 and $\hat{x}^2$ to consumer 2. If W and Z are convex, which occurs when firms' production sets and preferences are convex, then a common tangent to W and Z can be found. This makes $\hat{x}$ an equilibrium. Individual income allocations, the sum of the value of endowment plus profit income, can be placed anywhere on the budget lines tangent to the indifference curves at the individual allocations $\hat{x}_1$ and $\hat{x}_2$ provided that they sum to the total income of the economy. This decentralizes the consumption allocation $\hat{x}_1, \hat{x}_2$.

Before proceeding further, it is worth emphasizing that the proof of the Second Theorem requires more assumptions than the proof of the First, so there may be situations in which the First Theorem is applicable but the Second is not. The Second Theorem requires that a common tangent can be found that relies on preferences and production sets being convex. A competitive equilibrium can exist with some nonconvexity in the production sets of the individual firms or the preferences of the consumers, so the First Theorem will apply, but the Second Theorem will not apply.

2.5   Lump-Sum Taxation

The discussion of the Second Theorem noted that it does not describe the mechanism through which the decentralization is achieved. It is instead implicit in the statement of the theorem that the consumers are given sufficient income to purchase the consumption plans forming the Pareto-efficient allocation. Any practical value of the Second Theorem depends on the government being able to allocate the required income levels. The way in which the theorem sees this as being done is by making what are called *lump-sum transfers* between consumers.

A transfer is defined as lump sum if no change in a consumer's behavior can affect the size of the transfer. For example, a consumer choosing to work less hard or reducing the consumption of a commodity must not be able to affect the size of the transfer. This differentiates a lump-sum transfer from other taxes, such as income or commodity taxes, for which changes in behavior do affect the value of the tax payment. Lump-sum transfers have a very special role in the theoretical analysis of public economics because, as we will show, they are the idealized redistributive instrument.

The lump-sum transfers envisaged by the Second Theorem involve quantities of endowments and shares being transferred between consumers to ensure the necessary income levels. Some consumers would gain from the transfers; others would lose. Although the value of the transfer cannot be changed, lump-sum transfers do affect consumers' behavior because their incomes are either reduced or increased by the transfers—the transfers have an income effect but do not lead to a substitution effect between commodities. Without recourse to such transfers, the decentralization of the selected allocation would not be possible.

The illustration of the Second Theorem in an exchange economy in figure 2.15 makes clear the role and nature of lump-sum transfers. The initial endowment point is denoted ω, and this is the starting point for the economy. Assuming that the Pareto-efficient allocation at point e is to be decentralized, the income levels have to be modified to achieve the new budget constraint. At the initial point the income level of h is $\hat{p}\omega^h$ when evaluated at the equilibrium prices $\hat{p}$. The value of the transfer to consumer h that is necessary to achieve the new budget constraint is $M^h - \hat{p}\omega^h = \hat{p}\hat{x}^h - \hat{p}\omega^h$. One way of ensuring this is to transfer a quantity $\tilde{x}_1^1$ of good 1 from consumer 1 to consumer 2. But any transfer of commodities with the same value would work equally well.

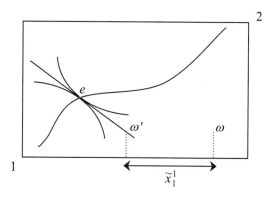

Figure 2.15
Lump-sum transfer

There is a problem, though, if we attempt to interpret the model this literally. For most people, income is earned almost entirely from the sale of labor so that their endowment is simply lifetime labor supply. This makes it impossible to transfer the endowment since one person's labor cannot be given to another. Responding to such difficulties leads to the reformulation of lump-sum transfers in terms of *lump-sum taxes*. Suppose that the two consumers both sell their entire endowments at prices $\hat{p}$. This generates incomes $\hat{p}\omega^1$ and $\hat{p}\omega^2$ for the two consumers. Now make consumer 1 pay a tax of amount $T^1 = \hat{p}\tilde{x}^1_1$ and give this tax revenue to consumer 2. Consumer 2 therefore pays a negative tax (or, in simpler terms, receives a subsidy) of $T^2 = -\hat{p}\tilde{x}^1_1 = -T^1$. The pair of taxes (T^1, T^2) moves the budget constraint in exactly the same way as the lump-sum transfer of endowment. The pair of taxes and the transfer of endowment are therefore economically equivalent and have the same effect on the economy. The taxes are also lump sum because they are determined without reference to either consumers' behavior and their values cannot be affected by any change in behavior.

Lump-sum taxes have a central role in public economics due to their efficiency in achieving distributional objectives. It should be clear from the discussion above that the economy's total endowment is not reduced by the application of the lump-sum taxes. This point applies to lump-sum taxes in general. As households cannot affect the level of the tax by changing their behavior, lump-sum taxes do not lead to any distortions in choice. There are also no resources lost due to the imposition of lump-sum taxes, so redistribution is achieved with no efficiency cost. In short, if they can be employed in the manner described they are the perfect taxes.

2.6   Discussion of Assumptions

The description of the competitive economy introduced a number of assumptions concerning the economic environment and how trade was conducted. These are important since they bear directly on the efficiency properties of competition. The interpretation and limitation of these assumptions is now discussed. This should help to provide a better context for evaluating the practical relevance of the efficiency theorems.

The most fundamental assumption was that of competitive behavior. This is the assumption that both consumers and firms view prices as fixed when they make their decisions. The natural interpretation of this assumption is that the individual economic agents are small relative to the total economy. When they are small, they naturally have no consequence. This assumption rules out any kind of market power such as monopolistic firms or trade unions in labor markets.

Competitive behavior leads to the problem of who actually sets prices in the economy. In the exchange model it is possible for equilibrium prices to be achieved via a process of barter and negotiation between the trading parties. However barter cannot be a credible explanation of price determination in an advanced economic environment. One theoretical route out of this difficulty is to assume the existence of a fictitious "Walrasian auctioneer" who literally calls out prices until equilibrium is achieved. Only at this point trade is allowed to take place. Obviously this does not provide a credible explanation of reality. Although there are other theoretical explanations of price setting, none is entirely consistent with the competitive assumption. How to integrate the two remains an unsolved puzzle.

The second assumption was symmetry of information. In a complex world there are many situations in which this does not apply. For instance, some qualities of a product, such as reliability (I do not know when my computer will next crash, but I expect it will be soon), are not immediately observable but are discovered only through experience. When it comes to re-sale, this causes an asymmetry of information between the existing owner and potential purchasers. The same can be true in labor markets where workers may know more about their attitudes to work and potential productivity than a prospective employer. An asymmetry of information provides a poor basis for trade because the caution of those transacting prevents the full gains from trade being realized.

When any of the assumptions underlying the competitive economy fail to be met, and as a consequence efficiency is not achieved, we say that there is *market failure*. Situations of market failure are of interest to public economics because they provide a potential role for government policy to enhance efficiency. A large section of this book is in fact devoted to a detailed analysis of the sources of market failure and the scope for policy response.

As a final observation, notice that the focus has been on positions of equilibrium. Several explanations can be given for this emphasis. Historically economists viewed the economy as self-correcting so that, if it were ever away from equilibrium, forces existed that move it back toward equilibrium. In the long run, equilibrium would then always be attained. Although such adjustment can be justified in simple single-market contexts, both the practical experience of sustained high levels of unemployment and the theoretical study of the stability of the price adjustment process have shown that the self-adjusting equilibrium view is not generally justified. The present justifications for focusing on equilibrium are more pragmatic. The analysis of a model must begin somewhere, and the equilibrium has much merit as a starting point. In addition, even if the final focus is on disequilibrium, there is much to be gained from comparing the properties of points of disequilibrium to those of the equilibrium. Finally, no positions other than those of equilibrium have any obvious claim to prominence.

2.7   Summary

This chapter described competitive economies and demonstrated the Two Theorems of Welfare Economics. To do this, it was necessary to introduce the concept of Pareto-efficiency. While Pareto-efficiency was simply accepted in this chapter, it will be considered very critically in chapter 12. The Two Theorems characterize the efficiency properties of the competitive economy and show how a selected Pareto-efficient allocation can be decentralized. It was also shown how prices are central to the achievement of efficiency through their role in coordinating the choices of individual agents. The role of lump-sum transfers or taxes in supporting the Second Theorem was highlighted. These transfers constitute the ideal tax system because they cause no distortions in choice and have no resource costs.

The subject matter of this chapter has very strong implications that are investigated fully in later chapters. An understanding of the welfare theorems, and of their limitations, is fundamental to appreciating many of the developments of public economics. Since claims about the efficiency of competition feature routinely in economic debate, it is important to subject it to the most careful scrutiny.

Further Reading

The two fundamental texts on the competitive economy are:

Arrow, K. J., and Hahn, F. H. 1971. *General Competitive Analysis*. Amsterdam: North-Holland.

Debreu, G. 1959. *The Theory of Value*. New Haven: Yale University Press.

A textbook treatment can be found in:

Ellickson, B. 1993. *Competitive Equilibrium: Theory and Applications*. Cambridge: Cambridge University Press.

The competitive economy has frequently been used as a practical tool for policy analysis. A survey of applications is in:

Shoven, J. B., and Whalley, J. 1992. *Applying General Equilibrium Theory*. Cambridge: Cambridge University Press.

A historical survey of the development of the model is given in:

Duffie, D., and Sonnenschein, H. 1989. Arrow and general equilibrium theory. *Journal of Economic Literature* 27: 565–98.

Some questions concerning the foundations of the model are addressed in:

Koopmans, T. C. 1957. *Three Essays on the State of Economic Science*. New York: McGraw-Hill.

The classic proof of the Two Theorems is in:

Arrow, K. J. 1951. An extension of the basic theorems of welfare economics. In J. Neyman, ed., *Proceedings of the Second Berkeley Symposium on Mathematical Statistics and Probability*. Berkeley: University of California Press.

A formal analysis of lump-sum taxation can be found in:

Mirrlees, J. A. 1986. The theory of optimal taxation. In K. J. Arrow and M. D. Intrilligator, eds., *Handbook of Mathematical Economics*. Amsterdam: North-Holland.

An extensive textbook treatment of Pareto-efficiency is:

Ng, Y.-K. 2003. *Welfare Economics*. Basingstoke: Macmillan.

Exercises

2.1.   Distinguish between partial equilibrium analysis and general equilibrium analysis. Briefly describe a model of each kind.

2.2.   Keynesian models in macroeconomics are identified by the assumption of a fixed price for output. Are such models partial or general equilibrium?

2.3.   You are requested to construct a model to predict the effect on the economy of the discovery of new oil reserves. How would you model the discovery? Discuss the number of goods that should be included in the model.

2.4.   Let a consumer have preferences described by the utility function

$$U = \log(x_1) + \log(x_2),$$

and an endowment of 2 units of good 1 and 2 units of good 2.

a. Construct and sketch the consumer's budget constraint. Show what happens when the price of good 1 increases.

b. By maximizing utility, determine the consumer's demands.

c. What is the effect of increasing the endowment of good 1 upon the demand for good 2? Explain your finding.

2.5.   How would you model an endowment of labor?

2.6.   Let two consumers have preferences described by the utility function

$$U^h = \log(x_1^h) + \log(x_2^h), \qquad h = 1, 2,$$

and the endowments described below:

	Good 1	Good 2
Consumer 1	3	2
Consumer 2	2	3

a. Calculate the consumers' demand functions.

b. Selecting good 2 as the numéraire, find the equilibrium price of good 1. Hence find the equilibrium levels of consumption.

c. Show that the consumers' indifference curves are tangential at the equilibrium.

2.7.   Consider an economy with two goods and two consumers with preferences

$$U^h = \min\{x_1^h, x_2^h\}, \qquad h = 1, 2.$$

Assume that the endowments are as follows:

	Good 1	Good 2
Consumer 1	1	2
Consumer 2	2	1

a. Draw the Edgeworth box for the economy.

b. Display the equilibrium in the Edgeworth box.

c. What is the effect on the equilibrium price of good 2 relative to good 1 of an increase in each consumer's endowment of good 1 by 1 unit?

2.8.   Consumer 1 obtains no pleasure from good 1, and consumer 2 obtains no pleasure from good 2. At the initial endowment point both consumers have endowments of both goods.

a. Draw the preferences of the consumers in an Edgeworth box.

b. By determining the trades that improve both consumers' utilities, find the equilibrium of the economy.

c. Display the equilibrium budget constraint.

2.9.   Demonstrate that the demands obtained in exercise 2.4 are homogeneous of degree zero in prices. Show that doubling prices does not affect the graph of the budget constraint.

2.10.   It has been argued that equilibrium generally exists on the basis that there must be a point where excess demand for good 2 is zero if excess demand is positive as the price of good 2 tends to zero and negative as it tends to infinity.

a. Select good 1 as numéraire and show that these properties hold when preferences are given by the utility function

$$U^h = \log(x_1^h) + \log(x_2^h),$$

and the consumer's endowment of both goods is positive.

b. Show that they do not hold if the consumer has no endowment of good 2.

c. Consider the implications of the answer to part b for proving the existence of equilibrium.

2.11.   Consider an economy with 2 consumers, A and B, and 2 goods, 1 and 2. The utility function of A is $U^A = \gamma \log(x_1^A) + [1 - \gamma] \log(x_2^A)$, where x_i^A is consumption of good i by A. A has endowments $\omega^A = (\omega_1^A, \omega_2^A) = (2, 1)$. For B, $U^B = \gamma \log(x_1^B) + [1 - \gamma] \log(x_2^B)$ and $\omega^B = (3, 2)$.

a. Use the budget constraint of A to substitute for x_2^A in U^A, and by maximizing over x_1^A, calculate the demands of A. Repeat for B.

b. Choosing good 2 as the numéraire, graph the excess demand for good 1 as a function of p_1.

c. Calculate the competitive equilibrium allocation by equating the demand for good 1 to the supply and then substituting for M^A and M^B. Verify that this is the point where excess demand is zero.

d. Show how the equilibrium price of good 2 is affected by a change in γ and in ω_1^A. Explain the results.

2.12.   A firm has a production technology that permits it to turn 1 unit of good 1 into 2 units of good 2. If the price of good 1 is 1, at what price for good 2 will the firm just break even? Graph the firm's profit as a function of the price of good 2.

2.13.   How can the existence of fixed costs be incorporated into the production set diagram? After paying its fixed costs a firm has constant returns to scale. Can it earn zero profits in a competitive economy?

2.14.   Consider an economy with 2 goods, H consumers and m firms. Each consumer, h, has an endowment of 2 units of good 1 and none of good 2, preferences described by

$U^h = x_1^h x_2^h$, and a share $\theta_j^h = \frac{1}{H}$ in firm $j = 1, \ldots, m$. Each firm has a technology characterized by the production function $y_2^j = [-y_1^j]^{1/2}$.

a. Calculate a firm's profit-maximizing choices, a consumer's demands and the competitive equilibrium of the economy.

b. What happens to $\frac{p_2}{p_1}$ as (i) m increases; (ii) H increases? Why?

c. Suppose that each consumer's endowment of good 1 increases to $2 + 2\delta$. Explain the change in relative prices.

d. What is the effect of changing:

i. The distribution of endowments among consumers;

ii. The consumers' preferences to $U^h = \alpha \log(x_1^h) + \beta \log(x_2^h)$?

2.15. Reproduce the diagram for the Robinson Crusoe economy for a firm that has constant returns to scale. Under what conditions will it be efficient for the firm not to produce? What is the consumption level of the consumer in such a case? Provide an interpretation of this possibility.

2.16. After the payment of costs, fishing boat captains distribute the surplus to the owner and crew. Typically the owner receives 50 percent, the captain 30 percent, and the remaining 20 percent is distributed to crew according to status. Is this distribution Pareto-efficient? Is it equitable?

2.17. A box of chocolates is to be shared by two children. The box contains ten milk chocolates and ten plain chocolates. Neither child likes plain chocolates. Describe the Pareto-efficient allocations.

2.18. As economists are experts in resource allocation, you are invited by two friends to resolve a dispute about the shared use of a car. By applying Pareto-efficiency, what are you able to advise them?

2.19. Two consumers have utility functions

$U^h = \log(x_1^h) + \log(x_2^h)$.

a. Calculate the marginal rate of substitution between good 1 and good 2 in terms of consumption levels.

b. By equating the marginal rates of substitution for the two consumers, characterize a Pareto-efficient allocation.

c. Using the solution to part b, construct the contract curve for an economy with 2 units of good 1 and 3 units of good 2.

2.20. A consumer views two goods as perfect substitutes.

a. Sketch the indifference curves of the consumer.

b. If an economy is composed of two consumers with these preferences, demonstrate that any allocation is Pareto-efficient.

c. If an economy has one consumer who views its two goods as perfect substitutes and a second that considers each unit of good 1 to be worth 2 units of good 2, find the Pareto-efficient allocations.

2.21.   Consider an economy in which preferences are given by

$$U^1 = x_1^1 + x_2^1 \quad \text{and} \quad U^2 = \min\{x_1^2, x_2^2\}.$$

Given the endowments $\omega^1 = (1, 2)$ and $\omega^2 = (3, 1)$, construct the set of Pareto-efficient allocations and the contract curve. Which allocations are also competitive equilibria?

2.22.   Take the economy in the exercise above, but change the preferences of consumer 2 to

$$U^2 = \max\{x_1^2, x_2^2\}.$$

Is there a Pareto-efficient allocation?

2.23.   Consider an economy with two consumers, A and B, and two goods, 1 and 2. Using x_i^h to denote the consumption of good i by consumer h, assume that both consumers have the utility function $U^h = \min\{x_1^h, x_2^h\}$.

a. By drawing an Edgeworth box, display the Pareto-efficient allocations if the economy has an endowment of 1 unit of each good.

b. Display the Pareto-efficient allocations if the endowment is 1 unit of good 1 and 2 units of good 2.

c. What would be the competitive equilibrium prices for parts a and b?

2.24.   Consider the economy in exercise 2.11.

a. Calculate the endowments required to make the equal-utility allocation a competitive equilibrium.

b. Discuss the transfer of endowment necessary to support this equilibrium.

2.25.   Provide an example of a Pareto-efficient allocation that cannot be decentralized.

2.26.   Let an economy have a total endowment of two units of the two available goods. If the two consumers have preferences

$$U^h = \alpha \log(x_1^h) + [1 - \alpha] \log(x_2^h),$$

find the ratio of equilibrium prices at the allocation where $U^1 = U^2$. Hence find the value of the lump-sum transfer that is needed to decentralize the allocation if the initial endowments are $\left(\frac{1}{2}, \frac{3}{4}\right)$ and $\left(\frac{3}{2}, \frac{5}{4}\right)$.

2.27.   Are the following statements true or false? Explain in each case.

a. If one consumer gains from a trade, the other consumer involved in the trade must lose.

b. The gains from trade are based on comparative advantage, not absolute advantage.

c. The person who can produces the good with less input has an absolute advantage in producing this good.

d. The person who has the smaller opportunity cost of producing the good has a comparative advantage in producing this good.

e. The competitive equilibrium is the only allocation where the gains from trade are exhausted.

II GOVERNMENT

3   Public Sector Statistics

3.1   Introduction

In 1913 the Sixteenth Amendment to the US Constitution gave Congress the legal authority to tax income. In so doing, it made income taxation a permanent feature of the US tax system and provided a significant source of additional tax revenues. Revenue collection passed the $1bil mark in 1918, increased to $5.4bil by 1920, and reached $43bil in 1945. It was not until the tax cut of 1981 that this process of growth showed any marked sign of slowing. This growth in tax revenue was matched by an equal growth in government expenditure. The US experience is typical of similar developments in all industrialized economies.

The purpose of this chapter is to provide a statistical overview of the public sector in modern market economies. Data are presented on government expenditure and revenue. This gives both a historical perspective and an insight into the current situation. Observing the numerous items of expenditure and sources of revenue emphasizes the extent and range of activities in which the public sector is involved.

A surprising feature that the data reveals is the similarity in public sector behavior in countries that are otherwise very diverse culturally. Specifically, the difference in the size of the public sector between the social-market economies of northern Europe and the free-market economies of North America and Asia is rather less than might be imagined.

3.2   Historical Development

The historical development of the public sector over the past century can be summarized as one of significant growth. For the typical industrially developed economy, government expenditure was only a small proportion of gross domestic product at the start of the twentieth century. Expenditure then rose steadily over the next sixty years, leveling out toward the end of the century. The details behind this broad-brush description are illustrated in the figures that follow.

Figure 3.1 shows the growth of public spending during the last century for five developed economies. This depicts expenditure as a percentage of gross domestic product to give an idea of the size of the public sector relative to the economy as a

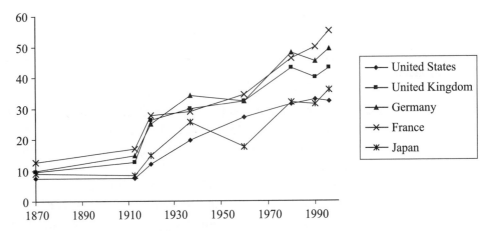

Figure 3.1
Total expenditure, 1870 to 1996 (% GDP)

whole. Only a selection of years are plotted, but the figure provides a clear impression of the overall trend. Although there is a persistent difference in the levels of expenditure between the three European countries (France, Germany, United Kingdom) and the non-European countries (Japan, United States) the pattern of growth is the same for all. These five economies had a clear long-run upward path in public spending relative to gross domestic product. Starting with a level of public spending around 10 percent of gross domestic product in 1870, this increased markedly around 1910 and then continued to rise afterward. In 1996 the United States had the lowest public spending level of the five countries at 32.4 percent, but even this is one-third of gross domestic product. France had the highest level at 55 percent. A number of explanations for this long-run increase have been proposed. These explanations are discussed in chapter 4.

A more detailed presentation of the changes in the level of expenditure in the last thirty years is provided in figure 3.2. This displays a picture of a slowing, or even a stagnation, of the growth in public sector expenditure, particularly over the past twenty years. Although expenditure is higher in 2002 than in 1970 for the six countries shown, the increases for the United Kingdom and the United States are very small (from 38.8 percent to 41.7 percent for the United Kingdom and from 31.7 to 35.6 percent for the United States). For the United Kingdom especially, expenditure was clearly higher in the early 1980s (peaking at 47.5 percent in 1981) than in 2002. The figure also suggests that there has been convergence in the level of expenditure between the countries. For example, in 1970, expenditure

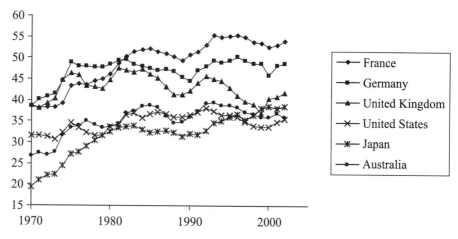

Figure 3.2
Total expenditure, 1970 to 2002 (% GDP)

in Japan was approximately half that in France, Germany, and the United Kingdom, but by 2002, it had reached 38.6 percent in Japan and almost matched that in the United Kingdom.

Figure 3.3 shows the path of expenditure in selected subcategories of public spending during the last century, again expressed as a percentage of gross domestic product. This breakdown into categories is helpful in understanding the composition of the long-run increase in figure 3.1. Defense spending constituted one of the largest items of public spending in the late nineteenth century. It has since been somewhat erratic and driven in large part by the history of international relations. In all cases, defense spending peaked in the midcentury and has fallen continually since. In 1996 the United States spent the largest proportion of gross domestic product on defense (4 percent).

The most marked rises have come from social spending on items such as education, health, and pensions. Expenditure on education and pensions has risen sharply as a share of gross domestic product in all five countries since the early twentieth century but particularly so since midcentury (and perhaps slightly earlier in the United Kingdom). In all five countries it is currently around 5 percent of gross domestic product. Health expenditure has risen more quickly. Even in the United States, which has a primarily private health care system, the public sector expenditure on health was 6.3 percent of gross domestic product in 1994. The significant increase in expenditure on pensions is important from a policy perspective. As discussed further in chapter 20, many countries are facing a "pensions

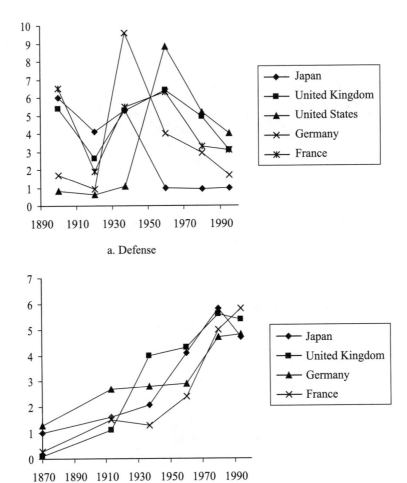

a. Defense

b. Education

Figure 3.3
Individual expenditure items (% GDP)

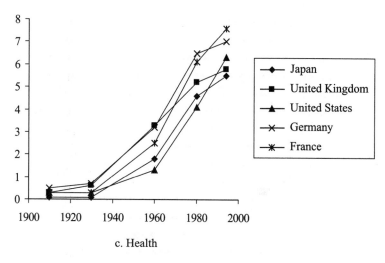

c. Health

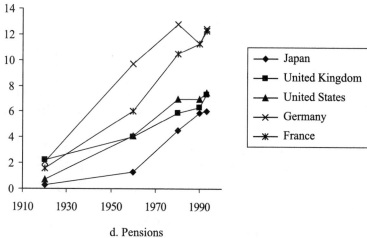

d. Pensions

Figure 3.3
(continued)

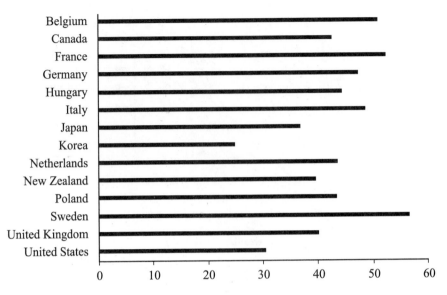

Figure 3.4
Government expenditure, 1998 (% GDP)

crisis" in which the current rate of expenditure on state pensions is unsustainable. The basis of this is clearly apparent in the rate of expenditure increase in France and Germany.

Data on public sector expenditure for a wide range of countries in 1998 is given in figure 3.4. This includes developed, developing, and transition economies. The figure clearly justifies the claim that the public sector is significant in countries across the world. Sweden has the highest level of public sector expenditure (at 56.6 percent) and Korea the lowest (at 25 percent). All have "mixed economies" characterized by substantial government involvement. They are clearly not free-market economies with minimal government intervention. These values for the size of the public sector emphasize the importance of studying how government should best choose its means of revenue collection and its allocation of expenditure.

As a final point, it is worth noting that data on expenditure typically understate the full influence of the public sector on the economy. For instance, regulations such as employment laws or safety standards affect economic activity but do not directly generate any measurable government expenditure or income. Analysis of statistics on government do not therefore capture the effects of such policies. This point is explored further in section 3.5.

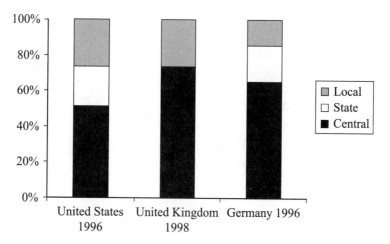

Figure 3.5
Share of expenditure by levels of government

3.3   Composition of Expenditure

The historical data display the broad trend in public expenditure. This section looks in more detail at the composition of expenditure. Expenditure is considered from the perspective of its allocation between various levels of government and its division into categories.

Figure 3.5 allocates expenditure between the different levels of government (net of all transfers between levels). The significant difference between the United Kingdom, which has no expenditures at the state level, and the other two countries is explained by political structure. Germany and the United States are *federal countries* that have central government, state government, and local government. In contrast, the United Kingdom is a *unitary country* that only has central and local government. The figures reveal that expenditure at the state level is similar in Germany and the United States (20 and 22 percent respectively), although local government is larger in the United States (26 percent compared to 15 percent). Despite the different political structure in the United Kingdom, the proportion of expenditure at the local level is identical to that in the United States (26 percent). By definition, central expenditure in the United Kingdom (73 percent) is then equal to the proportions of central plus state in the United States.

Figure 3.6 displays consolidated general spending for the United States, United Kingdom, and Germany. By "consolidated" we mean the combined expenditure

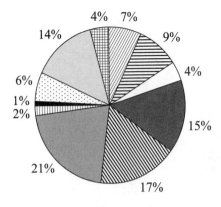

a. United States 1996

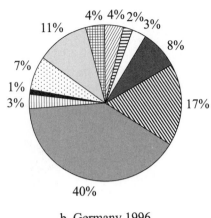

b. Germany 1996

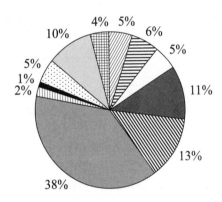

c. United Kingdom 1998

General public services
Defense
Public order and safety
Education
Health
Social security and welfare
Housing and community
Recreation, culture, etc.
Other economic affairs
Other
Transport and communication

Figure 3.6
Composition of consolidated general spending

of all levels of government. The figures avoid double counting by subtracting intergovernmental transfers. The diversity of public sector activity is clear from the list of spending categories. Interestingly spending on the goods associated with the core functions of the state, defense and public order, is relatively minor and forms about 10 percent of spending when averaged across the countries. Administrative and governmental costs are recorded under the heading of general public services and add no more than another 6 percent on average.

Health and education, despite providing benefits of an arguably largely private nature, are substantial in all three countries (e.g., education is 15 percent and health 17 percent in the United States). Spending on housing and community amenities, on recreation and culture, and on transport and communications sectors are comparatively small. Subsidies to agriculture, energy, mining, manufacturing, and the construction sector are brought together here under the heading of other economic affairs and also appear relatively minor. Social security and welfare spending is the largest single item in all countries under this classification. This is so even in the United States where, at 21 percent, it is noticeably smaller than in Germany and the United Kingdom (40 and 38 percent respectively). Averaged across the three countries it constitutes over a third of spending.

Figures 3.7 to 3.9 show how spending responsibilities are allocated between different tiers of government in the United States, United Kingdom, and Germany. This provides an interesting contrast between the two federal countries (Germany and the United States) and the unitary country (United Kingdom). Even though the political structures are significantly different, some common features can be observed. Certain items such as defense are always allocated to the center. Redistributive functions also tend to be concentrated centrally for the good reason that redistribution between poor and rich regions is only possible that way and also because attempts at redistribution at lower levels are vulnerable to frustration through migration of richer individuals away from localities with internally redistributive programs. Education, on the other hand, is largely devolved to lower levels, either to the states or to local government. Public order is also typically dealt with at lower levels. Health spending is always substantial at the central level but can also be important at lower tiers as, for example, in Germany.

The fact that spending is made at a lower level need not mean that it is financed from taxes levied locally. In most multiple-tier systems, central government partly finances lower tier functions by means of grants. These have many purposes, including correcting for imbalances in resources between localities and between tiers given the chosen allocation of tax instruments. Sometimes grants are lump

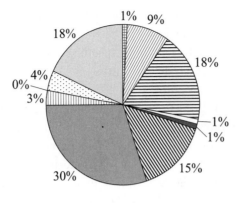

a. United States 1996

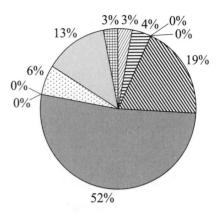

b. Germany 1996

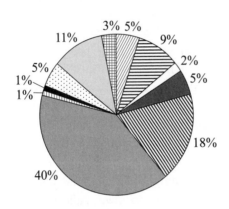

c. United Kingdom 1998

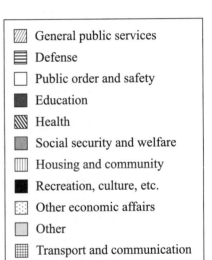

Figure 3.7
Composition of central spending

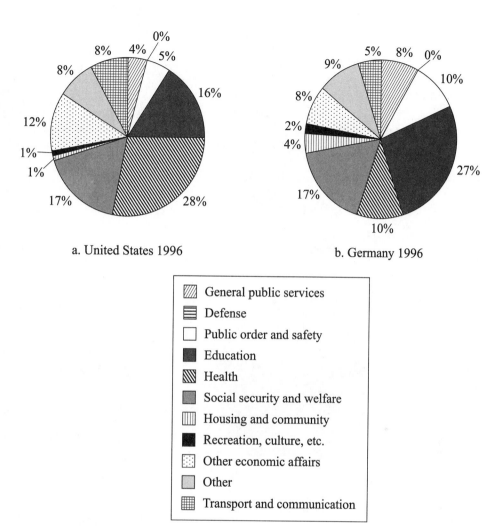

a. United States 1996   b. Germany 1996

General public services
Defense
Public order and safety
Education
Health
Social security and welfare
Housing and community
Recreation, culture, etc.
Other economic affairs
Other
Transport and communication

Figure 3.8
Composition of state spending

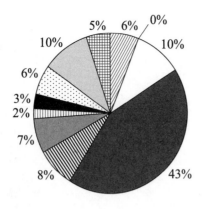

a. United States 1996

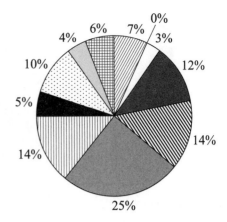

b. Germany 1996

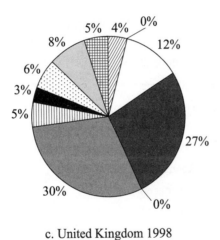

c. United Kingdom 1998

General public services	
Defense	
Public order and safety	
Education	
Health	
Social security and welfare	
Housing and community	
Recreation, culture, etc.	
Other economic affairs	
Other	
Transport and communication	

Figure 3.9
Composition of local spending

sum, and sometimes they depend on the spending activities of the lower tiers. In the latter case the incentives of lower tiers to spend can be changed by the design of the grant formula and central government can use this as a way to encourage recognition of externalities between localities.

3.4   Revenue

The discussion of public sector expenditure is now matched by a discussion of revenue. The following figures first trace the historical path tax of revenues and then relate revenues to different tax instruments and to alternative levels of government.

The first set of statistics consider the growth of total tax revenue from 1965 to 2000. Figure 3.10 charts total tax revenue for seven countries expressed as a percentage of gross domestic product. The general picture that emerges from this mirrors that drawn from the expenditure data. All of the countries have witnessed some growth in tax revenue, and there has also been a degree of convergence. In 2000 government revenue in these countries ranged between 27 and 45 percent of gross domestic product.

Looking more closely at the details, France (45 percent) and the United Kingdom (37 percent) have the highest percentage closely followed by Canada (36 percent) and Turkey (33 percent). The United States (30 percent) and Japan (27

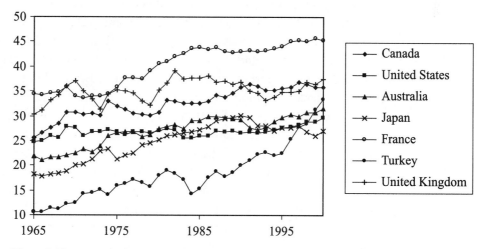

Figure 3.10
Tax revenues, 1965 to 2000 (% GDP)

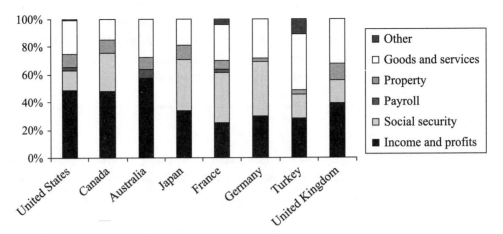

Figure 3.11
Tax revenue for category of taxation, 2000

percent) are somewhat lower. The country that has witnessed the most growth is Turkey, where tax revenue has risen from 11 percent of gross domestic product in 1965 to 33 percent in 2000. Tax revenue also grew strongly in Japan between 1965, when it was 11 percent, and 1990, when it reached 30 percent, but has leveled off since. Overall, these data are suggestive of surprising uniformity among these countries with all achieving a similar outcome. The figures that follow consider the details behind these aggregates.

Figure 3.11 looks at the proportion of tax revenue raised by six categories of tax instrument in 2000. The figure shows that income and profit taxes raise the largest proportion of revenue in Australia (57 percent), the United States (51 percent), Canada (49 percent), and the United Kingdom (39 percent). Social security taxes are the largest proportion in Japan (36 percent), France (36 percent), and Germany (39 percent). Among these countries Turkey is unique with taxes on goods and services the most significant item (41 percent). There is also noticeable division between the European countries, where taxes on goods and services are much more significant, and the United States. For instance, taxes on goods and services raise 32 percent of revenue in the United Kingdom but only 16 percent in the United States. This is a reflection of the importance of value-added taxation (VAT) in Europe where it has been a significant element of EU tax policy. Property taxes are significant in the majority of countries (12 percent in the United Kingdom and 10 percent in the United States and Japan). Payroll taxes are only really significant in Australia (6 percent).

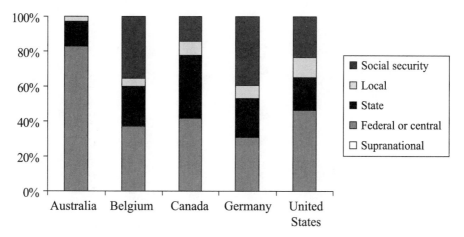

Figure 3.12
Tax revenue by level of government, federal countries, 2000

The next two figures display the proportion of tax revenue raised by each level of government. Figure 3.12 considers the proportions in five federal countries. In contrast, figure 3.13 considers five unitary countries. For all the federal countries the central government raises more revenue than state government. The two are closest in Canada, with the central government raising 42 percent and the provinces 36 percent, and in Germany, with the central government raising 31 percent and the Bundeslander 23 percent. The federal governments in the United States and Australia raise considerably more revenue than the states (46 and 20 percent for the United States and 83 and 14 percent for Australia). In all countries local government raises the smallest proportion of revenue. The US local government raises 11 percent of revenue, which is the largest value among these countries. The smallest proportion of revenue raised by local government is 3 percent in Australia.

The unitary countries in figure 3.13 display the same general feature that the central government raises significantly more revenue than local government. The largest value is 70 percent in Turkey and the smallest 37 percent in Japan. Local government is most significant in Japan (25 percent) and least significant in France (10 percent).

Comparing the federal and unitary countries, it can be seen that local government raises slightly more revenue on average in the unitary countries than the federal countries. What really distinguishes them is the size of central government. The figures suggest that the revenue raised by central government in the unitary

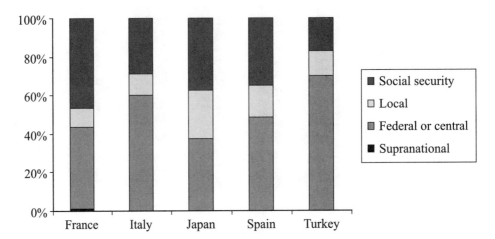

Figure 3.13
Tax revenue by level of government, unitary countries, 2000

countries is almost the same on average as that of central plus state in the federal countries. The absence of state government does not therefore put more emphasis on local government in the unitary countries. Instead, the role of the state government is absorbed within central government.

The final set of figures presents the share of revenue raised by each category of tax instrument at each level of government for two federal countries, the United States and Germany, and two unitary countries, Japan and the United Kingdom. Most of the previous figures have shown remarkable similarities in the behavior of a range of countries. In contrast, allocating revenues to tax instruments for the alternative levels of government reveals some interesting differences.

For the United States figure 3.14 shows that the importance of income and profits taxes falls as the progression is made from central to local government (91 percent for central, 7 percent for local). Their reduction is matched by an increase in importance of property taxes from 2 percent for central government up to 72 percent for local government. It would be easy to argue that this is the natural outcome since property is easily identified with a local area but income is not. However, figure 3.15 for Germany shows that the opposite pattern can also arise with income and profit taxes becoming more important for local government (78 percent of revenue) than for central government (42 percent of revenue). Despite this difference Germany and the United States do share the common feature that property taxes are more important for local government than for central government.

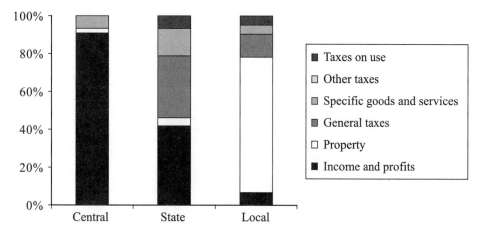

Figure 3.14
Tax shares at each level of government, United States, 2000

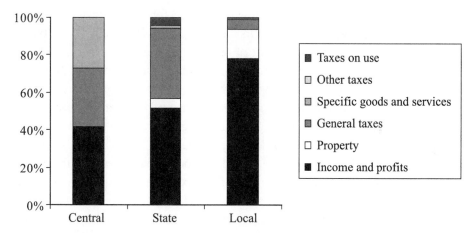

Figure 3.15
Tax shares at each level of government, Germany, 2000

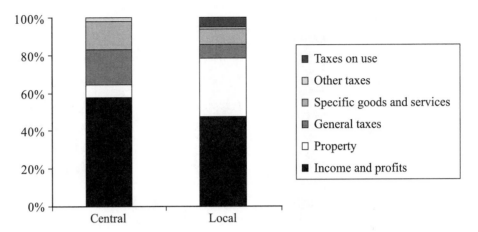

Figure 3.16
Tax shares at each level of government, Japan, 2000

The same data are now considered for two unitary countries. In Japan (figure 3.16) income and profits taxes are almost equally important for both central government (58 percent of revenue) and local government (47 percent). They are also more important for both levels of government than any other category of tax instrument. Where the difference arises is that property taxation is much more significant for local government (raising 31 percent of revenue) than for central (6 percent). For central government, general taxes (19 percent of revenue) make up the difference. The UK data, in figure 3.17, display an extreme version of the importance of property taxation for local government. As the figure shows, property taxes raise over 99 percent of all tax revenue for local government. No revenue is raised by local government in the United Kingdom from income and profit taxes.

Comparing between the unitary and federal countries does not reveal any standard pattern of revenues within each group. In fact the differences are as marked within the categories as they are across the categories. The one feature that is true for all four countries is that property taxes raise a larger proportion of revenue for local government than they do for central government.

This section has looked at data on tax revenues from an aggregate level down to the revenue raised from each category of tax instrument for different levels of government. What the figures show is that at an aggregate level there are limited differences among the countries. Those for which data are reported have converged on a mixed-economy solution with tax revenues at a similar percentage of gross domestic product. The most significant differences emerge when the source

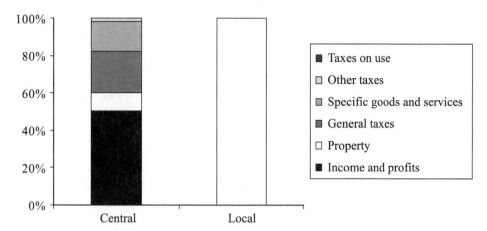

Figure 3.17
Tax shares at each level of government, United Kingdom, 2000

of revenue for the various levels of government is analyzed. Even countries that have adopted the same form of government structure (either unitary or federal) can have very different proportions of revenue raised by the various categories of tax instrument.

3.5   Measuring the Government

The figures given above have provided several different viewpoints on the public sector. They have traced both the division of expenditure and the level of expenditure. For the purpose of obtaining a broad picture of the public sector, these are interesting and informative statistics. However, they do raise two important questions that must be addressed in order to gain a proper perspective on their meaning.

The first issue revolves around the fact that the figures have expressed the size of the public sector relative to the size of the economy as a whole. To trace the implications of this, take as given that there exists an accurate measure of the expenditure level of the public sector. The basic question is then: What should this expenditure be expressed as a proportion of? The standard approach is to use nominal gross domestic product (i.e., gross domestic product measured using each year's own prices), but this is very much an arbitrary choice that can have a significant impact on the interpretation of the final figure.

Recall from basic national income accounting that the size of the economy can be measured in either nominal or real terms, using gross output or net output. Domestic or national product can be employed. Outputs can be valued at market prices or factor prices. For many purposes, as long as the basis of measurement is made clear, the choice of measure does not make much real difference. Where it can make a critical difference is in the impression it gives about the size of the public sector. By adopting the smallest measure of the size of the economy (which depends on a number of factors, e.g., the level of new investment relative to depreciation, the structure of the tax system, and income from abroad), the apparent size of the public sector can be increased by several percentage points over that when using the largest expenditure level.

While not changing anything of real economic significance, such manipulation of the figures can be very valuable in political debate. There is a degree of freedom for those who are supportive of the public sector, or are opponents of it, to present a figure that is more favorable for their purposes. This may be useful for those wishing to push a particular point of view, but it hinders informed discussion. Consequently, as long as the figures are calculated in a consistent way, it does not matter for comparative purposes which precise definition of output is used. In contrast, for an assessment of whether the public sector is "too large," it can matter significantly.

The second issue of measurement concerns what should be included within the definition of government. To see what is involved here, consider the question of whether state-run industries should be included. Assume that these are allowed to function as if they were private firms, so that they follow the objective of profit maximization, and simply remit their profits to the government. In this case they should certainly not be included, since the government is acting as if it were a private shareholder. The only difference between the state-run firm and any other private firm in which the government is a shareholder would be the extent of the shareholding. Conversely, assume that the state-run firm was directed by the government to follow a policy of investment in impoverished areas and to use cross-subsidization to lower the prices of some of its products. In this case there are compelling reasons to include the activities of the firm within the measure of government.

What this example illustrates is that it is not government expenditure per se that is interesting to the economist. Instead, what is really relevant is the degree of influence the government has over the economy. When the government is simply a shareholder, it is not directly influencing the firm's decisions. The converse is true when it directs the firm's actions. Looked at in this way, measuring the size of government via its expenditure is a means of estimating government influence using an easily observable statistic. In fact the extent of government influence is somewhat broader than just its expenditure. What must also be included are the economic consequences of government-backed regulations and restrictions on economic behavior. Minimum wage laws, weights and measures regulation, health and safety laws, are all examples of government intervention in the economy. However none of these would feature in any observation of government expenditure.

What this discussion shows is that there is a degree of flexibility in interpreting measures of government expenditure. Furthermore government influence on the economy is only approximately captured by the expenditure figure. The true extent, including all relevant laws and regulations, is most certainly much larger.

3.6   Conclusions

This chapter has reviewed the expenditures and revenues of the public sector using data from a range of countries. Despite their clear cultural differences the countries considered have all experienced the same phenomenon of significant public sector growth in the last century. From being only a minor part of the economy at the start of the last century, the public sector had grown to be significant proportion of gross domestic product in all developed countries by the end of the century. There is some variation within the figures for the precise level of public expenditure, but the pattern of growth is the same for all. There is also evidence that the growth has now ceased, and unless there is some major upheaval, the size of the public sector will now remain fairly constant.

In terms of the composition of public sector revenue and expenditure it can be noted that there are differences in the details among countries. However, there is common reliance on similar tax instruments. Spending patterns are also not too dissimilar. It is these commonalities that make the ideas and concepts of public economics so broadly applicable.

Further Reading

Detailed evaluations of the different areas of public expenditure can be found in:

Miles, D., Myles, G. D., and Preston, I. 2003. *The Economics of Public Spending*. Oxford: Oxford University Press.

The data for Figures 3.1 and 3.3 are taken from:

Tanzi, V., and Schuknecht, L. 2000. *Public Spending in the 20th Century: A Global Perspective.* Cambridge: Cambridge University Press.

Figure 3.2 is compiled using data from:

OECD *Economic Outlook*, vols. 51 and 73.

The expenditure data in figures 3.5 to 3.9 are from:

IMF. 1998. *Government Finance Statistics Manual.* Washington: IMF.

IMF. 2001a. *Government Finance Statistics Yearbook.* Washington: IMF.

IMF. 2001b. *Government Finance Statistics Manual.* Washington: IMF.

Data on revenues in figures 3.10 to 3.17 are from:

OECD. 2002. *Revenue Statistics 1965–2001.* Paris: OECD.

Exercises

3.1.   What factors might have been responsible for the growth of government expenditure between 1920 and 1940?

3.2.   Obtain data on public sector expenditure and estimate the growth trend:

a. Over the last 50 years.

b. Over the last 20 years.

Has there been a structural break (a point at which the rate of growth distinctly changed)?

3.3.   Why may expenditure data underestimate the influence of the public sector upon the economy?

3.4.   Does recent experience suggest that the growth of expenditure has now ceased?

3.5.   In the 1980s both the United Kingdom and the United States had governments that aimed to cut expenditure and reduce the role of government. Did they succeed? Could any government now cut expenditure?

3.6.   Is expenditure to combat market failure greater than expenditure for redistributive purposes?

3.7.   What is the "pensions crisis"? How can this be solved?

3.8.   Comparing figure 3.2 to figure 3.10 shows that taxation is a smaller proportion of gross domestic product than expenditure. How can this be so?

3.9.   Why is income taxed rather than wealth?

3.10.   What explains the limited revenue from property taxation?

3.11.   Should social security taxes be viewed as a second component of income taxation?

3.12.   Explain why defense spending is organized centrally and education locally.

3.13.   Is there any logic to the division of spending responsibilities between different levels of government?

3.14.   Does the division of political responsibility among different levels of government have any economic implications?

3.15.   Provide an interpretation of the EU structure from the perspective of the division of tax collection.

3.16.   How could a minimum wage law be evaluated as government intervention?

3.17.   Do increases in public expenditure cause an increase in national income, or vice versa? How would you test which is the case?

3.18.   The value of gross domestic product for several measures is given in the table. If public expenditure is $10bil, what are the largest and smallest proportional measures of the public sector? Does the difference matter?

Measure	Factor prices	Market prices	Domestic product	National product
Value ($bil)	30.2	32.3	31.2	31.5

4 Theories of the Public Sector

4.1 Introduction

The statistics of chapter 3 have described the size, growth, and composition of the public sector in a range of developed and developing countries. The data illustrated that the pattern of growth was similar across countries, as was the composition of expenditure. Although there is some divergence in the size of the public sector, it is significant in all the countries. Such observations raise two interrelated questions. First, why is there a public sector at all—would it not be possible for economic activity to function satisfactorily without government intervention? Second, is it possible to provide a theory that explains the increase in size of the public sector and the composition of expenditure? The purpose of this chapter is to consider possible answers to these questions.

The chapter begins with a discussion of the justifications that have been proposed for the public sector. These show how the requirements of efficiency and equity lead to a range of motives for public sector intervention in the economy. Alternative explanations for the growth in the size of the public sector are then assessed. As a by-product, they also provide an explanation for the composition of expenditure. Finally, some economists would argue that the public sector is excessively large. Several arguments for why this may be so are considered.

4.2 Justification for the Public Sector

Two basic lines of argument can be advanced to justify the role of the public sector. These can be grouped under the headings of *efficiency* and *equity*. Efficiency relates to arguments concerning the aggregate level of economic activity, whereas equity refers to the distribution of economic benefits. In considering these arguments, it is natural to begin with efficiency since this is essentially the more fundamental concept.

4.2.1 The Minimal State

The most basic motivation for the existence of a public sector follows from the observation that entirely unregulated economic activity cannot operate in a very sophisticated way. In short, an economy would not function effectively if there were no *property rights* (the rules defining the ownership of property) or *contract laws* (the rules governing the conduct of trade).

Without property rights, satisfactory exchange of commodities could not take place given the lack of trust that would exist between contracting parties. This argument can be traced back to Hobbes, who viewed the government as a social contract that enables people to escape from the anarchic "state of nature" where their competition in pursuit of self-interest would lead to a destructive "war of all against all." The institution of property rights is a first step away from this anarchy. In the absence of property rights, it would not be possible to enforce any prohibition against theft. Theft discourages enterprise, since the gains accrued may be appropriated by others. It also results in the use of resources in the unproductive business of theft prevention.

Contract laws determine the rules of exchange. They exist to ensure that the participants in a trade receive what they expect from that trade or, if they do not, have open an avenue to seek compensation. Examples of contract laws include the formalization of weights and measures and the obligation to offer product warranties. These laws encourage trade by removing some of the uncertainty in transactions.

The establishment of property rights and contract laws is not sufficient in itself. Unless they can be policed and upheld in law, they are of limited consequence. Such law enforcement cannot be provided free of cost. Enforcement officers must be employed and courts must be provided in which redress can be sought. In addition an advanced society also faces a need for the enforcement of more general criminal laws. Moving beyond this, once a country develops its economic activity, it will need to defend its gains from being stolen by outsiders. This implies the provision of defense for the nation. As the statistics made clear, national defense has at times been a very costly activity.

Consequently, even if only the minimal requirements of the enforcement of contract and criminal laws and the provision of defense are met, a source of income must be found to pay for them. This need for income requires the collection of revenue, whether these services are provided by the state or by private sector organizations. But they are needed in any economy that wishes to develop beyond the most rudimentary level. Whether it is most efficient for a central government to collect the revenue and provide the services could be debated. Since there are some good reasons for assuming this is the case, the coordination of the collection of revenue and the provision of services to ensure the attainment of efficient functioning of economic activity provides a natural role for a public sector.

This reasoning illustrates that to achieve even a most minimal level of economic organization, some unavoidable revenue requirements are generated and require financing. From this follows the first role of the public sector, which is to assist with the attainment of economic efficiency by providing an environment in which trade can flourish. The *minimal state* provides contract law, polices it, and defends the economy against outsiders. The minimal state does nothing more than this, but without it organized economic activity could not take place. These arguments provide a justification for at least a minimal state and hence the existence of a public sector and of public expenditure.

Having concluded that the effective organization of economic activity generates a need for public expenditure, one role for public economics is to determine how this revenue should be collected. The collection should be done with as little cost as possible imposed on the economy. Such costs arise from the distortion in choice that arise from taxation. Public economics aims to understand these distortions and to describe the methods of minimizing their impact.

4.2.2   Market versus Government

Moving beyond the basic requirements for organized economic activity, there are other situations where intervention in the economy can potentially increase welfare. Unlike the minimal provision and revenue requirements however, there will always be a degree of contentiousness about additional intervention whatever the grounds on which it is motivated. The situations where intervention may be warranted can be divided into two categories: those that involve market failure and those that do not.

When market failure is present, the argument for considering whether intervention would be beneficial is compelling. For example, if economic activity generated externalities (effects that one economic agent imposes on another without their consent), so that there is divergence between private and social valuations and the competitive outcome is not efficient, it may be felt necessary for the state to intervene to limit the inefficiency that results. This latter point can also be extended to other cases of market failure, such as those connected to the existence of public goods and of imperfect competition. Reacting to such market failures is intervention motivated on efficiency grounds.

It must be stressed that this reasoning does not imply that intervention will always be beneficial. In every case it must be demonstrated that the public sector actually has the ability to improve on what the unregulated economy can achieve.

This will not be possible if the choice of policy tools is limited or government information is restricted. It will also be undesirable if the government is not benevolent. These various imperfections in public intervention will be a recurrent theme of this book.

While some useful insights follow from the assumption of an omnipotent, omniscient, and benevolent policy-maker, in reality it can give us very misleading ideas about the possibilities of beneficial policy intervention. It must be recognized that the actions of the state, and the feasible policies that it can choose, are often restricted by the same features of the economy that make the market outcome inefficient. One role for public economics is therefore to determine the desirable extent of the public sector or the boundaries of state intervention. For instance, if we know that markets will fail to be efficient in the presence of imperfect information, to establish the merit of government intervention it is crucial to know if a government subject to the same informational limitations can achieve a better outcome.

Furthermore a government managed by nonbenevolent officials and subject to political constraints may fail to correct market failures and may instead introduce new costs of its own creation. It is important to recognize that this potential for government failure is as important as market failure and that both are often rooted in the same informational problems. At a very basic level the force of coercion must underlie every government intervention in the economy. All policy acts take place, and in particular, taxes are collected and industry is regulated, with this force in the background. But the very power to coerce raises the possibility of its misuse. Although the intention in creating this power is that its force should serve the general interest, nothing can guarantee that once public officials are given this monopoly of force, they will not try to abuse this power in their own interest.

4.2.3   Equity

In addition to market failure, government intervention can also be motivated by the observation that the economy may have widespread inequality of income, opportunity, or wealth. This can occur even if the economy is efficient in a narrow economic sense. In such circumstances the level of economic welfare as viewed by the government may well be raised by a policy designed to alleviate these inequalities. This is the reasoning through which the provision of state education, social security programs, and compulsory pension schemes are justified. It should be stressed that the gains from these policies are with respect to normative assessments of welfare, unlike the positive criterion lying behind the concept of economic efficiency.

In the cases of both market failure and welfare-motivated policies, policy intervention concerns more than just the efficient collection of revenue. The reasons for the failure of the economy to reach the optimal outcome have to be understood, and a policy that can counteract these has to be designed. Extending the scope of the public economics to address such issues provides the breadth to the subject.

4.2.4   Efficiency and Equity

When determining economic policy, governments are faced with two conflicting aims. All governments are concerned with organizing economic activity so that the best use is made of economic resources. This is the efficiency side of policy design. To varying degrees, governments are also concerned to see that the benefits of economic activity are distributed fairly. This is the equity aspect of policy design.

The difficulty facing the government is that the requirements of equity and efficiency frequently conflict. It is often the case that the efficient policy is highly inequitable, while the equitable policy can introduce significant distortions and disincentives. Given this fact, the challenge for policy design is to reach the correct trade-off between equity and efficiency. Quite where on the trade-off the government should locate is dependent on the relative importance it assigns to equity over efficiency.

In this context it is worth adding one final note concerned with the nature of the arguments often used in this book. A standard simplification is to assume that there is a single consumer or that all consumers are identical. In such a setting there can be no distributional issues, so any policy recommendations derived within it relate only to efficiency and not to equity. The reason for proceeding in this way is that it usually permits a much simpler analysis to be undertaken and for the conclusions to be much more precise. When interpreting such conclusions in terms of practical policy recommendations, their basis should never be overlooked.

4.3   Public Sector Growth

The data of chapter 3 showed quite clearly the substantial growth of the public sector in a range of countries during the past century. There are numerous theories that have been advanced to explain why this has occurred. These differ in their emphasis and perspective and are not mutually exclusive. In fact it is reasonable to argue that a comprehensive explanation would involve elements drawn from all.

4.3.1   Development Models

The basis of the development models of public sector growth is that the economy experiences changes in its structure and needs as it develops. Tracing the nature of the development process from the beginning of industrialization through to the completion of the development process, a story of why public sector expenditure increases can be told.

It is possible to caricature the main features of this story in the following way: The early stage of development is viewed as the period of industrialization during which the population moves from the countryside to the urban areas. To meet the needs that result from this, there is a requirement for significant infrastructural expenditure in the development of cities. The typically rapid growth experienced in this stage of development results in a significant increase in expenditure and the dominant role of infrastructure determines the nature of expenditure.

In what are called the middle stages of development, the infrastructural expenditure of the public sector becomes increasingly complementary with expenditure from the private sector. Developments by the private sector, such as factory construction, are supported by investments from the public sector, such as the building of connecting roads. As urbanization proceeds and cities increase in size, so does population density. This generates a range of externalities such as pollution and crime. An increasing proportion of public expenditure is then diverted away from spending on infrastructure to the control of these externalities.

Finally, in the developed phase of the economy, there is less need for infrastructural expenditure or for the correction of market failure. Instead, expenditure is driven by the desire to react to issues of equity. This results in transfer payments, such as social security, health, and education, becoming the main items of expenditure. Of course, once such forms of expenditure become established, they are difficult to ever reduce. They also increase with heightened expectations and through the effect of an aging population.

Although this theory of the growth of expenditure concurs broadly with the facts, it has a number of weaknesses. Most important, it is primarily a description rather than an explanation. From an economist's perspective, the theory is lacking in that it does not have any behavioral basis but is essentially mechanistic.

What an economist really would wish to see is an explanation in which expenditure is driven by the choices of the individuals that constitute the economy. In the development model the change is just driven by the exogenous process of economic progress. Changes in expenditure should be related to how choices change as preferences or needs evolve over time.

4.3.2 Wagner's Law

Adolph Wagner was a nineteenth-century economist who analyzed data on public sector expenditure for several European countries, Japan, and the United States. These data revealed the fact that was shown in chapter 3: the share of the public sector in gross domestic product had been increasing over time. The content of Wagner's law was an explanation of this trend and a prediction that it would continue. In contrast to the basic developments models, Wagner's analysis provided a theory rather then just a description and an economic justification for the predictions.

The basis for the theory consists of three distinct components. First, it was observed that the growth of the economy results in an increase in complexity. Economic growth requires continual introduction of new laws and the development of the legal structure. Law and order imply continuing increases in public sector expenditure. Second, there was the process of urbanization and the increased externalities associated with it. These two factors have already been discussed in connection with the development models.

The final component underlying Wagner's law is the most behavioral of the three and is what distinguishes it from other explanations. Wagner argued that the goods supplied by the public sector have a high income elasticity of demand. This claim appears reasonable, for example, for education, recreation, and health care. Given this fact, as economic growth raises incomes, there will be an increase in demand for these products. In fact from a high elasticity it can be inferred that public sector expenditure does rise as a proportion of income. This conclusion is the substance of Wagner's law. There have been many attempts at establishing whether Wagner's law is empirically valid. The problem that surfaces in all of these tests is how to disentangle the causality between public expenditure and the level of income. Wagner's law proposes that it is income that explains expenditure. In contrast, there is much macroeconomic theory in favor of the argument that government spending explains the level of income—this was the essential insight of Keynesian economics. Tests to date have not convincingly resolved this issue.

In many ways Wagner's law provides a good explanation of public sector growth. Its main failing is that it concentrates solely on the demand for public sector services. What must determine the level is some interaction between demand and supply. The supply side is explicitly analyzed in the next model.

4.3.3   Baumol's Law

Rather than work from the observed data, Baumol's law starts from an observation about the nature of the production technology in the public sector. The basic hypothesis is that the technology of the public sector is labor-intensive relative to that of the private sector. In addition the type of production undertaken leaves little scope for increases in productivity and that makes it difficult to substitute capital for labor. As examples, hospitals need minimum numbers of nurses and doctors for each patient, and maximum class sizes place lower limits on teacher numbers in schools.

Competition on the labor market ensures that labor costs in the public sector are linked to those in the private sector. Although there may be some frictions in transferring between the two, wage rates cannot be too far out of line. However, in the private sector it is possible to substitute capital for labor when the relative cost of labor increases. Furthermore technological advances in the private sector lead to increases in productivity. These increases in productivity result in the return to labor rising. The latter claim is simply a consequence of optimal input use in the private sector resulting in the wage rate being equated to the marginal revenue product.

Since the public sector cannot substitute capital for labor, the wage increases in the private sector feed through into cost increases in the public sector. Maintaining a constant level of public sector output must therefore result in public sector expenditure increasing. If public sector output/private sector output remain in the same proportion, public sector expenditure rises as a proportion of total expenditure. This is Baumol's law, which asserts the increasing proportional size of the public sector.

There are a number of problems with this theory. It is entirely technology-driven and does not consider aspects of supply and demand or political processes. There are also reasons for believing that substitution can take place in the public sector. For example, additional equipment can replace nurses, and less qualified staff can take on more mundane tasks. Major productivity improvements have also been witnessed in universities and hospitals. Finally, there is evidence of a steady decline in public sector wages relative to those in the private sector. This reflects lower skilled labor being substituted for more skilled.

4.3.4   A Political Model

A political model of public sector expenditure needs to capture the conflict in public preferences between those who wish to have higher expenditure and those who wish to limit the burden of taxes. It must also incorporate the resolution of this conflict and show how the size and composition of actual public spending reflects the preferences of the majority of citizens as expressed through the political process. The political model we now describe is designed to achieve these aims. The main point that emerges is that the equilibrium level of public spending can be related to the income distribution, and more precisely that the growth of government is closely related to the rise of income inequality.

To illustrate this, consider an economy with H consumers whose incomes fall into a range between a minimum of 0 and a maximum of $\hat{y}$. The government provides a public good that is financed by the use of a proportional income tax. The utility of consumer i who has income y_i is given by

$$u_i(t, G) = [1 - t]y_i + b(G), \tag{4.1}$$

where t is the income tax rate and G the level of public good provision. The function $b(\cdot)$ represents the benefit obtained from the public good and it is assumed to be increasing (so the marginal benefit is positive) and concave (so the marginal benefit is falling) as G increases. We denote by μ the mean income level in the population of consumers, so the government budget constraint is

$$G = tH\mu. \tag{4.2}$$

Using this budget constraint, a consumer with income y_i will enjoy utility from provision of a quantity G of the public good of

$$u_i(G) = \left[1 - \frac{G}{H\mu}\right]y_i + b(G). \tag{4.3}$$

The ideal level of public good provision for the consumer is given by the first-order condition

$$\frac{\partial u_i(G)}{\partial G} \equiv -\frac{y_i}{H\mu} + b'(G) = 0. \tag{4.4}$$

This condition relates the marginal benefit of an additional unit of the public good, $b'(G)$, to its marginal cost $\frac{y_i}{H\mu}$. The quantity of the public good demanded by the consumer depends on their income relative to the mean since this determines the marginal cost.

The marginal benefit of the public good has been assumed to be a decreasing function of G, so it follows that the preferred public good level is decreasing as income rises. The reason for this is that with a proportional income tax the rich pay a higher share of the cost of public good than the poor. Thus public good provision will disproportionately benefit the poor.

The usual way to resolve the disagreement over the desired level of public good is to choose by majority voting. If the level of public good is to be determined by majority voting, which level will be chosen? In the context of this model the answer is clear-cut because all consumers would prefer the level of public good to be as close as possible to their preferred level. Given any pair of alternatives, consumers will vote for that which is closest to their preferred alternative. The alternative that is closest for the largest number of consumers will receive maximal support. There is in fact only one option that will satisfy this requirement: the option preferred by the consumer with the median income. The reason is that exactly one-half of the electorate, above the median income (the rich), would like less public good and the other half, below the median (the poor), would like more public good. Any alternative that is better for one group would be opposed by the other group with opposite preferences. (We explore the theory of voting in detail in chapter 10.)

The political equilibrium G^*, determined by the median voter, is then the solution to

$$b'(G^*) = \frac{y_m}{H\mu},\tag{4.5}$$

where $\frac{y_m}{\mu}$ is the income of the median voter relative to the mean. Since the marginal benefits decrease as public good provision increases, the political equilibrium level of public good increases with income inequality as measured by the ratio of the median to mean income. Accordingly, more inequality as measured by a lower ratio of the median to mean income would lead the decisive median voter to require more public spending.

Government activities are perceived as redistributive tools. Redistribution can be explicit, such as social security and poverty alleviation programs, or it can take a more disguised form like public employment which is probably the main channel of redistribution from rich to poor in many countries. Because of its nature, and interaction with the tax system, the demand for redistribution will increase as income inequality increases as demonstrated by this political model.

4.3.5   Ratchet Effect

Models of the ratchet effect develop the modeling of political interaction in a different direction. They assume that the preference of the government is to spend money. Explanations of why this should be so can be found in the economics of bureaucracy, which is explored in the next section. For now the fact is just taken as given. In contrast, it is assumed that the public do not want to pay taxes. Higher spending can only come from taxes, so by implication the public partially resists this; they do get some benefit from the expenditure. The two competing objectives are moderated by the fact that governments desire re-election. This makes it necessary for government to take some account of the public's preferences.

The equilibrium level of public sector expenditure is determined by the balance between these competing forces. In the absence of any exogenous changes or of changes in preferences, the level of expenditure will remain relatively constant. In the historical data on government expenditure, the periods prior to 1914, between 1920 and 1940, and post-1945 can be interpreted as displaying such constancy. Occasionally, though, economies go through periods of significant upheaval such as occurs during wartime. During these periods normal economic activity is disrupted. Furthermore the equilibrium between the government and the taxpayers becomes suspended. Ratchet models argue that wartime permits the government to raise expenditure with the consent of the taxpayers on the understanding that this is necessary to meet the exceptional needs that have arisen.

The final aspect of the argument is that the level of expenditure does not fall back to its original level after the period of upheaval. Several reasons can be advanced for this. First, the taxpayers become accustomed to the higher level of expenditure and perceive this as the norm. Second, debts incurred during the period of upheaval have to be paid off later. This requires the raising of finance. Third, promises made by the government to the taxpayers during periods of upheaval then have to be met. These can jointly be termed *ratchet effects* that sustain a higher level of spending. Finally, there may occur an *inspection effect* after an upheaval whereby the taxpayers and government reconsider their positions and priorities. The discovery of previously unnoticed needs then provides further justification for higher public sector spending.

The prediction of the ratchet-effect model is that spending remains relatively constant unless disturbed by some significant external event. These events can trigger substantial increases in expenditure. The ratchet and inspection effects work together to ensure that expenditure remains at the higher level until the next upheaval.

The description of expenditure growth given by this political model is broadly consistent with the data of chapter 3. Before 1914, between 1918 and 1940, and post-1945 the level of expenditure is fairly constant but steps up between these periods. Whether this provides support for the explanation is debatable because the model was constructed to explain these known facts. In other words, the data cannot be employed as evidence that the model is correct, given that the model was designed to explain that data.

4.4   Excessive Government

The theories of the growth of public sector expenditure described above attempt to explain the facts but do not offer comment on whether the level of expenditure is deficient or excessive. They merely describe processes and do not attempt to evaluate the outcome. There are in fact many economists who argue that public sector expenditure is too large and represents a major burden on the economy. While the evidence on this issue is certainly not conclusive, there are a number of explanations of why this should be so. Several are now described that reach their conclusions not through a cost–benefit analysis of expenditure but via an analysis of the functioning of government.

4.4.1   Bureaucracy

A traditional view of bureaucrats is that they are motivated solely by the desire to serve the common good. They achieve this by conducting the business of government in the most efficient manner possible without political or personal bias. This is the idealistic image of the bureaucrat as a selfless public servant. There is a possibility that such a view may be correct. Having said this, there is no reason why bureaucrats should be any different than other individuals. From this perspective it is difficult to accept that they are not subject to the same motivations of self-serving.

Adopting this latter perspective, the theoretical analysis of bureaucracy starts with the assumption that bureaucrats are indeed motivated by maximization of their private utilities. If they could, they would turn the power and influence that their positions give them into income. But, due to the nature of their role, they face difficulties in achieving this. Unlike similarly positioned individuals in the private sector, they cannot exploit the market to raise income. Instead, they resort to obtaining utility from pursuing nonpecuniary goals. A complex theory of bureaucracy may include many factors that influence utility such as patronage, power, and reputation. However, to construct a basic variant of the theory, it is sufficient to observe that most of these factors can be related to the size of the bureau. The bureaucrat can therefore be modeled as aiming to maximize the size of his bureau in order to obtain the greatest nonpecuniary benefits. It is as a result of this behavior that the size of government becomes excessive.

To demonstrate excessive bureaucracy, let y denote the output of the bureau as observed by the government. In response to an output y, the bureau is rewarded by the government with a budget of size $B(y)$. This budget increases as observed output rises $(B'(y) > 0)$ but at a falling rate $(B''(y) < 0)$. The cost of producing output is given by a cost function $C(y)$. Marginal cost is positive $(C'(y) > 0)$ and increasing $(C''(y) > 0)$. It is assumed that the government does not know this cost structure—only the bureaucrat fully understands the production process. What restrains the behavior of the bureaucrat is the requirement that the budget received from the government is sufficient to cover the costs of running the bureau.

The decision problem of the bureaucrat is then to choose output to maximize the budget subject to the requirement that the budget is sufficient to cover costs. This optimization can be expressed by the Lagrangian

$$L = B(y) + \lambda[B(y) - C(y)], \tag{4.6}$$

where λ is the Lagrange multiplier on the constraint that the budget equals cost. Differentiating the Lagrangian with respect to y and solving characterizes the optimum output from the perspective of the bureaucrat, y^b, by

$$B'(y^b) = \frac{\lambda}{\lambda + 1} C'(y^b). \tag{4.7}$$

Since the Lagrange multiplier, λ, is positive, this expression implies that $B' < C'$ at the bureaucrats optimum choice of output.

We wish to contrast the bureaucracy outcome with the outcome that occurs when the government has full information. With full information there exists a variety of different ways to model efficiency. One way would be to place the bureau within a more general setting and consider its output as one component of overall

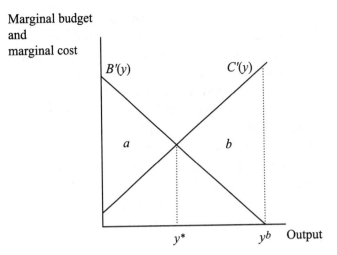

Figure 4.1
Excessive government

government intervention. A benefit–cost calculation for government intervention would then determine the efficient level of bureau output. A simpler alternative, and the one we choose to follow, is to determine the efficient output by drawing an analogy between the bureau and a profit-maximizing firm. The firm chooses its output to ensure that the difference between revenue and costs is made as large as possible. By this analogy, the bureau should choose output to maximize its budget less costs, $B(y) - C(y)$. For the bureau this is the equivalent of profit maximization.

Differentiating with respect to y, we equate the marginal effect of output on the budget to marginal cost to determine the efficient output y^*. The efficient output satisfies $B'(y^*) = C'(y^*)$. The output level chosen by the bureaucrat can easily be shown to be above the efficient level. This argument is illustrated in figure 4.1. The increasing marginal cost curve and declining marginal benefit curve are consequences of the assumptions already made. The efficient output occurs at the intersection of these curves. In contrast, the output chosen by the bureaucrat satisfies $B'(y^b) < C'(y^b)$, so it must lie to the right of y^*. In fact the budget covers costs when the area under the marginal budget curve a equals the area under the marginal cost curve b. It is clear from this figure that the size of the bureaucracy is excessive when it is determined by the choice of a bureaucrat.

This simple model shows how the pursuit of personal objectives by bureaucrats can lead to an excessive size of bureaucracy. Adding together the individual bureaus that comprise the public sector makes this excessive in aggregate. This excessive size is simply an inefficiency, since money is spent on bureaus that are not generating sufficiently valuable results.

The argument just given is enticing in its simplicity, but it is restricted by the fact that it is assumed that the bureaucrats have freedom to set the size of the bureau. There are various ways this limitation can be addressed. Useful extensions are to have the freedom constrained by political pressure or through a demand function. Although doing either of these would lessen the excess, the basic moral that bureaucrats have incentives to overly enlarge their bureaus would still remain. Whether they do so in practice is dependent on the constraints placed on them.

4.4.2   Budget-Setting

An alternative perspective on excessive bureaucracy can be obtained by considering a different process of budget determination. A motivation for this is the fact that each government department is headed by a politician who obtains satisfaction from the size of the budget. Furthermore, in many government systems, budgets for departments are determined annually by a meeting of cabinet. This meeting takes the budget bids from the individual departments and allocates a central budget on the basis of these. Providing a model incorporating these points then determines how departments' budgets evolve over time.

A simple process of this form can be the following: Let the budget for year t be given by B_t. The budget claim for year $t + 1$ is then given by

$$B^c_{t+1} = [1 + \alpha]B_t, \tag{4.8}$$

where $\alpha > 0$ is the rate at which departments inflate their budget claim. Such a rule represents a straightforward mechanical method of updating the budget claim— last year's is taken and a little more added. It is, of course, devoid of any basis in efficiency. The meeting of cabinet then takes these bids and proportionately reduces them to reach the final allocation. The agreed budget is written as

$$B_{t+1} = [1 - \gamma]B^c_{t+1} = [1 - \gamma][1 + \alpha]B_t, \tag{4.9}$$

where $0 < \gamma < 1$ is the rate at which the cabinet deflates each budget claim. The expression above gives a description of the change in the budget over time.

It can be seen that if $\alpha > \gamma$, then the budget will grow over time. Its development bears little relationship to needs, so there is every possibility that expenditure will eventually become excessive even if it initially begins at an acceptable level. When $\alpha < \gamma$, the budget will fall over time. Although either case is possible, the observed pattern of growth lends some weight to the former assumption.

This form of model could easily be extended to incorporate more complex dynamics but not really enhance the content of the simple story it tells. The modeling of budget determination as a process entirely independent of what is good for the economy provides an important alternative perspective on how the public sector may actually function. Even if the truth is not quite this stark, reasoning of this kind does put into context models that are based on the assumption that the government is informed and efficient.

4.4.3   Monopoly Power

The basis of elementary economics is that market equilibrium is determined via the balance of supply and demand. Those supplying the market are assumed to be distinct from those demanding the product. In the absence of monopoly power, the equilibrium that is achieved will be efficient. If the same reasoning could be applied to the goods supplied by the public sector, then efficiency would also arise there. Unfortunately, there are two reasons why efficiency is not possible. First, the public sector can award itself a monopoly in the supply of its goods and services. Second, this monopoly power may be extended into market capture.

Generally, a profit-maximizing monopolist will always want to restrict its level of output below the competitive level so that monopoly power will provide a tendency for too little government rather than the converse. This would be a powerful argument were it not for the fact that the government can choose not to exercise its monopoly power in this way. If it is attempting to achieve efficiency, then it will certainly not do so. Furthermore, since the government may not be following a policy of profit maximization, it might actually exploit its monopoly position to oversupply its output. This takes the analysis back in the direction of the bureaucracy model.

The idea of market capture is rather more interesting and arises from the nature of goods supplied by the public sector. Rather than being standard market goods, many of them are complex in nature and not fully understood by those consuming them. Natural examples of such goods would be education and health care. In both cases the consumer may not understand quite what the product is, nor what is best for them. Although this is important, it is also true of many other goods. The additional feature of the public sector commodities is that demand is not determined by the consumers and expressed through a market. Instead, it is delegated to specialists such as teachers and doctors. Furthermore these same specialists are also responsible for setting the level of supply. In this sense they can be said to capture the market.

The consequence of this market capture is that the specialists can set the level of output for the market that most meets their objectives. Naturally, since most would benefit from an expansion of their profession, within limits, this gives a mechanism that leads to supply in excess of the efficient level. The limits arise because they won't want to go so far that competition reduces the payment received or lowers standards too far. Effectively, they are reaching a trade-off between income and power, where the latter arises through the size of the profession. The resulting outcome has no grounds in efficiency and may well be too large.

4.4.4   Corruption

Corruption does not emerge as a moral aberration but as a general consequence of government officials using their power for personal gain. Corruption distorts the allocation of resources away from productive toward rent-seeking occupations. Rent-seeking (studied in chapter 11) is the attempt to obtain a return above what is judged adequate by the market. Monopoly profit is one example, but the concept is much broader. Corruption is not just redistributive (taking wealth from others to give it to some special interests), it can also have enormous efficiency costs. By discouraging the entrepreneurs on whom they prey, corruptible officials may have the effect of stunting economic growth.

Perhaps the most important form of corruption in many countries is predatory regulation. This is the process by which the government intentionally creates regulations that entrepreneurs have to pay bribes to get around. Because it raises the cost of productive activity, this form of corruption reduces efficiency. The damage is particularly large when several government officials, acting independently, create distinct obstacles to economic activity so that each can collect a separate bribe in return for removing the obstacle (e.g., creating the need for a license and then charging for it). When entrepreneurs face all these independent regulatory obstacles, they eventually cease trying, or else move into the underground economy to escape regulation altogether. Thus corruption is purely harmful from this perspective.

How could we give a positive role for a bribe-based corruption system? One possibility is that bribery is like an auction mechanism that directs resources to their best possible use. For example, corruption in procurement is similar to auctioning off the contract to the most efficient entrepreneur who can afford the highest bribe. However, there are some problems with this bribery-based system. First, we care about the means as well as the ends. Bribery is noxious. Allowing bribery will destroy much of the goodwill that supports the system. Second, people should not be punished for their honesty. Indeed, honest government officials can be used to create benchmarks by which to judge the performance of the more opportunistic officials. Third, it is impossible to optimize or even manage underground activities such as bribery.

4.4.5   Government Agency

Another explanation for excessive government is the lack of information available to voters. The imperfect information of voters enables the government to grow larger by increasing the tax burden. From this perspective government growth reflects the abuse of power by greedy bureaucrats. The central question is then how to set incentives that encourage the government to work better and to cost less, subject to the information available.

To illustrate this point, consider a situation in which the cost to the government of supplying a public good can vary. The unit cost is either low, at c_ℓ, or is high, at c_h. The gross benefit to the public from a level G of public good is given by the function $b(G)$ that is increasing and concave. The net benefit is $b(G) - t$, where t is the tax paid to the government for the public good provision. The chosen quantity of the public good will depend on the unit cost of the government. The benefit to the government of providing the public good is the difference between the tax and the cost. So, when the cost is c_i, the benefit is $t_i - c_i G_i$.

When the public is informed about the level of cost of the government, the quantity of public good will be chosen to maximize the net benefit subject to the government breaking even. For cost c_i, the public net benefit with the government breaking even is $b(G_i) - c_i G_i$. The public will demand a level of public good such that the marginal benefit is equal to the marginal cost, so $b'(G_i) = c_i$, and will pay the government $t_i = c_i G_i$, for $i = h, \ell$. This is shown in figure 4.2.

Now assume that the public cannot observe whether the government has cost c_ℓ or c_h. The government can then benefit by misrepresenting the cost to the public: for instance, it can exaggerate the cost by adding expenditures that benefit the government but not the public. When the cost is high, the government cannot exaggerate. When the cost is low, the government is better off pretending the cost

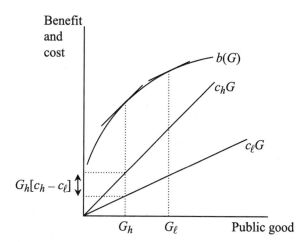

Figure 4.2
Government agency

is high to get tax t_h for the amount G_h of public good instead of getting t_ℓ for producing G_ℓ. Misrepresenting in this way leads to the benefit of $G_h[c_h - c_\ell]$ for the government, which is shown in figure 4.2.

To eliminate this temptation taxpayers must pay an extra amount $r > 0$ to the government in excess of its cost when the government pretends to have the low cost. This is called the *informational rent*. Since the truly high-cost government cannot further inflate its cost, the public pay $t_h = c_h G_h$ when the government reports a high cost. If the reported cost is low, the taxpayers demand the amount G_ℓ of public good defined by $b'(G_\ell) = c_\ell$ and pay the government $t_\ell = c_\ell G_\ell + r$, where r is exactly the extra revenue the government could have made if it had pretended to have high cost. To give a government with a low cost just enough revenue to offset its temptation to pretend to have higher cost, it is necessary that $r = [c_h - c_\ell]G_h$. This is the rent required to induce truthful revelation of the cost and have the provision of the public good equal to that when the public is fully informed.

It is possible for the taxpayers to reduce this excess payment by demanding that the high-cost government supply less than it would with full information. Assume that cost is low with probability p_ℓ and high with probability $p_h = 1 - p_\ell$. By maximizing their expected benefit subject to the government telling the truth, it can be shown that revelation can be obtained at the least cost by demanding an amount G_h of public services defined by

$$b'(G_h) = c_h + \frac{p_\ell}{1 - p_\ell}[c_h - c_\ell]. \qquad (4.10)$$

This quantity is lower than that with full information. The distortion of the quantity demanded from the high-cost government results from a simple cost–benefit argument. It trades off the benefit of reducing the rent, which is proportional to the cost difference $c_h - c_\ell$, and the probability p_ℓ that the government is of the low-cost type against the cost of imposing the distortion of the quantity on the high-cost government that occurs with probability $1 - p_\ell$.

Therefore, if the government is truly low cost, it need not be given the high tax. However, to eliminate the temptation for cost inflation, taxpayers have to provide the government just enough of the rent as a reward for reporting truthfully when its cost of public services is low. Because the ability of the government to misrepresent its costs allows it to earn rents and distort the level of provision, eventually the informational rent makes the government bigger than it should be.

4.4.6   Cost Diffusion

The last explanation we present for the possibility of excessively large government is the *common resource* problem. The idea is that spending authorities are dispersed while the treasury has the responsibility of collecting enough revenue to balance the overall budget. Each of the spending authorities has its own spending priorities, with little consideration for others' priorities, that it can be better met by raiding the overall budget. This is the common resource problem, just like that of several oil companies tapping into a common pool underground or fishermen netting in a single lake. In all cases it leads to excess pressure on the common resource. From this perspective a single committee with expenditure authority would have a much better sense of the opportunity cost of public funds, and could better compare the merits of alternative proposals, than the actual dispersed spending authorities. The current trend toward federalism and devolution aggravates this common-pool problem. The reason is essentially that each district can impose projects whose cost is shared by all other districts and so they support higher size projects than they would if they had to cover the full costs. We discuss in more detail the various aspects of federalism in chapter 17.

The problem can also be traced down to the individual level. Consider public services like pensions, health care, and schools and infrastructure work like bridges, roads, and railtracks. It is clear that for these public services, and many others, the government does not charge the direct users the full marginal cost but subsidizes the activities partly or wholly from tax revenues. There is an obvious equity concern behind this fact. But it is then natural that users who do not bear the full cost will support more public services than they would if they had to cover the full cost. The same argument applies in the opposite direction when contemplating some cut in public spending: contributors who are asked to make concessions are concentrated and possibly organized through a lobby with large per capita benefits from continued provision of specific public services. In contrast, the beneficiaries of downsizing public spending, the taxpayers as a whole, are diffuse with small per capita stakes. This makes it less likely that they can offer organized support for the reform. To sum up, many public services are characterized by the concentration of benefits to a small group of users or recipients and the diffusion of costs to the large group of taxpayers. This results in biases toward continuous demand for more public spending.

4.5   Conclusions

This chapter has provided a number of theories of public sector growth that are designed to explain the data exhibited in chapter 3. Each theory has some points to commend it, but none is entirely persuasive. It is fair to say that all provide a partial insight and have some element of truth. A more general story drawing together the full set of components, including the ratchet effect, income effect, political process, production technology, and bureaucracy would have much in its favor. This would be especially so if combined with the voting models of chapter 10.

The bureaucracy models are particularly attractive because they show how economic analysis can be applied to what appears to be a noneconomic problem. In doing so, they generate an interesting conclusion that casts doubt on the efficiency of government. This illustrates how the method of economic reasoning can be applied to understand the outcome of what is at first sight a noneconomic problem.

The perennial question of whether the government has grown too large is difficult to answer. The reason is that the government is both complementary to the market and a competitor of the market. As a major employer the government competes with businesses looking to hire talented people. The possibility that the best and brightest become public officials and politicians, rather than entrepreneurs, is considered by many as very costly to society, since they are seen as devoting their talents to taking wealth from others rather than creating it. When people pay taxes, they have less money to spend on other goods and services provided by the market. Likewise, when the government borrows money, it competes with companies looking to raise capital. In some areas like health care and education, public and private services compete with each other. But at the same time the government also serves as useful complement to every business activity by providing basic infrastructure and civil order. Every business depends on the government for things like protection of life and property, a transportation network, civil courts, and a stable currency. Without these things, people couldn't do business.

Finally, whether an activity is carried out in the public sector or the private sector is itself endogenous. As in architecture, the functions suggest the form. Take the example of education where the goals are multiple (literacy, vocational skills, citizenship, equality of chance, preparation for life) and not precisely measurable and where several stakeholders are involved (parents, employers, students, teachers, taxpayers) with possibly conflicting interests. It is not immediately clear that the market with its single-minded focus can cope adequately with all these aspects, and the risk is that the market could bias the activity toward dimensions that matter more for profit-making.

Further Reading

The concept of the minimal state is explored in:

Nozick, R. 1974. *Anarchy, State and Utopia*. Oxford: Basil Blackwell.

An account of Wagner's law can be found in:

Bird, R. M. 1971. Wagner's law of expanding state activity. *Public Finance* 26: 1–26.

Recent empirical tests are reviewed in:

Peacock, A. K., and A. Scott. 2000. The curious attraction of Wagner's Law. *Public Choice* 102: 1–17.

The classic study of public sector growth is:

Peacock, A. K., and Wiseman, J. 1961. *The Growth of Public Expenditure in the UK*. Princeton: Princeton University Press.

A nontechnical account on corruption and government is:

Rose-Ackerman, S. 1999. *Corruption and Government: Causes, Consequences and Reform*. Cambridge: Cambridge University Press.

The theory of bureaucracy was first developed in:

Niskanen, W. A. 1974. Non-market decision making: The peculiar economics of bureaucracy. *American Economic Review* 58: 293–305.

A fascinating book on bureaucracy from a political scientist is:

Wilson, J. Q. 1989. *Bureaucracy: What Government Agencies Do and Why They Do It*. New York: Basic Books.

The political theory of the size of the government is based on:

Meltzer, A., and Richard, S. 1981. A rational theory of the size of government. *Journal of Political Economy* 89: 914–27.

The main reference on government agency is:

Laffont, J.-J. 2001. *Incentives and Political Economy*. Oxford: Oxford University Press.

Exercises

4.1.   Can trade occur in a world with no rules? Is it ever possible to have no rules?

4.2.   If it takes four days of labor to produce a week's food, and one day of labor to steal a week's food, what will be the equilibrium outcome?

4.3.   Would a minimal state finance a fire service?

4.4.   Do the data of chapter 3 support the view that governments have expanded beyond the minimal state?

4.5.   Discuss whether provision of state education enhances efficiency or equity. What about health care?

4.6.   Would a minimal state:

a. Ensure that wage agreements are enforced?

b. Limit maximum working hours?

c. Prevent involuntary overtime?

4.7.   Will efficiency be achieved if:

a. No agent knows what the profit level of a firm will be next year?

b. One agent does know what the profit level will be?

4.8.   Can insider trading occur in the idealized competitive economy?

4.9.   All our sulphur emissions are blown into a neighboring country. Can our economy be efficient?

4.10.   Are the following policies conducted for efficiency or equity motives:

a. Provision of unemployment benefits?

b. Provision of primary education?

c. Provision of higher education?

d. Provision of retirement pensions?

e. Prohibiting smoking in public places?

f. Imposing higher marginal income tax rates on people with higher incomes?

In the case of efficiency motives, discuss the type of market failure involved.

4.11.   Should the government intervene with a redistributive policy if income inequality is due to:

a. Differences in work effort?

b. Differences in ability?

4.12.   Consider two consumers who each have a total of T hours to allocate between production and theft. Assume that production produces output $y_p = \log(t_p)$ for t_p units of time in production. If time t_f is devoted to theft, then a proportion $\frac{\alpha t_f}{T}$ of the other consumer's output can be stolen. Assuming that each unit of output has price p and both consumers attempt to maximize their wealth, what is the equilibrium? How does the equilibrium depend on the value of α? What is the equilibrium if there is no theft? What is the maximum that would be paid to prevent theft?

4.13.   Describe the expenditures at each stage of the development process in terms of efficiency and equity.

4.14.   a. Provide a graphical two-commodity (one private good and one public good) example of a preference relation generating an income elasticity of the demand for public good that is greater than one.

b. Show that in this case the fraction of the budget spent on public good increases as income increases. Explain also why the indifference curve in this two-commodity space is negatively sloped and convex (preferences are convex if for any two points on the same indifference curve the line segment between them is in the "weakly preferred" set, which is defined as the set of commodity bundles (weakly) preferred to any bundle that lies on the indifference curve.)

4.15.   In the same two-commodity economy as in the previous exercise, keeping constant the price of the private good:

a. Give a graphical illustration of a preference relation generating a price elasticity of demand for public good that is less than one in absolute value.

b. Show that in this case the fraction of the budget spent on the public good increases as the (relative) price of public good increases.

4.16.   Assume that the demand for public output at time t, G_t, is given by the demand function $G_t = [Y_t]^{\alpha}$, where Y_t is national income at time t.

a. What is the income elasticity of demand?

b. For what values α of does Wagner's law hold? Show that expenditure on public output rises as a fraction of income for these values.

c. Assume that national income growth is determined by $Y_{t+1} = \beta Y_t + [\bar{G} - G_t]$. Will an increase in G_t raise Y_t in the cases where Wagner's law applies? Explain the answer.

4.17.   Obtain data on public sector expenditure as a proportion of gross domestic product since 1970. Is expenditure still growing? Assess the answer relative to the arguments of the development model. Do the data describe a relation of demand to income that supports Wagner's law?

4.18.   Sketch a story of learning about preferences that supports the ratchet effect.

4.19.   Assume that the rental rate for capital is fixed at r. If the private sector has a production function $y = K^{1/2}[tL]^{1/2}$ and sells output at price p, what happens to the wage rate as technical progress increases t? What would happen if r were not fixed? Relate your answer to Baumol's law.

4.20.   Suppose that the production function is $y = \log(K) + \log(tL)$. If demand is constant and labor productivity doubles, what happens to labor demand? What will happen to the wage rate if the economy has many firms in this position? Does this analysis support Baumol's law?

4.21.   Consider a simplified setting for Baumol's law where there is no capital. Let the private sector have the production technology $y^p = tL$, where L is labor input and t denotes exogenous technical progress that occurs as time passes.

a. With output price p, use the condition of zero profit at the competitive equilibrium to determine the wage rate.

b. Calculate the cost function for the firm.

c. Let the public sector have production function $y^g = L$. Show that the ratio of marginal costs in the two sectors grows at rate t.

d. Find the equilibrium path for the economy if it has a single consumer, with preferences given by $U = \log(y^p) + \log(y^g)$, who can supply one unit of labor in each time period. Comment on the relative size of the public sector.

4.22.   Describe the benefits a bureaucrat can obtain from an increase in bureau size. Are there any private costs?

4.23.   Do regular changes in government assist or hinder bureaucrats in expanding their bureaus?

4.24.   Why might it be better to tolerate bureaus of excessive size rather than permit bureaucrats to seek rewards in cash?

4.25.   a. In the model of bureaucracy, let $B(y) = y^{1/2}$ and $C(y) = y^2$. Calculate the value y^* that maximizes $B(y) - C(y)$. For what values of y does $B(y) = C(y)$? Use this to find y^b. Show that $y^b > y^*$.

b. Now let the bureaucrat's income be given by $M = a + by$, and let his utility be given by $U = B(y) + M$. Does this alter the chosen value of y^b?

c. Is there any pay scale relating y to M that can lead the bureaucrat to choose y^*?

4.26.   How can right-wing and left-wing governments be modeled using the budget-setting framework?

4.27.   Consider a profession with n members and revenue determined by $r = bn - [\frac{1}{2}]n^2$. What value of n maximizes total revenue? What value maximizes revenue per member of the profession? If the benefit from the profession is vn, what is the efficient member-ship? Contrast these three membership levels.

4.28.   a. For the inverse demand function $p = a - by$ and cost function $C(y) = cy$, contrast the output choices of a profit-maximizing monopolist, an output-maximizing monopolist and a revenue-maximizing monopolist. Which is the best description of the public sector?

b. Now let the number of members in a profession be n. Given a fixed price p for output and a cost function $\frac{C(y)}{n}$, calculate the values of y and n that maximize per capita profit. What are the efficient values of y and n?

4.29.   Consider an economy with two goods (consumption and labor) in which individuals differ only in their income-generating ability a_i. Suppose that the distribution of abilities in the population is such that the median ability level, a_m, is strictly less than the average ability level, $\bar{a}$. Suppose that the income level of each individual i is $y_i = [1 - t]a_i$, where $t > 0$ is the proportional income tax rate. Suppose also that all tax revenues are redistributed through a uniform lump-sum grant g.

a. What is the tax rate which maximizes the lump-sum grant?

b. Using the fact that individual i's after-tax income is equal to $g + [1 - t]y_i$, show that income equality requires $t = 1$ and that the poorest ($a_i = 0$ and so $y_i = 0$) can be better off with a lower tax rate (and thus more inequality).

c. If every individual i's preference over (t, g) is $v_i = g + \frac{1}{2}[1 - t]^2 a_i$, then what will be the tax rate chosen by majority voting? (*Hint*: The median ability individual is the decisive voter in this model.)

d. Show that the majority voting tax rate is increasing with the difference between the average and the median ability levels, $\bar{a} - a_m > 0$. Does that mean that increasing inequality raises the relative size of the public sector (as measured by the tax rate)?

III DEPARTURES FROM EFFICIENCY

5 Public Goods

5.1 Introduction

When a government provides a level of national defense sufficient to make a country secure, all inhabitants are simultaneously protected. Equally, when a radio program is broadcast, it can be received simultaneously by all listeners in range of the transmitter. The possibility for many consumers to benefit from a single unit of provision violates the assumption of the private nature of goods underlying the efficiency analysis of chapter 2. The Two Theorems relied on all goods being private in nature, so they can only be consumed by a single consumer. If there are goods such as national defense in the economy, market failure occurs and the unregulated competitive equilibrium will fail to be efficient. This inefficiency implies that there is a potential role for government intervention.

The chapter begins by defining a public good and distinguishing between public goods and private goods. Doing so provides considerable insight into why market failure arises when there are public goods. The inefficiency is then demonstrated by analyzing the equilibrium that is achieved when it is left to the market to provide public goods. The Samuelson rule characterizing the optimal level of the public good is then derived. This permits a comparison of equilibrium and optimum.

The focus of the chapter then turns to the consideration of methods through which the optimum can be achieved. The first of these, the Lindahl equilibrium, is based on observation that the price each consumer pays for the public good should reflect their valuation of it. The Lindahl equilibrium achieves optimality, but since the valuations are private information, it generates incentives for consumers to provide false information. Mechanisms designed to elicit the correct statement of these valuations are then considered. The theoretical results are contrasted with the outcomes of experiments designed to test the extent of false statement of valuations and the use of market data to calculate valuations. These results are primarily static in nature. To provide some insight into the dynamic aspects of public good provision, the chapter is completed by the analysis of two different forms of fund-raising campaign that permit sequential contributions.

5.2   Definitions

The *pure public good* has been the subject of most of the economic analysis of public goods. In many ways the pure public good is an abstraction that is adopted to provide a benchmark case against which other, more realistic, cases can be assessed. A pure public good has the following two properties:

· *Nonexcludability*   If the public good is supplied, no consumer can be excluded from consuming it.

· *Nonrivalry*   Consumption of the public good by one consumer does not reduce the quantity available for consumption by any other.

In contrast, a *private good* is excludable at no cost and is perfectly rivalrous: if it is consumed by one person, then none of it remains for any other. Although they were not made explicit, these properties of a private good have been implicit in how we have analyzed market behavior in earlier chapters. As we will see, the efficiency of the competitive economy is dependent on them.

The two properties that characterize a public good have important implications. Consider a firm that supplies a pure public good. Since the good is non-excludable, if the firm supplies one consumer, then it has effectively supplied the public good to all. The firm can charge the initial purchaser but cannot charge any of the subsequent consumers. This prevents it from obtaining payment for the total consumption of the public good. The fact that there is no rivalry in consumption implies that the consumers should have no objection to multiple consumption. These features prevent the operation of the market equalizing marginal valuations as it does to achieve efficiency in the allocation of private goods.

In practice, it is difficult to find any good that perfectly satisfies both the conditions of nonexcludability and nonrivalry precisely. For example, the transmission of a television signal will satisfy nonrivalry, but exclusion is possible at finite cost by scrambling the signal. Similar comments apply, for example, to defense spending, which will eventually be rivalrous as a country of fixed size becomes crowded and from which exclusion is possible by deportation. Most public goods eventually suffer from congestion when too many consumers try to use them simultaneously. For example, parks and roads are public goods that can become congested. The effect of congestion is to reduce the benefit the public good yields to each user. Public goods that are excludable, but at a cost, or suffer from congestion beyond some level of use are called *impure*. The properties of impure public goods place them between the two extremes of private goods and pure public goods.

	Rivalrous	Non-rivalrous
Excludable	Private good	Club good
Non-excludable	Common property resource	Public good

Figure 5.1
Typology of goods

A simple diagram summarizing the different types of good and the names given to them is shown in figure 5.1. These goods vary in the properties of excludability and rivalry. In fact it is helpful to envisage a continuum of goods that gradually vary in nature as they become more rivalrous or more easily excludable.

The pure private good and the pure public good have already been identified. An example of a common property good is a lake that can be used for fishing by anyone who wishes, or a field that can be used for grazing by any farmer. This class of goods (usually called *the commons*) are studied in chapter 7. The problem with the commons is the tendency of overusing them, and the usual solution is to establish property rights to govern access. This is what happened in the sixteenth century in England where common land was enclosed and became property of the local landlords. The landlords then charged grazing fees, and so cut back the use. In some instances property rights are hard to define and enforce, as is the case of the control over the high seas or air quality. For this reason only voluntary cooperation can solve the international problems of overfishing, acid rain, and greenhouse effect. Club goods are public goods for which exclusion is possible. The terminology is motivated by sport clubs whose facilities are a public good for members but from which nonmembers can be excluded. Clubs are studied in chapter 6.

5.3   Private Provision

Public goods do not conform to the assumptions required for a competitive economy to be efficient. Their characteristics of nonexcludability and nonrivalry lead to the wrong incentives for consumers. Since they can share in consumption, each consumer has an incentive to rely on others to make purchases of the public good. This reliance on others to purchase is call *free-riding*, and it is this that leads to inefficiency.

To provide a model that can reveal the motive for free-riding and its consequences, consider two consumers who have to allocate their incomes between purchases of a private good and of a public good. Assume that the consumers take the prices of the two goods as fixed when they make their decisions. If the goods were both private, we could move immediately to the conclusion that an efficient equilibrium would be attained. What makes the public good different is that each consumer derives a benefit from the purchases of the other. This link between the consumers, which is absent with private goods, introduces strategic interaction into the decision processes. With the strategic interaction the consumers are involved in a game, so equilibrium is found using the concept of a Nash equilibrium.

The consumers have income levels M^1 and M^2. Income must be divided between purchases of the private good and the public good. Both goods are assumed to have a price of 1. With x^h used to denote purchase of the private good by consumer h and g^h to denote purchase of the public good, the choices must satisfy the budget constraint $M^h = x^h + g^h$. The link between consumers comes from the fact that the consumption of the public good for each consumer is equal to the total quantity purchased, $g^1 + g^2$. Hence, when making the purchase decision, each consumer must take account of the decision of the other.

This interaction is captured in the preferences of consumer h by writing the utility function as

$$U^h(x^h, g^1 + g^2). \tag{5.1}$$

The standard Nash assumption is now imposed that each consumer takes the purchase of the other as given when they make their decision. By this assumption, consumer 1 chooses g^1 to maximize utility given g^2, while consumer 2 chooses g^2 given g^1. This can be expressed by saying that the choice of consumer 1 is the best reaction to g^2 and that of consumer 2 the best reaction to g^1. The Nash equilibrium occurs when these reactions are mutually compatible, so that the choice of each is the best reaction to the choice of the other.

The Nash equilibrium can be displayed by analyzing the preferences of the two consumers over different combination of g^1 and g^2. Consider consumer 1. Using the budget constraint, we can write their utility as $U^1(M^1 - g^1, g^1 + g^2)$. The indifference curves of this utility function are shown in figure 5.2. These can be

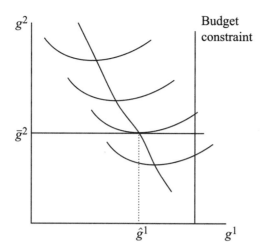

Figure 5.2
Preferences and choice

understood by noting that an increase in g^2 will always lead to a higher utility level for any value of g^1. For given g^2, an increase in g^1 will initially increase utility as more preferred combinations of private and public good are achieved. Eventually, further increases in g^1 will reduce utility as the level of private good consumption becomes too small relative to that of public good. The income level places an upper limit upon g^1.

Consumer 1 takes the provision of 2 as given when making their choice. Consider consumer 2 having chosen $\bar{g}^2$. The choices open to consumer 1 then lie along the horizontal line drawn at $\bar{g}^2$ in figure 5.2. The choice that maximizes the utility of consumer 1 occurs at the tangency of an indifference curve and the horizontal line—this is the highest indifference curve they can reach. This is shown as the choice $\hat{g}^1$. In the terminology we have chosen, $\hat{g}^1$ is the best reaction to $\bar{g}^2$. Varying the level of $\bar{g}^2$ will lead to another best reaction for consumer 1. Doing this for all possible $\bar{g}^2$ traces out the optimal choices of g^1 shown by the locus through the lowest point on each indifference curve. This locus is known as the *Nash reaction function* (or *best-response function*) and depicts the value of g^1 that will be chosen in response to a value of g^2. This construction can be repeated for consumer 2 and leads to figure 5.3. For consumer 2, utility increases with g^1, and thus indifference curves further to the right reflect higher utility levels. The best reaction for consumer 2 is shown by $\hat{g}^2$, which occurs where the indifference curve is tangential to the vertical line at $\bar{g}^1$. The Nash reaction function links the points where the indifference curves are vertical.

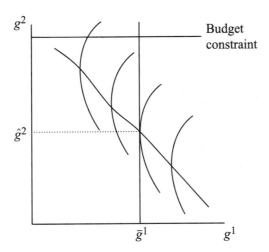

Figure 5.3
Best reaction for 2

The Nash equilibrium occurs where the choices of the two consumers are the best reactions to each other, so neither has an incentive to change their choice. This can only hold at a point where the Nash reaction functions cross. The equilibrium is illustrated in figure 5.4 in which the reaction functions are simultaneously satisfied at their intersection. By definition, $\hat{g}^1$ is the best reaction to $\hat{g}^2$ and $\hat{g}^2$ is the best reaction to $\hat{g}^1$. The equilibrium is privately optimal: if a consumer were to unilaterally raise or reduce his purchase, then he would move to a lower indifference curve.

Having determined the equilibrium, its welfare properties can now be addressed. From the construction of the reaction functions, it follows that at the equilibrium the indifference curve of consumer 1 is horizontal and that of consumer 2 is vertical. This is shown in figure 5.5. It can be seen that all the points in the shaded area are Pareto-preferred to the equilibrium—moving to one of these points will make both consumers better off. Starting at the equilibrium these points can be achieved by both consumers simultaneously raising their purchase of the public good. The Nash equilibrium is therefore not Pareto-efficient, although it is privately efficient. No further Pareto improvements can be made when a point is reached where the indifference curves are tangential. The locus of these tangencies, which constitutes the set of Pareto-efficient allocations, is also shown in figure 5.5.

The analysis has demonstrated that when individuals privately choose the quantity of the public goods they purchase, the outcome is Pareto-inefficient. A Pareto improvement can be achieved by all consumers increasing the purchases

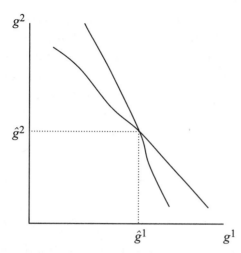

Figure 5.4
Nash equilibrium

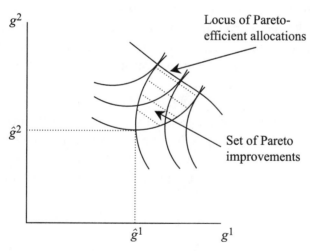

Figure 5.5
Inefficiency of equilibrium

of public goods. Consequently, compared to Pareto-preferred allocations, the total level of the public good consumed is too low. Why is this so? The answer can be attributed to strategic interaction and the free-riding that results. The free-riding emerges from each consumer relying on the other to provide the public good and thus avoiding the need to provide themselves. Since both consumers are attempting to free-ride in this way, too little of the public good is ultimately purchased. In the absence of government intervention or voluntary cooperation, inefficiency arises.

5.4   Efficient Provision

Efficiency in consumption for private goods is guaranteed by each consumer equating their marginal rate of substitution to the price ratio. The strategic interaction inherent with public goods does not ensure such equality. At a Pareto-efficient allocation with the public good, the indifference curves are tangential. However, this does not imply equality of the marginal rates of substitution because the indifference curves are defined over quantities of the public good purchased by the two consumers. As will soon be shown, the efficiency condition involves the sum of marginal rates of substitution and is termed the *Samuelson rule* in honor of its discoverer.

The basis for deriving the Samuelson rule is to observe that in figure 5.5 the locus of Pareto-efficient allocations has the property that the indifference curves of the two consumers are tangential. The gradient of these indifference curves is given by the rate at which g^2 can be traded for g^1 keeping utility constant. The tangency conditions can then be expressed by requiring that the gradients are equal, so

$$\left.\frac{dg^2}{dg^1}\right|_{U^1 const.} = \left.\frac{dg^2}{dg^1}\right|_{U^2 const.} \tag{5.2}$$

Calculating the derivatives using the utility functions (5.1), we write the efficiency condition (5.2) as

$$\frac{U_x^1 - U_G^1}{U_G^1} = \frac{U_G^2}{U_x^2 - U_G^2}. \tag{5.3}$$

The marginal rate of substitution between the private and the public good for consumer h is defined by $MRS_{G,x}^h = \frac{U_G^h}{U_x^h}$. This can be used to rearrange (5.3) in the form

$$\left[\frac{1}{MRS_{G,x}^1} - 1\right]\left[\frac{1}{MRS_{G,x}^2} - 1\right] = 1. \tag{5.4}$$

Multiplying across by $MRS_{G,x}^1 \times MRS_{G,x}^2$, we solve (5.4) and get the final expression

$$MRS_{G,x}^1 + MRS_{G,x}^2 = 1. \tag{5.5}$$

This is the two-consumer version of the Samuelson rule.

To interpret this rule, the marginal rate of substitution should be viewed as a measure of the marginal benefit of another unit of the public good. The marginal cost of a unit of public good is one unit of private good. Therefore the rule says that an efficient allocation is achieved when the total marginal benefit of another unit of the public good, which is the sum of the individual benefits, is equal to the marginal cost of another unit. The rule can easily be extended to incorporate additional consumers: the total benefit remains the sum of the individual benefits.

Further insight into the Samuelson rule can be obtained by contrasting it with the corresponding rule for efficient provision of two private goods. For two consumers, 1 and 2, and two private goods, i and j, this is

$$MRS_{i,j}^1 = MRS_{i,j}^2 = MRT_{i,j}, \tag{5.6}$$

where $MRT_{i,j}$ denotes the marginal rate of transformation, the number of units of one good the economy has to given up to obtain an extra unit of the other good (The $MRT_{G,x}$ between public and private good was assumed to be equal to 1 in the derivation of the Samuelson rule.) The difference between (5.5) and (5.6) arises because an extra unit of the public good increases the utility of all consumers so that the social benefit of this extra unit is found by summing the marginal benefits. This does not require equalization of the marginal benefit of all consumers. In contrast, an extra unit of private good can only be given to one consumer or another. Efficiency then occurs when it does not matter who the extra unit is given to so that the marginal benefits of all consumers are equalized.

The Samuelson rule provides a very simple description of the efficient outcomes, but this does not mean that efficiency is easily obtained. It was already shown that it will not be achieved if there is no government intervention and agents act noncooperatively (i.e., adopt Nash behavior). But what form should government intervention take? The most direct solution would be for the government to take total responsibility for provision of the public good and to finance it through lump-sum taxation. Because lump-sum taxes do not cause any distortions, this would ensure satisfaction of the rule. However, there are numerous difficulties in using lump-sum taxation, which will be explored in detail in chapter 12. The same shortcomings apply here, thus ruling out the employment of lump-sum taxes. The use of other forms of taxation would introduce their own distortions, and these would prevent efficiency being achieved. In addition, to apply the Samuelson rule, the government must know the individual benefits from public good provision. In practice, this information is not readily available, and the government must rely on what individuals choose to reveal.

The consequence of these observations is that efficiency will not be attained through direct public good provision if financed by distortionary taxes. Hence we have the motivation for considering alternative allocation mechanisms that can provide the correct level of public good by eliciting preferences from consumers.

5.5   Voting

The failure of private actions to provide a public good efficiently suggests that alternative allocation mechanisms need to be considered. There are a range of responses that can be adopted to counteract the market failure, ranging from intervention with taxation through to direct provision by the government. In practice, the level of provision for public goods is frequently determined by the political process, with competing parties in electoral systems differing in the level of public good provision they promise. The selection of one of the parties by voting then determines the level of public good provision.

We have already obtained a first insight into the provision of public goods by voting in chapter 4. That analysis focused on voting over the tax rate as a proxy for government size when people had different income levels. What we wish to do here is provide a contrast between the voting outcome and the efficient level of public good provision when people differ in tastes and income levels. Consider a population of consumers who determine the quantity of public good to be provided by a majority vote. The cost of the public good is shared equally among the consumers, so, if G units of the public good are supplied, the cost to each consumer is $\frac{G}{H}$. With income M^h, a consumer can purchase private goods to the value of $M^h - \frac{G}{H}$ after paying for the public good. This provides an effective price of $\frac{1}{H}$ for each unit of the public good and a level of utility $U^h(M^h - \frac{G}{H}, G)$. The budget constraint, the highest attainable indifference curves and the most preferred quantity of public good are shown in the upper part of figure 5.6.

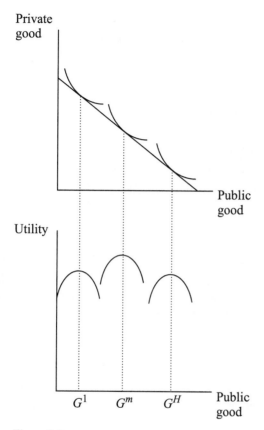

Figure 5.6
Allocation through voting

So that the Median Voter Theorem can be applied (see chapter 10 for details), assume that there is an odd number, H, of consumers, where $H > 2$, and that each of the consumers has single-peaked preferences for the public good. This second assumption implies that when the level of utility is graphed against the quantity of public good, there will be a single value of G^h that maximizes utility for consumer h. Such preferences are illustrated in the lower panel of figure 5.6. The consumers are numbered so that their preferred levels of public good satisfy $G^1 < G^2 < \cdots < G^H$.

By these assumptions, the Median Voter Theorem ensures that the consumer with the median preference for the public good will be decisive in the majority vote. The median preference belongs to the consumer at position $\frac{H+1}{2}$ in the ranking. We label the median consumer as m and denote their chosen quantity of the public good by G^m. A remarkable feature of the majority voting outcome is that nobody is able to manipulate the outcome to their advantage by misrepresenting their preference, so sincere voting is the best strategy. The reason is that anyone to the left of the median can only affect the final outcome by voting for a quantity to the right of the median that would move the outcome further away from their preferred position, and vice versa for anyone to the right of the median.

Having demonstrated that voting will reveal preferences and that the voting outcome will be the quantity G^m, it now remains to ask whether the voting outcome is efficient. The value G^m is the preferred choice of consumer m, so it solves

$$\max_{\{G\}} \ U^m\left(M^m - \frac{G}{H}, G\right), \tag{5.7}$$

where M^m denotes the income of the median voter that can differ from the median income with heterogeneous preferences. The first-order condition for the maximization can be expressed in terms of the marginal rate of substitution to show that the voting outcome is described by

$$MRS^m = \frac{1}{H}. \tag{5.8}$$

In contrast, because the marginal rate of transformation is equal to 1, the efficient outcome satisfies the Samuelson rule

$$\sum_{h=1}^{H} MRS^h = 1. \tag{5.9}$$

Contrasting these, the voting outcome is efficient only if

$$MRS^m = \sum_{h=1}^{H} \frac{MRS^h}{H}. \tag{5.10}$$

Therefore majority voting leads to efficient provision of the public good only if the median voter's MRS is equal to the mean MRS of the population of voters. There is no reason to expect that it will, so it must be concluded that majority voting will not generally achieve an efficient outcome. This is because the voting outcome does not take account of preferences other than those of the median voter: changing all the preferences except those of the median voter does not affect the voting outcome (although it would affect the optimal level of public good provision).

Can any comments be offered on whether majority voting typically leads to too much or too little public good? In general, the answer has to be no, since no natural restrictions can be appealed to and the median voter's *MRS* may be lower or higher than the mean. If it is lower, then too little public good will provided. The converse holds if it is higher. The only approach that might give an insight is to note that the distribution of income has a very long right tail. If the *MRS* is higher for lower income voters, then the nature of the income distribution suggests that the median *MRS* is higher than the mean. Thus voting will lead to an excess quantity of public good being provided. Alternatively, if the *MRS* is increasing with income, then voting would lead to underprovision.

5.6   Personalized Prices

We have now studied two allocation mechanisms that lead to inefficient outcomes. The private market fails because of free-riding, and voting fails because the choice of the decisive median voter need not match the efficient choice. What these have in common is that the consumers face incorrect incentives. In both cases the decision-makers take account only of the private benefit of the public good rather than the broader social benefit (i.e., that public good contribution also benefits others). As a rule, efficiency will only be attained by modifying the incentives to align private and social benefits.

The first method for achieving efficiency involves using an extended pricing mechanism for the public good. This mechanism uses prices that are "personalized," with each consumer paying a price that is designed to fit their situation. These personalized prices modify the actual price in two ways. First, they adjust the price of the public good in order to align social and private benefits. Second, they further adjust the price to capture each consumer's individual valuation of the public good.

This latter aspect can be understood by considering the differences between public and private goods. With a private good, consumers face a common price but choose to purchase different quantities according to their preferences. In contrast, with a pure public good, all consumers consume the same quantity. This can only be efficient if the consumers wish to purchase the same given quantity of the public good. They can be induced to do so by correctly choosing the price they face. For instance, a consumer who places a low value on the public good should face a low price, while a consumer with a high valuation should face a high price. This reasoning is illustrated in table 5.1.

Table 5.1
Prices and quantities

	Private good	Public good
Price	Same	Different
Quantity	Different	Same

The idea of personalized pricing can be captured by assuming that the government announces the share of the cost of the public good that each consumer must bear. For example, it may say that each of two consumers must pay half the cost of the public good. Having heard the announcement of these shares, the consumers then state how much of the public good they wish to have supplied. If they both wish to have the same level, then that level is supplied. If their wishes differ, the shares are adjusted and the process repeated. The adjustment continues until shares are reached at which both wish to have the same quantity. This final point is called a *Lindahl equilibrium*. It can easily be seen how this mechanism overcomes the two sources of inefficiency. The fact that the consumers only pay a share of the cost reduces the perceived unit price of the public good. Hence the private cost appears lower, and the consumers increase their demands for the public good. Additionally the shares can be tailored to match the individual valuations.

To make this reasoning concrete, let the share of the public good that has to paid by consumer h be denoted τ^h. The scheme must be self-financing, so, with two consumers, $\tau^1 + \tau^2 = 1$. Now let G^h denote the quantity of the public good that household h would choose to have provided when faced with the budget constraint

$$x^h + \tau^h G^h = M^h. \tag{5.11}$$

The Lindahl equilibrium shares $\{\tau^1, \tau^2\}$ are found when $G^1 = G^2$. The reason why efficiency is attained can be seen in the illustration of the Lindahl equilibrium in figure 5.7. The indifference curves reflect preferences over levels of the public good and shares in the cost. The shape of these captures the fact that each consumer prefers more of the public good but dislikes an increased share. The highest indifference curve for consumer 1 is to the northwest and the highest for consumer 2 to the northeast. Maximizing utility for a given share (which gives a vertical line in the figure) achieves the highest level of utility where the indifference curve is vertical. Below this point the consumer is willing to pay a higher share for more public good, and above it is just the other way around. Hence the indifference

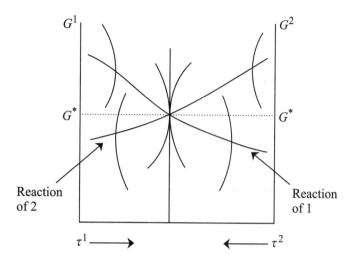

Figure 5.7
Lindahl equilibrium

curves are backward-bending. The *Lindahl reaction functions* are then formed as the loci of the vertical points of the indifference curve. The equilibrium requires that both consumers demand the same level of the public good; this occurs at the intersection of the reactions functions. At this point the indifference curves of the two consumers are tangential and the equilibrium is Pareto-efficient.

To derive the efficiency result formally, note that utility is given by the function $U^h(M^h - \tau^h G^h, G^h)$. The first-order condition for the choice of the quantity of public good is

$$\frac{U_G^h}{U_x^h} = \tau^h, \qquad h = 1, 2. \tag{5.12}$$

Summing these conditions for the two consumers yields

$$\frac{U_G^1}{U_x^1} + \frac{U_G^2}{U_x^2} \equiv MRS_{G,x}^1 + MRS_{G,x}^2 = \tau^1 + \tau^2 = 1. \tag{5.13}$$

This is the Samuelson rule for the economy, and it establishes that the equilibrium is efficient. The personalized prices equate the individual valuations of the supply of public goods to the cost of production in a way that uniform pricing cannot. They also correct for the divergence between private and social benefits.

Although personalized prices seem a very simple way of resolving the public good problem, when considered more closely a number of difficulties arise in actually applying them. First, there is the very practical problem of determining the prices in an economy with many consumers. The practical difficulties involved in announcing and adjusting the individual shares are essentially insurmountable. Second, there are issues raised concerning the incentives for consumers to reveal their true demands.

The analysis assumed that the consumers were honest in revealing their reactions to the announcement of cost shares, meaning they simply maximize utility by taking the share of cost as given. However, there will be a gain to any consumer who attempts to cheat, or *manipulate*, the allocation mechanism. By announcing preferences that do not coincide with their true preferences, it is possible for a consumer to shift the outcome in their favor, provided that the other does not do likewise. To see this, assume that consumer 1 acts honestly and that consumer 2 knows this and knows the reaction function of 1. In figure 5.8 an honest announcement on the part of consumer 2 would lead to the equilibrium e_L where the two Lindahl reaction functions cross. However, by claiming their preferences to be given by the dashed Lindahl reaction function rather than the true function, the equilibrium can be driven to point e_M that represents the maximization of 2's utility given the Lindahl reaction function of 1. This improvement for consumer 2 reveals the incentive for dishonest behavior.

The use of personalized prices can achieve efficiency but only if the consumers act honestly. If a consumers acts strategically, they are able to manipulate the

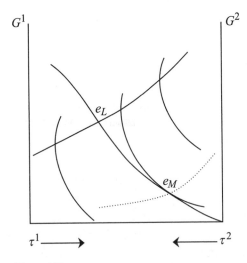

Figure 5.8
Gaining by false announcement

outcome to their advantage. This suggests that the search for a means of attaining the Samuelson rule should be restricted to allocation mechanisms that cannot be manipulated in this way. This is the focus of the next section.

5.7   Mechanism Design

The previous section showed how consumers have an incentive to reveal false information on demand when personalized prices are being determined. From the consistent application of the assumption of utility maximization we observed that a consumer will behave dishonestly if it is in their interests to do so. This fact has led to the search for allocation mechanisms that are immune from attempted manipulation. As will be shown, the design of some of these mechanisms leads households to reveal their true preferences. Because of this property these mechanisms are called *preference revelation mechanisms*.

5.7.1   Examples of Preference Revelation

The general problem of preference revelation is now illustrated by considering two simple examples. In both examples people are shown to gain by making false statements of their preferences. If they act rationally, then they will choose to make false statements. Since these situations have the nature of strategic games, we call the participants *players*.

Example 1: False Understatement

The decision that has to be made is whether to produce or not produce a fixed quantity of a public good. If the public good is not produced, then $G = 0$. If it is produced, $G = 1$. The cost of the public good is given by $C = 1$. The gross benefit of the public good for players 1 and 2 is given by $v^1 = v^2 = 1$. Since the social benefit of providing the good is $v^1 + v^2 = 2$, which is greater than the cost, it is socially beneficial to provide the public good.

Each player makes a report, r^h, of the benefit they receive from the public good. This report can either be false, in which case $r^h = 0$, or truthful so that $r^h = v^h = 1$. Based on the reports, the public good is provided if the sum of announced valuations is at least as high as the cost. This gives the collective decision rule to choose $G = 1$ if $r^1 + r^2 \geq C = 1$, and to choose $G = 0$ otherwise. The cost of the public good is shared between the two players, with the shares proportional to the announced valuations. In detail,

Player 2

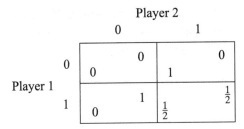

Figure 5.9
Announcements and payoffs

$$c^h = 1 \quad \text{if } r^h = 1 \text{ and } r^{h'} = 0, \tag{5.14}$$

$$c^h = \tfrac{1}{2} \quad \text{if } r^h = 1 \text{ and } r^{h'} = 1, \tag{5.15}$$

$$c^h = 0 \quad \text{if } r^h = 0 \text{ and } r^{h'} = 0 \text{ or } 1. \tag{5.16}$$

The net benefit, the difference between true benefit and cost, which is termed the *payoff* from the mechanism, is then given by

$$U^h = v^h - c^h \quad \text{if } r^1 + r^2 \geq 1, \tag{5.17}$$

$$= 0 \quad \text{otherwise.} \tag{5.18}$$

This information is summarized in the payoff matrix in figure 5.9.

From the payoff matrix it can be seen that the announcement $r^h = 0$ is a weakly dominant strategy for both players. For instance, if player 2 chooses $r^2 = 1$, then player 1 will choose $r^1 = 0$. Alternatively, if player 2 chooses $r^2 = 0$, then player 1 is indifferent between the two strategies of $r^1 = 0$ and $r^1 = 1$. The Nash equilibrium of the game is therefore $\hat{r}^1 = 0$, $\hat{r}^2 = 0$.

In equilibrium both players will understate their valuation of the public good. As a result the public good is not provided, despite it being socially beneficial to do so. The reason is that the proportional cost-sharing rule gives an incentive to underreport preferences for public good. With both players underreporting, the public good is not provided. To circumvent this problem, we can make contributions independent of the reports. This is our next example.

Example 2: False Overstatement
The second example is distinguished from the first by considering a public good that is socially nondesirable with a cost greater than the social benefit. The possible announcements and the charging scheme are also changed.

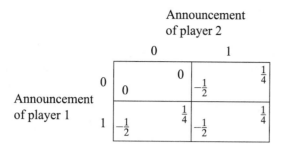

Figure 5.10
Payoffs and overstatement

It is assumed that the gross payoffs when the public good is provided are

$$v_1 = 0 < v_2 = \tfrac{3}{4}. \tag{5.19}$$

With the cost of the public good remaining at 1, these payoffs imply that

$$v_1 + v_2 = \tfrac{3}{4} < C = 1, \tag{5.20}$$

so the social benefit from the public good is less than its cost.

The possible announcements of the two players are given by $r^1 = 0$ or 1 and $r^2 = \tfrac{3}{4}$ or 1. These announcements permit the players to either tell the truth or overstate the benefit so as to induce public good provision. Assume that there is also a uniform charge for the public good if it is provided, so $c^h = \tfrac{1}{2}$ if $r^1 + r^2 \geq c = 1$, and $c^h = 0$ otherwise. These valuations and charges imply the net benefits

$$U^h = v^h - c^h \quad \text{if } r^1 + r^2 \geq 1, \tag{5.21}$$

$$U^h = 0 \quad \text{otherwise.} \tag{5.22}$$

These can be used to construct the payoff matrix in figure 5.10.

The weakly dominant strategy for player 1 is to play $r^1 = 0$ and the best response of player 2 is to select $r^2 = 1$ (which is also a dominant strategy). Therefore the Nash equilibrium is $\hat{r}^1 = 0$, $\hat{r}^2 = 1$, which results in the provision of a socially nondesirable public good. The combination of payoffs and charging scheme has resulted in overstatement and unnecessary provision. The explanation for this is that the player 2 is able to guarantee the good is provided by announcing $r^2 = 1$. Their private gain is $\tfrac{1}{4}$ but this is more than offset by the loss of $-\tfrac{1}{2}$ for player 1.

5.7.2   Clarke-Groves Mechanism

The preceding examples showed that true valuations may not be revealed for some mechanisms linking announcement to contribution. Even worse, it is possible for the wrong social decision to be made. The question then arises as to whether there is a mechanism that will always ensure that true values are revealed (as for voting), and at the same time that the optimal public good level is provided (which voting cannot do).

The potential for constructing such a mechanism, and the difficulties in doing so, can be understood by retaining the simple allocation problem of the examples that involves the decision on whether to provide a single public good of fixed size. The construction of a length of road or the erection of a public monument both fit with this scenario. It is assumed that the cost of the project is known, and it is also known how the cost is allocated among the consumers that make up the population. What needs to be found from the consumers is how much their valuation of the public good exceeds, or falls short of, their contribution to the cost. Each consumer knows the benefit they will gain if the public good is provided, and they know the cost they will have to pay. The difference between the benefit and the cost is called the *net benefit*. This can be positive or negative. The decision rule is that the public good is provided if the sum of reported net benefits is (weakly) positive.

Consider two consumers with true net benefits v^1 and v^2. The mechanism we consider is the following: Each consumer makes an announcement of their net benefit. Denote the report by r^h. The public good is provided if the sum of announced net benefits satisfies $r^1 + r^2 \geq 0$. If the public good is not provided, each consumer receives a payoff of 0. If the good is provided, then each consumer receives a *side payment* equal to the reported net benefit of the other consumer; hence, if the public good is provided, consumer 1 receives a total payoff of $v^1 + r^2$ and consumer 2 receives $v^2 + r^1$. It is these additional side payments that will lead to the truth being told by inducing each consumer to "internalize" the net benefit of the public good for the other. If the public good is not provided, no side payments are made.

To see how this mechanism works, assume that the true net benefits and the reports can take the values of either -1 or $+1$. The public good will not be provided if both report a value of -1, but if at least one reports $+1$ it will be provided. The payoffs to the mechanism are summarized in the payoff matrix in

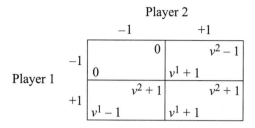

Figure 5.11
Clarke-Groves mechanism

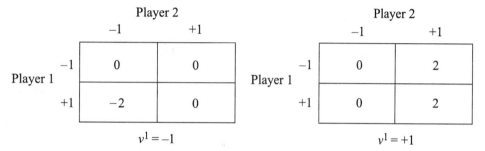

Figure 5.12
Payoffs for player 1

figure 5.11. The claim we now wish to demonstrate is that this mechanism provides no incentive to make a false announcement of the net benefit. To do this, it is enough to focus on player 1 and show that they will report truthfully when $v^1 = -1$ and when $v^1 = +1$. The payoffs relating to the true values are in the two payoff matrices in figure 5.12.

Take the case of $v^1 = -1$. Then consumer 1 finds the true announcement to be weakly dominant—the payoff from being truthful (the top row) is greater if $r^2 = -1$ and equal if $r^2 = +1$. Next take the case of $v^1 = +1$. Consumer 1 is indifferent between truth and nontruth. But the point is that there is now no incentive to provide a false announcement. Hence truth should be expected.

The problem with this mechanism is the side payments that have to be made. If the public good is provided and $v^1 = v^2 = +1$, then the total side payments are equal to 2—which is equal to the total net benefit of the public good. These side payments are money that has to be put into the system to support the telling of truth. Obtaining the truth is possible, but it is costly.

5.7.3   Clarke Tax

The problem caused by the existence of the side payments can be reduced but can never be eliminated. The reason it cannot be eliminated entirely is simply that the mechanism is extracting information, and this can never be done for free. The way in which the side payments can be reduced is to modify the structure of the mechanism.

One way to do this is for side payments to be made only if the announcement of a player *changes* the social decision. To see what this implies, consider calculating the sum of the announced benefits of all players but one. Whether this is positive or negative will determine a social decision for those players. Now add the announcement of the final player. Does this change the social decision? If it does, then the final player is said to be *pivotal,* and a set of side payments are implemented that requires taxing the pivotal agent for the cost inflicted on the other agent through the changed social decision. This process is repeated for each player in turn. These side payments are the *Clarke taxes* that ensure that the correct decision is made so that the public good is produced if it is socially desirable and not otherwise. The use of Clarke taxes reduces the number of circumstances in which the side payments are made.

In a game with only two players, the payoffs for player 1 when the Clarke taxes are used are given by

$$v^1 \quad \text{if} \quad r^1 + r^2 \geq 0 \quad \text{and} \quad r^2 \geq 0, \tag{5.23}$$

$$v^1 - t^1 \quad \text{if} \quad r^1 + r^2 \geq 0 \quad \text{and} \quad r^2 < 0, \quad \text{with } t^1 = -r^2 > 0, \tag{5.24}$$

$$-t^1 \quad \text{if} \quad r^1 + r^2 < 0 \quad \text{and} \quad r^2 \geq 0, \quad \text{with } t^1 = r^2 \geq 0, \tag{5.25}$$

$$0 \quad \text{if} \quad r^1 + r^2 < 0 \quad \text{and} \quad r^2 < 0. \tag{5.26}$$

Only in the second and third cases is player 1 pivotal (respectively, by causing provision and stopping provision of the public good), and for these cases a tax is levied on player 1 reflecting the cost to the other agent of changing public good provision ($t^1 = -r^2 > 0$ for the cost of imposing provision, and $t^1 = r^2 \geq 0$ for the cost of stopping provision).

The Clarke taxes induce truth-telling and guarantee that the public good is provided if and only if it is socially desirable. The explanation is that any misreport that changes the decision about the public good would induce the payment of a tax in excess of the benefit from the change in decision. Indeed, suppose that the public good is socially desirable, so $v^1 + v^2 \geq 0$, but that player 1 dislikes it, so

$v^1 < 0$. Then, given an honest announcement from player 2 with $r^2 = v^2$, by underreporting sufficiently to prevent provision of the public good (so $r^1 < -r^2$), player 1 becomes pivotal. Player 1 will have to pay a tax of $t^1 = r^2 = v^2$, which is in excess of the gain from nonprovision, $-v^1$ (since $v^1 + v^2 \geq 0 \Rightarrow v^2 \geq -v^1$). Hence player 1 is better off telling the truth, and given this truth-telling, player 2 is also better off telling the truth (although in this case he is the pivotal agent, inducing provision and paying a tax equal to the damage of public good provision for player 1, $t^2 = -r^1 = -v^1$).

The conclusion is that the Clarke tax induces preference revelation, and by restricting side payments to pivotal agents only, it lowers the cost of information revelation.

5.7.4　Further Comments

The theory of mechanism design shows that it is possible to construct schemes that ensure the truth will be revealed and correct social decision made. These mechanisms may work, but they are undoubtedly complex to implement. Putting this objection aside, it can still be argued that such revelation mechanisms are not actually needed in practice. Two major reasons can be provided to support this contention.

First, the mechanisms are built on the basis that the players will be rational and precise in their strategic calculations. In practice, many people may not act as strategically as the theory suggests. As in the theory of tax evasion we discuss in chapter 16, nonmonetary benefits may be derived simply from acting honestly. These benefits may provide a sufficient incentive that the true valuation is reported. In such circumstances the revelation mechanism will not be needed.

Second, the market activities of consumers often indirectly reveal the valuation of public goods. To give an example of what is meant by this, consider the case of housing. A house is a collection of characteristics, such as the number of rooms, size of garden, and access to amenities. The price that a house purchaser is willing to pay is determined by their assessment of the total value of these characteristics. Equally the cost of supplying a house is also dependent on the characteristics supplied. By observing the equilibrium prices of houses with different characteristics, it is possible to determine the value assigned to each characteristic separately. If one of the characteristics relates to a public good, for example, the closeness to a public park, the value of this public good can then be inferred. Such implicit valuation methods can be applied to a broad range of public goods by carefully choosing the related private good. Since consumers have no incentive to act strategically in purchasing private goods, the true valuations should be revealed.

The fact that consumers have an incentive to falsely reveal their valuations can also be exploited to obtain an approximation of the true value. This can be done by running two preference revelation mechanisms simultaneously. If one is designed to lead to an underreporting of the true valuation and the other one to overreporting, then the true value of the public good can be taken as lying somewhere between the over- and underreports. The Swedish economist Peter Bohm has conducted an experimental implementation of this procedure. In the experiment 200 people from Stockholm had to evaluate the benefit of seeing a previously unshown television program. The participants were divided into four groups which faced the following payment mechanisms: (1) pay stated valuation, (2) pay a fraction of stated valuation such that costs are covered from all payments, (3) pay a low flat fee, and (4) no payment. Although the first two provide an incentive to underreport and the latter two to overreport, the experiment found that there was no significant difference in the stated valuations, suggesting that misrevelation may not be as important as suggested by the theory.

5.8 More on Private Provision

The analysis of the private purchase of a public good in section 5.3 focused on the issue of efficiency. The analysis showed that a Pareto improvement can be made from the equilibrium point if both consumers simultaneously raise their contributions, so the equilibrium cannot be efficient. This finding was sufficient to develop the contrast with efficient provision and to act as a basis for investigating mechanism design.

Although useful, these are not the only results that emerge from the private purchase model. The model actually generates several remarkably precise predictions about the effect of income transfers and increases in the number of purchasers. These results are now described and then contrasted with empirical and experimental evidence.

5.8.1 Neutrality and Population Size

The first result concerns the effect of redistributing income. Consider transferring an amount of income Δ from consumer 1 to consumer 2 so that the income of consumer 1 falls to $M^1 - \Delta$ and that of consumer 2 rises to $M^2 + \Delta$. The objective

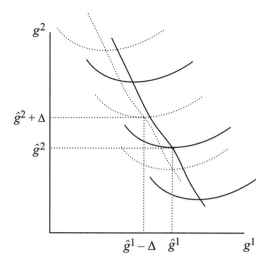

Figure 5.13
Effect of income transfer

is to calculate the effect that this transfer has on the equilibrium level of public good purchases. To do this, notice that the equilibrium in figure 5.5 is identified by the fact that it occurs where an indifference curve for consumer 1 crosses an indifference curve for consumer 2 at right angles. Hence the effect of the transfer on the equilibrium can be found by determining how it affects the indifference curves.

Consider consumer 1 who has their income reduced by Δ. If we reduce their public good purchase by Δ and raise that of consumer 2 by Δ, the utility of consumer 1 is unchanged because

$$U^1(M^1 - g^1, g^1 + g^2) = U^1([M^1 - \Delta] - [g^1 - \Delta], [g^1 - \Delta] + [g^2 + \Delta]). \qquad (5.27)$$

This transfer of income causes the indifference curves and the best-reaction function of consumer 1 to move as illustrated in figure 5.13. The indifference curve through any point g^1, g^2 before the income transfer shifts to pass through the point $g^1 - \Delta$, $g^2 + \Delta$ after the income transfer.

The transfer of income has the same effect on the indifference curves and best-reaction function of consumer 2. By considering the reduction in purchase of consumer 1 and the increase by consumer 2, it follows that

$$U^2(M^2 - g^2, g^1 + g^2) = U^2([M^2 + \Delta] - [g^2 + \Delta], [g^1 - \Delta] + [g^2 + \Delta]). \qquad (5.28)$$

For consumer 2 the indifference curve through g^1, g^2 before the income transfer, becomes that through $g^1 - \Delta$, $g^2 + \Delta$ after the transfer.

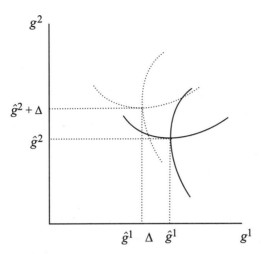

Figure 5.14
New equilibrium

These shifts in the indifference curves result in the equilibrium moving as in figure 5.14. The point where the indifference curves cross at right angles shifts in the same way as the individual indifference curves. If the equilibrium was initially at $\hat{g}^1$, $\hat{g}^2$ before the income transfer, it is located at $\hat{g}^1 - \Delta$, $\hat{g}^2 + \Delta$ after the transfer.

The important result now comes from noticing that in the move from the original to the new equilibrium, consumer 1 reduces their purchase of the public good by Δ, but consumer 2 increases their purchase by the same amount Δ. These changes in the value of purchases exactly match the change in income levels. The net outcome is that the levels of private consumption remain unchanged for the two consumers, and the total supply of the public good is also unchanged. As a consequence the income transfer does not affect the levels of consumption in equilibrium—all it does is to redistribute the burden of purchase. Income redistribution is entirely offset by an opposite redistribution of the responsibility for purchases of the public good. This result, known as *income distribution invariance*, is a consequence of the fact that the utility levels of the consumers are linked via the quantity of public good.

The second interesting result is that the transfer of income leaves the utility levels of the two consumers unchanged. This has to be so because, as we have just seen, the consumption levels do not change. Therefore the redistribution of income has not affected the distribution of welfare; the transfer is simply offset by the change in public good purchases. If the income redistribution was due to government policy, this becomes an example of *policy neutrality*: by changing their behavior the individuals in the economy are able to undo what the government is trying to do. Income redistribution will always be neutral until the point is reached at which one of the consumers no longer purchases the public good. Only then will further income transfers affect the distribution of utility.

A third result follows easily from income invariance. Let both consumers have the same utility function but possibly different income levels. Since the quantity of public good consumed by both must be the same, the first-order conditions require that both must also consume the same quantity of private good; hence $x^1 = x^2$. Further these common levels of consumption imply that the consumers must have the same utility levels even if there is an initial income disparity. The private purchase model therefore implies that when the consumers have identical utilities, the choices made by the consumers will equalize utilities even in the face of income differentials. The poor set their purchases sufficiently lower than the purchases of the rich to make them equally well off.

This model can also be used to consider the consequence of variations in the number of households. Maintaining the assumption that all the consumers are identical in terms of both preferences and income, for an economy with H consumers the total provision of the public good is $G = \sum_{h=1}^{H} g^h$ and the utility of h is

$$U^h = U(M - g^h, G) = U(M - g^h, \bar{G}^h + g^h). \tag{5.29}$$

Here $\bar{G}^h$ is the total contributions of all consumers other than h. Since all consumers are identical, it makes sense to focus on symmetric equilibria where all consumers make the same contribution. Hence let $g^h = g$ for all h. It follows that at at symmetric equilibrium

$$g = \frac{\bar{G}}{H - 1}. \tag{5.30}$$

In a graph of g against $\bar{G}$ an allocation satisfying (5.30) must lie on a ray through the origin with gradient $H - 1$. For each level of H, the equilibrium is given by the intersection of the appropriate ray with the best-reaction function. This is shown in figure 5.15.

The important point is what happens to the equilibrium level of provision as the number of consumer tends to infinity (the idealization of a "large" population). What happens can be seen by considering the consequence of the ray in figure 5.15 becoming vertical: the equilibrium will be at the point where the reaction function crosses the vertical axis. As this point is reached, the provision of each consumer will tend to zero, but aggregate provision will not since it is the sum of

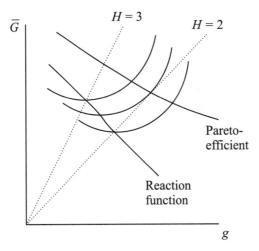

$\overline{G}$

$H = 3$

$H = 2$

Pareto-
efficient

Reaction
function

g

Figure 5.15
Additional consumers

infinitely many zeros. This result can be summarized by saying that in a large population each consumer will effectively contribute nothing.

5.8.2   Experimental Evidence

The analysis of private purchase demonstrated that the equilibrium will not be Pareto-efficient and that, compared to Pareto-preferred allocations, too little of the public good will be purchased. A simple explanation of this result can be given in terms of each consumer relying on others to purchase and hence deciding to purchase too little themselves. Each consumer is free-riding on others' purchases, and since all attempt to free-ride, the total value of purchases fails to reach the efficient level. This conclusion has been subjected to close experimental scrutiny.

The basic form of experiment is to give participants a number of tokens that can be invested in either a private good or a public good. Each participant makes a single purchase decision. The private good provides a benefit only to its purchaser while purchase of public good provides a benefit to all participants. The values are set so that the private benefit is less than the social benefit. The benefits are known to the participants and the total benefit from purchases is the payoff to the participant at the end of the experiment. It is therefore in the interests of each participant to maximize their payoff.

	Private good	Public good
Private benefit	5	1
Social benefit	5	10

Figure 5.16
Public good experiment

To see how this works in detail, assume that there are 10 participants in the game. Allow each participant to have 10 tokens to spend. A unit of the private good costs 1 token and provides a benefit of 5 units (private benefit = social benefit = 5). A unit of the public good also costs 1 token but provides a benefit of 1 unit to *all* the participants in the game (private benefit = 1 < social benefit = 10). The returns are summarized in figure 5.16.

If the game is played once (a one-shot game), the Nash equilibrium strategy is to purchase only the private good, since each token spent on the private good yields a return five times higher than for the public good. In equilibrium, the total return to each player is 50. In contrast, the socially efficient outcome is for all players to purchase only the public good and to generate a payoff of 100 to each player. The fact that the Nash equilibrium differs from the efficient outcome is because the private benefits diverge from the social benefits. Thus, in the one-shot game, all tokens should be spent on the private good.

In experimental implementations of this game the average value of purchases of the public good has been approximately 30 to 90 percent of tokens, with most observations falling in the 40 to 50 percent range. Interestingly, among student participants contributions have been lowest for those studying economics, and fall with the number of years of economics taken. Since the purchase of the public good is significantly different from 0, these results clearly do not support the predictions of the private-purchase model.

Some experiments have repeated the purchase decision over several rounds with the view that this should allow time for the participants to learn about free-riding and develop the optimal strategy. The results from such experiments are not as clear and a wider range of purchases occur. Free-riding is not completely supported, but instances have been reported in which it does occur. However, this finding should be treated with caution, since having several rounds of the game introduces aspects of repeated game theory. While it remains true that the only credible equilibrium of the repeated game is the private-purchase equilibrium of the corresponding single-period game, it is possible that in the experiments some participants may have been attempting to establish cooperative equilibria by playing in a fashion that invited cooperation. Additionally those not trained in game theory may have been unable to derive the optimal strategy even though they could solve the single-period game.

Other results show that increasing group size leads to increased divergence from the efficient outcome when accompanied by a decrease in marginal return from the public good but the results do not support a pure numbers-in-group effect. This finding is compatible with the theoretical finding that the effect of group size on the divergence from optimality is in general indeterminate.

These results indicate that there is little evidence of free-riding in single-period, or one-shot, games but in the repeated games the purchases fall toward the private-purchase level as the game is repeated. In total, these experiments do not provide great support for the equilibrium based on the private-purchase model with Nash behavior. In the single-period games free-riding is unambiguously rejected. Although it appears after several rounds in repeated games, the explanation for the strategies involved is not entirely apparent. Neither a strategic nor a learning hypothesis is confirmed. What seems to be occurring is that the participants are initially guided more by a sense of fairness than by Nash behavior. When this fairness is not rewarded, the tendency is then to move toward the Nash equilibrium. The failure of experimentation to support free-riding lends some encouragement to the views that although such behavior may be individually optimal, it is not actually observed in practice.

5.8.3   Modifications

The experimental evidence has produced a number of conflicts with the predictions of the theoretical model. The analysis of private-purchase was based on two fundamental assumptions. The utility of consumers was assumed to depend only on the consumption of the private good and the total supply of the public good. This ensures that consumers do not care directly about the size of their own contribution nor do they care about the behavior of other consumers, except for how it affects the total level of the public good. The second assumption was that the consumers acted noncooperatively and played according to the assumptions of Nash equilibrium.

The simplest modification that can be made to the model is to consider the game being played in a different way. The foundation of the Nash equilibrium is that each player takes the behavior of the others as given when optimizing. One way to change this is to consider "conjectural variations" so that each player forms an opinion as to how their choice will affect that of others. If the conjectural variation is positive, each player predicts that the others will respond to an increase in purchase by also making additional purchases. Such a positive conjecture can be interpreted as being more cooperative than the zero conjecture that arises in the Nash equilibrium and leads to the equilibrium having greater total public good supply than the Nash equilibrium.

Moving to non-Nash conjectures may alter the equilibrium level of the public good but it does not eliminate the neutrality properties. Furthermore the major objection to this approach is that it is entirely arbitrary. There are sensible reasons founded in game theory for focusing on the Nash equilibrium, and no other set of conjectures can appeal to similar justification. If the Nash equilibrium of the private-purchase model does not agree with observations, it would seem that the objectives of the consumers and the social rules they observe should be reconsidered, not the conjectures they hold when maximizing.

One approach to modified preferences is to assume that the consumer derives utility directly from the contribution they make. For instance, making a donation to charity can make a consumer feel good about themself; they are acting as a "good citizen." This is often referred to as the *warm glow* effect. With a warm glow, a purchase of the public good provides a return from direct consumption of the public good and a further return from the warm glow. The private warm glow effect increases the value of the purchase and so raises the equilibrium level of total purchases. The equilibrium also no longer has the same invariance properties. This would seem a significant advance were it not that the specification of the warm glow is entirely arbitrary.

A final modification is to remove the individualism and allow for social interaction by modifying the rules of social behavior. In the same way that social effects can arise with tax evasion, they can also occur with public goods. One way to do this is to introduce reciprocity, by which each consumer considers the contributions of others and contrasts them to what they feel they should have made. If the contributions of others match, or exceed, what is expected, then the consumer is assumed to feel under an obligation to make a similar contribution. This again raises the equilibrium level of contribution.

5.9   Fund-Raising Campaigns

The model of voluntary purchase that we have considered so far has involved a single one-off contribution decision. It is easy to appreciate that once these contributions have been made the consumers may look again at the situation and realize it is inefficient. This could give them an incentive to conduct a second round of contribution which will move the equilibrium closer to efficiency. Repeatedly applying this argument suggests that it may be possible to eventually reach efficiency. We now assess this claim by addressing it within a simple fund-raising game.

The basis of the fund-raising game is that a target level of funds must be achieved before a public good can be provided. For example, consider the target as the minimum cost of construction for a public library. Subscribers to the campaign take it in turn to make either a contribution or a pledge to contribute. Only when the target is met does the process cease. The basic question is whether such a fund-raising campaign can be successful given the possibility of free-riding.

We model a campaign as a game with an infinite horizon, meaning that solicitation for donations can continue until the goal is met. There is one public good (or joint project) whose production cost is C and two identical players X and Y. These players derive the same benefit, B, from the public good, so the total benefit is $2B$. Both also have the same discount rate δ, $0 < \delta < 1$, for delaying completion of the project by one period.

The players alternate in making contributions. The sequential (marginal) contributions are denoted $(\ldots, x_{t-1}, y_t, x_{t+1}, \ldots)$, where x_{t-1} denotes the contribution of player X at time $t-1$ and y_t denotes the contribution of player Y at time t. The game ends, and the public good is provided, only when the total contributions cover the cost of the public good. Individuals derive no benefits from the public good before completion of the fund-raising, so the marginal contributions yield no return until the cost is met. It follows that the incentive of each player to wait for the other one to contribute (free-riding) must be balanced against the cost of delaying completion of the project. We suppose that the public good is "socially desirable" ($C < 2B$) but that no single player values the public good enough to bear the full cost ($B < C$). We now contrast two different forms of fund-raising campaigns. In the first, the *contribution campaign*, the contributions are paid at the time they are made. In the second, the *subscription campaign*, players are asked in sequence to make donation pledges that are not be paid until the cost is met.

5.9.1   The Contribution Campaign

In the contribution campaign, contributions are sunk at the time they are made because a credible commitment cannot be made to make contributions later. The lack of commitment leads each player to back his contribution to ensure that the other players contribute their share. This is because past contributions are sunk and cannot influence the division of the remaining cost between the players. As a result we show that it is never possible to raise the money, even though the project is worthwhile.

The two players are asked in sequence to make a contribution. While there is no natural end period, there is a total contribution level that is close enough to the cost C that the contributor whose turn it is should complete the fund-raising rather than waiting for the other one to make up the difference. Suppose that it is player X's turn to make a contribution offer at that final round T. There exists a deficit sufficiently small that player X is indifferent between making up the difference and getting a payoff of $B - x_T$ or between waiting in the expectation (at best) that player Y will make up the difference in the next round and producing a payoff with delayed completion of δB. Hence the maximal contribution of player 1 in the final round T is

$$x_T = [1 - \delta]B, \tag{5.31}$$

so the contribution is equal to the benefit of speeding up completion of the project. We suppose that $[1 - \delta]B < C$ so that such a contribution cannot cover the full cost and a donation from player Y must be solicited. Working backward, it is now player Y's turn to make a contribution at time $T - 1$. Player Y anticipates that in bringing (total) contributions up to $C - x_T$ at date $T - 1$, player X will complete the project the next period. So there exists a sufficiently small deficit such that player Y is indifferent between bringing total contributions up to that level, giving a payoff $\delta B - y_{T-1}$, or waiting for the other player to make such contribution while making himself the final contribution x_T, which produces a payoff $\delta^2[B - x_T]$ (i.e., two periods later you get the completed project benefit B and pay the last contribution x_T). Hence, substituted for x_T, the contribution at time $T - 1$ that makes player Y indifferent is

$$y_{T-1} = \delta[1 - \delta^2]B. \tag{5.32}$$

Proceeding backward to date $T - 2$, it is now the turn of player X to make a contribution. Using the same line of argument, there exists a total contribution level at date $T - 2$ such that player X is indifferent between bringing total contribution up to that level to get a payoff $\delta^2[B - x_T] - x_{T-2}$ from completion in two periods or waiting and delaying completion to get a payoff $\delta^3 B - \delta^2 y_{T-1}$ (in which from the switching position it becomes worthwhile to contribute y_{T-1}). Substituting for x_T and y_{T-1} gives

$$x_{T-2} = \delta^3[1 - \delta^2]B. \tag{5.33}$$

Moving back to round $T - 3$ and following the same reasoning, the potential contribution at time $T - 3$ from player Y is

$$y_{T-3} = \delta^5[1 - \delta^2]B, \tag{5.34}$$

and the potential contribution at time $T - 4$ is

$$x_{T-4} = \delta^7[1 - \delta^2]B. \tag{5.35}$$

Going back further, it is possible to calculate how much each player is willing to contribute at each stage. This is illustrated in figure 5.17.

Summing these contributions by starting from the end of the campaign, we have the total potential for contributions as

$$[1 - \delta]B + \delta[1 - \delta^2]B + \delta^3[1 - \delta^2]B + \delta^5[1 - \delta^2]B + \delta^7[1 - \delta^2]B + \cdots = B. \tag{5.36}$$

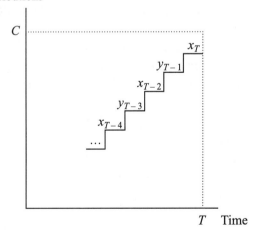

Figure 5.17
A contribution campaign

In (5.36) we used the geometric progression fact that $1 + \delta^2 + \delta^4 + \delta^6 + \cdots = \frac{1}{1-\delta^2}$. The remarkable feature is that the total potential for contributions never exceeds the individual benefit from the project, and because $B < C$, it is not possible to raise sufficient contributions for a successful campaign.

5.9.2   The Subscription Campaign

In the subscription game, agents alternate in making donation pledges and bear the cost of their contribution only *when* and *if* enough contributions are pledged to complete the project. In a sense, agents are able to make certain conditional commitments to contribute in the future. This possibility to commit modifies the strategic structure of the game and alters the total amount that can be raised. As we now show, in this case it becomes possible to raise an amount equal to the total valuation of all the contributors.

Once again, we start when the fund-raising operation is over and work backward. Fix an arbitrary end point T with player X's turn to make a donation pledge at date T. There must exists a contribution deficit sufficiently small to make player X indifferent between financing the deficit himself to obtain a payoff $B - x_T$ and waiting for player Y to make up the difference in the next period, with a delayed completion payoff of δB. So the potential pledge of player X at date T is

$$x_T = [1 - \delta]B. \tag{5.37}$$

We continue to assume that $[1 - \delta]B < C$ so that we can solicit player Y's donation. Working back, it is then up to player Y to pledge at date $T - 1$. Player Y anticipates that in bringing the total amount pledged up to $C - x_T$ at date $T - 1$, player X will complete the project in the next period. So there exists a sufficiently small deficit such that player Y is indifferent between making up the difference to get a payoff $\delta[B - y_{T-1}]$, or leaving player X to make up the difference and thereby delaying completion to get a payoff of $\delta^2[B - x_T]$ (in which case it becomes worthwhile for Y to pledge himself x_T at date T). Hence, substituting for x_T, we obtain

$$y_{T-1} = [1 - \delta^2]B. \tag{5.38}$$

Going back to date $T - 2$, it is then player X to pledge. Again, there exists a total amount pledged close enough to $C - x_T - y_{T-1}$ such that player X is indifferent between bringing the total contribution up to that level, anticipating completion in two rounds with a payoff $\delta^2[B - x_T - x_{T-2}]$ or waiting for Y to pledge instead with a payoff from switching position of $\delta^3[B - y_{T-1}]$. Substituting for x_T and y_{T-1} gives

$$x_{T-2} = \delta[1 - \delta^2]B. \qquad (5.39)$$

Proceeding likewise, we can go back further and calculate how much player Y will pledge at date $T - 3$ as

$$y_{T-3} = \delta^2[1 - \delta^2]B, \qquad (5.40)$$

and player X will pledge at date $T - 4$ the amount

$$x_{T-4} = \delta^3[1 - \delta^2]B.$$

Going back further, calculating how much each player is willing to pledge at each stage and summing up potential pledges, we get

$$[1 - \delta]B + [1 - \delta^2]B + \delta[1 - \delta^2]B + \delta^2[1 - \delta^2]B + \delta^3[1 - \delta^2]B + \cdots = 2B. \quad (5.41)$$

This is the maximum amount that can be raised and is equal to the total valuations of all the contributors. Hence it is always possible to raise enough money for any worthwhile project because $C < 2B$.

These results have shown how allowing contributions to be repeated may lead to efficient private provision of the public good. But this conclusion is sensitive to the assumptions made upon the ability of contributors to make binding commitments.

5.10   Conclusions

This chapter has reviewed the standard analysis of the efficient level of provision of a public good leading to the Samuelson rule. The analysis of private purchase emphasized the fact that this outcome will not be achieved without government intervention. The efficiency rule describes an allocation that can only be achieved if the government is unrestricted in its policy tools or, as the Lindahl equilibrium demonstrates, using prices that are personalized for each consumer.

One aspect of public goods that prevents the government from making efficient decisions is the government's lack of knowledge of consumers' preferences and their willingness to pay for public goods. Mechanisms were constructed that provide the right incentives for consumers to correctly reveal their true valuation of the public good. Experimental evidence suggests that consumer behavior when confronted with decision problems involving public goods does not fully conform with the theoretical prediction and that the private-purchase equilibrium may not be as inefficient as theory suggests. Furthermore misrevelation has not been confirmed as the inevitable outcome.

Further Reading

The classic paper on the efficient provision of public goods is:

Samuelson, P. A. 1954. The pure theory of public expenditure. *Review of Economics and Statistics* 36: 387–89.

The private provision model is developed fully in:

Cornes, R. C., and Sandler, T. 1996. *The Theory of Externalities, Public Goods and Club Goods.* Cambridge: Cambridge University Press.

The independence between income distribution and public good allocation is in:

Warr, P. 1983. The private provision of public goods is independent of the distribution of income. *Economic Letters* 13: 207–11.

Further developments of the model are in:

Bergstrom, T. C., Blume, L., and Varian, H. 1986. On the private provision of public goods. *Journal of Public Economics* 29: 25–49

Bergstrom, T. C., and Cornes, R. 1983. Independence of allocative efficiency from distribution in the theory of public goods. *Econometrica* 51: 1753–65.

Itaya, J.-I., de Meza, D., and Myles, G. D. 2002. Income distribution, taxation and the private provision of public goods. *Journal of Public Economic Theory* 4: 273–97.

The effect of group size on private provision is in:

Andreoni, J. 1988. Privately provided public goods in a large economy: The limits of altruism. *Journal of Public Economics* 35: 57–73.

Chamberlin, J. 1974. Provision of collective goods as a function of group size. *American Political Science Review* 68: 707–16.

The effect of altruism on private provision is in:

Hindriks, J., and Pancs, R. 2002. Free riding on altruism and group size. *Journal of Public Economic Theory* 4: 335–46.

Preference revelation for public goods was first described as a dominant strategy mechanism in:

Groves, T., and Ledyard, J. 1977. Optimal allocation of public goods: A solution to the "free rider" problem. *Econometrica* 45: 783–809.

A simple mechanism for preference revelation as a Nash equilibrium is the "round table" scheme in:

Walker, M. 1981. A simple incentive-compatible scheme for attaining Lindahl allocations. *Econometrica* 49: 65–71.

There is also a mechanism that induces truth-telling as a Bayesian-Nash equilibrium in:

d'Aspremont, C., and Gerard-Varet, L. A. 1979. Incentives and incomplete information. *Journal of Public Economics* 11: 25–45.

A very good survey of the preference revelation mechanisms is in:

Laffont, J.-J. 1987. Incentives and the allocation of public goods. In A. Auerbach and M. Feldstein, eds., *Handbook of Public Economics*. Amsterdam: North Holland, pp. 537–69.

The fund-raising campaign is based on private provision of discrete public good in:

Admati, A. R., and Perry, M. 1991. Joint projects without commitment. *Review of Economic Studies* 58: 259–76.

More on private provision of discrete public goods (such as the volunteer dilemma) is in:

Palfrey, T., and Rosenthal, H. 1984. Participation and the provision of discrete public goods: A strategic analysis. *Journal of Public Economics* 24: 171–93.

Experimental results are surveyed in:

Bohm, P. 1972. Estimating demand for public goods: An experiment. *European Economic Review* 3: 55–66.

Isaac, R. M., McCue, K. F., and Plott, C. R. 1985. Public goods in an experimental environment. *Journal of Public Economics* 26: 51–74.

Ledyard, J. O. 1993. Public goods: A survey of experimental research. In J. Kagel and R. Roth, eds., *Handbook of Experimental Economics*. Princeton: Princeton University Press.

Exercises

5.1.   Which of the following are public goods? Explain why.

a. Snowplowing services during the winter.

b. A bicycle race around France during the summer.

c. Foreign aid to Africa to feed its famine-stricken people.

d. Cable television programs.

e. Radio programs.

f. Back roads in the country.

g. Waste collection services.

h. Public schools.

What are their features with respect to the properties of rivalry and excludability?

5.2.   How does a nonrival good differ from a nonexcludable good?

5.3.   In the United Kingdom the lifeboat service is funded by charitable donations. How can this work? How are the rescue services funded in other countries?

5.4.   Discuss how television technology can turn a public good into a private good.

5.5.   What is a public good? How can one determine the efficient level of provision of a public good?

5.6.   Let each dollar spent on a private good give you 10 units of utility but each dollar spent on a public good give you and your two neighbors 5 units each. If you have a fixed income of $10, how much would you spend on the public good? What is the value of the total purchases at the Nash equilibrium if your neighbors also have $10 each? What level of expenditure on the public good maximizes the total level of utility?

5.7.   How many allocations satisfy the Samuelson rule?

5.8.   How do prices ensure that the efficiency condition is satisfied for private goods? Why is the same not true when there is a public good?

5.9.   Consider two consumers with the following demand functions for a public good:

$$p_1 = 10 - \frac{1}{10}G,$$

$$p_2 = 20 - \frac{1}{10}G,$$

where p_i is the price that i is willing to pay for quantity G.

a. What is the optimal level of the public good if the marginal cost of the public good is $25?

b. Suppose that the marginal cost of the public good is $5. What is the optimal level?

c. Suppose that the marginal cost of the public good is $40. What is the optimal level?

Should the consumers make an honest statement of their demand functions?

5.10.   There are three consumers of a public good. The demands for consumers are as follows:

$$p_1 = 50 - G,$$

$$p_2 = 110 - G,$$

$$p_3 = 150 - G,$$

where G measures the number of units of the good and p_i the price in dollars. The marginal cost of the public good is $190.

a. What is the optimal level of provision of the public good? Illustrate your answer with a graph.

b. Explain why the public good may not be supplied at all because of the free-rider problem.

c. If the public good is not supplied at all, what is the size of the deadweight loss arising from this market failure?

5.11.   Take an economy with 2 consumers, 1 private good, and 1 public good. Let each consumer have an income of M. The prices of public and private good are both 1. Let the consumers have utility functions

$$U^A = \log(x^A) + \log(G), \quad U^B = \log(x^B) + \log(G).$$

a. Assume that the public good is privately provided, so $G = g^A + g^B$. Eliminating x^A from the utility function using the budget constraint, show that along an indifference curve

$$dg^A \left[\frac{1}{g^A + g^B} - \frac{1}{M - g^A} \right] + dg^B \left[\frac{1}{g^A + g^B} \right] = 0,$$

and hence that

$$\frac{dg^B}{dg^A} = \frac{g^A + g^B}{M - g^A} - 1.$$

Solve the last equation to find the locus of points along which the indifference curve of A is horizontal and use this to sketch the indifference curves of A.

b. Consider A choosing g^A to maximize utility. Show that the optimal choice satisfies

$$g^A = \frac{M}{2} - \frac{g^B}{2}.$$

c. Repeat part b for B, and calculate the level of private provision of the public good.

d. Calculate the optimal level of provision for the welfare function

$$W = U^A + U^B.$$

Contrast this with the private provision level.

5.12.   Let there be H consumers all with the utility function $U^h = \log(x^h) + \log(G)$ and an income of 1. Noting that the utility with private purchase can be written

$$U^h = \log(x^h) + \log\left(g^h + \sum_{h' \neq h} g^{h'} \right),$$

and that the equilibrium must be symmetric, calculate the private purchase equilibrium and the social optimum for the welfare function

$$W = \sum_{h=1}^{H} U^h.$$

Comment on the effect of changing H on the contrast between the equilibrium and the optimum.

5.13.   Consider two consumers $(1, 2)$, each with income M to allocate between two goods. Good 1 provides 1 unit of consumption to its purchaser and α, $0 \leq \alpha \leq 1$, units of consumption to the other consumer. Each consumer i, $i = 1, 2$, has the utility function $U^i = \log(x_1^i) + x_2^i$, where x_1^i is consumption of good 1 and x_2^i is consumption of good 2.

a. Provide an interpretation of α.

b. Suppose that good 2 is a private good. Find the Nash equilibrium levels of consumption when both goods have a price of 1.

c. By maximizing the sum of utilities, show that the equilibrium is Pareto-efficient if $\alpha = 0$ but inefficient for all other values of α.

d. Now suppose that good 2 also provides 1 unit of consumption to its purchaser and α, $0 \leq \alpha \leq 1$, units of consumption to the other consumer. For the same preferences, find the Nash equilibrium and show that it is efficient for all values of α.

e. Explain the conclusion in part d.

5.14.   Consider four students deciding to jointly share a textbook. Describe a practical method for using the Lindahl equilibrium to determine how much each should pay.

5.15.   Let there be two identical consumers. What would be the share of the cost each should pay for a public good at the Lindahl equilibrium? Use this result to argue that there must be a subsidy to the price of the public good that makes the private purchase equilibrium efficient.

5.16.   What would be the equilibrium outcome if both consumers tried to manipulate the Lindahl equilibrium?

5.17.   Discuss the effect that an increase in the number of consumers involved in a mechanism has on the consequences of manipulation.

5.18.   Consider a two-good economy (one private good and one public good) and a large number H of individuals with single-peaked preferences for the public good. Suppose that the provision of the public good is decided by majority voting, and that it costs one unit of private good to produce one unit of public good. The cost is equally divided among the H individuals. Show that the majority voting outcome is Pareto-efficient if the median marginal rate of substitution is equal to the average marginal rate of substitution.

5.19.   Consider a collective decision by three individuals to produce, or not, one public good that costs $150. Suppose that if the public good is produced, the cost is equally shared among the three individuals, namely $50 each. Assume that the gross benefits from the public good differ among individuals and are respectively $20, $40, and $100 for individuals 1, 2, and 3. Each individual is asked to announce his own benefit for the public good, and the public good is produced only if the sum of reported benefits exceeds the total cost.

a. Show that the Groves-Clarke tax induces truth-telling as a dominant strategy if each individual reports independently his own benefit.

b. Show that the resulting provision of public good is optimal.

c. Show that the Groves-Clarke tax is not robust to collusion in the sense that two individuals could be better off by jointly misreporting their benefit from the public good.

d. What would be the provision of public good if the decision were taken by a majority vote, assuming that the cost is equally shared in the event of public good provision? Compare your answer with part b, and interpret the difference.

5.20.   Consider three consumers $(i = 1, 2, 3)$ who care about their consumption of a private good and their consumption of a public good. Their utility functions are respectively $u_1 = x_1 G$, $u_2 = x_2 G$, and $u_3 = x_3 G$, where x_i is consumer i's consumption of private good and G is the amount of public good jointly consumed by all of them. The unit cost of the private good is $1 and the unit cost of the public good is $10. Individual wealth levels in $ are $w_1 = 30$, $w_2 = 50$, and $w_3 = 20$. What is the efficient amount of public good for them to consume?

5.21.   Albert and Beth are thinking of buying a sofa. Albert's utility function is $u_a(s, m_a) = [1 + s]m_a$ and Beth's utility function is $u_b(s, m_b) = [2 + s]m_b$, where $s = 0$ if they don't get the sofa and $s = 1$ if they do, and m_a and m_b are the amounts of money they have respectively to spend on private consumption. Albert and Beth each have a total of $w = 100$ (in $) to spend. What is the maximum amount that they could pay for the sofa and still both be better off than without it?

5.22.   Are the following statements true or false? Explain why.

a. If the supply of public good is determined by majority vote, then the outcome must be Pareto-efficient.

b. If preferences are single-peaked, then everyone will agree about the right amount of public goods to be supplied.

c. Public goods are those goods that are supplied by the government.

d. The source of the free-rider problem is the absence of rivalry in the consumption of public goods.

e. The source of the preference revelation problem is the nonexcludability of public goods.

f. If a public good is provided by voluntary contributions, too little will be supplied relative to the efficient level.

5.23.   Why does the free-rider problem make it difficult for markets to provide the efficient level of public goods?

5.24.   Four people are considering whether to hire a boat for a day out. Describe questions that will elicit over- and undervaluations of the boat hire.

5.25.   People are observed traveling a long distance to visit an area of scenic countryside. How can this fact be used to place a lower bound on their valuation of the countryside?

6 Club Goods and Local Public Goods

6.1 Introduction

One of the defining features of the public goods of chapter 5 was nonrivalry: once the good was provided, its use by one consumer did not affect the quantity available for any other. This is clearly an extreme assumption. Many commodities, such as parks, roads, and sports facilities, satisfy nonrivalry to a point but are eventually subject to congestion. Although not pure public goods, these goods cannot be classed as private goods either.

A good that has some degree of nonrivalry but for which excludability is possible is called a *club good*. The name is intended to reflect the fact that there are benefits to groups of consumers forming a club to coordinate provision and that the group size may be less than the total population. The name also captures the fact that the clubs we observe in practice are formed by groups of consumers to coordinate the provision of such goods. For instance, a tennis club provides courts that are excludable and nonrival for users at different times. International bodies, such as NATO, can also be interpreted as clubs: NATO provides defense for its members which is again partly nonrivalrous and partly excludable (only partly because if the existence of NATO deters aggression generally, nonmembers will also benefit).

In our description of economic activity in the previous chapters we did not pay any attention to the geography of trade. In effect we assumed that there is either a single market place with consumers located close to it or that travel to markets is costless. It is a fact of actual economic activity that consumers and markets are dispersed, and that travel costs can be significant. As a consequence public goods provided in a particular geographical location need not be available except for those in the close vicinity. For instance, radio and television signals can only be received within range of the transmitter and a police service may only patrol a limited jurisdiction. Provided a consumer is located within the relevant area they can benefit from the public good; otherwise, the public good is unavailable to them because the cost of traveling to enjoy it exceeds the benefit. Such goods are again not pure public goods as defined in chapter 5 and are termed *local public goods*, with the name capturing the idea of geographical restriction. The geographical restriction on availability can also be accompanied by congestion within the region.

The issues that the chapter addresses are similar to those involved with pure public goods. It begins by defining club goods and local public goods and investigating the relationships between them. The efficiency question is then addressed for single-product clubs and is related to the charging scheme required to support efficiency. The clubs are then placed within an economy to consider whether efficiency is achieved at this level. Local public goods are introduced, and the efficiency question is again addressed. The extension is then made to consider heterogeneous consumers, which leads into a discussion of the influential *Tiebout hypothesis* of preference matching for local public goods. The chapter is completed by a review of the empirical evidence on this hypothesis.

6.2   Definitions

The purpose of this section is to provide precise definitions of the classes of goods under discussion. Once this is done, it is possible to describe how these classes are related.

The essential aspect of a club good is that it is possible for those who pay for its provision to exclude those who do not. This is in contrast to the pure public good, which was defined by the impossibility of exclusion. In addition club goods are often assumed to suffer from congestion but this is not strictly necessary. However, congestion provides a motive for exclusion and for the forming of a club to supply the good.

A formal definition can be given as follows:

Definition 2 (Club good)   A club good is a good that is either nonrivalrous or partly rivalrous but for which exclusion by the providers is possible.

The exclusion aspect of a club good can be taken literally, such as a check on membership credentials at the door to the club, or taken as representing some more general legal authority to bar nonmembers. Its consequence is that issues of preference revelation are not important for club goods. The benefits of the club can only be obtained by voluntarily choosing to become a member and doing so immediately reveals preferences. This observation is clearly important for the potential attainment of efficiency by the market.

The defining feature of a local public good is one of geography and the need to locate within a specific geographical area in order to benefit from the good. Once outside this area, the benefit of the good is no longer obtained. This geographical constraint may also be linked with congestion, which causes partial rivalry.

Definition 3 (Local public good)   A local public good can only benefit those within a given geographical area. It may be nonrivalrous within that area or it may be partially rivalrous.

This definition of a local public good makes clear that the unique feature is the geographic restriction. It leaves open the question of whether a local public good is excludable or not. This is important for the following reason: as will be seen, the focus of local public good theory is the analysis of local government and decisions on taxation and expenditure. Whether or not the local public goods provided are excludable then becomes a matter of policy rather than an inherent feature of the good. By this it is meant that local governments can use a variety of regulations to control access to the public goods they offer. As examples, registration at schools can be restricted by policy choice to pupils in the local area and the size of the local population can be controlled by prohibition on new building. Another example is immigration policy that aims to limit access to national public goods to native residents.

Consequently there are large overlaps between clubs and local public goods, and the terms have often been used interchangeably. What has mostly distinguished the two in the literature has been the issues that have been addressed using each concept. The discussion of club goods has focused more on issues of efficiency with homogeneous populations. In contrast, local public goods have found their most prominent use in the analysis of heterogeneous populations and preference revelation. Furthermore local public goods have been used to understand the role and structure of local government, whereas club goods have been more about the market. Even these distinctions are not always binding.

6.3   Single-Product Clubs

The analysis of efficiency for a pure public good involved determining how much of it should be provided. With a club good it is not just the quantity of the good that needs to be decided but also the size of the club membership. The latter is important because of the effect of congestion. Adding a new member allows the cost of providing a given quantity of public good to be spread among more members but reduces the benefit obtained by each existing member. With a club good that suffers from congestion there is a second efficiency condition involved concerning the correct level of membership.

6.3.1   Fixed Utilization

Consider now the simplest model of a club. There is a homogeneous population of consumers who are identical in terms of tastes and of income. One private good is available and one club good. The club good can potentially suffer from congestion. The focus of attention is on the decision of a single club. It is assumed that a club has formed with the intention of supplying the club good (imagine a small committee of founder members setting out its constitution) and is now in the process of deciding how much of the good to supply and how many member to admit.

To complete the description of the decision problem, it is necessary to consider the financing of the club. Since the club has the ability to exclude nonmembers, it is able to charge members for the privilege of membership. Unlike a pure public good, there is then no barrier to financing provision of the club good, provided enough potential members are willing to pay for membership. The most natural assumption to make on the method of charging is that the cost of the club is divided equally amongst the members. This charging policy will ensure the club just breaks even.

Let each consumer have the utility function $U(x, G, n)$, where x is the consumption of a private good, G provision of the club good, and n the number of club members. Utility increases in x and G, and decreases in n if there is congestion. If the cost of providing G units of the club good is $C(G)$, then the budget constraint of a member with income M when the cost of the club is shared equally between members will be

$$M = x + \frac{C(G)}{n}. \tag{6.1}$$

The decision problem for those in charge of the club involves choosing G and n to maximize the welfare of a typical member. Putting together the budget constraint and the utility function, this can be expressed as

$$\max_{\{G, n\}} U\left(M - \frac{C(G)}{n}, G, n\right). \tag{6.2}$$

The first-order conditions for this optimization produce the following pair of equations that characterize efficiency:

$$nMRS_{G,x} \equiv n\frac{U_G}{U_x} = C_G, \tag{6.3}$$

and

$$MRS_{n,x} \equiv \frac{U_n}{U_x} = -\frac{C}{n^2}. \tag{6.4}$$

The first of these conditions, (6.3), is a version of the Samuelson rule (5.5) and describes the level of public good, G, that the club should supply. It states that the sum of marginal rates of substitution between the public good and the private good for the n identical members of the club should be equated to the marginal rate of transformation (or the marginal cost), C_G, of another unit of the club good. What it is most important to observe from this condition is that the process of decision-making within the club ensures that this efficiency condition is satisfied. The ability to exclude nonmembers from consuming the club good permits the club to achieve the correct level of provision. A club therefore achieves efficient public good provision for its members.

To interpret (6.4), it should first be noted that $U_n \leq 0$. If there is congestion, $U_n < 0$ and an increase in the number of club members for a given level of provision will reduce the utility of each through congestion effects. We can treat $\frac{U_n}{U_x}$ as the marginal utility cost of another member of the club. This marginal utility cost is equated to the extent to which another club member reduces the share of the cost for each existing member.

With $U_n < 0$, (6.4) will determine an efficient level of membership for the club which is positive and finite. Again, the club will achieve efficiency through its internal decision-making. In the absence of congestion $U_n = 0$, so the optimal club membership will be infinite. In practice, this can be interpreted as the club encompassing the entire population. However, in contrast to the pure public good, the ability to exclude permits the levy of a membership fee that can finance the cost of the club. The club therefore achieves an efficient level of membership.

The arguments to this point can be summarized as follows. A club is able to exclude nonmembers from consumption of the public good and can levy a charge on members. If all consumers are identical, then the club will achieve an efficient level of the club good and an efficient level of membership. If the club good suffers from congestion, then the membership will be restricted. Without congestion, the entire population will be members of the club. The collection of membership fees by the club ensures that it breaks even in its financing of the provision of the club good. This fundamental insight that clubs can attain efficiency in the provision of public goods is attributed to the seminal work of Buchanan who was the first to develop the theory of clubs. In terms of the earlier discussion, Buchanan observed that joining a club constitutes an act of preference revelation that permits the attainment of efficiency.

6.3.2   Variable Utilization

The model of the club used above does not probe too deeply into the nature of the good that the club supplies. When this is considered further, it becomes apparent that it is not the number of club members that matters for congestion but how frequently the facilities of the club are used. Retaining the assumption that all club members are identical, the total use of the club is equal to the product of the number of members and the number of visits that each member makes to the club. In determining its provision, a club will wish to optimize the number of visits in addition to the size of facility and the membership.

The model can be easily extended to incorporate a variable rate of visitation into the analysis. Let v be the number of visits that each member makes to the club. An increase in the number of visits raises the utility of the member making those visits but causes congestion through the total number of visits of all members. Letting the total number of visits be $V = nv$, the utility function is written $U = U(x, G, v, V)$, with the marginal utility to a visit, U_v, positive and the marginal congestion effect, U_V, negative. The cost function for providing the club is also modified to make it dependent on the total number of visits, nv.

With this extension the optimization problem for the club becomes

$$\max_{\{x, G, v, n\}} U(x, G, v, V) \quad \text{subject to} \quad M = x + \frac{C(G, nv)}{n}. \tag{6.5}$$

The necessary condition for optimal provision of the public good by the club is

$$n\frac{U_G}{U_x} = C_G. \tag{6.6}$$

Condition (6.6) is again the Samuelson rule for the club equating the sum of marginal rates of substitution to the marginal cost of provision. The necessary condition for optimal club membership is

$$v\frac{U_V}{U_x} = -\frac{C}{n^2} + \frac{vC_V}{n}. \tag{6.7}$$

In this condition, $v\frac{U_V}{U_x}$ is the marginal loss of utility through the congestion caused by an additional club member. This is equated to the reduction in cost through increased membership, $-\frac{C}{n^2}$, offset by the increased cost of servicing additional visits, $\frac{vC_V}{n}$. The third optimality condition determines the number of visits to the club that each member should make. This is given by

$$\frac{U_v}{U_x} = C_V - n\frac{U_V}{U_x}, \tag{6.8}$$

which equates the marginal benefit of an additional visit to the marginal maintenance cost plus the marginal congestion cost an extra visit imposes upon all members of the club.

As with the case of fixed visits, if the decision-making of the club is guided by these three optimality conditions, then it will ensure an efficient allocation of resources for its members. It will accept the correct number of members, provide the correct quantity of public good, and set visit levels correctly. Therefore introducing a variable visitation rate does not affect the basic conclusion that clubs will supply excludable public goods efficiently.

However, there is a very important distinction between the cases of variable and fixed utilization. This analysis of variable utilization retained the assumption that there is a fixed charge for membership but no further charges for visits. Consequently, once someone has become a member of the club, the price for each additional visit is zero. In choosing visits, each member will only take account of the private cost of the increase in congestion and not the cost they impose on other members. Therefore they will make an excessive number of visits to the club. In brief, the fixed charge does not impose the correct incentives on members to decentralize the efficient outcome. To implement the optimum defined, it is therefore necessary for a club charging a fixed fee to directly regulate the number of visits. This is rather strong restriction on the behavior of the club and motivates the study of an alternative pricing scheme.

6.3.3   Two-Part Tariff

To provide a starting point for the study of a more sophisticated pricing scheme, it is worth formalizing the final comments of the previous subsection. Assume that the club has chosen its optimal provision, G^*, membership, n^*, and visits, v^*, and that its membership fee, which is based on all members abiding by the number of visits, is given by $F^* = \frac{C(G^*, n^* v^*)}{n^*}$. Now consider the incentives facing a member of the club who believes all other members will make v^* visits. Putting together the budget constraint, $M = x + F^*$, and the utility function, the club member faces the optimization

$$\max_{\{v\}} \; U(M - F^*, G^*, v, [n^* - 1]v^* + v). \tag{6.9}$$

The choice of v, taking the choices of G^*, $n^* v^*$, and F^* as given, then satisfies the necessary condition

$$U_v + U_V = 0. \tag{6.10}$$

Consequently the member will choose to make visits to the point at which the marginal utility of visits is completely offset by the marginal disutility of congestion. This is not the optimal condition as given by (6.8); it in fact leads to a number of visits in excess of the optimum because the member disregards the congestion cost imposed on others. This demonstrates how the membership fee fails to place the correct incentives in place, so it can only be optimal if visits are directly regulated.

Assume that instead of a membership fee, the club charges a price per visit (or user fee). If the price is denoted p and the membership fee is set at $F = 0$, then the number of visits is chosen to solve

$$\max_{\{x,v\}} \; U(x, G^*, v, [n^* - 1]v^* + v) \quad \text{subject to} \quad M = x + pv. \tag{6.11}$$

The necessary conditions for this optimization can be combined to give

$$p = \frac{U_v}{U_x} + \frac{U_V}{U_x}. \tag{6.12}$$

Given the price, visits will be made up to the point at which the price is equal to the marginal benefit of another visit less the additional congestion cost it causes. Contrasting this to (6.8) shows that the optimal number of visits will be sustained if the price is set so that

$$p = C_V - [n - 1]\frac{U_V}{U_x}. \tag{6.13}$$

However, it follows from optimal membership condition (6.7) that at this price the total revenue raised falls short of the cost of the club, since

$$nvp = C + nv\frac{U_V}{U_x} < C \tag{6.14}$$

by the fact that $U_V < 0$. This inequality shows the important result that a membership fee alone cannot both generate the correct number of visits and allow the club to break even.

The charging scheme that is required to finance the club and control visits is a two-part tariff consisting of a membership fee and a user fee. Let the fixed part of the two-part tariff be given by F and the user fee be p. With this tariff the club solves

$$\max_{\{x,v,G,n\}} U(x, G, v, nv)$$

subject to $M = x + F + pv$ and $nF + pnv = C(G, nv),$ $\tag{6.15}$

where both the individual budget constraint and the break-even constraint for the club have been imposed. The necessary conditions for this optimization readily yield the efficiency conditions (6.6) and (6.8), while the charging condition becomes

$$F + pv = vC_V - nv\frac{U_V}{U_x},$$

which is the analogue of (6.7). Taken together, these observations show that the two-part tariff allows the club to break even and attain efficiency.

This section has addressed the issue of charging when the number of visits to the club cannot be controlled directly. It has shown that with variable utilization a two-part tariff is required. The cost per visit is used to control the number of visits while the fixed fee covers any residual payment needed for the club to break even.

6.4   Clubs and the Economy

The analysis of the decision process of an individual club demonstrated that the club will ensure efficiency of provision for its membership. It is tempting to conclude from this observation that the argument can be extended to the economy as a whole, with efficiency in public good provision attained by the population of consumers separating themselves into a series of efficient clubs. This was the conclusion reached by Buchanan. We now argue that although this may sometimes be so, it is by no means guaranteed.

There are two settings in which the issue of economywide efficiency can be considered. The first setting, and the analytically simpler of the two, is to consider an economy where the efficient size of club is small relative to the total population. This situation applies when the club suffers from significant congestion, so its optimal size is relatively small, and population size is large. The second setting is when the efficient size of the club is large relative to the total population. This can arise either through limited congestion or through there being a small population. Either of these settings can potentially occur, and they give very different perspectives on the efficiency of clubs at the level of the economy.

6.4.1   Small Clubs

Consider first an economy in which the size of the efficient membership of a club is small relative to the size of the total population. This allows some very clear conclusions to be obtained.

To understand the effect of this assumption, consider what happens as population size increases. Initially, with a small population, there will either be some of the population who are not in an optimal-sized club or else every club will differ slightly in size from the optimum. In the first case, as the size of the population increases, the number of those not in an optimal size club becomes trivial compared to the total population, so the deviation from efficiency tends to zero. In the second case, as the population increases, the deviation of each club from the optimum size becomes less and less, so again the inefficiency tends to zero. Therefore increases in population size eventually wipe out the deviation from efficiency.

The limiting interpretation of a large population is one which is infinite in number. Assuming an infinite population allows the standard "tricks" that can be played with an infinity. In particular, if the population size is infinite, then it can be divided exactly into an infinite number of optimal size clubs. The provision of public goods by clubs is then efficient for each club and for the economy as a whole.

The conclusion of this analysis is that if the efficient membership of each club is small relative to the total population, then the outcome for the economy will be that a very large number of clubs will form each with the correct number of members and each providing the efficient level of service. Hence efficiency will be attained for the economy as a whole. In this case the efficiency of each individual club is reflected at the aggregate level.

6.4.2 Large Clubs

The second case, which is more interesting from both a practical and an analytical perspective, arises when the optimal membership of each club is relatively large compared to the total population. In this case the population size can support only a limited number of optimally sized clubs.

Two outcomes are then possible. It may be that the total population size is an integer multiple of the number of clubs. This allows the population to be divided neatly among the clubs and efficiency is achieved. However, such a neat match between club size and population is very unlikely. The more likely outcome is that there will be some remainder when the total population is divided by optimum club size. The outcome in this situation requires some careful analysis.

To focus the argument, assume that the total population is more than the optimum size of a club but less than twice the optimum. Denoting the total population by N and the optimum club size by n^*, utility as a function of the size of the club is graphed in figure 6.1. The assumptions imply that membership of a club of size $\frac{N}{2}$ produces less utility than that of a club of size n^*.

To determine the equilibrium, it is necessary to be clear about what is possible and what is not in terms of membership fees. For reasons that will become clear, a distinction must be made between cases where all members of a club must pay the

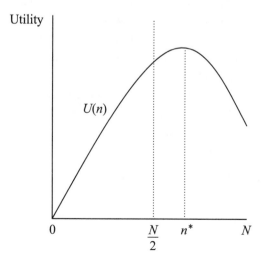

Figure 6.1
Utility and club size

same fee and cases where fees can be different among members. The latter case can be interpreted as all club members paying the same fee but making transfers, or "compensation" payments, among themselves. If this occurs, the fees net of transfers will differ.

Equal Fees

Let all members of each club pay the same fee. In this case it is easy to see that two clubs of size $\frac{N}{2}$ cannot be an equilibrium. Start from such a position and consider the decision problem of an individual. Assume all other club members remain in their initial clubs, which is an application of Nash equilibrium. The individual can stay in the same club or move to the other club. If individuals change clubs, the club they move to increases in membership from $\frac{N}{2}$ to $\frac{[N+1]}{2}$. This larger club provides greater utility, so moving is the preferred choice. Existing members of the club also benefit from an increase in membership and will welcome a new member. Because there is an incentive to change clubs, the initial position could not have been an equilibrium. For there to be equilibrium, one club must be of efficient size n^* and the other club of size $N - n^*$. In equilibrium the members of the larger club have a higher level of utility. Thus they have no motive to move to the smaller club, nor to accept members of the smaller club, because they will be made worse off by doing so.

The next question is whether this outcome is efficient from the viewpoint of society. The answer is dependent on the precise situation, and but for the example in figure 6.1, the possibilities can be grouped into four categories. To see this, note that the social decision must be to choose between having either one club or two clubs. When there is a single club, it may be beneficial to exclude some individuals from the club altogether. Alternatively, the single club may contain the entire population. If it is optimal to have two clubs, these may be equally sized or may be dissimilar. Summarizing this discussion gives the following breakdown of potential optimum configurations:

1. A single club, some of the population excluded
2. A single club containing the entire population
3. Two equally sized clubs
4. Two unequal clubs

Outcome 1 will occur if it is too costly to form a new club for a small number of members and additional membership of the single club reduces the benefit of existing members significantly. The contrast with outcomes 2, 3, and 4 depends on the costs of congestion relative to the gains from being closer to optimality. For instance, in outcome 3, with two equally sized clubs, both must have less than the optimum membership. The question then has to be asked whether it is better to take one closer to the optimum (moving to outcome 4). Those in the larger club will gain while those left in the smaller club will lose. Contrasting option 4 to option 2, the question has to be asked whether the smaller club in option 4 should be closed completely and the population all placed in a single club. This will cause a congestion cost for those initially in the larger club but may benefit those who were in the smaller club, since the per capita cost will be lower and public good provision higher.

At this level of generality it is not possible to proceed to identify the nature of the optimal allocation without being completely specific about the relationships (the utility function and congestion function) that underlie the model. What can be concluded is that there is no necessity for the equilibrium position with two dissimilar sized clubs to be the efficient outcome. So, from the perspective of the entire economy, the actions of the clubs though individually efficient do not guarantee social efficiency. The reason is that both clubs are competing to become larger, so when one club attracts new members in order to grow, it does not take into account the cost inflicted on the members of the other club that is becoming smaller.

To illustrate this point consider the following example: The total population, N, is normalized to have size one ($N = 1$), and this population has to be allocated between two clubs in proportions n and $1 - n$ (with $0 \leq n \leq 1$). The utility of being in a club of size n is given by

$$U(n) = n^3[1 - n], \tag{6.16}$$

so that the utility-maximizing club size is three-quarters of the population (which is greater than half the population, giving the situation illustrated in figure 6.1). Clubs with either the entire population as members or with no members provide zero utility.

We graph the utility of each club member for each partition of the population between the two clubs in figure 6.2. The figure measures the membership n in club A from the left corner and the membership $1 - n$ of club B from the right corner. The width of the figure is the total population, which is normalized to one. Utility in club A begins at 0 when $n = 0$ and rises to a maximum when $n = \frac{3}{4}$. Reading from the right corner, we see that utility in club B begins at 0 when $n = 1$ and rises

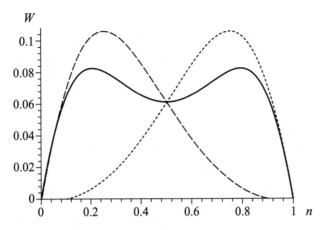

Figure 6.2
Optimum with unequally sized clubs

to a maximum at $n = \frac{1}{4}$. The equilibrium outcome occurs when one club is optimal, with $\frac{3}{4}$ of the population, and the other is inefficient, with just $\frac{1}{4}$.

The key feature of this example is that population is too small to allow both clubs to reach their utility maximizing size of $\frac{3}{4}$. The efficient outcome is obtained by maximizing total welfare

$$W(n) = nU(n) + [1 - n]U(1 - n). \tag{6.17}$$

The necessary condition for efficiency is then

$$U(n) + nU'(n) = U(1 - n) + [1 - n]U'(1 - n), \tag{6.18}$$

which requires that the marginal gains of another member are the same for both clubs. The average level of welfare, $\frac{W(n)}{n}$, is depicted by twin-peaked curve in figure 6.2. It is then readily seen that efficiency is achieved at one of the two peaks where there are two unequally sized clubs. Furthermore the membership allocation at either of these peaks has one club that exceeds the optimal membership and another club that falls below. The attainment of efficiency requires that the size of the larger club is pushed beyond the size that maximizes the utility of each member. The reason for this is that welfare is concerned with the product of n and $U(n)$, so there is always an incentive to raise the membership of the club generating the higher utility for its members.

Although this incentive always exists, it is not always the dominant effect. Changing the utility function can affect the efficient outcome, but it will preserve

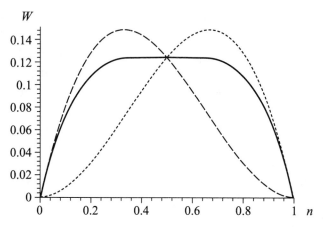

Figure 6.3
Optimum with equally sized clubs

the fundamental inefficiency of the equilibrium outcome. Figure 6.3 depicts the situation for the utility function

$$U(n) = n^2[1 - n]. \tag{6.19}$$

The equilibrium involves two unequal clubs, one with $\frac{2}{3}$ of the population and the other with $\frac{1}{3}$. The resulting average welfare function is single-peaked, with its maximum occurring with two equally sized clubs of size $n = 1 - n = \frac{1}{2}$. Hence efficiency is attained when both clubs are below the efficient membership.

Unequal Fees

The case where equal fees were paid by all members of a club was complex in terms of possible outcomes, but that where fees can be unequal is much more so. To gain some insight into this statement, we begin with a consideration of the determination of the equilibrium division of members between clubs.

As a starting point, let the allocation of members be the equilibrium found for the no-transfer case where there is one club of size n^* and one of $N - n^*$. It was previously argued that there was no incentive for those in the optimal club to move and no possibility of those in the smaller club being allowed to move. When unequal fees are allowable neither of these claims need be true. Consider first a member of the smaller club. If they were to move to the larger club, they would obtain a utility gain of $U(n^* + 1) - U(N - n^*)$. Their presence makes the previously optimal club too large so the welfare of its existing members will fall. However, it is a possibility that the gain of the new member is sufficiently great that they can more than compensate the existing members for their losses and yet still be better off. In other words, the new member pays a fee greater than that of the existing members and the fee of existing members is reduced more than sufficiently to compensate them for the additional crowding. If this compensation is possible, then the move between clubs will be allowed and the initial position cannot be an equilibrium.

Now consider reversing the argument and considering the incentive for a member of the optimal club to move to the smaller club. With equal fees this would never happen. Now let unequal fees be allowed. If the move did occur, the club member moving would lose utility of value $U(n^*) - U(N - n^* + 1)$, but the existing members of the smaller club would each gain $U(N - n^* + 1) - U(N - n^*)$. If they could collectively agree to pay compensation to the new member (meaning let them pay a lower membership fee), then it is possible that the existing members could more than compensate the new member for the loss incurred in their move while still remaining better off themselves.

These arguments reveal that members of the optimal club may be enticed to the smaller club and that members of the smaller club may be able to "buy" themselves into the optimal club. Both of these mechanisms may even be functioning simultaneously. The outcome of this reasoning is that it may not be possible to find any equilibrium, and even if an equilibrium exists, it is not easy to characterize. Furthermore there is even less reason to expect any equilibrium that is achieved to be efficient. All of this occurs because the population cannot be allocated to a set of clubs each with optimal membership except in the unlikely case of population size being a integer multiple of the optimal membership level. This problem does not diminish even when population size increases.

There is one situation in which this argument does not apply. Consider again the graph of utility as a function of club size drawn in figure 6.1. The problems of dividing the population into optimal clubs resulted from the fact that there was a unique value for optimal club membership. If the graph were instead like figure 6.4, with a flat section at its peak, then there would be a range of optimal sizes. To see the effect of this, let the optimal club size range from 2 to 3. Then a population of 11 consumers could be divided into three clubs of size 3 and one of size 2 and the economy would achieve efficiency. Of course, with a population of size 11, this could not be done if optimal club size was unique (unless it was 11). Furthermore any population size greater than 11 can be divided into optimal size clubs.

The general version of this argument is illustrated in figure 6.5. For a single club the range of optimal memberships is between n' and n''. When there are two clubs,

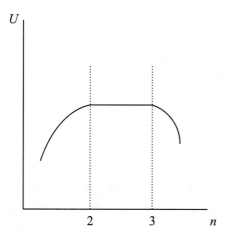

Figure 6.4
Non-unique club size

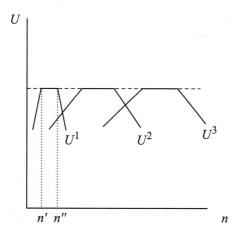

Figure 6.5
Achieving efficiency

optimality can occur for the range $2n'$ to $2n''$. This extension of the range continues as additional clubs are introduced. Eventually, if the total population is large enough, the ranges of values of total population for which optimality cannot be achieved shrink to zero (alternatively, the ranges of optimal size overlap) and all consumers can be placed in optimal clubs.

6.4.3   Conclusion

The conclusion of this section has to be that the efficiency of the individual club does not always translate into efficiency for the economy. In a large population approximate efficiency will be achieved, and individual utility will be virtually equal to maximal attainable utility. However, when there is a small-number problem, efficiency will not be achieved by the equilibrium allocation of members between clubs. This should not be surprising since small numbers introduces problems akin to those found in oligopoly markets. What occurs is that small groups of consumers are able to affect their own utility levels by choosing to form optimal size clubs. Therefore they possess market power, and this is reflected in the inefficiency. These problems are eliminated if there are a range of optimal club sizes.

6.5   Local Public Goods

The concept of a local public good was introduced in section 6.2. A local public good has the feature that its benefits are restricted to a particular geographical area and it cannot be enjoyed outside of that area. Relating this idea to the analysis of club goods, one can think of local communities as clubs that are formed to provide local public goods. To become a member of a local community, a consumer must move into the area (i.e., join the club) and pay whatever local taxes are levied in that community (i.e., pay the membership fee). Once they have done this, they can then enjoy the local public goods that are provided.

An important feature of the club good was that exclusion was possible, and it is interesting to discuss whether this is the case with local public goods. There are two points at which exclusion may be possible. First, a consumer must become resident in an area in order to benefit from the local public good. Although few (if any) local authorities have the right to prevent the resale of houses or to forcibly evict existing occupants, they do have the power to prevent additional new building. Consequently, although reductions in population may be hard to achieve (unlike expulsions in an ordinary club), the exclusion of additional members is possible. Second, there is the payment of taxes. Any resident who refuses to pay local taxes can be either forced to pay or excluded from the club, since local authorities have legal authority to collect taxation. If we impose the possibility of exclusion, then the analysis of local public goods becomes exactly that of the clubs we have already considered. However, the analysis of nonexclusion is also of interest with local public goods, since this captures the idea of a freely operating market in which individuals have the freedom to select their preferred residential location. We now focus on nonexclusion.

The concept of local public goods can be applied to the provision of public services by local regions in order to understand the allocation of a population between different localities. Intuitively we can think of localities competing for population by setting the package of public good provision and taxation they offer. Members of the population look at what is offered in different localities and select the one that offers the highest utility level. This will cause population flows until no one can gain by moving locality. This is similar to the adjustment process for club goods except for the fact that there is free access (i.e., no possibility of barring access to new migrants even if the existing population would lose from the immigration).

In this framework it is natural to question whether an efficient equilibrium will be attained. The localities are competing for population and no restrictions are imposed on the freedom of the population to move between regions. With clubs, efficiency was achieved at least within the clubs. To see whether the same is true for local public goods, it is necessary to construct a model of location choice.

Consider a total population of H consumers that is to be divided between two localities with h being the population of a locality (we use different notation to avoid confusion with club membership). Each locality provides a local public good financed through a charge on the population. As the population increases, the unit cost of the public good per resident is reduced. This is the benefit from increased population. There is also a cost to increasing population. This can be motivated by assuming that there is a fixed resource in each region so that income per person falls as the population rises and this resource has to be shared between a greater number.

These assumptions imply that income can be written as a decreasing function, $M(h)$, of the population of a locality. Think of wages or welfare benefits reducing with increased immigration. If the locality provides G units of the public good, the charge per resident is $\frac{G}{h}$. Combining these, the income left to spend on private goods is $M(h) - \frac{G}{h}$, and the resulting level of utility $U\left(M(h) - \frac{G}{h}, G\right)$.

It is assumed that localities choose the level of public good optimally given their population. This eliminates the possibility of inefficiency through a level of provision that does not satisfy the Samuelson rule. Given a population h, the level of public good provision satisfies the Samuelson rule

$$h\frac{U_G}{U_x} = 1. \tag{6.20}$$

This condition can be solved to find the level of public good, $G(h)$, which depends on the population of the locality. Substituting the level of the public good into the utility function determines the level of utility as a function of population. This relationship is written in brief as $U(h)$. The implications of the model follow from the fact that an increase in h can increase or decrease utility. Differentiating $U(h)$ with respect to h shows that

$$U' = U_x M' + U_x \left[\frac{G}{h^2}\right]. \tag{6.21}$$

The first term on the right-hand side is negative, since an increase in population reduces income M, while the second term is positive because the cost of the public good is reduced. It is therefore unclear what the net effect will be. To analyze the model further, assume that utility initially increases with the population until it reaches a maximum and then decreases. In addition let $U(H) > U(0)$ so that having all the population in a single locality leads to higher utility than having no population. This can be motivated by the fact that a small number of people find it very expensive to provide the public good but the income is not reduced too far when the entire population is in one locality.

The dynamics of migration are that the population always flows from the locality with the lower utility to the locality with the higher utility. An equilibrium is reached when both localities offer the same utility level or else all the population is in one region. Consequently, if $U(H) \geq U(0)$, an equilibrium can have all the population locating in one region or have the population divided between the two localities with utilities equalized. In the latter equilibrium $U(h^1) = U(h^2)$. The outcomes that can arise in this model can be illustrated by graphing the utility against the population in the two regions.

A possible structure of the utility function is shown in figure 6.6. This figure measures the population in locality 1 from the left corner and the population in locality 2 from the right corner. The width of the figure is the total population. The essential feature of this figure is that the population level that maximizes util-

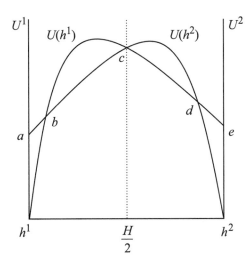

Figure 6.6
Stability of the symmetric equilibrium

ity is less than half the total population. There are five potential equilibria at a, b, c, d, and e. The equilibrium at c is symmetric with both regions having a population of $\frac{H}{2}$. This equilibrium is also stable and will arise from any starting point between b and d. The two asymmetric equilibria at b and d are unstable. For instance, starting just above b, the population will adjust to c. Starting just below b, the population will adjust to a. The two extremes points, a and e, where all the population are located within one of the two localities are stable but inefficient.

An alternative structure of utility is shown in figure 6.7. The change made is that the utility-maximizing population of a locality is now greater than one-half of the total population. There is still a symmetric and efficient equilibrium at b. But this equilibrium is now unstable: starting with a population below b, the flow of population will lead to the extreme outcome at a, whereas starting above b will lead to c. The two extreme equilibria are stable but inefficient. All consumers would prefer the symmetric equilibrium to either of the extreme equilibria.

What this simple model shows is that there is no reason why flows of population between localities will achieve efficiency. It is possible for the economy to get trapped in an inefficient equilibrium. In this case the market economy does not function efficiently. The reason for this is that the movement between localities of one consumer affects both the population left behind and the population the consumer joins. These nonmarket linkages lead to the inefficiency.

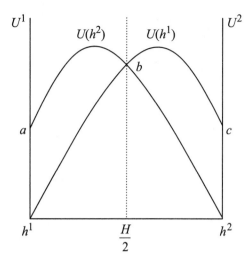

Figure 6.7
Inefficient stable equilibria

6.6   The Tiebout Hypothesis

The previous section has shown that inefficiency can arise when the population divides between two regions on the basis of their provision of local public goods. From this result it would be natural to infer that inefficiency will always be an issue with local public goods. It is therefore surprising that the Tiebout hypothesis asserts instead that efficiency will always be obtained with local public goods.

Tiebout observed that pure public goods lead to market failure because of the difficulties connected with information transmission. Since the true valuation by a consumer of a public good cannot be observed and a pure public good is nonexcludable, free-riding occurs and private provision is inefficient. This point was explored in the previous chapter. Now assume that there are a number of alternative communities where a consumer can choose to live and that these differ in their provision of local public goods. In contrast to the pure public good case, a consumer's choice of which location to live in provides a very clear signal of preferences. The chosen location is obviously the one offering the provision of local public goods closest to the consumer's ideal. Hence, through community choice, preference revelation takes place. Misrepresenting preference cannot help a consumer here, since the choice of a nonoptimal location merely reduces their welfare level. The only rational choice is to act honestly.

The final step in the argument can now be constructed. Since preference revelation is taking place, it follows that if there are enough different types of community and enough consumers with each kind of preference, then all consumers will allocate themselves to a community that is optimal for them and each community will be optimally sized. Thus the market outcome will be fully efficient, and the inefficiencies discussed in connection with pure public goods will not arise. Phrased more prosaically, consumers reveal their preferences by voting with their feet, and this ensures the construction of optimal communities. This also shows why the analysis of the previous section failed to find efficiency. The existence of at most two localities violated the large-number assumption employed in this argument.

The significance of this efficiency result, which is commonly called the *Tiebout hypothesis*, has been much debated. Supporters view it as another demonstration of the power of the market in allocating resources. Critics denounce it as simply another empty demonstration of what is possible under unrealistic assumptions. Certainly the Tiebout hypothesis has much the same foundations as the Two Theorems of Welfare Economics, since both concern economies with no rigidities and large numbers of participants. But there is one important difference between the two: formalizing the Tiebout hypothesis is a more difficult task.

To obtain an insight into this difficulty, some of the steps in the previous argument need to be retraced. It was assumed that consumers could move between communities or at least choose between them with no restrictions on their choice. If housing markets function efficiently, there should not be a problem in finding accommodation. Where problems do arise is in the link between income and location. An assumption that can justify the previous analysis is that consumers obtain all their income from "rents" such as from the ownership of land, property, or shares. In this case it does not matter where the consumers choose to reside, since the rents will accrue regardless of location. Once some income is earned from employment, then the Tiebout hypothesis only holds if all employment opportunities are replicated in all communities. Otherwise, communities with better employment prospects will appear more attractive even if they offer a slightly less appealing set of local public goods. If the two issues become entangled in this way, then the Tiebout hypothesis will naturally fail.

Further difficulties with the hypothesis arise when the numbers of communities and individuals is considered. When these are both finite, the problems already discussed above with achieving efficiency through market behavior arise again. These are compounded when individuals of different types are needed to make communities work. For example, assume that community A needs 10 doctors and 20 teachers to provide the optimal combination of local public goods while, community B requires 10 police officers and 20 teachers. If doctors, teachers, and police officers are not found in the proportions 1:4:1, then efficiency in allocation between the communities cannot be achieved. Furthermore, if all teachers have different tastes from doctors and from police officers, then none of the communities can supply the ideal local public good combination to meet all tastes.

The efficiency of the allocation can then be recovered in two steps. First, if we appeal again to the large population assumption, the issue of achieving the precise mix of different types is eliminated—there will always be enough people of each type to populate the localities in the correct proportions. Second, even if tastes are different, it is still possible to obtain agreement on the level of public good through the use of personalized prices. This issue has already been discussed for public goods in connection with the Lindahl equilibrium. The same idea can be applied to local public goods, in which case it would be the local taxes that are differentiated among residents to equalize the level of public good demand and to attain efficiency with a heterogeneous population.

The Tiebout hypothesis depends on the freedom of consumers to move to preferred locations. This is only possible if there are no transactions costs involved in changing location. In practice, such transactions costs arise in the commission that has to be paid to estate agents, in legal fees, and in the physical costs of shipping furniture and belongings. These can be significant and will cause friction in the movement of consumers to the extent that suboptimal levels of provision will be tolerated to avoid paying these costs.

To sum up, the Tiebout hypothesis provides support for allowing the market, by which is meant the free movement of consumers, to determine the provision of local public goods. By choosing communities, consumers reveal their tastes. They also have to abide by local tax law, so free-riding is ruled out. Hence efficiency is achieved. Although apparently simple, there are a number of difficulties when the practical implementation of this hypothesis is considered. The population may not partition neatly into the communities envisaged, and employment ties may bind consumers to localities whose local public good supply is not to their liking. Transactions costs in housing markets are significant, and these will limit the freedom of movement that is key to the hypothesis. The hypothesis provides an interesting insight into the forces at work in the formation of communities, but it does not guarantee efficiency.

6.7   Empirical Tests

The Tiebout hypothesis provides the reassuring conclusion that efficiency will be attained by local communities providing public goods efficiently. If correct, the forces of economics and local politics can be left to work unrestricted by government intervention. Given the strength of this conclusion, and some of the doubts cast on whether the Tiebout argument really works, it is natural to conduct empirical tests of the hypothesis.

In testing any hypothesis, it is first necessary to determine what the observational implications of the hypothesis will be. For Tiebout this means isolating what may be different between an economy in which the Tiebout hypothesis applies and one in which it does not. Empirical testing has been handicapped by the difficulty of establishing quite what this difference is.

The earlier empirical studies focused on property taxes, public good provision and house prices. The reason for this was made clear by Oates, who initiated this line of research in 1969: local governments fund their activities primarily through property taxes and the manner in which these taxes are reflected in house prices provides evidence on the Tiebout hypothesis. Assume that all local governments provide the same level of public goods. Then the jurisdictions with higher property tax rates will be less attractive and have lower house prices. Now let the provision of public goods vary. Holding tax rates constant, house prices should be higher in areas with more public good provision. These effects offset each other, and if the public good effect is sufficiently strong, jurisdictions with higher tax rates will actually have higher property prices. Oates considered evidence on house prices, property tax rates, and educational provision for 53 primarily residential municipalities in New Jersey. These municipalities were chosen because the majority of residents commuted to work and hence were not tied by employment to a particular location. The analysis showed that house prices were reduced by high property taxes but increased by greater public good provision.

Whether these results were evidence in favor of the Tiebout hypothesis became the subject of a debate that focused on the implications of the theory. Whereas Oates took differences in property prices as an indication of the Tiebout hypothesis at work (on the ground that more attractive locations would witness increased competition for the housing stock), an alternative argument suggests that a given quality of house would have the same price in all jurisdictions if Tiebout applied. The argument for uniform prices is based on the view that property taxes are the price paid for the bundle of public goods provided by the local government. If this price reflects the benefit enjoyed from the public goods, as it should if the Tiebout hypothesis is functioning, then it should not affect property prices. Uniform property prices should therefore be expected if the Tiebout hypothesis applies—an observation that lead to a series of studies looking for uniform house prices across jurisdictions with different levels of public good provision. Unfortunately, as Epple, Zelenitz, and Visscher show, the same conclusion is true even when the Tiebout hypothesis does not hold so that net-of-tax property prices should be uniform in all jurisdictions in all circumstances. Instead, they argue that when the Tiebout hypothesis applies, housing demand is not affected by the property tax rate, but when Tiebout does not apply, it is affected. Looking at prices, which are equilibrium conditions, cannot then provide a test of Tiebout. Instead, a test has to be based on the structural equations of housing demand and location demand and their dependence, or otherwise, on tax rates. This conclusion undermines the earlier work on property values but does not provide an easily implementable test.

As a response to these difficulties, alternative tests of the hypothesis have been constructed. One approach to determining whether the Tiebout hypothesis applies is to consider the level of demand for public goods from the residents of each locality. If the Tiebout hypothesis applies, residents should have selected a residential location that provides a level of public goods in line with their preferences. Hence within each locality there should be a degree of homogeneity in the level of demand for public goods. Note carefully that this does not assert that all residents have the same preferences but only that, given the taxes and other local charges they pay, their demands are equalized. The test of the hypothesis is then to consider the variance in demand within regions relative to the variance in demand across regions. Such a test was conducted by Gramlich and Rubinfeld who studied households in Michigan suburbs and provided compelling evidence that there was less variation within regions than across regions.

It is necessary to note that these results do not confirm that the Tiebout hypothesis is completely operating but only that some sorting of residents is occurring. It is supportive evidence for the hypothesis but not complete confirmation. This conclusion is only to be expected since, given the extent of frictions in the housing market, the freedom of movement necessary for the hypothesis to hold exactly is lacking.

Overall, the empirical work is suggestive that the right forces are at work to push the economy toward the efficient outcome of Tiebout but that there are residual frictions that prevent the complete sorting required for the efficiency.

Having said this, the tests have been limited to data from suburban areas that have the highest chance of producing the right outcome. In other locations, where the separation between work and location is not so simple, the hypothesis would have less chance of applying.

6.8   Conclusions

The chapter has discussed the nature of club goods and local public goods, and drawn the distinction between these and pure public goods. For a club good, the essential feature is the possibility of exclusion, and it has been shown how exclusion allows an individual club to attain efficiency. Although it is tempting to extend this argument to the economy as a whole, a series of new issues arise when the allocation of a population between clubs is analyzed. Efficiency may be attained, but it is not guaranteed.

Many of the same issues arise with local public goods whose benefits are restricted to a given geographical area. We have treated local public goods as a model of provision by localities where each locality is described by the package of public good and taxation that it offers. When there is no exclusion from membership, there is no implication that efficiency will be attained when residential choice can be made from only a small number of localities.

In contrast to this, the Tiebout hypothesis evokes a large-number assumption to argue that the population will be able to sort itself into a set of localities, each of which is optimal for its residents. At the heart of this argument is that choice of locality reveals preferences for public goods, so efficiency becomes attainable. The Tiebout hypothesis has been subjected to empirical testing, but the evidence is at best inconclusive. While it shows some degree of sorting and is certainly not a rejection of Tiebout, it does not go as far as confirming that the promised efficiency is delivered.

Further Reading

The potential for clubs to achieve efficiency in the provision of public goods was first identified in:

Buchanan, J. 1965. An economic theory of clubs. *Economica* 32: 1–14.

A more extensive discussion of many of these issues can be found in:

Cornes, R. C., and Sandler, T. 1996. *The Theory of Externalities, Public Goods and Club Goods.* Cambridge: Cambridge University Press.

Sandler, T., and Tschirhart, J. 1980. The economic theory of clubs: An evaluative survey. *Journal of Economic Literature* 18: 1481–1521.

A study of public goods with exclusion and user fees is in:

Drèze, J. H. 1980. Public goods with exclusion. *Journal of Public Economics* 13: 5–24.

The problems of attaining efficiency in a club economy are explored by:

Wooders, M. H. 1978. Equilibria, the core and jurisdiction structures in economies with a local public good. *Journal of Economic Theory* 18: 328–48.

The problem of attaining efficiency in a local public goods economy with mobility is in:

Greenberg, J. 1983. Local public goods with mobility: Existence and optimality of a general equilibrium. *Journal of Economic Theory* 30: 17–33.

Pestieau, P. 1983. Fiscal mobility and local public goods: A survey of the empirical and theoretical studies of the Tiebout model. In J. F. Thisse and H. G. Zoller, eds., *Locational Analysis of Public Facilities.* Amsterdam: North-Holland.

The influential Tiebout hypothesis was first stated in:

Tiebout, C. M. 1956. A pure theory of local expenditure. *Journal of Political Economy* 64: 416–24.

A strong critique of the hypothesis is in:

Bewley, T. F. 1981. A critique of Tiebout's theory of local public expenditure. *Econometrica* 49: 713–40.

Tests of the Tiebout hypothesis can be found in:

Epple, D., Zelenitz, A., and Visscher, M. 1978. A search for testable implications of the Tiebout hypothesis. *Journal of Political Economy* 86: 405–25.

Gramlich, E., and Rubinfield, D. 1982. Micro estimates of public spending demand and test of the Tiebout and median voter hypotheses. *Journal of Political Economy* 90: 536–60.

Hamilton, B. W. 1976. The effects of property taxes and local public spending on property values: A theoretical comment. *Journal of Political Economy* 84: 647–50.

Oates, W. E. 1969. The effects of property taxes and local public spending on property values: An empirical study of tax capitalization and the Tiebout hypothesis. *Journal of Political Economy* 77: 957–71.

Exercises

6.1.   If a tennis club does not limit membership, what will be the consequence?

6.2.   Is education a local public good?

6.3.   Can club theory be applied to analyze immigration policy?

6.4.   Consider a population of consumers. When a consumer is a member of a club providing a level of provision G and having n members, they obtain utility

$$U = M - \frac{G}{n} + \log(G) - \frac{n}{k},$$

where k is a positive constant and $\frac{G}{n}$ is the charge for club membership.

a. Derive the optimal membership for the club if it maximizes the utility of each member.

b. Assuming the club chooses G optimally given its membership, calculate the loss due to membership of a club with suboptimal size.

c. Assume that the total population is of size m, with $k < m < 2k$. Show that there is a continuum of Pareto-efficient allocations of population to clubs.

d. What club size maximizes total utility produced by the club? Contrast to the answer for part a.

6.5.   Will a club be efficient if it does not exercise exclusion?

6.6.   What will be the efficient membership level of a club if there is no congestion? Is it still appropriate to call it a club good if there is no congestion?

6.7.   Do all members of a club agree with the club's choices? What about nonmembers?

6.8.   Assume that a consumer receives a utility of $[a + bG - \beta n] + M - p$ when paying a price p to be in a club with n members and provision G of the public good and a utility of M if the consumer is not in a club. a, b, and β are positive constants.

a. Show that the willingness-to-pay of a consumer for club membership satisfies $p \le [a + bG - \beta n]$.

b. Assume that the club is provided by a monopolist who chooses membership and provision to maximize profit. If the cost of running the club is $G + n$, what are the profit-maximizing choices G and n?

c. What choice of G and n maximizes the welfare of a typical member if costs of the club are shared equally?

d. Compare the monopolistic and welfare-maximizing equilibrium values and discuss the contrasts.

6.9.   Theme parks do not use two-part tariffs. What is the consequence? Why do they choose not to use two-part tariffs?

6.10. How can a monopolist employ a two-part tariff to extract consumer surplus? Is the outcome efficient?

6.11. How does the design of two-part tariffs have to be modified when consumers are heterogeneous?

6.12. Assume an economy with 100 identical consumers. Assume that if consumers belong to a club with n members and the cost of the club is shared equally, they would obtain utility

$$U = \begin{cases} n & \text{for } n \le 5, \\ 5 & \text{for } 5 < n < 6, \\ (11 - n) & \text{for } n \ge 6. \end{cases}$$

a. Sketch this utility function and comment on the optimal club size.

b. Show that a population of size 14 cannot be allocated among optimal membership clubs. Beyond what population size is it possible to guarantee optimality?

c. How would your answers change if the utility function were instead

$$U = \begin{cases} n & \text{for } n \leq 5.5, \\ (11 - n) & \text{for } n \geq 5.5. \end{cases}$$

d. Discuss which of the two specifications you find most compelling. Does this lead you to believe clubs will attain efficiency for the economy?

6.13.   "A club will always seek to achieve the best outcome for its members. Therefore an economy with clubs achieves efficiency." Explain and critically appraise this statement.

6.14.   Consider a club where the utility function (incorporating the charge) of a member is $U = a + bn - cn^2$. Find the optimal membership of the club. What is the membership level that maximizes the total utility of the club? Contrast the two levels and explain the difference.

6.15.   Explain why the economy will be closer to an efficient equilibrium when congestion occurs with a small membership level.

6.16.   If the optimal club size is between 4 and 5, what is the smallest population beyond which efficiency is always achieved? What if the optimal size is between 3 and 4?

6.17.   Let $U = 40n - 2n^2$. Find the optimal club membership n^*. Graph the value of U against population size N when the population is divided between:

a. 1 club,

b. 2 clubs,

c. 3 clubs.

6.18.   What does the Tiebout hypothesis suggest for the organization of a city's structure?

6.19.   Should local communities be restricted in tax powers?

6.20.   (Bewley 1981) Imagine a world with 2 consumers and 2 potential jurisdictions. Each of the consumers has one unit of labor to supply and preferences described by

$$U = U(G^i),$$

where G^i is the quantity of public good provided in the jurisdiction i of residence. Denote labor supply in jurisdiction i by L^i; the public good is produced from labor with production function

$$G^i = L^i.$$

The regions both levy a tax on labor income to finance provision of their public good supply.

a. Assuming that consumers take taxes and public good provision as given when choosing their location, construct an inefficient equilibrium for this economy.

b. Discuss the inconsistency of consumer beliefs in this equilibrium.

c. How is the equilibrium modified if there is a continuum of consumers, each of whom is "small" relative to the economy?

6.21. (Scotchmer 1985) Suppose that consumers have income M, preferences represented by

$$U = x + 5 \log(G) - n,$$

and the public good produced with cost function

$$C(G) = G.$$

a. Show that the utility-maximizing membership is $n = 5$ with provision level $G = 25$.

b. Prove that if G is chosen optimally given n, utility as a function of n is

$$U = M + 10 \log(n) - 2n.$$

Hence for a total population of 18 calculate the efficient (integer) number of clubs and their (possibly noninteger) membership level. What price for membership will give zero profit with these values of n and G?

c. Given the utility achieved at the solution to part b, show that the willingness to pay is given by

$$p = 9.5 - 5 \log(22.5) + 5 \log(G) - n.$$

From this, find the profit maximizing choice of G and n and show that profit is positive. Comment on the possibility of an efficient, zero-profit equilibrium.

d. Discuss the integer issues in this analysis.

6.22. Consider two consumers with preferences

$$U^h = 1 - T^i + \alpha^h \log(G^i), \qquad h = 1, 2,$$

where T^i is the tax levied in jurisdiction i and G^i is public good provision. Assume $\alpha^2 > \alpha^1$. The level of public good in each region is decided by majority voting of its residents. If there are two residents, assume that the supply is the average of the preferred quantities of the residents.

a. Show that the preferred quantity of public good for consumer h if they locate in jurisdiction i is given by

$$G^h = n^i \alpha^h,$$

where n^i is the jurisdiction population.

b. Assuming consumers correctly predict the consequences of location choice, show that there is no equilibrium if

$$\alpha^2 > 1 + 2 \log(1 + \alpha^2).$$

c. Show that there is an equilibrium if consumers take provision levels as given.

6.23. Assume that there are three types of consumer with preferences $U_1 = \alpha_1 \log(G) + x$, $U_2 = \alpha_2 \log(G) + x$, and $U_3 = \alpha_3 \log(G) + x$. There is an equal number of each type and all consumers have the same income level. If there are two jurisdictions that levy a tax and provide the public good, what is the equilibrium allocation? What is the efficient allocation?

7 Externalities

7.1 Introduction

An externality is a link between economic agents that lies outside the price system of the economy. Everyday examples include the pollution from a factory that harms a local fishery and the envy that is felt when a neighbor proudly displays a new car. Such externalities are not controlled directly by the choices of those affected—the fishery cannot choose to buy less pollution nor can you choose to buy your neighbor a worse car. This prevents the efficiency theorems described in chapter 2 from applying. Indeed, the demonstration of market efficiency was based on the following two presumptions:

· The welfare of each consumer depended solely on her own consumption decision.

· The production of each firm depended only on its own input and output choices.

In reality, these presumptions may not be met. A consumer or a firm may be directly affected by the actions of other agents in the economy; that is, there may be external effects from the actions of other consumers or firms. In the presence of such externalities the outcome of a competitive market is unlikely to be Pareto-efficient because agents will not take account of the external effects of their (consumption/production) decisions. Typically the economy will generate too great a quantity of "bad" externalities and too small a quantity of "good" externalities.

The control of externalities is an issue of increasing practical importance. Global warming and the destruction of the ozone layer are two of the most significant examples, but there are numerous others, from local to global environmental issues. Some of these externalities may not appear immediately to be economic problems, but economic analysis can expose why they occur and investigate the effectiveness of alternative policies. Economic analysis can generate surprising conclusions and challenge standard policy prescriptions. In particular, it shows how government intervention that induces agents to internalize the external effects of their decisions can achieve a Pareto improvement.

The starting point for the chapter is to provide a working definition of an externality. Using this, it is shown why market failure arises and the nature of the resulting inefficiency. The design of the optimal set of corrective, or *Pigouvian*, taxes is then addressed and related to missing markets for externalities. The use of taxes is contrasted with direct control through tradable licenses. Internalization as a solution to externalities is considered. Finally these methods of solving the externality problem are set against the claim of the Coase theorem that efficiency will be attained by trade even when there are externalities.

7.2   Externalities Defined

An externality has already been described as an effect on one agent caused by another. This section provides a formal statement of this description, which is then used to classify the various forms of externality. The way of representing these forms of externalities in economic models is introduced.

There have been several attempts at defining externalities and of providing classifications of various types of externalities. From among these the following definition is the most commonly adopted. Its advantages are that it places the emphasis on recognizing externalities through their effects and it leads to a natural system of classification.

Definition 4 (Externality)   An externality is present whenever some economic agent's welfare (utility or profit) is "directly" affected by the action of another agent (consumer or producer) in the economy.

By "directly" we exclude any effects that are mediated by prices. That is, an externality is present if a fishery's productivity is affected by the river pollution of an upstream oil refinery but not if the fishery's profitability is affected by the price of oil (which may depend on the oil refinery's output of oil). The latter type of effect (often called a *pecuniary externality*) is present in any competitive market but creates no inefficiency (since price mediation through competitive markets leads to a Pareto-efficient outcome). We will present later an illustration of a pecuniary externality.

This definition of an externality implicitly distinguishes between two broad categories. A *production externality* occurs when the effect of the externality is on a profit relationship and a *consumption externality* whenever a utility level is affected. Clearly, an externality can be both a consumption and a production externality simultaneously. For example, pollution from a factory may affect the profit of a commercial fishery and the utility of leisure anglers.

Using this definition of an externality, it is possible to move on to how they can be incorporated into the analysis of behavior. Denote, as in chapter 2, the consumption levels of the households by $x = \{x^1, \ldots, x^H\}$ and the production plans of the firms by $y = \{y^1, \ldots, y^m\}$. It is assumed that consumption externalities enter the utility functions of the households and that production externalities enter the production sets of the firms. At the most general level, this assumption implies that the utility functions take the form

$$U^h = U^h(x, y), \qquad h = 1, \ldots, H, \tag{7.1}$$

and the production sets are described by

$$Y^j = Y^j(x, y), \qquad j = 1, \ldots, m. \tag{7.2}$$

In this formulation the utility functions and the production sets are possibly dependent upon the entire arrays of consumption and production levels. The expressions in (7.1) and (7.2) represent the general form of the externality problem, and in some of the discussion below a number of further restrictions will be employed.

It is immediately apparent from (7.1) and (7.2) that the actions of the agents in the economy will no longer be independent or determined solely by prices. The linkages via the externality result in the optimal choice of each agent being dependent on the actions of others. Viewed in this light, it becomes apparent why competition will generally not achieve efficiency in an economy with externalities.

7.3   Market Inefficiency

It has been accepted throughout the discussion above that the presence of externalities will result in the competitive equilibrium failing to be Pareto-efficient. The immediate implication of this fact is that incorrect quantities of goods, and hence externalities, will be produced. It is also clear that a non–Pareto-efficient outcome will never maximize welfare. This provides scope for economic policy to improve the outcome. The purpose of this section is to demonstrate how inefficiency can arise in a competitive economy. The results are developed in the context of a simple two-consumer model, since this is sufficient for the purpose and also makes the relevant points as clear as possible.

Consider a two-consumer, two-good economy where the consumers have utility functions

$$U^1 = x^1 + u_1(z^1) + v_1(z^2) \tag{7.3}$$

and

$$U^2 = x^2 + u_2(z^2) + v_2(z^1). \tag{7.4}$$

The externality effect in (7.3) and (7.4) is generated by consumption of good z by the consumers. The externality will be *positive* if $v_h(\cdot)$ is increasing in the consumption level of the other consumer and *negative* if it is decreasing.

To complete the description of the economy, it is assumed that the supply of good x comes from an endowment ω_h to consumer h, whereas good z is produced from good x by a competitive industry that uses one unit of good x to produce one unit of good z. Normalizing the price of good x at 1, the structure of production ensures that the equilibrium price of good z must also be 1. Given this, all that needs to be determined for this economy is the division of the initial endowment into quantities of the two goods.

Incorporating this assumption into the maximization decision of the consumers, the competitive equilibrium of the economy is described by the equations

$$u_h'(z^h) = 1, \qquad h = 1, 2, \tag{7.5}$$

$$x^h + z^h = \omega^h, \qquad h = 1, 2, \tag{7.6}$$

and

$$x^1 + z^1 + x^2 + z^2 = \omega^1 + \omega^2. \tag{7.7}$$

It is equations (7.5) that are of primary importance at this point. For consumer h these state that the private marginal benefit from each good, determined by the marginal utility, is equated to the private marginal cost. The external effect does not appear directly in the determination of the equilibrium. The question we now address is whether this competitive market equilibrium is efficient.

The Pareto-efficient allocations are found by maximizing the total utility of consumers 1 and 2, subject to the production possibilities. The equations that result from this will then be contrasted to (7.5). In detail, a Pareto-efficient allocation solves

$$\max_{\{x^h, z^h\}} U^1 + U^2 = [x^1 + u_1(z^1) + v_1(z^2)] + [x^2 + u_2(z^2) + v_2(z^1)] \tag{7.8}$$

subject to

$$\omega^1 + \omega^2 - x^1 - z^1 - x^2 - z^2 \geq 0. \tag{7.9}$$

The solution is characterized by the conditions

$$u_1'(z^1) + v_2'(z^1) = 1 \tag{7.10}$$

and

$$u_2'(z^2) + v_1'(z^2) = 1. \tag{7.11}$$

In (7.10) and (7.11) the externality effect can be seen to affect the optimal allocation between the two goods via the derivatives of utility with respect to the externality. If the externality is positive then $v_h' > 0$ and the externality effect will raise the value of the left-hand terms. It will decrease them if there is a negative externality, so $v_h' < 0$. It can then be concluded that at the optimum with a positive externality the marginal utilities of both consumers are below their value in the market outcome. The converse is true with a negative externality. The externality leads to a divergence between the private valuations of consumption given by (7.5) and the corresponding social valuations in (7.10) and (7.11). This observation has the implication that the market outcome is not Pareto-efficient.

In general, it can also be concluded that if the externality is positive then more of good z will be consumed at the optimum than under the market outcome. The converse holds for a negative externality. This situation is illustrated in figure 7.1. The market outcome is represented by equality between the private marginal benefit of the good (PMB) and its marginal cost (MC). The social marginal benefit (SMB) of the good is the sum of the private marginal benefit, $u_h'(z^h)$, and the marginal external effect, $v_h'(z^h)$. When $v_h'(z^h)$ is positive, SMB is above PMB. The converse holds when $v_h'(z^h)$ is negative. The Pareto-efficient outcome equates the social marginal benefit to marginal cost. The market failure is characterized by

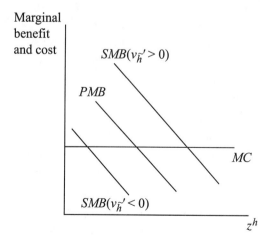

Figure 7.1
Deviation of private from social benefits

too much consumption of a good causing a negative externality and too little consumption of a good generating a positive externality.

7.4   Externality Examples

The previous section has discussed externalities at a somewhat abstract level. We now consider some more-concrete examples of externalities. Some of the examples are very simple because of the binary nature of the choice and the assumption of identical individuals. This modeling choice was widely used by Schelling to achieve an extremely simple exposition that brings out the line of the argument very clearly. In addition it will illustrate the range of situations that fall under the general heading of externalities.

7.4.1   River Pollution

This example, from Louis Gevers, is one of the simplest examples that can be described using only two agents. Assume that two firms are located along the same river. The upstream firm u pollutes the river, which reduces the production (e.g., the output of fish) of the downstream firm d. Both firms produce the same output, which they sell at a constant unit price of 1 so that total revenue coincides with production.

Labor and water are used as inputs. Water is free, but the equilibrium wage w on the competitive labor market is paid for each unit of labor. The production technologies of the firms are given by $F^u(L^u)$ and $F^d(L^d, L^u)$, with $\frac{\partial F^d}{\partial L^u} < 0$ to reflect that the pollution reduces downstream output. Decreasing returns to scale are assumed with respect to own labor input. Each firm acts independently and seeks to maximize its own profit $\pi^i = F^i(\cdot) - wL^i$, taking prices as given.

The equilibrium is illustrated in figure 7.2. The total stock of labor is allocated between the two firms. The labor input of the upstream firm is measured from the left, that of the downstream from the right. Each point on the horizontal axis represents a different allocation between the firms. The upstream firm's profit maximization process is represented in the upper part of the diagram and the downstream firm's in the lower part. As the input of the upstream firm increases the production function of the downstream firm moves progressively in toward the horizontal axis. Given the profit-maximizing input level of the upstream firm, denoted L^{u*}, the downstream firm can do no better than choose L^{d*}. At these choices the firms earn profits π^u and π^d respectively. This is the competitive equi-

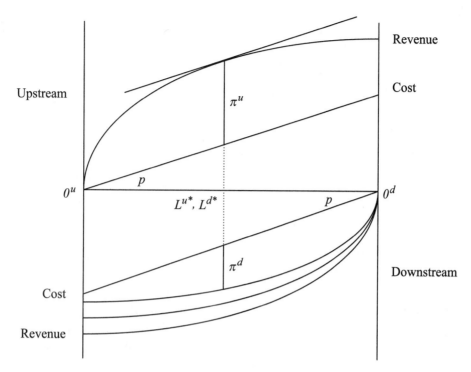

Figure 7.2
Equilibrium with river pollution

librium. We now show that this is inefficient and that reallocating labor between
the firms can increase total profit and reduce pollution.

Consider starting at the competitive equilibrium and make a small reduction in
the labor input to the upstream firm. Since the choice was optimal for the upstream firm, the change has no effect on profit for the upstream firm (recall that
$\frac{\partial \pi^u}{\partial L^u} = 0$). However, it leads to an outward shift of the downstream firm's production function. This raises its profits. Hence the change raises aggregate profit. This
demonstrates that the competitive equilibrium is not efficient and that the externality results in the upstream firm using too much labor and the downstream too
little. Shifting labor to the downstream firm raises total production and reduces
pollution.

7.4.2   Traffic Jams

The next example considers the externalities imposed by drivers on each other.
Let there be N commuters who have the choice of commuting by train or by

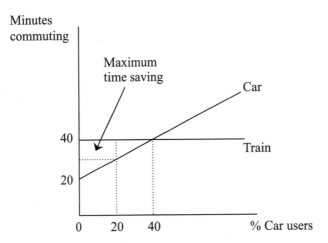

Figure 7.3
Choice of commuting mode

car. Commuting by train always takes 40 minutes regardless of the number of travelers. The commuting time by car increases as the number of car users increases. This congestion effect, which raises the commuting time, is the externality for travelers. Individuals must each make decisions to minimize their own transportation time.

The equilibrium in the choice of commuting mode is depicted in figure 7.3. The number of car users will adjust until the travel time by car is exactly equal to the travel time by train. For the travel time depicted in the figure, the equilibrium occurs when 40 percent of commuters travel by car. The optimum occurs when the aggregate time saving is maximized. This occurs when only 20 percent of commuters use a car.

The externality in this situation is that the car drivers take into account only their own travel time but not the fact that they will increase the travel time for all other drivers. As a consequence too many commuters choose to drive.

7.4.3   Pecuniary Externality

Consider a set of students each of whom must decide whether to be an economist or a lawyer. Being an economist is great when there are few economists, and not so great when the labor market becomes crowded with economists (due to price competition). If the number of economists grows high enough, they will eventually earn less than their lawyer counterparts. Suppose that each person chooses

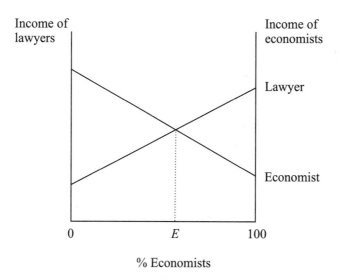

Figure 7.4
Job choice

the profession with the best earnings prospects. The externality (a pecuniary one!) comes from the fact that when one more person decides to become an economist, he lowers all other economists' incomes (through competition), imposing a cost on the existing economists. When making his decision, he ignores this external effect imposed on others. The question is whether the invisible hand will lead to the correct allocation of students across different jobs.

The equilibrium depicted in figure 7.4 determines the allocation of students between jobs. The number of economists will adjust until the earnings of an economist are exactly equal to the earnings of a lawyer. The equilibrium is given by the percentage of economists at point E. To the right of point E, lawyers would earn more and the number of economists would decrease. Alternatively, to the left of point E economists are relatively few in number and will earn more than lawyers, attracting more economists into the profession.

The laissez-faire equilibrium is efficient because the external effect is a change in price. The cost to an economists of a lower income is a benefit to employers. Since employers' benefits equals employees' costs, there is zero net effect. The policy implication is that there is no need for government intervention to regulate the access to professions. It follows that any public policy that aims to limit the access to some profession (like the *numerus clausus*) is not justified. Market forces will correctly allocate the right number of people to each of the different professions.

Player 2

		Low	High
Player 1	**Low**	1/2 1/2	1 − c 0
	High	0 1 − c	1/2 − c 1/2 − c

Figure 7.5
Rat race

7.4.4   The Rat Race Problem

The rat race problem is a contest for relative position as pointed out by George Akerlof. It can help explain why students work too hard when final marking takes the form of a ranking. It can also explain the intense competition for a promotion in the workplace when candidates compete with each other and only the best is promoted. We take the classroom example here. Assume that performance is judged not in *absolute* terms but in *relative* terms so that what matters is not how much is known but how much is known compared to what other students know.

In this situation an advantage over other students can only be gained by working harder than they do. Since this applies to all students, all must work harder. But since performance is judged in relative terms, all the extra effort cancels out. The result of this is an inefficient rat race in which each student works too hard to no ultimate advantage. If all could agree to work less hard, the same grades would be obtained with less work. Such an agreement to work less hard cannot be self-supporting, since each student would then have an incentive to cheat on the agreement and work harder.

A simple variant of the rat race with two possible effort levels is shown in figure 7.5. In this figure, c, $0 < c < \frac{1}{2}$, denotes the cost of effort. For both students high effort is a dominant strategy. In contrast, the Pareto-efficient outcome is low effort. This game is an example of the Prisoners' Dilemma in which a Pareto-improvement could be made if the players could make a commitment to the low-effort strategy.

Another example of rat race is the use of performance-enhancing drugs by athletes. In the absence of effective drug regulations, many athletes will feel compelled to enhance their performance by using anabolic steroids, and the failure to use steroids might seriously reduce their success in competition. Since the rewards in athletics are determined by performance relative to others, anyone that uses such drugs to increase their chance of winning must necessarily reduce the chances of others (an externality effect). The result is that when the stakes are high in the competition, unregulated contests almost always lead to a race for using more and more performance-enhancing drugs. However, when everyone does so, the use of such drugs yields no real benefits for the contestants as a whole: the performance-enhancing actions cancel each other. At the same time the race imposes substantial risks. Anabolic steroids have been shown to cause cancer of the liver and other serious health problems. Given what is at stake, voluntary restraint is unlikely to be an effective solution, and public intervention now requires strict drug testing of all competing athletes.

The rat race problem is present in almost every contest where something important is at stake and rewards are determined by relative position. In an electoral competition race, contestants spend millions on advertising, and governing bodies have now put strict limits on the amount of campaign advertising. Similarly a ban on cigarette advertising has been introduced in many countries. Surprisingly enough, this ban turned out to be beneficial to cigarette companies. The reason is that the ban helped them out of the costly rat race in defensive advertising where a company had to advertise because the others did.

7.4.5   The Tragedy of the Commons

The *Tragedy of the Commons* arises from the common right of access to a resource. The inefficiency to which it leads results again from the divergence between the individual and social incentives that characterizes all externality problems.

Consider a lake that can be used by fishermen from a village located on its banks. The fishermen do not own boats but instead can rent them for daily use at a cost c. If B boats are hired on a particular day, the number of fish caught by each boat will be $F(B)$, which is decreasing in B. A fisherman will hire a boat to fish if they can make a positive profit. Let w be the wage if they choose to undertake paid employment rather than fish, and let $p = 1$ be the price of fish so that total revenue coincide with fish catch $F(B)$. Then the number of boats that fish will be such as to ensure that profit from fishing activity is equal to the opportunity cost of fishing, which is the forgone wage w from the alternative job (if profit were greater, more boats would be hired and the converse if it were smaller). The equilibrium number of boats, B^*, then satisfies

$$\pi = F(B^*) - c = w. \tag{7.12}$$

The optimal number of boats for the community, B°, must be that which maximizes the total profit for the village, net of the opportunity cost from fishing. Hence B° satisfies

$$\max_{\{B\}} \; B[F(B) - c - w]. \tag{7.13}$$

This gives the necessary condition

$$F(B^\circ) - c - w + BF'(B^\circ) = 0. \tag{7.14}$$

Since an increase in the number of boats reduces the quantity of fish caught by each, $F'(B^\circ) < 0$. Therefore contrasting (7.12) and (7.14) shows that $B^\circ < B^*$ so the equilibrium number of boats is higher than the optimal number. This situation is illustrated in figure 7.6.

The externality at work in this example is that each fisherman is concerned only with their own profit. When deciding whether to hire a boat they do not take account of the fact that they will reduce the quantity of fish caught by every other fisherman. This negative externality ensures that in equilibrium too many boats

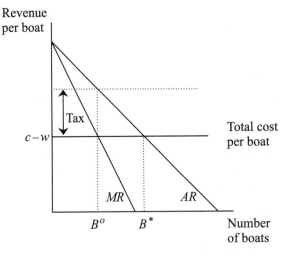

Figure 7.6
Tradegy of the Commons

are operating on the lake. Public intervention can take two forms. There is the price-based solution consisting of a tax per boat so as to internalize the external effect of sending a boat on the lake. As indicated in the figure a correctly chosen tax will reduce the number of boats so as to restore the optimal outcome. Alternatively, the quantity-based solution consists of setting a quota of fishing equal to the optimal outcome.

7.4.6   Bandwagon Effect

The bandwagon effect studies the question of how standards are adopted and, in particular, how it is possible for the wrong standard to be adopted. The standard application of this is the choice of arrangement for the keys on a keyboard.

The current standard, Qwerty, was designed in 1873 by Christopher Scholes in order to deliberately slow down the typist by maximizing the distance between the most used letters. The motivation for this was the reduction of key-jamming problems (remember this would be for mechanical typewriters in which metal keys would have to strike the ink ribbon). By 1904 the Qwerty keyboard was mass produced and became the accepted standard. The key-jamming problem is now irrelevant, and a simplified alternative keyboard (Dvorak's keyboard) has been devised that reduces typing time by 5 to 10 percent.

Why has this alternative keyboard not been adopted? The answer is that there is a switching cost. All users are reluctant to switch and bear the cost of retraining, and manufacturers see no advantage in introducing the alternative. It has therefore proved impossible to switch to the better technology.

This problem is called a *bandwagon effect* and is due to a *network externality*. The decision of a typist to use the Qwerty keyboard makes it more attractive for manufacturers to produce Qwerty keyboards, and hence for others to learn Qwerty. No individual has any incentive to switch to Dvorak. The nature of the equilibrium is displayed in figure 7.7. This shows the intertemporal link between the percentage using Qwerty at time t and the percentage at time $t + 1$. The natural advantage of Dvorak is captured in the diagram by the fact that the number of Qwerty users will decline over time starting from a position where 50 percent use Qwerty at time t. There are three equilibria. Either all will use Qwerty or Dvorak or else a proportion p^*, $p^* > 50$ percent, will use Qwerty and $1 - p^*$ Dvorak However, this equilibrium is unstable and any deviation from it will lead to one of the corner equilibria. The inefficient technology, Qwerty, can dominate in equilibrium if the initial starting point is to the right of p^*.

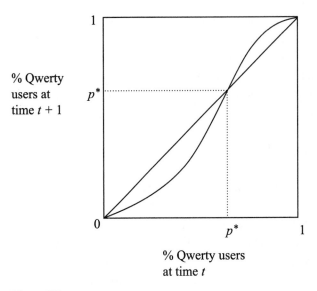

% Qwerty
users at
time $t + 1$

p^*

1

0

p^*

1

% Qwerty users
at time t

Figure 7.7
Equilibrium keyboard choice

7.5   Pigouvian Taxation

The description of market inefficiency has shown that its basic source is the divergence between social and private benefits (or between social and private costs). This fact has been reinforced by the examples. A natural means of eliminating such divergence is to employ appropriate taxes or subsidies. By modifying the decision problems of the firms and consumers these can move the economy closer to an efficient position.

To see how a tax can enhance efficiency, consider the case of a negative consumption externality. With a negative externality the private marginal benefit of consumption is always in excess of the social marginal benefit. These benefits are depicted by the *PMB* and *SMB* curves respectively in figure 7.8. In the absence of intervention, the equilibrium occurs where the *PMB* intersects the private marginal cost (*PMC*). This gives a level of consumption x^m. The efficient consumption level equates the *PMC* with the *SMB*; this is at point x^o. As already noted, with a negative externality the market outcome involves more consumption of the good than is efficient. The market outcome can be improved by placing a tax on consumption. What it is necessary to do is to raise the *PMC* so that it intersects

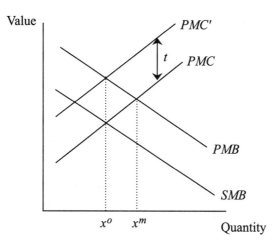

Figure 7.8
Pigouvian taxation

the SMB vertically above x^o. This is what happens for the curve PMC', which has been raised above PMC by a tax of value t. This process, often termed *Pigouvian taxation*, allows the market to attain efficiency for the situation shown in figure 7.8.

Based on arguments like that exhibited above, Pigouvian taxation has been proposed as a simple solution to the externality problem. The logic is that the consumer or firm causing the externality should pay a tax equal to the marginal damage the externality causes (or a subsidy if there is a marginal benefit). Doing so makes them take account of the damage (or benefit) when deciding how much to produce or consume. In many ways this is a compellingly simple conclusion.

The previous discussion is informative but leaves a number of issues to be resolved. Foremost among these is the fact that the figure implicitly assumes there is a single agent generating the externality whose marginal benefit and marginal cost are exhibited and that there is a single externality. The single tax works in this case, but will it still do so with additional externalities and agents? This is an important question to be answered if Pigouvian taxation is to be proposed as a serious practical policy.

To address these issues, we use our example from the market failure section again. This example involved two consumers and two goods with the consumption of one of the goods, z, causing an externality. The optimal structure of Pigouvian taxes is determined by characterizing the social optimum and inferring from that what the taxes must be. Recall from (7.10) and (7.11) that the social optimum is characterized by the conditions

$$u_1'(z^1) + v_2'(z^1) = 1 \tag{7.15}$$

and

$$u_2'(z^2) + v_1'(z^2) = 1. \tag{7.16}$$

It is from contrasting these conditions to those for individual choice that the optimal taxes can be derived.

Utility maximization by consumer 1 will equate their private marginal benefit, $u_1'(z^1)$, to the consumer price q_1. Given that the producer price is equal to 1 in this example, (7.15) shows that efficiency will be achieved if the price, q_1, facing consumer 1 satisfies

$$q_1 = 1 - v_2'(z^1). \tag{7.17}$$

Similarly from (7.16) efficiency will be achieved if the price facing consumer 2 satisfies

$$q_2 = 1 - v_1'(z^2). \tag{7.18}$$

These identities reveal that the taxes that ensure the correct difference between consumer and producer prices are given by

$$t_1 = -v_2'(z^1) \tag{7.19}$$

and

$$t_2 = -v_1'(z^2). \tag{7.20}$$

Therefore the tax on consumer 1 is the negative of the externality effect their consumption of good z inflicts on consumer 2. Hence, if the good causes a negative externality $(v_2'(z^1) < 0)$, the tax is positive. The converse holds if it causes a positive externality. The same construction and reasoning can be applied to the tax facing consumer 2, t_2, to show that this is the negative of the externality effect caused by the consumption of good z by consumer 2. The argument is now completed by noting that these externality effects will generally be different, and so the two taxes will generally not be equal. Another way of saying this is that efficiency can only be achieved if the consumers face personalized prices that fully capture the externalities that they generate.

So what does this say for Pigouvian taxation? Put simply, the earlier conclusion that a single tax rate could achieve efficiency was misleading. In fact the general outcome is that there must be a different tax rate for each externality-generating good for each consumer. Achieving efficiency needs taxes to be differentiated across consumers and goods. Naturally this finding immediately shows the practical difficulties involved in implementing Pigouvian taxation. The same arguments concerning information that were placed against the Lindahl equilibrium for public good provision with personalized pricing are all relevant again here. In conclusion, Pigouvian taxation can achieve efficiency but needs an unachievable degree of differentiation.

If the required degree of differentiation is not available, for instance, information limitations require that all consumers must pay the same tax rate, then efficiency will not be achieved. In such cases the chosen taxes will have to achieve a compromise. They cannot entirely correct for the externality but can go some way toward doing so. Since the taxes do not completely offset the externality, there is also a role for intervening in the market for goods related to that causing the externality. For instance, pollution from car use may be lessened by subsidizing alternative mode of transports. These observations are meant to indicate that once the move is made from full efficiency, many new factors become relevant, and there is no clean and general answer as to how taxes should be set.

A final comment is that the effect of the tax or subsidy is to put a price (respectively positive or negative) on the externality. This leads to the conclusion, which will be discussed in detail below, that if there are competitive markets for the externalities, efficiency will be achieved. In other words, efficiency does not require intervention but only the creation of the necessary markets.

7.6   Licenses

The reason why Pigouvian taxation can raise welfare is that the unregulated market will produce incorrect quantities of externalities. The taxes alter the cost of generating an externality and, if correctly set, will ensure that the optimal quantity of externality is produced. An apparently simpler alternative is to control externalities directly by the use of licenses. This can be done by legislating that externalities can only be generated up to the quantity permitted by licenses held. The optimal quantity of externality can then be calculated and licenses totaling this quantity distributed. Permitting these licenses to be traded will ensure that they are eventually used by those who obtain the greatest benefit.

Administratively, the use of licenses has much to recommend it. As was argued in the previous section, the calculation of optimal Pigouvian taxes requires considerable information. The tax rates will also need to be continually changed as the economic environment evolves. The use of licenses only requires information on the aggregate quantity of externality that is optimal. Licenses to this value are released and trade is permitted. Despite these apparently compelling arguments in favor of licenses, when the properties of licenses and taxes are considered in detail, the advantage of the former is not quite so clear.

The fundamental issue involved in choosing between taxes and licenses revolves around information. There are two sides to this. The first is what must be known to calculate the taxes or determine the number of licenses. The second is what is known when decisions have to be taken. For example, does the government know costs and benefits for sure when it sets taxes or issues licenses?

Taking the first of these, although licenses may appear to have an informational advantage this is not really the case. Consider what must be known to calculate the Pigouvian taxes. The construction of section 7.5 showed that taxation required the knowledge of the preferences of consumers and, if the model had included production, the production technologies of firms. Such extensive information is necessary to achieve the personalization of the taxes. But what of licenses? The essential feature of licenses is that they must total to the optimal level of externality. To determine the optimal level requires precisely the same information as is necessary for the tax rates. Consequently taxes and licenses are equivalent in their informational demands.

Now consider the issue of the information that is known when decisions must be made. When all costs and benefits are known with certainty by both the government and individual agents, licenses and taxation are equivalent in their effects. This result is easily seen by reconsidering figure 7.8. The optimal level of externality is x^o, which was shown to be achievable with tax t. The same outcome can also be achieved by issuing x^o licenses. This simple and direct argument shows there is equivalence with certainty.

In practice, it is more likely that the government must take decisions before the actual costs and benefits of an externality are known for sure. Such uncertainty brings with it the question of timing: Who chooses what and when? The natural sequence of events is the following. The government must make its policy decision (the quantity of licenses or the tax rate) before costs and benefits are known. In contrast, the economic agents can act after the costs and benefits are known. For example, in the case of pollution by a firm, the government may not know the cost of reducing pollution for sure when it sets the tax rate but the firm makes its abatement decision with full knowledge of the cost.

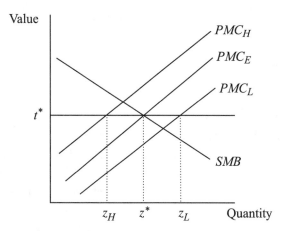

Figure 7.9
Uncertain costs

The effect of this difference in timing is to break the equivalence between the two policies. This can be seen by considering figure 7.9, which illustrates the pollution abatement problem for an uncertain level of cost. In this case the level of private marginal cost takes one of two values, PMC_L and PMC_H, with equal probability. Benefits are known for sure. When the government chooses its policy, it is not known whether private marginal cost is high or low, so it must act on the expected value, PMC_E. This leads to pollution abatement z^* being required (which can be supported by licenses equal in quantity to present pollution less z^*) or a tax rate t^*.

Under the license scheme, the level of pollution abatement will be z^* for sure—there is no uncertainty about the outcome. With the tax, the level of abatement will depend on the realized level of cost since the firm chooses after this is known. Therefore, if the cost turns out to be PMC_L, the firm will choose abatement level z_L. If its is PMC_H, abatement is z_H. This is shown in figure 7.9. Two observations emerge from this. First, the claim that licenses and taxation will not be equivalent when there is uncertainty is confirmed. Second, when cost is realized to be low, taxation leads to abatement in excess of z^*. The converse holds when cost is high.

The analysis of figure 7.9 may be taken as suggesting that licenses are better, since they do not lead to the variation in abatement that is inherent in taxation. However, it should also be realized that the choices made by the firm in the tax case are responding to the actual cost of abatement, so there is some justification for what the firm is doing. In general, there is no simple answer to the question of which of the two policies is better.

7.7   Internalization

Consider the example of a beekeeper located next door to an orchard. The bees pollinate the trees and the trees provide food for the bees, so a positive production externality runs in both directions between the two producers. According to the theory developed above, the producers acting independently will not take account of this externality. This leads to too few bees being kept and too few trees being planted.

The externality problem could be resolved by using taxation or insisting that both producers raise their quantities. Although both these would work, there is another simpler solution. Imagine the two producers merging and forming a single firm. If they were to do so, profit maximization for the combined enterprise would naturally take into account the externality. By so doing, the inefficiency is eliminated. The method of controlling externalities by forming single units out of the parties affected is called *internalization*, and it ensures that private and social costs become the same. It works for both production and consumption externalities whether they are positive or negative.

Internalization seems a simple solution, but it is not without its difficulties. To highlight the first of these, consider an industry in which the productive activity of each firm causes an externality for the other firms in the industry. In this situation the internalization argument would suggest that the firms become a single monopolist. If this were to occur, welfare loss would then arise due to the ability of the single firm to exploit its monopoly position, and this may actually be greater than the initial loss due to the externality. Although this is obviously an extreme example, the internalization argument always implies the construction of larger economic units and a consequent increase in market power. The welfare loss due to market power then has to be offset against the gain from eliminating the effect of the externality.

The second difficulty is that the economic agents involved may simply not wish to be amalgamated into a single unit. This objection is particularly true when applied to consumption externalities. That is, if a household generates an externality for their neighbor, it is not clear that they would wish to form a single household unit, particularly if the externality is a negative one.

In summary, internalization will eliminate the consequences of an externality in a very direct manner by ensuring that private and social costs are equated. However, it is unlikely to be a practical solution when many distinct economic agents contribute separately to the total externality and it has the disadvantage of leading to increased market power.

7.8   The Coase Theorem

After identifying externalities as a source of market failure, this chapter has taken the standard approach of discussing policy remedies. In contrast to this, there has developed a line of reasoning that questions whether such intervention is necessary. The focal point for this is the Coase theorem, which suggests that economic agents may resolve externality problems themselves without the need for government intervention. This conclusion runs against the standard assessment of the consequences of externalities and explains why the Coase theorem has been of considerable interest.

The Coase theorem asserts that if the market is allowed to function freely then it will achieve an efficient allocation of resources. This claim can be stated formally as follows.

Theorem 3 (Coase theorem)   In a competitive economy with complete information and zero transaction costs, the allocation of resources will be efficient and invariant with respect to legal rules of entitlement.

The legal rules of entitlement, or property rights, are of central importance to the Coase theorem. Property rights are the rules that determine ownership within the economy. For example, property rights may state that all agents are entitled to unpolluted air or the right to enjoy silence (they may also state the opposite). Property rights also determine the direction in which compensation payments will be made if a property right is violated.

The implication of the Coase theorem is that there is no need for policy intervention with regard to externalities except to ensure that property rights are clearly defined. When they are, the theorem presumes that those affected by an externality will find it in their interest to reach private agreements with those causing it to eliminate any market failure. These agreements will involve the payment of compensation to the agent whose property right is being violated. The level of compensation will ensure that the right price emerges for the externality and a Pareto-efficient outcome will be achieved. These compensation payments can be interpreted in the same way as the personalized prices discussed in section 7.5.

As well as claiming the outcome will be efficient, the Coase theorem also asserts the equilibrium will be invariant to the how property rights are assigned. This is surprising since a natural expectation would be, for example, that the level of pollution under a polluter-pays system (i.e., giving property rights to pollutees) will be less than that under a pollutee-pays (i.e., giving property rights to the polluter). To show how the invariance argument works, consider the example of a factory that is polluting the atmosphere of a neighboring house. When the firm has the right to pollute, the householder can only reduce the pollution by paying the firm a sufficient amount of compensation to make it worthwhile to stop production or to find an alternative means of production. Let the amount of compensation the firm requires be C. Then the cost to the householder of the pollution, G, will either be greater than C, in which case they will be willing to compensate the firm and the externality will cease, or it will be less than C and the externality will be left to continue. Now consider the outcome with the polluter pays principle. The cost to the firm for stopping the externality now becomes C and the compensation required by the household is G. If C is greater than G, the firm will be willing to compensate the household and continue producing the externality; if it is less than G, it stops the externality. Considering the two cases, it can be seen the outcome is determined only by the value of G relative to C and not by the assignment of property rights, which is essentially the content of the Coase theorem.

There is a further issue before invariance can be confirmed. The change in property rights between the two cases will cause differences in the final distribution of income due to the direction of compensation payments. Invariance can only hold if this redistribution of income does not cause a change in the level of demand. This requires there to be no income effects or, to put it another way, the marginal unit of income must be spent in the same way by both parties.

When the practical relevance of the Coase theorem is considered, a number of issues arise. The first lies with the assignment of property rights in the market. With commodities defined in the usual sense, it is clear who is the purchaser and who is the supplier and, therefore, the direction in which payment should be transferred. This is not the case with externalities. For example, with air pollution it may not be clear that the polluter should pay, with the implicit recognition of the right to clean air, or whether there is a right to pollute, with clean air something that should have to be paid for. This leaves the direction in which payment should go unclear. Without clearly specified property rights, the bargaining envisaged in the Coase theorem does not have a firm foundation: neither party would willingly accept that they were the party that should pay.

If the exchange of commodities would lead to mutually beneficial gains for two parties, the commodities will be exchanged unless the cost of doing so outweighs the benefits. Such transactions costs may arise from the need for the parties to travel to a point of exchange or from the legal costs involved in formalizing the transactions. They may also arise due to the search required to find a trading partner. Whenever they arise, transactions costs represent a hindrance to trade and, if sufficiently great, will lead to no trade at all taking place. The latter results in the economy having a missing market.

The existence of transactions costs is often seen as the most significant reason for the nonexistence of markets in externalities. To see how they can arise, consider the problem of pollution caused by car emissions. If the reasoning of the Coase theorem is applied literally, then any driver of a car must purchase pollution rights from all of the agents that are affected by the car emissions each time, and every time, that the car is used. Obviously this would take an absurd amount of organization, and since considerable time and resources would be used in the process, transactions costs would be significant. In many cases it seems likely that the welfare loss due to the waste of resources in organizing the market would outweigh any gains from having the market.

When external effects are traded, there will generally only be one agent on each side of the market. This thinness of the market undermines the assumption of competitive behavior needed to support the efficiency hypothesis. In such circumstances the Coase theorem has been interpreted as implying that bargaining between the two agents will take place over compensation for external effects and that this bargaining will lead to an efficient outcome. Such a claim requires substantiation.

Bargaining can be interpreted as taking the form of either a cooperative game between agents or as a noncooperative game. When it is viewed as cooperative, the tradition since Nash has been to adopt a set of axioms that the bargain must satisfy and to derive the outcomes that satisfy these axioms. The requirement of Pareto-efficiency is always adopted as one of the axioms so that the bargained agreement is necessarily efficient. If all bargains over compensation payments were placed in front of an external arbitrator, then the Nash bargaining solution would have some force as descriptive of what such an arbitrator should try and achieve. However, this is not what is envisaged in the Coase theorem, which focuses on the actions of markets free of any regulation. Although appealing as a method for achieving an outcome agreeable to both parties, the fact that Nash bargaining solution is efficient does not demonstrate the correctness of the Coase theorem.

The literature on bargaining in a noncooperative context is best divided between games with complete information and those with incomplete information, since this distinction is of crucial importance for the outcome. One of the central results of noncooperative bargaining with complete information is due to Rubinstein who considers the division of a single object between two players. The game is similar to the fund-raising game presented in the public goods chapter. The players take it in turns to announce a division of the object, and each period an offer and an acceptance or rejection are made. Both players discount the future, so they are impatient to arrive at an agreed division. Rubinstein shows that the game has a unique (subgame perfect) equilibrium with agreement reached in the first period. The outcome is Pareto-efficient.

The important point is the complete information assumed in this representation of bargaining. The importance of information for the nature of outcomes will be extensively analyzed in chapter 9, and it is equally important for bargaining. In the simple bargaining problem of Rubinstein the information that must be known are the preferences of the two agents, captured by their rates of time discount. When these discount rates are private information, the attractive properties of the complete information bargain are lost, and there are many potential equilibria whose nature is dependent on the precise specification of the structure of bargaining.

In the context of externalities it seems reasonable to assume that information will be incomplete, since there is no reason why the agents involved in bargaining an agreement over compensation for an external effect should be aware of each other's valuations of the externality. When they are not aware, there is always the incentive to try to exploit a supposedly weak opponent or to pretend to be strong and make excessive demands. This results in the possibility that agreement may not occur even when it is in the interests of both parties to trade.

To see this most clearly, consider the following bargaining situation. There are two agents: a polluter and a pollutee. They bargain over the decision to allow or not the pollution. The pollutee cannot observe the benefit of pollution B but knows that it is drawn from a distribution $F(B)$, which is the probability that the benefit is less or equal to B. On the other hand, the polluter cannot observe the cost of pollution C but knows that it is drawn from a distribution $G(C)$. Obviously the benefit is known to the polluter and the cost is known to the pollutee. Let us give the property rights to the pollutee so that he has the right to a pollution-free environment. Pareto-efficiency requires that pollution be allowed whenever $B \geq C$. Now the pollutee (with all the bargaining power) can make a take-it-or-leave-it offer to the polluter. What will be the bargaining outcome?

The pollutee will ask for compensation $T > 0$ (since $C > 0$) to grant permission to pollute. The polluter will only accept to pay T if his benefit from polluting exceeds the compensation he has to pay, so $B \geq T$. Hence the probability that the polluter will accept the offer is equal to $1 - F(T)$, that is, the probability that $B \geq T$. The best deal for the pollutee is to ask for compensation that maximizes her expected payoff defined as the probability that the offer is accepted times the net gain if the offer is accepted. Therefore the pollutee asks for compensation T^*, which solves

$$\max_{\{T\}}[1 - F(T)][T - C]. \tag{7.21}$$

Clearly, the optimal value, T^*, is such that

$$T^* > C. \tag{7.22}$$

But then bargaining can result (with strictly positive probability) in an inefficient outcome. This is the case for all realizations of C and B such that $C < B < T^*$, which implies that the offer is rejected (since the compensation demanded exceeds the benefit) and thus pollution is not allowed, while Pareto-efficiency requires permission to pollute to be granted (since its cost is less than its benefit).

The efficiency thesis of the Coase theorem relies on agreements being reached on the compensation required for external effects. The results above suggest that when information is incomplete, bargaining between agents will not lead to an efficient outcome.

7.9   Nonconvexity

One of the basic assumptions that supports economic analysis is that of convexity. Convexity gives indifference curves their standard shape, so consumers always prefer mixtures to extremes. It also ensures that firms have non-increasing returns so that profit-maximization is well defined. Without convexity, many problems

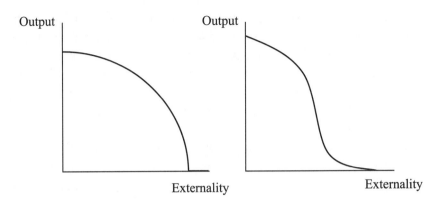

Figure 7.10
Nonconvexity

arise with the behavior of the decisions of individual firms and consumers, and with the aggregation of these decisions to find an equilibrium for the economy.

Externalities can be a source of nonconvexity. Consider the case of a negative production externality. The left-hand part of figure 7.10 displays a firm whose output is driven to zero by an externality regardless of the level of other inputs. An example would be a fishery where sufficient pollution of the fishing ground by another firm can kill all the fish. In the right-hand part of the figure a zero output level is not reached but output tends to zero as the level of the externality is increased. In both situations the production set of the firm is not convex.

In either case the economy will fail to have an equilibrium if personalized taxes are employed in an attempt to correct the externality. Suppose that the firm were to receive a subsidy for accepting externalities. Its profit-maximizing choice would be to produce an output level of zero and to offer to accept an arbitrarily large quantity of externalities. Since its output is zero, the externalities can do it no further harm, so this plan will lead to unlimited profits. If the price for accepting externalities were zero, the same firm would not accept any. The demand for externalities is therefore discontinuous, and an equilibrium need not exist.

There is also a second reason for nonconvexity with externalities. It is often assumed that once all inputs are properly accounted for, all firms will have constant returns to scale, since behavior can always be replicated. That is, if a fixed set of inputs (i.e., a factory and staff) produce output y, doubling all those inputs must produce output $2y$, since they can be split into two identical subunits (e.g., two factories and staff) producing an amount y each. Now consider a firm subject to a negative externality, and assume that it has constant returns to all inputs including the externality. From the perspective of society, there are constant returns to scale. Now let the firm double all its inputs but with the externality held at a constant level. Since the externality is a negative one, it becomes diluted by the increase in other inputs, and output must more than double. The firm therefore faces private increasing returns to scale. With such increasing returns, the firm's profit-maximizing decision may not have a well-defined finite solution and market equilibrium may again fail to exist.

These arguments provide some fairly powerful reasons why an economy with externalities may not share some of the desirable properties of economies without. The behavior that follows from nonconvexity can prevent some of the pricing tools that are designed to attain efficiency from functioning in a satisfactory manner. At worst, nonconvexity can even cause there to be no equilibrium in the economy.

7.10   Conclusions

Externalities are an important feature of economic activity. They can arise at a local level between neighbors and at a global level between countries. The existence of externalities can lead to inefficiency if no attempt is made to control their level. The Coase theorem suggests that well-defined property rights will be sufficient to ensure that private agreements can resolve the externality problem. In practice, property rights are not well defined in many cases of externality. Furthermore the thinness of the market and the incomplete information of market participants result in inefficiencies that undermine the Coase theorem.

The simplest policy solution to the externality problem is a system of corrective Pigouvian taxes. If the tax rate is proportional to the marginal damage (or benefit) caused by the externality then efficiency will result. However, for this argument to apply when there are many consumers and firms requires that the taxes are so differentiated between economic agents that they become equivalent to a system of personalized prices. The optimal system then becomes impractical due to its information limitations. An alternative policy response is the use of marketable licenses that limit the emission of externalities. These have some administrative advantages over taxes and will produce the same outcome when costs and benefits are known with certainty. With uncertainty, licenses and taxes have different effects and combining the two can lead to a superior outcome.

Further Reading

The classic analysis of externalities is in:

Meade, J. E. 1952. External economies and diseconomies in a competitive situation. *Economic Journal* 62: 54–76.

The externality analysis is carried further in a more rigorous and complete analysis in:

Buchanan, J. M. and Stubblebine, C. 1962. Externality. *Economica* 29: 371–84.

A persuasive argument for the use of corrective taxes is in:

Pigou, A. C. 1918. *The Economics of Welfare*. London: Macmillan.

The problem of social cost and the bargaining solution with many legal examples is developed in:

Coase, R. H. 1960. The problem of social cost. *Journal of Law and Economics* 3: 1–44.

An illuminating classification of externalities and non-market interdependences is in:

Bator, F. M. 1958. The anatomy of market failure. *Quarterly Journal of Economics* 72: 351–78.

A comprehensive and detailed treatment of the theory of externalities can be found in:

Lin, S., ed. 1976. *Theory and Measurement of Economic Externalities*. New York: Academic Press.

The efficient noncooperative bargaining solution with perfect information is in:

Rubinstein, A. 1982. Perfect equilibrium in a bargaining model. *Econometrica* 50: 97–110.

The general theory of bargaining with complete and incomplete information and many applications is in:

Muthoo, A. 1999. *Bargaining Theory with Applications*. Cambridge: Cambridge University Press.

An extremely simple exposition of the conflict between individual motives and collective efficiency is in:

Schelling, T. 1978. *Micromotives and Macrobehavior*. New York: Norton.

The bandwagon effect and technology adoption is in:

Arthur, B. 1988. Self-reinforcing mechanisms in economics. In P. Anderson, K. Arrow, and D. Pines, eds., *The Economy as an Evolving Complex System*. New York: Addison-Wesley.

David, P. 1985. Clio and the economics of Qwerty. *American Economic Review* 75: 332–37.

A summary of the arguments on the Tragedy of the Commons appears first in:

Hardin, G. 1968. The Tragedy of the Commons. *Science* 162: 1243–48.

The nonconvexity problem with externalities was first pointed out in:

Starrett, D. 1972. Fundamental non-convexities in the theory of externalities. *Journal of Economic Theory* 4: 180–99.

Exercises

7.1.   "Smoke from a factory dirties the local housing and poisons crops." Identify the nature of the externalities in this statement.

7.2.   How would you describe the production function of a laundry polluted by a factory?

7.3.   Let $U = [x_1]^\alpha [x_2 y]^{1-\alpha}$, where y is an externality. Is this externality positive or negative? How does it affect the demand for good 1 relative to the demand for good 2?

7.4.   If the two consumers in the economy have preferences $U_1 = [x_1^1]^\alpha [x_2^1 x_1^2]^{1-\alpha}$ and $U_2 = [x_1^2]^\alpha [x_2^2 x_1^1]^{1-\alpha}$, show that the equilibrium is efficient despite the externality. Explain this conclusion.

7.5.   Consider a group of n students. Suppose that each student i puts in h_i hours of work on her classes that involves a disutility of $\frac{h_i^2}{2}$. Her benefits depend on how she performs relative to her peers and take the form $u\left(\frac{h_i}{\bar{h}}\right)$ for all i, where $\bar{h} = \left(\frac{1}{n}\right)\sum_i h_i$ denotes the average number of hours put in by all students in the class and $u(\cdot)$ is an increasing and concave function.

   a. Calculate the symmetric Nash equilibrium.

   b. Calculate the Pareto-efficient level of effort.

   c. Explain why the equilibrium involves too much effort compared to the Pareto-efficient outcome.

7.6.   There is a large number of commuters who decide to use either their car or the tube. Commuting by train takes 70 minutes whatever the number of commuters taking the train. Commuting by car takes $C(x) = 20 + 60x$ minutes, where x is the proportion of commuters taking their cars, $0 \le x \le 1$.

   a. Plot the curves of the commuting time by car and the commuting time by train as a function of the proportion of car users.

   b. What is the proportion of commuters who will take their car if everyone is taking her decision freely and independently so as to minimize her own commuting time?

   c. What is the proportion of car users that minimizes the total commuting time?

   d. Compare this with your answer given in part b. Interpret the difference. How large is the deadweight loss from the externality?

   e. Explain how a toll could achieve the efficient allocation of commuters between train and car and be beneficial for everyone.

7.7.   Re-do the previous problem by replacing the train by a bus and assuming that commuting time by bus is increasing with the proportion of commuters using car (traffic congestion). Let the commuting time by bus be $B(x) = 40 + 20x$ and the commuting time by car be $C(x) = 20 + 60x$, where x is the proportion of commuters taking their car, $0 \le x \le 1$.

7.8.   Consider a binary choice to allow or not the emission of pollutants. The cost to consumers of allowing the pollution is $C = 2{,}000$, but this cost is only observable to the consumers. The benefit for the polluter of allowing the externality is $B = 2{,}300$, and only the polluter knows this benefit. Clearly, optimality requires this externality is allowed, since $B > C$. However, the final decision must be based on what each party chooses to reveal.

a. Construct a tax-subsidy revelation scheme such that it is a dominant strategy for each party to report truthfully their private information.

b. Show that this revelation scheme induces the optimal production of the externality.

c. Show that this revelation scheme is unbalanced in the sense that the given equilibrium reports the tax to be paid by the polluter is less than the subsidy paid to the pollutee.

7.9.   How can licenses be used to resolve the Tragedy of the Commons?

7.10.   If insufficient abatement is very costly, which of taxation or licenses is preferable?

7.11.   Are the following statements true or false? Explain why.

a. If your consumption of cigarettes produces negative externalities for your partner (which you ignore), then you are consuming more cigarettes than is Pareto-efficient.

b. It is generally efficient to set an emission standard allowing zero pollution.

c. A tax on cigarettes induces the market for cigarettes to perform more efficiently.

d. A ban on smoking is necessarily efficient.

e. A competitive market with a negative externality produces more output than is efficient.

f. A snob effect is a negative (network) externality from consumption.

7.12.   Consider two consumers with utility functions

$$U^A = \log(x_1^A) + x_2^A - \left[\tfrac{1}{2}\right] \log(x_1^B), \quad U^B = \log(x_1^B) + x_2^B - \left[\tfrac{1}{2}\right] \log(x_1^A).$$

Both consumers have income M and the (before-tax) price of both goods is 1.

a. Calculate the market equilibrium.

b. Calculate the social optimum for a utilitarian social welfare function.

c. Show that the optimum can be sustained by a tax placed on good 1 (so the after-tax price becomes $1 + t$) with the revenue returned equally to the consumers in a lump-sum manner.

d. Assume now that preferences are given by

$$U^A = \rho^A \log(x_1^A) + x_2^A - \left[\tfrac{1}{2}\right] \log(x_1^B), \quad U^B = \rho^B \log(x_1^B) + x_2^B - \left[\tfrac{1}{2}\right] \log(x_1^A).$$

Calculate the taxes necessary to decentralize the optimum.

e. For preferences of part d and income $M = 20$, contrast the outcome when taxes can and cannot be differentiated between consumers.

7.13.   A competitive refining industry releases one unit of waste into the atmosphere for each unit of refined product. The inverse demand function for the refined product is $p^d = 20 - q$, which represents the marginal benefit curve where q is the quantity consumed when the consumers pay price p^d. The inverse supply curve for refining is $MPC = 2 + q$, which represents the marginal private cost curve when the industry produces q units. The marginal external cost curve is $MEC = 0.5q$, where MEC is the marginal external cost when the industry releases q units of waste. Marginal social cost is given by $MSC = MPC + MEC$.

a. What are the equilibrium price and quantity for the refined product when there is no correction for the externality?

b. How much of the chemical should the market supply at the social optimum?

c. How large is the deadweight loss from the externality?

d. Suppose that the government imposes an emission fee of T per unit of emissions. How large must the emission fee be if the market is to produce the socially efficient amount of the refined product?

7.14. Discuss the following statement: "A tax is a fine for doing something right. A fine is a tax for doing something wrong."

7.15. Suppose that the government issues tradable pollution permits.

a. Is it better for economic efficiency to distribute the permits among polluters or to auction them?

b. If the government decides to distribute the permits, does the allocation of permits among firms matter for economic efficiency?

7.16. A chemical producer dumps toxic waste into a river. The waste reduces the population of fish, reducing profits for the local fishery industry by $150,000 per year. The firm could eliminate the waste at a cost of $100,000 per year. The local fishing industry consists of many small firms.

a. Apply the Coase theorem to explain how costless bargaining will lead to a socially efficient outcome, no matter to whom property rights are assigned (either to the chemical firm or the fishing industry).

b. Verify the Coase theorem if the cost of eliminating the waste is doubled to $200,000 (with the benefit for the fishing industry unchanged at $150,000).

c. Discuss the following argument: "A community held together by ties of obligation and mutual interest can manage the local pollution problems."

d. Why might bargaining not be costless?

7.17. It is often used as an objection to market-based policies of pollution abatement that they place a monetary value on cleaning up our environment. Economists reply that society implicitly places a monetary value on environmental cleanup even under command-and-control policies. Explain why this is true.

7.18. Use examples to answer whether the externalities related to common resources are generally positive or negative. Is the free-market use of common resources greater or less than the socially optimal use?

7.19. Why is there more litter along highways than in people's yards?

7.20. Evaluate the following statement: "Since pollution is bad, it would be socially optimal to prohibit the use of any production process that creates pollution."

7.21. Why is it not generally efficient to set an emissions standard allowing zero pollution?

7.22. Education is often viewed as a good with positive externalities.

a. Explain how education might produce positive external effects.

b. Suggest a possible action of the government to induce the market for education to perform more efficiently.

8 Imperfect Competition

8.1 Introduction

The analysis of economic efficiency in chapter 2 demonstrated the significance of the competitive assumption that no economic agent has the ability to affect market prices. Under this assumption prices reveal true economic values and act as signals that guide agents to mutually consistent decisions. As the Two Theorems of Welfare Economics showed, they do this so well that Pareto-efficiency is attained. Imperfect competition arises whenever an economic agent has the ability to influence prices. To be able to do so requires that the agent must be large relative to the size of the market in which they operate. It follows from the usual application of economic rationality that those agents who can affect prices will aim to do so to their own advantage. This must be detrimental to other agents and to the economy as a whole. This basic feature of imperfect competition, and its implications for economic policy, will be explored in this chapter.

Imperfect competition can take many forms. It can arise due to monopoly in product markets and through monopsony in labor markets. Firms with monopoly power will push price above marginal cost in order to raise their profits. This will reduce the equilibrium level of consumption below what it would have been had the market been competitive and will transfer surplus from consumers to the owners of the firm. Unions with monopoly power can ensure that the wage rate is increased above its competitive level and secure a surplus for their members. The increase in wage rate reduces employment and output. Firms (and even unions) can engage in non–price competition by choosing the quality and characteristics of their products, undertaking advertising, and blocking the entry of competitors.

Each of these forms of behavior can be interpreted as an attempt to increase market power and obtain a greater surplus. When they can occur, the assumption of price-taking behavior used to prove the Two Theorems is violated, and an economy with imperfect competition will not achieve an efficient equilibrium (with one special exception which is detailed later). It then becomes possible that policy intervention can improve on the unregulated outcome. The purpose of this chapter is to investigate how the conclusions derived in earlier chapters need to be modified and to look at some additional issues specific to imperfect competition.

The first part of the chapter focuses on imperfect competition in product markets. After categorizing types of imperfect competition, defining the market structure, and measuring the intensity of competition, the failure of efficiency is demonstrated when there is a lack of competition. This is followed by a discussion of tax incidence in competitive and imperfectly competitive markets. The effects of *specific* and *ad valorem* taxes are then distinguished, and their relative efficiency is assessed. The policies used to regulate monopoly and oligopoly in practice are also described. There is also a discussion of the recent European policy on the regulation of mergers. The final part of the chapter focuses on market power on the two sides of the labor market. Market power from the supply side (monopoly power of a labor union) is contrasted with monopsony power from the demand side. It is shown that both cases lead to inefficient underemployment with wages, respectively above and below competitive wages.

8.2   Concepts of Competition

Imperfect competition arises whenever an economic agent exploits the fact that they have the ability to influence the price of a commodity. If the influence on price can be exercised by the sellers of a product, then there is *monopoly power*. If it is exercised by the buyers, then there is *monopsony power,* and if by both buyers and sellers, there is *bilateral monopoly*. A single seller is a *monopolist* and a single buyer a *monopsonist*. *Oligopoly* arises with two or more sellers who have market power, with *duopoly* being the special case of two sellers.

An agent with market power can set either the price at which they sell, with the market choosing quantity, or can set the quantity they supply, with the market determining price. When there is either monopoly or monopsony, it does not matter whether price or quantity is chosen: the equilibrium outcome will be the same. If there is more than one agent with market power, then the choice variable does make a difference. In oligopoly markets *Cournot* behavior refers to the use of quantity as the strategic variable and *Bertrand* behavior to the use of prices. Typically Bertrand behavior is more competitive in that it leads to a lower market price. Entry by new firms may either be impossible so that an industry is composed of a fixed number of firms, or it may be unhindered, or incumbent firms may follow a policy of entry deterrence.

Forms of imperfect competition also vary with respect to the nature of products sold. These may be homogeneous so that the output of different firms is indistinguishable by the consumer, or differentiated so that each firm offers a different variant. With homogeneous products, at an equilibrium there must be a single price in the market. *Product differentiation* can either be *vertical* (so products can be unambiguously ranked in terms of quality) or *horizontal* (so consumers differ in which specification they prefer). Equilibrium prices can vary across specifications in markets with differentiated products. The notion of product differentiation captures the idea that consumers make choices among competing products on the basis of factors other than price. The exact nature of the differentiation is very important for the market outcome. What differentiation implies is that the purchases of a product do not fall off to zero when its price is raised above that of competing products. The greater the differentiation, the lower is the willingness of consumers to switch among sellers when one seller changes its price. The theory of *monopolistic competition* relates to this competition among many differentiated sellers who can enjoy some limited monopoly power if tastes differ markedly from one consumer to the next.

When products are differentiated, firms may engage in *non–price competition*. This is the use of variables other than price to gain profit. For example, firms may compete by choosing the specification of their product and the quantity of advertising used to support it. The level of investment can also be a strategic variable if this can deter entry by making credible a threat to raise output.

To limit the number of cases to be considered, this chapter will focus on Cournot behavior, so quantity is the strategic variable, with homogeneous products. Although only one of many possible cases, this perfectly illustrates most of the significant implications of imperfect competition. It also has monopoly as a special case (when there is a single firm) and competition as another (when the number of firms tends to infinity).

8.3   Market Structure

The structure of the market describes the number and size of firms that compete within it and the intensity of this competition. To describe the structure of the market, it is first necessary to define the market.

8.3.1   Defining the Market

A market consists of the buyers and sellers whose interaction determines the price and quantity of the good that is traded. Generally, two sellers will be considered to be in the same market if their products are close substitutes. Measuring the own-price elasticity of demand for a product tells us whether there are close substitutes available, but it does not identify what those substitutes might be. To identify the close substitutes, one must study cross-price elasticities of demand between products. When the cross-price elasticity is positive, it indicates that consumers increase their demand for one good when the price of the other good increases. The two products are thus close substitutes. Another approach to defining markets is to use the standard industry classification that identifies products as close competitors if they share the same product characteristics. Although products with the same classification number are often close competitors, this is not always true. For example, all drugs share the same classification number but not all drugs are close substitute for each other.

Markets are also defined by geographic areas, since otherwise identical products will not be close substitutes if they are sold in different areas and the cost of transporting the product from one area to another is large. Given this reasoning, one would expect close competitors to locate as far as possible from each other and it therefore seems quite peculiar to see them located close to one another in some large cities. This reflects a common trade-off between market size and market share. For instance, antique stores in Brussels are located next to one another around the Place du Grand Sablon. The reason is that the bunching effect helps to attract customers in the first place (market size), even if they become closer competitors in dividing up the market (market sharing). By locating close together, Brussels' antique stores make it more convenient for shoppers to come and browse around in search of some antiques. In other words, the bunching of sellers creates a critical mass that makes it easier to attract shoppers.

8.3.2   Measuring Competition

We now proceed on the basis that the market has been defined. What does it then mean to say that there is "more" or "less competition" in this market? Three distinct dimensions are widely used and need to be clearly distinguished.

The first dimension is *contestability*, which represents the freedom of rivals to enter an industry. It depends on legal monopoly rights (patent protection, operating licenses, etc.) or other barriers to entry (economies of scale and scope, the marketing advantage of incumbents, entry-deterring strategies, etc.). Entry barriers protect the market leader from serious competition from newcomers. Contestability theory shows how the threat of entry can constrain incumbents from raising prices even if there is only one firm currently operating in the market. However, when markets are not perfectly contestable, the threat of potential competition is limited, which allows the incumbents to reap additional profits.

Table 8.1
Market concentration in US manufacturing, 1987

Industry	Number of firms	Four-firm concentration ratio	Herfindahl index
Cereal breakfast foods	33	0.87	0.221
Pet food	130	0.61	0.151
Book publishing	2,182	0.24	0.026
Soap and detergents	683	0.65	0.170
Petroleum refining	200	0.32	0.044
Electronic computers	914	0.43	0.069
Refrigerators/freezers	40	0.85	0.226
Laundry machines	11	0.93	0.286
Greeting cards	147	0.85	0.283

Source: Concentration ratios in Manufacturing, 1992, US Bureau of the Census.

A second dimension is the degree of *concentration* that represents the number and distribution of rivals currently operating in the same market. As we will see, the performance of a market depends on whether it is concentrated (having few sellers) or unconcentrated (having many sellers). A widespread measure of market concentration is the *n-firm concentration ratio*. This is defined as the consolidated market share of the n largest firms in the market. For example, the four-firm concentration ratio in the US cigarette industry is 0.92, which means that the four largest cigarette firms have a total market share of 92 percent (with the calculation of market share usually based on sales revenue). Table 8.1 shows the four-firm concentration ratios for some US industries in 1987.

The problem with the n-firm concentration ratio is that it is insensitive to the distribution of market shares between the largest firms. For example a four-firm concentration ratio does not change if the first-largest firm increases its market share at the expense of the second-largest firm. To capture the relative size of the largest firms, another commonly used measure is the *Herfindahl index*. This index is defined as the sum of the squared market shares of all the firms in the market. Letting s_i be the market share of firm i, the Herfindahl index is given by $H = \sum_i s_i^2$. Notice that the Herfindahl index in a market with two equal-size firms is $\frac{1}{2}$ and with n equal-size firms is $\frac{1}{n}$. For this reason a market with Herfindahl index of 0.20 is also said to have a numbers-equivalent of 5. For example, if there is one dominant firm with a market share of 44 percent and 100 identical small firms with a total market share of 56 percent, the Herfindahl is

$$H = \sum_i s_i^2 = (0.44)^2 + 100 \left[\frac{0.56}{100} \right]^2 = 0.197. \tag{8.1}$$

This market structure is then interpreted as being equivalent to one with 5 identical firms. Herfindahls associated to some US industries are indicated in table 8.1. These numbers show that the market for laundry firms, which has a numbers-equivalent less than 4, is more concentrated than the market for book publishers, which has a numbers-equivalent of 38.

The third dimension of the market structure is *collusiveness*. This is related to the degree of independence of firms' strategies within the market or its reciprocal, which is the possibility for sellers to agree to raise prices in unison. Collusion can either be explicit (e.g., a cartel agreement) or tacit (when it is in each firm's interest to refrain from aggressive price cutting). Explicit collusion is illegal and more easily detected than tacit collusion. However, tacit collusion is more difficult to sustain. Experience has shown that it is unusual for more than a handful of sellers to raise prices much above costs for a sustained period. One common reason is that a small firm may view the collusive bargain among larger rivals as an opportunity to steal their market shares by undercutting the collusive price, which in turn triggers a price war. The airline industry is a good example in recent years of frequent price wars. The additional problem with the airline industry is that fixed cost is high relative to variable cost. This means that once a flight is scheduled, airlines face tremendous pressure to fill their planes, and they are willing to fly passengers at prices close to marginal cost but far below average cost. Thus with such pricing practices, airlines can take large financial losses during price wars.

The three dimensions of market structure and the resulting intensity of competition may be related. The freedom to enter a market may result in a larger number of firms operating and thus a less concentrated market, which in turn may lead to the breakdown of collusive agreement to raise prices.

8.4   Welfare

Imperfect competition, along with public goods, externalities, and asymmetric information, is one of the standard cases of market failure that lead to the inefficiency of equilibrium. It is the inefficiency that provides the motivation for economic policy in relation to imperfect competition. To provide the context for the discussion of policy, this section demonstrates the source of the inefficiency and reports measures of its extent.

8.4.1   Inefficiency

The most important fact about imperfect competition is that it invariably leads to inefficiency. The cause of this inefficiency is now isolated in the profit-maximizing behavior of firms that have an incentive to restrict output so that price is increased above the competitive level.

In a competitive economy equilibrium will involve the price of each commodity being equal to its marginal cost of production. This results from applying the argument that firms will always wish to increase supply whenever price is above marginal cost, since price is taken as given and additional supply will raise profit. Since all firms raise supply, price must fall until there is no incentive for further supply increases. This argument shows that the profit-maximizing behavior of competitive firms drives price down to marginal cost. If marginal cost is constant at value c, then competition results in a price, p, satisfying

$$p = c. \tag{8.2}$$

To see the cause of inefficiency with imperfect competition, consider first the case of monopoly. Assume that the monopolist produces with a constant marginal cost, c, and chooses its output level, y, to maximize profit. The market power of the monopolist is reflected in the fact that as their output is increased, the market price of the product will fall. This relationship is captured by the inverse demand function, $p(y)$, which determines price as a function of output. As y increases, $p(y)$ decreases. Using the inverse demand function, which the monopolist is assumed to know, the profit level of the firm is

$$\pi = [p(y) - c]y. \tag{8.3}$$

The first-order condition describing the profit-maximizing output level is

$$p + y\frac{dp}{dy} - c = 0, \tag{8.4}$$

which, since $\frac{dp}{dy} < 0$ (price falls as output increases), implies that $p > c$. The condition in (8.4) shows that the monopolist will set price above marginal cost and that the monopolist's price does not satisfy the efficiency requirement of being equal to marginal cost. The fact that the monopolist perceives that their output choice affects price (so $\frac{dp}{dy}$ is not zero) results directly in the divergence of price and marginal cost.

The condition describing the choice of output can be re-arranged to provide further insight into degree of divergence between price and marginal cost. Using the elasticity of demand, $\varepsilon = \frac{dy}{dp}\frac{p}{y} < 0$, the profit-maximization condition can be written as

$$\frac{p-c}{p} = \frac{1}{|\varepsilon|}. \tag{8.5}$$

This equilibrium condition for the monopoly is called the *inverse elasticity pricing rule*. In words, the condition says that the percentage deviation between the price and the marginal cost is equal to the inverse of the elasticity of demand. The expression $\frac{p-c}{p}$ is the *Lerner index*. The Lerner index will be shown shortly to be strictly between zero and one (i.e., $|\varepsilon| > 1$). The monopoly pricing rule can also be written as

$$p = \mu c, \tag{8.6}$$

where $\mu = \frac{1}{1-[1/|\varepsilon|]} > 1$ is called the *monopoly markup* and measures the extent to which price is raised above marginal cost. This pricing rule shows that the markup above marginal cost is inversely related to the absolute value of the elasticity of demand. The higher is the absolute value of the elasticity, the smaller is the monopoly markup.

In the extreme case of perfectly elastic demand, which equates to the firm having no market power, price would be equal to marginal cost. For the markup μ to be finite (so price is well-defined), it must be the case that $|\varepsilon| > 1$ so the monopolist locates on the elastic part of the demand curve. If demand is inelastic, with $|\varepsilon| \leq 1$, then the monopolist makes maximum profit by selling the smallest possible quantity at an arbitrarily high price. Since the monopolist operates on the elastic part of the demand curve with $|\varepsilon| > 1$, the Lerner index $\frac{p-c}{p} = \frac{1}{|\varepsilon|} \in (0, 1)$, and provides a simple measure of market power ranging from zero for a perfectly competitive market to one for maximal market power. Therefore a firm might have a monopoly, but its market power might still be low because it is constrained by competition from substitute products outside the market. By differentiating its product, a monopolist can insulate its product from the competition of substitute products and thereby expands its market power.

This relation of the monopoly markup to the elasticity of demand can be easily extended from monopoly to oligopoly. Assume that there are m firms in the market and denote the output of firm j by y_j. The market price is now dependent on the total output of the firms, $y = \sum_{j=1}^{m} y_j$. With output level y_j, the profit level of firm j is

$$\pi^j = [p - c]y_j. \tag{8.7}$$

Adopting the Cournot assumption that each firm regards its competitors' outputs as fixed when it optimizes, the choice of output for firm j satisfies

$$p + y_j \frac{dp}{dy} - c = 0. \tag{8.8}$$

Now assume that the firms are identical and each produces the same output level, $\frac{y}{m}$. The first-order condition for choice of output (8.8) can then be re-arranged to obtain the Lerner index

$$\frac{p - c}{p} = \frac{1}{m} \frac{1}{|\varepsilon|}, \tag{8.9}$$

and the oligopoly price is given by

$$p = \mu^\circ c, \tag{8.10}$$

where $\mu^\circ = \frac{m}{m - [1/|\varepsilon|]} > 1$ is the *oligopoly markup.* Thus, in the presence of several firms in the market, the Lerner index of market power is deflated according to the market share. As for monopoly, the value of the markup is related to the inverse of the elasticity of demand. The Lerner index can be used to show that an oligopoly becomes more competitive as the number of firms in the industry increases. This claim follows from the fact that $\frac{p-c}{p}$ must tend to zero as m tends to infinity. Hence, as the number of firms increases, the Cournot equilibrium becomes more competitive and price tends to marginal cost. The limiting position with an infinite number of firms can be viewed as the idealization of the competitive model.

There is one special case of monopoly for which the equilibrium is efficient. Let the firm be able to charge each consumer the maximum price that they are able to pay. To do so obviously requires the firm to have considerable information about its customers. The consequence is that the firm extracts all consumer surplus and translates it into profit. It will keep supplying the good until price falls to marginal cost and there is no more surplus to extract. So total supply will be equal to that under the competition. This scenario, known as *perfect price discrimination,* results in all the potential surplus in the market being turned into monopoly profit. No surplus is lost due to the monopoly, but all surplus is transferred from the consumers to the firm. Of course, this scenario can only arise with an exceedingly well-informed monopolist.

8.4.2   Incomplete Information

Monopoly inefficiency can also arise from the firm having incomplete information, even in situations where there would be efficiency with complete information. To see this, suppose that a monopolist with constant marginal cost c faces a buyer whose willingness to pay for a unit of the firm's output is v. If there was complete information, the firm and buyer would agree a price between c and v, and the product would be traded. The surplus from the transaction would be shared between the two and no inefficiency would arise.

The difference that imperfect information can make is that trade will sometimes not take place even though both parties would gain if they did trade. Suppose now that the monopolist cannot observe v but knows from experience that it is drawn from a distribution $F(v)$, which is the probability that the buyer's valuation is less or equal to v. The function $(1 - F(v))$ is analogous to the expected demand when a purchaser buys at most one unit because the probability that there is a demand at price v is the probability that the buyer's valuation is higher than the price. Assume that there are potential gains from trade so $v > c$ for at least a range of v. Pareto-efficiency requires trade to occur if and only if $v \geq c$.

The monopolist's problem is to offer a price p that maximizes its expected profit (anticipating that the buyer will not accept the offer if $v < p$). This price must fall between c and v for trade to occur. The monopolist sets a price p^* that solves

$$\max_{\{p\}} \underbrace{[1 - F(p)]}_{\substack{\text{Probability of} \\ \text{trade}}} \underbrace{[p - c]}_{\substack{\text{Profit if} \\ \text{trade}}}. \tag{8.11}$$

From the assumption that there is a potential gain from trade, there must be a range of values of v higher than c, and thus it is possible for the monopolist to charge a price in excess of the marginal cost with the offer being accepted. Clearly, the price that maximizes expected profit must be $p^* > c$, so the standard conclusion of monopoly holds that price is in excess of marginal cost. When trade takes place (so a value of v occurs with $c < p^* < v$), the outcome is an efficient trade. However, when a value of v occurs with $c < v < p^*$, trade does not take place. This is inefficient because trade should occur when the benefit exceeds the cost $(v > c)$. The effect of the monopolist setting price above marginal cost is to eliminate some of the potential trades.

For instance, assume the willingness to pay v is uniformly distributed on the interval $[0, 1]$ with the marginal cost $0 < c < 1$. Then the probability that trade

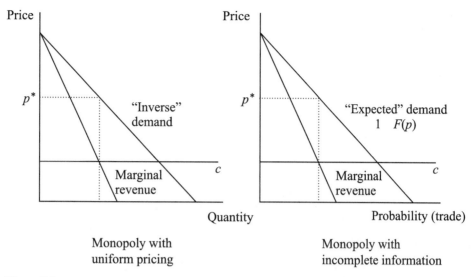

Figure 8.1
Monopoly pricing

takes place at price p (expected demand) is $1 - F(p) = 1 - p$, which gives expected revenue $[1 - F(p)]p = [1 - p]p$ and marginal revenue $MR = 1 - 2p$. The expected profit is $\pi = [1 - p][p - c]$, and the profit-maximizing pricing satisfies the first-order condition $[1 - 2p] + c = 0$, which can be re-arranged to give monopoly price of $p^* = \frac{1+c}{2} > c$. The parallel between this monopoly choice under incomplete information and the standard monopoly problem is illustrated in figure 8.1.

8.4.3   Measures of Welfare Loss

It has been shown that the equilibrium of an imperfectly competitive market is not Pareto-efficient, except in the special case of perfect price discrimination. This makes it natural to consider what the degree of welfare loss may actually be. The assessment of monopoly welfare loss has been a subject of some dispute in which calculations have provided a range of estimates from the effectively insignificant to considerable percentages of potential welfare.

The inefficiency of monopoly will be described in chapter 11 and part of that argument is now briefly provided. Figure 8.2 assumes that the marginal cost of production is constant at value c and that there are no fixed costs. The equilibrium

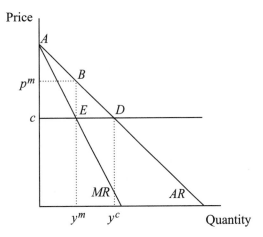

Figure 8.2
Deadweight loss with monopoly

price if the industry were competitive, p^c, would be equal to marginal cost, so $p^c = c$. This price leads to output level y^c and generates consumer surplus ADc. The inverse demand function facing the firm, $p(y)$, determines price as a function of output and is also the average revenue function for the firm. This is denoted by AR. The marginal revenue function is denoted MR. The monopolist's optimal output, y^m, occurs where marginal revenue and marginal cost are equal. At this output level, the price with monopoly is p^m. Consumer surplus is ABp^m and profit is $p^m BEc$.

Contrasting the competitive and the monopoly outcomes shows that some of the consumer surplus under competition is transformed into profit under monopoly. This is the area $p^m BEc$, and it represents a transfer from consumers to the firm. However, some of the consumer surplus is simply lost. This loss is the area BDE, which is termed the *deadweight loss of monopoly*. Since the total social surplus under monopoly ($ABp^m + p^m BEc$) is less than that under competition (ADc), the monopoly is inefficient. This inefficiency is reflected in the fact that consumption is lower under monopoly than competition.

When the demand function is linear so that the AR curve is a straight line, then the welfare loss area BDE is equal to half of the area $p^m BEc$. The area $p^m BEc$ is monopoly profit, which is equal to $[p^m - c]y^m$. This implies that the loss BDE is $\frac{1}{2}[p^m - c]y^m$. From the first-order condition for the choice of monopoly output, (8.5), $p^m - c = -\frac{1}{\varepsilon}p^m$. By this result it follows that a measure of the deadweight loss is

Table 8.2
Monopoly welfare loss

Author	Sector	Welfare loss (%)
Harberger	US manufacturing	0.08
Gisser	US manufacturing	0.11–1.82
Peterson and Connor	US food manufacturing	0.16–5.15
Masson and Shaanan	37 US industries	3
		16
McCorriston	UK agricultural inputs	1.6–2.5
		20–40
Cowling and Mueller	US corporate sector	4–13
	UK corporate sector	3.9–7.2

$$\text{Deadweight loss} = -\frac{p^m y^m}{2\varepsilon} = -\frac{R^m}{2\varepsilon}, \tag{8.12}$$

where R^m is the total revenue of the monopolist. This formula is especially simple to evaluate to obtain an idea of the size of the deadweight loss. For example, if the elasticity of demand is -2, then the welfare loss is 25 percent of sales revenue and is therefore quite large.

Numerous studies have been published that provide measures of the degree of monopoly welfare loss. A selection of these results is given in table 8.2. The smaller values are obtained by calculating only the deadweight loss triangle. If these were correct, then we could conclude that monopoly power is not a significant economic issue. This was the surprising conclusion of the initial study of Harberger in 1954, which challenged the conventional wisdom that monopoly must be damaging to the economy. In contrast, the larger values of loss are obtained by including the costs of defending the monopoly position. Chapter 11 considers the arguments proposed in the rent-seeking literature for the inclusion of these additional components of welfare loss. These values reveal monopoly loss to be very substantial.

It can be appreciated from table 8.2 that a broad range of estimates of monopoly welfare loss have been produced. Some studies conclude that welfare loss is insignificant; others conclude that it is very important. What primarily distinguishes these differing estimates is whether it is only the deadweight loss that is counted, or the deadweight loss plus the cost of defending the monopoly. Which one is correct is an unresolved issue that involves two competing perspectives on economic efficiency.

There is one further point that needs to be made. The calculations above have been based on a *static* analysis in which there is a single time period. The demand function, the product traded, and the costs of production are all given. The firm makes a single choice, and then the equilibrium is attained. What this ignores are all the *dynamic* aspects of economic activity such as investment and innovation. When these factors are taken into account, as Schumpeter forcefully argued, it is even possible for monopoly to generate dynamic welfare gains rather than losses. This claim is based on the argument that investment and innovation will only be undertaken if firms can expect to earn a sufficient return. In a competitive environment, any gains will be competed away so the incentives are eliminated. Conversely, holding a monopoly position allows gains to be realized. This provides the incentive to undertake investment and innovation. Furthermore the incentive is strengthened by the intention of maintaining the position of monopoly. The dynamic gains can more than offset the static losses, giving a positive argument for the encouragement of monopoly. We return to this issue in the discussion of regulation in section 8.7.

8.5   Tax Incidence

The study of tax incidence is about determining the changes in prices and profits that follow the imposition of a tax. The *formal* or *legal incidence* of a tax refers to who is legally responsible for paying the tax. The legal incidence can be very different from the *economic incidence*, which relates to who ultimately has to alter their behavior because of the tax.

To see this distinction, consider the following example. A tax of $1 is levied on a commodity that costs $10, and this tax must be paid by the retailer. The legal incidence is simple: for each unit sold the retailer must pay $1 to the tax authority. The economic incidence is much more complex. The first question has to be: What does the price of the commodity become after the tax? It may change to $11, but this would be an exception rather than the norm. It may, for example, rise instead only to $10.50. If it does, $0.50 of the tax falls on the consumer to pay. What of the other $0.50? This depends on how the producer responds to the tax increase. The producer may lower the price of the commodity to the retailer from $9 to $8.75 and then bear $0.25 of the tax. The remaining $0.25 of the tax is paid by the retailer. The economic incidence of the tax is then very distinct from the legal incidence.

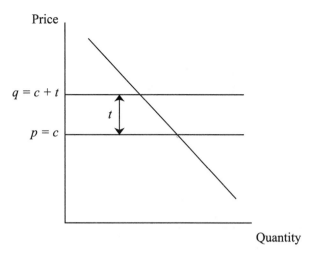

Figure 8.3
Tax incidence with perfectly elastic supply

This example raises the question of what determines the economic incidence. The answer is found in the demand and supply curves for the good that is taxed. Economic incidence will first be determined for the competitive case, and then it is shown how the conclusions are modified by imperfect competition. In fact imperfect competition can result in very interesting conclusions concerning tax incidence.

Tax incidence analysis is at its simplest when there is competition and the marginal cost of production is constant. In this case the supply curve in the absence of taxation must be horizontal at a level equal to marginal cost; see figure 8.3. This gives the before-tax price $p = c$. The introduction of a tax of amount t will raise this curve by exactly the amount of the tax. The after-tax price, q, is at the intersection of the demand curve and the new supply curve. It can be seen that $q = p + t$, so price will rise by an amount equal to the tax. Hence the tax is simply passed forward by the firms onto consumers since price is always set equal to marginal cost plus tax.

When marginal cost is not constant and the supply curve slopes upward, the introduction of a tax still shifts the curve vertically upward by the amount equal to the tax. The extent to which price rises is then determined by the slopes of the supply and demand curve. If the demand curve is vertical, price rises by the full amount of the tax; otherwise, it will rise by less. See figure 8.4.

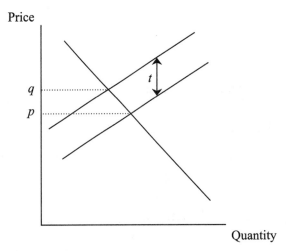

Figure 8.4
Tax incidence in the general case

In summary, if the supply curve is horizontal (so supply is infinitely elastic) or the demand curve is vertical (so demand is completely inelastic), then price will rise by exactly the amount of the tax. In all other cases it will rise by less, with the exact rise being determined by the elasticities of supply and demand. When the price increase is equal to the tax, the entire tax burden is passed by the firm onto the consumers. Otherwise, the burden of the tax is shared between firms and consumers. Consequently the extent to which the price is shifted forward from the producer onto the consumers is dependent on the elasticities of supply and demand.

There are two reasons why tax incidence with imperfect competition is distinguished from the analysis for the competitive case. First, prices on imperfectly competitive markets are set at a level above marginal cost. Second, imperfectly competitive firms may also earn nonzero profits so taxation can also affect profit. To trace the effects of taxation it is necessary to work through the profit-maximization process of the imperfectly competitive firms. Such an exercise involves characterizing the optimal choices of the firms and then seeing how they are affected by a change in the tax rate.

The incidence of a tax on output can be demonstrated by returning to the diagram for monopoly profit maximization. A tax of value t on output changes the tax-inclusive marginal cost from c to $c + t$. In figure 8.5 this is shown to move the intersection between the marginal revenue curve and the marginal cost curve from

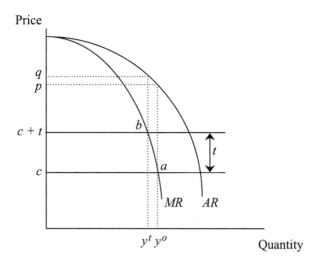

Figure 8.5
Tax undershifting

a to b. Output falls from y^o to y^t, and price rises from p to q. In this case price rises by less than the tax imposed—the difference between q and p is less than t. This is called the case of tax *undershifting*. What it means is that the monopolist is absorbing some of the tax and not passing it all on to the consumer.

With competition, the full value of the tax may be shifted to consumers but never more. With monopoly, the proportion of the tax that is shifted to consumers is determined by the shape of the AR curve (and hence the MR curve). In contrast to competition, for some shapes of AR curve it is possible for the imposition of a tax to be met by a price increase that exceeds the value of the tax. This is called the case of tax *overshifting* and is illustrated in figure 8.6. The imposition of the tax, t, leads to a price increase from p to q. As is clear in the figure, $q - p > t$. This outcome could never happen in the competitive case.

The feature that distinguishes the cases of overshifting and undershifting is the shape of the demand function. Figure 8.5 has a demand function that is convex— it becomes increasingly steep as quantity increases. In contrast, figure 8.6 involves a concave demand function with a gradient that decreases as output increases. Either of these shapes for the demand function is entirely consistent with the existence of monopoly.

The overshifting of taxation is also a possibility with oligopoly. To illustrate this, consider the constant elasticity demand function $X = p^\varepsilon$, where $\varepsilon < 0$ is the

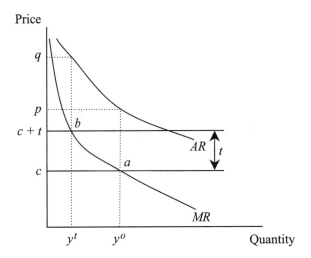

Figure 8.6
Tax overshifting

Table 8.3
Calculations of tax shifting

Baker and Brechling	UK beer 0.696	UK tobacco 0.568
Delipalla and O'Connell, tobacco	"Northern" EU 0.92	"Southern" EU 2.16
Tasarika	UK beer 0.665	

elasticity of demand. Since the elasticity is constant, so must be the mark-up at $\mu^o = \frac{m}{m-[1/|\varepsilon|]}$. Furthermore, because $\varepsilon < 0$ it follows that $\mu^o > 1$. Applying the markup to marginal cost plus tax, the equilibrium price of the oligopoly is $q = \mu^o[c + t]$. The effect of an increase in the tax is then

$$\frac{\partial q}{\partial t} = \mu^o > 1, \tag{8.13}$$

so there is always overshifting with the constant elasticity demand function. This holds for any value of $m \geq 1$, and hence applies to both monopoly ($m = 1$) and oligopoly ($m \geq 2$). In addition, as m increases and the market becomes more competitive, μ^o will tend to 1, as will $\frac{\partial q}{\partial t}$, so the competitive outcome of complete tax shifting will arise.

　　Some estimates of the value of the tax-shifting term are given in table 8.3 for the beer and tobacco industries. Both of these industries have a small number of dominant firms and an oligopolistic market structure. The figures show that although undershifting arises in most cases, there is evidence of overshifting in the tobacco industry.

There is an even more surprising effect that can occur with oligopoly: an increase in taxation can lead to an increase in profit. The analysis of the constant elasticity case can be extended to demonstrate this result. Since the equilibrium price is $q = \mu^o[c + t]$, we use the demand function to obtain the output of each firm as

$$x = \frac{[\mu^o]^\varepsilon[c + t]^\varepsilon}{m}. \tag{8.14}$$

Using these values for price and output results in a profit level for each firm of

$$\pi = \frac{[\mu^o - 1][\mu^o]^\varepsilon[c + t]^{\varepsilon+1}}{m}. \tag{8.15}$$

The effect of an increase in the tax on the level of profit is then given by

$$\frac{\partial \pi}{\partial t} = \frac{[\mu^o - 1][\mu^o]^\varepsilon[\varepsilon + 1][c + t]^\varepsilon}{m}. \tag{8.16}$$

The possibility of the increase in tax raising profit follows by observing that if $\varepsilon > -1$, then $[\varepsilon + 1] > 0$, so $\frac{\partial \pi}{\partial t} > 0$. When the elasticity satisfies this restriction, an increase in the tax will raise the level of profit. Put simply, the firms find the addition to their costs to be profitable.

It should be observed that such a profit increase cannot occur with monopoly because a monopolist must produce on the elastic part of the demand curve with $\varepsilon < -1$. With oligopoly the markup remains finite provided that $m - \frac{1}{|\varepsilon|} > 0$ or $\varepsilon < -\frac{1}{m}$. Therefore profit can be increased by an increase in taxation if there is oligopoly.

The mechanism that makes this outcome possible is shown in figure 8.7, which displays the determination of the Cournot equilibrium for a duopoly. The figure is constructed by first plotting the isoprofit curves. The curves denote sets of output levels for the two firms that give a constant level of profit. The profit of firm 1 is highest on the curves closest to the horizontal axis, and it reaches its maximum at the output level, m_1, which is the output firm 1 would produce if it were a monopolist. Similarly the level of profit for firm 2 is higher on the isoprofit curves closest to the vertical axis, and is maximized at its monopoly output level, m_2. The assumption of Cournot oligopoly is that each firm takes the output of the other as given when they maximize. So for any fixed output level for firm 2, firm 1 will

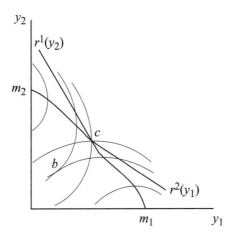

Figure 8.7
Possibility of a profit increase

maximize profit on the isoprofit curve that is horizontal at the output level of firm 2. Connecting the horizontal points gives the best-reaction function for firm 1 which is labeled $r^1(y_2)$. Similarly, setting a fixed output level for firm 1, we have that firm 2 maximizes profit on the isoprofit curve that is vertical at this level of 1's output. Connecting the vertical points gives its best-reaction function $r^2(y_1)$.

The Cournot equilibrium for the duopoly is where the best-reaction functions cross, and the isoprofit curves are locally horizontal for firm 1 and vertical for firm 2. This is point c in the figure. The Cournot equilibrium is not efficient for the firms and a simultaneous reduction in output by both firms, which would be a move from c in the direction of b, would raise both firms' profits. Further improvement in profit can be continued until the point that maximizes joint profit, $\pi_1 + \pi_2$, is reached. Joint profit maximization occurs at a point of tangency of the isoprofit curves, which is denoted by point b in figure 8.7. The firms could achieve this point if they were to collude, but such collusion would not be credible because both the firms would have an incentive to deviate from point b by increasing output.

It is this inefficiency that opens the possibility for a joint increase in profit to be obtained. Intuitively, how taxation raises profit is by shifting the isoprofit curves in such a way that the duopoly equilibrium moves closer to the point of joint profit maximization. Although total available production must fall as the tax increases, the firms secure a larger fraction of the gains from trade. Unlike collusion, the tax is binding on the firms and produces a credible reduction in output.

8.6   Specific and Ad valorem Taxation

The analysis of tax incidence has so far considered only *specific* taxation. With specific taxation, the legally responsible firm has to pay a fixed amount of tax for each unit of output. The amount that has to be paid is independent of the price of the commodity. Consequently the price the consumer pays is the producer price plus the specific tax. This is not the only way in which taxes can be levied. Commodities can alternatively be subject to ad valorem taxation so that the tax payment is defined as a fixed proportion of the producer price. Consequently, as price changes, so does the amount paid in tax.

The fact that tax incidence has been analyzed only for specific taxation in not a limitation when firms are competitive, since the two forms are entirely equivalent. The meaning of equivalence here is that a specific tax and an ad valorem tax that led to the same consumer price will raise the same amount of tax revenue. Their economic incidence is therefore identical.

This equivalence can be shown as follows: Let t be the specific tax on a commodity. Then the equivalent ad valorem tax rate τ must satisfy the equation

$$q = p + t = [1 + \tau]p. \tag{8.17}$$

Solving this equation, we have that $\tau = \frac{t}{p}$ is the ad valorem tax rate that leads to the same consumer price as the specific tax. In terms of the incidence diagrams, both taxes would shift the supply curve for the good in exactly the same way. The demonstration of equivalence is completed by showing that the taxes raise identical levels of tax revenue. The revenue raised by the ad valorem tax is $R = \tau p X$. Using the fact that $\tau = \frac{t}{p}$, we can write this revenue level as $\frac{t}{p} p X = tX$, which is the revenue raised by the specific tax. This completes the demonstration that the specific and ad valorem taxes are equivalent.

With imperfect competition this equivalence between the two forms of taxation breaks down: specific and ad valorem taxes that generate the same consumer price generate different levels of revenue. The reason for this breakdown of equivalence, and its consequences, are now explored.

The fact that specific and ad valorem taxes have different effects can be seen very easily in the monopoly case. Assume that the firm sells at price q and that each unit of output is produced at marginal production cost, c. With a specific tax the consumer price and producer price are related by $q = p + t$. This allows the profit level with a specific tax to be written as

$$\pi = [q - t]x - cx = qx - [c + t]x. \tag{8.18}$$

The expression for this profit level shows that the specific tax acts as an addition to the marginal cost for the firm. Now consider instead the payment of an ad valorem tax at rate τ. Since an ad valorem tax is levied as a proportion of the producer price, the consumer price and producer price are related by $q = [1 + \tau]p$; hence the consumers pay price q and the firm receives $p = \frac{1}{1+\tau}q$. The profit level with the ad valorem tax is then

$$\pi = \frac{1}{1 + \tau}qx - cx. \tag{8.19}$$

The basic difference between the two taxes can be seen by comparing these alternative specifications of profit. From the perspective of the firm, the specific tax raises marginal production cost from c to $c + t$. In contrast, the ad valorem tax reduces the revenue received by the firm from qx to $\frac{1}{1+\tau}qx$. Hence the specific tax works via the level of costs, whereas the ad valorem tax operates via the level of revenue. With competition this difference is of no consequence. But the very basis of imperfect competition is that the firms recognize the effect their actions has upon revenue—so the ad valorem tax interacts with the expression of monopoly power.

The consequence of this difference is illustrated in figure 8.8. In the left-hand figure, the effect of a specific tax is shown. In the right-hand figure, the effect of an ad valorem tax is shown. The specific tax leads to an upward shift in the tax-inclusive marginal cost curve. This moves the optimal price from p to q. The ad valorem tax leads to a downward shift in average and marginal revenue net of tax as shown in figure 8.8. The ad valorem tax leads from price p in the absence of taxation to q with taxation. The resulting price increase is dependent on the slope of the marginal revenue curve.

What is needed to make a firm comparison between the effects of the two taxes is some common benchmark. The benchmark chosen is a given consumer price. The values of the specific and ad valorem taxes that lead to this consumer price are found. The taxes are then contrasted by determining which raises the most tax revenue. This comparison is easily conducted by returning to the definition of profit in (8.19). With the ad valorem tax, the profit level can be expressed as

$$\pi = \frac{1}{1 + \tau}qx - cx = \frac{1}{1 + \tau}[qx - [c + \tau c]x]. \tag{8.20}$$

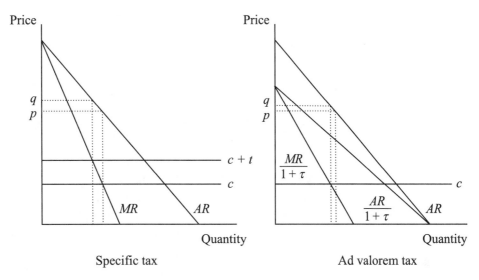

Figure 8.8
Contrasting taxes

The second term of (8.20) shows that the ad valorem tax is equivalent to the combined use of a specific tax of value τc plus a profit tax at rate $\frac{\tau}{1+\tau}$. A profit tax has no effect on the firm's choice, but it does raise revenue. Hence an ad valorem tax with its rate set so that

$$\tau c = t \tag{8.21}$$

must lead to the same after-tax price as the specific tax. However, the ad valorem tax raises more revenue. This is because the component τc collects the same revenue as the specific tax t but the ad valorem tax also collects revenue from the profit-tax component. Hence the ad valorem tax must collect more revenue for the same consumer price. This result can, alternatively, be expressed as the fact that for a given level of revenue, an ad valorem tax leads to lower consumer price than a specific tax.

In conclusion, ad valorem taxation is more effective than specific taxation when there is imperfect competition. The intuition behind this conclusion is that the ad valorem tax lowers marginal revenue, and this reduces the perceived market power of the firm. Consequently the ad valorem tax has the helpful effect of reducing monopoly power, offsetting some of the costs involved in raising revenue through commodity taxation.

8.7   Regulation of Monopoly

Up until this point the focus has been placed on the welfare loss caused by imperfect competition and on tax incidence. As we have shown, there are two competing views about the extent of the welfare loss, but even if the lower values are accepted, it is still beneficial to reduce the loss as far as possible. This raises the issue of the range of policies that are available to reduce the adverse effects of monopoly.

When faced with imperfect competition, the most natural policy response is to try to encourage an enhanced degree of competition. There are several ways in which this can be done. The most dramatic example is US antitrust legislation, which has been used to enforce the division of monopolies into separate competing firms. This policy was applied to the Standard Oil Company, which was declared a monopoly and broken up into competing units in 1911. More recently the Bell System telephone company was broken up in 1984. This policy of breaking up monopolists represents extreme legislation and, once enacted, leaves a major problem of how the system should be organized following the breakup. Typically the industry will require continuing regulation, a theme to which we return below.

Less dramatic than directly breaking up firms is to provides aids to competition. A *barrier to entry* is anything that allows a monopoly to sustain its position and prevent new firms from competing effectively. Barriers to entry can be legal restrictions such as the issue of a single license permitting only one firm to be active. They can also be technological in the sense of superior knowledge, the holding of patents, or the structure of the production function. Furthermore some barriers can be erected deliberately by the incumbent monopolist specifically to deter entry. For a policy to encourage competition, it must remove or at least reduce the barriers to entry. The appropriate policy response depends on the nature of the barrier.

If a barrier to entry is created by a legal restriction, it can equally be removed by a change to the law. But here it is necessary to inquire as to why the restriction was created initially. One possible answer would take us to the concept of rent-creation, which is discussed in chapter 11. In that chapter the introduction of a restriction is seen as a way of generating rent. An interesting example of the creation of such restrictions are the activities of MITI (the Ministry of International Trade and Industries) in Japan. In 1961 MITI produced its "Concentration Plan," which aimed to concentrate the mass-production automakers into two to three groups. The intention behind this was to cope with the international competition that ensued after the liberalization of auto imports into Japan and to place the Japanese car industry in a stronger position for exporting. These intentions were never fully realized, and the plan was ultimately undermined by developments in the auto industry, especially the emergence of Honda as a major manufacturer. Despite this the example still stands of a good illustration of a deliberate policy attempt to restrict competition.

If barriers to entry relate to technological knowledge, then it is possible for the government to insist on the sharing of this knowledge. Both the concern over the bundling of Internet Explorer with Windows in the United States and the bundling of Media Player with Windows in Europe are pertinent examples. In the United States the outcome has been that Microsoft is obliged to provide rival software firms with information that allows them to develop competing products, and to ensure that these products work with the Windows operating system. Microsoft's rivals are pushing for a similar solution in the European Union. The existence of patents to protect the use of knowledge is also a barrier to entry. The reasoning behind patents is that they allow a reward for innovation: new discoveries are only valuable if the products in which they are embedded can be exploited without competitors immediately copying them. The production of generic drugs is one of the better-known examples of product copying. Without patents the incentive to innovate would be much reduced, and aggregate welfare would fall. The policy issue then becomes the choice of the length of a patent. It must be long enough to allow innovation to be adequately rewarded but not so long that it stifles competition. Current practice in the United States is that the term of a patent is twenty years from the date at which the application is filed.

Barriers to entry can also be erected as a deliberate part of a corporate strategy designed to deter competitors. Entry barriers can be within the law, such as sustained advertising campaigns to build brand loyalty or the building of excess capacity to deter entry, or they can be illegal such as physical intimidation, violence, and destruction of property. Obviously the latter category can be controlled by recourse to the law if potential competitors wish to do so. Potentially limitations could be placed on advertising. The limitations on tobacco advertisements is an example of such a policy, but this has been motivated on health grounds and not competition reasons. The role of excess capacity is to provide a credible threat that the entry of a competitor will be met by an increase in output from the incumbent with a consequent reduction in market price. The reduction in price can

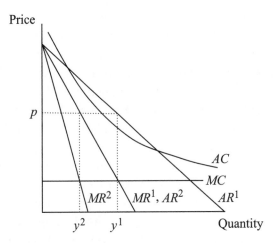

Figure 8.9
Natural monopoly

make entry unprofitable, so sustaining the monopoly position. Although the economic reasoning is clear, it is difficult to see how litigation could ever demonstrate that excess capacity was being held as an entry deterrent, and this limits any potential policy response.

The enhancement of competition only works if it is possible for competitors to be viable. The limits of the argument that monopoly can be tackled by the encouragement of competition are confronted when the market is characterized by *natural monopoly*. The essence of natural monopoly is that there are increasing returns in production and that the level of demand is such that only a single firm can be profitable. This is illustrated in figure 8.9 where the production technology of the two firms involves a substantial fixed cost but a constant marginal cost. Consequently the average cost curve, denoted AC, is decreasing while the marginal cost curve, MC, is horizontal. When there is a monopoly, the single firm faces the demand curve AR^1. Corresponding to this average revenue curve is the marginal revenue curve MR^1. The profit-maximizing price for the monopoly is p and output is y^1. It should be observed that the price is above the level of average cost at output y^1, so the monopolist earns a profit.

Now consider the consequence of a second firm entering the market. The cost conditions do not change, so the AC and MC curves are unaffected. Demand conditions do change since the firms have to share the market. The simplest assumption to make is that the two firms share exactly half the market each. This would hold if the total market consists of two geographical areas each of which could be served by one firm. Furthermore this is the most beneficial situation for the firms since it avoids them competing. Any other way of sharing the market will lead to them earning less profit. With the market shared equally, the demand facing each firm becomes AR^2 (equal to the old MR^1) and marginal revenue MR^2. The profit-maximizing price remains at p, but now at output y^2 this is below average cost. The two firms must therefore both make a loss. Since this market-sharing is the most profitable way for the two firms to behave, any other market behavior must lead to an even greater loss.

What this argument shows is that a market in which one firm can be profitable cannot support two firms. The problem is that the level of demand does not generate enough revenue to cover the fixed costs of two firms operating. The examples that are usually cited of natural monopolies involve utilities such as water supply, electricity, gas, telephones, and railways where a large infrastructure has to be in place to support the market and is very costly to replicate. If these markets do conform to the situation in the figure, then without government intervention only a single firm could survive in the market. Furthermore, any policy to encourage competition will not succeed unless the government can fundamentally alter the structure of the industry. It is not enough just to try to get another firm to operate.

The two policy responses to natural monopoly most widely employed have been public ownership and private ownership with a regulatory body controlling behavior. When the firm is run under public ownership, its price should be chosen to maximize social welfare subject to the budget constraint placed upon the firm—the resulting price is termed the *Ramsey price*. The budget constraint may require the firm to break even or to generate income above production cost. Alternatively, the firm may be allowed to run a deficit that is financed from other tax revenues. Assume that all other markets in the economy are competitive. The Ramsey price for a public firm subject to a break-even constraint will then be equal to marginal cost if this satisfies the constraint. If losses arise at marginal cost, then the Ramsey price will be equal to average cost. The literature on public sector pricing has extended this reasoning to situations where marginal cost and demand vary over time such as in the supply of electricity. Doing this leads into the theory of *peak-load pricing*. When other markets are not competitive, the Ramsey price will reflect the distortions elsewhere in the economy.

Public ownership was practiced extensively in the United Kingdom and elsewhere in Europe. All the major utilities including gas, telephones, electricity, water, and trains were taken into public ownership. This policy was eventually undermined by the problems of the lack of incentive to innovate, invest, or limit costs. Together, these produced a very poor outcome with the lack of market forces producing industries that were overmanned and inefficient. As a consequence the United Kingdom has undertaken a privatization program that has returned all these industries to private sector.

The treatment of the various industries since the return to private ownership illustrates different responses to the regulation of natural monopoly. The water industry is broken into regional suppliers that do not compete directly but are closely regulated. With telephones, the network is owned by British Telecom, but other firms are permitted access agreements to the network. This can allow them to offer a service without the need to undertake the capital investment. In the case of the railways, the ownership of the track, which is the fixed cost, has been separated from the rights to operate trains, which generates the marginal cost. Both the track owner and the train operators remain regulated. With gas and electricity, competing suppliers are permitted to supply using the single existing network.

The most significant difference between public ownership and private ownership with regulation is that under public ownership the government is as informed as the firm about demand and cost conditions. This allows the government to determine the behavior of the firm using the best available information. Policy can only maximize the objective function in an expected sense. So, although the available information may not be complete, the best that is possible will be achieved. As an alternative to public ownership, a firm may remain under private ownership but be made subject to the control of a regulatory body. This introduces possible asymmetries in information between the firm and the regulator. Faced with limited information, one approach considered in the theoretical literature is for the regulator to design an incentive mechanism that achieves a desirable outcome. An example of such a regulatory scheme is the two-part tariff in which the payment for a commodity involves a fixed fee to permit consumption followed by a price per unit of consumption, with these values being set by the regulator. Alternatively, the regulator may impose a constraint on some observable measure of the firm's activities such as that it must not exceed a given rate of return upon the capital employed. Even more simple are the regulatory schemes in the United Kingdom that involve restricting prices to rise at a slower rate than an index of the general price level.

The analysis has looked at a range of issues concerned with dealing with monopoly power and how to regulate industries. The essence of policy is to move the economy closer to the competitive outcome, but there can be distinct problems in achieving this. Monopoly can arise because of the combination of cost and demand conditions, and this can place limitations on what policies are feasible. Natural monopoly results in the need for regulation.

8.8   Regulation of Oligopoly

8.8.1   Detecting Collusion

In an oligopolistic market firms can collectively act as a monopolist and are consequently able to increase their prices. The problem for a regulatory agency is that such collusion is often tacit and so difficult to detect. However, from an economic viewpoint there is no real competition, and a high price is the prima facie evidence of collusion. The practical question for the regulator is whether a high price is the natural outcome of competition in a market where there is significant product differentiation (and so little pricing constraint from substitute products) or whether it reflects price collusion.

Nevo (2001) studied this question for the breakfast cereal industry where the four leaders Kellogg, Quaker, General Mills, and Post were accused by Congressman Schumer (March 1995) of charging "caviar prices for corn flakes quality." After estimating price elasticities of demand for each brand of cereal, Nevo used these price elasticities to calculate the Lerner index for each brand, $\frac{p-c}{p}$, that would prevail in the industry if producers were colluding and acting as a monopolist. Nevo then calculated the Lerner index for each brand if producers were really competing with each other.

Given the estimated demand elasticities, Nevo found that with collusion, the Lerner index of each brand would be on average around 65 to 75 percent. With the firms competing, the Lerner index would be on average around 40 to 44 percent. The next step was to compare these estimates of the Lerner index for the hypothetical collusive and competing industry with the actual Lerner index for the breakfast cereal industry to see which hypothesis is the most likely. According to Nevo, the actual Lerner index for the breakfast cereal market was about 45 percent in 1995. This market power index is far below the 65 to 75 percent hypothetical Lerner index that would prevail in a colluding industry and much closer to the Lerner index in the competing hypothesis. Nevo concludes that market power is significant in this industry, not because of collusion but because of product differentiation that limits competition from substitute products (after all, what is the substitute for a "healthy" cereal breakfast?).

8.8.2   Merger Policy

In its recent reform of Merger Regulation, the European Commission has recognized that in oligopolistic markets a merger may harm competition and consequently increase prices. Under the original European Commission Merger Regulation (ECMR) a merger was incompatible with the common market if and only if it "creates or strengthens a dominant position as a result of which competition would be significantly impeded." The problem with this two-part cumulative test was that unless a merger was likely to create or strengthen a dominant position, the question of whether it could lessen competition did not arise and so could not be used to challenge a merger. However, one can easily think of oligopoly situations where a merger would substantially lessen competition without giving any individual firm a dominant position. Moreover the concept of dominance is not easily established especially in the presence of tacit collusion. In practice, the concept of dominance had different meanings depending on the circumstances. In particular, when there was some presumption of collusion, the European Commission could use the concept of "collective" dominance taking as a single unit a group of sellers suspected to collude in their pricing policy. Just as Alice said in *Through the Looking Glass*, the question comes to "whether you *can* make words mean so many different things."

In the 2004 reform of merger policy the European Commission shifted the attention to the second part of the original regulation. The key article in the new ECMR says that "a concentration which would significantly impede effective competition, in the common market or in a substantial part of it, in particular as a result of the creation or strengthening of a dominant position, shall be declared incompatible with the common market" (Article 2). Thus the European Commission has recognized that reducing competition is not necessarily dominance but rather a result of how much competition is left. The fundamental idea is that in oligopolistic markets a merger of two or more rivals raises competitive concerns if the merging firms sell products that are close substitutes. By removing the competitive constraint, merging firms are able to increase their prices. This is the "unilateral effect" theory of competitive harm that has been commonly used in the US merger regulation.

Economists have developed a large number of simulation methods, mostly based on estimated demand elasticities, to determine the possible change in price resulting from a merger. Simulation models combine market data on market shares, the own-price elasticity of demand, and the cross-price elasticities of de-

Table 8.4
Estimating the effects of mergers in the bath tissue market

Bath tissue brand	Market share	Own-price elasticity	Price change (cost change)
Kleenex	7.5%	−3.38	+1.0% (−2.4%)
Cottonelle	6.7	−4.52	−0.3 (−2.4)
ScotTissue	16.7	−2.94	−2.6 (−4.0)
Charmin	30.9	−2.75	
Northern	12.4	−4.21	
Angel Soft	8.8	−4.08	
Private Label	7.6	−2.02	
Other	9.4	−1.98	
Market demand		−1.17	

Source: Data from tables 1 and 2 in Hausman and Leonard (1997).

mand with a model of firm behavior and anticipated reductions in cost from the merger to predict the likely price effects. A practical example will be useful to illustrate the method. The example is drawn from Hausman and Leonard (1997) and concerns the market for bath tissue. In 1995 the producer of the Kleenex brand acquired the producer of two competing brands (Cottonelle and Scot-Tissue). The market shares for these products and other brands are shown in table 8.4.

Using weekly retail scanner data that tracks household purchases in retail stores in major US cities, it was possible to estimate own-price elasticities as shown in table 8.4. The key cross-price elasticities were estimated to be 0.19 (Kleenex relative to Cotonelle), 0.18 (Kleenex relative to ScotTissue), 0.14 (Cottonelle relative to Kleenex), and 0.06 (ScotTissue relative to Kleenex). In addition it was anticipated that the acquisition would reduce the marginal cost of production for ScotTissue, Cottonelle, and Kleenex by 4 percent, 2.4 percent and 2.4 percent respectively. With these estimates of demand elasticities, information about market shares, and the anticipated cost saving from the acquisition of Cottonelle and ScotTissue by the Kleenex brand, it was possible to evaluate the price effects of the merger. A simulation model based on these market estimates and other assumptions about firm and market behavior (Nash equilibrium and constant marginal costs) produced the following prices changes. The acquisition would lead to a reduction in the price of ScotTissue and Cottonelle by 2.6 percent and 0.3 percent respectively, and an increase in the price of Kleenex by 1.0 percent. Not surprisingly the Antitrust did not challenge the merger.

8.9   Unions and Taxation

As well as monopoly on product markets, it is possible to have unions creating market power for their members on input markets. By organizing labor into a single collective organization, unions are able to raise the wage above the competitive level and generate a surplus for their members. The issue of tax incidence is also of interest when there are unions, since they can employ their market power to reduce the effect of a tax on the welfare of members.

The role of trade unions is to ensure that they secure the best deal possible for their members. In achieving this, the union faces a trade-off between the wage rate and the level of employment, since a higher wage will invariably lead to lower employment. This trade-off has to be resolved by the union's preferences.

A standard way of representing the preferences of a union is to assume that it has a fixed number, m, of members. Each employed member receives a wage $w[1 - t]$, where t is the tax on wage income. The unemployed members receive a payment of b, which can represent either unemployment benefit or the payment in a nonunionized occupation. The level of employment is determined by a labor demand function $n(w)$, with higher values of w leading to lower levels of employment. If the wage rate is w, the probability of any particular member being employed and receiving $w[1 - t]$ is $\frac{n(w)}{m}$. Consequently, if all members are assumed to have the same preferences, the expected utility of a typical union member is

$$U = \frac{n(w)}{m} u(w[1 - t]) + \frac{m - n(w)}{m} u(b). \tag{8.22}$$

Since all union members have identical preferences, this utility function can also be taken to represent the preferences of the union.

The union chooses the wage rate to maximize utility, so that the chosen wage satisfies the first-order condition

$$n'(w)[u(w[1 - t]) - u(b)] + n(w)[1 - t]u'(w[1 - t]) = 0. \tag{8.23}$$

The interpretation of this condition is that the optimal wage rate balances the marginal utility of a higher wage against the value of the marginal loss of employment. Now define the elasticity of labor demand by $\varepsilon_n = \frac{\Delta n}{\Delta w} \frac{w}{n} < 0$ and the elasticity of utility by $\varepsilon_u = \frac{\Delta u}{\Delta w[1-t]} \frac{w[1-t]}{u} > 0$. The first-order condition (8.23) can then be written as

$$u(w[1 - t]) = \mu^u u(b), \tag{8.24}$$

where $\mu^u = \frac{1}{1-[\varepsilon_u/|\varepsilon_n|]} > 1$ is the union markup relating the utility of an employed member to that of an unemployed member. This markup is a measure of the unions market power. Given a value for the utility elasticity, ε_u, the markup increases the lower is the elasticity of labor demand ε_n. As labor demand becomes perfectly elastic, as it does if the labor market is perfectly competitive, then μ^u tends to 1, and the union can achieve no advantage for its members.

The incidence of taxation can now be determined. To simplify, assume that the two elasticities—and hence the markup—are constant. Then the utility of the after-tax wage must always bear the same relation to the utility of unemployment benefit. Consequently $w[1 - t]$ must be constant whatever the tax rate. This can only be achieved if the union negates any tax increase by securing an increase in the wage rate that exactly offsets the tax change. Consequently those who retain employment are left unaffected by the tax change, but since the wage has risen, employment must fall. Overall, the union members must be worse off. This argument can easily be extended to see that if the elasticities are not constant, there is the potential for overshifting of the tax, or undershifting, of any tax increase. In this respect tax incidence with trade unions has very similar features to incidence with monopoly.

8.10   Monopsony

A monopsony market is a market consisting of a single buyer who can purchase from many sellers. The single buyer (or monopsonist) could be a firm that constitutes the only potential buyer of an input. It could also be an individual or public organization that is the only buyer of a product. For example, in many countries the government is the monopsonist in the teaching and nursing markets. In local markets with only one large employer, the local employer might literally be the only employment option in the local community (a coal mine, supermarket, government agency, etc.), so it might make sense that the local employer acts as a monopsonist in reducing the wage below the competitive level. In larger markets with more than one employer, employers association often have opportunities to coordinate their wage offers. This wage coordination allows employers to act as a "demand" cartel in the labor market and thus replicate the monopsony outcome. Just as monopoly results in supply reduction with a price or wage *above* competitive levels, monopsony will result in demand reduction with price or wage *below* competitive levels.

In a perfectly competitive market in which many firms purchase labor services, each firm takes the price of labor as given. Each firm maximizes its profits by choosing the employment level that equates the marginal revenue product of labor with the wage rate. In contrast, in a monopsony labor market, the monopsony firm pays a wage below the competitive wage. The result is a shortage of employment relative to the competitive level. The idea is that since the marginal revenue product from additional employment exceeds the wage cost in a monopsony labor market, the monopsonist employer might want to hire more people at the prevailing wage. However, it would not want to increase the wage to attract more workers because the gain from hiring additional workers (the marginal revenue product) is outweighed by the higher wage bill it would face for its existing workforce.

Figure 8.10 shows the equilibrium in a monopsony labor market. The competitive equilibrium occurs at a market clearing wage w^c, where the labor supply curve intersects the demand curve. Suppose now there is a single buyer on this labor market. The marginal revenue of labor is the additional revenue that the firm gets when it employs an additional unit of labor. Suppose that the firm's output as a function of its labor use is $Q(L)$ and that the firm is a price taker on the output market, so its output price p is independent of the amount of output Q. Then

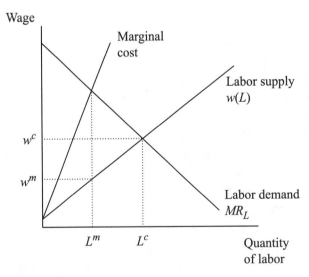

Figure 8.10
Monopsony in the labor market

the marginal revenue of labor is $MR_L = p\frac{dQ}{dL}$ which is decreasing due to decreasing returns to labor. This marginal revenue is depicted in figure 8.10 as the downward-sloping labor demand curve. The supply of labor is described by the "inverse" supply curve. The inverse supply curve $w(L)$ describes the wage required to induce any given quantity of labor to be supplied. Since the supply curve is upward sloping, $\frac{dw}{dL} > 0$. The total labor cost of the monopsonist is $Lw(L)$, and the marginal cost of labor is the extra cost that comes from hiring one more worker $MC_L = w + L\frac{dw}{dL}$. This additional cost can be decomposed into two parts: the cost from employing more workers at the existing wage (w) and the cost from raising the wage for all workers $\left(L\frac{dw}{dL}\right)$. Since $\frac{dw}{dL} > 0$, the marginal labor cost curve lies everywhere above the labor supply curve, as indicated in figure 8.10. The monopsonist will maximize profit $\pi = pQ(L) - w(L)L$ at the point where the marginal revenue of labor is equal to marginal cost $p\frac{dQ}{dL} = w + L\frac{dw}{dL}$.

The choice that gives maximum profit occurs in figure 8.10 at the intersection between the marginal cost curve and the labor demand curve, yielding employment level L^m and wage rate w^m. Therefore in a monopsony labor market, the monopsony firm pays a wage that is less than the competitive wage with employment level below the competitive level. The monopsony equilibrium condition can also be expressed as an inverse elasticity pricing rule. Indeed, the elasticity of labor supply is $\varepsilon_L = \frac{dL}{dw}\frac{w}{L}$ and the profit maximization condition $MR_L = MC_L$ can be re-arranged to give

$$\frac{MR_L - w}{w} = \frac{1}{\varepsilon_L}. \tag{8.25}$$

This inverse pricing rule says that the percentage deviation from the competitive wage is inversely proportional to the elasticity of labor supply. In contrast to monopoly, the key elasticity is the *supply* elasticity. Just as monopoly results in a deadweight loss, so does monopsony leading to underemployment and underpricing of the input (in this case labor) relative to the competitive outcome.

8.11   Conclusions

This chapter has shown how imperfect competition leads to a failure to attain Pareto-efficiency. As with all such failures, this opens a potential role for government intervention to promote efficiency. Estimates of the welfare loss due to imperfect competition vary widely from the almost insignificant to considerable proportions of welfare, depending on the perspective taken upon expenditures on securing the monopoly position. These static losses have to be set against the possible dynamic gains.

Economic tax incidence relates to whom ultimately has to change their behavior as a consequence of taxation. With competition the outcome is fairly straightforward: the cost of a commodity tax is divided between producers and consumers, with the division depending on the elasticities of supply and demand. Imperfect competition introduces two additional factors. Taxes may be overshifted so that price rises by more than the value of the tax. In addition an increase in taxation may even raise the profits of firms. In contrast to the competitive case, specific and ad valorem taxation are not equivalent with imperfect competition. In a choice between the instruments, ad valorem taxation is more effective, since it has the effect of reducing perceived monopoly power.

To reduce the welfare loss, policy should attempt to encourage competition. In some circumstances this can work, but when there is natural monopoly, this policy has to be carefully considered. A natural monopoly could be taken into public ownership or run as a private firm with regulation. Recent policy has concentrated on the latter.

Further Reading

The measurement of welfare loss began with:

Harberger, A. C. 1954. Monopoly and resource allocation. *American Economic Review* 45: 77–87.

The other values in table 8.1 are taken from:

Cowling, K. G., and Mueller, D. C. 1978. The social costs of monopoly power. *Economic Journal* 88: 727–48.

Gisser, M. 1986. Price leadership and welfare losses in U.S. manufacturing. *American Economic Review* 76: 756–67.

Masson, R. T., and Shaanan, J. 1984. Social costs of oligopoly and the value of competition. *Economic Journal* 94: 520–35.

McCorriston, S. 1993. The welfare implications of oligopoly in agricultural input markets. *European Review of Agricultural Economics* 20: 1–17.

Peterson, E. B., and Connor, J. M. 1995. A comparison of oligopoly welfare loss estimates for U.S. food manufacturing. *American Journal of Agricultural Economics* 77: 300–308.

The basics of oligopoly theory are covered in:

Waterson, M. 1983. *Oligopoly Theory*. Cambridge: Cambridge University Press.

The analysis of tax incidence with oligopoly can be traced back to:

Seade, J. 1985. Profitable cost increases. *Warwick Economic Research Paper*, no. 260.

The results in table 8.3 are compiled from:

Baker, P., and Brechling, V. 1992. The impact of excise duty changes on retail prices in the UK. *Fiscal Studies* 13: 48–65.

Delipalla, S., and O'Connell, O. 2001. Estimating tax incidence, market power and market conduct: The European cigarette industry. *International Journal of Industrial Organization* 19: 885–908.

Tasarika, E. 2001. *Aspects of International Taxation.* PhD dissertation. University of Exeter.

Results on comparison of specific and ad valorem tax are in:

Delipalla, S., and Keen, M. 1992. The comparison between ad valorem and specific taxation under imperfect competition. *Journal of Public Economics* 49: 351–67.

Myles, G. D. 1996. Imperfect competition and the optimal combination of ad valorem and specific taxation. *International Tax and Public Finance* 3: 29–44.

The example on detecting collusion is drawn from:

Nevo, A. 2001. Measuring market power in the ready-to-eat breakfast cereal industry. *Econometrica* 69: 307–42.

The merger simulation model for bath tissue is drawn from:

Hausman, J. A., and Leonard, G. K. 1997. Economic analysis of differentiated product mergers using real world data. *George Mason Law Review* 5: 321–46.

A further discussion of merger simulation analysis can be found in:

Epstein, R. J., and Rubinstein, D. L. 2002. Merger simulation: A simplified approach with new applications. *Antitrust Law Journal* 69: 883–919.

A presentation of the various concepts of competition is in:

Vickers, J. 1995. Concepts of competition. *Oxford Economic Papers* 47: 1–23.

A good perspective on the inefficiency resulting from market power with special attention on information problems is:

Vickers, J. 1996. Market power and inefficiency: A contract perspective. *Oxford Review of Economic Policy* 12: 11–26.

The basic and first paper on product differentiation is:

Hotelling, H. 1929. Stability in competition. *Economic Journal* 39: 41–47.

The other classic paper is:

d'Aspremont, C., Gabszewicz, J., and Thisse, J.-F. 1979. On Hotelling's stability in competition. *Econometrica* 17: 1145–51.

An economic analysis of regulation policies with special attention to the United Kingdom is:

Armstrong, M., Cowans, S., and Vickers, J. 1994. *Regulatory Reform: Economic Analysis and British Experience.* Cambridge: MIT Press.

Recent European merger regulation guidelines (28 January 2004) are available at: http://europa.eu.int/comm/competition/mergers/review.

A good account of antitrust law and economics is in:

Scherer, F. M. 1980. *Industrial Market Structure and Economic Performance*. Chicago: Rand McNally.

Exercises

8.1.   What should be the objective of a monopoly labor union?

8.2.   An industry is known to face market price elasticity of demand $\varepsilon = -3$. Suppose that this elasticity is approximately constant as the industry moves along its demand curve. The marginal cost in this industry is \$10 per unit, and there are five firms in the industry. What would the Lerner index be at the Cournot equilibrium in this industry?

8.3.   Consider a monopolist operating the underground in Europa city with a total cost curve given by $c(x) = 15 + 5x$. The monopolist sets two prices: a high price p_h and a low price p_l. Everyone is eligible for the high price, but only by taking the tube outside the peak hours is anyone eligible for the discount price. Suppose that the only off-peak travelers are those who are not willing to buy the ticket at p_h.

a. If the monopolist faces the inverse demand curve given by $p(x) = 20 - 5x$, what are the profit-maximizing values of p_h and p_l? [*Hint*: Let x_h and x_l denote the high-price and low-price quantities respectively. Then profit for the price discriminating monopolist is $p = p(x_h)x_h + p(x_h + x_l)x_l - c(x_h + x_l).$]

b. How much economic profit does the monopolist take?

c. How much profit would be made if the same price were charged to all buyers (no price discrimination)? Discuss the difference from part b.

8.4.   Demonstrate that monopoly is Pareto-inefficient. Must it always lead to a lower level of social welfare than competition?

8.5.   Consider an economy with one good and a linear inverse demand $p(x) = a - bx$. Suppose that there is a single firm operating in this market and that this firm faces a linear cost function $C(x) = cx$ (with $c < a$).

a. Show that the profit maximizing output with monopoly is $x^m = \frac{a-c}{2b}$ and the resulting price is $p^m = \frac{a+c}{2}$.

b. Show that the efficient competitive output level is $x^c = \frac{a-c}{b} = 2x^m$.

c. Calculate the monopoly profit and the monopoly deadweight loss, and show that these are respectively $\pi^m = \frac{1}{b}\left[\frac{a-c}{2}\right]^2$ and $\lambda^m = \frac{\pi^m}{2}$.

d. Consider a quantity subsidy s to the monopolist so that its cost function is $C(x) = [c - s]x$. Show that a subsidy rate of $s = a - c$ induces the monopolist to produce the efficient amount of output.

e. What is the monopolist's profit resulting from a government intervention imposing marginal cost pricing?

8.6.   Assume that a monopolist can identify two distinct markets. Find the profit-maximizing prices if the demand functions for the two markets are

$$x_1 = 100 - 2p_1, \quad x_2 = 120 - 3p_2.$$

What is the level of consumer surplus in each market? If the monopolist is forced by legislation to charge a single price, what will this price be? Contrast the level of consumer surplus with and without price discrimination.

8.7.   Consider two monopolists operating in separate markets with identical and constant marginal cost. Are the following statements true or false?

a. If both face different linear demand curves that are parallel, the monopolist that will have the higher markup is the one whose demand curve is farther from the origin.

b. If both face linear demand curves with identical vertical intercepts but different slopes, the monopolist with the higher markup is the one with the steeper demand curve.

c. If both face linear demand curves with identical horizontal intercepts but different slopes, the monopolist with the higher markup is the one with the steeper demand curve.

8.8.   Discuss how brand promotion can increase inefficiency. Is brand proliferation good or bad?

8.9.   Demand is assumed to be unit-elastic: $X(p) = \frac{1}{p}$. There are $m \geq 2$ firms operating in the market with constant marginal cost levels $c_1 \leq c_2 \leq \cdots \leq c_m$. They engage in Cournot competition.

a. Show that the equilibrium price implies Lerner indexes $\frac{p - c_i}{p} = s_i$, where s_i is the market share of firm i.

b. Using the equilibrium price, show that the profit of firm i is equal to $(s_i)^2$.

c. Show that the industry profit is equal to the Herfindahl index $H = \sum_i (s_i)^2$.

d. What is the effect of a specific tax t on equilibrium price? How does this tax affect the industry profit and the Herfindahl index?

8.10.   Consider a standard Cournot oligopoly with $n = 2k$ identical firms (with $k \geq 1$), an inverse demand $P(X)$, and a cost function $C(x)$ with no fixed costs. Consider only two possible cases: $C(x)$ convex and $C(x)$ concave. Assume that there is always a unique symmetric equilibrium with per firm output x_k and profit π_k. Assume that there are k two-firm mergers.

a. List all conditions on the primitives of the model such that each firm is better off after these mergers. Explain your answer (no proof needed).

b. Can such a set of mergers be expected to take place without regulatory intervention? Explain.

c. Under what conditions can such a set of mergers increase social welfare?

8.11.   Consider a standard Cournot oligopoly with $n \geq 2$ identical firms, $P(x) = a - bX$, $X \geq 0$, and $C(x) = cx^2$.

a. Find the Cournot equilibrium output and profit.

b. If m firms wish to merge, what would be their cost function, assuming that they can use all their m production plants but that they otherwise do not have any efficiency gains as a result of the merger?

c. Given the cost function from part b, when is an m-firm merger profitable to the merged entity? To the nonmerging firms?

d. Give a precise economic intuition explaining your answer relative to the usual (linear cost) case.

8.12.   Consider two firms, $i = 1, 2$, producing differentiated products and engaged in Cournot competition. The inverse demand for firm i is given by $p_i = a - bq_i - dq_j$, where q_i is the amount of its own output and q_j is firm j's level of output (with $a > c$, $b > \frac{1}{2}$ and $-1 < d < 1$). Similarly the inverse demand for firm j is given by $p_j = a - bq_j - dq_i$. The goods are substitutes for $d > 0$ and complements for $d < 0$. The marginal cost of each firm is zero.

a. Given the market demands, what are the best-response functions of the two firms?

b. Draw the best-response functions both for complements $(d < 0)$ and substitutes $(d > 0)$.

c. Compute the Cournot equilibrium quantities and prices in this market.

d. Compare the outcome between substitutes and complements goods.

e. What are the profit-maximizing quantities and prices if firm i is a monopolist in this market? Compare with part c.

8.13.   Consider a standard Cournot oligopoly with $n \geq 2$ identical firms, an inverse demand function $P(X) = a - bX$, and cost function $C(x) = K + cx$ if $x > 0$, and 0 if $x = 0$, meaning K is a fixed cost.

a. Find the Cournot equilibrium output and profit. How many firms (as a function of K) can survive at the equilibrium?

b. When is an m-firm merger profitable to the merged entity? To the nonmerging firms?

c. Give a precise economic intuition as to why most mergers are not profitable in the usual model with $K = 0$. How is it different when $K > 0$?

8.14.   Consider a homogeneous-good Cournot oligopoly with $n \geq 2$ identical firms with cost $C(x) = 0$ and inverse demand $P(X) = e^{-X}$.

a. Find a firm's best-response function, the Cournot equilibrium output, price, and profit. What type of equilibrium is this?

b. Find all the merger sizes m $(2 \leq m \leq n)$ that are profitable to the merged entity. Are these mergers also profitable to the nonmerging firms?

c. Give an economic intuition, and compare it to the case of linear demand.

8.15.   Consider Cournot competition with n identical firms. Suppose that the inverse demand function is linear with $P(X) = a - bX$, where X is total industry output, $a, b > 0$. Each firm has a linear cost function of the form $C(x) = cx$, where x stands for per firm output. It is assumed that $a > c$.

a. At the symmetric equilibrium, what are the industry output and price levels? What are the equilibrium per firm output and profit levels? What is the equilibrium social welfare (defined as the difference between the area under the demand function and total cost)?

b. Now let m out of n firms merge. Show that the merger is profitable for the m merged firms if and only if it involves a pre-merger market share of 80 percent.

c. Show that each of the $(n - m)$ nonmerged firms is better off after the merger.

d. Show that the m-firm merger increases industry price and also lowers consumer welfare.

8.16.   What is the difference between vertical and horizontal product differentiation? Provide an example of each.

8.17.   A monopolist faces the inverse demand function $P(x) = a - bx$ and produces with constant marginal cost c.

a. Determine the effect on equilibrium price of the introduction of a specific tax of value t. Is the tax overshifted?

b. Calculate the effect on profit of the tax. Show that $\frac{d\pi}{dt} = -x$, where x is the equilibrium output level. Explain this result.

c. Now replace the specific tax with an ad valorem tax at rate τ. Find a pair of taxes that lead to the same level of tax revenue. Which gives a lower price?

8.18.   (Mixed oligopoly) Consider a market with one public firm, denoted 0, and one private firm, denoted 1. Both firms produce a homogeneous good with identical and constant marginal c per unit of output, and face the same linear demand function $P(X) = a - bX$ with $X = x_0 + x_1$. It is assumed that $a > c$. The private firm maximizes profit $\pi_1 = P(X)x_1 - cx_1$, and the public firm maximizes a combination of welfare and profit $V_0 = \theta W + [1 - \theta]\pi_0$ with welfare given by consumer surplus less cost, $W = \int_0^X P(y)\,dy - c[x_0 + x_1]$. Both firms choose output as the strategic variable.

a. Calculate the best-response functions of the public and the private firms. Use a graph of the best-response functions to illustrate what would happen if θ changed from 0 to 1.

b. Calculate the equilibrium quantities for the private and public firms. Derive the aggregate output in equilibrium as a function of θ.

c. Calculate the socially optimal output level (by using the marginal cost pricing rule), and compare with the equilibrium outcome.

d. Show that an increase in θ must increase the equilibrium industry output, and so equilibrium price must fall and welfare increase. Verify that the equilibrium outcome converges to the socially optimal outcome when $\theta = 1$.

e. Consider $\theta < 1$ and calculate the quantity subsidy s (with marginal cost after subsidy $c - s$) such that the firms will produce the socially optimal output level. What impact does a change in θ have on the optimal subsidy? Why?

8.19.   Define natural monopoly. Draw the demand, marginal revenue, marginal cost, and average cost curves for a natural monopoly.

a. What does the size of a market have to do with whether an industry is a natural monopoly?

b. What are the two problems that arise when the government regulates a natural monopoly by limiting price to be equal to marginal cost?

c. Suppose that a natural monopoly is required to charge average total cost. On your diagram, label the price charged and the deadweight loss to society relative to marginal-cost pricing.

8.20.   What gives the government the power to regulate mergers between firms? From the view point of the welfare to society, give a good reason and a bad reason why two firms might want to merge.

8.21.   Assume that a monopolist's marginal cost is positive at all output levels. Are the following true or false?

a. When the monopolist operates on the inelastic part of the demand curve, it can increase profit by producing less.

b. When the monopolist operates on the inelastic part of the demand curve, it can increase profit by producing more.

c. The monopolist's marginal revenue can be negative for some levels of output.

8.22.   (Varian) A daily dose of the AIDS drug PLC sells for $18 in the United States and $9 in Uganda (*New York Times*, September 21, 2000). Even at $9 a dose the drug company makes a profit on additional sales. But if the drug were sold at $9 to everyone, profits would decline. Price discrimination is not popular with consumers, especially those paying the higher price. To evaluate whether differential pricing is good or bad, the critical question from the viewpoint of economics is whether uniform price or differential pricing leads to more people getting the drug. In general, there is no easy answer. Imagine that there are only two countries involved, the United States and Uganda:

a. Imagine the US market for the PLC drug is more than five times the Ugandan market, and the drug sells respectively for $18 and $9. What price is likely to prevail if only one price can be charged? What would be the effect on total consumption and, especially, for drug consumers in Uganda? What would be the effect on US drug consumers?

b. Imagine an anti-malarial drug that many people in Uganda would buy at $2 a dose and few people in the United States would buy at $10. If the Ugandan market is more than ten times the US market, what price is likely to prevail if drug company can set only one price? What would be the effect on total consumption and for drug consumers in United States and Uganda?

c. Based on this example, discuss when price discrimination is likely to be socially useful and when it does not have much to recommend it.

8.23.   A company is considering building a bridge across a river. The bridge would cost $3 million to build and nothing to maintain. The anticipated demand over the lifetime of the bridge is $x = 800 - 100p$, where x is the number of crossings (in thousands) given the price per crossing p.

    a. If the company builds the bridge, what will be the profit-maximizing price?

    b. Will that price lead to the efficient number of crossings? Why or why not?

    c. What will be the company's profit or loss? Should it build the bridge?

    d. If the government were to build the bridge, what price should it charge?

    e. Should the government build the bridge? Why or why not?

8.24.   The jazz singer Nora Jones has monopoly power over a scarce resource: herself on stage. She is the only person who can perform a Nora Jones concert. Does this fact imply that the government should regulate ticket prices for her concerts? Explain.

9 Asymmetric Information

9.1 Introduction

A key feature of the real world is asymmetric information. Most people want to find the right partner, one who is caring, kind, healthy, intelligent, attractive, trustworthy, and so on. While attractiveness may be easily verified at a glance, many other traits people seek in a partner are difficult to observe, and people usually rely on behavioral signals that convey partial information. There may be good reasons to avoid a potential mate who is too eager to start a relationship with you, as this may suggest unfavorable traits. Similarly it is hard not to infer that people who participate in dating services must be on average less worth meeting, and the consensus appears to be that these services are a bad investment. The reason is that the decision to resort to a dating agency identifies people who have trouble initiating their own relationships, which is indicative of other unwelcome traits. The lack of information causes caution in dating, which can result in good matches being missed.

Asymmetric information arises in economics when the two sides of the market have different information about the goods and services being traded. In particular, sellers typically know more about what they are selling than buyers do. This can lead to adverse selection where bad-quality goods drive out good-quality goods, at least if other actions are not taken. Adverse selection is the process by which buyers or sellers with "unfavorable" traits are more likely to participate in the exchange. Adverse selection is important in economics because it often eliminates exchange possibilities that would be beneficial to both consumers and sellers alike. There might seem some easy way to resolve the problem of information asymmetry: let everyone reveal what they know. Unfortunately, individuals do not necessarily have the incentive to tell the truth (think about the mating example or the market identification of high- and low-ability people).

Information imperfections are pervasive in the economy and, in some sense, it is an essential feature of a market economy that different people know different things. While such information asymmetries inevitably arise, the extent to which they do so and their consequences depends on how the market is organized. The anticipation that they will arise also affects market behavior. In this chapter we discuss the ways in which information asymmetries affect market functioning and how they can be partially overcome through policy intervention. We do not consider how the agents can *create* information problems, for example, in an attempt to exploit market power by differentiating products or by taking actions to increase information asymmetries as in the general governance problem.

One fundamental lesson of information imperfection is that *actions convey information*. This is a commonplace observation in life, but it took some time for economists to fully appreciate its profound effects on how markets function. Many examples can be given. A willingness to purchase insurance at a given price conveys information to an insurance company, because those most likely to decide the insurance is not worthwhile are those who are least likely to have an accident. The quality of a guarantee offered by a firm conveys information about the quality of its products as only firms with reliable products are willing to offer a good guarantee. The number of years of schooling may also convey information about the ability of an individual. More able people may go to school longer and the higher wage associated with more schooling may simply reflect the sorting that occurs rather than the ability-augmenting effect of schooling itself. The willingness of an investor to self-finance a large fraction of the cost of a project conveys information about his belief in the project. The size of deductibles and co-payments that an individual chooses in an insurance contract may convey information that he is less risk prone. The process by which individuals reveal information about themselves through the choices that they make is called *self-selection*.

Upon recognizing that actions convey information, two important results follow. First, when making decisions, agents will not only think about what they prefer, but they will also think about how their choice will affect others' beliefs about them. So I may choose longer schooling not because I value what is being taught, but because it changes others' beliefs concerning my ability. Second, it may be possible to design a set of choices that would induce those with different characteristics to effectively reveal their characteristics through their choices. As long as some actions are more costly for some types than others, it is an easy matter to construct choices that separate individuals into classes: self-selection mechanisms could, and would, be employed to screen. For example, insurance companies may offer a menu of transaction terms that will separate out different classes of risk into preferring different parts of the menu.

In equilibrium both sides of the market are aware of the informational consequences of their actions. In the case where the insurance company or employer takes the initiatives, self-selection is the main *screening* device. In the case where the insured, or the employee, takes the initiative to identify himself as a better type, then it is usually considered as a *signaling* device. So the difference between screening and signaling lies in whether the informed or uninformed side of the market moves first.

Whatever the actions taken, the theory predicts that the types of transactions that will arise in practice are different from those that would emerge in a perfect-information context. The fact that actions convey information affects equilibrium outcomes in a profound way. Since quality increases with price in adverse selection models, it may be profitable to pay a price in excess of the market-clearing price. In credit markets, the supply of loans may be rationed. In the labor market, the wage rate may be higher than the market-clearing wage, leading to unemployment. There may exist multiple equilibria. Two forms of equilibria are possible: *pooling* equilibria in which the market cannot distinguish among the types, and *separating* equilibria in which the different types separate out by taking different actions. On the other hand, under plausible conditions, equilibrium might not exist (in particular, if the cost of separation is too great).

Another set of issues arise when actions are not easily observable. An employer would like to know how hard his employee is working; a lender would like to know the actions the borrower will undertake that might affect the chance of reimbursement. These asymmetries of information about *actions* are as important as the situations of hidden knowledge. They lead to what is referred to as the *moral hazard problem*. This term originates from the insurance industry, which recognized early that more insurance reduces the precautions taken by the insured (and not taking appropriate precautions was viewed to be immoral, hence the name). One way to solve this problem is to try to induce desired behavior through the setting of contract terms. A borrower's risk-taking behavior may be controlled by the interest rate charged by the lender. The insured will exert more care when facing contracts with large deductibles. But, in competing for risk-averse customers, the insurance companies face an interesting trade-off. The insurance has to be complete enough so that the individual will purchase. At the same time deductibles have to be significant enough to provide adequate incentives for insured parties to take care.

This chapter will explore the consequences of asymmetric information in a number of different market situations. It will describe the inefficiencies that arise and discuss possible government intervention to correct these. Interpreted in this way, asymmetric information is one of the classic reasons for market failure and will prevent trading partners from realizing all the gains of trade. In addition to asymmetric information between trading parties, it can also arise between the government and the consumers and firms in the economy. When it does, it restricts the policies that the government can implement. Some aspects of how this affects the effectiveness of the government will be covered in this chapter; others will become apparent in later chapters. The main implication that will emerge for public intervention is that even if the government also faces informational imperfections, the incentives and constraints it faces often differ from those facing the private sector. Even when government faces exactly the same informational problems, welfare can be improved by market intervention. There are interventions in the market that can make all parties better off.

9.2   Hidden Knowledge and Hidden Action

There are two basic forms of asymmetric information that can be distinguished. *Hidden knowledge* refers to a situation where one party has more information than the other party on the quality (or "type") of a traded good or contract variable. *Hidden action* is when one party can affect the "quality" of a traded good or contract variable by some action, and this action cannot be observed by the other party.

Examples of hidden knowledge abound. Workers know more about their own abilities than the firm does; doctors know more about their own skills, the efficacy of drugs, and what treatment patients need than do either the patients themselves or the insurance companies; the person buying life insurance knows more about his health and life expectancy than the insurance firm; when an automobile insurance company insures an individual, the individual may know more than the company about her inherent driving skill and hence about her probability of having an accident; the owner of a car knows more about the quality of the car than potential buyers; the owner of a firm knows more about the firm than a potential investor; the borrower knows more about the riskiness of his project than the lender does; and not least, in the policy world, policy-makers know more about their competence than the electorate.

Hidden knowledge leads to the *adverse selection* problem. To introduce this, suppose that a firm knows that there are high-productivity and low-productivity workers and that it offers a high wage with the intention of attracting high-productivity workers. Naturally this high wage will also prove attractive to low-productivity workers, so the firm will attract a combination of both types. If the wage is above the average productivity, the firm will make a loss and be forced to lower the wage. This will result in high-productivity workers leaving and average productivity falling. Consequently the wage must again be lowered. Eventually the firm will be left with only low-productivity workers. The adverse selection problem is that the high wage attracts the workers the firm wants (the high-productivity) and the ones it does not (the low-productivity). The observation that the firm will eventually be left with only low-productivity workers reflects the old maxim that "The bad drives out the good."

There are also plenty of examples of hidden action. The manager of a firm does not seek to maximize the return for shareholders but instead trades off her remuneration for less work effort. Firms may find it most profitable to make unsafe products when quality is not easily observed. Employers also want to know how hard their workers work. Insurers want to know what care their insured take to avoid an accident. Lenders want to know what risks their borrowers take. Patients want to know if doctors provide the correct treatment or if, in an attempt to protect themselves from malpractice suits, they choose conservative medicine, ordering tests and procedures that may not be in the patient's best interests, and surely not worth the costs. The tax authority wants to know if taxing more may induce people to work less or to conceal more income. Government wants to know if more generous pension replacement rates may induce people to retire earlier. A welfaristic government will worry about the recipients of welfare spending too much and investing too little, thus being more likely to be in need again in the future. This concern will also be present among altruistic parents who cannot commit not to help out their children when needy and governments who cannot commit not to bail out firms with financial difficulties.

From hidden actions arises the *moral hazard* problem. This refers to the inefficiency that arises due to the difficulties in designing incentive schemes that ensure the right actions are taken. For instance, the price charged for insurance must take into account the fact that an insured person may become more careless once they have the safety net of insurance cover.

9.3   Actions or Knowledge?

Although the definitions given above make moral hazard and adverse selection seem quite distinct, in practice, it may be quite difficult to determine which is at work. The following example, due to Milgrom and Roberts, serves to illustrate this point.

A radio story in the summer of 1990 reported a study on the makes and models of cars that were observed going through intersections in the Washington, DC, area without stopping at the stop signs. According to the story, Volvos were heavily overrepresented: the fraction of cars running stop signs that were Volvos was much greater than the fraction of Volvos in the total population of cars in the DC area. This is initially surprising because Volvo has built a reputation as an especially safe car that appeals to sensible, safety-conscious drivers. In addition Volvos are largely bought by middle-class couples with children. How then is this observation explained?

One possibility is that people driving Volvos feel particularly safe in this sturdy, heavily built, crash-tested car. Thus they are willing to take risks that they would not take in another, less safe car. This implies that driving a Volvo leads to a propensity to run stop signs. This is essentially a moral hazard explanation: the car is a form of insurance, and having the insurance alters behavior in a way that is privately rational but socially undesirable.

A second possibility is that the people who buy Volvos know that they are bad drivers who are apt, for example, to be paying more attention to their children in the back seat than to stop signs. The safety that a Volvo promises is then especially attractive to people who have this private information about their driving, and so they buy this safe car in disproportionately large numbers. Hence a propensity for running stop signs leads to the purchase of a Volvo. This is essentially a self-selection story: Volvo buyers are privately informed about their driving habits and abilities and choose the car accordingly.

This self-selection is not necessarily adverse selection. It only becomes adverse selection if it imposes costs on Volvo. Quite the opposite may in fact be true, and the self-selection of customers can be very profitable.

It is also typically difficult to disentangle the moral hazard problem from the adverse selection problem in antipoverty programs because it is difficult to decide whether poverty is due to a lack of productive skill (adverse selection) or rather to a lack of effort from the poor themselves who know they will get welfare assistance anyway (moral hazard).

9.4   Market Unraveling

9.4.1   Hazard Insurance

In the Introduction we noted that asymmetric information can lead to a breakdown in trade as the less-informed party began to realize that the least desirable potential partners are those who are more willing to exchange. This possibility is now explored more formally in a model of the insurance market in which individuals differ in their accident probabilities. The basic conclusion to emerge is that in equilibrium some consumers do not purchase insurance, even though they could profitably be sold insurance if accident probabilities were observable to insurance companies.

Assume that there is a large number of insurance companies and that the insurance market is competitive. The insurance premium is based on the level of expected risk among those who accept offers of insurance. Competition ensures that profits are zero in equilibrium through entry and exit. Furthermore, if there is any new insurance contract that can be offered that will make a positive profit given the contracts already available, then one of the companies will choose to offer it.

The demand for insurance comes from a large number of individuals. These can be broken down into many different types of individual who differ in their probability of incurring damage of value $d = 1$. The probability of damage for an individual is given by θ. Different individuals have different values of θ, but all values lie between 0 and 1. If $\theta = 1$, the individual is certain to have an accident. Asymmetric information is introduced by assuming that each individual knows their own value of θ but that it is not observable by the insurance companies. The insurance companies do know (correctly) that risks are uniformly distributed in the population over the interval $[0, 1]$.

All of the individuals are risk averse, meaning that they are willing to pay an insurance premium to avoid facing the cost of damage. For each type the maximal insurance premium that they are willing to pay, $\pi(\theta)$ is given by

$$\pi(\theta) = [1 + \alpha]\theta, \tag{9.1}$$

where $\alpha > 0$ measures the level of risk aversion.

The assumption of competition between the insurance companies implies that in equilibrium they must earn zero profits. Now assume that insurance companies just offer a single insurance policy to all customers. Given the premium (or price) of the policy, π, the policy will be purchased by all the individuals whose expected value of damage is greater than or equal to this. That is, an individual will purchase the policy if

$$\pi(\theta) \geq \pi. \tag{9.2}$$

If a policy is to break even with zero profit, the premium for this policy must just equal the average value of damage for those who choose to purchase the policy. Hence (9.2) can be used to write the break-even condition as

$$\pi = E(\theta : \pi(\theta) \geq \pi),\tag{9.3}$$

which is just the statement that the premium equals expected damage. Returning to (9.1), the condition that $\pi(\theta) \geq \pi$ is equivalent to $[1 + \alpha]\theta \geq \pi$ or $\theta \geq \frac{\pi}{1+\alpha}$. Using the fact that the θ is uniformly distributed gives

$$E(\theta : \pi(\theta) \geq \pi) = E\left(\theta : \frac{\pi}{1+\alpha} \leq \theta \leq 1\right) = \frac{1}{2}\left[\frac{\pi}{1+\alpha} + 1\right].\tag{9.4}$$

The equilibrium premium then satisfies

$$\pi = \frac{1}{2}\left[\frac{\pi}{1+\alpha} + 1\right],\tag{9.5}$$

or

$$\pi = \frac{1+\alpha}{1+2\alpha}.\tag{9.6}$$

This equilibrium is illustrated in figure 9.1. It occurs where the curve $E(\theta : \pi(\theta) \geq \pi)$ crosses the 45° line—this intersection is the value given in (9.6). It can be seen from the figure that insurance is only taken by those with high risks, namely all those with risk $\theta \geq \frac{1}{1+2\alpha}$. This reflects the process of market unraveling through which only a small fraction of the potential consumers are actually served

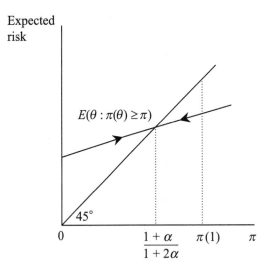

Figure 9.1
Equilibrium in the insurance market

in equilibrium. The level of the premium is too high for the low-risk to find it worthwhile to take out the insurance. This outcome is clearly inefficient, since the first-best outcome requires insurance for all consumers. To see this, note that the premium a consumer of type θ is willing to pay satisfies

$$\pi(\theta) = [1 + \alpha]\theta > \theta \qquad \text{for all } \theta. \tag{9.7}$$

Therefore everyone is willing to pay more than the price the insurance companies need to break even if they could observe probabilities of accident.

This finding of inefficiency is a consequence of the fact that the insurance companies cannot distinguish the low-risk consumers from the high-risk. When a single premium is offered to all consumers, the high-risk consumers force the premium up, and this drives the low-risk out of the market. This is a simple example of the mechanism of adverse selection in which the bad types always find it profitable to enter the market at the expense of the good. Without any intervention in the market, adverse selection will always lead to an inefficient equilibrium.

9.4.2   Government Intervention

There is a simple way the government can avoid the adverse selection process by which only the worst risks purchase insurance: it is by forcing all individuals to purchase the insurance. *Compulsory insurance* is then a policy that can make many consumers better off. With this, high-risk consumers benefit from a lower premium than the actual risk they face and lower than the level in (9.6)—it will actually be $\pi = \frac{1}{2} < \frac{1+\alpha}{1+2\alpha}$. The benefit for some of the low-risk is that they can now purchase a policy at a more favorable premium than that offered if only high-risk people purchased it. This benefits those close to the average who, although paying more for the policy than the level of their expected damage, prefer to have insurance at this price than no insurance at all. Only the very low-risk are made worse off—they would rather have no insurance than pay the average premium.

The imposition of compulsory insurance may seem to be a very strong policy, since in few circumstances are consumers forced by the government to make specific purchases. But it is the policy actually used for many insurance markets. For instance, both automobile insurance and employee protection insurance are compulsory. Health care insurance and unemployment insurance are also compulsory. Aircraft have to be insured. Pleasure boats have to be compulsorily insured in some countries (e.g., France) but not in others (e.g., the United Kingdom), despite their representing a much greater capital investment than automobiles. One argument that could be advanced to explain this difference is the operation of self-selection into boating as a leisure activity: those who choose to do it are by their nature either low-risk or sufficiently cautious to insure without compulsion.

There is another role for government intervention. So far the arguments have concentrated on one of the simplest cases. Particularly restrictive was the assumption that the probability of damage was uniformly distributed across the population. It was this assumption (together with the proportional reservation premium) that ensured that the curve $E(\theta : \pi(\theta) \geq \pi)$ is a straight line with a single intersection with the 45° line. When the uniform distribution assumption is relaxed, $E(\theta : \pi(\theta) \geq \pi)$ will have a different shape, and the nature of equilibrium may be changed. In fact there exist functions for the distribution of types that lead to multiple equilibria. Such a case is illustrated in figure 9.2. In this figure $E(\theta : \pi(\theta) \geq \pi)$ crosses the 45° line three times so that there are three equilibria that differ in the size of the premium. At the low-premium equilibrium, E_1, most of the population is able to purchase insurance but at the high-premium equilibrium, E_3, very few can.

Each of these equilibria is based on correct but different self-fulfilling beliefs. For example, if the insurance companies are pessimistic and expect that only high-risk consumers will take out insurance, they will set a high premium. Given a high premium, only the high-risk will choose to accept the policy. The beliefs of the insurance companies are therefore confirmed, and the economy becomes

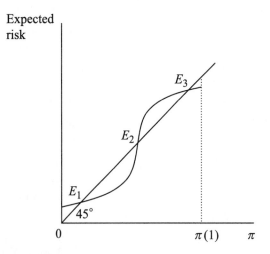

Figure 9.2
Multiple equilibria

trapped in a high-premium equilibrium with very few consumers covered by insurance. This is clearly a bad outcome for the economy, since there are also equilibria with lower premiums and wider insurance coverage.

When there are multiple equilibria, the one with the lowest premium is Pareto-preferred—it gives more consumers insurance cover and at a lower price. Consequently, if one of the other equilibria is achieved, there is a potential benefit from government intervention. The policy the government should adopt is simple: it can induce the best equilibrium (that with the lowest premium) by imposing a limit on the premium that can be charged. If we are at the wrong equilibrium, the corresponding premium reduction (from $E_2 \rightarrow E_1$ or $E_3 \rightarrow E_1$) will attract the good risks, making the cheaper insurance policy E_1 sustainable. This policy is not without potential problems. To see these, assume that the government slightly miscalculates and sets the maximum premium below the premium of policy E_1. No insurance company can make a profit at this price, and all offers of insurance will be withdrawn. The policy will then worsen the outcome. If set too high, one of the other equilibria may be established. To intervene successfully in this way requires considerable knowledge on the part of the government.

This analysis of the insurance market has shown how asymmetric information can lead to market unraveling with the bad driving out the good, and eventually to a position where fewer consumers participate in the market than is efficient. In addition asymmetric information can lead to multiple equilibria. These equilibria can also be Pareto-ranked. For each of these problems, a policy response was suggested. The policy of making insurance compulsory is straightforward to implement and requires little information on the part of the government. Its only drawback is that it cannot benefit all consumers, since the very low risk are forced to purchase insurance they do not find worthwhile. In contrast the policy of a maximum premium requires considerable information and has significant potential pitfalls.

9.5   Screening

If insurance companies are faced with consumers whose probabilities of having accidents differ, then it will be to the companies' advantage if they can find some mechanism that permits them to distinguish between the high-risk and low-risk. Doing so allows them to tailor insurance policies for each type and hence avoid the pooling of risks that causes market unraveling.

The mechanism that can be used by the insurance companies is to offer a menu of different contracts designed so that each risk type self-selects the contract designed for it. By self-select we mean that the consumers find it in their own interest to select the contract aimed at them. As we will show, self-selection will involve the high-risks being offered full insurance coverage at a high premium, while the low-risks are offered partial coverage at a low premium requiring them to bear part of the loss. The portion they have to bear consists of a deductible (an initial amount of the loss) and co-insurance (an extra fraction of the loss beyond the deductible). An equilibrium like this where different types purchase different contracts is called a *separating* equilibrium. This should be contrasted to the *pooling* equilibrium of the previous section in which all consumers of insurance purchased the same contract. Obviously the high-risks will lose from this separation, since they will no longer benefit from the lower premium resulting from their pooling with the low-risks.

To model self-selection, we again assume that the insurance market is competitive so that in equilibrium insurance companies will earn zero profits. Rather than have a continuous range of different types, we now simplify by assuming there are just two types of agents. The high-risk agents have a probability of an accident occurring of p_h, and the low-risks a probability p_ℓ, with $p_h > p_\ell$. The two types form proportions λ_h and λ_ℓ of the total population, where $\lambda_h + \lambda_\ell = 1$. Both types have the same fixed income, r, and suffer the same fixed damage, d, in the case of an accident.

If a consumer of type i buys an insurance policy with a premium π and payout (or coverage) δ, the expected utility of this consumer type is given by

$$V_i(\delta, \pi) = p_i u(r - d + \delta - \pi) + [1 - p_i]u(r - \pi). \tag{9.8}$$

When the consumer purchases no insurance (so $\pi = 0$ and $\delta = 0$), expected utility is

$$V_i(0,0) = p_i u(r - d) + [1 - p_i]u(r). \tag{9.9}$$

It is assumed that the consumer is risk averse, so the utility function, $u(\cdot)$, is concave.

The timing of the actions in the model is described by the following two stages:

Stage 1:   Firms simultaneously choose a menu of insurance contracts $S_i = (\delta_i, \pi_i)$ with contract i intended for consumers of type i.

Stage 2:   Consumers choose their most preferred contract (not necessarily the one the insurance companies intended for them!).

We now analyze the equilibrium of this insurance market under a number of different assumptions on information.

9.5.1   Perfect Information Equilibrium

In the perfect information equilibrium the insurance companies are assumed to be able to observe the type of each consumer; that is, they know exactly the accident probability of each customer. This case of perfect information is used as a benchmark to isolate the consequences of the asymmetric information that is soon to be introduced.

Figure 9.3 illustrates the equilibrium with perfect information. The curved lines are indifference curves—one curve is drawn for each type. The steeper curve is that of the high-risk. The indifference curves are positively sloped because consumers are willing to trade off greater coverage for a higher premium. They are concave because of risk aversion. It is assumed that willingness to pay for extra coverage increases with the probability of having an accident. This makes the indifference curves of the high-risk steeper at any point than those of the low-risk so that the indifference curves satisfy the *single-crossing* property. Single-crossing means that any pair of indifference curves—one for the low-risk and one for the high-risk—can only cross once. With full information the insurance companies know the accident probability. They can then offer contracts that trade off a

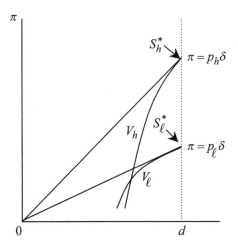

Figure 9.3
Perfect information equilibrium

higher premium for increased coverage at the rate of the accident probability. That is, low-risk types can be offered any contract $\{\pi, \delta\}$ satisfying $\pi = p_\ell \delta$, and the high-risk any contract satisfying $\pi = p_h \delta$. These equations give the two straight lines in figure 9.3. These are the equilibrium contracts that will be offered. To see this, note that if an insurance company offers a contract that is more generous (charges a lower premium for the same coverage), this contract must make a loss, and it will be withdrawn. Conversely, if a less generous contract is offered (so has a higher premium for the same coverage), other companies will be able to better it without making a loss. Therefore it will never be chosen.

Given this characterization of the equilibrium contracts, the final step is to observe that when these contracts are available, both types will choose to purchase full insurance cover. They will choose $\delta = d$ and pay the corresponding premium. Hence the competitive equilibrium when types are observable by the companies is a pair of insurance contracts S_h^*, S_ℓ^*, where

$$S_h^* = (d, p_h d) \tag{9.10}$$

and

$$S_\ell^* = (d, p_\ell d), \tag{9.11}$$

so there is full coverage and actuarially-fair premia are charged. As for any competitive equilibrium with full (hence symmetric) information, this outcome is Pareto-efficient.

9.5.2   Imperfect Information Equilibrium

Imperfect information is introduced by assuming that the insurance companies cannot distinguish a low-risk consumer from a high-risk. We also assume that it cannot employ any methods of investigation to elicit further information. As we will discuss later, insurance companies routinely do try to obtain further information. The reasons why they do and the consequences of doing so will become clear once it is understood what happens if they don't.

Given these assumptions, the insurance companies cannot offer the contracts that arose in the full-information competitive equilibrium. The efficient contract for the low-risk provides any given degree of coverage at a lower premium than the contract for the high-risk. Hence both types will prefer the contract intended for the low-risk (this is adverse selection again!). If offered, an insurance company will charge a premium based on the low-risk accident probability but have to pay claims at the population average probability. It will therefore make a loss and have to be withdrawn. This argument suggests what the insurance companies have to do: if they wish to offer a contract that will attract the low-risk type, the contract must be designed in such a way that it does not also attract the high-risk. This requirement places constraints on the contracts that can be offered and is what prevents the attainment of the efficient outcome.

Assume now that insurance companies offer a contract S_h designed for the high-risk and a contract S_ℓ designed for the low-risk. To formally express the comments in the previous paragraph, we say that when types are not observable, the contracts S_h and S_ℓ have to satisfy the self-selection (or incentive-compatibility) constraints. These constraints require the low-risk to find that the contract S_ℓ offers them at least as much utility as the contract S_h, with the converse holding for the high-risk. If these constraints are satisfied, the low-risk will choose the contract designed for them, as will the high-risk. The self-selection constraints can be written as

$$V_\ell(S_\ell) \geq V_\ell(S_h) \qquad (IC_u) \tag{9.12}$$

and

$$V_h(S_h) \geq V_h(S_\ell) \qquad (IC_d). \tag{9.13}$$

(These are labeled IC_u and IC_d because the first has the low-risk types looking "up" at the contract of the high-risk, the second has the high-risk looking "down" at the contract of the low-risk. This becomes clear in figure 9.4.) As we have already remarked, the contracts S_h^*, S_ℓ^* arising in the full-information equilibrium do not satisfy (IC_d): the high-risk will always prefer the low-risk's contract S_ℓ^*.

There is only one undominated pair of contracts that achieves the desired separation. By undominated we mean that no other pair of separating contracts can be introduced that makes a positive profit in competition with the undominated contracts. The properties of the pair are that the high-risk type receives full insurance at an actuarially fair rate. The low-risk do not receive full insurance. They are restricted to partial coverage, with the extent of coverage determined by where the indifference curve of the high-risk crosses the actuarially fair insurance line for the low-risk. In addition the constraint (9.13) is binding while the constraint (9.12) is not. This feature, that the "good" type (here the low-risk) are constrained by the "bad" type (here the high-risk), is common to all incentive problems of this kind.

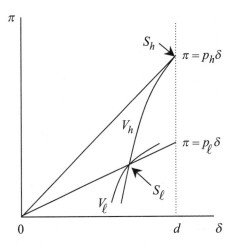

Figure 9.4
Separating contracts

It can easily be seen that the insurance contracts are undominated by any other pair of separating contracts and make zero profit for the insurance companies. To see that no contract can be introduced that will appeal to only one type and yield positive profit, assume that such a contract was aimed at the high-risk. Then it must be more favorable than the existing contract; otherwise, it will never be chosen. But the existing contract is actuarially fair, so any contract that is more favorable must make a loss. Alternatively, a contract aimed at the low-risk will either attract the high-risk too, and so not separate, or, if it attracts only low-risk, will be unprofitable. There remains, though, the possibility that a pooling contract can be offered that will attract both types and be profitable.

To see how this can arise, consider figure 9.5. A pooling contract will appeal to both types if it lies below the indifference curves attained by the separating contracts (lower premium and possibly greater coverage). Since the population probability of an accident occurring is $p = \lambda_h p_h + \lambda_\ell p_\ell$, an actuarially fair pooling contract $\{\pi, \delta\}$ will relate premium and coverage by $\pi = p\delta$. When λ_h is large, the pooling contract will lie close to the actuarially fair contract of the high-risk and hence will be above the indifference curve attained by the low-risks in the separating equilibrium. In this case the separating contracts will form an equilibrium. Conversely, when λ_ℓ is large, the pooling contract will lie close to the actuarially fair contract for the low-risk. It will therefore be below the indifference curves of both types in the separating equilibrium and, when offered, will attract both low- and high-risk types. When this arises, the separating contracts cannot constitute

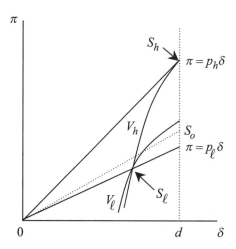

Figure 9.5
Separating and pooling contracts

an equilibrium, since an insurance company can offer a contract marginally less favorable than the actuarially fair pooling contract, attract all consumers, and make a profit.

To summarize, there exists a pair of contracts that separate the population and are not dominated by any other separating contracts. They constitute an equilibrium if the proportion of high-risk consumers in the population is sufficiently large (so that the low-risks prefer to separate and choose partial coverage rather than be pooled with many high-risks and pay a higher premium). On the other hand, if the proportion of low-risk is sufficiently large, there will be a pooling contract that is preferred by both types and profitable for an insurance company. In this latter case there can be no separating equilibrium.

By using the same kind of argument, it can be shown that there is no pooling equilibrium. Consider a pooling contract S with full coverage and average risk premium. Any contract $S^{\circ} = (\delta^{\circ}, \pi^{\circ})$ in the wedge formed by the two indifference curves in figure 9.6 attracts only low-risks and makes a positive profit. It will therefore be offered and attract the low-risk away from the pooling contract. Without the low-risk the pooling contract will make a loss.

In conclusion, there is no pooling equilibrium in this model of the insurance market. There may be a separating equilibrium, but this depends on the population proportions. When there is no separating equilibrium, there is no equilibrium at all. Asymmetric information either causes inefficiency by leading to a separating equilibrium in which the low-risk have too little insurance cover, or it results

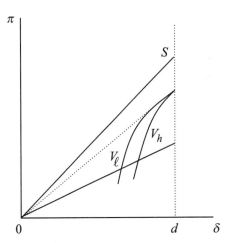

Figure 9.6
Nonexistence of pooling equilibrium

in there being no equilibrium at all. In the latter case we cannot predict what the outcome will be.

9.5.3   Government Intervention

Government intervention in this insurance market is limited by the same information restriction that affects firms: they cannot tell who is low-risk or high-risk directly but can only make inferences from observing choices. This has the consequence that it restricts policy intervention to be based on the same information as that available to the insurance companies. Even under these restrictions the government can achieve a Pareto-improvement by imposing a cross-subsidy from low-risks to high-risks. It does this by subsidizing the premium of the high-risk and taxing the premium of the low-risk. It can do that without observing risk by imposing a minimal coverage for all at the average risk premium.

The reason why this policy works is that the resulting transfer from the low-risks to the high-risks relaxes the incentive constraint (IC_d). This makes the set of insurance policies that satisfies the constraints larger and so benefits both types. This equilibrium cannot be achieved by the insurance companies because it would require them all to act simultaneously. This is an example of a coordination failure that prevents the attainment of a better outcome.

This policy is illustrated in figure 9.7. Let the subsidy to the high-risk be given by t_h and the tax on the low-risk be t_ℓ. The tax and subsidy are related to the

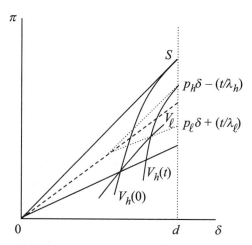

Figure 9.7
Market intervention

transfer, t, by the relationships $t_h = \frac{t}{\lambda_h}$ and $t_\ell = \frac{t}{\lambda_\ell}$. The premium for the low-risk then becomes $p_\ell\delta + t_\ell$ and for the high-risks $p_h\delta - t_h$. As figure 9.7 shows, the high-risks are strictly better off and the low-risks are as well as before because higher coverage is now incentive compatible. The policy intervention has therefore engineered a Pareto-improvement. It should be noted that the government has improved the outcome, even though it has the same information as the insurance companies. Government achieves this improvement through its ability to coordinate the transfer—something the insurance companies cannot do.

9.6 Signaling

The fundamental feature at the heart of asymmetric information is the inability to distinguish the good from the bad. This is to the detriment of both the seller of a good article, who fails to obtain its true value, and to the purchaser, who would rather pay a higher price for something that is known to be good. It seems natural that this situation would be improved if the seller could convey some information that convinces the purchaser of the quality of the product. For instance, the seller may announce the names of previous satisfied customers (employment references can be interpreted in this way) or provide an independent guarantee of quality (e.g., a report on the condition of a car by a motoring organization). Warranties can also serve as signals of quality for durable goods because, if a product is of higher quality, it is less costly for the seller to offer a longer warranty. Such information, generally termed *signals*, can be mutually beneficial.

It is worth noting the difference between screening and signaling. The less-informed players (like the insurance companies) use screening (different insurance contracts) to find out what the better-informed players (insurance customer) know (their own risk). In contrast, more-informed players use signals to help the less-informed players find out the truth.

For a signal to work it must satisfy certain criteria. First, it must be verifiable by the receiver (i.e., the less-informed agent). Being given the name of a satisfied customer is not enough—it must be possible to check back that they are actually satisfied. Second, it must be credible. In the case of an employment reference this is dependent partly on the author of the reference having a reputation to maintain and partly on the possibility of legal action if false statements are knowingly made. Finally the signal must also be costly for the sender (i.e., the better-informed agent) to obtain and the cost must differ between various qualities of sender. In the case of an employment reference this is obtained by a record of quality work. Something that is either costlessly obtainable by both the senders of low- and high-quality or equally costly cannot have any value in distinguishing between them. We now model such signals and see the effect that they have on the equilibrium outcome.

The modeling of signaling revolves around the timing of actions. The basic assumption is that the informed agent moves first and invests in acquiring a costly signal. The uninformed party then observes the signals of different agents and forms inferences about quality on the basis of these signals. An equilibrium is reached when the chosen investment in the signal is optimal for each informed agent and the inferences of the uninformed about the meaning of signals are justified by the outcomes. As we will see, the latter aspect involves self-supporting beliefs: they may be completely irrational, but the equilibrium they generate does not provide any evidence to falsify them.

9.6.1   Educational Signaling

To illustrate the consequences of signaling, we will consider a model of productivity signaling in the labor market. The model has two identical firms that compete for workers through the wages they offer. The set of workers can be divided into two types according to their productivity levels. Some of the workers are innately low-productivity in the form of employment offered by the firms, while the others are high-productivity. Without any signaling, the firms are assumed to be unable to judge the productivity of a worker.

The firms cannot directly observe a worker's type before hiring, but high-productivity workers can signal their productivity by being educated. Education itself does not alter productivity, but it is costly to acquire. Firms can observe the level of education of a potential worker and condition their wage offer on this. Hence education is a signal. Investment in education will be worthwhile if it earns a higher wage. To make it an effective signal, it must be assumed that obtaining education is more costly for the low-productivity than it is for the high-productivity; otherwise, both will have the same incentive for acquiring it.

Formally let θ_h denote the productivity of a high-productivity worker and θ_ℓ that of a low-productivity worker, with $\theta_h > \theta_\ell$. The workers are present in the population in proportions λ_h and λ_ℓ, so $\lambda_h + \lambda_\ell = 1$. The average productivity in the population is given by

$$E(\theta) = \lambda_h \theta_h + \lambda_\ell \theta_\ell. \tag{9.14}$$

Competition between the two firms ensures that this is the wage that would be paid if there were no signaling and the firms could not distinguish between workers. For a worker of productivity level θ, the cost of obtaining education level e is

$$C(e, \theta) = \frac{e}{\theta}, \tag{9.15}$$

which satisfies the property that any given level of education is more costly for a low-productivity worker to obtain.

The firms offer wages that are (potentially) conditional on the level of education; "potentially" is added because there may be equilibria in which the firms ignore the signal. The wage schedule is denoted by $w(e)$. Given the offered wage schedule, the workers aim to maximize utility, which is defined as wages less the cost of education. Hence their decision problem is

$$\max_{\{e\}} \ w(e) - \frac{e}{\theta}. \tag{9.16}$$

As shown in figure 9.8, the preferences in (9.16) satisfy the single-crossing property when defined over wages and education. Here V_ℓ denotes an indifference curve of a low-productivity worker and V_h that of a high-productivity. At any point the greater marginal cost of education for the low-productivity type implies that they have a steeper indifference curve.

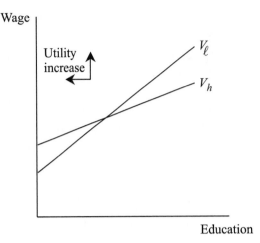

Figure 9.8
Single-crossing property

An equilibrium for this economy is a pair $\{e^*(\theta), w^*(e)\}$, where $e^*(\theta)$ determines the level of education as a function of productivity and $w^*(e)$ determines the wage as a function of education. In equilibrium these functions must satisfy three properties:

1. No worker wants to change his education choice given the wage schedule $w^*(e)$.

2. No firm wants to change its wage schedule given its beliefs about worker types and education choices $e^*(\theta)$.

3. Firms have correct beliefs given the education choices.

The first candidate for an equilibrium is a separating equilibrium in which low- and high-productivity workers choose different levels of education. Any separating equilibrium must satisfy

$$e^*(\theta_\ell) \neq e^*(\theta_h), \tag{i}$$

$$w^*(e^*(\theta_\ell)) = \theta_\ell,$$
$$w^*(e^*(\theta_h)) = \theta_h, \tag{ii}$$

$$w^*(e^*(\theta_\ell)) - \frac{e^*(\theta_\ell)}{\theta_\ell} \geq w^*(e^*(\theta_h)) - \frac{e^*(\theta_h)}{\theta_\ell}, \tag{iiia}$$

$$w^*(e^*(\theta_h)) - \frac{e^*(\theta_h)}{\theta_h} \geq w^*(e^*(\theta_\ell)) - \frac{e^*(\theta_\ell)}{\theta_h}. \tag{iiib}$$

Condition (i) is the requirement that low- and high-productivity workers choose different education levels, (ii) that the wages are equal to the marginal products, and (iii) that the choices are individually rational for the consumers. The values of the wages given in (ii) are a consequence of signaling and competition between firms. Signaling implies workers of different productivities are paid different wages. If a firm paid a wage above the marginal product, it would make a loss on each worker employed. This cannot be profit maximizing. Alternatively, if one firm paid a wage below the marginal productivity, the other would have an incentive to set its wage incrementally higher. This would capture all the workers of that productivity level and would be the more profitable strategy. Therefore the only equilibrium values for wages when signaling occurs are the productivity levels. This leaves only the levels of education to be determined.

The equilibrium level of education for the low-productivity workers is found by noting that if they choose not to act like the high-productivity, then there is no point in obtaining any education—education is simply a cost that does not benefit them. Hence $e^*(\theta_\ell) = 0$. By this fact and that wages are equal to productivities, the level of education for the high-productivity workers can be found from the incentive compatibility constraints. From (iiia),

$$\theta_\ell \geq \theta_h - \frac{e^*(\theta_h)}{\theta_\ell}, \tag{9.17}$$

or

$$e^*(\theta_h) \geq \theta_\ell[\theta_h - \theta_\ell]. \tag{9.18}$$

Condition (9.18) provides the minimum level of education that will ensure that the low-productivity workers choose not to be educated. Now from (iiib) it follows that

$$\theta_h - \frac{e^*(\theta_h)}{\theta_h} \geq \theta_\ell, \tag{9.19}$$

or

$$\theta_h[\theta_h - \theta_\ell] \geq e^*(\theta_h). \tag{9.20}$$

Hence a complete description of the separating equilibrium is

$$e^*(\theta_\ell) = 0, \qquad \theta_\ell[\theta_h - \theta_\ell] \leq e^*(\theta_h) \leq \theta_h[\theta_h - \theta_\ell], \tag{9.21}$$

$$w(e^*(\theta_\ell)) = \theta_\ell, \qquad w(e^*(\theta_h)) = \theta_h, \tag{9.22}$$

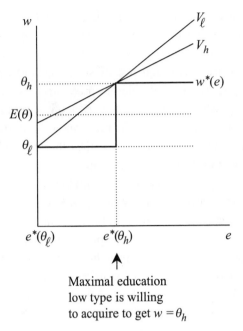

Figure 9.9
Separating equilibrium

so the low-productivity workers obtain no education, the high-productivity have education somewhere between the two limits and both are paid their marginal products. An equilibrium satisfying these conditions is illustrated in figure 9.9.

Since there is a range of possible values for $e^*(\theta_h)$, there is not a unique equilibrium but a set of equilibria differing in the level of education obtained by the high-productivity. This set of separating equilibria can be ranked according to criterion of Pareto-preference. Clearly, changing the level of education $e^*(\theta_h)$ within the specified range does not affect the low-productivity workers. On the other hand, the high-productivity workers always prefer a lower level of education, since education is costly. Therefore equilibria with lower $e^*(\theta_h)$ are Pareto-preferred, and the most preferred equilibrium is that with $e^*(\theta_h) = \theta_\ell[\theta_h - \theta_\ell]$. The Pareto-dominated separating equilibria are supported by the high-productivity worker's fear that choosing less education will give an unfavorable impression of their productivity to the firm and thus lead to a lower wage.

There are arguments (called refinements of equilibrium) to suggest that this most-preferred equilibrium will actually be the one that emerges. Let the equilibrium level of education for the high-productivity type, $e^*(\theta_h)$, be above the minimum required to separate. Denote this minimum e^0. Now consider the firm observing a worker with an education level at least equal to e^0 but less than $e^*(\theta_h)$. What should a firm conclude about this worker? Clearly, the worker cannot be low-productivity, since such a choice is worse for them than choosing no education. Hence the firm must conclude that the worker is of high productivity. Realizing this, it then pays the worker to deviate, since it would reduce the cost of an education. This argument can be repeated until $e^*(\theta_h)$ is driven down to e^0.

Signaling allows the high-productivity to distinguish themselves from the low-productivity. It might be thought that this improvement in information transmission would make signaling socially beneficial. However, this need not be the case, since the act of signaling is costly and does not add to productivity. The alternative to the signaling equilibrium is pooling where both types purchase no education and are paid a wage equal to the average productivity. The low-productivity would prefer this equilibrium as it raises their wage from θ_ℓ to $E(\theta) = \lambda_h \theta_h + \lambda_\ell \theta_\ell$. For the high-productivity pooling is preferred if

$$E(\theta) = \lambda_h \theta_h + \lambda_\ell \theta_\ell > \theta_h - \frac{\theta_\ell[\theta_h - \theta_\ell]}{\theta_h}. \tag{9.23}$$

Since $\lambda_\ell = 1 - \lambda_h$, this inequality will be satisfied if

$$\lambda_h > 1 - \frac{\theta_\ell}{\theta_h}. \tag{9.24}$$

Hence, when there are sufficiently many high-productivity workers so that the average wage is close to the high productivity level, the separating equilibrium is Pareto-dominated by the pooling equilibrium. In these cases signaling is individually rational but socially unproductive. Again, the Pareto-dominated separating equilibrium is sustained by the high-productivity workers' fear that lowering their education would give a bad impression of their ability to the firms and thus lead to lower wage. Actually the no-signaling pooling equilibrium is not truly available to the high-productivity workers. If they get no education, firms will believe they are low-productivity workers and then offer a wage of θ_ℓ. So we get the paradoxical situation that high-productivity workers choose to signal, although they are worse off when signaling.

If the government were to intervene in this economy, it has two basic policy options. The first is to allow signaling to occur but to place an upper limit on the level of education equal to $\theta_\ell[\theta_h - \theta_\ell]$. It might choose to do this in those cases where the pooling equilibrium does not Pareto-dominate the separating

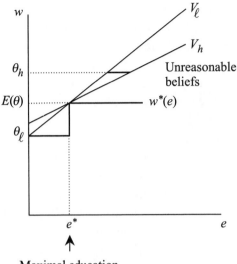

Figure 9.10
Unreasonable beliefs

equilibrium. There is, though, one problem with banning signaling and enforcing a pooling equilibrium. The pooling equilibrium requires the firms to believe that all workers have the same ability. If the firms were to "test" this belief by offering a higher wage for a higher level of education, they would discover that the belief was incorrect. This is illustrated in figure 9.10. A low-productivity worker would be better off getting no education than getting education above e^* whatever the firm's belief and the resulting wage. Therefore the firm should believe that any worker choosing an education level above e^* has high productivity and should be offered a wage θ_h. But, if this is so, the high-productivity worker could do better than the pooling equilibrium by deviating to an education level slightly in excess of e^* to get a wage θ_h. Therefore the pooling equilibrium is unlikely, since it involves unreasonable beliefs from the firms.

9.6.2   Implications

The model of educational signaling shows how an unproductive but costly signal can be used to distinguish between quality levels through a set of self-supporting beliefs. There will be a set of Pareto-ranked equilibria with the lowest level of signal the most preferred. Although there is an argument that the economy must achieve the Pareto-dominating signaling equilibrium, it is possible that this may not happen. If it does not, the economy may become settled in a Pareto-inferior separating equilibrium. Even if this does not happen, it is still possible for the pooling equilibrium to Pareto-dominate the separating equilibrium. This will occur when the high-productivity workers are relatively numerous in the population, since in that case almost every worker is getting unproductive but costly education to separate themselves from the few bad workers.

There are several policy implications of these results. In a narrow interpretation, they show how the government can increase efficiency and make everyone better off by restricting the size of signals that can be transmitted. Alternatively, the government could improve the welfare of everyone by organizing a cross-subsidy from the good to the bad workers. This can take the form of a minimum wage for the low-productivity workers in excess of their productivity financed by wage limit for the high-productivity workers that is below their productivity. Notice that a ban on signaling is an extreme form of such cross-subsidization, since it forces the same wage for all. When the pooling equilibrium is Pareto-preferred, signals should be eliminated entirely. More generally, the model demonstrates how market solutions may endogenously arise to combat the problems of asymmetric information. These solutions can never remove the problems entirely—someone must be bearing the cost of improving information flows—and can even exacerbate the situation.

The basic problem for the government in responding to these kinds of problems is that it does not have a natural informational advantage over the private agents. In the model of education there is no reason to suppose the government is any more able to tell the low-productivity workers from the high-productivity (in fact there is every reason to suspect that the firms would be better equipped to do this). Faced with these kinds of problems, the government may have little to offer beyond the cross-subsidization we have just mentioned.

9.7 Moral Hazard (Hidden Action)

A moral hazard problem arises when an agent can affect the "quality" of a traded good or contract variable by some action that is not observed by other agents. For instance, a houseowner once insured may become lax in her attention to security, such as leaving windows open, in the knowledge that if burgled she will be fully compensated. Or a worker, once in employment, may not fully exert himself, reasoning that his lack of effort may be hidden among the effort of the workforce as a whole. Such possibilities provide the motive for contracts to be designed that embody incentives to lessen these effects.

In the case of the worker, the employment contract could provide for a wage that is dependent on some measure of the worker's performance. Ideally the measure would be his exact productivity but, except for the simplest cases, this could be difficult to measure. Difficulties can arise because production takes place in teams (a production line can often be interpreted as a team) with the effort of the individual team member impossible to distinguish from the output of the team as a whole. They can also arise through randomness in the relation between effort and output. As examples, agricultural output is driven by the weather, maintenance tasks can depend on the (variable) condition of the item being maintained, and production can be dependent on the random quality of other inputs.

We now consider the design of incentive schemes in a situation with moral hazard. The model we choose embodies the major points of the previous discussion: effort cannot be measured directly, so a contract has to be based on some observable variable that roughly measures effort.

9.7.1   Moral Hazard in Insurance

The moral hazard problem that can arise in an insurance market is that effort on accident prevention is reduced when consumers become insured. If accident-prevention effort is costly, for instance, driving more slowly is time-consuming or eating a good diet is less enjoyable, then a rational consumer will seek to reduce such effort when it is beneficial to do so (and the benefits are raised once insurance is offered). Insurance companies must counteract this tendency through the design of their contracts.

To model this situation, assume an economy populated by many identical agents. The income of an agent is equal to r with probability $1 - p$ and $r - d$ with probability p. Here p is interpreted as the probability of an accident occurring and d the monetary equivalent of the accident damage. Moral hazard is introduced by assuming that the agents are able to affect the accident probability through their prevention efforts.

To simplify, it is assumed that effort, e, can take one of two values. If $e = 0$, an agent is making no effort at accident prevention and the probability of an accident is $p(0)$. Alternatively, if $e = 1$, the agent is making maximum effort at accident prevention and the probability is $p(1)$. In line with these interpretations, it is assumed that $p(0) > p(1)$, so the probability of the accident is higher when no effort is undertaken. The cost of effort for the agents, measured in utility terms, is $c(e) \equiv ce$.

In the absence of insurance, the preferences of the agent are described by the expected utility function

$$U^0(e) = p(e)u(r - d) + [1 - p(e)]u(r) - ce, \tag{9.25}$$

where $u(r - d)$ is the utility if there is an accident and $u(r)$ is the utility if there is no accident. It is assumed that the agent is risk averse, so the utility function $u(\cdot)$ is concave.

The value of e, either 0 or 1, is chosen to maximize this utility. Effort to prevent the accident will be undertaken ($e = 1$) if

$$U^0(1) > U^0(0). \tag{9.26}$$

Evaluating the utilities and rearranging shows that $e = 1$ if

$$c \leq c_0 \equiv [p(0) - p(1)][u(r) - u(r - d)]. \tag{9.27}$$

Here c_0 is the critical value of effort cost. If effort cost is below this value, effort will be undertaken. Therefore, in the absence of insurance, effort will be undertaken to prevent accidents if the cost of doing so is sufficiently small.

Consider now the introduction of insurance contracts. A contract consists of a premium π paid by the consumer and an indemnity $\delta, \delta \leq d$, paid to the consumer if they are subject to an accident. The consumer's preferences over insurance policies (meaning different combinations of π and δ) and effort are given by

$$U(e, \delta, \pi) \equiv p(e)u(r - \pi + \delta - d) + [1 - p(e)]u(r - \pi) - ce, \tag{9.28}$$

with $U(e, 0, 0) = U^0(e)$.

9.7.2   Effort Observable

To provide a benchmark from which to measure the effects of moral hazard, we first analyze the choice of insurance contract when effort is observable by the insurance companies. In this case there can be no efficiency loss, since there is no asymmetry of information.

If the insurance company can observe e, it will offer an insurance contract that is conditional on effort choice. The contract will therefore be of the form

$\{\delta(e), \pi(e)\}$, with $e = 0, 1$. Competition among the insurance companies ensures that the contracts on offer maximize the utility of a representative consumer subject to constraint that the insurance companies at least break even. To meet this latter requirement the premium must be no lower than the expected payment of indemnity. For a given e (recall this is observed) the policy therefore solves

$$\max_{\{\delta, \pi\}} \; U(e, \delta, \pi) \quad \text{subject to} \quad \pi \geq p(e)\delta. \tag{9.29}$$

The solution to this is a policy

$$\{\delta^*(e) = d, \pi^*(e) = p(e)d\} \tag{9.30}$$

so that the damage is fully covered and the premium is fair given the effort level chosen. This is illustrated in figure 9.11. The straight line is the set of contracts that are fair (so $\pi = p(e)\delta$), and I is the highest indifference curve that can be achieved given these contracts. (Note that utility increases with a lower premium and greater coverage.) The first-best contract is therefore full insurance with $\delta^*(e) = d$ and $\pi^*(e) = p(e)d$.

At the first-best contract, the resulting utility level is

$$U^*(e) = u(r - p(e)d) - ce. \tag{9.31}$$

Effort will be undertaken ($e = 1$) if

$$U^*(1) \geq U^*(0), \tag{9.32}$$

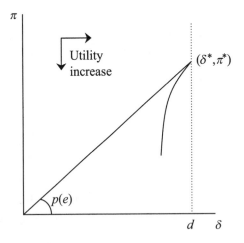

Figure 9.11
First-best contract

which holds if

$$c \leq c_1 \equiv u(r - p(1)d) - u(r - p(0)d). \tag{9.33}$$

That is, the cost of effort is less than the utility gain resulting from the lower premium.

An interesting question is whether the first-best contract encourages the supply of effort, in other words, whether the level of effort cost below which effort is supplied in the absence of the contract, c_0, is less than that with the contract, c_1. Calculations show that the outcome may go in either direction depending on the accident probabilities associated with effort and no effort.

9.7.3   Effort Unobservable

When effort is unobservable, the insurance companies cannot condition the contract on it. Instead, they must evaluate the effect of the policies on the choices of the consumers and choose the policy taking this into account.

The preferences of the consumer over contracts are determined by the highest level of utility they can achieve with that contract given that they have made the optimal choice of effort. Formally, the utility $V(\delta, \pi)$ arising from contract (δ, π) is determined by

$$V(\delta, \pi) \equiv \max_{\{e=0,1\}} U(e, \delta, \pi). \tag{9.34}$$

The basic analytical difficulty in undertaking the determination of the contract is the nonconvexity of preferences in the contract space (δ, π). This nonconvexity arises at the point in the contract space where the consumers switch from no effort $(e = 0)$ to full effort $(e = 1)$. When supplying no effort their preferences are determined by $U(0, \delta, \pi)$ and when they supply effort by $U(1, \delta, \pi)$. At any point $(\hat{\delta}, \hat{\pi})$ where $U(0, \hat{\delta}, \hat{\pi}) = U(1, \hat{\delta}, \hat{\pi})$, the indifference curve of $U(0, \hat{\delta}, \hat{\pi})$ is steeper than that of $U(1, \hat{\delta}, \hat{\pi})$ because the willingness to pay for extra coverage is higher when there is no effort and thus a high risk of accident. This is illustrated in figure 9.12, where $\delta^*(\pi)$ denotes the locus of points where the consumer is indifferent to $e = 0$ and $e = 1$. This locus separates those who make effort from those who make no effort. For each premium π, there is an indemnity level $\delta^*(\pi)$ such that if $\delta < \delta^*(\pi)$, then $e = 1$, but if $\delta \geq \delta^*(\pi)$, then $e = 0$. This indemnity level rises with the premium, so $\delta^*(\pi)$ is an increasing function of π. In words, if the coverage rate for any given premium is too high, agents will no longer find profitable to undertake effort.

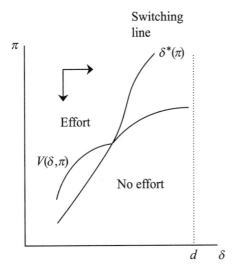

Figure 9.12
Switching line

9.7.4   Second-Best Contract

The second-best contract maximizes the consumer's utility subject to the constraint that it must at least break even. The optimization problem describing this can be written as that of maximizing $V(\delta, \pi)$ subject to the constraints that

$$\pi \geq p(1)\delta \quad \text{for } \delta < \delta^*(\pi), \tag{i}$$

$$\pi \geq p(0)\delta \quad \text{for } \delta^*(\pi) \leq \delta < d. \tag{ii}$$

The first constraint applies if the consumer chooses to supply effort $(e = 1)$ and requires that the contract break even. The second constraint is the break-even condition if the consumer chooses to supply no effort $(e = 0)$.

The problem is solved by calculating the solution under the first constraint and evaluating the resulting level of utility. Then the solution is found under the second constraint and utility is evaluated again. The two levels of utility are then compared, and the one yielding the highest utility is the optimal second-best contract. This reasoning provides two contracts that are candidates for optimality. These are illustrated in figure 9.13 by E_0 and E_1 and have the following properties:

Contract E_0:   No effort and full coverage at high price;

Contract E_1:   Effort and partial coverage at low price.

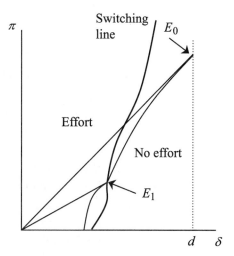

Figure 9.13
Second-best contract

Table 9.1
Categorization of outcomes

Cost of effort	c_2	c_1
First best	Effort, full coverage	No effort, full coverage
Second best	Effort, partial coverage	No effort, full coverage

Which of these contracts is optimal will depend on the cost, c, of effort. When this cost is low, contract E_1 will be optimal and partial coverage will be offered to consumers. Conversely, when the cost is high, then it will be optimal to have no effort and contract E_0 will be optimal. By this reasoning it follows that there must be some value of the cost of effort at which the switch is made between E_0 and E_1. Hence there exists a value of effort, c_2, with $c_2 < c_1$, such that $c \leq c_2$ implies that the second-best contract is E_1 and $c > c_2$ implies that the second-best contract is E_0.

It can now be shown that the second-best contract is inefficient. Since the critical level of cost, c, determining when effort is supplied satisfies $c < c_1$, the outcome has to be inefficient relative to the first-best. Furthermore there is too little effort if $c_2 < c < c_1$ and too little coverage if $c < c_2$. These results are summarized in table 9.1.

9.7.5   Government Intervention

The market failure associated with moral hazard is very profound. The moral hazard problem arises from the nonobservability of the level of care. When individuals are fully insured they tend to exert too little precaution but also over-use insurance. Consider, for instance, a patient who may be either sick with probability 0.09 or very sick with probability 0.01. In the two events his medical expenses will be $1,000 and $10,000. At a fair premium of $190 the patient will not have to pay anything if he gets sick and would buy such insurance if risk averse. But then suppose that when he is a little sick, there is some chance, however small, that he can be very sick. Then he would choose the expensive treatment given that there is no extra cost to the patient and all the extra cost is borne by the insurance company. Each individual ignores the effect of his reckless behavior and overconsumption on the premium, but when they all act like that, the premium increases. The lack of care by each inflates the premium, which generates a negative externality on others. An important implication is that market cannot be efficient.

Another way to see this generic market inefficiency is that the provision of insurance in the presence of moral hazard causes the insured individual to receive less than the full social benefit of his care. As a result not only will the individual expend less than the socially optimal level of care but also there will be an insurance-induced externality.

This implies that the potential scope for government intervention with moral hazard is substantial. Can the government improve efficiency by intervention when moral hazard is present? In answering this question it is important to specify what information is available to the government. For a fair evaluation of government intervention it is natural to assume that the government has the same information as the private sector. In this case it can be argued that efficient government intervention is still possible. The beneficial effects of government intervention stem from the government's capacity to tax and subsidize. For example, the government cannot monitor smoking, which has an adverse effect on health, any better than an insurance company. But the government can impose taxes, not only on cigarettes but also on commodities that are complements and subsidize substitutes that have a less adverse effect. Also the taxation of insurance induces firms to offer insurance at less than fair price. As a consequence individuals buy less insurance and expend more effort (as efficiency requires).

9.8   Public Provision of Health Care

9.8.1   Efficiency

Economists do not expect the private market for health care insurance to function well. Our previous discussion suggests that informational problems result in the private provision of health insurance having incomplete and inefficient coverage. The existence of asymmetric information between insurers and insured leads to adverse selection, which can result in the market breaking down, and the nonexistence of certain types of insurance. The moral hazard problem can lead to incomplete insurance in the form of co-payments and deductibles for those who have insurance. Another problem caused by the presence of moral hazard is that the insured who become sick will want to overconsume and doctors will want to oversupply health care, since it is a third party that pays. It is not surprising therefore that the government may usefully intervene in the provision of health care.

There is strong evidence that in the OECD countries the public sector plays an important role in the provision of insurance for health care. From OECD health data, in 1994 the proportion of publicly provided health expenses was 44 percent in the United States, 70 percent in Germany, 73 percent in Italy, 75 percent in France, and 83 percent in Sweden and the United Kingdom. The question is why the government intervenes so extensively in the health care field. In answering the question, one must bear in mind that the government faces many of same informational problems as the private sector. Like a private insurer, it faces the moral hazard of patients who get insurance exerting too little effort in risk-reducing activities and overconsuming health services, and doctors having the incentive to oversupply health services at too high a cost.

One advantage of public provision is to prevent the adverse selection problem by making health coverage compulsory and universal. It is tempting to believe that the actual provision of insurance need not be public to accomplish this effect. Indeed, the actual provision of health insurance could remain private and the government mandate that all individuals have to purchase health insurance and private insurers have to insure anyone who applies for insurance. However, mandates may be difficult to enforce at the individual level, and the incentive for private firms to accept only the good risks is a permanent concern. Another advantage of public provision is that as a predominant insurer it can exert monopsony power with considerable leverage over health suppliers in influencing the prices they set or the amount of services they prescribe.

The fact that private insurance is subject to the problem of moral hazard is less helpful in explaining government provision. Indeed, it is questionable whether the government has any advantage in dealing with the problem of moral hazard, since it cannot observe the (hidden) activities of the insured any better than private insurers. One possible form of advantageous government intervention is the taxing and subsidizing of consumption choices that influence the insured's demand for health care (e.g., a subsidy for health club membership and taxes on smoking). This argument, as noticed by Prescott and Townsend (1984), is based on a presumption that the government can monitor these consumption choices better than the private market; otherwise, private insurers could condition contracts on their clients' consumption choices and the government would have no advantage over the market. So the potential scope for government provision with moral hazard is seemingly limited.

However, there is a more subtle form of moral hazard that provides a reason for direct government delivery of health care: the time-consistency problem. Imagine that health insurance is provided by the private sector only. Each individual must decide how much insurance to purchase. In a standard insurance situation, risk-averse individuals would fully insure if they could get a fair price. However, in this case they may recognize that if they do not fully insure, a welfaristic government will provide for them should they become ill and uninsured. They have thus an incentive to buy too little insurance and to rely on the government to finance their health care when they become sick. This phenomenon is called the *Samaritan's Dilemma*, and it implies that people will underinvest resources available in the present, knowing that the truly welfaristic government will come to their rescue in the future. The problem is particularly acute for life-threatening diseases where denial of insurance is tantamount to a death sentence for the patient.

A similar time-consistency problem arises on the insurer's side: insurance companies cannot commit to guaranteeing that the rate charged for insurance will not change as they discover progressively more about the health conditions of their clients. Competition will force insurance companies to update their rate to reflect any new information about an individual's medical condition. Insurance could then become so expensive for some individuals that they could not afford it. With recent advances in genetic testing and other long-range diagnoses, this problem of the uninsured is likely to grow in the future. With no insurance against unfavorable test results or for the denial of insurance when a policy terminates, those more desperate to get insurance will find it increasingly hard to get it from the private market. The supply- and demand-side time-consistency problems were explicitly recognized in the United States by President Clinton, and used as a reason to make participation in health insurance compulsory. In response to the uninsured problem, the government provides a substitute for insurance by directly funding health care to the poor and long-term sick (Medicaid in the United States).

Another advantage of public provision of insurance is to achieve pooling on a much larger scale with improved risk sharing. In including every person in a nationwide insurance scheme and pooling health insurance with other forms of insurance (unemployment, pension, etc.) public insurance comes closer to the "ideal" optimal insurance that requires the pooling of all the risks faced by individuals and a single contract covering them jointly (with a single deductible against all risks).

Both adverse selection and moral hazard have been central in the debates over health care reform in Europe and North America. Consider, for example, the debate about medical savings accounts (MSA) in the United States. These were intended to encourage people to buy insurance with more deductibles and co-payments, thereby reducing the risk of moral hazard. But critics argued that they will trigger a process of adverse selection where those less likely to need medical care will avail themselves of MSA. So those opting for the MSA with larger deductibles might indeed face higher total medical costs despite the improved incentives (they take more care), simply because of the self-selection process. Another response to moral hazard problems in the United States is the mandatory pre-admission referral by Peer Review Organizations before hospitalization. The increasing popularity of Health Maintenance Organizations can also be viewed as a response to moral hazard by attracting cost-conscious patients who wish to lower the cost of insurance. Finally the increasing use of co-payments in many countries appears to be the effective method of cost containment.

9.8.2   Redistributive Politics

Government provision not only requires mandatory insurance to eliminate the adverse selection problem, but it also involves socializing insurance. Once insurance is compulsory and financed (at least partly) by taxation, redistributive considerations play a central role in explaining the extensive public provision of insurance. Government programs that provide the same amount of public services to all households may still be redistributive. In fact the amount of redistribution depends on how the programs are financed and how valuable the services are to individuals with different income levels.

First, a public health care program offering services that are available to all and financed by a proportional income tax will redistribute income from the rich to the poor. If there is not too much diversity of tastes and if consumption of health care is independent of income, all those with incomes below the average are subsidized by those above the average. Given the empirical fact that a majority of voters have incomes below the average, a majority of voters would approve of public provision. With diversity of tastes, different individuals prefer different levels of consumption even when incomes are the same and the "one-size-fits-all" public provision may no longer be desirable for the majority. So the trade-off is between income redistribution and preference-matching. However, in so far as consumption of medical care is mostly the responsibility of doctors, reflecting standard medical practices, the preference-matching concern is likely to be negligible.

The second way that redistribution occurs is from the healthy to the sick (or the young to the aged). The tax payments of any particular individual do not depend on that individual's morbidity. It follows that higher morbidity individuals receive insurance in the public system that is less expensive than the insurance they would get in the private market. So if a taxpayer has either high morbidity or low income, then his tax price of insurance is lower than the price of private insurance. This taxpayer will vote for public provision. The negative correlation between morbidity and income suggests that the majority below average income are also more likely to be in relatively poor health and so in favor of public insurance.

The third route to redistribution is through opting-out. Universal provision of health care by the government can redistribute welfare from the rich to the poor because the rich refuse the public health care and buy higher quality private health services financed by private insurance. For example, individuals may have to wait to receive treatment in the public system, whereas private treatment is immediate. In opting-out, they lose the value of the taxes they pay toward public insurance, and the resources available for those who remain in the public sector increases as the overall pressure on the system decreases (i.e., the waiting list shortens). So redistribution is taking place because the rich are more likely to use private health care, even though free public health care is available. This redistribution will arise even if everyone contributes the same amount to public health insurance.

Redistribution via health care is also more effective in targeting some needy groups than redistribution in cash. The majority may wish to redistribute from those who inherit good health to those who inherit poor health, which can be thought of as a form of social insurance. If individual health status could be observed, the government would simply redistribute in cash, and there would be no reason for public health insurance. But because it cannot observe an individual's poor state of health, providing health care in-kind is a better way to target those individuals. The healthy individuals are less likely to pretend to be unhealthy when health care is provided in-kind than if government were to offer cash compensation to everyone claiming to be in poor health. This is the self-selection benefit of in-kind redistribution.

9.9   Evidence

Information asymmetries have significant implications for the working of competitive markets and the scope for government intervention. Detailed policy recommendations for alleviating these problems also differ depending on whether we face the adverse selection or moral hazard problems. It is crucial to test in different markets the empirical relevance of adverse selection and moral hazard. Such a test is surprisingly simple in the insurance market because both adverse selection and moral hazard predict a positive correlation between the frequency of accident and insurance coverage. This prediction turns out to be very general and to extend to a variety of more general contexts (imperfect competition, multidimensional heterogeneity, etc.).

The key problem is that such correlation can be given two different interpretations depending on the direction of the causality. Under adverse selection high-risk agents, knowing they are more likely to have an accident, self-select by choosing more extensive coverage. Alternatively, under moral hazard agents with more extensive coverage are also less motivated to exert precaution, which may result in higher accident rates. The difference matters a lot for health insurance if we want to assess the impact of co-payments and deductibles on consumption and its welfare implications. Indeed, it is a well-documented fact that better coverage is correlated with higher medical expenses. Deductibles and co-payments are likely to be desirable if moral hazard is the main reason, since they reduce overconsumption. But, if adverse selection is the main explanation, then limiting coverage can only reduce the amount of insurance available to risk-averse agents with little welfare gain. Evidence on selection versus incentives can be tested in a number of ways, and we briefly describe some of them.

Manning et al. (1987) separate moral hazard from adverse selection by using a random experiment in which individuals are exogenously allocated to different contracts. Between 1974 and 1977 the Rand Health Insurance Experiment randomly assigned households in the United States to one out of 14 different insurance plans with different co-insurance rates and upper limits on annual out-of-pocket expenses. Compensation was paid in order to guarantee that no household would lose by participating in the experiment. Since individuals were randomly assigned to contracts, any differences in observed behavior can be interpreted as a response to the different incentive structures of the contracts. This experiment has provided some of the most interesting and robust tests of moral hazard and the sensitivity of the consumption of medical services to out-of-pocket expenditures. The demand for medical services was found to respond significantly to changes in the amount paid by the insuree. The largest decrease in the use of services arises between a free service and a contract involving a 25 percent co-payment rate.

Chiappori et al. (1998) exploit a 1993 change in French regulations to which health insurance companies responded by modifying their coverage rates in a non-uniform way. Some companies increased the level of deductibles, while others did not. They test for moral hazard by using groups of patients belonging to different companies who were confronted with different changes in co-payments and whose use of medical services was observed before and after the change in regulation. They find that the number of home visits by general practitioners significantly decreased for the patients who experienced the increase in co-payments but not for those whose coverage remained constant.

Another interesting study is by Cardon and Hendel (2001) who test for moral hazard versus adverse selection in the US employer-provided health insurance. As argued before, a contract with larger co-payments is likely to involve lower health expenditures, either because of the incentive effect of co-payments or because the high-risk self-select by choosing contracts with lower co-payments. The key identifying argument is that agents do not select their employer on the basis of the health insurance coverage. As a consequence the differences in behavior across employer plans can be attributed to incentive effects. They find strong evidence that incentives matter.

Another way to circumvent the difficulty in empirically distinguishing between adverse selection and moral hazard is to consider the annuity market. The annuity market provides insurance against the risk of outliving accumulated resources. It is more valuable to those who expect to live longer. In this market we can safely expect that individuals will not substantially modify their behavior in response to annuity income (e.g., exerting more effort to extend length of life). It follows that differential mortality rates for annuitants who purchase different types of annuities is convincing evidence that selection occurs. Finkesltein and Poterba (2004) obtain evidence of the following selection patterns: First, those who buy back-loaded annuities (annuities where payments increase over time) are longer-lived (controlling for all observables) than other annuitants, which is consistent with the fact that an annuitant with a longer life expectancy is more likely to be alive in later years when the back-loaded annuity pays out more than the flat annuity. Second, those who buy annuities making payments to the estate are shorter-lived than other annuitants, which is consistent with the fact that the possibility of payments to the annuitant's estate in the event of early death is more valuable to a short-lived annuitant.

9.10   Conclusions

The efficiency of competitive equilibrium is based on the assumption of symmetric information (or the very strong requirement of perfect information). This chapter has explored some of the consequences of relaxing this assumption. The basic points are that asymmetric information leads to inefficiency and that the inefficiency can take a number of different forms.

Under certain circumstances appropriate government intervention can make everyone better off, even though the government does not have better information than the private sector. The role of the government may also be limited by restrictions on its information. Welfare and public policy implications of the two main forms of information asymmetries are not the same, and it has been an empirical challenge to distinguish between adverse selection and moral hazard. Health insurance is a good illustration of the problems that arise and is characterized by extensive public intervention.

Further Reading

The main contributions on asymmetric information are:

Akerlof, G. 1970. The market for lemons: Quality uncertainty and the market mechanism. *Quarterly Journal of Economics* 89: 488–500.

Arrow, K. J. 1963. Uncertainty and the welfare economics of medical care. *American Economic Review* 53: 942–73.

Greenwald, B., and Stiglitz, J. E. 1986. Externalities in economies with imperfect information and incomplete markets. *Quarterly Journal of Economics* 100: 229–64.

Prescott, E., and Townsend, R. 1984. Pareto optima and competitive equilibrium with adverse selection and moral hazard. *Econometrica* 52: 21–46.

Rothschild, M., and Stiglitz, J. E. 1976. Equilibrium in competitive insurance markets: An essay in the economics of imperfect information. *Quarterly Journal of Economics* 80: 629–49.

Spence, M. 1973. Job market signaling. *Quarterly Journal of Economics* 87: 355–74.

Spence, M. 1974. *Market Signaling*. Cambridge: Harvard University Press.

A simple exposition of the moral hazard problem is in:

Arnott, R., and Stiglitz, J. E. 1988. The basic analytics of moral hazard. *Scandinavian Journal of Economics* 90: 383–413.

Applications of the self-selection concept in redistribution programs are:

Besley, T., and Coate, S. 1991. Public provision of private goods and the redistribution of income. *American Economic Review* 81: 979–84.

Blackorby, C., and Donaldson, D. 1988. Cash versus kind, self-selection, and efficient transfers. *American Economic Review* 78: 691–700.

Bruce, N., and Waldman, M. 1991. Transfer in kind: Why they can be efficient and nonpaternalistic. *American Economic Review* 81: 1345–51.

Buchanan, J. 1975. The Samaritan's Dilemma. In E. S. Phelps, ed., *Altruism, Morality and Economic Theory*. New York: Russell Sage Foundation, pp. 71–85.

Applications to health insurance are:

Besley, T., and Gouveia, M. 1994. Alternative systems of health care provision. *Economic Policy* 19: 199–258.

Cardon, J., and Hendel, I. 2001. Asymmetric information in health insurance: Evidence from the national health expenditure survey. *Rand Journal of Economics* 32: 408–27.

De Donder, P., and Hindriks, J. 2003. The politics of redistributive social insurance. *Journal of Public Economics* 87: 2639–60.

Poterba, J. 1994. Government intervention in the markets for education and health care: How and why? *NBER Working Paper* 4916.

Usher, D. 1977. The welfare economics of the socialization of commodities. *Journal of Public Economics* 8: 151–68.

Empirical testing of adverse selection and moral hazard is in:

Chiappori, P. A., Durand, F., and Geoffard, P. Y. 1998. Moral hazard and the demand for physicians services: First lessons from a French natural experiment. *European Economic Review* 42: 499–511.

Chiappori, P. A., and Salanié, B. 2003. Testing contract theory: A survey of some recent works. In M. Dewatripont, L. Hansen, and S. Turnovsky, eds., *Advances in Economics and Econometrics*, vol. 1. Cambridge: Cambridge University Press.

Finkesltein, A., and Poterba, J. 2004. Adverse selection in insurance markets: Policyholder evidence from the UK annuity market. *Journal of Political Economy* 112: 183–208.

Manning, W., Newhouse, J., Duan, N., Keeler, E., and Leibowitz, A. 1987. Health insurance and the demand for medical care: Evidence from the randomized experiment. *American Economic Review* 77: 257–77.

Exercises

9.1.   What is fair insurance? Why will a risk-averse consumer always buy full insurance when it is fair insurance?

9.2.   Should the government allow insurance companies to use genetic testing to better assess the health status of their applicants? Would this genetic testing help or hurt those who are in bad health? Would it exacerbate or mitigate the problem of adverse selection in the health insurance market? Would it increase or decrease the number of people without health insurance? Would it be a good thing?

9.3.   Are the following statements true or false?

a. An insurance company must be concerned about the possibility that someone will buy fire insurance on a building and then set fire to it. This is an example of moral hazard.

b. A life insurance company must be concerned about the possibility that the people who buy life insurance may tend to be less healthy than those who do not. This is an example of adverse selection.

c. In a market where there is separating equilibrium, different types of agents make different choices of actions.

d. Moral hazard refers to the effect of an insurance policy on the incentives of individuals to exercise care.

e. Adverse selection refers to how the magnitude of the insurance premium affects the types of individuals that buy insurance.

9.4.   Consider each of the following situations involving moral hazard. In each case identify the principal (uninformed party) and the agent (informed party) and explain why there is asymmetric information. How does the action described for each situation mitigate the moral hazard problem?

a. Car insurance companies offer discounts to customers who install anti-theft and speed-monitoring devices in their cars.

b. The International Monetary Fund conditions lending to developing countries upon the adoption of a structural adjustment plan.

c. Firms compensate top executives with options to buy company stock at a given price in the future.

d. Landlords require tenants to pay security deposits.

9.5.   Despite the negative stereotype of "women drivers," women under age of 25 are, on average, noticeably better drivers than men under 25. Consequently insurance companies have been willing to offer young women insurance with a discount of 60 percent over what they charge young men. Similar discrimination applies on the life insurance market given that women are expected to live longer. Sex-based discrimination for auto and life insurance is extremely controversial. Many people have argued that sex-based rates constitute unfair discrimination. After all some men live longer than some women, and there are some men who are better drivers than some women. In response several US states have laws mandating "unisex" insurance ratings.

a. What are the likely effects of such interference with the market forces?

b. Should the government allow insurance companies to base life insurance rates on sex? What are the risks for women and for men who were paying very different rates? Who gains and who loses?

c. Should insurance companies be allowed to base automobile insurance rates on sex, age, and marital status? What are the consequences of having some groups paying much less than they would if rates were based on actuarial differences in accident rates across sexes and ages?

9.6.   Discuss the argument that paying for human blood has the effect of lowering its average quality because people who are driven by the profit motive to provide blood are more likely to be drug addicts, alcoholics, and have serious infectious diseases than are voluntary donors.

9.7.   In California many insurance companies charge different rates depending on what part of the city you live in. Their rationale is that risk factors like theft, vandalism, and traffic congestion vary greatly from one place to the other. The result is that people who live close to each other but in adjacent zip codes may end up paying very different insurance premia.

a. What would happen to an insurance company that decided to sell insurance at the same price to all drivers with the same driving records no matter what part of the city they live in?

b. What would happen if the government decides to outlaw geographic rate differentials, given that the government cannot force private insurance companies to provide insurance against their will?

9.8.   The local government has hired someone to undertake a public project. If the project fails, it will lose $20,000. If it succeeds, the project will earn $100,000. The employee can choose to "work" or to "shirk." If she shirks, the project will fail for sure. If she works, the project will succeed half of the time but will still fail half of the time. The employee's utility is $10,000 lower if she works than if she shirks. In addition the employee could earn $10,000 in another job (where she would shirk). The government is choosing whether to pay the employee a flat wage of $20,000 (no matter how the project turns out) or performance-related pay under which the employee earns $0 if the project fails and $40,000 if it succeeds.

a. Assuming both parties are risk neutral, which compensation scheme should the government use?

b. Do you see any problem with the performance-related pay scheme when the employee is risk averse?

9.9.   Use the signaling model presented in section 9.6 to construct an example in which a government unaware of workers' productivities can improve the welfare of everyone compared to the (best) separating equilibrium by means of a cross-subsidization policy but not by banning signaling.

9.10.   A firm hires two kinds of workers, alphas and betas. One can't tell a beta from an alpha by looking at her, but an alpha will produce $3,000 worth of output per month and a beta will produce $2,500 worth of output in a month. The firm decides to distinguish alphas from betas by making them pass an examination. For each question that they get right on the exam, alphas have to spend half an hour studying and betas have to spend one hour. A worker will be paid $3,000 if she gets at least 40 answers right and $2,500 otherwise. For either type, an hour of studying is as bad as giving up $20 income. What is the equilibrium of this scheme?

9.11.   Consider a loan market to finance investment projects. All projects cost $1. Any project is either good (with probability ρ) or bad (with probability $1 - \rho$). Only investors know whether their project is good or bad. A good project yields profits of $\pi > 0$ with probability P_g and no profit with probability $1 - P_g$. A bad project makes profits of π with a lower probability P_b (with $P_b < P_g$) and no profit with a higher probability $1 - P_b$. Banks are competitive and risk neutral, which implies that banks offer loan contracts making expected profits of zero. A loan contract specifies a repayment R that is supposed to be repaid to the bank only if the project makes profit; otherwise, the investor defaults on her loan contract. The opportunity cost of funds to the bank is $r > 0$. Suppose

$$P_g \pi - [1 + r] > 0 > P_b \pi - [1 + r].$$

a. Find the equilibrium level of R and the set of projects financed. How does this depend on P_g, P_b, ρ, π, and r?

b. Now suppose that the investor can signal the quality of her project by self-financing a fraction of the project. The opportunity cost of funds to the investor is δ (with $\delta > r$ implying a costly signal). Describe the investor's payoff as a function of the type of her project, the loan repayment R and her self-financing rate. Derive the indifference curve for each type of investor in the (s, R) space. Show that the single-crossing property holds.

c. What is the best separating equilibrium of the signaling game where the investor first chooses s and banks then respond by a repayment schedule $R(s)$? How does the self-financing rate of good projects change with small changes of P_g, P_b, ρ, π, and r?

d. Compare this (best) separating equilibrium with part a.

9.12.   (Akerlof) Consider the following market for used cars. There are many sellers of used cars. Each sellers has exactly one used car to sell and is characterized by the quality of the used car he wishes to sell. Let θ, $0 \le \theta \le 1$, index the quality of a used car, and suppose that θ is uniformly distributed on the interval $[0, 1]$. If a seller of type θ sells his car at price p, his utility is $u_s(p, \theta)$. With no sale his utility is 0. Buyers receive utility $\theta - p$ if they buy a car of quality θ at price p, and receive utility 0 if they do not purchase. The quality of the car is only known to sellers, and there are enough cars to supply all potential buyers.

a. Explain why the competitive equilibrium outcome under asymmetric information requires that the average quality of cars that are put for sale conditional on price is just equal to price, $E(\theta|p) = p$. Describe the equilibrium outcome in words. In particular, describe which cars are traded in equilibrium.

b. Show that if $u_s(p, \theta) = p - \frac{\theta}{2}$, then every price $0 < p \leq \frac{1}{2}$ is an equilibrium price.

c. Find the equilibrium price when $u_s(p, \theta) = p - \sqrt{\theta}$.

d. How many equilibrium prices are there when $u_s(p, \theta) = p - \theta^3$?

e. Which (if any) of the preceding outcomes are Pareto-efficient? Describe Pareto-improvements whenever possible.

9.13.   It is known that some fraction d of all new cars are defective. Defective cars cannot be identified as such except by those who own them. Each consumer is risk neutral and values a nondefective car at $16,000. New cars sell for $14,000 each, and used ones for $2,000. If cars do not depreciate physically with use, what is the proportion d of defective new cars?

9.14.   In the preceding question, assume that new cars sell for $18,000 and used cars sell for $2,000. If there is no depreciation and risk-neutral consumers know that 20 percent of all new cars are defective, how much do the consumers value a nondefective car?

9.15.   There are two types of jobs in the economy, good and bad, and two types of workers, qualified and unqualified. The population consists of 60 percent qualified and 40 percent unqualified. In a bad job, either type of worker produces the same 10 units of output. In a good job, a qualified worker produces 100 and an unqualified worker produces 0. There are numerous job openings of each type, and companies must pay for each type of job what they expect the appointee to produce. The worker's type is unknown before hiring, but the qualified workers can signal their type (e.g., by getting educated or some other means). The cost of signaling to level s for a qualified worker is $\frac{s^2}{2}$ and for an unqualified worker is s^2. The signaling costs are measured in the same units as output, and s must be an integer (e.g., number of years of education).

a. What is the minimum level of s that will achieve separation?

b. Suppose that the signal is no longer available. Which kinds of job will be filled by which types of workers, and at what wages? Who gains and who loses?

9.16.   The government can help those people most in need by either giving them cash or providing free meals. What is the argument for giving cash? What kind of argument based on asymmetric information could support the claim that free meals (an in-kind transfer) are better than the cash handout? Can such an argument apply to free education?

9.17.   Explain why an automaker's willingness to offer a resale guarantee for its cars may serve as a signal of their quality.

9.18.   The design of the health care system involves issues of information at several points. The potential users (patients) are better informed about their own state of health and lifestyle than insurance companies. The health providers (doctors and hospitals) know more about what patients need than do either the patients themselves or the insurance companies. Providers also know more about their own skills and efforts. Insurance companies have statistical information about outcomes of treatments and surgical procedures from past records. The drug companies know more about the efficacy of drugs than do others. As is usual, the parties have different interests, so they do not have a natural inclination to share their information fully or accurately with others.

a. From this perspective, consider the relative merits of the following payments schemes:

i. A fee for service versus capitation fees to doctors.

ii. Comprehensive premiums per year versus payment for each visit for patients.

b. Which payments schemes are likely to be most beneficial to the patients and which to the providers?

c. What are the relative merits of private insurance compared to coverage of costs from general tax revenues?

IV POLITICAL ECONOMY

10 Voting

10.1 Introduction

Voting is the most commonly employed method of resolving a diversity of views or eliciting expressions of preference. It is used to determine the outcome of elections from local to supra-national level. Within organizations, voting determines who is elected to committees, and it governs the decision-making of those committees. Voting is a universal tool that is encountered in all spheres of life. The prevalence of voting, its use in electing governments, and its use by those governments elected to reach decisions, is the basis for the considerable interest in the properties of voting.

The natural question to ask of voting is whether it is a good method of making decisions. There are two major properties to look for in a good method. First is the success or failure of the method in achieving a clear-cut decision. Second is the issue of whether voting always produces an outcome that is efficient. Voting would be of limited value if it frequently left the choice of outcome unresolved or led to a choice that was clearly inferior to other alternatives. Whether voting satisfies these properties is shown to be somewhat dependent on the precise method of voting adopted. Ordinary majority voting is very familiar, but it is only one among a number of ways of voting. Several of these methods of voting will be introduced and analyzed alongside the standard form of majority voting.

10.2 Stability

Voting is an example of collective choice—the process by which a group (or collective) reaches a decision. A major issue of collective choice is *stability*. By stability we mean the tendency of the decision-making process to eventually reach a settled conclusion, and not to keep jumping around between alternatives. We begin this chapter by a simple illustration of the central fact that when you have a large group of people, with conflicting preferences, stability in matching preferences is not guaranteed.

The example involves three married couples living as neighbors on a remote island. Initially the couples are comprised of Alil and Alice, Bob and Beth, and Carl and Carol. We assume that each husband has his own preference list of the women as potential wives and each wife has a list of preferences among husbands, each ranking partners from best to worst. We also make the assumption that the top preference for any given wife may or may not be her own husband, and similarly for the men. To avoid untenable frustrations developing, the island society introduces a rule that if two people prefer each other to their existing partners they can reform as a new couple. For example, if Alil prefers Beth to his own wife, Alice, and Beth prefers Alil to her own husband, Bob, then Alil can join Beth, leaving Bob and Alice to console each other. (It is forbidden on this island to live alone or to form a couple with someone of the same sex.)

Now consider the lists of preferences for the participants given in table 10.1. It follows from these preferences that Beth will join Alil (she prefers him to Bob, and Alil prefers her to Alice), then she will continue her ascension to Carl (who prefers her to Carol, while he is her first choice). By then Alice has been left with Bob, her worst choice, so she will go to Carl, and finally back to Alil, her favorite. In every case the leaving male is also improving his own position. But now the end result is that this round of spouse trading leaves us back exactly with the initial situation, so the cycle can begin again, and go on forever. The attempt to prevent frustration has lead to an unstable society.

The example has shown that stability may not be achieved. One argument for wanting stability is that it describes a settled outcome in which a final decision has been reached. If the process of changing position is costly, as it would be in our example, then stability would be beneficial. It can also be argued that there are occasions when stability is not necessarily desirable. In terms of the example, consider the extreme case where each man is married to his first choice but each husband is at the bottom of his wife's preference list. This would be a stable outcome because no man would be interested in switching and no wife can switch either because she cannot find an unhappy man who prefers her. So it is stable but not necessarily desirable, since the stability is forcing some of the participants to remain with unwanted choices.

Table 10.1
Stability

Alil	Alice	Bob	Beth	Carl	Carol
Beth	Alil	Beth	Carl	Alice	Bob
Alice	Carl	Alice	Alil	Beth	Carl
Carol	Bob	Carol	Bob	Carol	Alil

10.3   Impossibility

Determining the preferences of an individual is just a matter of accepting that an individual's judgment cannot be open to dispute. In contrast, determining the preferences of a group of people is not a simple matter. And that is what social choice theory (including voting as one particular method) is all about. Social choice takes a given set of individual preferences and tries to aggregate them into a social preference.

The central result of the theory of social choice, *Arrow's Impossibility Theorem*, says that there is no way to devise a collective decision-making process that satisfies a few commonsense requirements and works in all circumstances. If there are only two options, majority voting works just fine, but with more than two we can get into trouble. Despite all the talk about the "will of the people," it is not easy—in fact the theorem proves it impossible—to always determine what that will is. This is the remarkable fact of Arrow's Impossibility Theorem.

Before presenting the theorem, a taste of it can be obtained with the simplest case of three voters with the (conflicting) rankings over three options shown in table 10.2. Every voter has transitive preferences over the three options. For example, voter 1 prefers *a* to *b* to *c*, and therefore *a* to *c*. As individuals, the voters are entirely self-consistent in their preferences.

Now suppose that we use majority rule to select one of these options. We see that two out of three voters prefer *a* to *b*, while two out of three prefer *b* to *c*, and two out of three prefer *c* to *a*. At the collective level there is a cycle in preference and no decision is possible. We say that such collective preferences are intransitive, meaning that the preference for *a* over *b* and for *b* over *c* does not imply *a* is preferred to *c*. As the example shows, intransitivity of group preferences can arise even when individual preferences are transitive. This generation of social intransitivity from individual transitivity is called the *Condorcet paradox*.

Table 10.2
Condorcet paradox

Voter 1	Voter 2	Voter 3
a	*c*	*b*
b	*a*	*c*
c	*b*	*a*

The general problem addressed by Arrow in 1951 was to seek a way of aggregating individual rankings over options into a collective ranking. In doing so, difficulties such as the Condorcet paradox had to be avoided. Arrow's approach was to start from a set of requirements that a collective ranking must satisfy and then consider if any ranking could be found that met them all. These conditions are now listed and explained.

Condition *I* (Independence of irrelevant alternatives) Adding new options should not affect the initial ranking of the old options, so the collective ranking over the old options should be unchanged.

For example, suppose that a group prefers option *A* to option *C*, and the new option *B* is introduced. Wherever it fits into each individual's ranking, condition *I* requires that the group preference should not switch to *C* over *A*. They may like or dislike the new option *B*, but their relative preferences for other options should not change. If this condition was not imposed on collective decision-making, any decision could be invalidated by bringing in new irrelevant (inferior) options. Since it is always possible to add new options, no decision would ever be made.

Condition *N* (Nondictatorship) The collective preference should not be determined by the preferences of one individual.

This is the weakest equity requirement. Having a dictatorship as a collective decision process may solve transitivity problems, but it is manifestly unfair to the other individuals. Any conception of democracy aspires to some form of equity among all the voters.

Condition *P* (Pareto criterion) If everybody agrees on the ranking of all the possible options, so should the group; the collective ranking should coincide with the common individual ranking.

The Pareto condition requires that unanimity should prevail where it arises. It is hardly possible to argue with this condition.

Condition *U* (Unrestricted domain) The collective choice method should accommodate any possible individual ranking of options.

This is the requirement that the collective choice method should work in all circumstances so that the method is not constructed in such a way as to rule out (arbitrarily), or fail to work on, some possible individual rankings of alternatives.

Condition *T* (Transitivity)   If the group prefers *A* to *B* and *B* to *C*, then the group cannot prefer *C* to *A*.

This is merely a consistency requirement that ensures that a choice can always be made from any set of alternatives. The Condorcet paradox shows that majority voting fails to meet this condition and can lead to cycles in collective preference.

That is it, and one can hardly disagree with any of these requirements. Each one seems highly reasonable taken individually. Yet the remarkable result that Arrow discovered is that there is no way to devise a collective choice method that satisfies them all simultaneously.

Theorem 4 (Arrow's Impossibility Theorem)   When choosing among more than two options, there exists no collective decision-making process that satisfies the conditions *I, N, P, U, T*.

The proof is slightly, rather than very, complicated and is quite formal. We will not reproduce it here. The intuition underlying the proof is clear enough and follows this reasoning:

1. The unrestricted domain condition allows for preferences such that no option is unanimously preferred.

2. The independence of irrelevant alternatives forces the social ranking over any two options to be based exclusively on the individual preferences over those two options only.

3. From the Condorcet paradox we know that a cycle can emerge from three successive pairwise comparisons.

4. The transitivity requirement forces a choice among the three options.

5. The only method for deciding must give one individual all the power, thus contradicting the nondictatorship requirement.

The implication of Arrow's Impossibility Theorem is that any search for a "perfect" method of collective decision-making is doomed to failure. Whatever process is devised, a situation can be constructed in which it will fail to deliver an outcome that satisfies one or more of the conditions *I, N, P, U, T*. As a consequence all collective decision-making must make the most of imperfect decision rules.

10.4   Majority Rule

In any situation involving only two options, majority rule simply requires that the option with the majority of votes is chosen. Unless unanimity is possible, asking that the few give way to the many is a very natural alternative to dictatorship. The process of majority voting is now placed into context and its implications determined.

10.4.1   May's Theorem

Nondictatorship is a very weak interpretation of the principles of democracy. A widely held view is that democracy should treat all the voters in the same way. This symmetry requirement is called *Anonymity*. It requires that permuting the names of any two individuals does not change the group preference. Thus Anonymity implies that there cannot be any dictator. Another natural symmetry requirement is that the collective decision-making process should treat all possible options alike. No apparent bias in favor of one option should be introduced. This symmetric treatment of the various options is called *Neutrality*.

Now a fundamental result due to May is that majority rule is the obvious way to implement these principles of democracy (Anonymity and Neutrality) in social decision-making when only two options are considered at a time. The theorem asserts that majority rule is the unique way of doing so if the conditions of *Decisiveness* (i.e., the social decision rule must pick a winner) and *Positive Responsiveness* (i.e., increasing the vote for the winning option should not lead to the declaration of another option the winner) are also imposed.

Theorem 5 (May's theorem)   When choosing among only two options, there is only one collective decision-making process that satisfies the requirements of Anonymity, Neutrality, Decisiveness, and Positive Responsiveness. This process is majority rule.

Simple majority rule is the best social choice procedure if we consider only two options at a time. Doing so is not at all unusual in the real world. For instance, when a vote is called in a legislative assembly, there are usually only two possible options: to approve or to reject some specific proposal that is on the floor. Also in a situation of two-party political competition voters again face a binary choice. Therefore interest in other procedures arises only when there are more than two options to consider.

10.4.2   Condorcet Winner

When there are only two options, majority rule is a simple and compelling method for social choice. When there are more than two options to be considered at any time, we can still apply the principle of majority voting by using binary agendas that allow us to reduce the problem of choosing among many options to a sequence of votes over two alternatives at a time.

For example, one simple binary agenda for choosing among the three options $\{a, b, c\}$ in the Condorcet paradox is as follows. First, there is a vote on a against b. Then, the winner of this first vote is opposed to c. The winner of this second vote is the chosen option. The most famous pairwise voting method is the *Condorcet method*. This consists of a complete round-robin of majority votes, opposing each option against all of the others. The option that defeats all others in pairwise majority voting is called a *Condorcet winner*, after Condorcet suggested that such an option should be declared the winner. That is, using the symbol $\succ$ to denote majority preference, a Condorcet winner is an option x such that $x \succ y$ for every other option y in the set of possible options X.

The problem is that the existence of a Condorcet winner requires very special configurations of individual preferences. For instance, with the preferences given in the Condorcet paradox, there is no Condorcet winner. So a natural question to ask is under what conditions a Condorcet winner does exist.

10.4.3   Median Voter Theorems

When the policy space is one-dimensional, sufficient (but not necessary) conditions for the existence of a Condorcet winner are given by the *Median Voter Theorems*. One version of these theorems refers to single-peaked preferences, while the other version refers to single-crossing preferences. The two conditions of single-peaked and single-crossing preferences are logically independent, but both conditions give the same conclusion that the median position is a Condorcet winner.

$$1 \quad 2 \quad 3 \quad 4 \qquad \text{................} \qquad n-3 \; n-2 \; n-1 \; n$$

Figure 10.1
Location of households

As an example of single-peaked preferences, consider figure 10.1 depicting a population of consumers who are located at equally spaced positions along a straight road. A bus stop is to be located somewhere on this road. It is assumed that all consumers prefer the stop to be located as close as possible to their own homes. If the location of the bus stop is to be determined by majority voting (taking pairwise comparisons again), which location will be chosen?

When there is an odd number of houseowners, the answer to this question is clear-cut. Given any pair of alternatives, a household will vote for that which is closest to their own location. The location that is the closest choice for the largest number of voters will receive a majority of votes.

Now consider a voting process in which votes are taken over every possible pair of alternatives. This is very much in the form of a thought-process rather than a practical suggestion, since there must be many rounds of voting and the process will rapidly becomes impractical if there are many alternatives. Putting this difficulty aside, it can easily be seen that this process will lead to the central outcome being the chosen alternative. This location wins all votes and is the Condorcet winner. Expressed differently, the location preferred by the median voter (i.e., the voter in the center) will be chosen. At least half the population will always vote for this.

This result is the basis of the Median Voter Theorem. When there is an even number of voters, there is no median voter but the two locations closest to the center will both beat any other locations in pairwise comparisons. They will tie when they are directly compared. The chosen location must therefore lie somewhere between them.

The essential feature that lies behind the reasoning of the example is that each consumer has single-peaked preferences, and that the decision is one-dimensional. Preferences are termed single-peaked when there is a single preferred option. Figure 10.2b illustrates preferences that satisfy this condition, whereas those in figure 10.2a are not single-peaked. In the bus stop example, each consumer most prefers a location close to home and ranks the others according to the how close they are to the ideal. Such preference looks exactly like those in figure 10.2b. The choice variable is one-dimensional because it relates to locations along a line.

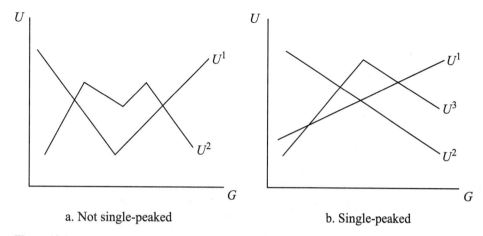

a. Not single-peaked   b. Single-peaked

Figure 10.2
Single-peaked preferences

The first general form of the Median Voter Theorem can be stated as follows:

Theorem 6 (Median Voter Theorem I: Single-peaked version)   Suppose that there is an odd number of voters and that the policy space is one-dimensional (so that the options can be put in a transitive order). If the voters have single-peaked preferences, then the median of the distribution of voters' preferred options is a Condorcet winner.

The idea of median voting has also been applied to the analysis of politics. Instead of considering the line in figure 10.1 as a geographical identity, view it as a representation of the political spectrum running from left to right. The houseowners then becomes voters and their locations represent political preferences. Let there be two parties who can choose their location upon the line. A location in this sense represents the manifesto on which they stand. Where will the parties choose to locate? Assume as above that the voters always vote for the party nearest to their location. Now fix the location of one party at any point other than the center and consider the choice of the other. Clearly, if the second party locates next to the first party on the side containing more than half the electorate, it will win a majority of the vote. Realizing this, the first party would not be content with its location. It follows that the only possible equilibrium set of locations for the parties is to be side by side at the center of the political spectrum.

This agglomeration at the centre is called *Hotelling's principle of minimal differentiation* and has been influential in political modeling. The reasoning underlying it can be observed in the move of the Democrats in the United States and the Labor party in the United Kingdom to the right in order to crowd out the Republicans and Conservatives respectively. The result also shows how ideas developed in economics can have useful applications elsewhere.

Although a powerful result, the Median Voter Theorem does have significant drawbacks. The first is that the literal application of the theorem requires that there be an odd number of voters. This condition ensures that there is a majority in favor of the median. When there is an even number of voters, there will be a tie in voting over all locations between the two central voters. The theorem is then silent on which of these locations will eventually be chosen. In this case, though, there is a median tendency. The second, and most significant drawback, is that the Median Voter Theorem is applicable only when the decision over which voting is taking place has a single dimension. This point will be investigated in the next section. Before doing that let us consider the single-crossing version of the Median Voter Theorem.

The single-crossing version of the Median Voter Theorem assumes not only that the policy space is transitively ordered, say from left to right (and thus one-dimensional), but also that the voters can be transitively ordered, say from left to right in the political spectrum. The interpretation is that voters at the left prefer left options more than voters at the right. This second assumption is called the single-crossing property of preferences. Formally,

Definition (Single-crossing property)   For any two voters i and j such that $i < j$ (voter i is to the left of voter j), and for any two options x and y such that $x < y$ (x is to the left of y).

Definition 5   (i) If $u^j(x) > u^j(y)$, then $u^i(x) > u^i(y)$, and (ii) if $u^i(y) > u^i(x)$, then $u^j(y) > u^j(x)$.

The median voter is characterized as the median individual on the left to right ordering of voters, so that half the voters are to the left of the median voter and the other half is to the right. Therefore, according to the single-crossing property, for any two options x and y, with $x < y$, if the median voter prefers x, then all the voters to the left also prefer x, and if the median voter prefers y, then all the voters to the right also prefer y. So there is always a majority of voters who agree with the median voter, and the option preferred by the median voter is a Condorcet winner.

Theorem 7 (Median Voter Theorem II: Single-crossing version)   Suppose that there is an odd number of voters and that the policy space is one-dimensional (so that the options can be put in a transitive order). If the preferences of the set of voters satisfy the single-crossing property, then the preferred option of the median voter is a Condorcet winner.

Single-crossing and single-peakedness are different conditions on preferences. But both give us the same result that the median voter's preferred option is a Condorcet winner. However, there is a subtle difference. With the single-peakedness property, we refer to the median of the voters' preferred options, but with the single-crossing property, we refer to the preferred option of the median voter. Notice that single-crossing and single-peakedness are logically independent as the example in figure 10.3 illustrates. The options are ranked left to right along the horizontal axis, and the individual 3 is to the left of 2 who is to the left of 1. It can be checked that single-crossing holds for any pair of options but single-peakedness does not hold for individual 2. So one property may fail to hold when the other is satisfied.

An attractive aspect of the Median Voter Theorem is that it does not depend on the intensity of preferences, and thus nobody has an incentive to misrepresent

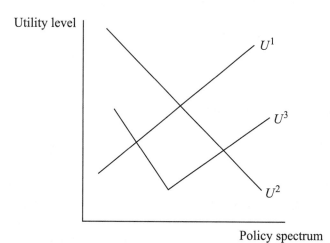

Figure 10.3
Single-crossing without single-peakedness

their preferences. This implies that honest, or sincere, voting is the best strategy for everyone. Indeed, for a voter to the left of the median, misrepresenting preference more to the left does not change the median and therefore the final outcome, whereas misrepresenting preferences more to the right either does nothing or moves the final outcome further away from his preferred outcome. Following the same reasoning, a voter to the right of the median has no incentive to misrepresent his preferences either way. Last, the median gets his most-preferred outcome and thus cannot benefit from misrepresenting his preferences.

Having seen how the Median Voter Theorem leads to a clearly predicted outcome, we can now inquire whether this outcome is efficient. The chosen outcome reflects the preferences of the median voter, so the efficient choice will only be made if this is the most preferred alternative for the median voter. Obviously there is no reason why this should be the case. Therefore the Median Voter Theorem will not in general produce an efficient choice. In addition, without knowing the precise details, it is not possible to predict whether majority voting will lead, via the Median Voter Theorem, to a choice that lies to the left or to the right of the efficient choice.

A further problem with the Median Voter Theorem is its limited applicability. It always works when policy choices can be reduced to one dimension but only works in restricted circumstances where there is more than one dimension. We now demonstrate this point.

10.4.4   Multidimensional Voting

The problem of choosing the location of the bus stop was one-dimensional. A second dimension could be introduced into this example by extending the vote to determine both the location of the bus stop and the time at which the bus is to arrive. The important observation for majority voting is that when this extension is made there is no longer any implication that single-peaked preferences will lead to a transitive ranking of alternatives.

This finding can be illustrated by considering the indifference curves of a consumer over the two-dimensional space of location and time. To do this, consider location as the horizontal axis and time as the vertical axis with the origin at the far left of the street and midnight respectively. The meaning of single-peaked preferences in this situation is that a consumer has a most-preferred location and any move in a straight line away from this must lead to a continuous decrease in utility. This is illustrated in figure 10.4 where x_i denotes the most preferred loca-

Time

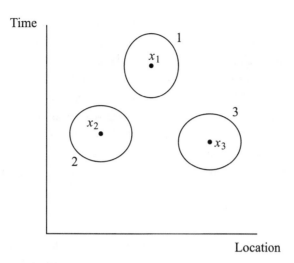

Location

Figure 10.4
Single-peakedness in multidimensions

Table 10.3
Rankings

Voter 1	Voter 2	Voter 3
x_1	x_2	x_3
x_2	x_3	x_1
x_3	x_1	x_2

tion of i and the oval around this point is one of the consumer's indifference curves.

Using this machinery, it is now possible to show that the Median Voter Theorem does not apply and majority voting fails to generate a transitive outcome. The three voters, denoted 1, 2, and 3, have preferred locations x_1, x_2, and x_3. Assume that voting is to decide which of these three locations is to be chosen (this is not necessary for the argument, as will become clear, but it does simplify it). The rankings of the three consumers of these alternatives in table 10.3 are consistent with the preferences represented by the ovals in figure 10.4. Contrasting these to table 10.2, one can see immediately that these are exactly the rankings that generate an intransitive social ordering through majority voting. Consequently, even though preferences are single-peaked, the social ordering is intransitive and the

Median Voter Theorem fails. Hence the theorem does not extend beyond one-dimensional choice problems. It is worth noting that if voting was carried out on each dimension separately, then voter 1 would be the median voter on the location dimension and voter 2 would be the median voter on the time dimension. So the time voting outcome will be given by the projection of x_2 on the vertical axis and the location voting outcome will be given by the projection of x_1 on the horizontal axis. The problem with this *item-by-item voting* is that it can generate, for some preferences, an inefficient voting outcome. This is the case when the chosen point lies outside the triangle formed by the voters' blisspoints x_1, x_2, and x_3.

10.4.5   Agenda Manipulation

In a situation in which there is no Condorcet winner, the door is opened to agenda manipulation. This is because changing the agenda, meaning the order in which the votes over pairs of alternatives are taken, can change the voting outcome. Thus the agenda-setter may have substantial power to influence the voting outcome. To determine the degree of the agenda-setter's power, we must find the set of outcomes that can be achieved through agenda manipulation.

To see how agenda-setting can be effective, suppose that there are three voters with preferences as in the Condorcet paradox (described in table 10.2). Then there is a majority (voters 1 and 2) who prefer a over b, there is a majority (voters 2 and 3) who prefer c over a, and there is a majority (voters 1 and 3) who prefer b over c. Given these voters' preferences, what will be the outcome of different binary agendas? The answer is that when voters vote sincerely, then it is possible to set the agenda so that any of the three options can be the ultimate winner. For example, to obtain option a as the final outcome, it suffices to first oppose b against c (knowing that b will defeat c) and then at the second stage to oppose the winner b against a (knowing that a will defeat b). Similarly, to get b as the final outcome, it suffices to oppose a against c at the first stage (given that c will defeat a) and then the winner c against b (given that b will defeat c). These observations show how the choice of agenda can affect the outcome.

This reasoning is based on the assumption that voters vote sincerely. However, the voters may respond to agenda manipulation by misrepresenting their preferences. That is, they may vote strategically. Voters can choose to vote for options that are not actually their most-preferred options if they believe that such behavior in the earlier ballots can affect the final outcome in their favor. For example, if we first oppose b against c, then voter 2 may vote for c rather than b. This ensures that c goes on to oppose a. Option c will win, an outcome preferred by voter 2 to the victory for a that emerges with sincere voting. So voters may not vote for their preferred option in order to prevent their worst option from winning. The question is then how strategic voting affects the set of options that could be achieved by agenda-manipulation. Such outcomes are called *sophisticated outcomes* of binary agendas, because voters anticipate what the ultimate result will be, for a given agenda, and vote optimally in earlier stages.

A remarkable result, due to Miller, is that strategic voting (relative to sincere voting) does not alter the set of outcomes that can be achieved by agenda manipulation when the agenda-setter can design any binary agendas, provided only that every option must be included in the agenda. Miller called the set that can be achieved the *top cycle*.

When there exists a Condorcet winner, the top cycle reduces to that single option. With preferences as in the Condorcet paradox, the top cycle contains all three options $\{a, b, c\}$. For example, option b can be obtained by the following agenda (different from the agenda under sincere voting): at the first stage, a is opposed to b, then the winner is opposed to c. This binary agenda is represented in figure 10.5.

The agenda begins at the top, and at each stage the voters must vote with the effect of moving down the agenda tree along the branch that will defeat the other with a sophisticated majority vote. To resolve this binary agenda, sophisticated voters must anticipate the outcome of the second stage and vote optimally in the first stage. Either the second stage involves c against a, and thus c will beat a, or the second stage involves c against b, and thus b will beat c (as voters will vote sincerely in this last stage). So the voters should anticipate that in the first stage voting for a will in fact lead to the ultimate outcome c, whereas voting for b will

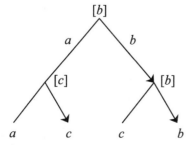

Figure 10.5
Binary agenda

Table 10.4
Top cycle

Voter 1	Voter 2	Voter 3
a	c	b
b	d	c
c	a	d
d	b	a

lead to the ultimate outcome b (as displayed in parentheses). So, in voting for a in the first stage, they vote in effect for c, whereas voting for b in the first stage effectively leads to the choice of b as the ultimate outcome. Because b is preferred by a majority to c, it follows that a majority of voters should vote for b at the first stage (even though a majority prefers a over b).

The problem with the top cycle is that it can contain options that are Pareto-dominated. To see this, suppose that the preferences are as in the Condorcet paradox, and add a fourth alternative d that falls just below c in every individual's preference. The resulting rankings are give in table 10.4. Note that there is a cycle: two out of three prefer b to c, while two out of three prefer a to b, and two out of three prefer d to a, and last all prefer c to d, making it a full circle. So d is included in the top cycle, even though d is Pareto-dominated by c.

The situation is in fact worse than this. An important theorem, due to McKelvey, says that if there is no Condorcet winner, then the top cycle is very large and can even coincide with the full set of alternatives. There are two implications of this result. First, the agenda-setter can bring about any possible option as the ultimate voting outcome. So the power of the agenda-setter may be substantial. Such dependence implies that the outcome chosen by majority rule cannot be characterized, in general, as the expression of the voters' will. Second, the existence of a voting cycle makes the voting outcome arbitrary and unpredictable, with very little normative appeal.

We know that the existence of a Condorcet winner requires very special conditions on voters' preferences. In general, with preferences that do not have the single-peakedness or single-crossing properties on a simple one-dimensional issue space, we should not generally expect that a Condorcet winner exists. For example, Fishburn has shown us that when voters' preferences are drawn randomly and independently from the set of all possible preferences, then the probability of a Condorcet winner existing tends to zero as the number of possible options goes to infinity.

Before embarking on the alternatives to majority rule, let us present some Condorcet-consistent selection procedures; that is, procedures that select the Condorcet winner as the single winner when it exists. The first, due to Miller, is the *uncovered set*. An option x is covered if there exists some other option y such that (1) y beats x (with a majority of votes) and (2) y beats any option z that x can beat. If x is Pareto-dominated by some option, then x must be covered. The uncovered set is the set of options that are not covered. For the preferences such as in top cycle example above, d is covered by c because d is below c in everyone's ranking. Thus the uncovered set is a subset of the top cycle.

If more restrictions are imposed on the agenda, then it is possible to reduce substantially the set of possible voting outcomes. One notable example is the successive-elimination agenda according to which all options are put into an ordered list, and voters are asked to eliminate the first or second option, and thereafter the previous winner or the next option. The option surviving this successive elimination is the winner, and all eliminations are resolved by sophisticated majority votes. The *Bank's set* is the set of options that can be achieved as (sophisticated) outcomes of the successive-elimination agendas. It is a subset of the uncovered set.

10.5 Alternatives to Majority Rule

Even if one considers the principle of majority rule to be attractive, the failure to select the Condorcet winner when one exists may be regarded as a serious weakness of majority rule as a voting procedure. This is especially relevant because many of the most popular alternatives to majority rule also do not always choose the Condorcet winner when one does exist, although they always pick a winner even when a Condorcet winner does not exist. This is the case for all the *scoring rule methods*, such as plurality voting, approval voting, and Borda voting.

Each scoring rule method selects as a winner the option with the highest aggregate score. The difference is in the score voters can give to each option. Under *plurality voting*, voters give 1 point to their first choice and 0 points to all other options. Thus only information on each voter's most preferred option is used. Under *approval voting*, voters can give 1 point to more than one option, in fact to as many or as few options as they want. Under *Borda voting*, voters give the

Table 10.5
Borda voting

(3)	(2)	(2)
a	c	b
b	a	c
c	b	a

highest possible score to their first choice, and then progressively lower scores to worse choices.

10.5.1 Borda Voting

Borda voting (or weighted voting) is a scoring rule. With n options each voter's first choice gets n points, the second choice gets $n - 1$ points, and so forth, down to a minimum of 1 point for the the worst choice. Then the scores are added up, and the option with the *highest* score wins. It is very simple, and almost always picks a winner (even if there is no Condorcet winner). So a fair question is: Which requirements of Arrow's theorem does it violate?

Suppose there are seven voters whose preferences over three options $\{a, b, c\}$ are as shown in table 10.5 (with numbers in parentheses representing the number of voters). Thus three voters have a as their first choice, b as their second, and c as their third.

Clearly, there is no Condorcet winner: five out of the seven voters prefer a to b, and five out of seven prefer b to c, and then four out of seven prefer c to a, which leads to a voting cycle. Applying the Borda method as described above, it is easy to see that a with three first places, two second places, and two third places will be the Borda winner with 15 points (while b gets 14 points and c gets 13 points). So we get the Borda ranking $a \succ b \succ c$, where the symbol $\succ$ denotes strict preference. But now let us introduce a new option d. This becomes the first choice of three voters but a majority prefer c, the worst option under Borda rule, to the new alternative d. The new preference lists are given in table 10.6.

If we compute the scores with the Borda method (now with points from one to four), the election results are different: d will be the Borda winner with 22 points, c will be second with 17 points, b will be third with 16 points and a will be fourth with 15 points. So the introduction of the new option d has reversed the Borda

Table 10.6
Independence of irrelevant alternatives

(3)	(2)	(2)
d	c	b
a	d	c
b	a	d
c	b	a

Table 10.7
Plurality voting

(2)	(3)	(4)
a	b	c
b	a	a
c	c	b

ranking between the original alternatives to $a \prec b \prec c$. This reversal of the ranking shows that the Borda rule violates the independence of irrelevant alternatives and should be unacceptable in a voting procedure.

This example illustrates the importance of Arrow's condition I. Without imposing this requirement it would be easy to manipulate the voting outcome by adding or removing irrelevant alternatives without any real chance of them winning the election in order to alter the chance of real contenders winning.

10.5.2   Plurality Voting

Under *plurality voting* only the first choice of each voter matters and is given one point. Choices other than the first do not count at all. These scores are added and the option with the highest score is the plurality winner. Therefore the plurality winner is the option that is ranked first by the largest number of voters.

Consider the voters' preferences over the three options given in table 10.7. Clearly, a majority of voters rate c as worst option but it also has a dedicated minority who rate it best (four out of nine voters). Under plurality voting c is the winner, with four first-place votes, while b and a have three and two respectively.

The example illustrates the problem that the plurality rule fails to select the Condorcet winner, which in this case is a (a beats both b and c with majority votes). The reason for this is that plurality voting dispenses with all information other than about the first choices.

10.5.3   Approval Voting

One problem with plurality rule is that voters don't always have an incentive to vote sincerely. Any rule that limits each voter to cast a vote for only one option forces the voters to consider how likely it is that their first-choice will win the election. If the first choice option is unlikely to win, the voters may instead vote for a second (or even lower) choice to prevent the election of a worse option.

In response to this risk of misrepresentation of preferences (i.e., strategic voting), Brams and Fishburn have proposed the *approval voting* procedure. They argue that this procedure allows voters to express their true preferences. Under approval voting voters may each vote (approve) for as many options as they like. Approving one option does not exclude approving any other options. So there is no cost in voting for an option that is unlikely to win. The winning option is the one that gathers the most votes. This procedure is simpler than Borda rule because instead of giving a score for all the possible options, voters only need to separate the options they approve of from those they do not. Approval voting also has the advantage over pairwise voting procedures that voters need only vote once, instead of engaging in a repetition of binary votes (as in the Condorcet method).

The problem with approval voting is that it may fail to pick the Condorcet winner when one exists. Suppose that there are five voters with the preferences shown in table 10.8. With pairwise majority voting, a beats both b and c with a majority of 3 and 4 votes out of 5 respectively, making a a Condorcet winner. Now consider approval voting, and suppose that each voter gives his approval votes to the

Table 10.8
Approval voting

(3)	(1)	(1)
a	b	c
b	a	b
c	c	a

first and second choices on his list but not the bottom choice. Then b will be the winner with 5 approval votes (everyone gives it an approval vote), a will be second with 4 approval votes (one voter does not approve this option), and c will be third with 1 vote. So approval voting fails to pick the Condorcet winner.

10.5.4   Runoff Voting

The *runoff* is a very common scheme used in many presidential and parliamentary elections. Under this scheme only first-place votes are counted, and if there is no majority, there is a second runoff election involving only the two strongest candidates. The purpose of a runoff is to eliminate the least-preferred options. Runoff voting seems fair, and it is very widely used. However, runoff has two drawbacks. First, it may fail to select a Condorcet winner when it exists; second, it can violate *positive responsiveness*, which is a fundamental principle of democracy. Let us consider these two problems in turn.

The failure to select a Condorcet winner is easily seen by considering the same set of voters' preferences as for the plurality voting example (table 10.7). Recall that in this example, a is the Condorcet winner. In the first round, c has 4 votes, b has 3 votes, and a has 2 votes. So a is eliminated and the second runoff election is between b and c. Supporters of the eliminated option, a, move to their second choice, b; that would give b an additional two votes in the runoff, and a decisive victory over c (with 5 votes against 4). So this runoff voting fails to select the Condorcet winner, a.

To illustrate the violation of positive responsiveness, consider the example in table 10.9, which is due to Brams, with 4 options and 17 voters. There is no Condorcet winner: a beats b, c beats a, and b beats c. Under runoff voting, the result of the first election is a tie between options a and b, with 6 votes each, while c is eliminated, with only 5 votes. There is no majority, and a runoff is necessary.

Table 10.9
Runoff voting

(6)	(5)	(4)	(2)
a	c	b	b
b	a	c	a
c	b	a	c

In the runoff between a and b, the supporters of c move to their second choice, a, giving a an extra 5 votes and and a decisive victory for a over b. This seems fair: c is the least-preferred option and there is a majority of voters who prefer a over b.

Now suppose that preferences are changed so that option a attracts extra supporters from the two voters in the last column who switch their first choice from b to a. Then a will lose! Indeed, the effect of this switch in preferences is that b is now the option eliminated in the first election, and there is still no majority. Thus a runoff is necessary between a and c. The disappointed supporters of b move to their second choice giving 5 more votes to c and the ultimate victory over a. The upshot is that by attracting more supports, a can lose a runoff election it would have won without that extra support.

10.6   The Paradox of Voting

The working assumption employed in analyzing voting so far has been that all voters choose to cast their votes. It is natural to question whether this assumption is reasonable. Although in some countries voting is a legal obligation, in others it is not. The observation that many of the latter countries frequently experience low voter turnouts in elections suggests that the assumption is unjustified.

Participation in voting almost always involve costs. There is the direct cost of traveling to the point at which voting takes place, and there is also the cost of the time employed. If the individuals involved in voting are rational utility-maximizers, then they will only choose to vote if the expected benefits of voting exceed the costs.

To understand the interaction of these costs and benefits, consider an election that involves two political parties. Denote the parties by 1 and 2. Party 1 delivers to the voter an expected benefit of E^1 and party 2 a benefit of E^2. It is assumed that $E^1 > E^2$, so the voter prefers party 1. Let $B = E^1 - E^2 > 0$ be the value of party 1 winning versus losing. If the voter knows that party 1 will win the election, then they will choose not to vote. This is because they gain no benefit from doing so but still bear a cost. Similarly they will also not vote if they expect party 2 to win. In fact the rational voter will only ever choose to vote if they expect that they can affect the outcome of the election. Denoting the probability of breaking a tie occurring by P, then the expected benefit of voting is given by PB. The voting decision is then based on whether PB exceeds the private cost of voting C. Intuition suggests that the probability of being pivotal decreases with the size of the voting population and increases with the predicted closeness of the election. This can be demonstrated formally by considering the following coin-toss model of voting.

There is a population of potential voters of size N. Each of the voters chooses to cast a vote with probability p (so they don't vote with probability $1 - p$). This randomness in the decision to vote is the "coin-toss" aspect of the model. Contesting the election are two political parties, which we will call party 1 and party 2. A proportion σ_1 of the population supports party 1, meaning that if this population did vote they would vote for party 1. Similarly a proportion σ_2 of the population supports party 2. It must be the case that $0 \le \sigma_1 + \sigma_2 \le 1$. If $\sigma_1 + \sigma_2 < 1$, then some of the potential voters do not support either political party and abstain from the election. The number of votes cast for party 1 is denoted X_1 and the number for party 2 by X_2.

Now assume that the election is conducted. The question we want to answer is: What is the probability that an additional voter can affect the outcome? An additional person casting a vote can affect the outcome in two circumstances:

· If the vote had resulted in a tie with $X_1 = X_2$. The additional vote can then break the tie in favor of the party they support.

· If the party the additional person supports was 1 vote short of a tie. The additional vote will then lead to a tie.

Now assume that the additional voter supports party 1. (The argument is identical if they support party 2.) The first case arises when $X_1 = X_2$, so the additional vote will break the tie in favor of party 1. The second case occurs if $X_1 = X_2 - 1$, so the additional vote will ensure a tie. The action in the event of a tie is now important. We assume, as is the case in the United Kingdom, that a tie is broken by the toss of a fair coin. Then when a tie occurs each party has a 50/50 chance of winning the vote.

Putting these points together, the probability of being pivotal can be calculated. If the original vote resulted in a tie, the additional vote will lead to a clear victory. Without the additional vote the tie would have been broken in favor of party 1 just $\frac{1}{2}$ of the time so the additional vote leads to a reversal of the outcome with probability $\frac{1}{2}$. If the original vote had concluded with party 1 having 1 less vote than party 2, the addition of another vote for party 1 will lead from defeat to a tie. The tie is won by party 1 just $\frac{1}{2}$ of the time. The probability, P, of being pivotal and affecting the outcome can then be calculated as

$$P = \tfrac{1}{2} \Pr(X_1 = X_2) + \tfrac{1}{2} \Pr(X_1 = X_2 - 1). \tag{10.1}$$

	$X_2 = 0$	$X_2 = 1$	$X_2 = 2$
$X_1 = 0$	$\dfrac{1}{8}$	$\dfrac{2}{8}$	$\dfrac{1}{8}$
$X_1 = 1$	$\dfrac{1}{8}$	$\dfrac{2}{8}$	$\dfrac{1}{8}$

Figure 10.6
Probabilities of election outcomes

To see the implication of this formula, take the simple case of $N = 3$, $\sigma_1 = \frac{1}{3}$, $\sigma_2 = \frac{2}{3}$, and $p = \frac{1}{2}$. The probabilities of the various outcomes of the election are summarized in figure 10.6. These are calculated by observing that with 3 voters and 2 alternatives for each voter (vote or not vote), there are 8 possible outcomes. Since 2 of the 3 voters prefer party 2, the probability of party 2 receiving 1 vote is twice that of party 1 receiving 1 vote.

Using these probabilities, we can calculate the probability of the additional voter affecting the outcome as

$$P = \tfrac{1}{2}[\Pr(X_1 = X_2 = 0) + \Pr(X_1 = X_2 = 1)]$$
$$\quad + \tfrac{1}{2}[\Pr(X_1 = 0, X_2 = 1) + \Pr(X_1 = 1, X_2 = 2)]$$
$$= \tfrac{1}{2}\left[\tfrac{1}{8} + \tfrac{2}{8}\right] + \tfrac{1}{2}\left[\tfrac{2}{8} + \tfrac{1}{8}\right]$$
$$= \tfrac{3}{8}. \tag{10.2}$$

With this probability the voter will choose to vote in the election if

$$V = \tfrac{3}{8}B - C > 0. \tag{10.3}$$

In an election with a small number of voters the benefit does not have to be much higher than the cost to make it worthwhile to vote.

The calculation of the probability can be generalized to determine the dependence of P on the values of N, σ_1, σ_2, and p. This is illustrated in the following two figures. Figure 10.7 displays the probability of being pivotal against the number of potential voters for three values of p given that $\sigma_1 = \sigma_2 = 0.5$. We can interpret the value of p as being the willingness to participate in the election. The

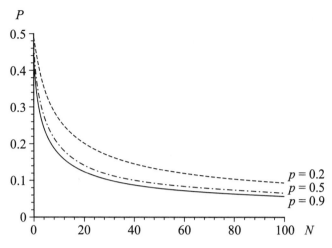

Figure 10.7
Participation and the probability of being pivotal

figures show clearly how an increase in the number of voters reduces the probability of being pivotal. Although the probability tends to zero as N becomes very large, it is still significantly above zero at $N = 100$.

Figure 10.8 confirms the intuition that the probability of being pivotal is highest when the population is evenly divided between the parties. If the population is more in favor of party 2 (the case of $\sigma_1 = 0.25$, $\sigma_2 = 0.75$), then the probability of the additional voter being pivotal in favor of party 1 falls to 0 very quickly. If the initial population is evenly divided, the probability of a tie remains significant for considerably larger values of N.

The probability of a voter being pivotal can be approximated by a reasonably simple formula if the number of potential voters, N, is large and the probability of each one voting, p, is small. Assume that this is so, and that the value of pN tends to the limit of n. The term n is the number of potential voters that actually choose to vote. The probability of being pivotal is then

$$P = \frac{e^{n(2\sqrt{\sigma_1\sigma_2}-\sigma_1-\sigma_2)}}{4\sqrt{\pi n(\sigma_1\sigma_2)^{1/2}}}\left[\frac{\sqrt{\sigma_1}+\sqrt{\sigma_2}}{\sqrt{\sigma_1}}\right], \tag{10.4}$$

where π is used in its standard mathematical sense. From this equation can be observed three results:

• The probability is a decreasing function of n. This follows from the facts that $2\sqrt{\sigma_1\sigma_2} - \sigma_1 - \sigma_2 \leq 0$, so the power on the exponential is negative, and that n

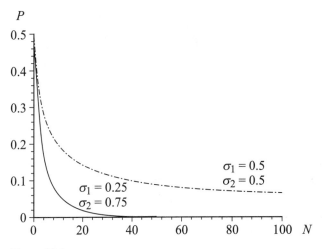

Figure 10.8
Closeness and the probability of being pivotal

is also in the denominator. Hence as the number of voters participating in the election increases, the probability of being pivotal falls.

· For any given value of σ_1, the probability increases the closer is σ_2 to σ_1. Hence the probability of being pivotal is increased the more evenly divided is the support for the parties.

· For a given value of n, the probability of being pivotal is at its maximum when $\sigma_1 = \sigma_2 = \frac{1}{2}$, and the expression for P simplifies to $P = \frac{1}{\sqrt{2\pi n}}$. In this case the effect of increasing n is clear.

The bottom line of this analysis is that the probability that someone's vote will change the outcome is essentially zero when the voting population is large enough. So, if voting is costly, the cost–benefit model should imply almost no participation. The small probability of a large change is not enough to cover the cost of voting. Each person's vote is like a small voice in a very large crowd.

Table 10.10 presents the results of an empirical analysis of voter turnout to test the basic implications of the pivotal-voter theory (i.e., that voting should depend on the probability of a tie). It uses a linear regression over aggregate state-by-state data for 11 US presidential elections (1948–1988) to estimate the empirical correlation between the participation rate and the strategic variables (population size and electoral closeness). The analysis also reveals the other main variables relevant for participation. As the table shows, there is strong empirical support for the

Table 10.10
Testing the paradox of voting

Variable	Coefficients[a]	Standard error
Constant	0.4033	0.0256
Closeness	0.1656	0.0527
Voting population	−0.0161	0.0036
Blacks (%)	−0.4829	0.0357
Rain on election day	−0.0349	0.0129
New residents (%)	−0.0127	0.0027

Source: Shachar and Nalebuff (1999), table 6.
a. All coefficients are significantly different from zero at the 1 percent level.

pivotal-agent argument: a smaller population and a closer election are correlated with higher participation. It also reveals that black participation is 48 percent lower, that new residents are 1.2 percent less likely to vote, and that rain on the election day decreases participation by 3.4 percent.

The paradox of voting raises serious questions about why so many people actually vote. Potential explanations for voting could include mistaken beliefs about the chance of affecting the outcome or feelings of social obligation. After all, every democratic society encourages its citizens to take civic responsibilities seriously and to participate actively in public decisions. Even if the act of voting is unlikely to promote self-interest, citizens feel they have a duty to vote. And this is exactly the important point made by the cost–benefit model of voting. Indeed, economists are suspicious about trying to explain voting only by the civic responsibility argument. This is because the duty model cannot explain what the cost–benefit model can, namely that many people do not vote and that turnout is higher when the election is expected to be close.

10.7   The "Alabama" Paradox

The Alabama paradox is associated with the apportionment problem. Many democratic societies require representatives to the parliament to be apportioned between the states or regions according to their respective population shares. Such a rule for proportional representation apportionment arises in the EU context where representation in European institutions is based on the population shares of member states. At the level of political parties there is also the proportional representation assignment of seats to different parties based on their respective

Table 10.11
Apportionment of seats

Party	Vote share	Exact apportionment	Hamilton apportionment
Left	0.45	11.25	11
Right	0.41	10.25	10
Center	0.14	3.5	4
Total	1	25	25

vote shares. For instance, with the party "list system" in Belgium electors vote for the list of candidates provided by each party. Then the number of candidates selected from each list is determined by the share of the vote a party receives. The selection is made according to the ordering of the candidates on the list from top to the bottom.

In all these forms of apportionment the solutions may involve fractions, but the number of representatives has to be an integer. How can these fractions be handled? With only two parties, rounding off will do the job. But rounding off loses simplicity once there are more than two parties, and it can produce an unexpected shift in power. To illustrate, suppose that 25 seats are to be allocated among three political parties (or states) based on their voting (population) shares as given in table 10.11. The exact apportionment for a party is obtained by allocating the 25 seats in proportion of the vote shares. However, such a scheme requires that the three parties should share one seat (hardly feasible!). The obvious solution is to allocate the contested seat to the party with the largest fractional part. This solution seems reasonable and was proposed by the American statesman Alexander Hamilton (despite the strong opposition of Thomas Jefferson). It was then used for a long period of time in the United States. Applying this solution to our problem gives the contested seat to the small Center party (with a fractional part of 0.5 against 0.25 for the two other parties).

Now what is the problem? Recall the runoff voting problem that more support for a candidate can make this candidate lose the election. A similar paradox arises with the Hamilton's apportionment scheme: increasing the number of seats available can remove seats from some parties. And it did happen in practice: when the size of the US House of Representatives grew, some states lost representation. The first to lose seats was Alabama (hence the name of Alabama paradox). To see this paradox with our simple example, suppose that one extra seat has to be allocated bringing the total number of seats to 26. Recalculating the Hamilton apportion-

Table 10.12
The paradox

Party	Vote share	Exact apportionment	Hamilton apportionment
Left	0.45	11.7	12 (+1 seat)
Right	0.41	10.66	11 (+1 seat)
Center	0.14	3.64	3 (−1 seat)
Total	1	26	26

ment accordingly, it follows that the small party loses out by one seat, which implies a 25 percent loss of its representation. The large parties have benefited from this expansion in the number of seats. It is unfair that one party loses one seat when more seats become available. The explanation for this paradox is that larger parties have their fractional part quickly jumping to the top of the list when extra seat becomes available.

10.8   Conclusions

Voting is one of the most common methods used to make collective decisions. Despite its practical popularity, it is not without its shortcomings. The theory of voting that we have described carefully catalogs the strengths and weaknesses of voting procedures. The major result is due to Arrow who pointed out the impossibility of finding the perfect voting system. Although there are many alternative systems of voting, none can always deliver in every circumstance.

Voting is important, but we should never forget its limitations. When discussing the various alternative voting schemes (Borda rule, approval voting, runoff voting, and plurality voting), we have mentioned their respective drawbacks in terms of the violation of some of the conditions of Arrow's theorem. However, such violations are inevitable given the content of the Impossibility Theorem. Thus violation of one condition does not rule out the use of a particular voting scheme. Whatever scheme we choose will have some problem associated with it.

Further Reading

Some of the fundamental work on collective choice can be found in:

Arrow, K. J. 1963. *Social Choice and Individual Values*. New York: Wiley.

Black, D. 1958. *The Theory of Committees and Elections*. Cambridge: Cambridge University Press.

Brams, S. J., and Fishburn, P. C. 1978. Approval voting. *American Political Science Review* 72: 831–47.

Farquharson, R. 1969. *Theory of Voting.* New Haven: Yale University Press.

Grandmont, J. M. 1978. Intermediate preferences and the majority rule. *Econometrica* 46: 317–30.

May, K. 1952. A set of independent, necessary and sufficient conditions for simple majority decision. *Econometrica* 20: 680–84.

McKelvey, R. D. 1976. Intransitivities in multidimensional voting models and some implications for agenda control. *Journal of Economic Theory* 12: 472–82.

Riker, W. H. 1986. *The Art of Political Manipulation*. New Haven: Yale University Press.

The two fundamental papers on the inevitable manipulability of voting schemes are:

Gibbard, A. 1973. Manipulation of voting schemes: A general result. *Econometrica* 41: 587–602.

Satterthwaite, M. 1975. Strategy-proofness and Arrow's condition. *Journal of Economic Theory* 10: 187–217.

Two excellent books providing comprehensive surveys of the theory of voting are:

Mueller, D. C. 1989. *Public Choice II*. Cambridge: Cambridge University Press.

Ordeshook, P. C. 1986. *Game Theory and Political Theory*. Cambridge: Cambridge University Press.

Two very original presentations of voting theory are:

Saari, D. G. 1995. *Basic Geometry of Voting*. Berlin: Springer-Verlag.

Saari, D. G. 2001. *Decision and Elections: Explaining the Unexpected*. Cambridge: Cambridge University Press.

A quite simple and striking proof of the impossibility result is in:

Taylor, A. D. 1995. *Mathematics and Politics: Strategy, Voting Power and Proof*. New York: Springer-Verlag.

There is also a nice proof of the impossibility theorem in:

Feldman, A. 1980. *Welfare Economics and Social Choice*. Boston: Martinus Nijhoff.

The voting paradox is based on:

Feddersen, T. J. 2004. Rational choice theory and the paradox of not voting. *Journal of Economic Perspectives* 18: 99–112.

Myerson, R. B. 2000. Large Poisson games. *Journal of Economic Theory* 94: 7–45.

Shachar, R., and Nalebuff, B. 1999. Follow the leader: Theory and evidence on political participation. *American Economic Review* 89: 525–47.

Some Condorcet-consistent alternatives to majority rule are presented and discussed in:

Banks, J. 1989. Equilibrium outcomes in two stage amendment procedures. *American Journal of Political Science* 33: 25–43.

McKelvey, R. D. 1986. Covering, dominance and the institution free properties of social choice. *American Journal of Political Science* 30: 283–314.

Miller, N. R. 1980. A new solution set for tournaments and majority voting. *American Journal of Political Science* 24: 68–96.

Exercises

10.1. Show that unidimensional median voting wth single-peaked preferences satisfies the conditions of theorem 5.

10.2. Suppose that to overthrow the status quo, an alternative requires 70 percent or more of the vote. Which property of voting is violated? In many committees the chairman has the casting vote. Which property of voting is violated?

10.3. With sincere voting can an example be given in which an agenda is constructed so that a Condorcet winner is defeated? Is the same true with strategic voting?

10.4. Consider five people with the preference rankings over four projects a, b, c, and d as follows:

b	a	c	a	d
c	d	b	c	b
d	c	d	b	c
a	b	a	d	a

a. Draw the preferences by ranking the projects by alphabetical order from left to right.

b. Who has single-peaked preferences and who has not?

c. Which project will be selected by majority voting? If none is selected, explain why.

10.5. Is condition U acceptable when some voters hold extreme political preferences?

10.6. Let G be the number of hours of television broadcast each day. Consider three individuals with preferences:

$$U^A = \frac{G}{4}, \quad U^B = 2 - G^{3/4}, \quad U^C = G - \frac{G^2}{2}.$$

a. Show that the three consumers have single-peaked preferences.

b. If the government is choosing G from the range $0 \leq G \leq 2$, what is the majority voting outcome?

c. Does this outcome maximize the sum of utilities $W = U^A + U^B + U^C$?

d. How are the answers to parts a through c altered if the preferences of C become $U^C = \frac{G^2}{2} - G$?

10.7. Consider the Cobb-Douglas utility function $U = [Y^i - T^i]^{[1-\alpha]} G^\alpha$ with $0 < \alpha < 1$. Suppose that a poll tax $T = T^i$ for all i is levied on each of N members of society. Tax revenues are used to finance a public good G.

a. Show that the majority voting outcome involves the amount of public good $G = \alpha N Y^m$, where Y^m denotes the before-tax income of the median voter.

b. Now suppose that a proportional income tax $T^i = t Y^i$ is levied. Show that the majority voting outcome involves the amount of public good $G = \alpha N \bar{Y}$, where $\bar{Y}$ is the mean income level.

c. When income is uniformly distributed, which outcome is closest to the efficient outcome?

10.8. Construct an example of preferences for which the majority voting outcome is not the median. Given these preferences, what is the median voting outcome? Is there a Pareto-preferred outcome?

10.9. If preferences are not single-peaked, explain why the Median Voter Theorem fails.

10.10. Show that the preferences used in section 4.3.4 are single-peaked.

10.11. Consider a scoring rule in which the preferred option is given one point and all others none.

a. Show that this need not select the Condorcet winner.

b. Demonstrate the scope for false voting.

10.12. Which of Arrow's conditions does approval voting violate?

10.13. Discuss the individual benefits that may arise from a preferred party winning. How large are these likely to be relative to the cost of voting?

10.14. Assume that all voters have an hourly wage of $10 and that it takes half an hour to vote. They stand to gain $50 if their party wins the election (in a two-party system where support is equal). What is the number of voters at which voting no longer becomes worthwhile?

10.15. Has there been any national election where a single vote affected the outcome?

10.16. Which of Arrow's conditions is removed to prove the Median Voter Theorem? Which condition does the Borda rule violate? Which condition does the Condorcet method fail? Why do we wish to exclude dictatorship?

10.17. In a transferable voting system each voter provides a ranking of the candidates. The candidate with the lowest number of first-choice votes is eliminated, and the votes are transferred to the second-choice candidates. This process proceeds until a candidate achieves a majority.

a. Can the Condorcet winner lose under a transferable vote system?

b. Is it possible for a candidate that is no one's first choice to win?

c. Show how strategic voting can affect the outcome.

10.18. Consider four people with preference rankings over three projects a, b, and c as follows:

a	a	b	c
b	b	c	b
c	c	a	a

a. Assume that voters cast their votes sincerely. Find a Borda rule system (scores to be given to first, second, and third choices) where project a wins.

b. Find a Borda weighting system where b wins.

c. Under plurality voting, which proposal wins?

10.19. The Hare procedure was introduced by Thomas Hare in 1861. It is also called the "single transferable vote system." The Hare system is used to elect public officials in Australia, Malta, and the Republic of Ireland. The system selects the Condorcet winner if it exists. If not, then it will proceed to the successive deletion of the least-desirable alternative or alternatives until a Condorcet winner is found among the remaining alternatives. Consider the following preference profile of five voters on five alternatives:

a	b	c	d	e
b	c	b	c	d
e	a	e	a	c
d	d	d	e	a
c	e	a	b	b

a. What social choice emerges from this profile under the Hare procedure? Explain in detail the successive deletions.

b. Repeat the exercise for the opposite procedure proposed by Clyde Coombs. The Coombs system operates exactly as the Hare system does, but instead of deleting alternatives with the fewest first places, it deletes alternatives with the most last places.

c. Which of Arrow's conditions are violated in the Coombs and Hare procedures?

10.20. Define a collective choice procedure as satisfying the "top condition" if an alternative is never among the social choices unless it is on top of at least one individual preference list. Prove or disprove each of the following:

a. Plurality voting satisfies the top condition.

b. The Condorcet method satisfies the top condition.

c. Sequential pairwise voting satisfies the top condition.

d. A dictatorship satisfies the top condition.

e. Approval voting satisfies the top condition.

f. Runoff voting satisfies the top condition.

g. If a procedure satisfies the top condition, then it satisfies the Pareto condition.

h. If a procedure satisfies the top condition, then it selects the Condorcet winner (if any).

10.21. Consider the following preference profile of three voters and four alternatives:

a	c	b
b	a	d
d	b	c
c	d	a

a. Show that if the social choice method used is sequential pairwise voting with a fixed agenda, and if you have agenda-setting power, then you can arrange the order to ensure whichever alternative you want to be chosen.

b. Define an alternative as a "Condorcet loser" if it is defeated by every other alternative in pairwise voting. Prove that there is no Condorcet loser in this preference profile.

c. Modify the preference profile for one voter to ensure that there exists a Condorcet loser.

d. Modify the preference profile for one voter to ensure that there exists a Condorcet winner.

10.22. Show that for an odd number of voters and a given preference profile over a fixed number of alternatives, an alternative is a Condorcet winner if and only if it emerges as the social choice in sequential pairwise voting with a fixed agenda, no matter what the order of the agenda.

11 Rent-Seeking

11.1 Introduction

The *United States National Lobbyist Directory* records there to be over 40,000 state-registered lobbyists and a further 4,000 federal government lobbyists registered in Washington. Some estimates put the total number, including those who are on other registers or are unregistered, as high as 100,000. Although the number of lobbyists in the United States dwarfs those elsewhere, there are large numbers of lobbyists in all major capitals. These lobbyists are not engaged in productive activity. Instead, their role is to seek favorable government treatment for the organizations that employ them. Viewed from the US perspective, the country has at least 40,000 (presumably skilled) individuals who are contributing no net value to the economy but are merely attempting to influence government policy and shift the direction of income flow.

The behavior that the lobbyists are engaged in has been given the name of *rent-seeking* in the economic literature. Loosely speaking, rent-seeking is the act of trying to seize an income flow rather than create an income flow. What troubles economists about rent-seeking is that it uses valuable resources unproductively and can push the government into inefficient decisions. This places the economy inside its production possibility frontier and implies that efficiency improvements will be possible. As such, rent-seeking can be viewed as a potential cause of economic inefficiency.

The chapter will first consider the nature and definition of rent-seeking. It will then proceed onto the analysis of a simple game that demonstrates the essence of rent-seeking. This game generates the fundamental results on the consequences of rent-seeking and forms the basis on which the later analysis is developed. The insights from the game are then applied to rent-seeking in the context of monopoly. The basic point made there is that the standard measure of monopoly welfare loss understates the true loss to society if rent-seeking behavior is present. This partial equilibrium analysis of monopoly is then extended to a general equilibrium setting. Following this, the emphasis turns to how and why rents are created. Government policy is analyzed and the relationship between lobbying and economic welfare is characterized in detail. The reasons why a government might allow itself to be swayed by lobbyists are then discussed. Finally possible policies for containing rent-seeking are considered.

11.2   Definitions

Rent-seeking has received a number of different definitions in the literature. These vary only in detail, particularly, in whether the resources used in rent-seeking are directly wasted and in whether the term can be applied only to rents created by government. It is not the purpose here to catalog these definitions but instead to motivate the concept of rent-seeking by example and to draw out the common strands of the definitions.

The ideas that lie behind rent-seeking can be seen by considering the following two situations:

• A firm is engaged in research intended to develop a new product. If the research is successful, the product will be unique, and the firm will have a monopoly position, and extract some rent from this, until rival products are introduced.

• A firm has introduced a new product to the home market. A similar product is manufactured overseas. The firm hires lawyers to lobby the government to prevent imports of the overseas product. If it is successful, it will enjoy a monopoly position from which it will earn rents.

What is the difference between these two situations? Both will give the firm a monopoly position, at least in the short run, from which it can earn monopoly rents. The first, though, would be seen by many economists as something to be praised, but the second as something to be condemned. In fact the fundamental difference is that the first case, with the firm expending resources to develop a new product, will lead to monopoly rent only if the product is successful and valued by consumers. Hence the resources used in research may ultimately lead to an increase in economic welfare. In contrast, the resources used in the second case are reducing economic welfare. If the lawyers are successful, consumers will be denied a choice between products, and the lack of competition will mean that they face higher prices. Their welfare is reduced and some of their income, via the higher prices, is diverted to the monopolist. There is also (implicitly) a transfer from the overseas producers to the monopolist. Some of the monopoly rents are transferred to the lawyers via their fees (we will clarify how much in section 11.3). In short, although the research and the lawyers are both directed to attaining a monopoly position, in the first case research potentially increases economic welfare, but in the second the lawyers reduce it.

These comments now allow us to distinguish between two concepts:

• *Profit-seeking* is the expenditure of resources to create a profitable position that is ultimately beneficial to society. Profit-seeking, as exemplified by the example of research, is what drives progress in the economy and is the motivating force behind competition.

• *Rent-seeking* is the expenditure of resources to create a profitable opportunity that is ultimately damaging to society. Rent-seeking, as exemplified by the use of lawyers, hinders the economy and limits competition.

There are some other points that can be drawn out of these definitions. Notice that the scientists and engineers employed in research are being productive. If their work is successful, then new products will emerge that raise the economy's output. On the other hand, the lawyers engaged in lobbying the government are doing nothing productive. Their activity does not raise output. At best it simply redistributes what there already is, and generally it reduces it. Furthermore output would be higher if they were usefully employed in a productive capacity rather than working as lawyers. In this respect rent-seeking always reduces total output, since the resources engaged in rent-seeking can be expected to have alternative productive uses.

It can be inferred from this discussion that rent-seeking can take many forms. All lobbying of government for beneficial treatment, be it protection from competition or the payment of subsidies, is rent-seeking. Expenditure on advertising is rent-seeking and so is arguing for tariffs to protect infant industries. These activities are rife in most economies, so rent-seeking is a widespread and important issue.

One of the factors that will feature strongly in the discussion below is the level of resources wasted in the lobbying process. At first sight there appears to be a clear distinction between the time a lobbyist uses talking to a politician and a bribe passed to a politician. The time is simply lost to the economy—it could have been used in some productive capacity but has not. This is a resource wasted. In contrast, the bribe is just a transfer of resources. Beyond the minimal costs needed to deliver the bribe, there appear to be no other resource costs. Hence it is tempting to conclude that lobbying time has a resource cost whereas bribes do not. Thus, if rent-seeking is undertaken entirely by bribes, it appears to have no resource cost.

Before reaching this conclusion, it is necessary to take a further step back. Consider the position of the politician receiving the bribe. How did they achieve their position of authority? Clearly, resources would have been expended to obtain election. If potential politicians believed they would receive bribes once elected, they would be willing to expend more resources to become politicians—they are in fact rent-seeking themselves. Much of the resources used in seeking election will simply be a cost to the economy with no net output resulting from them. Through this process a bribe, which is just a transfer, actually becomes transformed further down the line into a resource loss caused by rent-seeking. These arguments suggest that caution is required in judging between lobby costs that seem to be transfers and those that are clearly resource costs.

So far the discussion has concentrated on rent-seeking. The economic literature has also dealt with the very closely related concept of *directly unproductive activities*. The distinction between the two is not always that clear, and many economists use them interchangeably. If there is a precise distinction, it is in the fact that directly unproductive activities are by definition a waste of resources whereas the activity of rent-seeking may not always involve activities that waste resources. The focus below will be placed on rent-seeking, though almost all of what is said could be rephrased in terms of directly unproductive activities.

11.3   Rent-Seeking Games

This section considers several variants of a simple game that is designed to capture the essential aspects of rent-seeking. From the analysis emerge several important conclusions that will form the basis of more directly economic applications in the following sections. The game may appear at first sight to be extreme, but on reflection, its interpretation in terms of rent-seeking will become clear.

The basic structure of the game is as follows: Consider the offer of a prize of $10,000. Competitors enter the game by simultaneously placing a sum of money on a table and setting it alight. The prize is awarded to the competitor that burns the most money. Assuming that the competitors are all identical and risk-neutral, how much money will each one burn? This question will be answered when there is either a fixed number of competitors or the number of competitors is endogenously determined through free-entry into the competition.

Before conducting the analysis, it is worth detailing how this game relates to rent-seeking. The prize to be won is the rent—think of this as the profit that will accrue if awarded a monopoly in the supply of a product. The money that is burned represents the resources used in lobbying for the award of the monopoly. Instead of burning money, it could be fees paid to a lobby company for the provision of their services. The game can then be seen as representing a number of companies each wishing to be granted the monopoly and employing lobbyists to make their case. We consider two different games. In the deterministic game, the prize is awarded to the firm that spends most on lobbying. In the probabilistic game, the chance of obtaining the prize is an increasing function of one's share in the total spending on lobbying, so spending the most does not necessarily secure a win.

11.3.1   Deterministic Game

A game of this form is solved by constructing its equilibrium. In this case we look for the *Nash equilibrium*, which occurs when each competitor's action is optimal given the actions of all other competitors. Consequently at a Nash equilibrium no variation in one competitor's choice can be beneficial for that competitor. It is this latter property that allows potential equilibria to be tested.

Say initially that there are two competitors for the prize. To apply the Nash equilibrium argument, the method is to fix the strategy choice of one competitor and to consider what the remaining competitor will do. Strategies for the game can be of two types. There are *pure strategies* that involve the choice of a single quantity of money to burn. There are also *mixed strategies* where the competitor uses a randomizing device to select its optimal strategy. The benefit of randomizing is that if one player engages in any determinate behavior, the rival can take advantage of it. The only sensible thing for each to do is to mix its action randomly to act in an unpredictable way for its rival. For instance, labeling six possible strategies from 1 to 6 and then using the roll of a die to choose which one to play is a mixed strategy. The central component of finding a mixed strategy equilibrium is to determine the mixing rule described by the probabilities assigned to each pure strategy. The argument will first show that there can be no pure strategy equilibrium for the game. The mixed strategy equilibrium will then be constructed.

To show that there can be no pure strategy equilibrium, let competitor 1 burn an amount B^*. Then, if competitor 2 burns $B^* + \epsilon$, this competitor will win the contest and receive the prize of value V. The same argument applies for any value of $B^* < V$ and any positive value of ϵ, no matter how small. Since competitor 1 has lost the contest, burning B^* cannot be an equilibrium choice: competitor 1 will wish to burn slightly more than $B^* + \epsilon$. By this reasoning, no amount of burning less than V can be an equilibrium. The only way a competitor can prevent this "leapfrogging" argument is by burning exactly V. The other competitor must then also burn V.

However, burning V each is still not an equilibrium. If both competitors burn V, then each has an equal chance of winning. This chance of winning is $\frac{1}{2}$, so their expected payoff, EP, is equal to the expected value of the prize minus the money burned,

$$EP = \tfrac{1}{2} V - V = -\tfrac{1}{2} V < 0. \tag{11.1}$$

Clearly, given that the other burns V, a competitor would be better off to burn 0 and make an expected payoff of 0 rather than burn V and make an expected loss of $-\frac{V}{2}$. So the strategies of both burning V are not an equilibrium. The conclusion of this reasoning is that the game has no equilibrium in pure strategies. Therefore, to find an equilibrium, it becomes necessary to look for one in mixed strategies.

The calculation of the mixed strategy for the game is easily motivated. It is first noted that each player can obtain a payoff of at least 0 by burning nothing. Therefore the equilibrium strategy must yield a payoff of at least 0. No player can ever burn a negative amount of money, nor is there any point in burning more than V. Hence the strategy must assign positive probability only to amounts in the range 0 to V.

It turns out that the equilibrium strategy is to assign the same probability to all amounts in the range 0 to V. This probability, denoted $f(B)$, must then be given by $f(B) = \frac{1}{V}$. Given that the other competitor also plays this mixed strategy, the probability of winning when burning an amount B is the probability that the other competitor burns less than B. This can be calculated as $F(B) = \frac{B}{V}$. Burning B then gives an expected payoff of

$$EP = \left[\frac{B}{V} \right] V - B = 0. \tag{11.2}$$

Therefore, whatever amount the random device suggests should be played, the expected payoff from that choice will be zero. In total the mixed strategies used in this equilibrium give both players an expected payoff of zero.

In the context of rent-seeking the important quantity is the total sum of money burned, since this can be interpreted as the value wasted. The mixed strategy makes each value between 0 and V equally likely so the expected burning for each player is $\frac{V}{2}$. Adding these together, the total amount burnt is V—which is exactly equal to the value of the prize. This conclusions forms the basis of the important result that the effort put into rent-seeking will be exactly equal to the rent to be won.

The argument can now be extended to any number of players. With three players the strategy of giving the same probability to each value between 0 and V is not the equilibrium. To see this, observe that with this mixed strategy the average amount burned remains at $\frac{V}{2}$, but the probability of winning with three players is reduced to $\frac{1}{3}$. The expected payoff is therefore

$$EP = \left[\frac{1}{3}\right] V - \frac{V}{2} = -\frac{V}{6}, \tag{11.3}$$

so an expected loss is made. This strategy gives too much weight to higher levels of burning now that there are three players. Consequently the optimal strategy must give less weight to higher values of burning so that the level of expected burning must match the expected winnings.

The probability distribution for the mixed strategy equilibrium when there are n players can be found as follows: Let the probability of beating one of the other competitors when B is burned be $F(B)$. There are $n - 1$ other competitors, so the probability of beating them all is $[F(B)]^{n-1}$. The expected payoff in equilibrium must be zero, so $[F(B)]^{n-1} V = B$ for any value of B between 0 and V. Solving this equation for $F(B)$ gives the equilibrium probability distribution as

$$F(B) = \left[\frac{B}{V}\right]^{1/[n-1]}. \tag{11.4}$$

This distribution has the property that the probability applied to higher levels of B falls relative to that for lower levels as n increases. It can also be seen that when $n = 2$, it gives the solution found earlier.

What is important for the issue of rent-seeking is the expected amount burned by each competitor. Given that the expected payoff in equilibrium is zero and that everyone is equally likely to win V with probability $\frac{1}{n}$, the expected amount burnt by each competitor is

$$EB = \frac{V}{n}. \tag{11.5}$$

By this result the expected amount burned by all the competitors is $nEB = V$, which again is exactly equal to the prize being competed for. This finding is summarized as a theorem.

Theorem 8 (Complete Dissipation Theorem)   If there are two or more competitors in a deterministic rent-seeking game, the total expected value of resources expended by the competitors in seeking a prize of V is exactly V.

The interpretation of this theorem is that between them the set of competitors will burn (in expected terms) a sum of money exactly equal to the value of the prize. The theorem is just a restatement of the fact that the expected payoff from the game is zero. The theorem has been very influential in the analysis of rent-seeking. Originally demonstrated in the context of monopoly (we will look at its application in this context later), the theorem provides the conclusion that from a social perspective there is nothing gained from the existence of the prize. Instead, all the possible benefits of the prize are wasted through the burning of money. In the circumstances where it is applicable, the finding of complete dissipation provides an exact answer to the question of what quantity of resources is expended in rent-seeking.

It is important to note before proceeding that the theorem holds whatever the value of n (provided it is at least 2). Early analyses of rent-seeking concluded that rents would be completely dissipated only if there were large numbers of competitors for the rent. This conclusion was founded on standard arguments that competition between many would drive the return down to zero. Prior to the proof of the Complete Dissipation Theorem it had been suspected that this would not be the case with only a small number of competitors and that some rent would be undissipated. However, the theorem proves that this reasoning is false and that even with only two competitors attempting to win the prize, rents are completely dissipated.

11.3.2   Probabilistic Game

The key feature of the Complete Dissipation Theorem is that it takes only a slight advantage over one's competitors to obtain a sure win. This is the situation where the rent-seeking contest takes the form of a race or an auction with maximal competition. However, in many cases there is inevitably uncertainty in rent-seeking, so higher effort increases the probability of obtaining the prize but does not ensure a win. A natural application is political lobbying where lobbying expenditures involve real resources that seek to influence public decisions. Even if a lobby can increase its chance of success by spending more, it cannot obtain a sure win by simply spending more than its competitors. We now show that such uncertainty will reduce the equilibrium rent-seeking efforts, preventing full dissipation of the rent.

Consider modifying the payoff function to let the probability of anyone obtaining the prize be equal to their share of the total rent-seeking expenditures of all contestants,

$$EP_i = \left[\frac{B_i}{B_i + [n-1]B_{-i}} \right] V - B_i,\tag{11.6}$$

where $[n-1]B_{-i}$ is the total effort of the other contestants. So the expected payoff of contestant i is the probability of obtaining the prize, which is their spending as a proportion of the total amount spent in the competition, times the value of the rent, V, minus their own spending.

A Nash equilibrium in this game is an expenditure level for each contestant such that nobody would want to alter their expenditure given that of the other contestants. Because all contestants are identical, we should expect a symmetric Nash equilibrium in which rent-seeking activities are the same for all and everyone is equally likely to win the prize. To find this Nash equilibrium, we proceed in two steps. First, we derive the optimal response of contestant i as a function of the total efforts of the other contestants. Second, we use the symmetry property to obtain the Nash equilibrium.

To find player i's best response when the others are choosing B_{-i}, we must take the derivative of player i's expected payoff and set it equal to zero (this is the first-order condition). To facilitate the derivative, express the probability of winning as a power function in the expected payoff,

$$EP_i = B_i[B_i + [n-1]B_{-i}]^{-1} V - B_i.\tag{11.7}$$

Using the product rule for the derivative of the first term (the derivative of the first function times the second, plus the first function times the derivative of the second), the first-order condition is given by

$$[B_i + [n-1]B_{-i}]^{-1} V - B_i[B_i + [n-1]B_{-i}]^{-2} V - 1 = 0.\tag{11.8}$$

Next we use the fact that in a symmetric equilibrium $B_i = B_{-i} = B$. Making this substitution in the first-order condition gives

$$[B + [n-1]B]^{-1} V - B[B + [n-1]B]^{-2} V - 1 = 0,\tag{11.9}$$

or

$$[nB]^{-1} V - B[nB]^{-2} V = 1.\tag{11.10}$$

Finally, multiplying both sides by $n^2 B$, we obtain

$$nV - V = n^2 B.\tag{11.11}$$

Hence the equilibrium level of rent-seeking expenditure is

$$B = \frac{[n-1]}{n^2} V,\tag{11.12}$$

and the total expenditure of all contestants in equilibrium is

$$nB = \frac{[n-1]}{n} V. \tag{11.13}$$

Thus the fraction of the rent that is dissipated is $\frac{n-1}{n} < 1$, which is an increasing function of the number of contestants. With two contestants only one-half of the rent is dissipated in a Nash equilibrium, and the fraction increases to one as the number of contestants gets large. In equilibrium each contestant is equally likely to obtain the prize (with probability $\frac{1}{n}$) and, using the equilibrium value of B, their expected payoff is $EP = \left[\frac{1}{n}\right] V - B = \frac{V}{n^2}$.

Theorem 9 (Partial Dissipation Theorem)   If there are two or more competitors in a probabilistic rent-seeking game, the total expected value of resources expended by the competitors in seeking a prize of V is a fraction $\frac{n-1}{n}$ of the prize value V, and is increasing with the number of competitors.

It follows that the total costs of rent-seeking activity are significant, and are greater than one-half of the rent value in all cases. Notice that the rate of rent dissipation is independent of the value of the rent. It is also worth mentioning that in the Nash equilibrium contestants play a pure strategy and do not randomize as in the previous deterministic rent-seeking game. This is because the probability of obtaining the rent is a *continuous* function of the person's own rent-seeking activity. Finally in equilibrium, no single person spends more on rent-seeking than the prize is worth, but the total expenditure on rent-seeking activities may dissipate a substantial fraction of the prize value. This destruction of value is often innocuous because the contestants participate willingly expecting to gain. However, as in any competition where the *winner takes all*, there is only one winner who may earn large profits but many losers who bear the full cost of the destruction of value.

11.3.3   Free-Entry

Beginning with a fixed number of competitors does not capture the idea of a potential pool of competitors who may opt to enter the competition if there is a rent to be obtained. It is therefore of interest to consider what the equilibrium will be if there is free-entry into the competition. In the context of the game, free-entry means that competitors enter to bid for the prize until there is no expected benefit from further entry. This has the immediate implication that the expected payoff has to be driven to zero in any free-entry equilibrium.

How can the game be solved with free-entry? The analysis of the deterministic game showed that the expected payoff of each competitor is zero in the mixed strategy equilibrium. From this it follows that once at least two players have entered the competition, the expected payoff is zero. The free-entry equilibrium concept is therefore compatible with any number of competitors greater than or equal to two, and all competitors who enter play the mixed strategy.

There is an important distinction between this equilibrium and the one considered for fixed numbers. In the former case it was assumed (but without being explicitly stated) that all competitors played the same strategy and only such symmetric equilibria were considered. If this is applied to the free-entry case, it means that the entire (unlimited) set of potential competitors must enter the game and play the mixed strategy given by (11.4) as $n \to \infty$. An alternative to this cumbersome equilibrium is to consider an asymmetric equilibrium in which different competitors play different strategies. An asymmetric equilibrium of the game is for some competitors to choose not to enter while some (at least 2) enter and play the mixed strategy in (11.4). All competitors (both those who enter and those who do not) have an expected payoff of 0. The other important feature of the both the symmetric and asymmetric free-entry equilibria is that there is again complete dissipation of the rent. This finding is less surprising in this case than it is with no-entry, since the entry could be expected to reduce the net social value of the competition to zero.

In the probabilistic game contestants get a positive expected payoff from their rent-seeking activities of $\frac{V}{n}$. Such a gain from rent-seeking will attract new contestants until the rent value is fully dissipated, that is, $n \to \infty$ and $\frac{V}{n} \to 0$. So free-entry will make the two games equivalent with full dissipation of the rent.

11.3.4   Risk Aversion

The analysis so far has relied on the assumption that competitors for the prize care only about the expected amount of money with which they will leave the contest. This is a consequence of the assumption that they are risk neutral and hence indifferent about accepting a fair gamble. Although risk neutrality may be appropriate in some circumstances, such as for governments and large firms that can diversify risk, it is not usually felt to correctly describe the behavior of individual consumers. It is therefore worth reflecting on how the results are modified by the incorporation of risk aversion.

The first effect of risk aversion is that the expected monetary gain from entering the contest must be positive in order for a competitor to take part—this is the compensation required to induce the risk-averse competitors to take on risk. In terms of the deterministic game with a mixed strategy equilibrium, for a given number of competitors this means that less probability must be given to high levels of money burning and more to lower levels. However, the expected utility gain of the contest will be zero, since competition will bid away any excess utility. In contrast to the outcome with risk neutrality, there will not be complete dissipation of the rent. This is a consequence of the expected monetary gain being positive, which implies that something must be left to be captured. With risk aversion the resources expended on rent-seeking will be strictly less than the value of the rent. But note carefully that this does not say that society has benefited. Since the expected utility gain of each competitor is zero, the availability of the rent still does not raise society's welfare.

The same reasoning applies to the probabilistic game with more risk-averse individuals tending to expend less on rent-seeking activities. As a result a lower fraction of the rent will be dissipated. The effect of free-entry will be to drive the expected utility gain of each contender to zero.

11.3.5   Conclusions

This section has analyzed a simple game that can be interpreted as modeling the most basic of rent-seeking situations. The burning of money captures the use of resources in lobbying and the fact that these resources are not used productively. The fundamental conclusion is that when competitors are risk neutral, competition leads to the complete dissipation of the rent. This applies no matter how many competitors there are (provided there are at least two) and whether or not the number of competitors is fixed or variable. This fundamental conclusion of the rent-seeking literature shows that the existence of a rent does not benefit society, since resources (possibly equal in value to that rent) will be exhausted in capturing it. This conclusion has to be slightly modified with risk aversion. In this case there is less expenditure on rent-seeking and thus less rent dissipation. However, the expected utility gain of the competition is zero. In welfare terms, society does not benefit from the rent.

11.4   Social Cost of Monopoly

Monopoly is one of the causes of economic inefficiency. A monopolist restricts output below the competitive level in order to raise price and earn monopoly

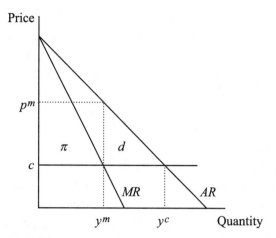

Figure 11.1
Monopoly deadweight loss

profits. This causes some consumer surplus to be turned into profit and some to become deadweight loss. Standard economic analysis views this deadweight loss to be the cost of monopoly power. The application of rent-seeking concepts suggests that the cost may actually be much greater.

Consider figure 11.1. This depicts a monopoly producing with constant marginal cost c and no fixed costs. Its average revenue is denoted AR and marginal revenue MR. The monopoly price and output are p^m and y^m respectively, while the competitive output would be y^c. Monopoly profit is the rectangle π, and deadweight loss the triangle d. In a static situation the deadweight loss d is the standard measure of the cost of monopoly. (The emphasis on "static" is necessary here because there may be dynamic gains through innovation from the monopoly that offset the deadweight loss.)

How can the introduction of rent-seeking change this view of the cost of monopoly? There are two scenarios in which it can do so. First, the monopoly position may have been created by the government. An example would be the government deciding that an airline route can be served only by a single carrier. If airlines must then compete in lobbying for the right to fly this route the situation is just like the money-burning competition of section 11.3. The rent-seeking here comes from the bidders for the monopoly position. Another example is the allocation in the late 1980s by the US Federal Communications Commission of regional cell phone licenses. The lure of extremely high potential profits was strong enough to attract many contenders. There were about 320,000 contestants competing for 643 licenses. Hazlett and Michaels (1993) estimated the total cost of all applications (due to the technical expertise required) to be about $400 million. Each winner earned very large profits well in excess of their application costs. However, the costs incurred by others were lost, and the total cost of the allocation of licenses was estimated to be about 40 percent of the market value of the license. Second, the monopoly may be already in existence but in a position where it has to defend itself from potential competitors. Such defense could involve lawyers or an effective lobbying presence attempting to prevent the production of similar goods using copyright or patent law, or it could mean advertising to stifle competition. It could even mean direct action to intimidate potential competitors.

Whichever case applies, the implications are the same. The value of having the monopoly position is given by the area π. If there are a number of potential monopolists bidding for the monopoly, then the analysis of money-burning can be applied to show that if they are risk neutral, the entire value will be dissipated in lobbying. Alternatively, if an incumbent monopolist is defending their position, they will expend resources up to value π to do so. In both cases the costs of rent-seeking will be π.

Combining these rent-seeking costs with the standard deadweight loss of monopoly, the conclusion of the rent-seeking approach is that the total cost of the monopoly to society is at least d and may be as high as $\pi + d$. What determines the total cost is the nature of the rent-seeking activity. We can conclude that resources of value π will be expended but not how much is actually wasted. As the discussion of section 11.2 noted, some of the costs may be transfer payments (or, more simply, bribes) to officials. These are not directly social costs but, again referring to section 11.2, may become so if they induce rent-seeking in obtaining official positions. In contrast, if all the rent-seeking costs are expended on unproductive activities, such as time spent lobbying, then the total social cost of the monopoly is exactly $\pi + d$.

These results demonstrate one of the most basic insights of the rent-seeking literature: the social costs of monopoly may be very much greater than measurement through deadweight loss would suggest. To see the extent of the difference that this can make, reconsider the measurements of welfare loss given in chapter 8. Harberger, using just the deadweight loss d, calculated the cost of monopolization in US manufacturing industry for the period 1924 to 1928 as equal to 0.08 percent of national income. In contrast, the 1978 calculations by Cowling and Mueller followed the rent-seeking approach and included the cost of advertising in the measure of welfare loss. Their analysis of US industry concluded that welfare loss was between 4 and 13 percent of gross corporate product. The difference between these measures reflects the additional loss through rent-seeking.

This discussion of monopoly has shown that rent-seeking does have important implications. In particular, it strongly alters our assessment of the social costs of monopoly and shows that the standard deadweight loss measure seriously understates the true loss. This conclusion does not apply just to monopoly. Rent-seeking has the same effect when applied to any distortionary government policy. This includes regulation, tariffs, taxes, and spending. It also shows that the net costs of a distortionary policy may be much higher than an analysis of benevolent government suggests. Attempts at quantifying the size of these effects show that they can be very dramatic.

11.5   Equilibrium Effects

The discussion of monopoly welfare loss in the previous section is an example of partial equilibrium analysis. It considered the monopolist in isolation and did not consider any potential spillovers into related markets nor the consequences of rent-seeking for the economy as a whole. This section will go some way toward remedying these omissions. The analysis here will be graphical; an algebraic development of similar arguments will be given in section 11.6.1.

Consider an economy that produces two goods and has a fixed supply of labor. The production possibility frontier depicting the possible combinations of output of the two goods is denoted by *ppf* in figure 11.2. The competitive equilibrium prices ratio $p^c = \frac{p_1}{p_2}$ determines the gradient of the line tangent to the *ppf* at point *a*. This will be the equilibrium for the competitive economy in the absence of lobbying.

The form of lobbying that we consider is for the monopolization of industry 1. If this lobbying is successful it will have two effects. The first effect will be to change the relative prices in the economy. The second will be to use some labor in the lobbying process that could be used productively elsewhere. The consequences of these effects will now be traced on the production possibility diagram. Let the monopoly price for good 1 be given by p_1^m and the monopoly price ratio be denoted by $p^m = \frac{p_1^m}{p_2}$. Since $p^m > p^c$, the monopoly price line will be steeper than the competitive price line. This change in the relative prices will move the economy from point *a* to point *b* around the initial production possibility frontier (see figure 11.2). Evaluated at the competitive prices, the value of output has fallen (point *b* lies below the extension of the competitive price line).

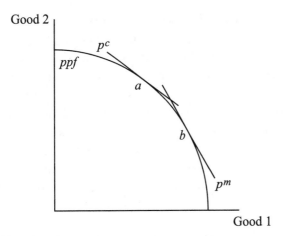

Figure 11.2
Competitive and monopoly equilibria

The consequence of accounting for the labor used in lobbying is derived by observing that the labor of lobbyists produces neither good 1 nor good 2 but is effectively lost to the economy. This loss of labor reduces the potential output of the economy. Hence the production possibility frontier with lobbying must lie inside that without lobbying. This is shown in figure 11.3 where the production possibility frontier with lobbying is denoted ppf^L. With the monopoly price line the equilibrium with both monopoly and lobbying will be at point c in figure 11.3. The outcome in figure 11.3 shows that the move to monopoly pricing shifts the equilibrium around the frontier and lobbying shifts the frontier inward. The value at competitive prices of output at a is higher than at b, and the value at b is higher than at c. Hence successful lobbying has reduced the value of output by altering the price ratio and by causing an inward move of the production possibility frontier. At the aggregate level this is damaging for the economy. At the micro level there will be a transfer of income to the owners of the monopoly and the lobbyists, and away from the consumers, so the outcome is not necessarily bad for all individuals.

A further comparison that can be made is between the equilibrium with un-successful lobbying where the resource cost of lobbying is incurred but the prices remain at the competitive level (point d in figure 11.4) and monopoly with no lobbying (point b). As figures 11.4a and 11.4b show, either outcome b or d could have the highest value of output when computed using the competitive prices. From this it can be concluded that there may be situations (as shown in figure 11.4b) when it is better to concede to the threat of lobbying and allow the

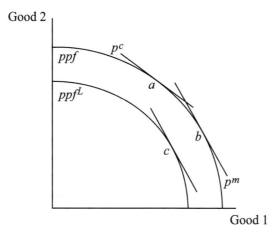

Figure 11.3
Monopoly and lobbying

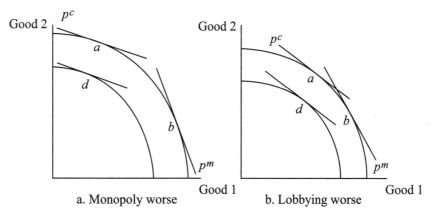

Figure 11.4
Threat of lobbying

monopoly (without the lobbying taking place) rather than refuse to concede to the lobby.

This section has extended the partial equilibrium analysis of lobbying to a general equilibrium setting to illustrate the combined effects of the distortions generated by successful lobbying and the waste of the resources used in the lobbying process. The switch from the competitive to the monopoly price reduces the value of output. Including lobbying moves the production possibility frontier inward. Moving the equilibrium onto this new frontier can lower the value of output even further.

11.6   Government Policy

Rent-seeking may be important for the study of private-sector monopoly, but most proponents of rent-seeking would see its application to government as being far more significant. Much analysis of policy choice views the government as benevolent and trying to make the best choices it can. The rent-seeking model of government is very different. This takes the view of the government as a creator of rents and those involved in government as seeking rent wherever possible. Chapter 4 touched on some of these issues in the discussion of bureaucracy, but that discussion can be extended much further.

There are two channels through which the government is connected with rent-seeking. These are:

· *Lobbying*   We began this chapter by noting that the United States may have up to 100,000 professional lobbyists. These lobbyists attempt to change government policy in favor of the interests that employ them. If the lobbyists are successful, rents are created.

· *Bureaucrats and politicians*   Bureaucrats and politicians in government are able to create rents through their policy choices. These rents can be "sold" to the parties that benefit. Selling rents generates income for the seller and gives an incentive for careers to be made in politics and bureaucracy.

These two channels of rent-seeking are now discussed in turn.

11.6.1   Lobbying

The discussion so far has frequently referred to lobbying but without going into great detail about its economic effects. Section 11.4 showed graphically how the use of labor in lobbying shifted the production possibility frontier inward, but a graphical analysis of that kind could not provide an insight into the size of the effects. The purpose now is to analyze an example that can quantify the potential size of the economic loss resulting from the use of labor in lobbying.

Many of the implications of lobbying can be found by analyzing the use of productive labor to lobby for a tariff. The effect of a tariff is to make imports more expensive, so allowing the home firm to charge a higher price and earn greater profits. The potentially higher profit gives an incentive for lobbying. For example, the owners of textile firms will benefit from a lobby-induced tariff on imported clothing. Also the US steel industry is a well-organized group and has long been active in encouraging tariffs on competing imports. The resources used for lobbying have a social value (equal to their productivity elsewhere in the economy), so the lobbying is not without cost. The calculations below will reveal the extent of this cost.

Consider a small economy in which two consumption goods are produced. In the absence of tariffs, the world prices of these commodities are both equal to 1, and the assumption that the economy is small means that it treats these prices as fixed. Some output is consumed and some is exported. A quantity $\bar{\ell}$ of labor is supplied inelastically by consumers. This is divided between production of the two goods and lobbying. Good 2 is produced with constant returns to scale, and one unit of labor produces one unit of output. This implies that the wage rate, w, must equal 1 (if it were higher, the firms would make a loss producing good 2; if it were lower, their profit would be unlimited since the price is fixed at the world level).

The cost function for the firm producing good 1 is assumed to be $C(y_1) = \frac{1}{2}y_1^2$, where y_1 is output. With a tariff τ, which may be zero, the price of good 1 on the domestic market becomes $1 + \tau$. Assuming that all of the output of the firm is sold on the domestic market, the profit level of the firm is

$$\pi_1(\tau) = y_1[1 + \tau] - \frac{1}{2}y_1^2. \tag{11.14}$$

Profit is maximized at output level

$$y_1 = 1 + \tau. \tag{11.15}$$

It can be seen from (11.15) that the output of good 1 is increasing in the value of the tariff. The monopolist therefore produces a higher output if they succeed in obtaining tariff protection. The level of profit that results from this output is given by

$$\pi_1(\tau) = \tfrac{1}{2}[1+\tau]^2, \tag{11.16}$$

so profit increases as the square of the tariff. This indicates the benefits that are obtained from protection.

Equilibrium on the labor market requires that labor supply must equal the use of labor in the production of good 1, ℓ_1, plus that used in the production of good 2, ℓ_2, plus that used for lobbying, ℓ_L. Hence $\bar{\ell} = \ell_1 + \ell_2 + \ell_L$. The labor demand from the firm 1 is $\ell_1 = \tfrac{1}{2}[1+\tau]^2$. To determine the labor used in lobbying the Complete Dissipation Theorem of section 11.3 is applied. That is, it is assumed that resources are used in lobbying up to the point at which the extra profit they generate is exactly equal to the resource cost. Without lobbying, profit is $\pi_1(0)$. After a successful lobby with a tariff implemented, it becomes $\pi_1(\tau)$. The value of labor that the firm will devote to lobbying is therefore

$$\ell_L = \pi_1(\tau) - \pi_1(0) = \tfrac{1}{2}[2\tau + \tau^2]. \tag{11.17}$$

Hence the value of labor wasted in lobbying is increasing as the square of the tariff. Finally, since the production of each unit of good 2 requires one unit of labor, the output of good 2 equals the labor input into the production of that good, so $\ell_2 = y_2$ or

$$y_2 = \bar{\ell} - \tfrac{1}{2}[1 + 4\tau + 2\tau^2]. \tag{11.18}$$

This shows that the output of good 2 is decreasing as the square of the tariff.

From these observations it can be judged that the rent-seeking is damaging the economy, since the production of good 2 falls at a faster rate than the production of good 1 increases. One method for quantifying the effect of this process is to determine the value of national output at world prices. World prices are used since these are the true measure of value. Doing this gives

$$y_1 + y_2 = \bar{\ell} - \tfrac{1}{2}[2\tau^2 + 2\tau - 1]. \tag{11.19}$$

Hence national income is reduced at the rate of the tariff squared. The conclusion in (11.19) shows just how damaging rent-seeking can be. The possible availability of a tariff causes resources to be devoted to lobbying. These resources are withdrawn from the production of good 2 and national income, evaluated at world prices, declines.

11.6.2   Rent Creation

The analysis so far has focused primarily on the effects of rent-seeking in the presence of preexisting rents. We now turn to study the other side of the issue: the motives for the deliberate creation of rents. Such rent-creation is important because the existence of a rent implies a distortion in the economy. Hence the economic cost of a created rent is the total of the rent-seeking costs plus the cost of the economic distortion. This is the sum of deadweight loss plus profit identified in the section 11.4.

To be in a position to create rents requires the power to make policy decisions. In most political systems this authority is formally vested in politicians. Assuming that they are solely responsible for decision-making would, though, be short-sighted. Politicians are advised and informed by bureaucrats. Many of the responsibilities for formulating policy options and for clarifying the vague policy notions of politicians are undertaken by bureaucrats. By carefully limiting the policies suggested or by choosing their advice carefully, a bureaucrat may well be able to wield implicit political power. It therefore cannot be judged in advance whether it is the politicians or the bureaucrats who actually make policy decisions. This does not matter unduly. For the purpose of the analysis all that is necessary is that there is someone in a position to make decisions that can create rents, be it a politician or a bureaucrat. When the arguments apply to both politicians and bureaucrats, the generic term "policy-maker" will be adopted.

How are rents created? To see this most clearly, consider an initial position where there is a uniform rate of corporation tax applicable to all industries. A rent can then be created by making it known that sufficient lobbying will be met by a reduction in the rate of tax. For instance, if the oil sector were to expend resources on lobbying, then it would be made a special case and permitted a lower corporation tax. The arguments already applied several times show that the oil sector will be willing to lobby up to a value equal to the benefit of the tax reduction. The creation of a monopoly airline route mentioned in section 11.4 is another example of rent-creation.

The reason for the rent-creation can now be made clear. By ensuring that the nature of the lobbying is in a form that they find beneficial, the policy-maker will personally gain. Such benefits could take many forms, ranging from meals to gifts through to actual bribes in the form of cash payments. Contributions to campaign funds are an especially helpful form of lobbying for politicians, as are lucrative appointments after a term of office is completed. All of these forms of lobbying are observed to greater or lesser degrees in political systems across the world.

It has already been noted that this rent-creation leads to the economic costs of the associated rent-seeking. There are also further costs. Since there are rents to be gained from being a politician or a bureaucrat (the returns from the lobbying), there will be excessive resources devoted to securing these positions. Political office will be highly sought after with too many candidates spending too much money in seeking election. Bureaucratic positions will be valued far in excess of the contribution that bureaucrats make to economic welfare. Basically, if politicians or bureaucrats can earn rents, then this will generate its own rent-seeking as these positions are competed for. In short, the ability to create rents has cumulative effects throughout the system. The Complete Dissipation Theorem can again be applied here: in expected terms these rents are dissipated. It is important to bear in mind that the winner of the rent does gain: the politician who is elected or the bureaucrat who secures their position will personally benefit from the rent. Losses arise for those who competed but failed to win.

Two further effects arise. First, there will be an excessive number of distortions introduced into the economy. Distortions will be created until there is no further potential for the decision-maker to extract additional benefits from lobbyists. Second, there will be an excessive number of changes in policy. Decision-makers will constantly seek new methods of creating rents and this will involve policy being continually revised. One simple way for a new policy-maker to obtain rents is to make tax rates uniform with a broad base on appointment, and then gradually auction off exemptions throughout the term of office. The broader the chosen base, the greater the number of exemptions that can be sold.

11.6.3   Conclusions

The discussion of this section has presented a very negative view of government and economic policy-making. The rent-seeking perspective argues that decisions are not made for reasons of economic efficiency but are made on the basis of how much can be earned for making them. As a result the economy is damaged by inefficient and distortionary policies. In addition resources are wasted in the process of rent-seeking. Both lobbying and attempting to obtain decision-making positions waste resources. When these are combined, the damage to the economy is significant. It suggests that political power is sought after not as an end in itself but simply as a means to access rent.

11.7   Informative Lobbying

The discussion so far has presented a picture of lobbyists as a group who contribute nothing to the economy and are just a source of welfare loss. To provide some balance, it is important to note that circumstances can arise in which lobby-ists do make a positive contribution. Lobbyists may be able to benefit the econ-omy if they, or the interest groups they represent, have superior information about the policy environment than the policy-maker. By transmitting this infor-mation to the policy-maker, they can assist in the choice of a better policy.

Several issues arise in this process of information transmission. To provide a simple description of these, assume that a policy has to be chosen for the next economic period. At the time the policy has to be chosen, the policy-maker is un-certain about the future economic environment. This uncertainty is modeled by assuming that the environment can be described by one of several alternative "states of the world." Here a state of the world is a summary of all relevant eco-nomic information. The policy-maker knows that different states of the world re-quire different policy choices to be made, but they do not know the future state of the world. Without additional information, the policy-maker would have to base policy choice upon some prior beliefs about the probability of alternative states of the world. Unfortunately, if the chosen policy is not correct for the state of the world that is realized, welfare will not be maximized.

Now assume that there is a lobbyist who knows which state of the world will occur. It seems that if they were just to report this information to the policy-maker, then the correct policy would be chosen and welfare maximized. But this misses the most important point: the objectives of the lobbyist. If the lobbyist had the same preferences as the policy-maker, there would be no problem. The policy-maker would accept the information that was offered knowing that the lobbyist was pursuing the same ends. In contrast, if lobbyists have different preferences, then they may have an incentive to reveal false information about the future state of the world with the intention of distorting policy in a direction that they find beneficial. Therefore the policy-maker faces the problem of determining when the information they receive from lobbyists is credible and correct, and when it repre-sents a distortion of the truth.

To see how these issues are resolved, consider a model where there are only two possible values for the future state of the world. Let these values be denoted θ_h and θ_ℓ with $\theta_\ell < \theta_h$, where we term θ_h the "high state" and θ_ℓ is the "low state." The policy-maker seeks to maximize a social welfare function that depends on the state of the world and the policy choice, π. Suppose that this objective function takes the form

$$W(\pi, \theta) = -[\pi - \theta]^2, \tag{11.20}$$

which implies that welfare loss is minimized when the policy choice is adapted to the state of the world. If the policy-maker had perfect information, then when the state was known to be high, a high policy level $\pi_h = \theta_H$ would be chosen. In contrast, when the state was known to be low, a low policy level $\pi_\ell = \theta_\ell$ would be chosen. Now assume that the policy-maker is uninformed about the state of the world and initially regards the two states as equally likely. In this case the policy-maker will choose a policy based on the expected state of the world, so

$$\pi^e = \frac{\theta_\ell + \theta_h}{2}. \tag{11.21}$$

That is, the policy-maker sets the policy equal to the expected value of θ.

Now we introduce a lobbyist who knows what the state of the world will be. The welfare of the lobbyist also depends on the policy level and the state of the world. However, the lobbyist does not share the same view as the policy-maker about the ideal policy level in each state. We assume that the ideal policy for the lobbyist exceeds the ideal policy of the policy-maker by an amount Δ in both states of the world. We can refer to such a difference in the ideal policy as the *extent of the disagreement* between the policy-maker and the lobbyist. Such a lack of agreement can be obtained by adopting preferences for the lobbyist given by

$$U(\pi, \theta) = -[\pi - \theta - \Delta]^2. \tag{11.22}$$

To find the conditions under which the lobbyist can credibly transmit information about the state of the world, we must investigate the incentives the lobbyist has to truthfully report the state of the world. The lobbyist can only report either θ_h or θ_ℓ, and if he is trusted by the policy-maker, the policy choice will be, respectively, π_h or π_ℓ. If the true state is θ_h the lobbyist has no incentive to misreport the information. Indeed, the lobbyist has a bias toward a high policy level; misreporting the state as being low would lead to a policy π_ℓ, which is worse than the lobbyist's ideal policy of $\pi_h + \Delta$ when the state is high. On the other hand, if the state is θ_ℓ the lobbyist has a potential incentive to misreport because a truthful report, if trusted by the policy-maker, leads to a policy level π_ℓ that is below the ideal policy of the lobbyist $\pi_\ell + \Delta$. The lobbyist may prefer to claim that the state is high to exploit the trust and obtain policy π_h instead of π_ℓ. However, it may be that π_h is too large for the lobbyist when the state is θ_ℓ, in which case the lobbyist will report truthfully. The latter is the case if π_ℓ is closer to the ideal policy of the lobbyist in the low state than π_h, which occurs if the following inequality is satisfied:

$$[\theta_\ell + \Delta] - \theta_\ell \le \theta_h - [\theta_\ell + \Delta]. \tag{11.23}$$

This inequality reduces to

$$\Delta \leq \frac{\theta_h - \theta_\ell}{2}. \tag{11.24}$$

This condition says that policy-maker can expect the lobbyist to truthfully report the state of the world if the extent of the disagreement is not too large. The equilibrium that results is fully revealing because the lobbyist can credibly transmit information about the state of the world. Lobbying is then informative and desirable for the society. If, in contrast, the above inequality is not satisfied, the extent of the disagreement is too large for the policy-maker to expect truthful reporting when the state is low. The lobbyist's report lacks credibility because the policy-maker knows that the lobbyist prefers reporting the high state no matter what the true state happens to be. The report is then uninformative, and the policy-maker will rightly ignore it. So the policy-maker sets the policy equal to the expected value $\pi^e = \frac{\theta_\ell + \theta_h}{2}$. This policy choice is suboptimal for society because it is too large when the state is low and too small when the state is high. Note that the lobbyist is also worse off with the uninformative outcome because the policy choice π^e is smaller than their ideal policy $\pi_h + \Delta$ when the state is high.

The problem of securing credibility is magnified when there are more than two states of the world. As the number of possible states increases, honest information revelation becomes ever more difficult to obtain. This is easily demonstrated. For a lobbyist to credibly report the true state, Δ must be smaller than one-half of the distance between any two adjacent states—this is the content of (11.24). With n states, $\theta_1 < \cdots < \theta_i < \cdots < \theta_n$, the conditions for truth-telling are for all $i = 1, \ldots, n-1$,

$$\Delta \leq \frac{\theta_{i+1} - \theta_i}{2}. \tag{11.25}$$

Evidently, as the number of states grows, intermediate states are added, and this reduces the distance between any two states. Eventually the states become too close to each other for the lobbyist to be able to credibly communicate the true state, even if Δ is small. Full revelation is then impossible. What can the lobbyist do in such a situation? The answer is to reveal partial information, as pointed out by Crawford and Sobel (1982).

Suppose that the states are partitioned into two intervals, $L = (\theta_1, \ldots, \theta_i)$ and $H = (\theta_{i+1}, \ldots, \theta_n)$. Then the lobbyist can report the interval in which the true state falls, instead of reporting the precise state—we term this *partial revelation*.

If he reports Θ_L, then it means that $\theta_1 \leq \theta \leq \theta_i$. If all states are equally likely and equally spaced, then a trusty policy-maker sets the policy equal to the expected value on this interval $\pi(L) = \frac{\theta_1 + \theta_i}{2}$. Similarly, the report Θ_H induces a policy choice $\pi(H) = \frac{\theta_{i+1} + \theta_n}{2}$. The question is whether the lobbyist has any incentive to lie.

Among the states in the interval L, the greatest temptation to lie (by reporting Θ_H) is when the true state is close to θ_i: if the lobbyist does not want to claim H when $\theta = \theta_i$ then he will not wish to do so when $\theta < \theta_i$, since this would push the policy choice further away from his ideal policy. Hence we can restrict attention to the incentive to report truthfully L when the true state is θ_i. Truthful reporting induces policy $\pi(L)$ and misreporting induces policy $\pi(H)$. The lobbyist will report truthfully if the former policy is closer than the latter to his ideal policy $\theta_i + \Delta$ given the true state θ_i. This is the case if

$$[\theta_i + \Delta] - \pi(L) \leq \pi(H) - [\theta_i + \Delta], \tag{11.26}$$

which reduces to

$$\theta_i + \Delta \leq \frac{\pi(H) + \pi(L)}{2}. \tag{11.27}$$

Now suppose that θ actually is in H. We must check the incentive of the lobbyist to truthfully report H instead of L. The temptation to misreport is highest when the true state is close to θ_{i+1}. In such a case, to sustain truthful reporting, it is required that the lobbyist induce a policy $\pi(H)$ that is closer to the ideal policy $\theta_{i+1} + \Delta$ than the policy that would be induced by misreporting $\pi(L)$. That is,

$$[\theta_{i+1} + \Delta] - \pi(L) \geq \pi(H) - [\theta_{i+1} + \Delta], \tag{11.28}$$

which reduces to

$$\theta_{i+1} + \Delta \geq \frac{\pi(H) + \pi(L)}{2}. \tag{11.29}$$

Combining the two incentive constraints (11.27) and (11.29), truth-telling requires that

$$\frac{\pi(H) + \pi(L)}{2} - \theta_{i+1} \leq \Delta \leq \frac{\pi(H) + \pi(L)}{2} - \theta_i. \tag{11.30}$$

This condition puts both a lower bound and an upper bound on the extent of the disagreement for the lobbyist to be able to communicate credibly partial information about the state to the policy-maker.

The outcome of this analysis is that lobbyists can raise welfare if they are able to credibly report information to the policy-maker. Unfortunately, this argument is limited by the potential incentive to report false information when there is divergence between the preferences of the lobbyist and the preferences of the policy-maker. With a limited number of states, credible correct transmission can be sustained if the divergence is not too great. However, as the number of states of the world increases, credible transmission cannot be sustained if there is any divergence at all in preferences. In this latter case, though, it is possible to have partial information credibly released—again, provided that the divergence is limited. In conclusion, informed lobbyists can be beneficial through the advice they can offer a policy-maker, but this can be undermined by their incentives to reveal false information.

11.8   Controlling Rent-Seeking

Much has been made of the economic cost of rent-seeking. These insights are interesting (and also depressing for those who may believe in benevolent government) but are of little value unless they suggest methods of controlling the phenomenon. This section gathers together a number of proposals that have been made in this respect. There are two channels through which rent-seeking can be controlled. The first channel is to limit the efforts that can be put into rent-seeking. The second is to restrict the process of rent-creation.

Beginning with the latter, rent-creation relies on the unequal treatment of economic agents. For instance, the creation of a monopoly is based on one economic agent being given the right to operate in the market and all other agents being denied. Equally, offering a tax concession for one industry treats the agents in that industry more favorably than those outside. Consequently a first step in controlling rent-seeking is to disallow policies that discriminate among economic agents. Restricting the policy-maker to the implementation of *nondiscriminatory policies* would eliminate the creation of tax breaks for special interests or the imposition of tariffs on particular imports. If restricted in this way, the decision-maker cannot auction off rents—if all parties gain, none has the incentive to pay.

The drawback of a rule preventing discrimination is that it is sometimes economically efficient to discriminate. For example, the theory of optimal commodity taxation (see chapter 14) describes circumstances where it is efficient for necessities to be taxed more heavily than luxuries. This would not be possible with nondiscrimination because the industries producing necessities would have grounds for complaint. Similarly the theory of income taxation (see chapter 15) finds that, in general, it is optimal to have a marginal rate of income tax that is not uniform. If implemented, the taxpayers facing a higher marginal rate would have ground for alleging discrimination. Hence a nondiscrimination ruling would result in uniform commodity and income taxes. These would not usually be efficient, so there would be a trade-off between economic losses through restrictions on feasible policy choices and losses through rent-seeking. It is not unlikely that the latter will outweigh the former.

There are other ways in which the process of rent-seeking can be lessened, but all of these are weaker than a nondiscrimination rule. These primarily focus on ensuring that the policy-making process is as *transparent* as possible. Among them would be policies such as limiting campaign budgets, insisting on the revelation of names of donors, requiring registration of lobbyists, regulating and limiting gifts, and reviewing bureaucratic decisions. Policing can be improved to lessen the use of bribes. Unlike nondiscrimination, none of these policies has any economic implications other than their direct effect on rent-seeking.

11.9 Conclusions

Lobbyists are very numerous in number; they are also engaged in an activity that is not productive. The theory of rent-seeking provides an explanation for this apparent paradox and looks at the consequences for the economy. The fundamental insight of the literature is the Complete Dissipation Theorem: competition for a rent will result in resources being expended up until the expected gain of society from the existence of the rent is zero. If competitors for the rent are risk-neutral, this implies that the resources used in rent-seeking are exactly equal in value to the size of the rent. The application of these rent-seeking ideas show that the losses caused by distortions are potentially much larger than the standard measure of deadweight loss.

The other aspect of rent-seeking is that economic policy-makers have an incentive to create distortions. They do this in order to receive benefits from the resulting rent-seeking. This leads to a perspective of policy driven not by what is good for the economy but by what the policy-maker can get out of it and of a politics corrupted by self-interest. If this view is the correct description of the policy-making process, the response should be to limit the discretion for policy-makers. Last, lobbying can be desirable when the lobbyists have better information about a policy-relevant variable than the policy-maker. The question is then how the lobbyists can credibly communicate this information when there is some disagreement about the ideal policy choice.

Further Reading

The classic analysis of rent-seeking is in:

Krueger, A. O. 1974. The political economy of the rent-seeking society. *American Economic Review* 64: 291–303.

Tullock, G. 1967. The welfare costs of tariffs, monopolies and theft. *Western Economic Journal* 5: 224–32.

The second article is reprinted in:

Buchanan, J. M., Tollison, R. D., and Tullock, G. 1980. *Towards a Theory of the Rent-Seeking Society*. College Station: Texas A & M Press.

This book also contains other interesting reading.

For more discussion of the definition of rent-seeking and a survey of the literature see:

Brooks, M. A., and Heijdra, B. J. 1989. An exploration of rent-seeking. *Economic Record* 65: 32–50.

The complete analysis of the rent-seeking game is in:

Hillman, A., and Samet, D. 1987. Dissipation of contestable rents by small numbers of contenders. *Public Choice* 54: 63–82.

An alternative and very simple treatment of the rent-seeking game as an aggregative game is in:

Cornes, R., and Hartley, R. 2003. Risk aversion, heterogeneity and contests. *Public Choice* 115: 1–25.

Estimates of the social costs of monopoly are taken from:

Cowling, K. G., and Mueller, D. C. 1978. The social costs of monopoly power. *Economic Journal* 88: 727–48.

Harberger, A. C. 1954. Monopoly and resource allocation. *American Economic Review* 45: 77–87.

Hazlett, T. W., and Michaels, R. J. 1993. The cost of rent-seeking—Evidence from cellular telephone license lotteries. *Southern Economic Journal* 59: 425–35.

Another important paper in this area is:

Posner, R. A. 1975. The social cost of monopoly and regulation. *Journal of Political Economy* 83: 807–27.

More on interest groups and lobbying can be found in:

Austen-Smith, D. 1997. Interest groups: Money, information and influence. In D. Mueller, ed., *Perspectives on Public Choice*. Cambridge: Cambridge University Press.

Crawford, V., and Sobel, J. 1982. Strategic information transmission. *Econometrica* 50: 1431–51.

Grossman, G., and Helpman, E. 2001. *Special Interest Politics.* Cambridge: MIT Press.

A debate about the relative merits of rent-seeking and the traditional public finance approach is found in:

Buchanan, J. M., and Musgrave, R. A. 1999. *Public Finance and Public Choice: Two Contrasting Visions of the State.* Cambridge: MIT Press.

Exercises

11.1. One country invades another to create a demand for its construction industry. Is this rent-seeking?

11.2. IBM assembled its first personal computers from standard components to lower the cost. Was this rent-seeking?

11.3. A computer software company refuses to release its code to other developers. Is this rent-seeking?

11.4. Construct a variation of the rent-seeking game without the discontinuity in winning/losing. Find the pure strategy equilibrium.

11.5. If demand is linear, show that profit and monopoly deadweight loss are related by $\pi = 2d$. Hence contrast the total loss with rent-seeking to the deadweight loss.

11.6. Should advertising be banned?

11.7. Does the observation that profit is positive show that the rent-seeking argument does not apply?

11.8. Using figure 11.3, locate the points where monopoly welfare loss (in units of good 2) occurs in the diagram. Show that this increases the higher the monopoly price is relative to the competitive price.

11.9. You are competing for a rent with one rival. Your valuation and your competitor's valuation are private information. You believe that the other bidder's valuation is equally likely to lie anywhere in the interval between 0 and \$5,000. Your own valuation is \$2,000. Suppose that you expect your rival will submit a bid that is exactly one-half of his valuation. Thus you believe that your rival is equally likely to bid anywhere between 0 and \$2,500 (depending on the realized valuation between 0 and \$5,000).

a. Show that if you submit a bid of B, the probability that you win the contest is the probability that your bid B will exceed your rival's bid, and that this probability of winning is $\frac{B}{250}$.

b. Your expected profit from bidding B is $[200 - B] \times$ Probability of winning. Show that the profit-maximizing strategy consists of bidding half your valuation.

11.10. Three firms have applied for the franchise to operate the cable TV system during the coming year. The annual cost of operating the system is \$250 and the demand curve for its services is $P = 500 - Q$, where P is the price per subscriber per year and Q is the expected number of subscribers. The franchise is assigned for only one year, and it allows the firm with the franchise to charge whatever price it chooses. The government will choose the applicant that spends the most money lobbying the government members. If the applicants cannot collude, how much will each spend on lobbying? (*Hint:* The winner will set the monopoly price for the service.)

11.11. In exercise 11.10 the rent goes to the firm with the highest lobbying activity, and it takes only a small advantage to obtain a sure win. Now suppose that a higher lobbying activity increases the probability of getting the rent but does not ensure a win. If firm i spends the amount x_i on lobbying activity, it will get the franchise with probability $p_i = \frac{x_i}{\sum_{j=1}^{3} x_j}$.

a. What is the optimal spending of firm i in response to the total spending of the two other firms $x_{-i} = \sum_{j \neq i} x_j$? Draw the best-response function of firm i to x_{-i}.

b. Suppose a symmetric equilibrium in lobbying where $x_i = x^*$ for all i. How much will each firm will spend on lobbying?

c. How does your answer change if there are N extra firms competing for the franchise (assuming again all firms are identical)?

11.12. Consider a rent-seeking game with $N \geq 2$ contestants. The effort for person i is denoted by x_i for $i = 1, \ldots, N$. The cost per unit of effort is C. All contestants are identical. They value the rent at V and each contestant can win the prize with a probability equal to their effort relative to the total effort of all contestants. Thus the payoff function of person i exerting effort x_i is given by $U = \left[\frac{x_i}{X}\right] V - C x_i$, where $X = \sum x_j$. Note that the cost must be paid whether or not the prize is obtained. A Nash equilibrium is a lobbying effort for each contestant such that nobody would want to alter their expenditure given that of the other competitors.

a. Find the derivative of player i's expected utility and then set it equal to zero. Draw the resulting best-response function for player i when the $N - 1$ each of the others chooses x.

b. In a symmetric equilibrium it must be the case that all contestants choose the same effort $x_i = x^*$. Using this symmetry condition and the best-response function in part a, show that the equilibrium outcome is $x^* = \left[\frac{N-1}{N^2}\right]\frac{V}{C}$. Show that the total cost $NCx^* = \frac{[N-1]V}{N}$ and that the fraction of the rent that is dissipated (i.e., total cost relative to the value of the prize) is an increasing function of N.

c. Suppose that there are four contenders ($N = 4$), the value of the prize is $V = 20,000$, and the cost of effort is $C = 5,000$. What is the equilibrium level of rent-seeking activity x^*? What is the fraction of rent dissipation?

d. Suppose that the cost of rent-seeking effort reduces from 5,000 to 2,500 with four competitors and a prize of 20,000. What is the impact on the common equilibrium level of rent-seeking activity? Does it affect the fraction of rent dissipation? Why or why not?

11.13. There is a given rent of R. Each of two players spends resources competing for the rent. If player 1 spends x_1, the probability that he wins the rent is $p_1 = \frac{\phi x_1}{\phi x_1 + x_2}$ when player 2 spends the amount x_2, where $\phi > 1$.

a. What is the optimal spending of player 1 in response to a given spending level of player 2? What is the optimal response of player 2 to player 1? Draw the best-response functions. Discuss the effect of changing ϕ on the function.

b. How much will each player spend on lobbying? Which player is more likely to win the rent in equilibrium?

c. Compare the total equilibrium spending for $\phi > 1$ and $\phi = 1$. Should we expect more spending in rent-seeking activities when players are identical? Why or why not?

11.14. Consider the following situation: There are $N > 2$ players competing for a chance to win benefits from the government of R. The rent is given to the highest bidder. The second-highest bidder gets nothing but must also spend the amount he bids. What is the likely outcome of such a situation? Where will the process stop? Is it possible that the first- and second-highest bidder could together bid more than the value of the rent? Could each of them spend more than the value of the rent? Why or why not?

V EQUITY AND DISTRIBUTION

12.1   Introduction

On April 17, 1975, the Khmer Rouge seized power in Cambodia. Pol Pot began to implement his vision of Year Zero in which all inequalities—of class, money, education, and religion—would be eliminated. Driven by their desire to achieve what they perceived as the social optimum, the Khmer Rouge attempted to engineer a return to a peasant economy. In the process they slaughtered an estimated two million people, approximately one-quarter of Cambodia's population. The actions of the Khmer Rouge are an extreme example of the pursuit of equality and the willingness to accept an immense loss in order to achieve it. In normal circumstances governments impose a limit on the cost they are willing to pay for an improvement in equality.

When it comes to the efficiency/equity trade-off the Second Theorem of Welfare Economics has very strong policy implications. These were touched on in chapter 2 but were not developed in detail at that point. This was because the primary value of the theorem is what it says about issues of distribution. To fully appreciate the Second Theorem, it is necessary to view it from an equity perspective and to assess it in the light of its distributional implications.

This chapter will begin by investigating the implications of the Second Theorem for economic policy. This is undertaken accepting that a social planner is able to make judgments between different allocations of utility. The concept of an optimal allocation is developed and the Second Theorem is employed to show how this can be achieved. Once this has been accomplished, questions will be raised about the applicability of lump-sum taxes and the value of Pareto-efficiency as a criterion for social decision-making. This provides a basis for re-assessing the interpretation of the First Theorem of Welfare Economics.

The major deficiency of Pareto-efficiency is identified as its inability to trade utility gains for one consumer against losses for another. To proceed further, the informational basis for making welfare comparisons has to be addressed. We describe different forms of utility and different degrees of comparability of utility between consumers. These concepts are then related to Arrow's Impossibility Theorem and the construction of social welfare functions.

12.2   Social Optimality

The importance of the Second Theorem for policy analysis is very easily explained. In designing economic policy, a policy-maker will always aim to achieve a Pareto-efficient allocation. If an allocation that was not Pareto-efficient was selected, then it would be possible to raise the welfare of at least one consumer without harming any other. It is hard to imagine why any policy-maker would want to leave such gains unexploited. Applying this argument, the set of allocations from which a policy-maker will choose reduces to the Pareto-efficient allocations.

Suppose that a particular Pareto-efficient allocation has been selected as the policy-maker's preferred outcome. The Second Theorem shows that this allocation can be achieved by making the economy competitive and providing each consumer with the level of income needed to purchase the consumption bundle assigned to them in the chosen allocation. In achieving this, only two policy tools are employed: the encouragement of competition and a set of lump-sum taxes to ensure that each consumer has the required income. If this approach could be applied in practice, then economic policy analysis would reduce to the formulation of a set of rules that guarantee competition and the calculation and redistribution of the lump-sum taxes. The subject matter of public economics, and economic policy, in general, would then be closed.

Looking at this process in detail, the first point that arises is the question of selecting the most preferred allocation. There are a number of ways to imagine this being done. An obvious one would be to consider voting, either over the alternative allocations directly or else for the election of a body (a "government"), to make the choice. Alternatively, the consumers could agree for it to be chosen at random or else they might hold unanimous views, perhaps via conceptions of fairness, about what the outcome should be. The method that is adopted here is to assume that there is a social planner (which could be the elected government). This planner forms preferences over the alternative allocations by taking into account the utility levels of the consumers. The most preferred allocation according to these preferences is the one that is chosen.

To see how this method functions, consider the set of Pareto-efficient allocations described by the contract curve in the left-hand part of figure 12.1. Each point on the contract curve is associated with an indifference curve for consumer 1 and an indifference curve for consumer 2. These indifference curves correspond

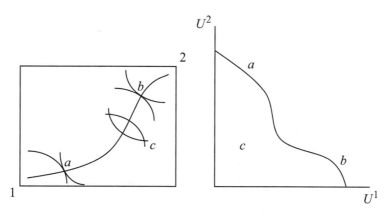

Figure 12.1
Utility possibility frontier

to a pair of utility levels $\{U^1, U^2\}$ for the two consumers. As the move is made from the southwest corner of the Edgeworth box to the northeast corner, the utility of consumer 1 rises and that of 2 falls. In plotting these utility changes, the utility levels on the contract curve can be represented as loci in utility space—usually called the *utility possibility frontier*. This is shown in the right-hand part of figure 12.1 where the utility values corresponding to the points *a*, *b*, and *c* are plotted. Points such as *a* and *b* lie on the frontier: they are Pareto-efficient, so it is not possible to raise both consumers' utilities simultaneously. Point *c* is off the contract curve and is inefficient according to the Pareto criterion. It therefore lies inside the utility possibility frontier.

The utility possibility frontier describes the options from which the social planner will choose. It is now necessary to describe how the choice is made. To do this, it is assumed that the social planner measures the welfare of society by aggregating the individual consumers' welfare levels. Given the pair of welfare levels $\{U^1, U^2\}$, the function determining the aggregate level of welfare is denoted by $W(U^1, U^2)$. This is termed a *Bergson-Samuelson social welfare function*. Basically, given individual levels of happiness, it imputes a social level of happiness. Embodied within it are the equity considerations of the planner. Two examples of social welfare functions are the *utilitarian* $W = U^1 + U^2$ and the *Rawlsian* (or maxi-min) $W = \min\{U^1, U^2\}$.

Given the welfare function, the social planner considers the attainable allocations of utility described by the contract curve and chooses the one that provides the highest level of social welfare. Indifference curves of the welfare function can

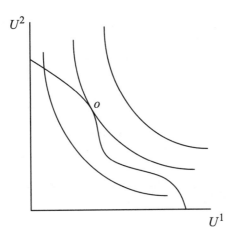

Figure 12.2
Social optimality

be drawn as in figure 12.2. These curves show combinations of the two consumers'
utilities that give constant levels of social welfare. The view on equity taken by the
social planner translates into their willingness to trade off the utility of one consumer against the utility of the other. This determines the shape of the indifference
curves. The social planner then selects the outcome that achieves the highest indifference curve. This optimal point on the utility possibility locus, denoted by point
o, can then be traced back to an allocation in the Edgeworth box. This allocation
represents the socially optimal division of resources for the economy given the
preferences captured by the social welfare function. If these preferences were to
change, so would the optimal allocation.

Having chosen the socially optimal allocation, the reasoning of the Second Theorem is applied. Lump-sum taxes are imposed to ensure that the incomes of the
consumers are sufficient to allow them to purchase their allocation conforming to
point o. Competitive economic trading then takes place. The chosen socially optimal allocation is then achieved through trade as the equilibrium of the competitive economy. This process of using lump-sum taxes and competitive trade to
reach a chosen equilibrium is called *decentralization*.

This construction shows that the use of the Second Theorem allows the economy to achieve the outcome most preferred by its social planner. Given the economy's limited initial stock of resources, the socially optimal allocation reaches the
best trade-off between efficiency and equity as measured by the social welfare
function. In this way the application of the Second Theorem can be said to solve

the economic problem, since the issues of both efficiency and equity are resolved to the greatest extent possible and there is no better outcome attainable. Clearly, if this reasoning is applicable, all that a policy-maker has to do is choose the allocation, implement the required lump-sum taxes, and ensure that the economy is competitive. No further policy or action is required. Once the incomes are set, the economy will take itself to the optimal outcome.

12.3   Lump-Sum Taxes

The role of lump-sum taxes has been made very explicit in describing the application of the Second Theorem. In the economic environment envisaged, lump-sum taxes are the only tool of policy that is required beyond an active competition policy. To justify the use of policies other than lump-sum taxes, it must be established that such taxes are either not feasible or else are restricted in the way in which they can be employed. This is the purpose of the next two sections. The results described are important in their own right, but they also provide important insights into the design of other forms of taxation.

In order for a tax to be lump sum, the consumer on whom the tax is levied must not be able to affect the size of the tax by changing their behavior. Most tax instruments encountered in practice are not lump sum. Income taxes cannot be lump sum by this definition because a consumer can work more or less hard and vary income in response to the tax. Similarly commodity taxes cannot be lump sum because consumption patterns can be changed. Estate duties are lump sum at the point at which they are levied (since, by definition, the person on which they are levied is dead and unable to choose any other action) but can be affected by changes in behavior prior to death (e.g., by making gifts earlier in life).

There are some taxes, though, that are close to being lump sum. For example, taxing every consumer some fixed amount imposes a lump-sum tax. Setting aside minor details, this was effectively the case of the UK Poll Tax levied in the late 1980s as a source of finance for local government. This tax was unsuccessful for two reasons. First, taxpayers could avoid paying the tax by ensuring that their names did not appear on any official registers. Usually this was achieved by moving house and not making any official declaration of the new address. It appears large numbers of taxpayers did this (unofficial figures put the number as high as 1 million). This "disappearance" is a change in behavior that reduces the tax burden. Second, the theoretical efficiency of lump-sum taxes rests partly on the fact that their imposition is costless, though this was far from the case with the Poll

Tax. As it turned out, the difficulty of actually collecting and maintaining information on the residential addresses of all households made the imposition of a uniform lump-sum tax prohibitively expensive. The mobility of taxpayers proved to be much greater than had been expected. Therefore, although the structure of lump-sum taxes makes them appear deceptively simple to collect, this may not be the case in practice, since the tax base (people) is highly mobile and keen to evade. Consequently, in practice, even a uniform lump-sum tax has proved difficult and costly to administer.

However, the costs of collection are only part of the issue. What is the primary policy concern is the use of *optimal* lump-sum taxes. Optimal here means a tax that is chosen, via application of the Second Theorem, to achieve the income distribution necessary to decentralize a certain allocation. The optimal lump-sum tax system is unlikely to be a uniform tax on each consumer. This is because the role of the taxes is fundamentally redistributive, so taxes will be highly differentiated across consumers. Since even uniform lump-sum taxes are implemented with difficulty, the use of differentiated taxes presents even greater problems.

The extent of these problems can be seen by considering the information needed to calculate the taxes. First, the social planner must be able to construct the contract curve of Pareto-efficient allocations so that the social optimum can be selected. Second, the planner needs to predict the equilibrium that will emerge for all possible income levels so that the incomes needed to decentralize the chosen allocation can be determined. Both of these steps require knowledge of the consumers' preferences. Finally the social planner must also know the value of each consumer's endowment in order to calculate their incomes before taxes and hence the lump-sum taxes that must be imposed. The fundamental difficulty is that these economic characteristics, preferences and endowments, are *private information*. As such they are known only to the individual consumers and are not directly observed by the social planner. The characteristics may be partly revealed through market choices, but these choices can be changed if the consumers perceive any link with taxation. The fact that lump-sum taxes are levied on private information is the fundamental difficulty that hinders their use.

Some characteristics of the consumers are public information, or at least can be directly observed. Lump-sum taxes can then be levied on these characteristics. For example, it may be possible to differentiate lump-sum taxes according to characteristics of the consumers such as sex, age, or eye-color. However, these characteristics are not those that are directly economically relevant as they convey neither preference information nor relate to the value of the endowment. Although we could differentiate taxes on this basis, there is no reason why we should want to do so.

This returns us to the problem of private information. Since the relevant characteristics such as ability are not observable, the social planner must either rely on consumers honestly reporting their characteristics or infer them from the observed economic choices of consumers. If the planner relies on the observation of choices, there is invariably scope for consumers to change their market behavior, which then implies that the taxes cannot be lump sum. When reports are the sole source of information, unobserved characteristics cannot form a basis for taxation unless the tax scheme is such that individuals are faced with incentives to report truthfully.

As an example of the interaction between taxes and reporting, consider the following: Let the quality of a consumer's endowment of labor be determined by their IQ level. Given a competitive market for labor, the value of the endowment is then related to IQ. Assume that there are no economically relevant variables other than IQ, so that any set of optimal lump-sum taxes must be levied on IQ. If the level of lump-sum tax was inversely related to IQ and if all households had to complete IQ tests, then the tax system would not be cheated because the incentive would always be to maximize the score on the test. In this case the lump-sum taxes are said to be *incentive compatible*, meaning that they give incentives to behave honestly. In contrast, if the taxes were positively related to IQ, a testing procedure could easily be manipulated by the high-IQ consumers who would intentionally choose to perform poorly. If such a system were put into place, the mean level of tested IQ would be expected to fall considerably. This indicates the potential for misrevelation of characteristics, and the system would not be incentive compatible. Clearly, if a high-IQ results in higher earnings and, ultimately, greater utility, a redistributive policy would require the use of lump-sum taxes that increased with IQ. The tax policy would not be incentive compatible. As the next section shows such problems will always be present in any attempt to base lump-sum taxes on unobservable characteristics.

12.4 Impossibility of Optimality

Imagine that each individual in a society can be described by a list of personal attributes on which the society wishes to condition taxes and transfers (e.g., tastes, needs, talents, and endowments). Individuals are also identified by their names and possibly other publicly observable attributes (such as eye color) that are not judged to be relevant attributes for taxation. The list of personal attributes associated to every agent is not publicly known but is the private information of each individual. This implies that the lump-sum taxes the government would like to implement must rely on information about personal attributes that individuals must either report or reveal indirectly through their actions.

Lump-sum taxes are not incentive compatible when at least one individual who understands how the reported information will be used chooses to report falsely. We have already argued that there can be incentive problems in implementing optimal lump-sum taxes. What we now wish to demonstrate is that these problems are fundamental ones and will always afflict any attempt to implement optimal lump-sum taxes. In brief, optimal lump-sum taxes are not incentive compatible. This does not mean that lump-sum taxes cannot be used—for instance, all individuals could be taxed the same amount—but only that the existence of private information places limits on the extent to which taxes can be differentiated before incentives for the false revelation of information come into play. These issues are first illustrated for a particular example and then a general result is provided.

A good illustration of the failure of incentive compatibility is provided in the following example due to Mirrlees. Assume that individuals can have one of two levels of ability: low or high. The low-ability level is denoted by s_l and the high-ability level by s_h with $s_l < s_h$. For simplicity suppose that the number with high ability is equal to the number with low. The two types have the same preferences over consumption, x, and labor, ℓ, as represented by the utility function $U(x, \ell) = u(x) - v(\ell)$. It is assumed that the marginal utility of consumption is decreasing in x and the marginal disutility of labor is increasing in ℓ.

To determine the optimal lump-sum taxes, suppose that the government can observe the ability of each individual and impose taxes that are conditioned on ability. Let the tax on an individual of ability level i be $T_i > 0$ (or a subsidy if $T_i < 0$). The budget constraint of a type i is

$$x_i = s_i \ell_i - T_i, \tag{12.1}$$

where earnings are $s_i \ell_i$. Given the lump-sum taxes, each type chooses labor supply to maximize utility subject to this budget constraint. The choice of labor supply equates the marginal utility of additional consumption to the disutility of labor:

$$s_i \frac{\partial u}{\partial x_i} - \frac{\partial v}{\partial \ell_i} = 0. \tag{12.2}$$

This provides a labor supply function $\ell_i = \ell_i(T_i)$.

Now suppose the government is utilitarian and chooses the lump-sum taxes to maximize the sum of utilities. Then the optimal lump-sum taxes solve

$$\max_{\{T_l, T_h\}} \sum_{l,h} u(s_i \ell_i(T_i) - T_i) - v(\ell_i(T_i)) \tag{12.3}$$

subject to the government budget balance, which requires

$$T_h + T_l = 0, \tag{12.4}$$

since there are equal numbers of the two types. This budget constraint can be used to substitute for T_l in (12.3). Differentiating the resulting expression with respect to the tax T_h and using the first-order condition (12.2) for the choice of labor supply, we can characterize the optimal lump-sum taxes by the condition

$$\frac{\partial u}{\partial x_h} = \frac{\partial u}{\partial x_l}. \tag{12.5}$$

Since the marginal utility of consumption is decreasing in x_i, the optimality condition (12.5) implies that there is equality of consumption for the two types: $x_h = x_l$. When this conclusion is combined with (12.2) and the fact $s_l < s_h$, it follows that

$$\frac{\partial v}{\partial \ell_l} = s_l \frac{\partial u}{\partial x_l} < s_h \frac{\partial u}{\partial x_h} = \frac{\partial v}{\partial \ell_h}. \tag{12.6}$$

Under the assumption of an increasing marginal disutility of labor, this inequality shows that the optimal lump-sum taxes should induce the outcome $\ell_h > \ell_l$, so the more able work harder than the less able. The motivation for this outcome is that working the high-ability type harder is the most efficient way to raise the level of total income for the society, which can then be redistributed using the lump-sum taxes. Thus the high-ability type works harder than the low-ability type but only gets to consume the same. Therefore the high-ability type is left with a lower utility level than the low-ability type after redistribution.

Now suppose that the government can observe incomes but cannot observe the ability of each individual. Assume that it still attempts to implement the optimal lump-sum taxes. The taxes are obviously not incentive compatible because, if the high-ability type understand the outcome, she can always choose to earn as little as the low-ability type. Doing so then qualifies the high-ability type for the redistribution aimed at the low-ability type. This will provide them with a higher utility level than if they did not act strategically. The optimal lump-sum taxes cannot then be implemented with private information.

Who would work hard if the government stood ready to tax away the resulting income? Optimal (utilitarian) lump-sum redistribution makes the more able individuals worse off because it requires them to work harder but does not reward them with additional consumption. In this context it is profitable for the more able individuals to make themselves seem incapable. Many people believe there is something unfair about inequality that arises from the fact that some people are born with superior innate ability or similar advantage over others. But many people also think it morally right that one should be able to keep some of the fruits of one's own effort. This example may have been simple, but its message is far-reaching. The Soviet Union and other communist economies have shown us that it is impossible to generate wealth without offering adequate material incentives. Incentive constraints inevitably limit the scope for redistribution.

The observations of the example are now shown to reflect a general principle concerning the incentive compatibility of optimal lump-sum taxes. We state the formal version of this result for a "large economy," which is an economy where the actions of a single individual are insignificant relative to the economy as a whole. In other words, there is a continuum of different agents, which is the mathematical form of the idealized competitive economy with a very large number of small agents with no market power. The theorem shows that optimal lump-sum taxation is never incentive compatible.

Theorem 10 (Hammond)   In a large economy, redistribution through optimal lump-sum taxes is always incentive incompatible.

The logic behind this theorem is surprisingly simple. A system of optimal lump-sum taxes is used to engineer a distribution of endowments that will decentralize the first-best allocation. The endowments after redistribution must be based on the agents' characteristics (recall that in the analysis of the Second Theorem the taxes were based on knowledge of endowments and preferences), so assume that the endowment given to an agent with characteristics θ_i is $e^i = e(\theta_i)$. For those characteristics that are not publicly observable, the government must rely on an announcement of the values by the agents. Assume, for simplicity, that none of the characteristics can be observed. Then the incentive exists for each agent to announce the set of characteristics that maximize the value of the endowment at the equilibrium prices p. This is illustrated in figure 12.3 where θ_1 and θ_2 are two potential announcements, with related endowments $e(\theta_1)$ and $e(\theta_2)$, and θ^* is the announcement that maximizes $pe(\theta)$. The announcement of θ^* leads to the highest

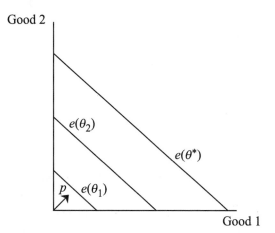

Figure 12.3
Optimal lump-sum taxes and incentive compatibility

budget constraint from among the set of possible announcements and, by giving the agent maximum choice, allows the highest level of utility to be attained. Consequently all agents will announce θ^*, and the optimal lump-sum taxes are not incentive compatible.

The main points of the argument can now be summarized. To implement the Second Theorem as a practical policy tool it is necessary to employ optimal lump-sum taxes. Such taxes are unlikely to be available in practice or to satisfy all the criteria required of them. The taxes may be costly to collect and the characteristics on which they need to be based may not be observable. When characteristics are not observable, the relationship between taxes and characteristics can give consumers the incentive to make false revelations. It is therefore best to treat the Second Theorem as being of considerable theoretical interest but of very limited practical relevance. The theorem shows us what *could* be possible, not what *is* possible.

Lump-sum taxes can achieve the optimal allocation of resources provided all information is public. If some of the characteristics that are relevant for taxation are private information, then the optimal lump-sum taxes are not incentive compatible. Information limitations therefore place a limit on the extent to which redistribution can be undertaken using lump-sum taxation. It is the impracticality of lump-sum taxation that provides the motive for studying the properties of other tax instruments. The income taxes and commodity taxes that are analyzed in chapters 14 and 15 are second-best solutions and are used because the first-best solution, lump-sum taxation, is not available. Lump-sum taxes are used as a benchmark from which to judge the relative success of these alternative instruments. Lump-sum taxes also help clarify what it is that we are really trying to tax.

12.5   Non–Tax Redistribution

The lump-sum taxes we have been discussing are a very immediate form of redistribution. In practice, there are numerous widely used methods of redistribution that do not directly involve taxation. Governments frequently provide goods such as education or health services at less than their cost, which may be viewed as a redistributional policy. One may expect that a cash transfer of the same value would have more redistributional power than such in-kind transfer programs. This is mistaken. There are three reasons why transfers in-kind may be superior to the cash transfers achieved through standard tax-transfer programs.

One reason is *political*. Political considerations dictate that many governments ensure that the provision of programs like education, pension, and basic health insurance is universal. Without this feature the programs would not have the political support required to be adopted or continued. For instance, public pensions and health care would be far more vulnerable politically if they were targeted to the poor and not available to others. Redistribution through cash would be even more vulnerable. It should be noted that because a government program is universal, it does not follow that there is no redistribution. First, if the program is financed by proportional income taxation, the rich will contribute more to its finance than the poor. Second, even if everyone contributes the same to the program, it is possible that the rich will not use the publicly provided good to the same extent as the poor. Consider, for example, a program of public provision of basic health care that is available to everyone for free and financed by a uniform tax on all households. Assume that there exists a private health care alternative with higher quality than the public system but only available at a cost. Since the rich can afford the higher quality, they will use the private health care, even though free public health care is available. These rich households still pay their contribution to the public program, and thus the poor households derive a net benefit from this cross-subsidization.

Another reason for preferring in-kind redistribution is *self-selection*. What ultimately limits redistribution is that it will eventually become advantageous for higher ability people to earn lower incomes by expending less effort and thereby paying the level of taxes (or receiving the transfers) intended for the lower ability groups. The self-selection argument is that anything that makes it less attractive for people to mimic those with lesser ability will extend the limit to redistribution. The use of in-kind transfers can obtain a given degree of redistribution more efficiently because of differences in preferences among different income groups. Consider two individuals who differ not only in their ability but also in their health status. Suppose that lesser ability means also poorer health, so the less able spend relatively more on health. Then both income and health expenditures act as a signal of ability. It follows that the limits to redistribution can be relaxed if transfers are made partly in the form of provision of health care (or equivalently with full subsidization of health expenditures). The reason is simply that the more able individual (with less tendency to become ill) is less likely to claim in-kind benefits in the form of health care provision than he would be to claim cash benefits. To take another example, suppose the government is considering redistribution either in cash or in the form of low-quality housing. All households, needy or not, would like the cash transfer. However, few non-needy households would want to live in low-quality housing as they can afford better housing. Thus self-selection occurs, and the non-needy drop out of the housing program, which is taken up only by the needy. In short, transfers in-kind invite people to self-select in a way that reveals their neediness. When need is correlated with income-earning ability, then in-kind transfers can relax incentive and selection constraints, thereby improving the government's ability to redistribute income.

A third reason is *time consistency*. Here the argument for in-kind transfers relies on the inability of government to commit to its future actions. Unlike the argument of Strotz (1956) on government time inconsistency, this does not arise from a change in government objective over time (e.g., because of elections) nor from the fact that the government is not welfaristic or rational. The time-consistency problem arises from a perfectly rational government that fully respects individual preferences but that does not have the power to commit to its policy in the long run. The time-consistency problem is obvious with regard to pensions. To the extent that households expect governments to provide some basic pension to those with too little savings, their incentive to save for retirement consumption and provide for themselves is reduced. Anticipating this, the government may prefer to provide public pensions. A related time-consistency problem can explain why transfer programs, such as social security, education, and job training are in-kind. If a welfaristic government cannot commit not to come to the rescue of those in need in the future, potential recipients will have little reason to invest in their education or to undertake job training, because the government will help them out anyway. Again, the government can improve both economic efficiency and redistribution by making education and job training available at less than their cost, rather than making cash transfers of equivalent value.

12.6   Aspects of Pareto-Efficiency

The analysis of lump-sum taxation has raised questions about the practical value of the Second Theorem. Although the theorem shows how an optimal allocation can be decentralized, the means to achieve the decentralization may be absent. If the use of lump-sum taxes is restricted, the government must resort to alternative policy instruments. All alternative instruments will be distortionary and will not achieve the first-best.

These criticisms do not extend to the First Theorem, which states only that a competitive equilibrium is Pareto-efficient. Consequently the First Theorem implies no policy intervention, so it is safe from the restrictions on lump-sum taxes. However, at the heart of the First Theorem is the use of Pareto-efficiency as a method for judging the success of an economic allocation. The value of the First Theorem can only be judged once a deeper understanding of Pareto-efficiency has been developed.

The Pareto criterion was introduced into economics by the Italian economist Vilfredo Pareto at the beginning of the twentieth century. This was a period of reassessment in economics during which the concept of utility as a measurable entity was rejected. Alongside this rejection of measurability, the ability to compare utility levels between consumers also had to be rejected. Pareto-efficiency was therefore constructed explicitly to allow comparisons of allocations without the need to make any interpersonal comparisons of utility. As will be seen, this avoidance of interpersonal comparisons is both its strength and its main weakness.

To assess Pareto-efficiency, it is helpful to develop the concept in three stages. The first stage defines the idea of making a *Pareto improvement* when moving from one allocation to another. From this can be constructed the *Pareto preference* order that judges whether one allocation is preferred to another. The final stage is to use Pareto preference to find the most preferred states, which are then defined as *Pareto-efficient*. Reviewing each of these steps allows us to assess the meaning and value of the concept.

Consider a move from economic state s_1 to state s_2. This is defined as a Pareto improvement if it makes some consumers strictly better off and none worse off. If there are H consumers, this definition can be stated formally by saying a Pareto improvement is made in going from s_1 to s_2 if

$$U^h(s_2) > U^h(s_1) \qquad \text{for at least one consumer } h, \tag{12.7}$$

and

$$U^h(s_2) \geq U^h(s_1) \qquad \text{for all consumers } h = 1, \ldots, H. \tag{12.8}$$

The idea of a Pareto improvement can be used to construct a preference order over economic states. If a Pareto improvement is made in moving from s_1 to s_2, then state s_2 is defined as being *Pareto-preferred* to state s_1. This concept of Pareto preference defines one state as preferred to another if all consumers are at least as well off in that state and some are strictly better off. It is important to note that this stage of the construction has converted the set of individual preferences of the consumers into social preferences over the states.

The final stage is to define Pareto-efficiency. The earlier definition can be rephrased as saying that an economic state is *Pareto-efficient* if there is no state that is Pareto-preferred to it. That is, no move can be made from that state to another that achieves a Pareto improvement. From this perspective, we can view Pareto-efficient states as being the "best" relative to the Pareto preference order. The discussion now turns to assessing the usefulness of Pareto preference in selecting an optimal state from a set of alternatives. By analyzing a number of examples, several deficiencies of the concepts will become apparent.

The simplest allocation problem is to divide a fixed quantity of a single commodity between two consumers. Let the commodity be a cake, and assume that both consumers prefer more cake to less. The first observation is that no cake should be wasted—it is always a Pareto improvement to move from a state where some is wasted to one with the wasted cake given to one, or both, of the consumers. The second observation is that any allocation in which no cake is wasted is Pareto-efficient. To see this, start with any division of the cake between the two consumers. Any alternative allocation must give more to one consumer and less to the other; therefore, since one must lose, no change can be a Pareto improvement.

From this simple example two deficiencies of Pareto-efficiency can be inferred. First, since no improvement can be made on an allocation where none is wasted, extreme allocations such as giving all of the cake to one consumer are Pareto-efficient. This shows that even though an allocation is Pareto-efficient, there is no implication that it need be good in terms of equity. This illustrates quite clearly

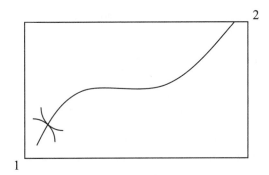

Figure 12.4
Efficiency and inequity

that Pareto-efficiency is not concerned with equity. The cake example also illustrates a second point: there can be a multiplicity of Pareto-efficient allocations. This was shown in the cake example by the fact that every nonwasteful allocation is Pareto-efficient. This multiplicity of efficient allocations limits the value of Pareto-efficiency as a tool for making allocative decisions. For the cake example, Pareto-efficiency gives no guidance whatsoever in deciding how the cake should be shared, other than showing that none should be thrown away. In brief, Pareto-efficiency fails to solve even this simplest of allocation problems.

The points made in the cake division example are also relevant to allocations within a two-consumer exchange economy. The contract curve in figure 12.4 shows the set of Pareto-efficient allocations, and there is generally an infinite number of these. Once again the Pareto preference ordering does not select a unique optimal outcome. In addition the competitive equilibrium may be as the one illustrated in the bottom left corner of the box. This has the property of being Pareto-efficient, but it is highly inequitable and may not find much favor using other criteria for judging optimality.

Another failing of the Pareto preference ordering is that it is not always able to compare alternative states. In formal terms, it does not provide a *complete ordering* of states. This is illustrated in figure 12.5 where the allocations s_1 and s_2 cannot be compared, although both can be compared to s_3 (s_3 is Pareto-preferred to both s_1 and s_2). When faced with a choice between s_1 and s_2, the Pareto preference order is silent about which should be chosen. It should be noted that this incomparability is not the same as indifference. If the preference order were indifferent between two states, then they are judged as equally good. Incomparability means the pair of states simply cannot be ranked.

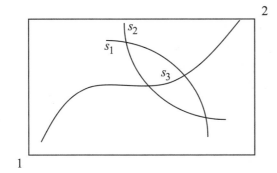

Figure 12.5
Incompleteness of Pareto ranking

The basic mechanism at work behind this example is that the Pareto preference order can only rank alternative states if there are only gainers or only losers as the move is made between the states. If some gain and some lose, as in the choice between s_1 and s_2 in figure 12.5, then the preference order is of no value. Such gains and losses are invariably a feature of policy choices and much of policy analysis consists of weighing up the gains and losses. In this respect Pareto-efficiency is insufficient as a basis for policy choice.

To summarize these arguments, Pareto-efficiency does not embody any concept of justice, and highly inequitable allocations can be efficient under the criterion. In many situations there are very many Pareto-efficient allocations, in which case the criterion provides little guidance for policy choice. Finally Pareto-efficiency may not provide a complete ordering of states, so some states will be incomparable under the criterion. The source of all these failing is that the Pareto criterion avoids weighing gains against losses, but it is just such judgments that have to be made in most allocation decisions. To make a choice of allocation, the evaluation of the gains and losses has to be faced directly.

12.7   Social Welfare Functions

The social welfare function was employed in section 12.2 to introduce the concept of a socially optimal allocation. At that point it was simply described as a means by which different allocations of utility between consumers could be socially ranked. What was not done was to provide a convincing description of where such a ranking could come from or of how it could be constructed. Three alternative interpretations will now be given, each of which provides a different perspective on the social welfare function.

The first possibility is that the social welfare function captures the distributive preferences of a central planner or dictator. Under this interpretation there can be two meanings of the individual utilities that enter the function. One is that they are the planner's perception of the utility achieved by each consumer at their level of consumption. This provides a consistent interpretation of the social welfare function, but problems arise in its relation to the underlying model. To see why this is so, recall that the Edgeworth box and the contract curve within it were based on the actual preferences of the consumers. There is then a potential inconsistency between this construction and the evaluation using the planner's preferences. For example, what is Pareto-efficient under the true preferences may not be one under the planner's (it need not even be an equilibrium).

The alternative meaning of the utilities is that they are the actual utilities of the consumers. This leads directly into the central difficulty faced in the concept of social welfare. In order to evaluate all allocations of utility it must be possible to determine the social value of an increase in one consumer's utility against the loss in another's. This is only possible if the utilities are comparable across the consumers. More will be said about this below.

The second interpretation of the social welfare function is that it captures some ethical objective that society should be pursuing. Here the social welfare function is determined by what is viewed as the just objective of society. There are two major examples of this. The *utilitarian philosophy* of aiming to achieve the greatest good for society as a whole translates into a social welfare function that is the sum of individual utilities. In this formulation only the total sum of utilities counts, so it does not matter how utility is distributed among consumers in the society. Alternatively, the *Rawlsian philosophy* of caring only for the worst-off member of society leads to a level of social welfare determined entirely by the minimum level of utility in that society. With this objective the distribution of utility is of paramount importance. Gains in utility achieved by anyone other than the worst-off consumer do not improve social welfare.

Although this approach to the social welfare function is internally consistent, it is still not entirely satisfactory. The utilitarian approach requires that the utilities of the consumers be added in order to arrive at the total sum of social welfare. The Rawlsian approach necessitates the utility levels being compared in order to find the lowest. The nature of the utility comparability is different for the two approaches (being able to add utilities is different to being able to compare), but both rely on some form of comparability. This again leads directly into the issue of utility comparisons.

The final view that can be taken of the social welfare function is that it takes the preferences of the individual consumers (represented by their utilities) and aggregates these into a social preference. This aggregation process would be expected to obey certain rules; for instance, if all consumers prefer one state to another, it should be the case that the social preference also prefers the same state. The structure of the social welfare function then emerges as a consequence of the rules the aggregation must obey.

Although this arrives at the same outcome as the other two interpretations, it does so by a distinctly different process. In this case it is the set of rules for aggregation that are foremost rather than the form of social welfare. That is, the philosophy here would be that if the aggregation rules are judged as satisfactory, then society should accept the social welfare function that emerges from their application, whatever its form. An example of this is that if the rules of majority voting are chosen as the method of aggregating preferences (despite the failings already identified in chapter 10), then the minority must accept what the majority chooses.

The consequences of constructing a social welfare function by following this line of reasoning are of fundamental importance in the theory of welfare economics. In fact doing so leads straight back into Arrow's Impossibility Theorem, which was described in chapter 10. The next section is dedicated to interpreting the theorem and its implications in this new setting.

12.8   Arrow's Theorem

Although they appear very distinct in nature, both majority voting and the Pareto criterion are examples of procedures for aggregating individual preferences into a social preference. It has been shown that neither is perfect. The Pareto preference order can be incomplete and is unable to rank some of the alternatives. Majority voting always leads to a complete social preference order but this may not be transitive. What Arrow's Impossibility Theorem has shown is that such failings are not specific to these aggregation procedures. All methods of aggregation will fail to meet one or more of its conditions, so the Impossibility Theorem identifies a fundamental problem at the heart of generating social preferences from individual preferences.

The conditions of Arrow's theorem were stated in terms of the rankings induced by individual preferences. However, since individual preferences can usually be

represented by a utility function, the theorem also applies to the aggregation of individual utility functions into a social welfare function. The implication behind
applying the theorem is that a social welfare function does not exist that can aggregate individual utilities without conflicting with one, or more, of the conditions
I, N, P, U, T. This means that whatever social welfare function is proposed, there
will be some set of utility functions for which it conflicts with at least one of the
conditions. In other words, no ideal social welfare function can be found. No
matter how sophisticated the aggregation mechanism is, it cannot overcome this
theorem.

Since the publication of Arrow's theorem there has been a great deal of research
attempting to find a way out of the dead-end into which it leads. One approach
that has been tried is to consider alternative sets of aggregation rules. For instance, transitivity of the social preference ordering can be relaxed to quasi-
transitivity (only strict preference is transitive) or weaker versions of condition I
and condition P can be used. Most such changes just lead to further impossibility
theorems for these different sets of rules. Modifying the rules does not therefore
really seem to be the way forward out of the impossibility.

What is at the heart of the impossibility is the limited information contained in
individual utility functions. Effectively all that is known is the individuals' rankings of the alternatives—which is best, which is worst, and how they line up in between. What the rankings do not give is any strength of feeling either between
alternatives for a given individual or across individuals for a given option. Such
strength of feeling is an essential art of any attempt to make social decisions. Consider, for instance, a group of people choosing where to dine. In this situation a
strong preference in one direction ("I really don't want to eat fish") usually counts
for more than a mild preference ("I don't really mind, but I would prefer fish").
Arrow's theorem rules out any information of this kind.

Using information on how strongly individuals feel about the alternatives can
be successful in choosing where to dine. It is interesting that the strength of preference comparisons can be used in informal situations, but this does not demonstrate that it can be incorporated within a scientific theory of social preferences.
This issue is now addressed in detail.

12.9   Interpersonal Comparability

Earlier in this chapter it was noted that Pareto-efficiency was originally proposed
because it provided a means by which it was possible to compare alternative allo-

cations without requiring interpersonal comparisons of welfare. It is also from this avoidance of comparability that the failures of Pareto-efficiency emerge. This point is also at the core of the impossibility theorem. To proceed further, this section first reviews the development of utility theory in order to provide a context and then describes alternative degrees of utility comparability.

Nineteenth-century economists viewed utility, the level of happiness of an individual, as something that was potentially measurable. Advances in psychology were expected to deliver the machinery for conducting the actual measurement. If utility were measurable, it follows naturally that it would be comparable between individuals. This ability to measure utility, combined with the philosophy that society should aim for the greatest good, came to provide the underpinnings of utilitarianism. The measurability of utility permitted social welfare to be expressed by the sum of individual utilities. Ranking states by the value of this sum then gave a means of aggregating individual preferences that satisfied all of the conditions of the impossibility theorem except for the information content. If the envisaged degree of measurability could be achieved, then the restrictions of the impossibility theorem are overcome.

This concept of measurable and comparable utility began to be dispelled in the early twentieth century. There were two grounds for this rejection. First, no means of measuring utility had been discovered, and it was becoming clear that the earlier hopes would not be realized. Second, advances in economic theory showed that there was no need to have measurable utility in order to construct a coherent theory of consumer choice. In fact the entire theory of the consumer could be derived by specifying only the consumer's preference ordering. The role of utility then became strictly secondary—it could be invoked to give a convenient function to represent preferences if necessary but was otherwise redundant. Since utility had no deeper meaning attached to it, any increasing monotonic transformation of a utility function representing a set of preferences would also be an equally valid utility function. Utility was simply an ordinal concept, with no natural zero or units of measurement. By the very construction of utility, comparability between different consumers' utilities was a meaningless concept. This situation therefore left no scientific basis on which to justify the comparability of different consumer's utility levels.

This perspective on utility, and the consequent elimination of utility comparisons among consumers, created the need to develop concepts for social comparisons, such as Pareto-efficiency, that were free of interpersonal comparisons. However, the weaknesses of these criteria soon became obvious. The analytical trend since the 1960s has been to explore the consequences of re-admitting interpersonal comparability into the analysis. The procedure adopted is basically to assume that comparisons are possible. This permits the derivation of results from which interpretations can be obtained. These are hoped to provide some general insights into policy that can be applied, even though utility is not actually comparable in the way assumed.

There are even some economists who would argue that comparisons are possible. One basis for this is the claim that all consumers have very similar underlying preference orderings. All prefer to have more income to less, and consumers with equal incomes make very similar divisions of expenditures between alternative groups of commodities. For example, expenditure on food is similar, even though the actual foodstuffs purchased may be very different. In modeling such consumers, it is possible to assert that they all have the same utility function guiding their choices. This makes their utilities directly comparable.

So far comparability has been used as a catch-all phrase for being able to draw some contrast between the utility levels of consumers. In fact many different degrees of comparability can be envisaged. For instance, the claim that one household has a higher level of utility than another requires rather less comparability than claiming it has 15 percent more utility. Different degrees of comparability have implications for the way in which individual utilities can be aggregated into a social preference ordering.

The starting point for discussing comparability is to define the two major forms of utility. The first is *ordinal utility*, which is the familiar concept from consumer theory. Essentially an ordinal utility function is no more than just a numbering of a consumer's indifference curves, with the numbering chosen so that higher indifference curves have higher utility numbers. These numbers can be subjected to any form of transformation without altering their meaning, provided that the transformation leaves the ranking of the numbers unchanged—higher indifference curves must still have larger utility numbers attached. Because they can be so freely transformed, there is no meaning to differences in utility levels between two situations for a single consumer except which of the two provides the higher utility.

The second form of utility is *cardinal utility*. Cardinal utility imposes restrictions beyond those of ordinal utility. With cardinal utility one can only transform utility numbers by multiplying by a constant and then adding a constant, so an initial utility function U becomes the transformed utility $\tilde{U} = a + bU$, where a and b are the constants. Any other form of transformation will affect the meaning of a cardinal utility function. The typical place where cardinal utility is found is in the economics of uncertainty, since an expected utility function is cardinal. This cardinality is a consequence of the fact that an expected utility function must provide a consistent ranking for different probability distributions of the outcomes. (A noneconomic example of a cardinal scale is temperature. It is possible to convert Celsius to Fahrenheit by multiplying by $\frac{9}{5}$ and adding 32. The converse transformation from Fahrenheit to Celsius is to multiply by $\frac{5}{9}$ and subtract 32.) With these definitions it now becomes possible to talk in detail about comparability and noncomparability.

Noncomparability can arise with both ordinal and cardinal utility. What noncomparability means is that we can apply different transformations to different consumers' utilities. To express this in formal terms, let U^1 be the utility function of consumer 1 and U^2 the utility function of consumer 2. Then noncomparability arises if the transformation f^1 can be applied to U^1 and a different transformation f^2 to U^2, with no relationship between f^1 and f^2. Why is this noncomparable? The reasoning is that by suitably choosing f^1 and f^2, it is always possible to start with one ranking of the initial utilities and to arrive at a different ranking of the transformed utilities. The utility information therefore does not provide sufficient information to make a comparison of the two utility levels.

Comparability exists when the transformations that can be applied to the utility functions are restricted. With ordinal utility there is only one possible degree of comparability. This occurs when the ordinal utilities for different consumers can be subjected only to the same transformation. The implication of this is that the transformation preserves the ranking of utilities among different consumers. So if one consumer has a higher utility than another before the transformation, the same consumer will have a higher utility after the transformation. Letting this transformation be denoted by f, then if $U^1 \geq U^2$, it must be the case that $f(U^1) \geq f(U^2)$. This form of comparability is called *ordinal level comparability*.

If the underlying utility functions are cardinal, there are two forms of comparability that are worth discussing. The first form of comparability is to assume that the constant multiplying of utility in the transformation must be the same for all consumers, but the constant that is added can differ. Hence for two consumers the transformed utilities are $\tilde{U}^1 = a^1 + bU^1$ and $\tilde{U}^2 = a^2 + bU^2$, so the constant b is the same for both. This is called *cardinal unit comparability*. The implication of this transformation is that it now becomes meaningful to talk about the effect of changes in utility, meaning that gains to one consumer can be measured against losses to another—and whether the gain exceeds the loss is not affected by the transformation. The second degree of comparability for cardinal utility is to further restrict the constant a in the transformation to be the same for both consumers. For all consumers the transformed utility becomes $\tilde{U}^h = a + bU^h$. It is now possible for both changes in utility and levels of utility to be compared. This form of comparability is called *cardinal full comparability*.

The next step is to explore the implications of these comparabilities for the construction of social welfare functions. It will be shown that each form of comparability implies different permissible social welfare functions.

12.10   Comparability and Social Welfare

The discussion of Arrow's Impossibility Theorem showed that the failure to successfully generate a social preference ordering from a set of individual preference orderings was the result of limited information. The information content of an individual's preference order involves nothing more than knowing how they rank the alternatives. A preference order does not convey any information on the strength of preferences or allow comparison of utility levels across consumers. When more information is available, it becomes possible to find social preference orderings that satisfy the conditions I, N, P, U, T. Such information can be introduced by building social preferences on individual utility functions that allow for comparability.

What this section shows is that for each form of comparability there is a specification of social welfare function that is consistent with the information content of the comparable utilities. To explain what is meant by consistent, recall that comparability is described by a set of permissible transformations of utility. A social welfare function is *consistent* if it ranks the set of alternative social states in the same way for all permissible transformations of the utility functions. Since increasing the degree of comparability reduces the number of permissible transformations, it has the effect of increasing the set of consistent social welfare functions.

Let the utility obtained by consumer h from allocation s be $U^h(s)$. A transformation of this basic utility function is denoted by $\tilde{U}^h(s) = f^h(U^h(s))$. The value of social welfare at allocation s using the basic utilities is $W(s) = W(U^1(s), \ldots, U^H(s))$, and that from using the transformed utilities is $\tilde{W}(s) = W(\tilde{U}^1(s), \ldots, \tilde{U}^H(s))$. Given alternative allocations A and B, the social welfare function is consistent with the transformation (and hence the form of comparability) if

Table 12.1
Allocations and utility

	x^1	y^1	U^1	x^2	y^2	U^2
A	4	9	6	3	2	5
B	16	1	4	2	5	7

$W(A) \geq W(B)$ implies $\tilde{W}(A) \geq \tilde{W}(B)$. In words, if A generates higher social welfare than B for the basic utilities, it will also do so for the transformed utilities.

To demonstrate these points, assume there are two consumers with the basic utility functions $U^1 = [x]^{1/2}[y]^{1/2}$ and $U^2 = x + y$, where x and y are the consumption levels of the two goods. Further assume that there are two allocations A and B with the consumption levels, and the resulting utilities, as shown in table 12.1.

The first point to establish is that it is possible to find a social welfare function that is consistent with ordinal level comparability but none that is consistent with ordinal noncomparability. What level comparability allows is the ranking of consumers by utility level (think of placing the consumers in a line with the lowest utility level first). A position in this line (e.g., the first, or the tenth, or the nth) can be chosen, and the level of utility of the consumer in that position used as the measure of social welfare. This process generates a *positional* social welfare function. The best known example is the Rawlsian social welfare function, $W = \min\{U^h\}$, which judges social welfare by the minimum level of utility in the population. An alternative that shows other positions can be employed (though not one that is often used) is to measure social welfare measure by the maximum level of utility, $W = \max\{U^h\}$.

That such positional welfare functions are consistent with ordinal level comparability but not with ordinal noncomparability is shown in table 12.2 using the allocations A and B introduced above. For the social welfare function $W = \min\{U^h\}$, the welfare level in allocation A is 5 and that in allocation B is 4. Therefore allocation A is judged superior using the basic utilities. An example of a pair of transformations that satisfy ordinal noncomparability are $\tilde{U}^1 = f^1(U^1) = 3U^1$ and $\tilde{U}^2 = f^2(U^2) = 2U^2$. The levels of utility and resulting social welfare are displayed in the upper part of table 12.2. The table shows that the preferred allocation is now B, so the transformation has changed the preferred social outcome. With ordinal level comparability, the transformations $f^1(U^1)$ and $f^2(U^2)$ must be the same. For example, let the transformation be given by

Table 12.2
Noncomparability and level comparability

	A	B
Noncomparability		
$\tilde{U}^1 = f^1(U^1) = 3U^1$	18	12
$\tilde{U}^2 = f^2(U^2) = 2U^2$	10	14
$W = \min\{\tilde{U}^h\}$	10	12
Level comparability		
$\tilde{U}^1 = f(U^1) = (U^1)^2$	36	16
$\tilde{U}^2 = f(U^2) = (U^2)^2$	25	49
$W = \min\{\tilde{U}^h\}$	25	16

$\tilde{U}^h = f(U^h) = (U^h)^2$. The values of the transformed utilities in the lower part of the table confirm that allocation A is preferred—as it was with the basic utilities. The positional social welfare function is therefore consistent with ordinal level comparability.

Although cardinal utility is often viewed as stronger concept than ordinal utility, cardinality alone does not permit the construction of a consistent social welfare function. Recalling that transformations of the form $f^h = a^h + b^h U^h$ can be applied with noncomparability, it can be seen that even positional welfare functions will not be consistent since a^h can always be chosen to change the social ranking generated by the transformed utilities compared to that generated by the basic utilities. In contrast, if utility satisfies cardinal unit comparability, it is possible to use social welfare functions of the form

$$W = \sum_{h=1}^{H} \alpha^h U^h, \tag{12.9}$$

where the α^h are constants. To demonstrate this, and to show that social welfare function is not consistent with cardinal noncomparability, assume that $\alpha^1 = 2$ and $\alpha^2 = 1$. Then under the basic utility functions the social welfare levels in the two allocations are $W(A) = 2 \times 6 + 5 = 17$ and $W(B) = 2 \times 4 + 7 = 15$, so allocation A is preferred. The upper part of table 12.3 displays two transformations satisfying non-comparability and the implied value of social welfare. This shows that allocation B will be preferred with the transformed utility. Therefore the social welfare function is not consistent with the transformations. With cardinal unit comparability, the transformations are restricted to have a common value for b^h, so $\tilde{U}^h = a^h + bU^h$. Two such transformations are selected, and the result-

Table 12.3
Cardinal utility

	A	B
Noncomparability		
$\tilde{U}^1 = f^1(U^1) = 2 + 2U^1$	14	10
$\tilde{U}^2 = f^2(U^2) = 5 + 6U^2$	35	47
$W = 2\tilde{U}^1 + \tilde{U}^2$	63	67
Level comparability		
$\tilde{U}^1 = f^1(U^1) = 2 + 3U^1$	20	14
$\tilde{U}^2 = f^2(U^2) = 5 + 3U^2$	20	26
$W = 2\tilde{U}^1 + \tilde{U}^2$	60	54

ing utility levels are given in the lower part of the table. Calculation of the social welfare shows the preferred allocation to be A as it was with the basic utilities. Therefore with cardinal level comparability, social welfare functions of the form (12.9) are consistent and provide a social ranking that is invariant for the permissible transformations.

With cardinal full comparability the transformations must satisfy $\tilde{U}^h = a + bU^h$. One interesting example of the forms of social welfare function that are consistent with such transformations is

$$W = \overline{U} + \gamma \min\{U^h - \overline{U}\}, \quad \overline{U} = \frac{\sum_{h=1}^{H} U^h}{H}, \tag{12.10}$$

where γ is a parameter that can be chosen. This form of social welfare function is especially interesting because it is the utilitarian social welfare function when $\gamma = 0$ and Rawlsian when $\gamma = 1$. To show that this function is not consistent for cardinal unit comparability, assume $\gamma = \frac{1}{2}$. For the basic utilities it follows for allocation A that $\overline{U} = \frac{6+5}{2} = 5.5$ and for allocation B, $\overline{U} = \frac{4+7}{2} = 5.5$. The social welfare levels are then $W = 5.5 + \frac{1}{2} \min\{6 - 5.5, 5 - 5.5\} = 5.25$ for allocation A and $W = 5.5 + \frac{1}{2} \min\{4 - 5.5, 7 - 5.5\} = 4.75$ for allocation B. The social welfare function would select allocation A. The upper part of table 12.4 displays the welfare levels for two transformations that satisfy cardinal level comparability. With these transformed utilities the welfare function would select allocation B, so the social welfare function is not valid for these transformations. The lower part of the table displays a transformation that satisfies cardinal full comparability. For this transformation the social welfare function selects allocation A for both the basic and the transformed utilities. This demonstrates the consistency.

Table 12.4
Full comparability

	A	B
Level comparability		
$\tilde{U}^1 = f^1(U^1) = 7 + 3U^1$	25	19
$\tilde{U}^2 = f^2(U^2) = 1 + 3U^2$	16	22
$W = \bar{U} + \frac{1}{2}\min\{U^h - \bar{U}\}$	18.25	19.75
Full comparability		
$\tilde{U}^1 = f^1(U^1) = 1 + 3U^1$	19	13
$\tilde{U}^2 = f^2(U^2) = 1 + 3U^2$	16	22
$W = \bar{U} + \frac{1}{2}\min\{U^h - \bar{U}\}^2$	16.75	15.25

These calculations have demonstrated that if we can compare utility levels among consumers then a consistent social welfare function can be constructed. The resulting social welfare function must agree with the information content in the utilities, so each form of comparability leads to a different consistent social welfare function. As the information increases, so does the range of consistent social welfare functions. Expressed differently, for each of the cases of comparability the problem of aggregating individual preferences leads to a well-defined form of social welfare function. All these social welfare functions will generate a social preference ordering that completely ranks the alternative states. They are obviously stronger in content than majority voting or Pareto-efficiency. The drawback is that they are reliant on stronger utility information that may simply not exist.

12.11   Conclusions

This chapter has cast a critical eye over the efficiency theorems of chapter 2. Although these theorems are important for providing a basic framework in which to think about policy, they are not an end in their own right. This perspective is based on the limited practical applicability of the lump-sum transfers needed to support the decentralization in the Second Theorem and the weakness of Pareto-efficiency as a method of judging among economic states.

Although at first sight the theorems apparently have very strong policy implications, they become weakened when placed under critical scrutiny. But they are not without value. Much of the subject matter of public economics takes as its starting point the practical shortcomings of these theorems and attempts to find a way forward to something that is applicable. A knowledge of what could be achieved if the optimal lump-sum transfers were available provides a means of assessing the success of what can be achieved and shows ways in which improvements in policy can be made.

The other aspect involved in the Second Theorem is the selection of the optimal allocation to be decentralized. This choice requires a social welfare function that can be used to judge different allocations of utility among consumers. Such a social welfare function can only be constructed if the consumers' utilities are comparable. The chapter described several different forms of comparability and of the social welfare functions that are consistent with them.

Further Reading

Arrow's Impossibility Theorem was first demonstrated in:

Arrow, K. J. 1950. A difficulty in the concept of social welfare. *Journal of Political Economy* 58: 328–46.

The theorem is further elaborated in:

Arrow, K. J. 1951. *Social Choice and Individual Values*. New York: Wiley.

A comprehensive textbook treatment is given by:

Kelly, J. 1987. *Social Choice Theory: An Introduction*. Berlin: Springer Verlag.

The concept of a social welfare function was first introduced by:

Bergson, A. 1938. A reformulation of certain aspects of welfare economics. *Quarterly Journal of Economics* 68: 233–52.

An analysis of limitations on the use of lump-sum taxation is contained in:

Mirrlees, J. A. 1986. The theory of optimal taxation. In K. J. Arrow and M. D. Intrilligator, eds., *Handbook of Mathematical Economics*. Amsterdam: North-Holland.

An economic assessment of the UK poll tax is conducted in:

Besley, T., Preston, I., and Ridge, M. 1997. Fiscal anarchy in the UK: Modelling poll tax noncompliance. *Journal of Public Economics* 64: 137–52.

For a more complete theoretical treatment of the information constraint on redistribution see:

Guesnerie, R. 1995. *A Contribution to the Pure Theory of Taxation*. Cambridge: Cambridge University Press.

Hammond, P. 1979. Straightforward incentive compatibility in large economies. *Review of Economic Studies* 46: 263–82.

Roberts, K. 1984. The theoretical limits to redistribution. *Review of Economic Studies* 51: 177–95.

Two excellent reviews of the central issues that arise with redistribution:

Boadway, R., and Keen, M. 2000. Redistribution. In A. B. Atkinson and F. Bourguignon, eds., *Handbook of Income Distribution*, vol. 1. Amsterdam: North Holland, pp. 677–789.

Stiglitz, J. 1987. Pareto-efficient and optimal taxation and the new welfare economics. In A. Auerbach and M. Feldstein, eds., *Handbook of Public Economics*, vol. 2. Amsterdam: North Holland, pp. 991–1042.

The self-selection argument for in-kind redistribution is in:

Akerlof, G. 1978. The economics of tagging as applied to the optimal income tax, welfare programs and manpower planning. *American Economic Review* 68: 8–19.

Besley, T., and Coate, S. 1991. Public provision of private goods and the redistribution of income. *American Economic Review* 81: 979–84.

Blackorby, C., and Donaldson, D. 1988. Cash versus kind, self-selection and efficient transfers. *American Economic Review* 78: 691–700.

Garfinkel, I. 1973. Is in-kind redistribution efficient? *Quarterly Journal of Economics* 87: 320–30.

Estimates of the incentive effects of welfare programs are in:

Eissa, N., and Liebman, J. 1996. Labour supply response to the earned income tax credit. *Quarterly Journal of Economics* 111: 605–37.

Gruber, J. 2000. Disability, insurance benefits and labor supply. *Journal of Political Economy* 108: 1162–83.

The government time-consistency problem is in:

Bruce, N., and Waldman, M. 1991. Transfers in kind: Why they can be efficient and nonpaternalistic. *American Economic Review* 81: 1345–51.

Hillier, B., and Malcomson, J. M. 1984. Dynamic inconsistency, rational expectations and optimal government policy. *Econometrica* 52: 1437–52.

Strotz, R. H. 1956. Myopia and inconsistency in dynamic utility maximization. *Review of Economic Studies* 24: 165–80.

Comparability of utility is discussed in:

Ng, Y.-K. 2003. *Welfare Economics*. Basingstoke: Macmillan.

A discussion of the relation between social welfare functions and Arrow's theorem can be found in:

Samuelson, P. A. 1977. Reaffirming the existence of "reasonable" Bergson-Samuelson social welfare functions. *Economica* 44: 81–88.

Several of Sen's papers that discuss these issues are collected in:

Sen, A. K. 1982. *Choice, Welfare and Measurement*. Oxford: Basil Blackwell.

Exercises

12.1.   Should a social planner be concerned with the distribution of income or the distribution of utility? How does the answer relate to needs and abilities?

12.2.   Sketch the indifference curves of the Bergson-Samuelson social welfare function $W = U^1 + U^2$. What do these indifference curves imply about the degree of concern for equity of the social planner? Repeat for the welfare function $W = \min\{U^1, U^2\}$.

12.3.   Show that an anonymous social welfare function must have indifference curves that are symmetric about the 45° line. Will an optimal allocation with an anonymous social welfare function and a symmetric utility possibility frontier always be equitable?

12.4.   Assume that the preferences of the social planner are given by the function $W = \frac{[U^1]^\varepsilon}{\varepsilon} + \frac{[U^2]^\varepsilon}{\varepsilon}$. What effect does an increase in ε have on the curvature of a social indifference curve? Use this result to relate the value of ε to the planner's concern for equity.

12.5.   There are H consumers who each have utility function $U^h = \log(M^h)$. If the social welfare function is given by $W = \sum U^h$, show that a fixed stock of income will be allocated equitably. Explain why this is so.

12.6.   For a social welfare function $W = W(U^1(M^1), \dots, U^H(M^H))$, where M^h is income, the "social marginal utility of income" is defined by $\frac{\partial W}{\partial U^h} \frac{\partial U^h}{\partial M^h}$. If $U^h = [M^h]^{1/2}$ for all h, show that the social marginal utility of income is decreasing in M^h for a utilitarian social welfare function. Use this to argue that a fixed stock of income will be distributed equally. Show that the argument extends to any anonymous and concave social welfare function when all consumers have the same utility function.

12.7.   The two consumers that constitute an economy have utility functions $U^1 = x_1^1 x_2^1$ and $U^2 = x_1^2 x_2^2$.

a. Graph the indifference curves of the consumers, and show that at every Pareto-efficient allocation $\frac{x_1^1}{x_2^1} = \frac{x_1^2}{x_2^2}$.

b. Employ the feasibility conditions and the result in part a to show that Pareto-efficiency requires $\frac{x_1^2}{x_2^2} = \frac{\omega_1}{\omega_2}$, where ω_1 and ω_2 denote the endowments of the two goods.

c. Using the utility function of consumer 2, solve for x_1^2 and x_2^2 as functions of ω_1, ω_2, and U^2.

d. Using the utility function of consumer 1, express U^1 as a function of ω_1, ω_2, and U^2.

e. Assuming that $\omega_1 = 1$ and $\omega_2 = 1$, plot the utility possibility frontier.

f. Which allocation maximizes the social welfare function $W = U^1 + U^2$?

12.8.   Consider three individuals with utility indicators $U^A = M^A$, $U^B = \nu M^B$, and $U^C = \gamma M^C$.

a. Show that there are values of ν and γ that can generate any social ordering of the income allocations $a = (5, 2, 5)$, $b = (4, 6, 1)$, and $c = (3, 4, 8)$ when evaluated by the social welfare function $W = U^A + U^B + U^C$.

b. Assume instead that $U^A = v + \gamma M^A$, $U^B = v + \gamma M^B$, and $U^C = v + \gamma M^C$. Show that the evaluation via the utilitarian social welfare function is unaffected by the choices of v and γ.

c. Now assume $U^h = [M^h]^\gamma$, where $h = A, B, C$. Show that the preferred outcome under the social welfare function $W = \min_{\{h\}}\{U^A, U^B, U^C\}$ is unaffected by choice of γ but that for the welfare function $W = U^A + U^B + U^C$ is affected.

d. Explain the answers to parts a through c in terms of the comparability of utility.

12.9.   Provide an argument to establish that the optimal allocation must be Pareto-efficient. What assumptions have you placed upon the social welfare function?

12.10. The most general form of a social welfare function (SWF) can be written as $W = W(U^1, \ldots, U^H)$.

a. Explain the following properties that a SWF may satisfy: nonpaternalism, Pareto principle, anonymity (the names of the agents do not matter), and concavity (aversion to inequality).

b. Consider two agents $h = 1, 2$ with utilities U^1 and U^2. Depict the social indifference curve of the utilitarian SWF in (U^1, U^2)-space. Which of the properties in part a does it satisfy?

c. Depict the social indifference curves of the maximin or Rawlsian SWF. Contrast to the utilitarian SWF with respect to the aversion to inequality. Which properties does the Rawlsian SWF satisfy?

d. The Bernoulli-Nash social welfare function is given by the product of individual utilities. Discuss the distributional properties of the Bernoulli-Nash SWF.

12.11. Consider the SWF of the form $W = [\sum_h [U^h]^\eta]^{1/\eta}$ with $-\infty < \eta \le 1$. Show that this SWF reduces to the utilitarian SWF when $\eta = 1$, to the Bernoulli-Nash SWF when $\eta = 0$, and to the maximin Rawlsian SWF when $\eta \to -\infty$.

12.12. A fixed amount $\bar{x}$ of a good has to be allocated between two individuals, $h = 1, 2$ with utility functions $U^h = \alpha^h x^h$ (with $\alpha^h > 0$), where x^h is the amount of the good allocated to consumer h.

a. How should $\bar{x}$ be allocated to maximize a utilitarian SWF? Illustrate the answer graphically. How do the optimal values of x^1 and x^2 change among the cases $\alpha^1 < \alpha^2$, $\alpha^1 = \alpha^2$, and $\alpha^1 > \alpha^2$?

b. What is the allocation maximizing the Bernoulli-Nash SWF? Illustrate graphically. How do the optimal values of x^1 and x^2 change with the preference parameters α^1 and α^2?

c. What is the allocation maximizing the maximin-Rawlsian SWF? Illustrate graphically. How does the allocation change with preference parameters α^1 and α^2?

12.13. Show how the results of the previous exercise change if we assume a utility function of the form $U^h = \alpha^h \sqrt{x^h}$.

12.14. Consider a two-good exchange economy with two types of consumers. Type A have the utility function $U^A = 2\log(x_1^A) + \log(x_2^A)$ and an endowment of 3 units of good 1 and k units of good 2. Type B have the utility function $U^B = \log(x_1^B) + 2\log(x_2^B)$ and an endowment of 6 units of good 1 and $21 - k$ units of good 2.

a. Find the competitive equilibrium outcome and show that the equilibrium price $p^* = \frac{p_1}{p_2}$ of good 1 in terms of good 2 is $p^* = \frac{21+k}{15}$.

b. Find the income levels (M^A, M^B) of both types in equilibrium as a function of k.

c. Suppose that the government can make a lump-sum transfer of good 2, but it is impossible to transfer good 1. Use your answer to part b to describe the set of income distributions attainable through such transfers. Draw this in a diagram.

d. Suppose that the government can affect the initial distribution of resources by varying k. Find the optimal distribution of income if (i) the *SWF* is $W = \log(M^A) + \log(M^B)$ and (ii) $W = M^A + M^B$.

12.15. Are the following true or false? Explain your answer.

a. Cardinal utilities are always interpersonally comparable.

b. A Rawlsian social welfare function can be consistent with ordinal utility.

c. The optimal allocation with a utilitarian social welfare function is always inequitable.

12.16. The purpose of this exercise is to illustrate the potential conflict between personal liberty and the Pareto principle (first studied by Sen). Assume there is a copy of *Lady Chatterley's Lover* available to be read by two persons, A and B. There are three possible options: (a) A reads the book and B does not; (b) B reads the book and A does not; (c) neither reads the book. The preference ordering of A (the prude) is $c \succ_A a \succ_A b$ and the preference ordering of B (the lascivious) is $a \succ_B b \succ_B c$. Hence c is the worst option for one and the best option for the other; while both prefer a to b. Define the personal liberty rule as allowing everyone to choose freely on personal matters (like the color of one's own hair) with society as a whole accepting the choice, no matter what others think.

a. Apply the personal liberty rule to the example to derive social preferences $b \succ c$ and $c \succ a$.

b. Show that by the Pareto principle we must have a social preference cycle $a \succ b \succ c \succ a$.

c. Suppose that liberalism is constrained by the requirement that the prude A decides to respect B's preferences such that A's preference for c over b is ignored. Similarly for B, only his preference for b over c is relevant but not his preference for a over c. What are the modified preference orderings of each person? Show that it leads to acyclic (transitive) social preference.

d. The second possibility to solve the paradox is to suppose that each is willing to respect the other's choice. Thus A respects B's preference for b over c and B respects A's preference for c over a. What are the modified preference orderings of each person? Show that it leads to acyclic social preference. What is then the best social outcome?

13.1   Introduction

A social welfare function permits the evaluation of economic policies that cause redistribution between consumers—a task that Pareto-efficiency can never accomplish. Although the concept of a social welfare function is a simple one, previous chapters have identified numerous difficulties on the path between individual utility and aggregate social welfare. The essence of these difficulties is that if the individual utility function corresponds with what is theoretically acceptable, then its information content is too limited for social decision making.

The motivation for employing a social welfare function was to be able to address issues of equity as well as issues of efficiency. Fortunately a social welfare function is not the only way to do this, and as this chapter will show, we can construct measures of the economic situation that relate to equity and that are based on observable and measurable information. This provides a set of tools that can be, and frequently are, applied in economic policy analysis. They may not meet some of the requirements of the ideal social welfare function, but they have the distinct advantage of being practically implementable.

Inequality and poverty provide two alternative perspectives on the equity of the income distribution. Inequality of income means that some households have higher incomes than others—which is a basic source for an inequity in welfare. Poverty exists when some households are too poor to achieve an acceptable standard of living. An inequality measure is a means of assigning a single number to the observed income distribution that reflects its degree of inequality. A poverty measure achieves the same for poverty. Although measures of inequality and poverty are not themselves social welfare functions, the chapter will reveal the closeness of the link between the measures and welfare.

The starting point of the chapter is a discussion of income. There are two aspects to this: the definition of income and the comparison of income across families with different compositions. In a setting of certainty, income is a clearly defined concept. When there is uncertainty, differences can arise between *ex ante* and *ex post* definitions. Given this, we look at alternative definitions and relate these to the treatment of income for tax purposes. If two households differ in their composition (e.g., one household is a single person and the other is a family of four), a direct comparison of their income levels will reveal little about the standard of living they achieve. Instead, the incomes must be adjusted to take account of composition and then compared. The tool used to make the adjustment is an equivalence scale. We review the use of equivalence scales and some of the issues that they raise.

Having arrived at a set of correctly defined income levels that have been adjusted for family composition using an equivalence scale, it becomes possible to evaluate inequality and poverty. A number of the commonly used measures of each of these concepts are discussed and their properties investigated. Importantly, the link is drawn between measures of inequality and the welfare assumptions that are implicit within them. This leads into the idea of making the welfare assumptions explicit and building the measure up from these assumptions. To measure poverty, it is necessary to determine who is "poor," which is achieved by choosing a level of income as the poverty line and labeling as poor all those who fall below it. As well as discussing measures of poverty, we also review issues concerning the definition of the poverty line and the concept of poverty itself.

Although the aim of this chapter is to move away from utility concepts toward practical tools, it is significant that we keep returning to utility in the assessment and improvement of the tools. In attempting to refine, for example, an equivalence scale or a measure of inequality it is found that it is necessary to comprehend the utility basis of the measure. Despite intentionally starting in a direction away from utility, the theory returns us back to utility on every occasion.

13.2   Measuring Income

What is income? The obvious answer is that it is the additional resources a consumer receives over a given period of time. The reference to a time period is important here, since income is a flow, so the period over which measurement takes place must be specified. Certainly evaluating the receipt of resources is the basis of the definition used in the assessment of income for tax purposes. This definition works in a practical setting but only in a backward-looking sense. What an economist needs in order to understand behavior, especially when choices are made in advance of income being received, is a forward-looking measure of income. If the flow of income is certain, then there is no distinction between backward- and forward-looking measures. It is when income is uncertain that differences emerge.

The relevance of this issue is that both inequality and poverty measures use income data as their basic input. The resulting measures will only be as accurate as the data that is employed to evaluate them. The data will be accurate when information is carefully collected and a consistent definition is used of what is to be measured. To evaluate the level of inequality or poverty, a necessary first step is to resolve the issues surrounding the definition of income.

The classic backward-looking definition of income was provided by Simons in 1938. This definition is "Personal income may be defined as the algebraic sum of (1) the market value of rights exercised in consumption and (2) the change in the value of the store of property rights between the beginning and end of the period in question." The essential feature of this definition is that it makes an attempt to be inclusive so as to incorporate all income regardless of the source.

Although income definitions for tax purposes also adopt the backward-looking viewpoint, they do not precisely satisfy the Simons's definition. The divergence arises through the practical difficulties of assessing some sources of income especially those arising from capital gains. According to the Simons's definition, the increase in the value of capital assets should be classed as income. However, if the assets are not liquidated, the capital gain will not be realized during the period in question and will not be received as an income flow. For this reason capital gains are taxed only on realization. In the converse situation when capital losses are made, most tax codes place limits on the extent to which they can be offset against income.

We have so far worked with the natural definition of income as the flow of additional resources. To proceed further, it becomes more helpful to adopt a different perspective and to view the level of income by the benefits it can deliver. Since income is the means to achieve consumption, the flow of income during a fixed time period can be measured as the value of consumption that can be undertaken, while leaving the household with the same stock of wealth at the end of the period as it had at the start of the period. The benefit of this perspective is that it extends naturally to situations where the income flow is uncertain. Building on it, in 1939 Hicks provided what is generally taken as the standard definition of income with uncertainty. This definition states that "income is the maximum value which a man can consume during a week and still expect to be as well-off at the end of the week as he was at the beginning."

This definition can clearly cope with uncertainty, since it operates in expectational terms. But this advantage is also its major shortcoming when a move is made toward applications. Expectations may be ill-defined or even irrational, so evaluation of the expected income flow may be unreasonably high or low. A literal application of the definition would not count windfall gains, such as unexpected gifts or lottery wins, as income because they are not expected despite such gains clearly raising the potential level of consumption. For these reasons the Hicks definition of income is informative but not perfect.

These alternative definitions of income have highlighted the distinctions between ex ante and ex post measures. Assessments of income for tax purposes use the backward-looking viewpoint and measure income as all relevant payments received over the measurement period. Practical issues limit the extent to which some sources of income can be included, so the definition of income in tax codes does not precisely satisfy any of the formal definitions. This observation just reflects the fact that there is no unambiguously perfect definition of income.

13.3   Equivalence Scales

The fact that households differ in size and age distribution means that welfare levels cannot be judged just by looking at their income levels. A household of one adult with no children needs less income to achieve a given level of welfare than a household with two adults and one child. In the words of the economist Gorman, "When you have a wife and a baby, a penny bun costs threepence." A larger household obviously needs more income to achieve a given level of utility, but the question is how much more income? Equivalence scales are the economist's way of answering this question and provide the means of adjusting measured incomes into comparable quantities.

Differences between households arise in the number of adults and the number and ages of dependants. These are called *demographic variables*. The general problem in designing equivalence scales is to achieve the adjustment of observed income to take account of demographic differences in household composition. Several ways exist to do this, and these are now discussed.

The first approach to equivalence scales is based on the concept of *minimum needs*. A bundle of goods and services that is seen as representing the minimum needs for the household is identified. The exact bundle will differ among households of varying size but typically involves only very basic commodities. The cost of this bundle for families with different compositions is then calculated and the ratio of these costs for different families provides the equivalence scale. The first application of this approach was by Rowntree in 1901 in his pioneering study of poverty. The bundle of goods employed was just a minimum acceptable quantity of food, rent, and a small allowance for "household sundries." The equivalence scale was constructed by assigning the expenditure for a two-adult household

Table 13.1
Minimum needs equivalence scales

	Rowntree (1901)	Beveridge (1942)	US Poverty Scale (2003)
Single person	60	59	78
Couple	100	100	100
+1 child	124	122	120
+2 children	161	144	151
+3 children	186	166	178
+4 children	223	188	199

Sources: B. S. Rowntree (1901), *Poverty: A Study of Town Life* (New York: Macmillan); W. H. Beveridge (1942), *Social Insurance and Allied Services* (London: HMSO); US Bureau of the Census (2003), *www.census.gov/hhes/poverty/threshld/thresh03.html*.

with no children the index of 100 and measuring costs for all other household compositions relative to this. The scale obtained from expenditures calculated by Rowntree is given in the first column of table 13.1. The interpretation of these figures is that the minimum needs of a couple with one child cost 24 percent more than for a couple with no children.

A similar approach was taken by Beveridge in his construction of the expenditure requirements that provided the foundation for the introduction of social assistance in the United Kingdom. In addition to the goods in the bundle of Rowntree, Beveridge added fuel, light, and a margin for "inefficiency" in purchasing. Also the cost assigned to children increased with their age. The values of the Beveridge scale in the second column of table 13.1 are for children in the 5 to 10 age group.

The final column of the table is generated from the income levels that are judged to represent poverty in the United States for families with different compositions. The original construction of these poverty levels was undertaken by Orshansky in 1963. The method she used was to evaluate the cost of food for each family composition using the 1961 Economy Food Plan. Next it was observed that if expenditure upon food, F, constituted a proportion θ of the family's budget, then total needs would be $\left(\frac{1}{\theta}\right)F$. For a family of two, $\frac{1}{\theta}$ was taken as 3.7 and for a family of three or more $\frac{1}{\theta}$ was 3. The exception to this process was to evaluate the cost for a single person as 80 percent of that of a couple. The minimum expenditures obtained have been continually updated, and the third column of the table gives the equivalence scale implied by the poverty line used in 2003.

Table 13.1 shows that these equivalence scales all assume that there are returns to scale in household size so that, for example, a family of two adults does not require twice the income of a single person. Observe also that the US poverty scale is relatively generous for a single person compared to the other two scales. The fact that the single-person value was constructed in a different way to the other values for the poverty scale (as a fixed percentage of that for a couple rather than as a multiple of food costs) has long been regarded as a contentious issue. Furthermore only for the Beveridge scale is the cost of additional children constant. The fact that the cost of children is nonmonotonic for the poverty scale is a further point of contention.

There are three major shortcomings of this method of computing equivalence scales. First, by focusing on the cost of meeting a minimum set of needs, they are inappropriate for applying to incomes above the minimum level. Second, they are dependent on an assessment of what constitutes minimum needs—and this can be contentious. Most important, the scales do not take into account the process of optimization by the households. The consequence of optimization is that as income rises, substitution between goods can take place, and the same relativities need no longer apply. Alternative methods of constructing equivalence scales that aim to overcome these difficulties are now considered.

In a similar way to the Orshansky construction of the US poverty scale, the Engel approach to equivalence scales is based on the hypothesis that the welfare of a household can be measured by the proportion of its income that is spent on food. This is a consequence of Engel's law, which asserts that the share of food in expenditure falls as income rises. If this is accepted, equivalence scales can be constructed for households of different compositions by calculating the income levels at which their expenditure share on food is equal. This is illustrated in figure 13.1 in which the expenditure share on food, as a function of income, is shown for two households with family compositions d^1 and d^2. For example, d^1 may refer to a couple and d^2 to a couple with one child. Incomes M^1 and M^2 lead to the same expenditure share, s, and so are equivalent for the Engel method. The equivalence scale is then formed from the ratio $\frac{M^2}{M^1}$.

Although Engel's law may be empirically true, it does not necessarily provide a basis for making welfare comparisons, since it leaves unexplored the link between household composition and food expenditure. In fact there is ground for believing that the Engel method overestimates the cost of additional children because a child is largely a food-consuming addition to a household. If this is correct, a household compensated sufficiently to restore the share of food in its expenditure

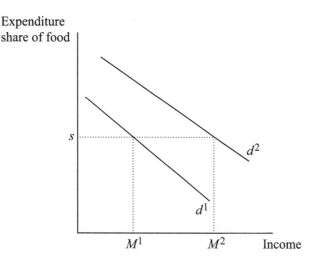

Figure 13.1
Construction of Engel scale

to its original level after the addition of a child would have been overcompensated with respect to other commodities. The approach of Engel has been extended to the more general iso-prop method in which the expenditure shares of a basket of goods, rather than simply food, becomes the basis for the construction of scales. However, considering a basket of goods does not overcome the basic shortcomings of the Engel method.

A further alternative is to select for attention a set of goods that are consumed only by adults, termed "adult goods," and such that the expenditure on them can be treated as a measure of welfare. Typical examples of such goods that have been used in practice are tobacco and alcohol. If these goods have the property that changes in household composition only affect their demand via an income effect (so changes in household composition do not cause substitution between commodities), then the extra income required to keep their consumption constant when household composition changes can be used to construct an equivalence scale. The use of adult goods to construct an equivalence scale is illustrated in figure 13.2. On the basis that they generate the same level of demand, $\bar{x}$, as family composition changes, the income levels M^1 and M^2 can be classed as equivalent, and the equivalence scale can be constructed from their ratio.

There are also a number of difficulties with this approach. It rests on the hypotheses that consumption of adult goods accurately reflects welfare and that household composition affects the demand for these goods only via an income

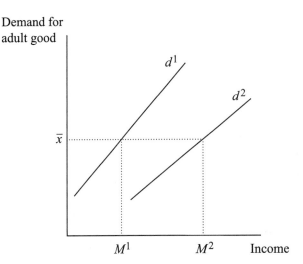

Figure 13.2
Adult good equivalence scale

effect. Furthermore the ratio of M^1 to M^2 will depend on the level of demand chosen for the comparison except in the special case where the demand curves are straight lines through the origin. The ratios may also vary for different goods. This leads into a further problem of forming some average ratio out of the ratios for the individual goods.

All of the methods described so far have attempted to derive the equivalence scale from an observable proxy for welfare. A general approach that can, in principal, overcome the problems identified in the previous methods is illustrated in figure 13.3. To understand this figure, assume that there are just two goods available. The outer indifference curve represents the consumption levels of these two goods necessary for a family of composition d^2 to obtain welfare level U^*, and the inner indifference curve the consumption requirements for a family with composition d^1 to obtain the same utility. The extent to which the budget line has to be shifted outward to reach the higher curve determines the extra income required to compensate for the change in family structure. This construction incorporates both the potential change in preferences as family composition changes and the process of optimization subject to budget constraint by the households.

To formalize this process, let the household have preferences described by the utility function $U(x_1, x_2; d)$, where x_i is the level of consumption of good i and d denotes information on family composition. For example, d will describe the number of adults, the number and ages of children, and any other relevant in-

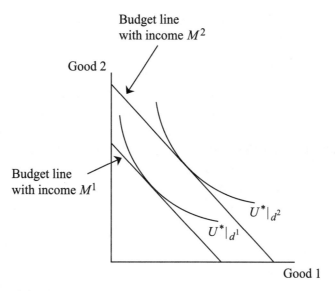

Figure 13.3
General equivalence scale

formation. The consumption plan needed to attain a given utility level, U, at least cost is the solution to

$$\min_{\{x_1, x_2\}} p_1 x_1 + p_2 x_2 \quad \text{subject to} \quad U(x_1, x_2; d) \geq U^*. \tag{13.1}$$

Denoting the (compensated) demand for good i by $x_i(U^*, d)$, the minimum cost of attaining utility U with characteristics d is then given by

$$M(U^*, d) = p_1 x_1(U^*, d) + p_2 x_2(U^*, d). \tag{13.2}$$

The equivalent incomes at utility U^* for two households with compositions d^1 and d^2 are then given by $M(U^*, d^1)$ and $M(U^*, d^2)$. The equivalence scale is derived by computing their ratio. The important point obtained by presenting the construction in this way is the observation that the equivalence scale will generally depend on the level of utility at which the comparison is made. If it does, there can be no single equivalence scale that works at all levels of utility.

The construction of an equivalence scale from preferences makes two further issues apparent. First, the minimum needs and budget share approaches do not take account of how changes in family structure may shift the indifference map. For instance, the pleasure of having children may raise the utility obtained from any given consumption plan. With the utility approach it then becomes cheaper to attain each indifference curve, so the value of the equivalence scale falls as family size increases. This conclusion, of course, conflicts with the basic sense that it is more expensive to support a larger family.

The second problem centers around the use of a household utility function. Many economists would argue that a household utility function cannot exist; instead, they would observe that households are composed of individuals with individual preferences. Under the latter interpretation, the construction of a household utility function suffers from the difficulties of preference aggregation identified by Arrow's Impossibility Theorem. Among the solutions to this problem now being investigated is to look within the functioning of the household and to model its decisions as the outcome of an efficient resource allocation process.

13.4   Inequality Measurement

Inequality is a concept that has immediate intuitive implications. The existence of inequality is easily perceived: differences in living standards between the rich and poor are only too obvious both across countries and, sometimes to a surprising extent, within countries. The obsession of the media with wealth and celebrity provides a constant reminder of just how rich the rich can be. An increase in inequality can also be understood at a basic level. If the rich become richer, and the poor become poorer, then inequality must have increased.

The substantive economic questions about inequality arise when we try to move beyond these generalizations to construct a quantitative measure of inequality. Without a quantitative measure it is not possible to provide a precise answer to questions about inequality. For example, a measure is required to determine which of a range of countries has the greatest level of inequality and to determine whether inequality has risen or fallen over time.

What an inequality measure must do is to take data on the distribution of income and generate a single number that captures the inequality in that distribution. A first approach to constructing such a measure is to adopt a standard statistical index. We describe the most significant of these indexes. Looking at the statistical measures reveals that there are properties, particularly how the measure is affected by transfers of income between households, that we may wish an inequality measure to possess. These properties can also be used to assess the acceptability of alternative measures. It is also shown that implicit within a statistical measure are a set of welfare implications. Rather than just accept these implications, the alternative approach is explored of making the welfare assumptions explicit and building the inequality measure on them.

13.4.1   The Setting

The intention of an inequality measure is to assign a single number to an income distribution that represents the degree of inequality. This section sets out the notation employed for the basic information that is input into the measure and defines precisely what is meant by a measure.

We assume that there are H households and label these $h = 1, \ldots, H$. The labeling of the households is chosen so that the lower is the label, the lower is the household's income. The incomes, M^h, then form an increasing sequence with

$$M^1 \leq M^2 \leq M^3 \leq \cdots \leq M^H. \tag{13.3}$$

The list $\{M^1, \ldots, M^H\}$ is the income distribution whose inequality we wish to measure. Given the income distribution, the mean level of income, μ, is defined by

$$\mu = \frac{1}{H} \sum_{h=1}^{H} M^h. \tag{13.4}$$

The purpose of an inequality measure is to assign a single number to the distribution $\{M^1, \ldots, M^H\}$. Let $I(M^1, \ldots, M^H)$ be an inequality measure. Then income distributions $\{\tilde{M}^1, \ldots, \tilde{M}^H\}$ has greater inequality than distribution $\{\hat{M}^1, \ldots, \hat{M}^H\}$ if $I(\tilde{M}^1, \ldots, \tilde{M}^H) > I(\hat{M}^1, \ldots, \hat{M}^H)$. Typically the inequality measure is constructed so that a value of 0 represents complete equality (the position where all incomes are equal) and a value of 1 represents maximum inequality (all income is received by just one household).

The issues that arise in inequality measurement are encapsulated in determining the form that the function $I(M^1, \ldots, M^H)$ should take. We now investigate some alternative forms and explore their implications.

13.4.2   Statistical Measures

Under the heading of "statistical" fall inequality measures that are derived from the general statistical literature. That is, the measures have been constructed to characterize the distribution of a set of numbers without thought of any explicit economic application or motivation. Even so, the discussion will later show that these statistical measures make implicit economic value judgments. Accepting any one of these measures as the "correct" way to measure inequality means the acceptance of these implicit assumptions. The measures that follow are presented in approximate order of sophistication. Each is constructed to take a value between 0 and 1, with a value of 0 occurring when all households have identical income levels.

Probably the simplest conceivable measure, the *range* calculates inequality as being the difference between the highest and lowest incomes expressed as a proportion of total income. As such, it is a very simple measure to compute. The definition of the range, R, is

$$R = \frac{M^H - M^1}{H\mu}.$$
(13.5)

The division by $H\mu$ in (13.5) is a normalization that ensures the index is independent of the scale of incomes (or the units of measurement of income). Any index that has this property of independence is called a *relative index*.

As an example of the use of the range, consider the income distribution $\{1, 3, 6, 9, 11\}$. For this distribution $\mu = 6$ and

$$R = \frac{11 - 1}{5 \times 6} = 0.3333.$$
(13.6)

The failure of the range to take account of the intermediate part of the distribution can be illustrated by taking income from the second household in the example and giving it to the fourth to generate new income distribution $\{1, 1, 6, 11, 11\}$. This new distribution appears to be more unequal than the first, yet the value of the range remains at $R = 0.3333$.

Given the simplicity of its definition, it is not surprising that the range has deficiencies. Most important, the range takes no account of the dispersion of the income distribution between the highest and the lowest incomes. Consequently it is not sensitive to any features of the income distribution between these extremes. For instance, an income distribution with most of the households receiving close to the maximum income would be judged just as unequal as one in which most received the lowest income. An ideal measure should possess more sensitivity to the value of intermediate incomes than the range.

The *relative mean deviation, D*, takes account of the deviation of each income level from the mean so that it is dependent on intermediate incomes. It does this by calculating the absolute value of the deviation of each income level from the mean and then summing. This summation process gives equal weight to deviations both above and below the mean and implies that D is linear in the size of deviations. Formally, D is defined by

$$D = \frac{\sum_{h=1}^{H} |\mu - M^h|}{2[H-1]\mu}.$$

(13.7)

The division by $2[H-1]\mu$ again ensures that D takes values between 0 and 1.

The advantage of the relative mean deviation over the range is that it takes account of the entire income distribution and not just the endpoints. Taking the example used for the range, the inequality in the distribution $\{1, 3, 6, 9, 11\}$ as measured by D is

$$D = \frac{|-5| + |-3| + |0| + |3| + |5|}{2 \times 4 \times 6} = 0.3333,$$

(13.8)

and the inequality of $\{1, 1, 6, 11, 11\}$ is

$$D = \frac{|-5| + |-5| + |0| + |5| + |5|}{2 \times 4 \times 6} = 0.4167.$$

(13.9)

Unlike the range, the relative mean deviation measures the second distribution as having more inequality. Due to the division by $2[H-1]\mu$ it is easily seen that $D = 1$ with the maximum inequality distribution $\{0, 0, 0, 0, 30\}$ where all income is received by just one household.

Although it does take account of the entire distribution of income, the linearity of D has the implication that it is insensitive to transfers from richer to poorer households when the households involved in the transfer remain on the same side of the mean income level. To see an example of this, assume that the mean income level is $\mu = 20,000$. Now take two households with incomes 25,000 and 100,000. Transferring 4,000 from the poorer of these two households to the richer, so the income levels become 21,000 and 104,000, does not change the value of D—one term in the summation rises by 4,000 and the other falls by 4,000. (Notice that if the two households were on different sides of the mean, then a similar transfer would raise two terms in the summation by 4,000 and increase inequality.) The fact that D can be insensitive to transfers seems unsatisfactory, since it is natural to expect that a transfer from a poorer household to a richer one should raise inequality.

This line of reasoning is enshrined in the *Pigou-Dalton Principle of Transfers*, which is a central concept in the theory of inequality measurement. The basis of this principle is precisely the requirement that any transfer from a poor household to a rich one must increase inequality regardless of where the two households are located in the income distribution.

Definition (Pigou-Dalton Principle of Transfers)   The inequality index must decrease if there is a transfer of income from a richer household to a poorer household that preserves the ranking of the two households in the income distribution and leaves total income unchanged.

Any inequality measure that satisfies this principle is said to be *sensitive to transfers*. The Pigou-Dalton Principle is generally viewed as a feature that any acceptable measure of inequality should possess and is therefore expected in an inequality measure. Neither the range nor the relative mean deviation satisfy this principle.

The reason why D is not sensitive to transfers is its linearity in deviations from the mean. The removal of the linearity provides the motivation for considering the *coefficient of variation*, which is defined using the sum of squared deviations. The procedure of forming the square places more weight on incomes that are further away from the mean and so introduces a sensitivity to transfers. The coefficient of variation, C, is defined by

$$C = \frac{\sigma}{\mu[H-1]^{1/2}}, \tag{13.10}$$

where $\sigma^2 = \frac{\sum_{h=1}^{H}[M^h - \mu]^2}{H}$ is the variance of the income distribution, so σ is its standard deviation. The division by $\mu[H-1]^{1/2}$ ensures the C lies between 0 and 1. For the income distribution $\{1, 3, 6, 9, 11\}$, $\sigma^2 = \frac{[-5]^2 + [-3]^2 + [0]^2 + [3]^2 + [5]^2}{5} = 13.6$, so

$$C = \frac{[13.6]^{1/2}}{6[4]^{1/2}} = 0.3073, \tag{13.11}$$

and for $\{1, 1, 6, 11, 11\}$, $\sigma^2 = 20.0$ giving

$$C = \frac{[20]^{1/2}}{6[4]^{1/2}} = 0.3727. \tag{13.12}$$

To see that the coefficient of variation satisfies the Pigou-Dalton Principle, consider a transfer of an amount of income $d\epsilon$ from household i to household j, with the households chosen so that $M^i < M^j$. Then

$$\frac{dC}{d\epsilon} = \frac{1}{\mu[H-1]^{1/2}} \frac{d\sigma}{d\epsilon} = \frac{2[M^i - M^j]}{\sigma H \mu[H-1]^{1/2}} < 0, \qquad (13.13)$$

so the transfer from the poorer household to the richer household decreases measured inequality as required by the Pigou-Dalton Principle. It should be noted that the value of the change in C depends on the difference between the incomes of the two households. This has the consequence that a transfer of 100 units of income from a household with an income of 1,000,100 to one with an income of 999,900 produces the same change in C as a transfer of 100 units between households with incomes 1,100 and 900. Most interpretations of equity would suggest that the latter transfer should be of greater consequence for the index because it involves two households of relatively low incomes. This reasoning suggests that satisfaction of the Pigou-Dalton Principle may not be a sufficient requirement for an inequality measure; the manner in which the measure satisfies it may also matter.

Before moving on to further inequality measures, it is worth describing the Lorenz curve. The Lorenz curve is a helpful graphical device for presenting a summary representation of an income distribution, and it has played an important role in the measurement of inequality. Although not strictly an inequality measure as defined above, Lorenz curves are considered because of their use in illustrating inequality and the central role they play in the motivation of other inequality indexes.

The Lorenz curve is constructed by arranging the population in order of increasing income and then graphing the proportion of income going to each proportion of the population. The graph of the Lorenz curve therefore has the proportion of population on the horizontal axis and the proportion of income on the vertical axis. If all households in the population had identical incomes the Lorenz curve would then be the diagonal line connecting the points $(0,0)$ and $(1,1)$. If there is any degree of inequality, the ordering in which the households are taken ensures that the Lorenz curve lies below the diagonal since, for example, the poorest half of the population must have less than half the total income.

To see how the Lorenz curve is plotted, consider a population of 10 with income distribution $\{1, 2, 3, 4, 5, 6, 7, 8, 9, 10\}$. The total quantity of income is 55, so the first household (which represents 10 percent of the population) receives $\frac{1}{55} \times 100$ percent of the total income. This is the first point plotted in the lower-left corner of figure 13.4. Taking the two lowest income households (which are 20 percent of the population), we have their combined income as $\frac{3}{55} \times 100$ percent of the total. Adding the third household awards 30 percent of the population $\frac{6}{55} \times 100$ percent

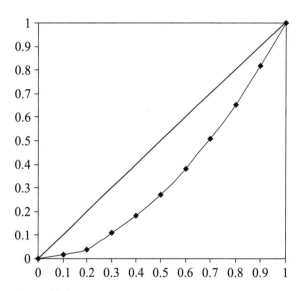

Figure 13.4
Construction of a Lorenz curve

of total income. Proceeding in this way, we plot the ten points in the figure. Joining them gives the Lorenz curve. In summary, the larger the population, the smoother is this curve.

The Lorenz curve can be employed to unambiguously rank some income distributions with respect to income inequality. This claim is based on the fact that a transfer of income from a poor household to a richer household moves the Lorenz curve farther away from the diagonal. (This can be verified by re-plotting the Lorenz curve in figure 13.4 for the income distribution $\{1, 1, 3, 4, 5, 6, 7, 8, 10, 10\}$, which is the same as the original except for the transfer of one unit from household 2 to household 9.) Because of this property the Lorenz curve satisfies the Pigou-Dalton Principle, with the curve farther from the diagonal indicating greater inequality.

Income distributions that can, and cannot, be ranked are displayed in figure 13.5. In the left-hand figure, the Lorenz curve for income distribution B lies entirely outside that for income distribution A. In such a case distribution B unambiguously has more inequality than A. One way to see this is to observe that distribution B can be obtained from distribution A by transferring income from poor households to rich households. Applying the Pigou-Dalton Principle, we see that this raises inequality. If the Lorenz curves representing the distributions A and B cross, it is not possible to obtain an unambiguous conclusion by the Lorenz

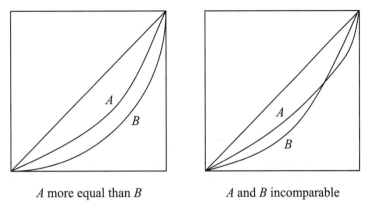

A more equal than B   A and B incomparable

Figure 13.5
Lorenz curves as an incomplete ranking

curve alone. The Lorenz curve therefore provides only a partial ranking of income distributions. Despite this limitation the Lorenz curve is still a popular tool in applied economics, since it presents very convenient and easily interpreted visual summary of an income distribution.

The next measure, the *Gini*, has been the subject of extensive attention in discussions of inequality measurement and has been much used in applied economics. The Gini, *G*, can be expressed by considering all possible pairs of incomes and out of each pair selecting the minimum income level. Summing the minimum income levels and dividing by $H^2\mu$ to ensure a value between 0 and 1 provides the formula for the Gini:

$$G = 1 - \frac{1}{H^2\mu} \sum_{i=1}^{H} \sum_{j=1}^{H} \min\{M^i, M^j\}. \tag{13.14}$$

It should be noted that in the construction of this measure, each level of income is compared to itself as well as all other income levels. For example, if there are three income levels $\{3, 5, 10\}$, the value of the Gini is

$$G = 1 - \frac{1}{3^2 \times 6} \begin{bmatrix} \min\{3,3\} + \min\{3,5\} + \min\{3,10\} \\ + \min\{5,3\} + \min\{5,5\} + \min\{5,10\} \\ \min\{10,3\} + \min\{10,5\} + \min\{10,10\} \end{bmatrix}$$

$$= 1 - \frac{1}{54}[3 + 3 + 3 + 3 + 5 + 5 + 3 + 5 + 10]$$

$$= 0.259. \tag{13.15}$$

By counting the number of times each income level appears, we can also write the Gini as

$$G = 1 - \frac{1}{H^2\mu}[[2H-1]M^1 + [2H-3]M^2 + [2H-5]M^3 + \cdots + M^H]. \quad (13.16)$$

This second form of the Gini makes its computation simpler but hides the construction behind the measure.

The Gini also satisfies the Pigou-Dalton Principle. This can be seen by considering a transfer of income of size $\Delta > 0$ from household i to household j, with the households chosen so that $M^j > M^i$. From the ranking of incomes this implies $j > i$. Then

$$\Delta G = \frac{2}{H^2\mu}[j-i]\Delta > 0, \quad (13.17)$$

as required. In the case of the Gini, the effect of the transfer of income on the measure depends only on the locations of i and j in the income distribution. For example, a transfer from the household at position $i = 1$ to the household at position $j = 11$ counts as much as one from position $i = 151$ to position $j = 161$. It might be expected that an inequality should be more sensitive to transfers between households low in the income distribution.

There is an important relationship between the Gini and the Lorenz curve. As shown in figure 13.6, the Gini is equal to the area between the Lorenz curve and the line of equality as a proportion of the area of the triangle beneath the line of equality. As the area of the triangle is $\frac{1}{2}$, the Gini is twice the area between the Lorenz curve and the equality line. This definition makes it clear that the Gini, in

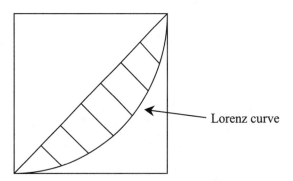

Figure 13.6
Relating Gini to Lorenz

common with R, C, and D, can be used to rank distributions when the Lorenz curves cross, since the relevant area is always well defined. Since all these measures provide a stronger ranking of income distributions than the Lorenz curve, they must each impose additional restrictions that allow a comparison to be made between distributions even when their Lorenz curves cross.

A final statistical measure that displays a different form of sensitivity to transfers is the *Theil entropy measure*. This measure is drawn from information theory and is used in that context to measure the average information content of a system of information. The definition of the Theil entropy measure, T, is given by

$$T = \frac{1}{\log(H)} \sum_{h=1}^{H} \frac{M^h}{H\mu} \left[\log\left(\frac{M^h}{H\mu}\right) - \log\left(\frac{1}{H}\right) \right]$$

$$= \frac{1}{H\log(H)} \sum_{h=1}^{H} \frac{M^h}{\mu} \log\left(\frac{M^h}{\mu}\right). \tag{13.18}$$

In respect of the Pigou-Dalton Principle, the effect of an income transfer, $d\epsilon$, between households i and j on the entropy index is given by

$$\frac{dT}{d\epsilon} = \frac{1}{H\log(H)} \log\left(\frac{M^j}{M^i}\right) < 0, \tag{13.19}$$

so the entropy measure also satisfies the criterion. For the Theil entropy measure, the change is dependent on the relative incomes of the two households involved in the transfer. This provides an alternative form of sensitivity to transfers.

13.4.3   Inequality and Welfare

The analysis of the statistical measures of inequality has made reference to "acceptable" criteria for a measure to possess. One of these was made explicit in the Pigou-Dalton Principle, while other criteria relating to additional desirable sensitivity properties have been implicit in the discussion. To be able to say that something is acceptable or not implies that there is some notion of distributive justice or social welfare underlying the judgment. It is then interesting to consider the relationship between inequality measures and welfare.

The first issue to address is the extent to which income distributions can be ranked in terms of welfare with minimal restrictions imposed on the social welfare function. To investigate this, let the level of social welfare be determined by the function $W = W(M^1, \ldots, M^H)$. It is assumed that this social welfare function is symmetric and concave. Symmetry means that the level of welfare is unaffected by changing the ordering of the households. This is just a requirement that all households are treated equally. Concavity ensures that the indifference curves of the welfare function have the standard shape with mixtures preferred to extremes. This assumption imposes a concern for equity on the welfare function.

The critical theorem relating the ranking of income distributions to social welfare is now given.

Theorem 11   Consider two distributions of income with the same mean. If the Lorenz curves for these distributions do not cross, every symmetric and concave social welfare function will assign a higher level of welfare to the distribution whose Lorenz curve is closest to the main diagonal.

The proof of this theorem is very straightforward. Since the welfare function is symmetric and concave, it follows that $\frac{\partial W}{\partial M^i} \geq \frac{\partial W}{\partial M^j}$ if $M^i < M^j$. Hence the marginal social welfare of income is greater for a household lower in the income distribution. If the two Lorenz curves do not cross, the income distribution represented by the inner one (that closest to the main diagonal) can be obtained from that of the outer one by transferring income from richer to poorer households. Since the marginal social welfare of income to the poorer households is never less than that from richer, this transfer must raise welfare as measured by any symmetric and concave social welfare function.

The converse of this theorem is that if the Lorenz curves for two distributions cross, then two symmetric and concave social welfare functions can be found that will rank the two distributions differently. This is because the income distributions of two Lorenz curves that cross are not related by simple transfers from rich to poor. So, if the Lorenz curves do cross, the income distributions cannot be unambiguously ranked without specifying the social welfare function.

Taken together, the theorem and its converse show that the Lorenz curve provides the most complete ranking of income distributions that is possible without our making assumptions on the form of the social welfare function other than symmetry and concavity. To achieve a complete ranking when the Lorenz curves cross requires restrictions to be placed on the structure of the social welfare function. In addition any measure of inequality is necessarily stronger than the Lorenz curve because it generates a complete ranking of distributions. This is true of all the statistical measures, which is why it can be argued that they all carry implicit welfare judgments.

This argument can be taken a stage further. It is in fact possible to construct the social welfare function that is implied by an inequality measure. To see how this can be done, consider the Gini. Assume that the total amount of income available is constant. Any redistribution of this that leaves the Gini unchanged must leave the implied level of welfare unchanged. A redistribution of income will not affect the Gini if the term $[[2H - 1]M^1 + \cdots + M^H]$ remains constant. The welfare function must thus be a function of this expression. Furthermore the Gini is defined to be independent of the total level of income, but a welfare function will increase if total income rises and distribution is unaffected. This can be incorporated by not dividing through by the mean level of income. Putting these arguments together, the welfare function implied by the Gini is given by

$$W_G(M) = \frac{1}{H^2}[[2H - 1]M^1 + [2H - 3]M^2 + \cdots + M^H]. \tag{13.20}$$

The form of $W_G(M)$ is interesting, since it shows that the Gini implies a social welfare function that is linear in incomes. It also shows a clear structure of increasing welfare weights for lower income consumers. The welfare function further has indifference curves that are straight lines above and below the line of equal incomes but kinked on this line. This is illustrated in figure 13.7.

In the same way a welfare function can be constructed for all the statistical measures. Therefore acceptance of the measure is acceptance of the implied

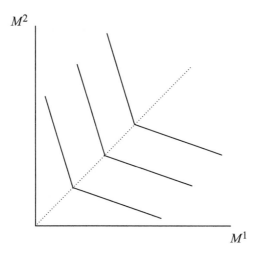

Figure 13.7
Gini social welfare function

welfare function. As shown by the linear social indifference curves and increasing welfare weights for the Gini social welfare function, the implied welfare functions can have a very restrictive form. We do not need to merely accept such welfare restrictions. The fact that each inequality measure implies a social welfare function suggests that the relationship can be inverted to move from a social welfare function to an inequality measure. By assuming a social welfare function at the outset, it is possible to make welfare judgments explicit and, by deriving the inequality measure from the social welfare function, to ensure that these judgments are incorporated in the inequality measure.

To implement this approach, assume that the social welfare function is utilitarian with

$$W = \sum_{h=1}^{H} U(M^h). \tag{13.21}$$

The household utility of income function, $U(M)$, is taken to satisfy the conditions that $U'(M) > 0$ and $U''(M) < 0$. The utility function $U(M)$ can either be the households' true cardinal utility function or be chosen by the policy analyst as in the evaluation of the utility of income to each household. In this second interpretation, since social welfare is obtained by summing the individual utilities, the importance given to equity can be captured in the choice of $U(M)$. This is because increasing the concavity of the utility function places a relatively higher weight on low incomes in the social welfare function.

A measure of inequality can be constructed from the social welfare function by defining M_{EDE} as the solution to

$$\sum_{h=1}^{H} U(M^h) = HU(M_{EDE}). \tag{13.22}$$

M_{EDE} is called the *equally distributed equivalent* income and is the level of income that, if given to all households, would generate the same level of social welfare as the initial income distribution. Using M_{EDE}, the *Atkinson* measure of inequality is defined by

$$A = 1 - \frac{M_{EDE}}{\mu}. \tag{13.23}$$

For the case of two households the construction of M_{EDE} is illustrated in figure 13.8. The initial income distribution is given by $\{M^1, M^2\}$, and this determines

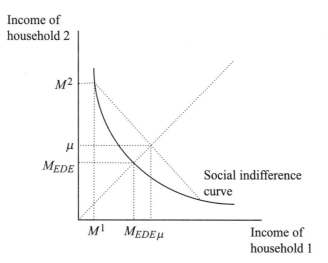

Figure 13.8
Equally distributed equivalent income

the relevant indifference curve of the social welfare function. M_{EDE} is found by moving around this indifference curve to the 45° line where the two households' incomes are equal. The figure makes clear that because of the concavity of the social indifference curve, M_{EDE} is less than the mean income, μ. This fact guarantees that $0 \leq A \leq 1$. Furthermore, for a given level of mean income, a more diverse income distribution will achieve a lower social indifference curve and be equivalent to a lower M_{EDE}.

The flexibility in this measure lies in the freedom of choice of the household utility of income function. Given the assumption of a utilitarian social welfare function, it is the household utility that determines the importance attached to inequality by the measure. One commonly used form of utility function is

$$U(M) = \frac{M^{1-\varepsilon}}{1 - \varepsilon}, \qquad \varepsilon \neq 1, \tag{13.24}$$

which allows the welfare judgments of the policy analyst to be contained in the chosen value of the parameter ε. The value of ε determines the degree of concavity of the utility function: it becomes more concave as ε increases. An increase in concavity raises the relative importance of low incomes because it causes the marginal utility of income to decline at a faster rate. The utility function is isoelastic, and concave if $\varepsilon \geq 0$. When $\varepsilon = 1$, $U(M) = \log(M)$, and when $\varepsilon = 0$, $U(M) = M$.

The Atkinson measure can be illustrated using the example of the income distribution $\{1,3,6,9,11\}$. If $\varepsilon = \frac{1}{2}$ the household utility function is $U = \frac{M^{1/2}}{2}$ so the level of social welfare is

$$W = \frac{1^{1/2}}{2} + \frac{3^{1/2}}{2} + \frac{6^{1/2}}{2} + \frac{9^{1/2}}{2} + \frac{11^{1/2}}{2} = 5.7491. \tag{13.25}$$

The equally distributed equivalent income then solves

$$5 \times \frac{[M]^{1/2}}{2} = 5.7491, \tag{13.26}$$

so $M_{EDE} = 5.2883$. This gives the value of the Atkinson measure as

$$A = 1 - \frac{5.2883}{6} = 0.1186. \tag{13.27}$$

13.4.4   An Application

As has been noted in the discussion, inequality measures are frequently used in practical policy analysis. Table 13.2 summarizes the results of an OECD study into the change in inequality over time in a wide range of countries. This is under-

Table 13.2
Inequalities before and after taxes and transfers

Measure	SCV[a]		Gini		Atkinson[b]	
	Before	After	Before	After	Before	After
Denmark 1994	0.671	0.229	0.420	0.217	0.209	0.041
% Change 1983–1994	4.9	2.0	11.2	−4.9	25.3	−11.1
Italy 1993	1.19	0.584	0.570	0.345	0.299	0.105
% Change 1984–1993	59.6	44.7	20.8	12.8	43.8	33.1
Japan 1994	0.536	0.296	0.340	0.265	0.124	0.059
% Change 1984–1994	33.7	21.7	14.0	4.9	47.3	10.9
Sweden 1995	0.894	0.217	0.487	0.230	0.262	0.049
% Change 1975–1995	49.1	36.9	17.2	−1.0	28.7	3.2
United States 1995	0.811	0.441	0.455	0.344	0.205	0.100
% Change 1974–1995	32.0	25.4	13.1	10.0	19.6	18.6

Source: OECD ECO/WKP(98)2.
a. The squared coefficient of variation (SCV) is defined by $SCV = [H-1]C$.
b. For the Atkinson measure, $\varepsilon = 0.5$.

taken by calculating inequality at two points in time and determining the percentage change in the measure. If the change is positive, then inequality has increased. The converse holds if it is negative. The study also calculates inequality for income before taxes and transfers, and for income after taxes and transfers. The difference between the inequality levels in these two situations gives an insight into the extent to which the tax and transfer system succeeds in redistributing income.

Looking at the results, in all cases inequality is smaller after taxes and transfers than before, so the tax systems in the countries studied are redistributive. For instance, in Denmark inequality is 0.0420 when measured by Gini before taxes and transfers but only 0.0217 after. The second general message of the results is that inequality has tended to rise in these countries—only in three cases has it been reduced, and in every case this is after taxes and transfers.

It is also interesting to look at the rankings of inequality and changes in inequality under the different measures. If there is general agreement for different measures, then we can be reassured that the choice of measure is not too critical for what we observe. For the level of inequality all four measures are in agreement for both the before-tax and after-tax cases except for the SCV (squared coefficient of variation), which reverses the after-taxes and transfers ranking of Denmark and Sweden, and the Atkinson, which reverses the before-taxes and transfers ranking of Denmark and the United States. For these four measures there is a considerable degree of consistency in the rankings. Taking the majority opinion, observe that before taxes and transfers the ranking (with the highest level of inequality first) is Italy, Sweden, United States, Denmark, and Japan. After the operation of taxes and transfers this ranking becomes Italy, United States, Japan, Sweden, and Denmark. This change in rankings is evidence of the highly redistributive tax and transfer systems operated in the Nordic countries.

The rankings for the change in inequality are not quite as consistent across the four measures, but there is still considerable agreement. The majority order for the before taxes and transfers case (with the greatest increase in inequality first) is Italy, Sweden, Japan, United States, and Denmark. The Atkinson measure places Japan at the top and reverses Denmark and the United States. For the after-taxes and transfers ranking, the Gini and the Atkinson measures produce the same ranking, but the SCV places Sweden above the United States and Japan. But what is clear is the general agreement on an increase in inequality.

The review of this application has shown that the different measure can produce a fairly consistent picture about ranking by inequality, about the changes in inequality, and on the effect of taxes and transfers. Despite the differences emphasized in the analysis of the measures, when put into practice in this way, the differences need not lead to widespread disagreement between the measures. In fact a fairly harmonious picture can emerge.

13.5   Poverty

The essential feature of poverty is the possession of fewer resources than are required to achieve an acceptable standard of living. What constitutes poverty can be understood in the same intuitive way as what constitutes inequality, but similar issues about the correct measure arise again once we attempt to provide a quantification. This section first discusses concepts of poverty and the poverty line, and then proceeds to review a number of common poverty measures.

13.5.1   Poverty and the Poverty Line

Before measuring poverty, it is first necessary to define it. It is obvious that poverty refers to a situation involving a lack of income and a consequent low level of consumption and welfare. What is not so clear is the standard against which the level of income should be judged. Two possibilities arise in this context: an absolute conception of poverty and a relative one. The distinction between these has implications for changes in the level of poverty over time and the success of policy in alleviating poverty.

The concept of *absolute poverty* assumes that there is some fixed minimum level of consumption (and hence of income) that constitutes poverty and is independent of time or place. Such a minimum level of consumption can be a diet that is just sufficient to maintain health and limited housing and clothing. Under the concept of absolute poverty, if the incomes of all households rise, there will eventually be no poverty. Although a concept of absolute poverty was probably implicit in early studies of poverty, such as that of Rowntree in 1901, the appropriateness of absolute poverty has since generally been rejected. In its place has been adopted the notion of relative poverty.

Relative poverty is not a recent concept. Even in 1776 Adam Smith was defining poverty as the lack of necessities, where necessities are defined as "what ever the custom of the country renders it indecent for creditable people, even of the lowest order, to be without." This definition makes it clear that relative poverty is defined in terms of the standards of a given society at a given time and that the level that represents poverty rises as does the income of that society. Operating under a relative standard, it becomes much more difficult to eliminate poverty. Relative poverty has also been defined in terms of the ability to "participate" in society. Poverty then arises whenever a household possesses insufficient resources to allow it to participate in the customary activities of its society.

The starting point for the measurement of poverty is to set a poverty line that separates those viewed as living in poverty from those who are not. Of course, this poverty line applies to the incomes levels after application of an equivalence scale. Whether poverty is viewed as absolute or relative matters little for setting a poverty line at any particular point in time (though advocates of an absolute poverty concept may choose to set it lower). Where the distinction matters is whether and how the poverty line is adjusted over time. If an absolute poverty standard were adopted, then there would be no revision. Conversely, with relative poverty the level of the line would rise or fall in line with average incomes.

In practice, poverty lines have often been determined by following the minimum needs approach that was discussed in connection with equivalence scales. As noted in section 13.3, this is the case with the US poverty line that was fixed in 1963 and has since been updated annually. As the package of minimum needs has not changed, the underlying concept is that of an absolute poverty measure. In the United Kingdom the poverty line has been taken as the level of income that is 120 or 140 percent of the minimum supplementary benefit level. As this level of benefit is determined by minimum needs, a minimum needs poverty line is implied. In addition benefits have risen with increases in average income, so causing the poverty line to rise. The UK poverty line thus represents the use of a relative concept of poverty.

The assumption that there is a precise switch between poverty and nonpoverty as the poverty line is crossed is very strong. It is much more natural for there to be a gradual move out of poverty as income increases. The precision of the poverty line may also lead to difficulty in determining where it should lie if the level of poverty is critically dependent on the precise choice. Both of these difficulties can be overcome by observing that often it is not the precise level of poverty that matters but changes in the level of poverty over time and across countries. In these instances the poverty value is not too important but only the rankings. This suggest the procedure of calculating poverty for a range of poverty lines. If poverty is higher today for all poverty lines than it was yesterday, then it seems unambiguous that poverty has risen. In this sense the poverty line may not actually be of critical importance for the uses to poverty measurement is often put. An application illustrating this argument is given below.

13.5.2   Poverty Measures

The poverty line is now taken as given, and we proceed to discuss alternative measures of poverty. The basic issue in this discussion is how best to combine two pieces of information (how many households are poor, and how poor they are) into a single quantitative measure of poverty. By describing a number of measures, the discussion will draw out the properties that are desirable for a poverty measure to possess.

Throughout the discussion the poverty line is denoted by the income level z so that a household with an income level below or equal to z is classed as living in poverty. For a household with income M^h the *income gap* measures how far their income is below the poverty line. Denoting the income gap for household h by g_h, it follows that $g_h = z - M^h$. Given the poverty line z and an income distribution $\{M^1, \ldots, M^H\}$, where $M^1 \leq M^2 \leq \cdots \leq M^H$, the number of households in poverty is denoted by q. The value of q is defined by the facts that the income of household q is on or below the poverty line, so $M^q \leq z$, but that of the next household is above $M^{q+1} > z$.

The simplest measure of poverty is the *head-count ratio*, which determines the extent of poverty by counting the number of households whose incomes are not above the poverty line. Expressing the number as a proportion of the population, the head-count ratio is defined by

$$E = \frac{q}{H}. \tag{13.28}$$

This measure of poverty was first used by Rowntree in 1901 and has been employed in many subsequent studies. The major advantage of the head-count ratio is its simplicity of calculation.

The head-count ratio is clearly limited because it is not affected by how far below the poverty line the households are. For example, with a poverty line of $z = 10$ the income distributions $\{1, 1, 20, 40, 50\}$ and $\{9, 9, 20, 40, 50\}$ would both have a headcount ratio of $E = \frac{2}{5}$. A policy-maker may well see these income distributions differently, since the income required to alleviate poverty in the second case (2 units) is much less then that required for the first (18 units). The head-count ratio is also not affected by any transfer of income from a poor household to one that is richer if both households remain on the same side of the poverty line. Even worse, observe that if we change the second distribution to $\{7, 11, 20, 40, 50\}$ the head-count ratio falls to $E = \frac{1}{5}$, so a regressive transfer has actually reduced the head-count ratio. This will happen whenever a transfer takes the income of the recipient of the transfer above the poverty line.

The head-count uses only one of the two pieces of information on poverty. A measure that uses only information on how far below the poverty line are the incomes of the poor households is the *aggregate poverty gap*. This is defined as the simple sum of the income gaps of the households that are in poverty. Recalling that it is the first q households that are in poverty, the aggregate poverty gap is

$$V = \sum_{h=1}^{q} g_h. \tag{13.29}$$

The interpretation of this measure is that it is the additional income for the poor that is required to eliminate poverty. It provides some information but is limited by the fact that it is not sensitive to changes in the number in poverty. In addition the aggregate poverty gap gives equal weight to all income shortfalls regardless of how far they are from the poverty line. It is therefore insensitive to transfers unless the transfer takes one of the households out of poverty. To see this latter point, for the poverty line of $z = 10$ the income distributions $\{5, 5, 20, 40, 50\}$ and $\{1, 9, 20, 40, 50\}$ have an aggregate poverty gap of $V = 10$. The distribution between the poor is somewhat different in the two cases.

One direct extension of the aggregate poverty gap is to adjust the measure by taking into account the number in poverty. The *income gap ratio* does this by calculating the aggregate poverty gap and then dividing by the number in poverty. Finally the value obtained is divided by the value of the poverty line, z, to obtain a measure whose value falls between 0 (the absence of poverty) and 1 (all households in poverty have no income):

$$I = \frac{1}{z} \frac{\sum_{h=1}^{q} g_h}{q}. \tag{13.30}$$

For the income distribution $\{1, 9, 20, 40, 50\}$, the income gap ratio when $z = 10$ is

$$I = \frac{1}{10} \frac{9 + 1}{2} = 0.5. \tag{13.31}$$

However, when this income distribution changes to $\{1, 10, 20, 40, 50\}$, so only one household is now in poverty, the measure become

$$I = \frac{1}{10} \frac{9}{1} = 0.9. \tag{13.32}$$

This example reveals that the income gap ratio has the unfortunate property of being able to report increased poverty when the income of household crosses the poverty line and the number in poverty is reduced.

These observations suggest that it is necessary to reflect more carefully on the properties that a poverty measure should possess. In 1976 Sen suggested that a poverty measure should have the following properties:

· Transfers of income between households above the poverty line should not affect the amount of poverty.
· If a household below the poverty line becomes worse off, poverty should increase.
· The poverty measure should be anonymous, meaning it should not depend on who is poor.
· A regressive transfer among the poor should raise poverty.

These are properties that have already been highlighted by the discussion. Two further properties were also proposed:

· The weight given to a household should depend on their ranking among the poor, meaning more weight should be given to those furthest below the poverty line.
· The measure should reduce to the headcount if all the poor have the same level of income.

One poverty measure that satisfies all of these conditions is the *Sen measure*

$$S = E\left[I + [1 - I]G_p\left[\frac{q}{q+1}\right]\right], \tag{13.33}$$

where G_p is the Gini measure of income inequality among the households below the poverty line. This poverty measure combines a measure of the number in poverty (the head-count ratio), a measure of the shortfall in income (the income gap ratio), and a measure of the distribution of income among the poor (the Gini). Applying this to the income distribution $\{1, 9, 20, 40, 50\}$, when $z = 10$, we have $E = \frac{2}{5}$ and $I = 0.5$. The Gini is calculated for the distribution of income of the poor $\{1, 9\}$, so $G_p = 1 - \frac{1}{2^2 \times 5}[3 \times 1 + 9] = \frac{4}{10}$. These values give

$$S = \frac{2}{5}\left[0.5 + [1 - 0.5]\frac{4}{10}\left[\frac{2}{2+1}\right]\right] = 0.2533. \tag{13.34}$$

In contrast, for the distribution $\{1, 10, 20, 40, 50\}$ that was judged worse using the income gap ratio, there is no inequality among the poor (since there is a single poor person), so the Sen measure is

$$S = \frac{1}{5}\left[0.9 + [1 - 0.9]0\left[\frac{1}{1 + 1}\right]\right] = 0.18, \tag{13.35}$$

which is simply the head-count ratio and records a lower level of poverty.

There is a further desirable property that leads into an alternative and important class of poverty measures. Consider a population that can be broken down into distinct subgroups. For instance, imagine dividing the population into rural and urban dwellers. The property we want is for the measure to be able to assign a poverty level for each of the groups and to aggregate these group poverty levels into a single level of the total society. Further we will also want the aggregate measure to increase if poverty rises in one of the subgroups and does not fall in any of the others. So, if rural poverty rises while urban poverty remains the same, aggregate poverty must rise. Any poverty measures that satisfies this condition is termed *subgroup consistent*.

Before introducing a form of measure that is subgroup consistent, it is worth providing additional discussion of the effect of transfers. The measures discussed so far have all had the property that the effect of a transfer has been independent of the income levels of the loser and gainer (except when the transfer was between households on different sides of the poverty line or changed the number in poverty). In the same way that in inequality measurement we argued for magnifying the effect of deviations far from the mean, we can equally argue that the effect of a transfer in poverty measurement should be dependent on the incomes of those involved in the transfer. For example, a transfer away from the lowest income household should have more effect on measured poverty than a transfer away from a household close to the poverty line. A poverty measure will satisfy this *sensitivity to transfers* if the increase in measured poverty caused by a transfer of income from a poor household to a poor household with a higher income is smaller, the larger the income is of the lowest income household.

Let the total population remain at H. Assume that this population can be divided into Γ separate subgroups. Let g_h^γ be the income gap of a poor member of subgroup γ and q^γ be the number of poor in that subgroup. Using this notation, a poverty measure that satisfies the property of subgroup consistency is the Foster-Greer-Thorbecke (FGT) class given by

$$P_\alpha = \frac{1}{H} \sum_{\gamma=1}^{\Gamma} \sum_{h=1}^{q^\gamma} \left[\frac{g_h^\gamma}{z} \right]^\alpha. \tag{13.36}$$

The form of this measure depends on the value chosen for the parameter α. If $\alpha = 0$, then

$$P_0 = \frac{\sum_{\gamma=1}^{\Gamma} q^\gamma}{H} = E, \tag{13.37}$$

the head-count ratio. If instead $\alpha = 1$, then

$$P_1 = \frac{1}{H} \sum_{\gamma=1}^{\Gamma} \left[\sum_{h=1}^{q^\gamma} \frac{g_h^\gamma}{z} \right] = EI, \tag{13.38}$$

the product of the head-count ratio and the income gap ratio. Note that P_0 is insensitive to transfers, while the effect of a transfer for P_1 is independent of the incomes of the households involved. For higher values of α the FGT measure satisfies sensitivity to transfers, and more weight is placed on the income gaps of lower income households.

13.5.3   Two Applications

The use of these poverty measures is now illustrated by reviewing two applications. The first application, taken from Foster, Greer, and Thorbecke, shows how subgroup consistency can give additional insight into the sources of poverty. The second application is extracted from an OECD working paper and illustrates how a range of poverty lines can be used as a check on consistency. It also reveals that there can be a good degree of agreement between different measures of poverty.

Table 13.3 reports an application of the FGT measure. The data are from a household survey in Nairobi and groups the population according to their length of residence in Nairobi. The measure used is the P_2 measure, so $\alpha = 2$. As already discussed, the use of the FGT measure allows the contribution of each group to total poverty to be identified. For example, those living in Nairobi between 6 and 10 years have a level of poverty of 0.0343 and contribute 12.1 percent to total poverty—this is also the percentage by which total poverty would fall if this group were all raised above the poverty line. This division into groups also allows identification of where the major contribution to poverty arises. In this case the major contribution is made by those in the 21 to 70 group. Although the actual poverty

Table 13.3
Poverty using the FGT P_2 measure

Years in Nairobi	Level of poverty	% Contribution to total poverty
0	0.4267	5.6
0.01–1	0.1237	6.5
2	0.1264	6.6
3–5	0.0257	5.1
6–10	0.0343	12.1
11–15	0.0291	9.4
16–20	0.0260	6.6
21–70	0.0555	23.8
Permanent resident	0.1659	8.7
Don't know	0.2461	15.5
Total	0.0558	99.9

Source: Foster, Greer, and Thorbecke (1985).

level in this group is quite low, the number of households in this group causes them to have a major effect on poverty.

The second application is reported in table 13.4. This OECD analysis studies the change in poverty over (approximately) a ten-year period from the mid-1980s to the mid-1990s. The numbers given are therefore the percentage change in the measure and not the value of the measure. What the results show is that the direction of change in poverty as measured by the head-count ratio is not sensitive to the choice of the poverty line—the only inconsistency is the value for Australia with the poverty line as 40 percent of median income. In detail, there has been a decrease in poverty in Australia, Belgium, and the United States but an increase in Germany, Japan, and Sweden. The results in the three central columns report the calculations for three different poverty measures. These show that the Sen measure and the head-count are always in agreement about the direction of change. This is not true of the income gap which disagrees with the other two for Australia and the United States.

13.6   Conclusions

The need to quantify is driven by the aim of making precise comparisons. What economic analysis contributes is an understanding of the bridge between intuitive

Table 13.4
Evolution of poverty (% change in poverty measure)

Poverty line (% of median income)	40%	50%	50%	50%	60%
Measure	Head-count	Head-count	Income Gap	Sen Index	Head-count
Australia, 1984–1993/94	0.0	−2.7	5.0	−4.2	−1.4
Belgium, 1983–1995	−1.4	−2.8	1.1	−27.1	−2.3
Germany, 1984–1994	1.8	2.9	2.5	20.8	3.8
Japan, 1984–1994	0.6	0.8	2.5	23.1	1.0
Sweden, 1983–1995	0.9	0.4	7.9	23.7	0.4
United States, 1985–1995	−1.2	−1.2	0.2	−4.9	−0.1

Source: OECD ECO/WKP(98)2.

concepts of inequality and poverty, and specific measures of these phenomena. Analysis can reveal the implications of alternative measures and provide principles that a good measure should satisfy.

The first problem we challenged in this chapter was the comparison of incomes between households of different compositions. It is clearly more expensive to support a large family than a small family, but exactly how much more expensive is more difficult to determine. Equivalence scales were introduced as the analytical tool to solve this problem. These scales were initially based on the cost of achieving a minimum standard of living. Though simple, such an approach does not easily generalize to higher income levels, nor does it take much account of economic optimization. In principle, equivalence scales could be built directly from utility functions, but to do so, issues must be addressed of how the preferences of the individual members of a household are aggregated into a household preference order.

Inequality occurs when some households have a higher income (after the incomes have been equivalized for household composition) than others. The Lorenz curve provides a graphical device for contrasting income distributions. Some income distributions can be ranked directly by the Lorenz curve, in which case there is no ambiguity about which has more inequality, but not all distributions can be. Inequality measures provide a quantitative assessment of inequality by imposing restrictions beyond those incorporated in the Lorenz curve. The chapter investigated the properties of a number of measures of inequality. Of particular importance was the observation that all inequality measures embody implicit welfare judgments. Given this, the Atkinson measure is constructed on the basis that the welfare judgments should be made explicit and the inequality measure constructed on these judgments. In principle, alternative measures can generate different rankings of income distributions, but in practice, as the application showed, they can yield very consistent rankings.

In many ways the measurement of poverty raises similar issues to that of inequality. The additional feature of poverty is the necessity to determine whether households can be classed as living in poverty or not. The poverty line, which provides the division between the two groups, plays a central role in poverty measurement. Where and how to locate this poverty line is important, but more fundamental is how it should be adjusted over time. At stake here is the key question of whether poverty should be viewed in absolute or relative terms. The practice in developed countries is to use relative poverty. The chapter reviewed a number of poverty measures from the headcount ratio to the Foster-Greer-Thorbecke measure. These measures are also distinguished by a range of sensitivity properties. The applications showed how they could be used and that the different measures could provide a consistent picture of the development of poverty despite their different conceptual bases.

The chapter has revealed how economic analysis is able to provide insights into what we are assuming when we employ a particular inequality or poverty measure. It has also revealed how we can think about the process of improving our measures. Inequality and poverty are significant issues, and better measurement is a necessary starting point for better policy.

Further Reading

The relationship between inequality measures and social welfare was first explored in:

Atkinson, A. B. 1970. On the measurement of inequality. *Journal of Economic Theory* 2: 244–63.

A comprehensive survey of the measurement of inequality is given by:

Sen, A. K. 1997. *On Economic Inequality*. Oxford: Oxford University Press.

A textbook treatment is in:

Lambert, P. 1989. *The Distribution and Redistribution of Income: A Mathematical Analysis*. Oxford: Basil Blackwell.

Issues surrounding the definition and implications of the poverty line are treated in:

Atkinson, A. B. 1987. On the measurement of poverty. *Econometrica*. 55: 749–64.

Callan, T., and Nolan, B. 1991. Concepts of poverty and the poverty line. *Journal of Economic Surveys* 5: 243–61.

The derivation of the Sen measure, and a general discussion of constructing measures from a set of axioms is given by:

Sen, A. K. 1976. Poverty: An ordinal approach to measurement. *Econometrica* 44: 219–31.

The FGT measure was first discussed in:

Foster, J. E., Greer, J., and Thorbecke, E. 1984. A class of decomposable poverty measures. *Econometrica* 52: 761–67.

An in-depth survey of poverty measure is:

Foster, J. E. 1984. On economic poverty: A survey of aggregate measures. *Advances in Econometrics* 3: 215–51.

Exercises

13.1.   In many countries lottery prizes are not taxed. Is this consistent with Hicks's definition of income?

13.2.   Let the utility function be $U = 40d^{1/2}\log(M)$, where d is family size. Construct the equivalence scale for the value of $U = 10$. How is the scale changed if $U = 20$?

13.3.   What economies of scale are there in family size? Are these greater or smaller at low incomes?

13.4.   Take the utility function $U = \log\left(\frac{x_1}{d}\right) + \log\left(\frac{x_2}{d}\right)$, where d is family size and good 1 is food.

   a. What proportion of income is spent on food? Can this provide the basis for an equivalence scale? Calculate the exact equivalence scale. Does it depend on U?

   b. Repeat part a for the utility function $U = \left[\frac{x_1}{d}\right]^{1/2} + [x_2]^{1/2}$.

13.5.   If children provide utility for their parents, show on a diagram how an equivalence scale can decrease as family size increases.

13.6.   Consider a community with ten persons.

   a. Plot the Lorenz curve for the income distribution

   $(2, 4, 6, 8, 10, 12, 14, 16, 18, 20)$.

   b. Consider an income redistribution that takes two units of income from each of the four richest consumers and gives two units to each of the four poorest. Plot the Lorenz curve again to demonstrate that inequality has decreased.

   c. Show that the Lorenz curve for the income distribution

   $(2, 3, 5, 9, 11, 12, 15, 17, 19, 20)$,

   crosses the Lorenz curve for the distribution in part a.

   d. Show that the two social welfare functions $W = \sum M^h$ and $W = \sum \log(M^h)$ rank the income distributions in parts a and c differently.

13.7. What is the Gini index, and how can it be used to determine the impact of taxes and transfers on income inequality?

13.8. Calculate the Gini index for the income distributions used in parts a through c of exercise 13.6. Discuss the values obtained.

13.9. For a utilitarian social welfare function construct M_{EDE} for the distributions used in exercise 13.6 if the utility of income is logarithmic. Find the Atkinson inequality measure. Repeat the exercise for the Rawlsian social welfare function. Compare and discuss.

13.10. What drawbacks are there to eliminating inequality?

13.11. Should we be concerned with inequality if it is due to differences in ability? What if it is due to differences in effort levels?

13.12. Define inequality aversion. Explain how it is related to the concept of risk aversion.

13.13. Discuss the following quote from Cowell (1995): "The main disadvantage of G[ini] is that an income transfer from a rich to a poorer man has a much greater effect on G if the men are near the middle rather than at either end of the parade." Do you agree? Why or why not? (*Hint*: Use the formula for the Gini coefficient to determine the effect of a fixed transfer at different points in the income distribution.) Does the Gini have other "disadvantages"?

13.14. Consider a hypothetical island with only ten people. Eight have income of $10,000, one has income of $50,000, and one has income of $100,000.

a. Draw the Lorenz curve for this income distribution. What is the approximate value of the Gini coefficient?

b. Suppose that a wealthy newcomer arrives on this island with an income of $500,000. How does it change the Lorenz curve? What is the impact on the Gini coefficient?

13.15. Have a look at actual income distribution in the United States available on the Web site ⟨http://www.census.gov/hhes/income/histinc/histinctb.html⟩. Select Households, and then Table H-2.

a. Plot the Lorenz curve for 1981 and 2001. Clearly label each curve. What can you say about the evolution of inequality over time?

b. Based on your diagram, can we conclude that the Gini coefficient was higher in 1981 or 2001? Explain. Check your answer by consulting Table H-4 on the Web site.

c. Can we conclude from the diagram that the poor were necessarily worse off in either 1981 or 2001? Why or why not? Use Table H-1 on the Web site to refine your answer.

d. Now suppose that people with similar incomes are more likely to get married than people with dissimilar incomes. How would this change affect the Lorenz curve drawn in part a?

13.16. There are two senior advisors to the government, *A* and *B*, both of whom agree that the poverty line is at $4,000 for a single person. However, they have different equivalence scales. Mr. *A* believes that the scale factor in determining equivalent income should be 0.25 for each additional family member. Mrs. *B* suggests that the scale factor should be 0.75.

a. Find the poverty line for families of two, three, and four under both values of the scale factors 0.25 and 0.75.

b. Explain how Mr. A and Mrs. B must have very different views about income sharing within a family to end up with such different answers.

c. Suppose that the government is committed to providing welfare eligibility to every family below the poverty line. If this government wishes to keep total spending to a minimum, which of the two views should it support?

13.17. Given the income distributions

$$(1, 2, 2, 5, 5, 5, 7, 11, 11, 12, 20, 21, 22, 24),$$

$$(2, 3, 3, 4, 4, 5, 7, 7, 11, 11, 12, 20, 21, 24),$$

and a poverty line of $z = 6$, calculate the Sen poverty measure. Explain the values obtained for the two distributions.

13.18. Use the two income distributions in exercise 13.17 to evaluate the Foster-Greer-Thorbecke poverty measure for $\alpha = 2$. Pool the distributions to evaluate the poverty measure for the total population. Show that the measure is a weighted sum of the measures for the individual distributions.

13.19. (Decoster) The Pareto distribution is a popular functional form for describing income distributions. It is a two-parameter specification for which the frequency density function reads as follows: $f(x) = \alpha x_0^\alpha x^{-[1+\alpha]}$ for $x \geq x_0$, where $x_0 > 0$ is the lowest income level and $\alpha > 1$ is a parameter.

a. Show that the mean income for the Pareto distribution is $\bar{x} = \frac{\alpha x_0}{\alpha - 1}$.

b. Show that the distribution function for the Pareto distribution is $F(x) = 1 - \left[\frac{x_0}{x}\right]^\alpha$ for $x \geq x_0$. Discuss the effect of changing the parameter α.

c. The Pareto distribution parameterized by α can easily be used to construct a very simple inequality measure, which is defined as follows: Take an arbitrary income level, say x. Calculate the mean income of the subpopulation of all income earners who have an income larger than x. The ratio of this mean income to the income x is given by $I = \frac{\alpha}{\alpha - 1}$. Calculate the values of this inequality index for some different values of α (e.g., $\alpha = 1.5, 2, 3$). Does α represent equality or inequality? What is the limiting value of I for very large α? Interpret this result.

d. Show that the Lorenz curve for the Pareto distribution is $L(p) = 1 - [1 - p]^{[\alpha - 1]/\alpha}$, where $p = F(x)$ and $p \in [0, 1]$. What is the shape of the curve for very large α?

e. Draw the Lorenz curve for two values $\alpha_1 > \alpha_2$, and verify that the two Lorenz curves will never cross.

f. Show that the Gini coefficient for the Pareto distribution (with parameter α) is $G = \frac{1}{2\alpha - 1}$. How does it compare with your answer in part e?

VI TAXATION

14.1 Introduction

Commodity taxes are levied on transactions involving the purchase of goods. The necessity for keeping accounts ensures that such transactions are generally public information. This makes them a good target for taxation. The drawback, however, is that commodity taxation distorts consumer choices and causes inefficiency. Some striking historical examples can be found in the United Kingdom where there have been window taxes and hearth taxes. The window tax was introduced in 1696 in the reign of William III and lasted until 1851. The tax was paid on any house with more than six windows (increased to eight in 1825), which gave an incentive to brick up any windows in excess of the allowable six. Even today, old houses can be found with windows still bricked up. The hearth tax was levied between 1662 and 1689 at the rate of two shillings (two days' wages for a ploughman) per annum on each hearth in a building. This induced people to brick up their chimneys and shiver through the winter. In the market place, commodity taxes drive a wedge between the price producers receive and the price consumers pay. This leads to inefficiency and reduces the attainable level of welfare compared to what could be achieved using lump-sum taxes. This is the price that has to be paid for implementable taxation.

The effects of commodity taxes are quite easily understood—the imposition of a tax raises the price of a good. On the consumer side of the market, the standard analysis of income and substitution effects predicts what will happen to demand. For producers, the tax is a cost increase, and they respond accordingly. What is more interesting is the choice of the best set of taxes for the government. There are several interesting settings for this question. The simplest version can be described as follows: There is a given level of government revenue to be raised that must be financed solely by taxes on commodities. How must the taxes be set so as to minimize the cost to society of raising the required revenue? This is the Ramsey problem of efficient taxation, first addressed in the 1920s. The insights its study gives are still at the heart of the understanding of setting optimal commodity taxes. More general problems introduce equity issues in addition to those of efficiency.

The chapter begins by discussing the deadweight loss that is caused by the introduction of a commodity tax. A diagrammatic analysis of optimal commodity taxation is then presented. This diagram is also used to demonstrate the Diamond-Mirrlees Production Efficiency result. Following this, the Ramsey rule is derived and an interpretation of this is provided. The extension to many consumers is then made and the resolution of the equity–efficiency trade-off is emphasized. This is followed by a review of some numerical calculations of optimal taxes based on empirical data.

14.2   Deadweight Loss

Lump-sum taxation was described as the perfect tax instrument because it does not cause any distortions. The absence of distortions is due to the fact that a lump-sum tax is defined by the condition that no change in behavior can affect the level of the tax. Commodity taxation does not satisfy this definition. It is always possible to change a consumption plan if commodity taxation is introduced. Demand can shift from goods subject to high taxes to goods with low taxes and total consumption can be reduced by earning less or saving more. It is these changes at the margin, which we call *substitution effects*, that are the tax-induced distortions.

The introduction of a commodity tax raises tax revenue but causes consumer welfare to be reduced. The *deadweight loss* of the tax is the extent to which the reduction in welfare exceeds the revenue raised. This concept is illustrated in figure 14.1. Before the tax is introduced, the price of the good is p and the quantity consumed is X^0. At this price the level of consumer surplus is given by the triangle abc. A specific tax of amount t is then levied on the good, so the price rises to $q = p + t$ and quantity consumed falls to X^1. This fall in consumption together with the price increase reduces consumer surplus to aef. The tax raises revenue equal to tX^1, which is given by the area $cdef$. The part of the original consumer surplus that is not turned into tax revenue is the deadweight loss, DWL, given by the triangle bde.

It is possible to provide a simple expression that approximates the deadweight loss. The triangle ebd is equal to $\frac{1}{2}t\,dX$, where dX is the change in demand $X^0 - X^1$. This formula could be used directly, but it is unusual to have knowledge of the level of demand before and after the tax is imposed. Accepting this, it is possible to provide an alternative form for the formula. This can be done by noting that the elasticity of demand is defined by $\varepsilon^d = \frac{p}{X}\frac{dX}{dp}$, so it implies that $dX = \varepsilon^d \frac{X^0}{p}\,dp$. Substituting this into deadweight loss gives

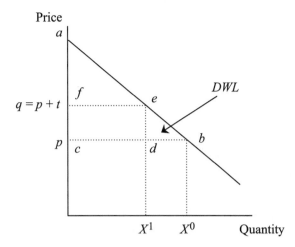

Figure 14.1
Deadweight loss

$$DWL = \frac{1}{2}|\varepsilon^d|\frac{X^0}{p}t^2, \tag{14.1}$$

since the change in price is $dp = t$. The measure in (14.1) is approximate because it assumes that the elasticity is constant over the full change in price from p to $q = p + t$.

The formula for deadweight loss reveals two important observations. First, deadweight loss is proportional to the square of the tax rate. The deadweight loss will therefore rise rapidly as the tax rate is increased. Second, the deadweight loss is proportional to the elasticity of demand. For a given tax change the deadweight loss will be larger the more elastic is demand for the commodity.

An alternative perspective on commodity taxation is provided in figure 14.2. Point a is the initial position in the absence of taxation. Now consider the contrast between a lump-sum tax and a commodity tax on good 1 when the two tax instruments raise the same level of revenue. In the figure the lump-sum tax is represented by the move from point a to point b. The budget constraint shifts inward, but its gradient does not change. Utility falls from U_0 to U_1. A commodity tax on good 1 increases the price of good 1 relative to the price of good 2 and causes the budget constraint to become steeper. At point c the commodity tax raises the same level of revenue as the lump-sum tax. This is because the value of consumption at c is the same as that at b, so the same amount must have been taken off the consumer by the government in both cases. The commodity tax causes utility to fall

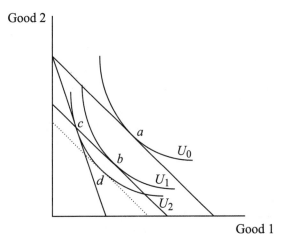

Figure 14.2
Income and substitution effects

to U_2, which is less than U_1. The difference between $U_1 - U_2$ is the deadweight loss measured directly in utility terms.

Figure 14.2 illustrates two further points to which it is worth drawing attention. Notice that commodity taxation produces the same utility level as a lump-sum tax that would move the consumer to point d. This is clearly a larger lump-sum tax than that which achieved point a. The difference in the size of the two lump-sum taxes provides a monetary measure of the deadweight loss. The effect of the commodity tax can now be broken down into two separate components. First, there is the move from the original point a to point d. In line with the standard terminology of consumer theory, this is called an *income effect*. Second, there is a *substitution effect* due to the increase in the price of good 1 relative to good 2 represented by a move around an indifference curve. This shifts the consumer's choice from point d to point c.

This argument can be extended to show that it is the substitution effect that is responsible for the deadweight loss. To do this, note that if the consumer's indifference curves are all L-shaped so that the two commodities are perfect complements, then there is no substitution effect in demand—a relative price change with utility held constant just pivots the budget constraint around the corner of the indifference curve. As shown in figure 14.3, the lump-sum tax and the commodity tax result in exactly the same outcome, so the deadweight loss of the commodity tax is zero. The initial position without taxation is at a and both tax

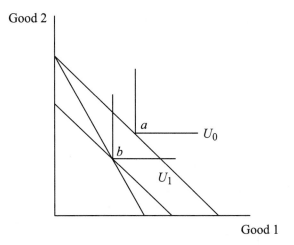

Figure 14.3
Absence of deadweight loss

instruments lead to the final equilibrium at b. Hence the deadweight loss is caused by substitution between commodities.

14.3   Optimal Taxation

The purpose of optimal tax analysis is to find the set of taxes that gives the highest level of welfare while raising the revenue required by the government. The set of taxes that do this are termed *optimal*. In determining these taxes, consumers must be left free to choose their most preferred consumption plans at the resulting prices and firms to continue to maximize profits. The taxes must also lead to prices that equate supply to demand. This section will consider the problem for the case of a single consumer. This restriction ensures that only efficiency considerations arise. The more complex problem involving equity, as well as efficiency, will be addressed in section 14.6.

To introduce a number of important aspects of commodity taxation in a simple way, it is best to begin with a diagrammatic approach. Among the features that this makes clear are the second-best nature of commodity taxes relative to lump-sum taxes. In other words, the use of commodity taxes leads to a lower level of welfare compared to the optimal set of lump-sum taxes. Despite this effect, the observability of transactions makes commodity taxes feasible whereas optimal lump-sum taxes are generally not, for the reasons explored in chapter 12.

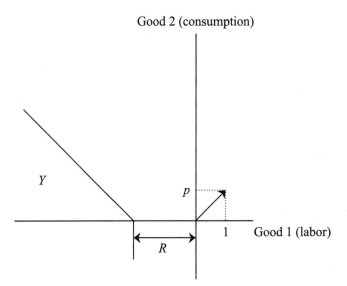

Figure 14.4
Revenue and production possibilities

Consider a two-good economy with a single consumer and a single firm (the Robinson Crusoe economy of chapter 2). One of the goods, labor, is used as an input (so it is supplied by the consumer to the firm), and the output is sold by the firm to the consumer. In figure 14.4 the horizontal axis measures labor use and the vertical axis output. The firm's production set, marked Y in the figure, is also the production set for the economy. This is displaced from the origin by a distance R that equals the tax revenue requirement of the government. The interpretation is that the government takes out of the economy R units of labor for its own purposes. After the revenue requirement has been met, the economy then has constant returns to scale in turning labor into output. The commodity taxes have to be chosen to attain this level of revenue. Normalizing the wage rate to 1, the only output price for the firm that leads to zero profit is shown by p. This is the only level of profit consistent with the assumption of competitive behavior, and p must be the equilibrium price for the firm. Given this price, the firm is indifferent to where it produces on the frontier of its production set.

Figure 14.5 shows the budget constraint and the preferences of the consumer. With the wage rate of 1, the budget constraint for the consumer is constructed by setting the consumer's price for the output to q. The difference between q and p is the tax on the consumption good. It should be noticed that labor is not taxed. As

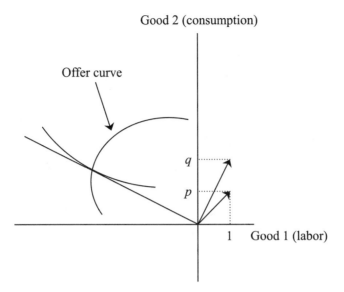

Figure 14.5
Consumer choice

will become clear, this is not a restriction on the set of possible taxes. With these prices the consumer's budget constraint can be written $qx = \ell$, where x denotes units of the output and ℓ units of labor. The important properties of this budget constraint are that it is upward sloping and must pass through the origin. The preferences of the consumer are represented by indifference curves. The form of these follows from noting that the supply of labor causes the consumer disutility, so an increase in labor supply must be compensated for by further consumption of output in order to keep utility constant. The indifference curves are therefore downward sloping. Given these preferences, the optimal choice is found by the tangency of the budget constraint and the highest attainable indifference curve. Varying the price, q, faced by the consumer gives a series of budget constraints whose slopes increase as q falls. Forming the locus of optimal choices determined by these budget constraints traces out the consumer's offer curve. Each point on this offer curve can be associated with a budget constraint that runs through the origin and an indifference curve tangential to that budget constraint. The interpretation given to the offer curve is that the points on the curve are the only ones consistent with utility maximization by the consumer in the absence of lump-sum taxation. It should also be noted that the consumer's utility rises as the move is made up the offer curve.

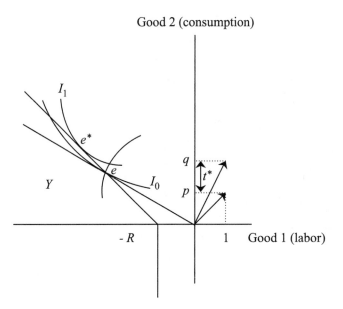

Good 2 (consumption)

Figure 14.6
Optimal commodity taxation

Figures 14.4 and 14.5 can be superimposed to represent the production and consumption decisions simultaneously. This is done in figure 14.6, which can be used to find the optimal tax rate on the consumption good. The only points that are consistent with choice by the consumer are those on the offer curve. The maximal level of utility achievable on the offer curve is at the point where it intersects the production frontier. Any level higher than this is not feasible. This optimum is denoted by point e, and here the consumer is on indifference curve I_0. At this optimum the difference between the consumer price and the producer price for the output, $t^* = q - p$, is the optimal tax rate. That is, it is the tax that ensures that the consumer chooses point e. By construction, this tax rate must also ensure that the government raises its required revenue so that $t^*x^* = R$, where x^* is the level of consumption at point e.

This discussion has shown how the optimal commodity tax is determined at the highest point of the offer curve in the production set. This is the solution to the problem of finding the optimal commodity taxes for this economy. The diagram also shows why labor can remained untaxed without affecting the outcome. The choices of the consumer and the firm are determined by the ratio of prices they face or the direction of the price vector (which is orthogonal to the budget constraint). By changing the length (but not the direction) of either p or q, one can introduce a tax on labor, but it does not alter the fact that e is the optimum. This reasoning can be expressed by saying that the zero tax on labor is a normalization, not a real restriction on the system

Figure 14.6 also illustrates the second-best nature of commodity taxation relative to lump-sum taxation. It can be seen that there are points above the indifference curve I_0 (the best achievable by commodity taxation) that are preferred to e and that are also productively feasible. The highest attainable indifference curve for the consumer given the production set is I_1 with utility maximized at point e^*. This point would be chosen by the consumer if they faced a budget constraint that is coincident with the production frontier. A budget constraint of this form would cross the horizontal axis to the left of the origin and would have equation $qx = \ell - R$, where R represents a lump-sum tax equal to the revenue requirement. This lump-sum tax would decentralize the first-best outcome at e^*. Commodity taxation can only achieve the second-best at e.

14.4   Production Efficiency

The diagrammatic illustration of optimal taxation in the one-consumer economy also shows another important result. This result, known as the *Diamond-Mirrlees Production Efficiency Lemma*, states that the optimal commodity tax system should not disrupt production efficiency. In other words, the optimum with commodity taxation must be on the boundary of the production set and all distortions are focused on consumer choice. This section provides a demonstration of the efficiency lemma and discusses its implications.

Production efficiency occurs when an economy is maximizing the output attainable from its given set of resources. This can only happen when the economy is on the boundary of its production possibility set. Starting at a boundary point, no reallocation of inputs among firms can increase the output of one good without reducing that of another (compare this with the conditions for Pareto-efficiency in chapter 2). In the special case where each firm employs some of all the available inputs, a necessary condition for production efficiency is that the marginal rate of substitution (*MRS*) between any two inputs be the same for all firms. Such a position of equality is attained, in the absence of taxation, by the profit maximization of firms in competitive markets. Each firm sets the marginal rate of substitution equal to the ratio of factor prices, and since factor prices are the same for all firms,

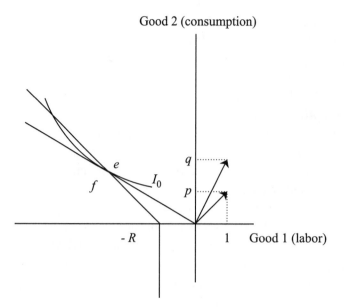

Figure 14.7
Production efficiency

this induces the necessary equality in the *MRS*s. The same is true when there is taxation, provided that all firms face the same after-tax prices for inputs, meaning inputs taxes are not differentiated among firms.

To see that the optimum with commodity taxation must be on the frontier of the production set, consider the interior point f in figure 14.7. If the equilibrium were at f, the consumer's utility could be raised by reducing the use of the input while keeping output constant. Since this is feasible, f cannot be an optimum. Since this reasoning can be applied to any point that is interior to the production set, the optimum must be on the boundary.

Although figure 14.7 was motivated by considering the input to be labor, a slight re-interpretation can introduce intermediate goods. Assume that there is an industry that uses one unit of labor to produce one unit of an intermediate good and that the intermediate good is then used to produce final output. Figure 14.7 then depicts the intermediate good (the input) being used to produce the output. Although the household actually has preferences over labor and final output, and acts only on the markets for these goods, the direct link between units of labor and of intermediate good allows preferences and the budget constraint to be depicted as if they were defined directly on those variables. The production efficiency argument then follows directly as before and now implies that intermediate goods should not be taxed, since this would violate the equalization of *MRS*s between firms.

The logic of the single-consumer economy can be adapted to show that the efficiency lemma still holds when there are many consumers. What makes the result so obvious in the single-consumer case is that a reduction in labor use or an increase in output raises the consumer's utility. With many consumers, such a change would have a similar effect if all consumers supply labor or prefer to have more, rather than less, of the consumption good. This will hold if there is some agreement in the tastes of the consumers. If this is so, a direction of movement can be found from an interior point in the production set to an exterior point that is unanimously welcomed. The optimum must then be exterior.

In summary, the Diamond-Mirrlees Production Efficiency Lemma provides a persuasive argument for the nontaxation of intermediate goods and the nondifferentiation of input taxes among firms. These are results of immediate practical importance, since they provide a basic property that an optimal tax system must possess. As will become clear, it is rather hard to make precise statements about the optimal levels of tax, but what the efficiency lemma provides is a clear and simple statement about the structure of taxation.

14.5   Tax Rules

The diagrammatic analysis has shown the general principle behind the determination of the optimal taxes. What is not shown is how the tax burden is allocated across different commodities. The optimal tax problem is to set the taxes on commodities to maximize social welfare subject to raising a required level of revenue. This section looks at tax rules that characterize the solution to this problem.

To derive the rules, it is first necessary to precisely specify a model of the economy. Let there be n goods, each produced with constant returns to scale by competitive firms. Since the firms are competitive, the price of the commodity they sell must be equal to the marginal cost of production. Under the assumption of constant returns, this marginal cost is also independent of the scale of production. Labor is assumed to be the only input into production.

With the wage rate as numéraire, these assumptions imply that the producer (or before-tax) price of good i is determined by

$$p_i = c_i, \qquad i = 1, \ldots, n, \tag{14.2}$$

where c_i denotes the number of units of labor required to produce good i. The consumer (or after-tax) prices are equal to the before-tax prices plus the taxes. For good i the consumer price q_i is

$$q_i = p_i + t_i, \qquad i = 1, \ldots, n. \tag{14.3}$$

Writing x_i for the consumption level of good i, the tax rates on the n consumption goods must be chosen to raise the required revenue. With the revenue requirement denoted by R, the revenue constraint can be written

$$R = \sum_{i=1}^{n} t_i x_i. \tag{14.4}$$

In line with this numbering convention, labor is denoted as good 0, so x_0 is the supply of labor (labor is the untaxed good, so $t_0 = 0$).

   This completes the description of the economy. The simplifying feature is that the assumption of constant returns to scale fixes the producer prices via (14.2) so that equilibrium prices are independent of the level of demand. Furthermore constant returns also implies that whatever demand is forthcoming at these prices will be met by the firms. If the budget constraints are satisfied (both government and consumer), any demand will be backed by sufficient labor supply to carry out the necessary production.

14.5.1   The Inverse Elasticity Rule

Figure 14.6 shows some of the features that the optimal set of commodity taxes will have. What the single-good formulation cannot do is give any insight into how that tax burden should be spread across different goods. For example, should all goods have the same rate of tax or should taxes be related to the characteristics of the goods? The first tax rule considers a simplified situation that delivers a very precise answer to this question. This answer, the *inverse elasticity rule*, provides a foundation for proceeding to the more general case. The simplifying assumption is that the goods are independent in demand so that there are no cross-price effects between the taxed goods. This independence of demands is a strong assumption, so it is not surprising that a clear result can be derived. The way the analysis works is to choose the optimal allocation and infer the tax rates from this. This was the argument used in the diagram when the intersection of the offer curve and the frontier of the production set was located and the tax rate derived from the implied budget constraint.

Consider a consumer who buys the two taxed goods and supplies labor. The consumer's preferences are described by the utility function $U(x_0, x_1, x_2)$, and his budget constraint is $q_1 x_1 + q_2 x_2 = x_0$. The utility-maximizing consumption levels of the two consumption goods are described by the first-order conditions $U_i = \alpha q_i$, $i = 1, 2$, where U_i is the marginal utility of good i and α is the marginal utility of income. The choice of labor supply satisfies the first-order condition $U_0 = -\alpha$.

With taxes t_1 and t_2 the government revenue constraint is $R = t_1 x_1 + t_2 x_2$. Since producer and consumer prices are related by $t_i = q_i - p_i$, this can be written as

$$q_1 x_1 + q_2 x_2 = R + p_1 x_1 + p_2 x_2. \tag{14.5}$$

The optimal tax rates are inferred from an optimization whereby the government chooses the consumption levels to maximize the consumer's utility while meeting the revenue constraint. This problem is summarized by the constrained maximization

$$\max_{\{x_1, x_2\}} L = U(x_0, x_1, x_2) + \lambda[q_1 x_1 + q_2 x_2 - R - p_1 x_1 - p_2 x_2]. \tag{14.6}$$

In this maximization the quantity of labor supply, x_0, is determined endogenously by x_1 and x_2 from the consumer's budget constraint, $x_0 = q_1 x_1 + q_2 x_2$.

The basic assumption that the demands are independent can be used to write the (inverse) demand function $q_i = q_i(x_i)$. Using these demand functions and the consumer's budget constraint to replace x_0, we write the first-order condition for the quantity of good i as

$$U_i + U_0 \left[q_i + x_i \frac{\partial q_i}{\partial x_i} \right] + \lambda \left[q_i + x_i \frac{\partial q_i}{\partial x_i} - p_i \right] = 0. \tag{14.7}$$

The conditions $U_i = \alpha q_i$ and $U_0 = -\alpha$ can be used to write this as

$$-\alpha x_i \frac{\partial q_i}{\partial x_i} + \lambda t_i + \lambda x_i \frac{\partial q_i}{\partial x_i} = 0, \tag{14.8}$$

where $t_i = q_i - p_i$. Now note that $\frac{x_i}{q_i} \frac{\partial q_i}{\partial x_i} = \frac{1}{\varepsilon_i^d}$, where ε_i^d is the elasticity of demand for good i. The first-order condition can then be solved to write

$$\frac{t_i}{p_i + t_i} = -\left[\frac{\lambda - \alpha}{\lambda} \right] \frac{1}{\varepsilon_i^d}. \tag{14.9}$$

Equation (14.9) is the inverse elasticity rule. This is interpreted by noting that α is the marginal utility of another unit of income for the consumer and λ is the utility cost of another unit of government revenue. Since taxes are distortionary, $\lambda > \alpha$. Since ε_i^d is negative, this makes the tax rate positive.

The inverse elasticity rule states that the proportional rate of tax on good i should be inversely related to its price elasticity of demand. Furthermore the constant of proportionality is the same for all goods. Recalling the discussion of the deadweight loss of taxation, it can be seen that this places more of the tax burden on goods where the deadweight loss is low. Its implication is clearly that necessities, which by definition have low elasticities of demand, should be highly taxed. It is this latter aspect that emphasizes the fact that the inverse elasticity rule describes an efficient way to tax commodities but not an equitable way. Placing relative high taxes on necessities will result in lower income consumers bearing relatively more of the commodity tax burden than high-income consumers.

14.5.2   The Ramsey Rule

The inverse elasticity rule is restricted by the fact that the demand for each good depends only on the price of that good. This rules out all cross-price effects in demand, meaning that the goods can be neither substitutes nor complements. When this restriction is relaxed, a more general tax rule is derived. The general result is called the *Ramsey rule*, and it is one of the oldest results in the theory of optimal taxation. It provides a description of the optimal taxes for an economy with a single consumer and with no equity considerations.

To derive the Ramsey rule, it is necessary to change from choosing the optimal quantities to choosing the taxes. Assume that there are just two consumption goods in order to simplify the notation, and let the demand function for good i be $x_i = x_i(q)$, where $q = (q_1, q_2)$. The fact that the prices of all the commodities enter this demand function shows that the full range of interactions between the demands and prices are allowed. Using these demand functions, the preferences of the consumer can be written

$$U = U(x_0(q), x_1(q), x_2(q)). \tag{14.10}$$

The optimal commodity taxes are those that give the highest level of utility to the consumer while ensuring that the government reaches its revenue target of $R > 0$. The government's problem in choosing the tax rates can then be summarized by the Lagrangean

$$\max_{\{t_1, t_2\}} L = U(x_0(q), x_1(q), x_2(q)) + \lambda \left[\sum_{i=1}^{2} t_i x_i(q) - R \right], \tag{14.11}$$

where it is recalled that $q_i = p_i + t_i$. Differentiating (14.11) with respect to the tax on good k, the first-order necessary condition is

$$\frac{\partial L}{\partial t_k} \equiv \sum_{i=0}^{2} U_i \frac{\partial x_i}{\partial q_k} + \lambda \left[x_k + \sum_{i=1}^{2} t_i \frac{\partial x_i}{\partial q_k} \right] = 0. \tag{14.12}$$

This first-order condition needs some manipulation to place it in the form we want. The first step is to note that the budget constraint of the consumer is

$$q_1 x_1(q) + q_2 x_2(q) = x_0(q). \tag{14.13}$$

Any change in price of good k must result in demands that still satisfy this constraint so that

$$q_1 \frac{\partial x_1}{\partial q_k} + q_2 \frac{\partial x_2}{\partial q_k} + x_k = \frac{\partial x_0}{\partial q_k}. \tag{14.14}$$

In addition the conditions for optimal consumer choice are $U_0 = -\alpha$ and $U_i = \alpha q_i$. Using these optimality conditions and (14.14), we rewrite the first-order condition for the optimal tax, (14.12), as

$$\alpha x_k = \lambda \left[x_k + \sum_{i=1}^{2} t_i \frac{\partial x_i}{\partial q_k} \right]. \tag{14.15}$$

Notice how this first-order condition involves quantities rather than the prices that appeared in the inverse elasticity rule. After rearrangement (14.15) becomes

$$\sum_{i=1}^{2} t_i \frac{\partial x_i}{\partial q_k} = - \left[\frac{\lambda - \alpha}{\lambda} \right] x_k. \tag{14.16}$$

The next step in the derivation is to employ the Slutsky equation, which breaks the change in demand into the income and substitution effects. The effect of an increase in the price of good k upon the demand for good i is determined by the Slutsky equation as

$$\frac{\partial x_i}{\partial q_k} = S_{ik} - x_k \frac{\partial x_i}{\partial I}, \tag{14.17}$$

where S_{ik} is the substitution effect of the price change (the move around an indifference curve) and $-x_k \frac{\partial x_i}{\partial I}$ is the income effect of the price change (I denotes lumpsum income). Substituting from (14.17) into (14.16) gives

$$\sum_{i=1}^{2} t_i \left[S_{ik} - x_k \frac{\partial x_i}{\partial I} \right] = -\left[\frac{\lambda - \alpha}{\lambda} \right] x_k. \tag{14.18}$$

Equation (14.18) is now simplified by extracting the common factor x_k, which yields

$$\sum_{i=1}^{2} t_i S_{ik} = -\left[1 - \frac{\alpha}{\lambda} - \sum_{i=1}^{2} t_i \frac{\partial x_i}{\partial I} \right] x_k. \tag{14.19}$$

The substitution effect of a change in the price of good i on the demand for good k is exactly equal to the substitution effect of a change in the price of good k on the demand for good i because both are determined by movement around the same indifference curve. This symmetry property implies $S_{ki} = S_{ik}$, which can be used to rearrange (14.19) to give the expression

$$\sum_{i=1}^{2} t_i S_{ki} = -\theta x_k, \tag{14.20}$$

where $\theta = \left[1 - \frac{\alpha}{\lambda} - \sum_{i=1}^{2} t_i \frac{\partial x_i}{\partial I} \right]$ is a positive constant. Equation (14.20) is the Ramsey rule describing a system of optimal commodity taxes and an equation of this form must hold for all goods, $k = 1, \ldots, n$.

The optimal tax rule described by (14.20) can be used in two ways. If the details of the economy are specified (the utility function and production parameters), then the actual tax rates can be calculated. Naturally the precise values would be a function of the structure chosen. Although this is the direction that heads toward practical application of the theory (and more is said later), it is not the route that will be currently taken. The second use of the rule is to derive some general conclusions about the determinants of tax rates. This is done by analyzing and understanding the different components of (14.20).

To proceed with this, the focus on the typical good k is maintained. Recall that a substitution term measures the change in demand with utility held constant. Demand defined in this way is termed *compensated demand*. Now begin in an initial position with no taxes. From this point the tax t_i is the change in the tax rate on good i. Then $t_i S_{ki}$ is a first-order approximation to the change in compensated demand for good k due to the introduction of the tax t_i. If the taxes are small, this will be a good approximation to the actual change. Extending this argument to take account of the full set of taxes, it follows that $\sum_{i=1}^{2} t_i S_{ki}$ is an approximation to the total change in compensated demand for good k due to the introduction of the tax system from the initial no-tax position. In employing this approximation, the Ramsey rule can be interpreted as saying that the optimal tax system should be such that the *compensated demand for each good is reduced in the same proportion* relative to the before-tax position. This is the standard interpretation of the Ramsey rule.

The importance of this observation is reinforced when it is set against the alternative, but incorrect, argument that the optimal tax system should raise the prices of all goods by the same proportion in order to minimize the distortion caused by the tax system. This is shown by the Ramsey rule to be false. What the Ramsey rule says is that it is the distortion in terms of quantities, rather than prices, that should be minimized. Since it is the level of consumption that actually determines utility, it is not surprising that what happens to prices is secondary to what happens to quantities. Prices only matter so far as they determine demands.

Although the actual tax rates are only implicit in the Ramsey rule, some general comments can still be made. Employing the approximation interpretation, the rule suggests that as the proportional reduction in compensated demand must be the same for all goods, those goods whose demand is unresponsive to price changes must bear higher taxes in order to achieve the same reduction. Although broadly correct, this statement can only be completely justified when all cross-price effects are accounted for. One simple case that overcomes this difficulty is that in which there are no cross-price effects among the taxed goods. This is the special case that led to the inverse elasticity rule.

Returning to the general case, goods that are unresponsive to price changes are typically necessities such as food and housing. Consequently using the Ramsey rule leads to a tax system that bears most heavily on necessities. In contrast, the lowest tax rates would fall on luxuries. If put into practice, such a tax structure would involve low-income consumers paying disproportionately larger fractions of their incomes in taxes relative to high-income consumers. The inequitable nature of this is simply a reflection of the single-consumer assumption: the optimization does not involve equity and the solution reflects only efficiency criteria.

The single-consumer framework is not accurate as a description of reality, and it leads to an outcome that is unacceptable on equity grounds. The value of the Ramsey rule therefore arises primarily through the framework and method of analysis it introduces. This can easily be generalized to more relevant settings. It shows how taxes are determined by efficiency considerations and hence gives a baseline from which to judge the effects of introducing equity.

14.6   Equity Considerations

The lack of equity in the tax structure determined by the Ramsey rule is inevitable given its single-consumer basis. The introduction of further consumers who differ in incomes and preferences makes it possible to see how equity can affect the conclusions. Although the method that is now discussed can cope with any number of consumers, it is sufficient to consider just two. Restricting the number in this way has the merit of making the analysis especially transparent.

Consider then an economy which consists of two consumers. Each consumer h, $h = 1, 2$, is described by their (indirect) utility function

$$U^h = U^h(x_0^h(q), x_1^h(q), x_2^h(q)). \tag{14.21}$$

These utility functions may vary between the consumers. Labor remains the untaxed numéraire, and all consumers supply only the single form of labor service.

The government revenue constraint is now given by

$$R = \sum_{i=1}^{2} t_i x_i^1(q) + \sum_{i=1}^{2} t_i x_i^2(q), \tag{14.22}$$

where the first term on the right-hand side is the total tax payment of consumer 1 and the second term is the total tax payment of consumer 2. The government's policy is guided by a social welfare function that aggregates the individual consumers' utilities. This social welfare function is denoted by

$$W = W(U^1(x_0^1, x_1^1, x_2^1), U^2(x_0^2, x_1^2, x_2^2)). \tag{14.23}$$

Combining (14.22) and (14.23) into a Lagrangean expression (as in equation 14.11), the first-order condition for the choice of the tax on good k is

$$\frac{\partial L}{\partial t_k} \equiv -\frac{\partial W}{\partial U^1}\alpha^1 x_k^1 - \frac{\partial W}{\partial U^2}\alpha^2 x_k^2 + \lambda\left[\sum_{h=1}^{2}\left[x_k^h + \sum_{i=1}^{2} t_i \frac{\partial x_i^h}{\partial q_k}\right]\right] = 0, \tag{14.24}$$

where from the consumer's first-order condition $\frac{\partial U^h}{\partial q_k} = \alpha^h x_k^h$. To obtain a result that is easily comparable to the Ramsey rule, define

$$\beta^h = \frac{\partial W}{\partial U^h}\alpha^h. \tag{14.25}$$

β^h is formed as the product of the effect of an increase in consumer h's utility on social welfare and their marginal utility of income. It measures the increase in social welfare that results from a marginal increase in the income of consumer h. Consequently β^h is termed the *social marginal utility of income* for consumer h. Employing the definition of β^h and the substitutions used to obtain the Ramsey rule, we write the first-order condition (14.24) as

$$\frac{\sum_{i=1}^2 t_i S_{ki}^1 + \sum_{i=1}^2 t_i S_{ki}^2}{x_k^1 + x_k^2} = \frac{1}{\lambda}\frac{\beta^1 x_k^1 + \beta^2 x_k^2}{x_k^1 + x_k^2} - 1$$
$$+ \frac{[\sum_{i=1}^2 t_i[\partial x_i^1/\partial I^1]]x_k^1 + [\sum_{i=1}^2 t_i[\partial x_i^2/\partial I^2]]x_k^2}{x_k^1 + x_k^2}. \tag{14.26}$$

The tax structure that is described by (14.26) can be interpreted in the same way as the Ramsey rule. The left-hand side is approximately the proportional change in aggregate compensated demand for good k caused by the introduction of the tax system from an initial position with no taxes. When a positive amount of revenue is to be raised (so that $R > 0$), the level of demand will be reduced by the tax system, so this term will be negative.

The first point to observe about the right-hand side is that unlike the Ramsey rule, the proportional reduction in compensated demand is not the same for all goods. It is therefore necessary to discuss the factors that influence the extent of the reduction, and it is by doing this that the consequences of equity can be seen. The essential component in this regard is the first term on the right-hand side. The proportional reduction in demand for good k will be smaller the larger is the value of $\beta^1\frac{x_k^1}{x_k^1+x_k^2} + \beta^2\frac{x_k^2}{x_k^1+x_k^2}$. The value of this will be large if a high β^h is correlated with a high $\frac{x_k^h}{x_k^1+x_k^2}$. The meaning of this is clear, since a consumer will have a high value of β^h when their personal marginal utility of income, α^h, is large and when $\frac{\partial W}{\partial U^h}$ is also large so that the social planner gives them a high weight in social welfare. If the social welfare function is concave, both of these will be satisfied by low-utility consumers with low incomes. The term $\frac{x_k^h}{x_k^1+x_k^2}$ will be large when good k is consumed primarily by consumer h. Putting these points together, we have that the proportional reduction in the compensated demand for a good will be smaller if it is consumed primarily by the poor consumer. This is the natural reflection of equity considerations.

The second term on the right-hand side shows that the proportional reduction in demand for good k will be smaller if its demand comes mainly from the consumer whose tax payments change most as income changes. This term is related to the efficiency aspects of the tax system. If taxation were to be concentrated on goods consumed by those whose tax payments fell rapidly with reductions in income, then increased taxation, and consequently greater distortion, would be required to meet the revenue target.

This has shown how the introduction of equity modifies the conclusions of the Ramsey rule. Rather than all goods having their compensated demand reduced in the same proportion, equity results in the goods consumed primarily by the poor facing less of a reduction. In simple terms, this should translate into lower rates of tax on the goods consumed by the poor relative to those determined solely by efficiency. Equity therefore succeeds in moderating the hard edge of the efficient tax structure.

14.7   Applications

At this point in the discussion it should be recalled that the fundamental motive for the analysis is to provide practical policy recommendations. The results that have been derived do give some valuable insights: the need for production efficiency and the non-uniformity of taxes being foremost among them. Accepting this, the analysis is only of real merit if the tax rules are capable of being applied to data and the actual values of the resulting optimal taxes calculated. The numerical studies that have been undertaken represent the development of a technology for achieving this aim and also provide further insights into the structure of taxation.

Referring back to (14.26), it can be seen that two basic pieces of information are needed in order to calculate the tax rates. The first is knowledge of the demand functions of the consumers. This provides the levels of demand x_k^h and the demand derivatives $\frac{\partial x_k^h}{\partial q_i}$. The second piece of information is the social marginal utilities of income, β^h. Ideally these should be calculated from a specified social welfare function and individual utility functions for the consumers. The problem here is the same as that raised in previous chapters: the construction of some meaningful utility concept. The difficulties are further compounded in the present case by the requirement that the demand functions also be consistent with the utility functions.

In practice, the difficulties are circumvented rather than solved. The approach that has been adopted is to first ignore the link between demand and utility and then impose a procedure to obtain the social welfare weights. The demand functions are then estimated using standard econometric techniques. One common procedure to find the social welfare weights is to employ the utility function defined by (13.24) to measure the social utility of income to each consumer. That is, $U^h = K \frac{[M^h]^{1-\varepsilon}}{1-\varepsilon}$. The social marginal utility is then given by

$$\beta^h = K[M^h]^{-\varepsilon}. \qquad (14.27)$$

The value of the parameter K can be fixed by, for instance, setting the value of β^h equal to 1 for the lowest income consumer. With $\varepsilon > 0$ the social marginal utility declines as income rises. It decreases faster as ε rises, so relatively more weight is given to low-income consumers. This way the value of ε can be treated as a measure of the concern for equity.

14.7.1   Reform

The first application of the analysis is to consider marginal reforms of tax rates. By a marginal reform it is meant a small change from the existing set of tax rates that moves the system closer to optimality. This should be distinguished from an optimization of tax rates that might imply a very significant change from the initial set of taxes.

Marginal reforms are much easier to compute than optimal taxes, since it is only necessary to evaluate effect of changes not of the whole move. An analogy can be drawn with hill-climbing: to climb higher, you only need to know which direction leads upward and do not need to know where the top is. Essentially studying marginal reforms reduces the informational requirement.

Return to the analysis of the optimal taxes in the economy with two consumers. The effect on welfare of a marginal increase in the tax on good k is

$$\frac{\partial W}{\partial t_k} = -\sum_{h=1}^{2} \beta^h x_k^h, \qquad (14.28)$$

and the effect on revenue is

$$\frac{\partial R}{\partial t_k} = \sum_{h=1}^{2} \left[x_k^h + \sum_{i=1}^{2} t_i \frac{\partial x_i^h}{\partial q_k} \right] = X_k + \sum_{i=1}^{2} t_i \frac{\partial X_i}{\partial q_k}, \qquad (14.29)$$

where X_i is the aggregate demand for good i. The marginal revenue benefit of taxation of good k is defined as the extra revenue generated relative to the welfare change of a marginal increase in a tax. This can be written as

$$MRB_k = -\frac{\partial R/\partial t_k}{\partial W/\partial t_k}. \tag{14.30}$$

At the optimum all goods should have the same marginal revenue benefit. If that was not the case, taxes could be raised on those with a high marginal revenue benefit and reduced for those with a low value. This is exactly the process we can use to deduce the direction of reform.

From the marginal revenue benefit the economy of information can be clearly seen. All that is needed to evaluate MRB_k are the social marginal utilities, β^h, the individual commodity demands, x_k^h, and the aggregate derivatives of demand $\frac{\partial X_i}{\partial q_k}$ (or, equally, the aggregate demand elasticities). The demands and the elasticities are easily obtainable from data sets on consumer demands.

Table 14.1 displays the result of a calculation of the MRB_k using Irish data for ten commodity categories in 1987. Two different values of ε are given, with $\varepsilon = 5$ representing a greater concern for equity. The interpretation of these figures is that the tax levied on the goods toward the top of the table should be raised and the tax should be lowered on the goods at the bottom. Hence services should be more highly taxed and the tax on tobacco should be reduced! The rankings are fairly consistent for both values of ε; there is some movement, but no good moves

Table 14.1
Tax reform

Good	$\varepsilon = 2$	$\varepsilon = 5$
Other goods	2.316	4.349
Services	2.258	5.064
Petrol	1.785	3.763
Food	1.633	3.291
Alcohol	1.566	3.153
Transport and equipment	1.509	3.291
Fuel and power	1.379	2.221
Clothing and footwear	1.341	2.837
Durables	1.234	2.514
Tobacco	0.420	0.683

Source: Madden (1995).

very far. Therefore a reform based on these data would be fairly robust to changes in the concern for equity.

14.7.2 Optimality

The most developed implementation of the optimal tax rule for an economy with many consumers uses data from the Indian National Sample Survey. Defining θ to be the wage as a proportion of expenditure, a selection of these results are given in table 14.2 for $\varepsilon = 2$. The table shows that these tax rates achieve some redistribution, since cereals and milk products, both basic foodstuffs, are subsidized. Such redistribution results from the concern for equity embodied in a value of ε of 2. Interesting as they are, these results are limited, as are other similar analyses, by the degree of commodity aggregation that leads to the excessively general other nonfood category.

The same dataset has been used to analyze the redistributive impact of Indian commodity taxes. The redistributive impact is found by calculating the total payment of commodity tax, T^h, by consumer h relative to the expenditure, μ^h, of that consumer. The net gain from the tax system for h is then defined by $-\frac{T^h}{\mu^h}$. The consumer gains from the tax system if $-\frac{T^h}{\mu^h}$ is positive, since this implies that a net subsidy is being received. Contrasting the gain of a consumer from the existing tax system with the gain under the optimal system provides an indication of both the success of the existing system and the potential gains from the optimal system. The calculations for the existing Indian tax system give the gains shown

Table 14.2
Optimal tax rates

Item	$\theta = 0.05$	$\theta = 0.1$
Cereals	−0.015	−0.089
Milk and milk products	−0.042	−0.011
Edible oils	0.359	0.342
Meat, fish, and eggs	0.071	0.083
Sugar and tea	0.013	0.003
Other food	0.226	0.231
Clothing	0.038	0.014
Fuel and light	0.038	0.014
Other nonfoods	0.083	0.126

Source: Ray (1986a).

Table 14.3
Redistribution of Indian commodity taxes

	Rural	Urban
	$-T^h/\mu^h$	$-T^h/\mu^h$
Expenditure level		
Rs 20	0.105	0.220
Rs 50	0.004	0.037

Source: Ray (1986b).

Table 14.4
Optimal redistribution

	$\varepsilon = 0.1$	$\varepsilon = 1.5$	$\varepsilon = 5$
$-T/\mu$	0.07	0.343	0.447

Source: Ray (1986b).

in table 14.3. The expenditure levels of Rs. 20 and Rs. 50 place consumers with these incomes in the lower 30 percent of the income distribution. The table shows a net gain to consumers at both income levels from the tax system, with the lower expenditure consumer making a proportionately greater gain.

The same calculations can be used to find the redistributive impact of the optimal tax system for a consumer with expenditure level $\mu = 0.5\bar{\mu}$, where $\bar{\mu}$ is mean expenditure, is given in table 14.4. For $\varepsilon = 1$ or more, it can be seen that the potential gains from the tax system, relative to the outcome that would occur in the absence of taxation, are substantial. This shows that with sufficient weight given to equity considerations, the optimal set of commodity taxes can effect significant redistribution and that the existing Indian tax system does not attain these gains.

This section has discussed a method for calculating the taxes implied by the optimal tax rule. The only difficulty in doing this is the specification of the social welfare weights. To determine these, it is necessary to know both the private utility functions and the social welfare function. In the absence of this information, a method for deriving the weights is employed that can embody equity criteria in a flexible way. Although these weights are easily calculated, they are not entirely consistent with the other components of the model. The numbers derived demonstrate clearly that when equity is embodied in the optimization, commodity taxes can secure a significant degree of redistribution. This is very much in contrast to what occurs with efficiency alone.

14.8   Efficient Taxation

The tax rules in the previous section have only considered the competitive case. When there is imperfect competition, additional issues have to be taken into account. The basic fact is that imperfectly competitive firms produce less than the efficient output level, so the equilibrium without intervention is not Pareto-efficient. This gives a reason to use commodity taxes to subsidize the output of imperfectly competitive firms relative to that of competitive firms. However, the strength of this argument depends on the degree of tax-shifting, as identified in chapter 8.

The issues involved in tax design can be understood by determining the direction of welfare-improving tax reform starting from an initial position with no commodity taxation. This is undertaken for an economy with a single consumer and a zero-revenue requirement. The fact that no revenue is raised implies that the taxes are used merely to correct for the distortion introduced by the imperfect competition. There are two consumption goods, each produced using labor alone. Good 1 is produced with constant returns to scale by a competitive industry with after-tax price $q_1 = p_1 + t_1$. There is a single household in the economy whose (indirect) utility function is

$$U = U(x_0(q_1, q_2), x_1(q_1, q_2), x_2(q_1, q_2)). \tag{14.31}$$

Tax revenue, R, is defined by

$$R = t_1 x_1 + t_2 x_2. \tag{14.32}$$

Good 2 is produced by a monopolist who chooses their output to maximize profit

$$\pi_2 = [q_2 - c - t_2] x_2(q_1, q_2), \tag{14.33}$$

where c is the constant marginal cost. The profit-maximizing price depends on the tax, t_2, and the price of good 1, q_1. This relationship is denoted $q_2 = q_2(q_1, t_2)$. The derivative $\frac{\partial q_2}{\partial t_2}$ measures the rate of shifting of the tax. In the terminology of chapter 8, there is undershifting if $\frac{\partial q_2}{\partial t_2} < 1$ and overshifting if $\frac{\partial q_2}{\partial t_2} > 1$. The dependence of the demand for good 2 on the price of good 1 is reflected in the profit-maximizing price. The derivative $\frac{\partial q_2}{\partial q_1}$ is the cross-price effect of taxation. It can be positive or negative, and since $q_1 = p_1 + t_1$, it follows that $\frac{\partial q_2}{\partial q_1} = \frac{\partial q_2}{\partial t_1}$.

The tax reform problem searches for a pair of tax changes that raise welfare while collecting zero revenue. The initial position is taken to be one where both commodity taxes are zero initially, so the intention is to find a pair of tax changes

dt_1, dt_2, starting from an initial position with $t_1 = t_2 = 0$ such that $dU > 0$ and $dR = 0$. The formulation ensures that one of the taxes will be negative and the other positive. The aim is to provide a simple characterization of the determination of the relative rates. It should be noted that if both industries were competitive the initial equilibrium would be Pareto-efficient and the solution to the tax problem would have $dt_1 = dt_2 = 0$. So nonzero tax rates will be a consequence of the distortion caused by the imperfect competition.

Totally differentiating the utility function and using the first-order conditions for consumer choice, the effect of the tax changes on utility is

$$dU = -\alpha x_1 \frac{\partial q_1}{\partial t_1} dt_1 - \alpha x_2 \frac{\partial q_2}{\partial t_1} dt_1 - \alpha x_2 \frac{\partial q_2}{\partial t_2} dt_2, \tag{14.34}$$

where α is the consumer's marginal utility of income. Totally differentiating the revenue constraint and using the fact that the initial values of the taxes are $t_1 = t_2 = 0$ gives

$$dR = 0 = x_1 \, dt_1 + x_2 \, dt_2. \tag{14.35}$$

Solving (14.35) for dt_1 and substituting into the derivative of utility determines the utility change as dependent on dt_2 alone:

$$dU = \left[-\alpha x_2 \frac{\partial q_2}{\partial t_2} + \alpha x_2 + \alpha \frac{x_2^2}{x_1} \frac{\partial q_2}{\partial t_1} \right] dt_2. \tag{14.36}$$

It is condition (14.36) that provides the key to understanding the determination of the relative tax rates. Since we wish to choose the tax change dt_2 to ensure that $dU > 0$, it follows that the sign of the tax change must be the same as the bracketed term in (14.36). From this observation follows the conclusion that

$$x_1 \left[1 - \frac{\partial q_2}{\partial t_2} \right] + x_2 \frac{\partial q_2}{\partial t_1} < 0 \Rightarrow dt_2 < 0. \tag{14.37}$$

From (14.37) the output of the imperfectly competitive industry should be subsidized and the competitive industry taxed when $\frac{\partial q_2}{\partial t_2}$ is large, so that overshifting is occurring and $\frac{\partial q_2}{\partial t_1}$ is negative. These are, of course, sufficient conditions. In general, the greater the degree of tax shifting, the more likely is subsidization. The explanation for this result is that if firms overshift taxes, they will also do the same for any subsidy. Hence a negative dt_2 will be reflected by an even greater reduction in price. If $\frac{\partial q_2}{\partial t_1}$ is also negative, the tax on the competitive industry secures a further reduction in the price of good 2.

The conclusion of this analysis is that the rate of tax shifting is important in the determination of relative rates of taxation. Although the economy is simplified, it does demonstrate that with imperfect competition commodity taxation can be motivated on efficiency grounds alone to mitigate the inefficiency cost of market power.

14.9   Public Sector Pricing

The theory that was developed in the previous sections also has a second application. This arises because there are close connections between the theory of commodity taxation and that of choosing optimal public sector prices. Firms operated by the public sector can be set the objective of choosing their pricing policy to maximize social welfare subject to a revenue target. If the firms have increasing returns to scale, which is often the reason they are operated by the public sector, then marginal cost pricing will lead to a deficit (because marginal cost is below the decreasing average cost). The government will then want to find the optimal deviation from marginal-cost pricing that ensures that the firms break even.

For both commodity taxation and public sector pricing, the government is choosing the set of consumer prices that maximize welfare subject to a revenue constraint. Under the commodity taxation interpretation, these prices are achieved by setting the level of tax to be included in each consumer price, whereas with public sector pricing, the prices are chosen directly. However, the choice of tax rate is equivalent to the choice of consumer price.

In the context of public sector pricing, the optimal prices are generally known as *Ramsey prices*. The constraint on the optimization with commodity taxation requires the raising of a specified level of revenue. With public sector pricing this can be reinterpreted as the need to raise a given level of revenue in excess of marginal cost. The tax rates of the commodity taxation problem then translate into the markup over marginal cost in the public sector pricing interpretation. The rules for optimal taxation derived above then characterize the public sector prices.

14.10   Conclusions

This chapter has reviewed the determination of optimal commodity taxes. It has been shown how an efficient system places the burden of taxation primarily on necessities. If implemented, such a system would be very damaging to low-income consumers. When equity is introduced, this outcome is modified to reduce the extent to which goods consumed primarily by those with low incomes are affected by the tax system. These interpretations were borne out by the numerical calculations.

As well as providing these insights into the structure of taxes, the chapter has also been shown that the optimal tax system should ensure production efficiency. The implication of this finding is that there should be no taxes on intermediate goods. This is a very strong and clear prediction. It is also a property that actual value-added tax systems satisfy.

Further Reading

The theory of optimal commodity taxation was given its modern form in:

Diamond, P. A., and Mirrlees, J. A. 1971. Optimal taxation and public production 1: Production efficiency and 2: Tax rules. *American Economic Review* 61: 8–27 and 261–78.

A simplified version of the optimal tax rule for a many-consumer economy is developed in:

Diamond, P. A. 1975. A many-person Ramsey tax rule. *Journal of Public Economics* 4: 227–44.

An argument for uniform taxation is presented by:

Deaton, A. S., and Stern, N. H. 1986. Optimally uniform commodity taxes, taste difference and lump-sum grants. *Economics Letters* 20: 263–66.

The welfare effects of tax reform are analyzed in:

Madden, D. 1995. An analysis of indirect tax reform in Ireland in the 1980s. *Fiscal Studies* 16: 18–37.

Murty, M. N., and Ray, R. 1987. Sensitivity of optimal commodity taxes to relaxing leisure/goods separability and to the wage rate. *Economics Letters* 24: 273–77.

Ray, R. 1986a. Sensitivity of "optimal" commodity tax rates to alternative demand functional forms. *Journal of Public Economics* 31: 253–68.

Ray, R. 1986b. Redistribution through commodity taxes: The non-linear Engel curve case. *Public Finance* 41: 277–84.

The extension of efficient taxation to imperfect competition is described in:

Myles, G. D. 1987. Tax design in the presence of imperfect competition: An example. *Journal of Public Economics* 34: 367–78.

Public sector pricing is described in:

Drèze, J. H. 1964. Some postwar contributions of French economists to theory and public policy with special emphasis on problems of resource allocation. *American Economic Review* 54: 1–64.

Exercises

14.1.   For the linear demand function $x = a - bp$ calculate the deadweight loss of introducing a commodity tax t when the marginal cost of production is constant at c. How is the deadweight loss affected by changes in a and b? How does a change in b affect the elasticity of demand at the equilibrium without taxation?

14.2.   Assume that the demand function is given by $x = p^{-\varepsilon_d}$ and the supply function by $y = p^{\varepsilon_s}$. Find the equilibrium price. What is the effect on the equilibrium price of the introduction of a tax $t = \frac{1}{10}$ if $\varepsilon_d = \varepsilon_s = \frac{1}{2}$? Describe how the incidence of the tax is divided between consumers and suppliers.

14.3.   The analysis of taxation in the single-consumer economy used labor as an untaxed numéraire. Show that the optimal allocation with commodity taxation is unchanged when the consumption good becomes the untaxed numéraire. Then establish that it does not matter which good is numéraire and which is taxed.

14.4.   The value-added tax system requires all goods to be sold at a price that includes tax. Any firm purchasing a good to use as an input can reclaim the tax it has paid. Assess this tax structure using the Diamond-Mirrlees Production Efficiency Lemma.

14.5.   Consider an economy with a single consumer whose preferences are given by $U = \log(x) - \ell$, where x is consumption and ℓ labor supply. Assume that the consumption good is produced using labor alone with a constant-returns-to-scale technology. Units of measurement are chosen so that the producer prices of both the consumption good and the wage rate are equal to 1.

a. Let the consumer's budget constraint be $qx = \ell$, where the consumer price is $q = 1 + t$, and t is the commodity tax. By maximizing utility, find the demand function and the labor supply function.

b. Assume the revenue requirement of the government is $\frac{1}{10}$ of a unit of labor. Draw the production possibilities for the economy and the consumer's offer curve.

c. By using the offer curve and the production possibilities, show that the optimal allocation with commodity taxation has $x = \frac{9}{10}$ and $\ell = 1$.

d. Calculate the optimal commodity tax.

e. By deriving the first-best allocation, show that the commodity tax optimum is second-best.

14.6.   For an economy with one consumption good that is produced using only labor, show that at the optimal allocation with commodity taxation tax revenue, tx, is equal to the government use of labor, R.

14.7.   Assume that the production technology is such that each unit of output requires one unit of labor and that the government has a revenue requirement of one unit of labor. Also assume that there is a single consumer.

a. Using a diagram, describe how the optimal tax on the consumption good is determined.

Now assume that the consumer has preferences given by $U = \log(x) + \log(10 + \ell)$, where x is consumption and ℓ is labor supply.

b. By maximizing utility subject to the budget constraint $qx + w\ell = 0$, construct the consumer's offer curve.

c. Treating the equations of the production frontier and the offer curve as a simultaneous system, determine the optimal tax rate.

14.8.   An economy has a single consumption good produced using labor and a single consumer. The production process has decreasing returns to scale. Explain the derivation of the optimal commodity tax when profit is not taxed.

14.9.   Consider the utility function $U = \alpha \log(x_1) + \beta \log(x_2) - \ell$ and budget constraint $w\ell = q_1 x_1 + q_2 x_2$.

a. Show that the price elasticity of demand for both commodities is equal to -1.

b. Setting producer prices at $p_1 = p_2 = 1$, show that the inverse elasticity rule implies $\frac{t_1}{t_2} = \frac{q_1}{q_2}$.

c. Letting $w = 100$ and $\alpha + \beta = 1$, calculate the tax rates required to achieve revenue of $R = 10$.

14.10. Let the consumer have the utility function $U = x_1^{\rho_1} + x_2^{\rho_2} - \ell$.

a. Show that the utility maximizing demands are $x_1 = \left[\frac{\rho_1 w}{q_1}\right]^{1/[1-\rho_1]}$ and $x_2 = \left[\frac{\rho_2 w}{q_2}\right]^{1/[1-\rho_2]}$.

b. Letting $p_1 = p_2 = 1$, use the inverse elasticity rule to show that the optimal tax rates are related by $\frac{1}{t_2} = \left[\frac{\rho_2 - \rho_1}{1-\rho_2}\right] + \left[\frac{1-\rho_1}{1-\rho_2}\right]\frac{1}{t_1}$.

c. Setting $w = 100$, $\rho_1 = 0.75$, and $\rho_2 = 0.5$, find the tax rates required to achieve revenue of $R = 0.5$ and $R = 10$.

d. Calculate the proportional reduction in demand for the two goods comparing the no-tax position with the position after imposition of the optimal taxes for both revenue levels. Comment on the results.

14.11. "If all commodities are taxed at the same rate, the distortion in prices is minimized." Explain why this statement does not act as a guide for setting optimal commodity taxes.

14.12. Consider an economy with a single consumer whose preferences are given by $U = \log(x_1) + \log(x_2) - \ell$, where x_1 and x_2 are the consumption levels of goods 1 and 2 and ℓ is leisure. Assume that both goods are produced using labor alone, subject to a constant-returns-to-scale technology. Units of measurement are chosen so that the producer prices of both goods and the wage rate are equal to 1.

a. Using L to denote the consumer's endowment of time and ℓ to denote leisure, explain the budget constraint

$$q_1 x_1 + q_2 x_2 + w\ell = wL.$$

b. Show that the consumer's demands satisfy the conditions required for the inverse elasticity rule to apply.

c. Use the inverse elasticity rule to conclude that both goods should be subject to the same level of tax.

d. Calculate the tax required to obtain a level of revenue of $R = 1$.

e. Show that the commodity taxes are second-best.

14.13. Show how the impact of a commodity tax upon a consumer's optimal demand can be separated into an "income effect" and a "substitution effect."

14.14. In the absence of taxation a consumer has the budget constraint $p_1 x_1 + p_2 x_2 - w\ell = 0$. Show that an ad valorem tax levied at rate t on both commodities and on labor raises no revenue. Explain this fact.

14.15. (Ramsey rule) Consider a three-good economy ($k = 1, 2, 3$) in which every consumer has preferences represented by the utility function $U = x_1 + g(x_2) + h(x_3)$, where the functions $g(\cdot)$ and $h(\cdot)$ are increasing and strictly concave. Suppose that each good is produced with constant returns to scale from good 1, using one unit of good 1 per unit of good $k \neq 1$. Let good 1 be the numéraire, and normalize the price of good 1 to equal 1. Let t_k denote the (specific) commodity tax on good k so that the consumer price is $q_k = (1 + t_k)$.

a. Consider two commodity tax schemes $t = (t_1, t_2, t_3)$ and $t' = (t'_1, t'_2, t'_3)$. Show that if $1 + t'_k = \phi[1 + t_k]$ for $k = 1, 2, 3$ for some scalar $\phi > 0$, then the two tax schemes raise the same amount of tax revenue.

b. Argue from part a that the government can without cost restrict tax schemes to leave one good untaxed.

c. Set $t_1 = 0$, and suppose that the government must raise revenue of R. What are the tax rates on goods 2 and 3 that minimize the welfare loss from taxation?

d. Show that the optimal taxes are inversely proportional to the elasticity of the demand for each good. Discuss this tax rule.

e. When should both goods be taxed equally? Which good should be taxed more?

14.16. Consider a three-good economy ($k = 1, 2, 3$) in which every consumer has preferences represented by the utility function $U = x_1 + g(x_2, x_3)$, where the function $g(.)$ is increasing and strictly concave. Suppose that each good is produced with constant returns to scale from good 1, using one unit of good 1 per unit of good $k \neq 1$. Let good 1 be the numéraire and normalize the price of good 1 to equal 1. Let t_k denote the (specific) commodity tax on good k so that the consumer price is $q_k = 1 + t_k$. Suppose that a tax change is restricted to only good 2 so that $t'_2 = t_2 + \Delta$ with $\Delta > 0$.

a. What is the correct measure of the welfare loss arising from this tax increase if $t_3 = 0$?

b. Show that if $t_3 > 0$, then the measure of welfare loss in part a overestimates the welfare loss if good 3 is a substitute for good 2. What is then the correct measure of the welfare change?

c. Show that if $t_3 > 0$, then the measure of welfare loss in part a underestimates the welfare loss if good 3 is a complement for good 2. What is the correct welfare change?

d. Show that if good 3 is subsidized, $t_3 < 0$, then the the measure of welfare loss in part a underestimates the welfare loss if good 3 is a substitute for good 2. How can you explain this result?

e. Show that if good 3 is subsidized, $t_3 < 0$, then the the measure of welfare loss in part a overestimates the welfare loss if good 3 is a complement for good 2.

14.17. The purpose of this exercise is to contrast the incidence of a commodity tax under different market structures. Consider an economy with identical households and identical firms. The representative household receives labor income for its labor supply ℓ and profit income π for its ownership of the firm. The utility function of the household is $U = 2\sqrt{x} - \ell$. The firm produces one unit of final consumption good x with one unit of labor input. Labor is the numéraire good: the price of labor is normalized to 1, and labor is the untaxed good. The producer price is p and the consumer price is $q = p + t$, where $t > 0$ is the (specific) commodity tax.

a. Describe the household's optimization program treating profit income and the consumer prices in the budget constraint as fixed. Find the demand for good x as a function of consumer price q.

b. Calculate the elasticity of the slope of the inverse demand function.

c. Suppose that the firms act in unison like a monopolist. Find the supply of the monopoly as a function of t.

d. What is the equilibrium price charged by the monopolist? What is the producer price? What is the division of the tax burden between the producer and the consumer?

e. Suppose that the firms act independently maximizing their own profit-taking prices as given. What is the equilibrium producer price? What is the division of the tax burden between producer and consumer? Compare with the result in part d.

14.18. Consider an economy with two representative households ($h = 1, 2$) that supply labor ℓ^h to the one representative firm and buy a consumption good x^h. Labor supply is inelastic (with $\ell^1 = 4$ and $\ell^2 = 2$) and perfectly substitutable in production. There is no disutility of labor. The utility function is $U = x^h$, and the firm produces one unit of x with one unit of labor. Labor is the numeraire good with its price normalized to 1. The producer price of x is p. The government can levy individualized commodity tax t^h on good x. Thus the consumer price facing household h is $q^h = p + t^h$. There is no revenue requirement so $R = t^1 x^1 + t^2 x^2 = 0$.

a. What is the equilibrium producer price?

b. What is the demand for good x as a function of the tax rate for each household?

c. Use the demand function to express the utility of each household as a function of the price of the consumption good.

d. Show that government budget balance implies that the taxes are related by $t^2 = -\frac{2t^1}{3t^1 + 1}$.

e. Use the budget balance condition in part d to find the tax rates maximizing the Rawlsian social welfare function $W = \min\{U^1, U^2\}$.

f. Why individualized commodity taxes are not used in practice?

14.19. Are the following statements true or false?

a. The theory of optimal commodity taxation argues that equal tax rates should be set across all commodities so as to maximize efficiency by "smoothing taxes."

b. In the United States prescription drugs and CDs are taxed at the same rate of 10 percent. The Ramsey rule suggests that this is the optimal tax policy.

c. Some economists have proposed replacing the income tax with a consumption tax to avoid taxing savings twice. This is a good policy both in terms of efficiency and equity.

14.20. Consider two consumers with preferences

$$U^1 = \alpha \log(x_1^1) + [1 - \alpha] \log(x_2^1),$$

$$U^2 = \beta \log(x_1^2) + [1 - \beta] \log(x_2^2),$$

and incomes $M^1 < M^2$. What is the maximum amount of redistribution that can be obtained by levying commodity taxes on goods 1 and 2? Why is it zero if $\alpha = \beta$?

15 Income Taxation

15.1 Introduction

In 1799 an income tax was introduced for the first time in the United Kingdom to pay for the Napoleonic war. The tax was levied at a rate of 10 percent on income above £60 and survived until it was repealed in 1816 following major public opposition. Part of the opposition was due to concerns about privacy, and this was reflected in the decision of Parliament to pulp all documents relating to the income tax. The tax returned in 1842 as a temporary measure (imposed for three years with the possibility of a two-year extension) to cover a major budget deficit. It has remained in place ever since, although it is still temporary and Parliament has to re-apply it every year.

The income tax has remained controversial. As the discussion of chapter 3 showed, the taxation of income is a major source of government revenue. This fact, coupled with the direct observation by taxpayers of income tax payments, explains why the structure of income tax is the subject of much political discussion. The arguments that are aired in such debate reflect the two main perspectives on income taxation. The first views the tax primarily as a disincentive to effort and enterprise. On this ground, it follows that the rate of tax should be kept as low as possible in order to avoid such discouragement. This is essentially the expression of an efficiency argument. The competing perspective is that income taxation is well suited for the task of redistributing income. Hence notions of equity require that high earners should pay proportionately more tax on their incomes than low earners. The determination of the optimal structure of income taxation involves the resolution of these contrasting views.

The chapter begins by conducting an analysis of the interaction between income taxation and labor supply. A number of theoretical results are derived, and these are related to the empirical evidence. This evidence makes clear the extent of the difference between the responses of male and female labor supply to taxation. A model that permits the efficiency and equity aspects of taxation to be incorporated into the design of the optimal tax is then described. A series of results characterizing properties of the optimal tax function are derived using this model, and these properties are interpreted in terms of practical policy recommendations. Calculations of the optimal tax rates that emerge from the model are then reviewed. The chapter is completed by a discussion of political economy aspects of income taxation.

15.2   Equity and Efficiency

There are two major issues involved in the taxation of income. The first is the effect of taxation on the supply of labor. Taxation alters the choices that consumers make by affecting the trade-off between labor and leisure. In this respect a particularly important question is whether an increase in the rate of tax necessarily reduces the supply of labor. If this is the case, support would be provided for the argument that taxes should be kept low to meet the needs of efficiency. Both theoretical and empirical results addressing this question will be discussed. The second issue that has been studied is the determination of the optimal level of income taxation. For reasons that will become clear, this is a complex problem, since it can only be addressed in a model with a meaningful trade-off between efficiency and equity. Having said this, the search for the right trade-off has proved to be a fruitful avenue of investigation.

The essential idea we wish to convey in this chapter is that it is a major mistake to design the income tax structure to meet equity motives without taking into account the impact on work effort. To see why, consider the naïve solution of setting the marginal tax rate at one hundred percent for all incomes above some threshold level z^0 and at a rate of zero for all incomes below this threshold. We might expect that such a tax structure will maximize the redistribution possible from the rich (those above the income threshold) to the poor (those below). However, this conclusion is incorrect when taxpayers respond to the tax structure. The confiscatory tax above the threshold removes the incentive to earn more than z^0 and everyone previously above this level will choose to earn exactly that amount of income. This sets a vicious circle in motion. The government must lower the threshold, inducing everyone above the new level to lower their incomes again, and so forth, until no one chooses to work and income is zero.

It therefore stands to reason that we must analyze the equity of the tax structure in tandem with its effect on work incentives. The idea is to find the tax schedule that meets social objectives, as captured by the social welfare function (see chapter 12), given the adjustment in work effort and labor market participation by taxpayers. Such a tax scheme is said to be optimal conditional on the given objective. The results need to be interpreted with caution, however, because they are very sensitive to the distribution of abilities in the population and to the form of the utility function. More important, they depend on the equity objective as built into the social welfare function.

In this chapter we will only consider welfaristic equity criteria (of which the utilitarian and Rawlsian social welfare functions are noteworthy examples). Hence, in so far as the social objective is entirely based on individual welfare levels, we are not assessing the tax structure on the basis of its capacity for either redressing inequality or eliminating poverty. Neither do we consider egalitarian social objectives like equal sacrifice or equality of opportunities. There is, indeed, an interesting literature on "fair" income taxation that examines the distribution of taxes that impose the same loss of utility on everyone, either in absolute or relative terms. Such arguments are related to the ability-to-pay principle according to which $1 of tax is less painful for a rich person than for a poor person (due to the decreasing marginal value of income). This equal sacrifice approach predicts that the resulting tax structure must be progressive (in the sense that everyone sacrifices equally if they pay an increasing percentage of their income in tax as their income rises). It was John Stuart Mill in his *Principles of Political Economy* who first pointed out this principle of equal sacrifice. He suggested that "Equality of taxation, therefore as a maxim of politics, means equality of sacrifice. It means apportioning the contribution of each person towards the expenses of government so that he shall feel neither more nor less inconvenience from his share of the payment than every other person experiences from his" (bk. V, ch. 2, p. 804).

15.3   Taxation and Labor Supply

The effect of income taxation on labor supply can be investigated using the standard model of consumer choice. The analysis will begin with the general question of labor supply and then move on to a series of specific analyses concerning the effect of variations in the tax system. The major insight this gives will be to highlight the importance of competing income and substitution effects.

As is standard, it is assumed that the consumer has a given set of preferences over allocations of consumption and leisure. The consumer also has a fixed stock of time available which can be divided between labor supply and time spent as leisure. The utility function representing the preferences can then be defined by

$$U = U(x, L - \ell) = U(x, \ell), \tag{15.1}$$

where L is the total time endowment, ℓ is labor supply, and x is consumption. Consequently leisure time is $L - \ell$. Labor is assumed to be unpleasant for the worker, so utility is reduced as more labor is supplied, implying that $\frac{\partial U}{\partial \ell} < 0$. Let each hour of labor earn the wage rate w so that income, in the absence of taxation

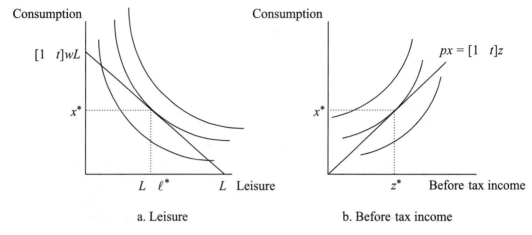

Figure 15.1
Labor supply decision

is $w\ell$. Letting the (constant) rate of tax be t, the budget constraint facing the consumer is $px = [1 - t]w\ell$, where p is the price of the consumption good.

The choice problem is shown in figure 15.1a, which graphs consumption against leisure. The indifference curves and budget constraint are as standard for utility maximization. The optimal choice is at the tangency of the budget constraint and the highest attainable indifference curve. This results in consumption x^* and leisure $L - \ell^*$.

There is an alternative way to write the utility function. Let before-tax income be denoted by z, so $z = w\ell$. Since $\ell = \frac{z}{w}$, utility can then be written in terms of before-tax income as

$$U = U\left(x, \frac{z}{w}\right).$$ (15.2)

These preferences can be depicted on a graph of before-tax income against consumption. Expressed in terms of income, the budget constraint becomes $px = [1 - t]z$. This is shown in figure 15.1b. The optimal choice occurs at the point of tangency between the highest attainable indifference curve and the budget constraint, with consumption x^* and before-tax income z^*. The important feature of this alternative representation is that the budget constraint is not affected as w changes, so it is the same whatever wage the consumer earns, but the indifference curves do change, since it is $\frac{z}{w}$ that enters the utility function. How they change is described below.

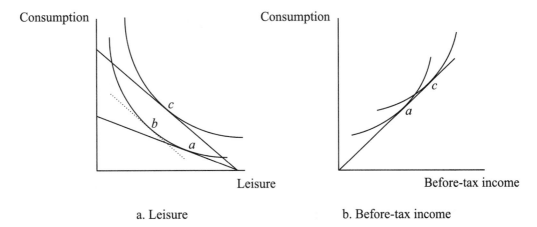

Figure 15.2
Effect of a wage increase

This model can now be used to understand the effects of variations in the wage rate or tax rate. Consider the effect of an increase in the wage rate (or a decrease in the tax rate), which is shown in figure 15.2a by the move to the higher budget line and the new tangency at c. The move from a to c can be broken down into a substitution effect $(a \rightarrow b)$ and an income effect $(b \rightarrow c)$. The direction of the substitution effect can always be signed, since it is given by a move around the indifference curve. In contrast, the income effect cannot be signed: it may be positive or negative. Consequently the net effect is ambiguous so an increase in the wage can raise or lower labor supply. This is the basic ambiguity that runs throughout the analysis of labor supply.

The effect of a wage increase (or a tax decrease) when preferences are written as in (15.2) is shown in figure 15.2b. An increase in the wage rate means that less additional labor is required to achieve any given increase in consumption. This change in the trade-off between labor and consumption causes the indifference curve through a point to pivot round and become flatter. This flattening of the indifference curves causes the optimal choice to move along the budget constraint. The level of before-tax income will rise, but the effect on hours worked is ambiguous.

It is also helpful to consider more complex tax systems using this approach. A common feature of the income tax in many countries is that there is a threshold level of income below which income is untaxed. This is shown in figures 15.3a and b. The threshold level of income is z^* so at wage rate w this arises at $\frac{z^*}{w}$ hours

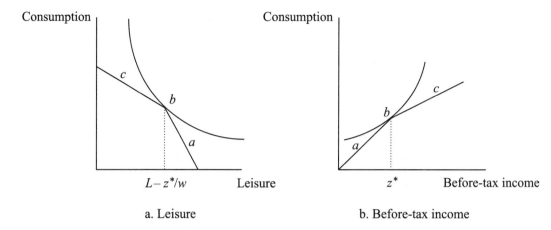

Figure 15.3
A tax threshold

of labor supply. The economic importance of this threshold is that it puts a kink into the budget constraint. If a set of consumers with differing preferences are considered, some may locate at points such as a and pay no tax, and some may locate at points like c. However, it can be expected that a number of consumers will cluster or "bunch" at the kink point b. The observation that consumers will bunch at a kink point is a common feature and reflects the fact that an extra unit of labor will receive net pay $[1 - t]w$, whereas the previous unit received w. It is therefore helpful to distinguish between interior solutions, such as a and c, and corner solutions such as b. The consumer at an interior solution will respond to changes in the tax rate in the manner illustrated in figure 15.2. In contrast, a consumer at a corner solution may well be left unaffected by a marginal tax change. Their choice will only be affected if the change is sufficient to allow the attainment of a utility level higher than at the kink.

More generally, an income tax system may have a number of thresholds with the marginal tax rate rising at each. Such a tax system appears as in figure 15.4. Again, with preferences varying across consumers, the expectation is that there will tend to be collections of consumers at each kink point.

The final issue that is worth investigating in this framework is that of participation in the labor force. The basic assumption so far has been that the worker can continuously vary the number of working hours in order to arrive at the most preferred outcome. In practice, it is often the case that either hours are fixed or else there is a minimum that must be undertaken with the possibility of more. Either

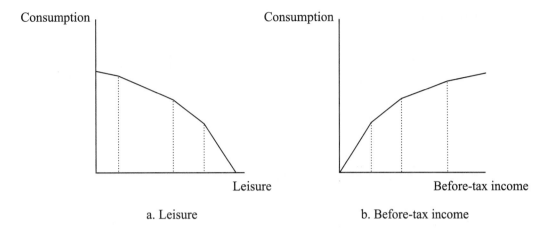

Figure 15.4
Several thresholds

case leads to a discontinuity in the budget constraint at the point of minimum hours. The choice for the consumer is then between either undertaking no work or working at least the minimum. This is the participation decision: whether or not to join the workforce.

The participation decision and its relation to taxation is shown in figure 15.5 where ℓ^m denotes the minimum working time. The effect of an increase in taxation is to lower the budget constraint. A consumer that was previously indifferent between working and not (both points being on the same indifference curve) now strictly prefers not to do so. At this margin there is no conflict between income and substitution effects. An increase in taxation strictly reduces participation in the labor force.

15.4   Empirical Evidence

The theoretical analysis of section 15.3 has identified the three major issues in the study of labor supply. These are the potential conflict between income and substitution effects that make it impossible to provide any clear-cut results for those consumers at an interior solution, kinks in the budget constraint that make behavior insensitive to taxes, and a participation decision that can be very sensitive to taxation. How important each of these factors is in determining the actual level of labor supply can only be discovered by reference to the empirical evidence.

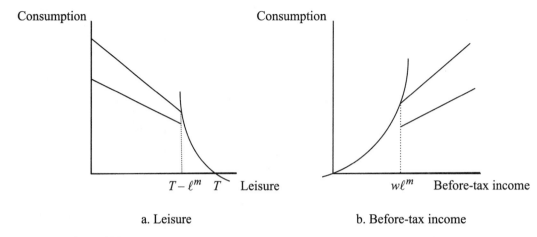

Figure 15.5
Taxation and the participation decision

Empirical evidence on labor supply and the effect of income taxes can be found in both the results of surveys and in econometric estimates of labor supply functions. In considering what evidence is useful, it is best to recall that labor supply will be insensitive to taxation if working hours are determined by the firm or by union and firm agreement. When this is the case, only the participation decision is of real interest. The effect of taxation at interior solutions can only be judged when the evidence relates to workers who have the freedom to vary their hours of labor. This is most commonly the position for those in self-employment rather than employment. For those in employment, variations in hours can sometimes be achieved by undertaking overtime, so this dimension of choice can be considered.

These comments also draw attention to the fact that the nature of labor supply may well be different between males and females, especially married females. It still remains a fact that males continue to be the dominant income earner in most families. This leaves the married female as typically a secondary income earner, and for them there is often no necessity to work. From this position it is the participation decision that is paramount. In contrast, most males consider work to be a necessity, so the participation decision is an irrelevance. It can therefore be expected that the labor supply of males and females will show different degrees of sensitivity to taxation.

Surveys on labor supply have normally arrived at the conclusion that changes in the tax rate have little effect on the labor-supply decision. For instance, a survey

Table 15.1
Labor-supply elasticities

	Married women		Married men		Lone mothers	
	United States	United Kingdom	United States	United Kingdom	United States	United Kingdom
Uncompensated wages	0.45	0.43	0.03	−0.23	0.53	0.76
Compensated wages	0.90	0.65	0.95	0.13	0.65	1.28
Income	−0.45	−0.22	−0.98	−0.36	−0.18	−0.52

Source: Blundell (1992).

of the disincentive effect of high tax rates on solicitors and accountants in the United Kingdom, 63 percent of whom were subject to marginal tax rates above 50 percent, concluded that as many of the respondents were working harder because of the tax rates as were working less hard. Groups such as these are ideal candidates for study for the reasons outlined above: they can be expected to have flexibility in the choice of working hours and should be well informed about the tax system. A similar conclusion was also found in a survey of the effect of income taxation on the level of overtime worked by a sample of weekly paid workers: little net effect of taxation on working hours was found.

These results suggest the conclusion that labor supply does not vary significantly with the tax rate. If this were correct, the labor supply function would be approximately vertical. In terms of the theoretical analysis the survey results point to an income effect that almost entirely offsets the substitution effect. However, the discussion has already suggested that different groups in the population may have different reactions to changes in the tax system. This issue is now investigated by considering evidence from econometric analysis.

Table 15.1 presents some summary econometric estimates of labor supply elasticities. These are divided into those for married men, married women, and unmarried women. Each gives the overall elasticity and its breakdown into substitution and income effects. Estimates for both the United Kingdom and the United States are given.

Since these results relate to the effect of a wage increase, theory would predict that the substitution effect should be positive. This is what is found in all cases. The income effect, which theoretically can be positive or negative, is found to be always negative. Consequently the negativity offsets the substitution effect, sometimes more than completely. While there are a range of estimates for each category, some general observations can be made. The estimated elasticity for married men is the lowest and is the only one that is ever estimated to be negative. This implies that the labor supply curve for married men is close to vertical and may even slope backward. One explanation for this result could be that the working hours of this group are constrained by collective agreements that leave little flexibility for variation.

The labor supply elasticity of unmarried women is on average the largest of the three sets. This result is probably a consequence of the participation effect. For single women part-time work is an unattractive option, since this usually implies the loss of state benefits. Consequently labor supply becomes an all or nothing decision. Married women represent the intermediate case. For them part-time work is quite common, and this often opens the way to some degree of flexibility in hours of work. As expected, these factors lead to a labor supply elasticity greater than that of married men but lower than that of unmarried women.

Although the estimates vary widely within the groups, indicating some imprecision in the estimates, some general conclusions can still be drawn. First, the elasticity of labor supply is not uniform across the population of workers. It clearly varies among the three groups identified in this discussion and probably varies within these groups. Despite this variation it is still clearly apparent that the uncompensated labor-supply elasticity for married men is small with estimates grouped around zero. In contrast, the elasticity of women is higher and reflects the participation effect and the greater flexibility they have in the choice of hours.

15.5   Optimal Income Taxation

The analysis to this point has considered the positive question of how income taxation affects labor supply. Having understood this, it is now possible to turn to the normative question of how the income tax structure should be determined. This is by nature a complex issue. As has already been noted, in practice, income tax systems generally have a number of thresholds at which the marginal tax rate rises. An investigation of the optimal system must at least be flexible enough to consider such tax systems without limiting the number of thresholds or the rates of tax at each. In fact it must do more much than this. The model of income taxation introduced by Mirrlees has several important attributes. First, there is an unequal distribution of income, so there are equity motivations for taxation. Second, the income tax affects the labor supply decisions of the consumers so that it has efficiency consequences. Third, in view of the comments above, the structure is sufficiently flexible that no prior restrictions are placed on the optimal tax functions that may arise.

In the model all consumers have identical preferences but differ in their level of skill in employment. The hourly wage received by each consumer is determined by their level of skill. This combines with the labor-supply decision to determine income. The economy is competitive, so the wage rate is also equal to the marginal product of labor and firms price their output at marginal cost. A tax levied on skill would be the first-best policy as it would be a lump-sum tax on the unalterable characteristic that differentiates consumers. But this first-best is not feasible, since the level of skill is assumed to be private information and so unobservable by the government. As the discussion of chapter 12 showed, this makes it impossible to tax skill directly. Since the government cannot observe a consumer's skill level (which is essentially the initial endowment of the consumer), it employs an income tax as a second-best policy. The income tax function is chosen to maximize social welfare subject to it raising enough revenue to meets the government's requirements.

There are two commodities: a consumption good and labor. A consumer's labor supply is denoted by ℓ, and consumption by x. Each consumer is characterized by their skill level s. The value of s measures the hourly output of the consumer, and since the economy is competitive, it is equal to the wage rate. If a consumer of ability s supplies ℓ hours of labor, they earn income of $s\ell$ before tax. Denote the income of a consumer with skill s by $z(s) = s\ell(s)$. The amount of tax paid on an income z is given by $T(z)$. This is the tax function that the analysis aims to determine. Equivalently, denoting the consumption function by $c(z)$, a consumer who earns income z can consume

$$x = c(z) = z - T(z). \tag{15.3}$$

The relationship between income, the tax function, and consumption is depicted in figure 15.6. In the absence of taxation, income would be equal to consumption and this is depicted by the 45° line. Where the consumption function lies above the 45° line, the tax payment is negative. It is positive when the consumption function is below the line. For example, the consumer earning $\hat{z}$ in the figure pays an amount of tax $T(\hat{z})$ and can consume $\hat{x}$. The gradient of the consumption function is equal to one minus the marginal rate of tax.

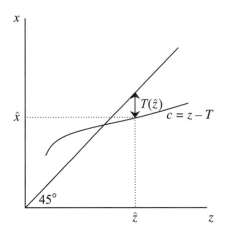

Figure 15.6
Taxation and the consumption function

All consumers have the same utility function (so that the possibility of workers displaying different aversion to work is ruled out)

$$U = U\left(x, \frac{z}{s}\right). \tag{15.4}$$

The indifference curves are dependent on the skill level of the consumer, since a high-skill consumer takes less labor time to achieve a given level of income than a low-skill consumer. This is reflected in the fact that at any income and consumption pair $\{\hat{x}, \hat{z}\}$ the indifference curve of a high-skill consumer passing through that point is flatter than the indifference curve of a low-skill consumer. This single-crossing property is termed *agent monotonicity* and is illustrated in figure 15.7.

An immediate consequence of agent monotonicity is that high-skill consumers will never earn less income than low-skill. Generally, they will earn strictly more. This result is shown in figure 15.8. It arises because at the point where the indifference curve of the low-skill consumer is tangential to the consumption function (and so determines the optimal choice for that consumer), the indifference curve of the high-skill consumer is flatter and so cannot be at a tangency. Recall that all consumers face the same tax function and thus the same consumption function no matter what their skills are. The optimal choice for the high-skill consumer therefore has to be to the right of a, which implies a higher level of income.

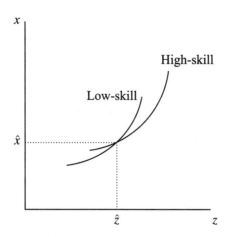

Figure 15.7
Agent monotonicity

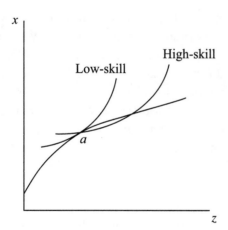

Figure 15.8
Income and skill

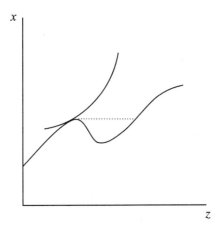

Figure 15.9
Upper limit on tax rate

The first property of the optimal tax function relates to the maximum tax rate that will be charged. If the consumption function slopes downward, as shown in figure 15.9, then the shape of the indifference curves ensures that no consumer will choose to locate on the downward-sloping section. This part of the consumption function is therefore redundant and can be replaced by the flat-dashed section without altering any of the consumers' choices. Economically along the downward-sloping section increased work effort is met with lower consumption. Hence there is no incentive to work harder, and such points will not be chosen. Since $c(z) = z - T(z)$, it follows that $c'(z) = 1 - T'(z)$. The argument has shown that $c'(z) \geq 0$, which implies $T'(z) \leq 1$, so the marginal tax rate is less than 100 percent.

It is also possible to put a lower limit on the marginal tax rate. If the gradient of the consumption function is greater than one, meaning $c'(z) > 1$, then $T'(z) < 0$. A negative tax rate represents a marginal subsidy to the tax payer from the tax system. That is, the after-tax wage for additional work will be greater than the before-tax wage. Figure 15.10 illustrates the argument that a negative marginal rate can never be optimal. To see this, start with the tax function denoted $c^1(z)$, which has gradient greater than one. Along this are located a high-skill consumer at h_1 and a low-skill consumer at l_1. Now consider the effect of moving to the new tax function $c^2(z)$ where the gradient is less than one. Under this tax function the high-skill consumer moves to h_2 and the low-skill to l_2. The new tax function is chosen so the the extra before-tax income earned by the high-skill is exactly equal to the reduction in earning by the low and the consumption of the low-skill rises

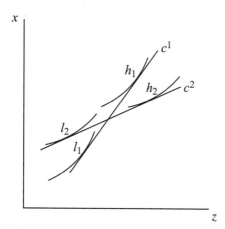

Figure 15.10
Lower limit on tax rate

by exactly the amount that of the high-skill falls. The net effect of these changes is to transfer consumption to the low-skill and work effort to the high-skill. This change must raise welfare because the marginal utility of consumption for the low-skill is higher than that for the high-skill, and because of their greater skill, the extra work is less arduous for the high-skill consumer. The sum of these effects ensures that consumption function $c^2(z)$ leads to a higher welfare level than consumption function $c^1(z)$. Consumption function $c^1(z)$ with a negative marginal rate of tax cannot therefore be optimal. From this it follows that the marginal tax rate must be nonnegative so $T'(z) \geq 0$. It should be noted that this result does not restrict the average rate of tax, $\frac{T(z)}{z}$, to be nonnegative. The average rate of tax is negative whenever the consumption function is above the 45° line, and if the system is redistributive, this will be the case at low incomes.

The final result determines the marginal tax rate faced by the highest skill consumer. Let the consumption function ABC in figure 15.11 be a candidate for optimality. It is now shown that ABC cannot be optimal unless its gradient is one (so the marginal rate of tax is zero) at point B where the highest skill consumer locates. To prove this result, assume that the gradient is less than one (so the marginal tax rate is positive) at point B. A better consumption function than ABC will now be constructed. To do this, define ABD by following the old consumption function up to point B, and then let the new section BD have gradient of one. The highest ability consumer will now relocate to point b. Consequently the highest ability consumer is better off, but their actual tax payment (the vertical distance from the consumption point to the 45° line) is unchanged. So replacing ABC with

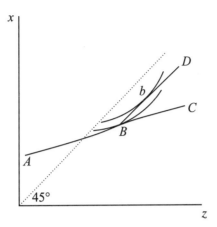

Figure 15.11
Zero marginal rate of tax

ABD leaves aggregate tax revenue unchanged, makes one person better off, and makes no one worse off. This must be an improvement for society, so no consumption function, like *ABC*, that has the highest ability person facing a positive marginal rate of tax can be optimal. In other words, the optimal tax function must have a zero marginal rate of tax for the highest skill consumer.

This result is important for assessing the optimality of actual tax schedules. Those observed in practice invariably have a marginal rate of tax that rises with income. This leaves the highest income consumers facing the highest marginal tax rate rather than a zero rate. Accordingly such tax systems cannot be optimal. The result also carries implications for discussions about how progressive the income tax system should be. A tax system displays marginal rate progressivity if the marginal rate of tax increases with income. Since it has been shown that the marginal rate of tax should be zero at the top of the income distribution, the optimal tax system cannot be a fully (marginal rate) progressive one.

There has been considerable debate about this result due partly to its contrast with what is observed in practice. There are several points that can be made in this respect. The result is valid only for the highest skill consumer, and it makes no prediction about the tax rate that will be faced by consumer with the second-highest skill. Therefore it does not demonstrate that those close to the top of the skill range should face a tax rate of zero or even close to zero. For them the tax rate may have to be significantly different to zero. If this is the case, observed tax systems may only be "wrong" at the very top, which will not result in too great a divergence from optimality. The result also relies on the fact that the highest skill person can be identified and the tax system adjusted around his needs. Putting this into practice is clearly an impossible task. In summary, the result is important in that it questions preconceptions about the structure of taxes, but it has limited immediate policy relevance.

The results described in this section capture the general properties of an optimal income tax system that can be derived within this framework. They have shown that the marginal tax rate should be between zero and one and that the highest skill consumer should face a zero marginal rate. Moreover they have established that the tax system should not involve marginal rate progressivity everywhere. It is possible to derive further results only by adding further specification. The next section looks at two special cases that give alternative routes for proceeding in this direction. However, even these do not provide entirely transparent insights into the level of optimal tax rates. This can only be done through the use of numerical results, and these are the subject matter of section 15.7.

15.6   Two Specializations

To provide some further insight into the optimal income tax, two specializations of the model are worth considering. These are noteworthy for the very clear view they give into the trade-offs involved in setting the tax rate.

15.6.1   Quasi-Linearity

The first specialization is to consider a special form for the utility function. It is assumed in this section that utility is quasi-linear with respect to labor income,

$$U\left(x, \frac{z}{s}\right) = u(x) - \frac{z}{s}, \tag{15.5}$$

so that the marginal disutility of labor $\ell = \frac{z}{s}$ is constant. The utility of consumption, $u(x)$, is increasing and concave (so $u' > 0$ and $u'' < 0$). For this utility function the marginal rate of substitution between consumption and income is $MRS_{x,\ell} = \frac{1}{su'(x)}$. Since the marginal rate of substitution is decreasing in s, the gradient of the indifference curve through any value of x falls as s rises. This makes the utility function consistent with agent monotonicity.

We simplify further by assuming that there are just two consumers, one with a high level of skill, s_h, and the other with a low level, s_l. It is assumed that

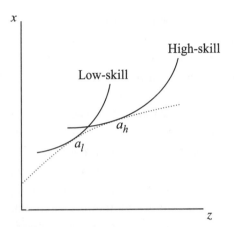

Figure 15.12
Allocations and the consumption function

$s_l < s_h < 3s_l$ (the reason for this is explained later). With only two consumers the problem of choosing the optimal tax (or consumption) function can be given the following formulation: Whatever consumption function is selected by the government, the fact that there are only two consumers ensures that at most two locations on it will ever be chosen. For example, in figure 15.12, a_l is the allocation chosen by the low-skill consumer and a_h the chosen allocation of the high-skill. Having observed this, it is apparent that selecting the consumption function is equivalent to specifying the two allocations. The rest of the consumption function can then be chosen to ensure that no point on it is better for the consumers than the two chosen allocations. Essentially the consumption function just needs to link the two points, while elsewhere remaining below the indifference curves through the points. Following this reasoning reduces the choice of tax function to a simple maximization problem involving the two locations.

A consumer will only choose the allocation intended for them if they prefer their own location to that of the other consumer. In other words, the allocations must be *incentive compatible*. Since the high-skill consumer can mimic the low-skill, but not vice versa, the incentive compatibility constraint must be binding on the high-skill consumer. Denoting the location intended for low-skill consumer by $\{x_l, z_l\}$ and that for high-skill by $\{x_h, z_h\}$, the incentive compatibility constraint is

$$u(x_h) - \frac{z_h}{s_h} = u(x_l) - \frac{z_l}{s_h}. \tag{15.6}$$

495   Chapter 15   Income Taxation

The optimization facing a government that maximizes a utilitarian social welfare function is

$$\max_{\{x_l, x_h, z_l, z_h\}} u(x_l) - \frac{z_l}{s_l} + u(x_h) - \frac{z_h}{s_h} \tag{15.7}$$

subject to the incentive compatibility constraint (15.6) and the resource constraint

$$x_l + x_h = z_l + z_h. \tag{15.8}$$

The resource constraint makes the simplifying assumption that no revenue is to be raised so the tax system is purely redistributive. What is now shown is that the quasi-linearity of utility allows this maximization problem to be considerably simplified. The simplification then permits an explicit solution to be given.

Given that (15.6) is an equality, it can be solved to write

$$z_h = s_h[u(x_h) - u(x_l)] + z_l. \tag{15.9}$$

Combining this equation with the resource constraint and eliminating z_h by using (15.9), the income of the low-skill consumer can be written

$$z_l = \tfrac{1}{2}[x_l + x_h - s_h[u(x_h) - u(x_l)]]. \tag{15.10}$$

Using the resource constraint again gives the income of the high-skill consumer as

$$z_h = \tfrac{1}{2}[x_l + x_h + s_h[u(x_h) - u(x_l)]]. \tag{15.11}$$

These solutions for the income levels can then be substituted into the objective function (15.7). Collecting terms shows that the original constrained optimization is equivalent to

$$\max_{\{x_l, x_h\}} \beta_l u(x_l) + \beta_h u(x_h) - \left[\frac{s_l + s_h}{2 s_l s_h}\right][x_l + x_h], \tag{15.12}$$

where $\beta_l = \frac{3s_l - s_h}{2s_l}$ and $\beta_h = \frac{s_l + s_h}{2s_l}$. (The assumption that $s_h < 3s_l$ ensures that β_l is greater than zero so that the low-skill consumer has a positive social weight. Without this assumption the analysis becomes more complex.)

Comparing (15.7) and (15.12) allows a new interpretation of the optimal tax problem. The construction undertaken has turned the maximization of the utilitarian social welfare function subject to constraint into the maximization of a weighted welfare function without constraint. The incentive compatibility and resource constraints have been incorporated by placing a greater weight on the welfare of the high-skill consumer (since $\beta_h > \beta_l$), which in turn ensures that their consumption level must be higher at the optimum. From (15.10) and (15.11) this feeds back into a higher level of income for the high-skill consumer. It can also be seen that as the skill difference between the two consumers increases, so does the relative weight given to the high-skill.

Carrying out the optimization in (15.12), the consumption levels of the consumers satisfy the first-order conditions

$$\beta_i u'(x_i) - \frac{s_l + s_h}{2 s_l s_h} = 0, \qquad i = l, h, \tag{15.13}$$

so the consumption levels are proportional to the welfare weights. For the high-skill consumer, substituting in the value of β_h gives

$$u'(x_h) = \frac{1}{s_h}. \tag{15.14}$$

Consequently the marginal utility of the high-skill consumer is inversely proportional to their skill level. With $u'' < 0$ (decreasing marginal utility) this implies that consumption is proportional to skill. Combining this result with the fact that $MRS^h_{x,\ell} = \frac{1}{su'}$, it follows that at the optimum allocation $MRS^h_{x,\ell} = 1$. The finding that the marginal rate of substitution is unity shows that the high-skill consumer faces a zero marginal tax rate. This is the no-distortion-at-the-top result we have already seen. For the low-skill consumer

$$u'(x_l) = \frac{s_l + s_h}{s_h [3 s_l - s_h]}, \tag{15.15}$$

and $MRS^l_{x,\ell} = \frac{s_h[3s_l - s_h]}{s_l[s_l + s_h]} < 1$. These show that consumer l faces a positive marginal rate of tax.

The use of quasi-linear utility allows the construction of an explicit solution to the optimal income tax problem, which shows how the general findings of the previous section translate into this special case. It is interesting to note the simple dependence of consumption levels on the relative skills and the manner in which the constraints become translated into a higher effective welfare weight for the high-skill consumer. This shows that this consumer needs to be encouraged to supply more labor through the reward of additional consumption.

15.6.2   Rawlsian Taxation

The second specialization restricts the form of the social welfare function. In chapter 12 we introduced the Rawlsian social welfare function, which represents a society that is concerned only with the utility of the worst-off individual. The worst-off person is typically at the bottom of the income distribution and his welfare depends on the extent of redistribution. We now assume that tax revenue is entirely redistributed in the form of lump-sum grants. Consequently, for a Rawlsian government, the optimal income tax is simply that which maximizes the lump-sum grant or, equally, that which maximizes the revenue extracted from taxpayers.

Given a tax schedule $T(z)$, a consumer of skill level s makes the choice of income, z (which is equivalent to choosing labor supply $\ell = \frac{z}{s}$) and consumption, x, to maximize their utility subject to satisfying the budget constraint $x = z - T(z)$. Let $z(s)$ denote the optimal income choice of type s (conditional on the tax function T). It has been seen that agent monotonicity implies that high-skill consumers never earn less income than low-skill. So $z(s)$ is increasing in s and can be inverted to give the increasing inverse function $z^{-1}(s)$ that represents the skill level s associated to each income choice. Different tax schemes will induce different relationships between skill and income from the same underlying distribution of skills.

Assume that skill levels are continuously distributed in the population according to a cumulative distribution function $F(s)$ (indicating the proportion of the population below any skill level s) with associated density function $f(s) > 0$ (representing the probability associated with a small interval of the continuous skill). The tax scheme $T(z)$ induces the income distribution $G(z) = F(z^{-1}(s))$ with density $g(z) = f(z^{-1}(s))$.

Now we are in a position to derive the optimal income tax associated to a Rawlsian social welfare function following a simple method originally proposed by Piketty. The Rawlsian optimal tax structure maximizes tax revenue, so no alternative tax structure must exist that can raise more revenue from the taxpayers given their optimal labor supply response to that new tax structure. From the first-order condition of the revenue maximization problem, a small deviation from the optimal tax scheme must have no effect on total tax revenue (and larger deviations must lower tax revenue). It follows that a small change of the tax rate at any given income level z must not change total revenue. Using this simple argument, we can derive the optimal tax structure.

Take income level z, and consider a small increase in the marginal tax rate at that point of amount $\Delta T'$. This change has two effects on tax revenue. First, holding labor supply constant, it will increase the tax payment by amount $z\Delta T'$ for all those taxpayers with an income above or equal to the level, z, at which the higher marginal tax rate applies. These taxpayers represent a proportion $1 - G(z)$ of the population. Therefore the revenue gain from this marginal tax change is

$$[1 - G(z)]z\Delta T'. \tag{15.16}$$

Obviously labor supply is not fixed, and it is expected to vary in response to a change in the tax rate. Let ε_s denote the elasticity of labor supply with respect to the net price of labor (the percentage change in labor supply in response to a 1 percent reduction in the net price of labor). With perfect competition on the labor market, the price of labor decreases by the amount of the tax rate (i.e., there is no shifting of the tax burden to employers in the form of a higher gross wage). Now the marginal tax rate increase $\Delta T'$ at income level z induces a percentage reduction $\frac{\Delta T'}{1-T'}$ in the price of labor. Those facing this marginal tax rate change will reduce their labor supply by $\frac{\varepsilon_s \Delta T'}{1-T'}$, inducing a reduction of their taxable income equal to $\frac{z\varepsilon_s \Delta T'}{1-T'}$. They represent a proportion $g(z)$ of the population (since those with an income level above the level at which higher marginal tax rate applies continue to face the same marginal tax rate). Therefore the revenue loss associated with the incentive effect of the tax change is

$$[g(z)]T'z\varepsilon_s \frac{\Delta T'}{1 - T'}. \tag{15.17}$$

The revenue maximizing tax scheme (Rawlsian tax) is found by equating the revenue loss to the revenue gain from a marginal tax change for every income level. This yields

$$[1 - G(z)]z\Delta T' = [g(z)]T'z\varepsilon_s \frac{\Delta T'}{1 - T'}, \tag{15.18}$$

and the Rawlsian tax structure is easily seen to be such that for all income level z,

$$\frac{T'(z)}{1 - T'(z)} = \frac{1 - G(z)}{\varepsilon_s g(z)}. \tag{15.19}$$

This expression has the following interpretation. High marginal tax rates over some middle-income interval $[z, z + dz]$ mean that for those middle-income individuals, but also for the upper-income individuals, the government is collecting more taxes. All together they represent a proportion $1 - G(z)$ that is decreasing with z and converging to zero for the highest income level (hence the zero marginal tax rate at the top). The cost of the high marginal tax rate over this interval is a greater distortion for those with income in the range $[z, z + dz]$. The total distortion (and revenue loss) will be low, however, if there are relatively few tax-payers in this interval (low $g(z)$), or if those in it have a relatively low labor supply elasticity (low ε_s).

Interestingly, even though the redistributive motive is maximal under the Rawlsian social welfare function, the optimal tax structure does not require marginal rate progressivity. Indeed, since we do not really know how the labor supply elasticity changes with income. Suppose that it is constant. Next take the Pareto distribution of income, which is supposed to be a good fit to the empirical distribution of income. For the Pareto distribution, the *hazard rate* $\frac{g(z)}{1-G(z)}$ is increasing almost everywhere. Therefore, from the optimal tax structure given above, it follows that marginal tax rate must decrease everywhere. Maximal redistribution is better achieved when the tax schedule is regressive (concave) instead of progressive (convex).

15.7   Numerical Results

The standard analysis of optimal income taxation has been introduced above, and a number of results have been derived that provide some characterization of the shape of the tax schedule. It has been seen that the marginal rate is between zero and one but as yet no idea has been developed, except for the upper end point, of how close it should be to either. Similarly, although equity considerations are expected to raise the marginal rate, this has not been demonstrated formally nor has consideration been given to how efficiency criteria, particularly the effect of taxation on labor supply, affects the choice of tax schedule. Due to the analytical complexity of the model these questions are best addressed via numerical analysis.

The numerical results (from Mirrlees 1971) are based on a social welfare function that takes the form

$$W = \begin{cases} \int_0^S \frac{1}{\varepsilon} e^{-\varepsilon U} f(s)\, ds, & \varepsilon > 0, \\ \int_0^S U f(s)\, ds, & \varepsilon = 0, \end{cases} \tag{15.20}$$

where S is the maximum level of skill in the population and 0 the lowest, and $f(s)$ is the density function for the skill distribution. The form of this social welfare function permits variations in the degree of concern for equity by changes in ε. Higher values of ε represent greater concern for equity, with $\varepsilon = 0$ representing

Table 15.2
Utilitarian case ($\varepsilon = 0$)

Income	Consumption	Average tax (%)	Marginal tax (%)
0	0.03	—	23
0.05	0.07	−34	26
0.10	0.10	−5	24
0.20	0.18	9	21
0.30	0.26	13	19
0.40	0.34	14	18
0.50	0.43	15	16

Table 15.3
Some equity considerations ($\varepsilon = 1$)

Income	Consumption	Average tax (%)	Marginal tax (%)
0	0.05	—	30
0.05	0.08	−66	34
0.10	0.12	−34	32
0.20	0.19	7	28
0.30	0.26	13	25
0.40	0.34	16	22
0.50	0.41	17	20

the utilitarian case. (This is an alternative specification to that of equation 13.24). The individual utility function is the Cobb-Douglas form

$$U = \log(x) + \log(1 - \ell). \tag{15.21}$$

The skill distribution is lognormal with a standard deviation of 0.39. This value of the standard deviation corresponds approximately to a typical value for the income distribution. If the skill distribution matches the income distribution then this is a value of particular interest.

A selection of the numerical results obtained from this model are given in tables 15.2 and 15.3. In table 15.2, $\varepsilon = 0$, so this is the case of a utilitarian social welfare function. Table 15.3 introduces equity considerations by using $\varepsilon = 1$. In both cases the government revenue requirement is set at 10 percent of national income.

The first fact to be noticed from these results is that the average rate of tax for low-skill consumers is negative. These consumers are receiving an income supplement from the government. This is in the nature of a negative income tax where incomes below a chosen cut-off are supplemented by the government through the tax system. The average rate of tax then increases with skill. The maximum average rate of tax is actually quite small. The value of 34 percent in table 15.3 is not far out of line with the actual rate in many countries.

The behavior of the marginal rate of tax is rather different from that of the average rate. It first rises and then falls. The maximum rate is reached around the median of the skill distribution. Except at the extremes of the skill distribution, there is not actually much variation in the marginal tax rate. To a first approximation, the optimal tax systems reported in these tables have a basically constant marginal rate of tax so that the consumption function is close to being a straight line. This is one of the most surprising conclusions of the analysis of income taxation: the model allows nonconstancy in the marginal tax rate, but this does not feature to a great degree in the optimal solution. Finally the zero tax rate for the highest skill consumer is reflected in the fall of the marginal rate at high skills, but this is not really significant until close to the top of the skill distribution.

These results provide an interesting picture of the optimal income tax function. They suggest that it should subsidize low-skill consumers through a negative income tax but should still face them with a high marginal rate of tax. The maximum marginal rate of tax should not be at the top of the skill distribution but should occur much lower. Generally, the marginal rate should be fairly constant.

15.8   Tax Mix: Separation Principle

As the discussion of chapter 12 showed, tax systems must be based on observable variables. In practice, governments use income and consumption as the basis of taxation, even if they are imperfect measures of individual earning ability. From a lifetime perspective, savings are future consumption, and thus as consumption must equal income, a tax on the value of consumption is equivalent to a tax on income. From this perspective it does not matter whether taxes are levied on income or on the value of consumption.

In the simple models we have used so far in this chapter, we have assumed that there is a single consumption good so the observations above apply. When there are two or more consumption goods, the commodity taxes levied on them need not be uniform. As we showed in chapter 14, when there is no income tax, the commodity taxes should be inversely related to the elasticity of demand for each commodity. We now consider how this conclusion can be modified when income and commodity taxes are employed simultaneously.

The central question is whether there should be differential commodity taxation in combination with a nonlinear income tax. There is a sense in which commodity taxation can usefully supplement income taxation by reducing the distortion in the labor-consumption choice induced by income tax. If we tax commodities that are substitutes for work and subsidize those that are complements, we can encourage people to work more and thus reduce the work-discouraging effect of the income tax. The optimal differentiation depends on how the preferences for some goods vary with labor supply. Turning this argument around, if the preference between commodities does not vary with labor supply, then there seems to be no argument for differential commodity taxes.

Preferences over commodities are independent of labor supply if the utility function is *separable*. What separable means is that utility can be written as $U = U(u(x), \ell)$, where x is a vector of consumption goods, so that the marginal rate of substitution between any pair of consumption goods depends only on $u(x)$ and is independent of labor supply. We now demonstrate that if labor and goods are separable in utility, then there is no need to supplement an optimal nonlinear income tax with differential commodity taxation.

The result that commodity taxation is not needed with separability between labor and goods is easily demonstrated in a model with two skill levels. We assume there are two goods, with the consumption plan of a consumer with skill level i denoted $x_i = (x_1^i, x_2^i)$. We already know that the optimal allocation $\{x_i^*, z_i^*\}$ is constrained by the incentive of high-skill individuals to "disguise" themselves as low-skill. That is, the downward incentive constraint, $U\left(u(x_h^*), \frac{z_h^*}{s_h}\right) \geq U\left(u(x_l^*), \frac{z_l^*}{s_h}\right)$, is binding at the optimum. Because it requires less work for a high-skill individual to earn the income z_l^* of a low-skill individual, then $\ell_h = \frac{z_l^*}{s_h} < \ell_l = \frac{z_l^*}{s_l}$. The only difference between the two types at any given level of income arises from this difference in labor supplies. This feeds into a utility difference, $U(u(x_l^*), \ell_l) \neq U(u(x_l^*), \ell_h)$, when the high-skill mimic the low-skill. With separable preferences, such a difference does not affect the indifference curves between commodities (since $u(x_l^*)$ is the same for both types), so we cannot use differential taxation to separate the types (i.e., to make the consumption bundle of the low-skill individual less attractive to high-skill individual). The fact that differential taxes do not help in relaxing the incentive constraint renders their use unnecessary.

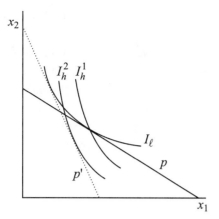

Figure 15.13
Differential taxation and nonseparability

With a nonseparable utility function, $U(x, \ell)$, the indifference curves between commodities differ and the good that the high-skill person values more in the consumption bundle of the low-skill can be taxed more heavily. This reduces the incentive for the high-skill to mimic the low-skill. Figure 15.13 illustrates how differential commodity taxation (changing prices from p to p') can be used to make the consumption bundle of the low-skill type less attractive for the high-skill type. The change in prices from the budget constraint labeled p to the budget constraint labeled p' does not affect the utility of the low-skill (the budget constraint pivots around their indifference curve I_ℓ), but it causes a reduction in utility of the high-skill (shown by the new budget constraint changing the location of the choice from initial indifference curve I_h^1 to the lower indifference curve I_h^2). This reduction in utility for the high-skill type relaxes the incentive constraint, which in turn expands the set of allocations attainable.

15.9   Voting over a Flat Tax

Having identified the properties of the optimal tax structure, we now consider the tax system that emerges from the political process. To do this, we consider people voting over tax schedules that have some degree of redistribution. Because it is difficult to model voting on nonlinear tax schemes given the high dimensionality of the problem, we will restrict attention to a linear tax structure as originally proposed by Romer (1975). We specify the model further with quasi-linear preferences to avoid unnecessary complications and to simplify the analysis of the voting equilibrium.

Assume, as before, that individuals differ only in their level of skill. We assume that skills are distributed in the population according to a cumulative distribution function $F(s)$ that is known to everyone, with mean skill $\bar{s}$ and median s_m. Individuals work and consume. They also vote on a linear tax scheme that pays a lump-sum benefit b to each individual financed by a proportional income tax at rate t. The individual utility function has the quasi-linear form

$$u\left(x, \frac{z}{s}\right) = x - \frac{1}{2}\left[\frac{z}{s}\right]^2,$$ (15.22)

and the individual budget constraint is

$$x = [1 - t]z + b.$$ (15.23)

It is easy to verify that in this simple model the optimal income choice of a consumer with skill level s is

$$z(s) = [1 - t]s^2.$$ (15.24)

The quasi-linear preferences imply that there is no income effect on labor supply (i.e., $z(s)$ is independent of the lump-sum benefit b). This simplifies the expression of the tax distortion and makes the analysis of the voting equilibrium easier. Less surprisingly a higher tax rate induces taxpayers to work less and earn less income.

The lump-sum transfer b is constrained by the government budget balance condition

$$b = tE(z(s)) = t[1 - t]E(s^2),$$ (15.25)

where $E(\cdot)$ is the mathematical expectation, and we used the optimal income choice to derive the second equality. This constraint says that the lump-sum benefit paid to each individual must be equal to the expected tax payment $tE(z(s))$. This expression is termed the *Dupuit-Laffer curve* and describes tax revenue as a function of the tax rate. In this simple model the Dupuit-Laffer curve is bell-shaped with a peak at $t = \frac{1}{2}$ and no tax collected at the ends $t = 0$ and $t = 1$. We can now derive individual preferences over tax schedules by substituting (15.23) and (15.24) into (15.22). After re-arrangement (indirect) utility can be written

$$v(t, b, s) = b + \frac{1}{2}[1 - t]^2 s^2.$$ (15.26)

Taking the total differential of (15.26) gives

$$dv = db - [1 - t]s^2 \, dt \tag{15.27}$$

so that along an indifference curve where $dv = 0$,

$$\frac{db}{dt} = [1 - t]s^2. \tag{15.28}$$

It can be seen from this that for given t, the indifference curve becomes steeper in (t, b) space as s increases. This monotonicity is a consequence of the single-crossing property of the indifference curves. As we saw in chapter 10, the single-crossing property is a sufficient condition for the Median Voter Theorem to apply. It follows that there is only one tax policy that can result from majority voting: it is the policy preferred by the median voter (half the voters are poorer than the median and prefer higher tax rates, and the other half are richer and prefer lower tax rates). Letting t_m be the tax rate preferred by the median voter, then we have t_m implicitly defined by the solution to the first-order condition for maximizing the median voter's utility. We differentiate (15.26) with respect to t, taking into account the government budget constraint (15.25) to obtain

$$\frac{\partial v}{\partial t} = [1 - 2t]E(s^2) - [1 - t]s^2. \tag{15.29}$$

Setting this expression equal to zero for the median skill level s_m yields the tax rate preferred by the median voter

$$t_m = \frac{E(s^2) - s_m^2}{2E(s^2) - s_m^2}, \tag{15.30}$$

or, using the optimal income choice (15.24),

$$t_m = \frac{E(z) - z_m}{2E(z) - z_m}. \tag{15.31}$$

This simple model predicts that the political equilibrium tax rate is determined by the position of the median voter in the income distribution. The greater is income inequality as measured by the distance between median and mean income, the higher the tax rate. If the median voter is relatively worse off, with income well below the mean income, then equilibrium redistribution is large. In practice, the income distribution has a median income below the mean income, so a majority of voters would favor redistribution through proportional income taxation. More general utility functions would also predict that the extent of this redistribution decreases with the elasticity of labor supply.

15.10   Conclusions

This chapter introduced the issues surrounding the design of the income tax structure. It was first shown how income and substitution effects left the theoretical impact of a tax increase on labor supply indeterminate. If the income effect is sufficiently strong, it is possible for a tax increase to lead to more labor being supplied. The participation decision was also discussed, and it was argued that taxation could be significant in affecting this choice.

This lack of theoretical predictions places great emphasis on empirical research for determining the actual effects of taxation. The labor-supply responses of different groups in the population to tax changes were discussed. The observations made were borne out by the empirical results that showed a very small or negative elasticity of supply for married men but a much large positive elasticity for unmarried women. The latter can be interpreted as a reflection of the participation decision.

A model that was able to incorporate the important issues of efficiency and equity in income taxation was then introduced. A number of results were derived capturing general features of the optimal tax system. Most notably, the marginal rate of tax facing the highest skill person should be zero and the optimal tax rate is bounded between zero and one. This model was then specialized to quasi-linear utility and to a Rawlsian social welfare function and some further insights obtained. Numerical simulation results were given that showed that the marginal rate of tax should remain fairly constant while the average rate of tax should be negative for low-skill consumers. Finally the political economy of taxation was presented by means of a simple model of voting over linear income tax schedules.

Further Reading

For a comprehensive survey of recent income tax policy in the United States see:

Pechman, J. E. 1987. *Federal State Policy*, 5th ed. Washington: Brookings Institution.

The economics of taxation and labor supply are surveyed in:

Blundell, R. 1992. Labour supply and taxation: A survey. *Fiscal Studies* 13: 15–40.

Feldstein, M. 1995. The effect of marginal tax rates on taxable income: A panel study of the 1986 tax reform act. *Journal of Political Economy* 103: 551–72.

The initial analysis of the problem of nonlinear income taxation was given in:

Mirrlees, J. A. 1971. An exploration in the theory of optimum income tax. *Review of Economic Studies* 38: 175–208.

Be warned, the analytical parts of this paper are exceptionally complex. Even so, the numerical simulation is easily understood.

Further numerical simulations are discussed in:

Kanbur, S. M. R., and Tuomala, M. 1994. Inherent inequality and the optimal graduation of marginal tax rates. *Scandinavian Journal of Economics* 96: 275–82.

Tuomala, M. 1990. *Optimal Income Tax and Redistribution*. Oxford: Clarendon Press.

The zero marginal tax rate at the top was first presented in:

Seade, J. K. 1977. On the shape of optimal tax schedules. *Journal of Public Economics* 7: 203–35.

The properties of the quasi-linear model are explored in:

Weymark, J. A. 1986. A reduced-form optimal income tax problem. *Journal of Public Economics* 30: 199–217.

An alternative form of quasi-linearity is used to discuss potential patterns of marginal tax rates in:

Diamond, P. A. 1998. Optimal income taxation: An example with a U-shaped pattern of optimal marginal tax rates. *American Economic Review* 88: 83–95.

Further analysis of the pattern of marginal rates of tax is given in:

Myles, G. D. 2000. On the optimal marginal rate of income tax. *Economics Letters* 66: 113–19.

Saez, E. 2001. Using elasticities to derive optimal tax rates. *Review of Economic Studies* 68: 205–29.

The role of indirect taxation in supplementing the income tax is in:

Atkinson, A. B., and Stiglitz, J. E. 1976. The design of the tax structure: Direct versus indirect taxation. *Journal of Public Economics* 6: 55–75.

Christiansen, V. 1984. Which commodity taxes should supplement the income tax? *Journal of Public Economics* 24: 195–220.

Cremer, H., Pestieau, P., and Rochet, J.-C. 2001. Direct versus indirect taxation: The design of the tax structure revisited. *International Economic Review* 42: 781–800.

Voting over linear income tax was originally developed in:

Roberts, K. 1977. Voting over income tax schedules. *Journal of Public Economics* 8: 329–40.

Romer, T. 1975. Individual welfare, majority voting and the properties of a linear income tax. *Journal of Public Economics* 7: 163–68.

Voting over a nonlinear income tax schedule is in:

Hindriks, J. 2001. Is there a demand for income tax progressivity? *Economics Letters* 73: 43–50.

Marhuenda, F., and Ortuno-Ortin, I. 1995. Popular support for progressive taxation. *Economics Letters* 48: 319–24.

Snyder, J., and Kramer, G. 1988. Fairness, self-interest and the politics of the progressive income tax. *Journal of Public Economics* 36: 197–230.

A comprehensive and more advanced presentation of the optimal taxation theory is:

Salanié, B. 2003. *Economics of Taxation*. Cambridge: MIT Press.

A bargaining approach to the income tax problem is in:

Aumann, R. J., and Kurz, M. 1977. Power and taxes. *Econometrica* 45: 1137–61.

For the relationship between existing income tax systems and the equal sacrifice principle see:

Young, H. P. 1990. Progressive taxation and equal sacrifice. *American Economic Review* 80: 2531–66.

Exercises

15.1. Consider the budget constraint $x = b + [1 - t]w\ell$. Provide an interpretation of b. How does the average rate of tax change with income? Let utility be given by $U = x - \ell^2$. How is the choice of ℓ affected by increases in b and t? Explain these effects.

15.2. Assume that a consumer has preferences over consumption and leisure described by $U = x[1 - \ell]$, where x is consumption and ℓ is labor. For a given wage rate w, which leads to a higher labor supply: an income tax at constant rate t or a lump-sum tax T that raises the same revenue as the income tax?

15.3. Let the utility function be $U = \log(x) - \ell$. Find the level of labor supply if the wage rate, w, is equal to 10. What is the effect of the introduction of an overtime premium that raises w to 12 for hours in excess of that worked at the wage of 10?

15.4. Assume that utility is $U = \log(x) + \log(1 - \ell)$. Calculate the labor supply function. Explain the form of this function by calculating the income and substitution effects of a wage increase.

15.5. (Stern 1976) The utility function of a consumer has the constant elasticity of substitution form

$$U = [\alpha[L - \ell]^{-\mu} + [1 - \alpha]x^{-\mu}]^{-1/\mu}.$$

Let the budget constraint be $x = b + w\ell$, where $b \geq 0$ is a lump-sum grant received from the government.

a. Show that the first-order condition for utility maximization can be written as

$$\left[\frac{[L - \ell]}{b + w\ell}\right]^{\mu+1} = \frac{\alpha}{[1 - \alpha]w}.$$

b. Totally differentiate the first-order condition to find $d\ell/dw$. Under what conditions is this negative?

15.6.   Show that a tax function is average-rate progressive (the average rate of tax rises with income) if $MRT > ART$.

15.7.   Which is better: a uniform tax on consumption or a uniform tax on income?

15.8.   Consider the utility function $U = x - \ell^2$.

a. For $U = 10$, plot the indifference curve with ℓ on the horizontal axis and x on the vertical axis.

b. Now define $z = s\ell$. For $s = 0.5$, 1, and 2 plot the indifference curves for $U = 10$ with z on the horizontal axis and x on the vertical.

c. Plot the indifference curves for $s = 0.5$, 1, and 2 through the point $x = 20$, $z = 2$.

d. Prove that at any point (x, z) the indifference curve of a high-skill consumer is flatter than that of a low-skill.

15.9.   Consider an economy with two consumers who have skill levels $s_1 = 1$ and $s_2 = 2$ and utility function $U = 10x^{1/2} - \ell^2$. Let the government employ an income tax function that leads to the allocation $x = 4$, $z = 5$ for the consumer of skill $s = 1$ and $x = 9$, $z = 8$ for the consumer of skill $s = 2$.

a. Show that this allocation satisfies the incentive compatibility constraint that each consumer must prefer his allocation to that of the other.

b. Keeping incomes fixed, consider a transfer of 0.01 units of consumption from the high-skill to the low-skill consumer.

i. Calculate the effect on each consumer's utility.

ii. Show that the sum of utilities increases.

iii. Show that the incentive compatibility constraint is still satisfied.

iv. Use parts i through iii to prove that the initial allocation is not optimal for a utilitarian social welfare function.

15.10.   For the utility function $U = x - \ell^2$ and two consumers of skill levels s_1 and s_2, $s_2 > s_1$, show that the incentive compatibility constraints imply that the income and consumption levels of the high-skill consumer cannot be lower than those of the low-skill consumer.

15.11.   Assume that skill is uniformly distributed between 0 and 1 and that total population size is normalized at 1. If utility is given by $U = \log(x) \log(1 - \ell)$ and the budget constraint is $x = b + (1 - t)s\ell$, find the optimal values of b and t when zero revenue is to be raised. Is the optimal tax system progressive?

15.12.   Consider the tax function $T(z) = az + bz^2 - c$, with consumption given by $x = z - az + bz^2 + c$.

a. For a consumer of skill s, find the level of income that maximizes $U = x - \ell^2$. (*Hint*: Substitute for x using the above and for ℓ using $z = s\ell$.)

b. Hence calculate labor supply and describe its relation to s.

c. Show that at income level z, the marginal rate of tax is $a + 2bx$.

d. Substitute the answer from part b into the expression for the marginal rate of tax and calculate the limiting marginal tax rate as $z \to \infty$.

e. Use the answer to part d to show that the tax function is not optimal.

15.13. Consider an economy with two consumers of skill levels s_1 and s_2, $s_2 > s_1$. Denote the allocation to the low-skill consumer by x_1, z_1 and that to the high-skill consumer by x_2, z_2.

a. For the utility function $U = u(x) - \frac{z}{s}$ show that incentive compatibility requires that $z_2 = z_1 + [u(x_2) - u(x_1)]$.

b. For the utilitarian social welfare function

$$W = u(x_1) - \frac{z_1}{s_1} + u(x_2) - \frac{z_2}{s_2},$$

express W as a function of x_1 and x_2 alone.

c. Assuming $u(x_h) = \log(x_h)$, derive the optimal values of x_1 and x_2 and hence of z_1 and z_2.

d. Calculate the marginal rate of substitution for the two consumers at the optimal allocation. Comment on your results.

15.14. How is the analysis of section 15.6.1 modified if $s_2 > 3s_1$? (*Hint:* Think about what must happen to the before-tax income of consumer 1.)

15.15. Suppose two types of consumers with skill levels 10 and 20. There is an equal number of consumers of both types. If the social welfare function is utilitarian and no revenue is to be raised, find the optimal allocation under a nonlinear income tax for the utility function $U = \log(x) - \ell$. Contrast this to the optimal allocation if skill was publicly observable.

15.16. Tax revenue is given by $R(t) = tB(t)$, where $t \in [0,1]$ is the tax rate and $B(t)$ is the tax base. Suppose that the tax elasticity of the tax base is $\varepsilon = -\frac{\gamma t}{1-\gamma t}$ with $\gamma \in \left[\frac{1}{2}, 1\right]$.

a. What is the revenue-maximizing tax rate?

b. Graph tax revenue as a function of the tax rate both for $\gamma = \frac{1}{2}$ and $\gamma = 1$. Discuss the implications of this Dupuit-Laffer curve.

15.17. Consider an economy populated by a large number of workers with utility function $U = x^\alpha [1 - \ell]^{1-\alpha}$, where x is disposable income, ℓ is the fraction of time worked ($0 \le \ell \le 1$), and α is a preference parameter (with $0 < \alpha < 1$). Each worker's disposable income depends on his fixed "skill" as represented by wage w and a tax-transfer scheme (t, B) such that $x = B + [1 - t]w\ell$, where $t \in (0,1)$ is the marginal tax rate and $B > 0$ is the unconditional benefit payment.

a. Find the optimal labor supply for someone with ability w. Will the high-skill person work more than the low-skill person? Will the high-skill person have higher disposable income than the low-skill person? Show that the condition for job market participation is $w > \frac{[[1-\alpha]/\alpha]B}{1-t}$.

b. If tax proceeds are only used to finance the benefit B, what is the government's budget constraint?

c. Suppose that the mean skill in the population is $\bar{w}$ and that the lowest skill is a fraction $\gamma < 1$ of the mean skill. If the government wants to redistribute all tax proceeds to finance the cash benefit B, what condition should the tax-transfer scheme (t, B) satisfy?

d. Find the optimal tax rate if the government seeks to maximize the disposable income of the lowest skill worker subject to everyone working.

15.18. Under the negative income tax all individuals are guaranteed a minimum standard of living by being awarded a grant, and the grant is reduced as their earnings rise (though by less than one for one). Alternatively, under wage subsidies, for each dollar of earnings up to some level, the government pays each person a refundable tax credit for each dollar earned up to some level. This tax credit is then phased out after reaching a maximum, so the credit goes to zero for middle-income taxpayers.

a. Compare the work incentives of the wage subsidy and the negative income tax for the entire income distribution. Use a diagram and explain.

b. Assume that the poverty line is fixed at $20,000. Design a negative income tax to combat poverty by choosing a basic grant level and an implicit tax rate at which this grant is reduced as incomes rise. What are the trade-offs involved in setting grant level and tax rate? What are the efficiency and equity effects of choosing different grant levels and tax rates? How will the program affect people with different incomes?

c. Now consider the possibility of using categorical welfare grants. Under categorical welfare grants all individuals possessing certain characteristics are guaranteed a minimum standard of living, and the grant is taken away one for one as income rises. How should the government choose the right categories for targeting grants to some welfare groups?

d. What are the advantages and disadvantages of categorical grants relative to negative income tax?

15.19. Consider a single mother with the utility function $U = \frac{2}{3}\log(x) + \frac{1}{3}\log(l)$, where x is consumption and l is leisure. The mother can work up to 100 hours per month. Any of the 100 hours that are not worked are leisure hours. She earns a wage of $10 per hour and pays no taxes. The consumption price is normalized to $1. To be able to work, she has to incur a child care cost of $5 for every hour worked.

a. Suppose that there is no tax and welfare benefits. How many hours will she work and what will be her consumption level? Draw the graph depicting her budget set with consumption on the vertical axis and leisure on the horizontal axis.

b. Suppose that the government introduces a negative income tax (NIT) that guarantees an income of $200 per month. The benefit is taken away one for one as earnings increase. Draw the new budget set. Compute the new number of hours worked and consumption level. Has consumption increased and is the mother better off? Why or why not?

c. Now suppose the income guarantee is reduced by one-half to the amount of $100 per month. What is the new number of hours worked and the consumption level? Compare with your result in part b.

d. Now consider again the income guarantee in part b of $200 per month, and suppose that the government complements this benefit by offering free child care. Draw the new budget set and calculate the number of hours worked and consumption level. Calculate the total cost of the program for the government. How does it compare with the program in part b? Define program efficiency as the ratio of the mother's consumption to government expenditure. Which program dominates on efficiency grounds?

15.20. (Stern 1976) The numerical analysis of income taxation has often assumed that the skill distribution is identical to the income distribution. This need not be the case. Assume that the utility function is defined as

$$U(x, \ell) = \begin{cases} 1 - \ell & \text{if } x \geq \bar{x}, \\ -\infty & \text{otherwise.} \end{cases}$$

a. Provide an interpretation of this utility function.

b. Assume that the skill level of all consumers is strictly positive. What will be the observed distribution of income?

c. Will this distribution be identical to the skill distribution?

d. Comment on the practice of assuming that the income and skill distributions are identical.

16   Tax Evasion

16.1   Introduction

It is not unusual to be offered a discount for payment in cash. This is almost routine in the employment of the services of builders, plumbers, and decorators. It is less frequent, but still occurs, when major purchases are made in shops. While the expense of banking checks and the commissions charged by credit card companies may explain some of these discounts, the usual explanation is that payment in cash makes concealment of the transaction much easier. Income that can be concealed need not be declared to the tax authorities.

The same motivation can be provided for exaggeration in claims for expenses. By converting income into expenses that are either exempt from tax or deductible from tax, the total tax bill can be reduced. Second jobs are also a lucrative source of income that can be concealed from the tax authorities. A tax return that reports no income, or at least a very low level, is likely to attract more attention than one that declares earnings from primary employment but fails to mention income from secondary employment.

In contrast to these observations on tax evasion, the analysis of taxation in the previous chapters assumed that firms and consumers reported their taxable activities honestly. Although acceptable for providing simplified insights into the underlying issues, this assumption is patently unacceptable when confronted with reality. The purpose of this chapter can be seen as the introduction of practical constraints on the free choice of tax policy. Tax evasion, the intentional failure to declare taxable economic activity, is pervasive in many economies as the evidence given in the following section makes clear and is therefore a subject of practical as well as theoretical interest.

The chapter begins by considering how tax evasion can be measured. Evidence on the extent of tax evasion in a range of countries is reviewed. The chapter then proceeds to try to understand the factors involved in the decision to evade tax. Initially this decision is represented as a choice under uncertainty. The analysis predicts the relationship among the level of evasion, tax rates, and punishments. Within this framework the optimal degree of auditing and of punishment is considered. Evidence that can be used to assess the model's predictions is then discussed. In the light of this, some extensions of the basic model are considered. A game-theoretic approach to tax compliance is presented where taxpayers and governments interact strategically. The last section emphasizes the importance of social interaction on compliance decisions.

16.2   The Extent of Evasion

Tax evasion is illegal, so those engaging in it have every reason to seek to conceal what they are doing. This introduces a fundamental difficulty into the measurement of tax evasion. Even so, the fact that the estimates that are available show evasion to constitute a significant part of total economic activity underlines the importance of measurement. The lost revenue due to tax evasion also emphasizes the value of developing a theory of evasion that can be used to design a tax structure that minimizes evasion and ensures that policy is optimal given that evasion occurs.

Before proceeding, it is worth making some distinctions. First, *tax evasion* is the failure to declare taxable activity. Tax evasion should be distinguished from *tax avoidance*, which is the reorganization of economic activity, possibly at some cost, to lower tax payment. Tax avoidance is legal, whereas tax evasion is not. In practice, the distinction is not as clear-cut, since tax avoidance schemes frequently need to be tested in court to clarify their legality. Second, the terms *black*, *shadow*, or *hidden economy* refer to all economic activities for which payments are made but are not officially declared. Under these headings would be included illegal activities, such as the drug trade, and unmeasured activity, such as agricultural output by smallholders. Added to these would also be the legal, but undeclared, income that constitutes tax evasion. Finally the *unmeasured* economy would be the shadow economy plus activities such as do-it-yourself jobs that are economically valuable but do not involve economic transaction.

This discussion reveals that there are several issues concerning how economic activity should be divided between the regular economy and the shadow economy. For instance, most systems of national accounts do not include criminal activity (Italy, however, does make some adjustment for smuggling). In principle, the UN System of National Accounts includes both legal and illegal activities, and it has been suggested that criminal activity should be made explicit when the system is revised. Although this chapter is primarily about tax evasion, when an attempt is made at the measurement of tax evasion, the figures obtained may also include some or all of the components of the shadow economy.

The essential problem involved in the measurement of tax evasion is that its illegality provides an incentive for individuals to keep the activity hidden. Furthermore, by its very nature, tax evasion does not appear in any official statistics. This implies that the extent of tax evasion cannot be measured directly but must be inferred from economic variables that can be observed.

A first method for measuring tax evasion is to use survey evidence. This can be employed either directly or indirectly as an input into an estimation procedure. The obvious difficulty with survey evidence is that respondents who are active in the hidden economy have every incentive to conceal the truth. There are two ways in which the problem of concealment can be circumvented. First, information collected for purposes other than the measurement of tax evasion can be employed. One example of this is the use that has been made of data from the Family Expenditure Survey in the United Kingdom. This survey involves consumers recording their incomes and expenditures in a diary. Participants have no reason to falsely record information. The relation between income and expenditure can be derived from the respondents whose entire income is obtained in employment that cannot escape tax. The expenditures recorded can then be used to infer the income of those who do have an opportunity to evade. Although these records are not surveys in the normal sense, studies of taxpayer compliance conducted by revenue collection agencies, such as the Internal Revenue Service in the United States, can be treated as survey evidence and have some claim to accuracy.

The second general method is to infer the extent of tax evasion, or the hidden economy generally, from the observation of another economic variable. This is done by determining total economic activity and then subtracting measured activity, which gives the hidden economy. The *direct input* approach observes the use of an input to production and from this predicts what output must be. An input that is often used for this purpose is electricity, since this is universally employed and accurate statistics are kept on energy consumption. The *monetary* approach employs the demand for cash to infer the size of the hidden economy on the basis that transactions in the hidden economy are financed by cash rather than checks or credit cards. Given a relationship between the quantity of cash and the level of economic activity, this allows estimation of the hidden economy. What distinguishes alternative studies that fall under the heading of monetary approaches is the method used to derive the total level of economic activity from the observed use of cash. One way to do this is to assume that there was a base year in which the hidden economy did not exist. The ratio of cash to total activity is then fixed by that year. This ratio allows observed cash use in other years to be compounded up into total activity. An alternative has been to look at the actual use of banknotes. The issuing authorities know the expected lifespan of a note (i.e., how

Table 16.1
Hidden economy as percentage of GDP, average over 1990 to 1993

Developing	Transition	OECD
Egypt 68–76%	Georgia 28–43%	Italy 24–30%
Thailand 70%	Ukraine 28–43%	Spain 24–30%
Mexico 40–60%	Hungary 20–28%	Denmark 13–23%
Malaysia 38–50%	Russia 20–27%	France 13–23%
Tunisia 39–45%	Latvia 20–27%	Japan 8–10%
Singapore 13%	Slovakia 9–16%	Austria 8–10%

Source: Schneider and Enste (2000).

many transactions it can finance). Multiplying the number of notes used by the number of transactions gives the total value of activity financed.

Table 16.1 presents estimates of the size of the hidden economy for a range of countries. These figures are based on a combination of the direct input (actually use of electricity as a proxy for output) and money demand approaches. Further details can be found in the source reference. The table clearly indicates that the hidden economy is a significant issue, especially in the developing and transition economies. Even for Japan and Austria, which have the smallest estimated size of hidden economy, the percentage figure is still significant.

As already noted, these estimates are subject to error and must be treated with a degree of caution. Having said this, there is a degree of consistency running through them. They indicate that a value for the hidden economy of at least 10 percent is not an unreasonable approximation. Therefore the undeclared economic activity is substantial relative to total economic activity. Tax evasion is clearly an important phenomenon that merits extensive investigation.

16.3   The Evasion Decision

The estimates of the hidden economy have revealed that tax evasion is a significant part of overall economic activity. We now turn to modeling the decision to evade in order to understand how the decision is made and the factors that can affect that decision.

The simplest model of the evasion decision considers it to be just a gamble. If taxpayers declare less than their true income (or overstate deductions), there is a chance that they may do so without being detected. This leads to a clear benefit over making an honest declaration. However, there is also a chance that they may be caught. When they are, a punishment is inflicted (usually a fine but sometimes imprisonment) and they are worse off than if they had been honest. In deciding how much to evade, the taxpayer has to weigh up these gains and losses, taking account of the chance of being caught and the level of the punishment.

A simple formal statement of this decision problem can be given as follows: Let the taxpayer have an income level Y, which they know but is not known to the tax collector. The income declared by the taxpayer, X, is taxed at a constant rate t. The amount of unreported income is $Y - X \geq 0$ and the unpaid tax is $t[Y - X]$. If the taxpayer evades without being caught, their income is given by $Y^{nc} = Y - tX$. When the taxpayer is caught evading, all income is taxed and a fine at rate F is levied on the tax that has been evaded. This gives an income level $Y^c = [1 - t]Y - Ft[Y - X]$. If income is understated, the probability of being caught is p.

Assume that the taxpayer derives utility $U(Y)$ from an income Y. After making declaration X, the income level Y^c occurs with probability p and the income level Y^{nc} with probability $1 - p$. In the face of such uncertainty the taxpayer should choose the income declaration to maximize expected utility. Combining these facts, the declaration X solves

$$\max_{\{X\}} E[U(X)] = [1 - p]U(Y^{nc}) + pU(Y^c). \tag{16.1}$$

The solution to this choice problem can be derived graphically. To do this, observe that there are two states of the world. In one state of the world, taxpayers are not caught evading and have income Y^{nc}. In the other state of the world, they are caught and have income Y^c. The expected utility function describes preferences over income levels in these two states. The choice of a declaration X determines an income level in each state, and by varying X, the taxpayer can trade off income between the two states. A high value of X provides relatively more income in the state where the taxpayer is caught evading and a low value of X relatively more where they are not caught.

The details of this trade-off can be identified by considering the two extreme values of X. When the maximum declaration is made so that $X = Y$, the taxpayer's income will be $[1 - t]Y$ in both states of the world. Alternatively, when the minimum declaration of $X = 0$ is made, income will be $[1 - t(1 + F)]Y$ if caught and Y if not. These two points are illustrated in figure 16.1, which graphs income when not caught against income when caught. The other options available

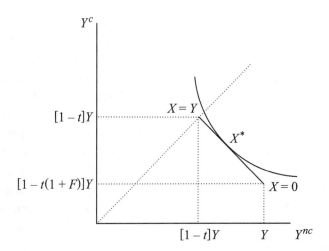

Figure 16.1
Interior choice: $0 < X^* < Y$

to the consumer lie on the line joining $X = 0$ and $X = Y$; this is the opportunity set showing the achievable allocations of income between the two states. From the utility function can be derived a set of indifference curves—the points on an indifference curve being income levels in the two states that give the same level of expected utility. Including the indifference curves of the utility function completes the diagram and allows the taxpayer's choice to be depicted. The taxpayer whose preferences are shown in figure 16.1 chooses to locate at the point with declaration X^*. This is an interior point with $0 < X^* < Y$—some tax is evaded but some income is declared.

Besides the interior location of figure 16.1 it is possible for corner solutions to arise. The consumer whose preferences are shown in figure 16.2a chooses to declare his entire income, so $X^* = Y$. In contrast the consumer in figure 16.2b declares no income, so $X^* = 0$.

The interesting question is what condition guarantees that evasion will occur rather than the no-evasion corner solution with $X = Y$. Comparing the figures it can be seen that evasion will occur if the indifference curve is steeper than the budget constraint where it crosses the dashed 45° line. The condition that ensures that this occurs is easily derived. Totally differentiating the expected utility function (16.1) at a constant level of utility gives the slope of the indifference curve as

$$\frac{dY^c}{dY^{nc}} = -\frac{[1-p]U'(Y^{nc})}{pU'(Y^c)}, \tag{16.2}$$

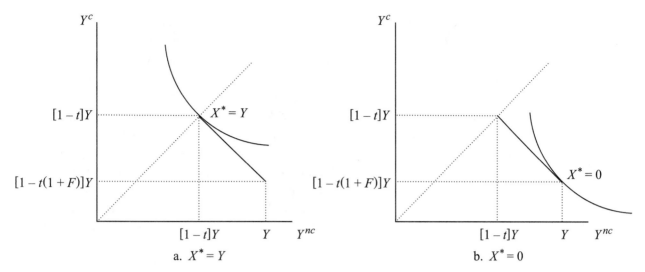

Figure 16.2
Corner solutions

where $U'(Y)$ is the marginal utility of income level Y. On the 45° line $Y^{nc} = Y^c$, so the marginal utility of income is the same whether or not the tax evader is caught. This implies that

$$\text{Slope of indifference curve} = -\frac{1-p}{p}. \tag{16.3}$$

What this expression suggests is that all the indifference curves have the same slope, $-\frac{1-p}{p}$, where they cross the 45° line. The slope of the budget constraint is seen in figure 16.1 to be given by the ratio of the penalty $Ft[Y - X]$ to the unpaid tax $t[Y - X]$. Thus

$$\text{Slope of budget constraint} = -F \tag{16.4}$$

Because of these features the indifference curve is steeper than the budget constraint on the 45° line if $\frac{1-p}{p} > F$, or

$$p < \frac{1}{1+F}. \tag{16.5}$$

This result shows that evasion will arise if the probability of detection is too small relative to the fine rate.

Several points can be made about this condition for evasion. First, this is a trigger condition that determines whether or not evasion will arise, but it does not say anything about the extent of evasion. Second, the condition is dependent only on the fine rate and the probability of detection, so it applies for all taxpayers regardless of their utility-of-income function $U(Y)$. Consequently if one taxpayer chooses to evade, all taxpayers should evade. Third, this condition can be given some practical evaluation. Typical punishments inflicted for tax evasion suggest that an acceptable magnitude for F is between 0.5 and 1. In the United Kingdom the Taxes Management Act specifies the maximum fine as 100 percent of the tax lost, which implies the maximum value of $F = 1$. This makes the ratio $\frac{1}{1+F}$ greater or equal to $\frac{1}{2}$. Information on p is hard to obtain, but a figure between 1 in a 100 or 1 in a 1,000 evaders being caught is probably a fair estimate. Therefore $p < \frac{1}{2} < \frac{1}{1+F}$ and the conclusion is reached that the model predicts all taxpayers should be evading. In the United States, taxpayers who understate their tax liabilities may be subjected to penalties at a rate between 20 to 75 percent of the under-reported taxes, depending on the gravity of the offence. The proportion of all individual tax returns that are audited was 1.7 percent in 1997. This is clearly not large enough to deter cheating, and everyone should be underreporting taxes. In fact the Taxpayer Compliance Measurement Program reveals that 40 percent of US taxpayers underpaid their taxes. This is a sizable minority but not as widespread evasion as the theoretical model would predict. So taxpayers appears to be more honest than might be expected.

The next step is to determine how the amount of tax evasion is affected by changes in the model's variables. There are four such variables that are of interest: the income level Y, the tax rate t, the probability of detection p, and the fine rate F. These effects can be explored by using the figure depicting the choice of evasion level.

Take the probability of detection first. The probability of detection does not affect the opportunity set but does affect preferences. The effect of an increase in p is to make the indifference curves flatter where they cross the 45° line. As shown in figure 16.3, this moves the optimal choice closer to the point $X = Y$ of honest declaration. The amount of income declared rises, so an increase in the probability of detection reduces the level of evasion. This is a clearly expected result, since an increase in the likelihood of detection lowers the payoff from evading and makes evasion a less attractive proposition.

A change in the fine rate only affects income when the taxpayer is caught evading. The consequence of an increase in F is that the budget constraint pivots round the honest report point and becomes steeper. Since the indifference curve is unaffected by the penalty change, the optimal choice must again move closer to

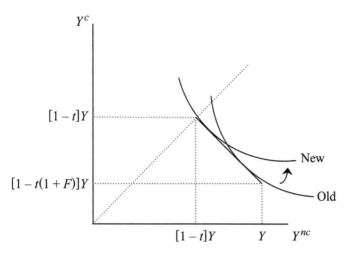

Figure 16.3
Increase in detection probability

the honest declaration point. This is shown in figure 16.4 by the move from the initial choice of X^{old} when the fine rate is F to the choice X^{new} when the fine rate increases to $\hat{F}$. An increase in the fine rate therefore leads to a reduction in the level of tax evasion. This, and the previous result, shows that the effects of the detection and punishment variables on the level of evasion are unambiguous.

Now consider the effect of an increase in income from the initial level Y to a higher level $\hat{Y}$. This income increase causes the budget constraint to move outward. As already noted the slope of the budget constraint is equal to $-F$, which does not change with income, so the shift is a parallel one. The optimal choice then moves from X^{old} to X^{new} in figure 16.5. How the evasion decision is affected depends on the degree of absolute risk aversion, $R_A(Y) = -\frac{U''(Y)}{U'(Y)}$, of the utility function. What absolute risk aversion measures is the willingness to engage in small bets of fixed size. If $R_A(Y)$ is constant as Y changes, the optimal choices will be on a locus parallel to the 45° line. There is evidence, though, that in practice, $R_A(Y)$ decreases as income increases, so wealthier individuals are more prone to engage in small bets, in the sense that the odds demanded to participate diminish. This causes the locus of choices to bend away from the 45° line, so that the amount of undeclared income rises as actual income increases. This is the outcome shown in figure 16.5. Hence, with decreasing absolute risk aversion, an increase in income increases tax evasion.

The final variable to consider is the tax rate. An increase in the tax rate from t to $\hat{t}$ moves the budget constraint inwards. As can be seen in figure 16.6 the

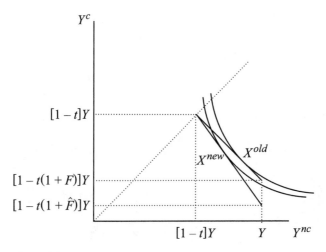

Figure 16.4
Increase in the fine rate

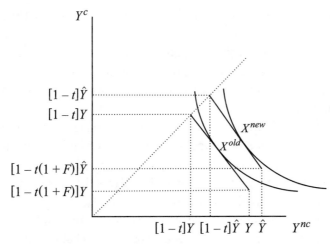

Figure 16.5
Income increase

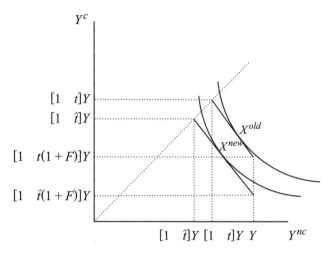

Figure 16.6
Tax rate increase

outcome is not clear-cut. However, when absolute risk aversion is decreasing, the effect of the tax increase is to reduce tax evasion. This final result has received much discussion because it is counter to what seems reasonable. A high tax rate is normally seen as providing a motive for tax evasion, whereas the model predicts precisely the converse. Why the result emerges is because the fine paid by the consumer is determined by t times F. An increase in the tax rate thus has the effect of raising the penalty. This takes income away from the taxpayer when they are caught—the state in which they have least income. It is through this mechanism that a higher tax rate can reduce evasion.

This completes the analysis of the basic model of tax evasion. It has been shown how the level of evasion is determined and how this is affected by the parameters of the model. The next section turn to the issue of determining the optimal levels of auditing and punishment when the behavior of taxpayers corresponds to the predictions of this model. Some empirical and experimental evidence is then considered and used to assess the predictions of the model.

16.4   Auditing and Punishment

The analysis of the tax evasion decision assumed that the probability of detection and the rate of the fine levied when caught evading were fixed. This is a satisfactory assumption from the perspective of the individual taxpayer. From the government's perspective, though, these are variables that can be chosen. The probability of detection can be raised by the employment of additional tax inspectors, and the fine can be legislated or set by the courts. The purpose of this section is to analyze the issues involved in the government's decision.

It has already been shown that an increase in either p or F will reduce the amount of undeclared income. The next step is consider how p and F affect the level of revenue raised by the government. Revenue in this context is defined as taxes paid plus the money received from fines. From a taxpayer with income Y the expected value (it is expected, since there is only a probability the taxpayer will be fined) of the revenue collected is

$$R = tX + p(1 + F)t[Y - X]. \tag{16.6}$$

Differentiating with respect to p shows that the effect on revenue of an increase in the probability of detection is

$$\frac{\partial R}{\partial p} = (1 + F)t[Y - X] + t[1 - p - pF]\frac{\partial X}{\partial p} > 0 \tag{16.7}$$

whenever $pF < 1 - p$. Recall from (16.5) that if $pF \geq 1 - p$, there is no evasion, so p has no effect on revenue. Carrying out the differentiation for the fine rate shows that if $pF < 1 - p$

$$\frac{\partial R}{\partial F} = pt[Y - X] + t[1 - p - pF]\frac{\partial X}{\partial F} > 0. \tag{16.8}$$

An increase in the fine will therefore raise revenue if tax evasion is taking place. Again, the fine has no effect if $pF \geq 1 - p$ and there is no evasion. These expressions show that if evasion is taking place, an increase in the probability of either detection or the fine will increase the revenue the government receives.

The choice problem of the government can now be addressed. It has already been noted that an increase in the probability of detection can be achieved by the employment of additional tax inspectors. Tax inspectors require payment; as a consequence an increase in p is costly. In contrast, there is no cost involved in raising or lowering the fine. Effectively, increases in F are costless to produce. From these observations the optimal policy can be determined.

Since p is costly and F is free, the interests of the government are best served by reducing p close to zero while raising F toward infinity. This has been termed the policy of "hanging taxpayers with probability zero." Expressed in words, the government should put virtually no effort into attempting to catch tax evaders but should severely punish those it apprehends. This is an extreme form of policy, and nothing like it is observed in practice. Surprising as it is, it does follow from the logical application of the model.

Numerous comments can be made about this conclusion. The first begins with the objective of the government. In previous chapters it was assumed that the government is guided in its policy choice by a social welfare function. There will be clear differences between a policy designed to maximize revenue and one that maximizes welfare. For instance, inflicting an infinite fine on a taxpayer caught evading will have a significantly detrimental effect on welfare. Even if the government does not pursue welfare maximization, it may be constrained by political factors such as the need to ensure re-election. A policy of severely punishing tax evaders may be politically damaging especially if tax evasion is a widely established phenomenon.

One could think that such an argument is not relevant because, if the punishment is large enough to deter cheating, it should not matter how dire it is. If fear keeps everyone from cheating, the punishment never actually occurs and its cost is irrelevant. The problem with this argument is that it ignores the risk of mistakes. The detection process may go wrong, or the taxpayer can mistakenly understate taxable income. If the punishment is as large as possible, even for small tax underpayments, then mistakes will be very costly. To reduce the cost of mistakes, the punishment should be of the smallest size required to deter cheating. Minimal deterrence accomplishes this purpose.

A further observation, and one whose consequences will be investigated in detail, concerns the policy instruments under the government's control. The view of the government so far is that it is a single entity that chooses the level of all its policy instruments simultaneously. In practice, the government consists of many different departments and agencies. When it comes to taxation and tax policy, a reasonable breakdown would be to view the tax rate as set by central government as part of a general economic policy. The probability of detection is controlled by a revenue service whose objective is the maximization of revenue. Finally, the punishment for tax evasion is set by the judiciary.

This breakdown shows why the probability and fine may not be chosen in a cohesive manner by a single authority. What it does not do is provide any argument for why the fine should not be set infinitely high to deter evasion. An explanation for this can be found by applying reasoning from the economics of crime. This would view tax evasion as just another crime, and the punishment for it should fit with the scheme of punishments for other crimes. The construction of these punishments relies on the argument that they should provide incentives that lessen the overall level of crime. To see what this means, imagine that crimes can be ranked from least harmful to most harmful. Naturally, if someone is going to commit a crime, the authorities wish that they commit a less harmful one rather than a more harmful one. If more harmful ones are also more rewarding (think of robbing a bank while armed compared to merely attempting to snatch cash), then a scheme of equal punishments will not provide any incentive for committing the less harmful crime. What will provide the right incentive is for the more harmful crime to also have a heavier punishment. So the extent of punishment should be related to the harmfulness of the crime. Punishment should fit the crime.

This framework has two implications. First of all, the punishment for tax evasion will not be varied freely in order to maximize revenue. Instead, it will be set as part of a general crime policy. The second implication is that the punishment will also be quite modest, since tax evasion is not an especially harmful crime. Arguments such as these are reflected in the fact that the fine rate on evasion is quite low—a figure in the order of 1.5 to 2 would not be unrealistic. As already noted, the maximum fine in the United Kingdom is 100 percent of the unpaid tax, but the Inland Revenue may accept a lesser fine depending on the "size and gravity" of the offense.

Putting all of these arguments together suggests adopting a different perspective on choosing the optimal probability of detection. With the tax rate set as a tool of economic policy and the fine set by the judiciary, the only instrument under the control of the revenue service is the probability of detection. As already seen, an increase in this raises revenue but only does so at a cost. The optimal probability is found when the marginal gain in revenue just equals the marginal cost—and this could occur at a very low value of the probability of detection.

16.5   Evidence on Evasion

The model of tax evasion has predicted the effect that changes in various parameters will have on the level of tax evasion. In some cases, such as the effect of the probability of detection and the fine, these are unambiguous. In others, particularly the effect of changes in the tax rate, the effects depend on the precise specification of the tax system and on assumptions concerning attitudes toward risk. These uncertainties make it valuable to investigate further evidence to see how

Table 16.2
Declaration of income

Income interval	17–20	20–25	25–30	30–35	35–40
Midpoint	18.5	22.5	27.5	32.5	37.5
Assessed income	17.5	20.6	24.2	28.7	31.7
Percentage	94.6	91.5	88.0	88.3	84.5

Source: Mork (1975).

the ambiguities are resolved in practice. The analysis of evidence also allows the investigation of the relevance of other parameters, such as the source of income, and other hypotheses on tax evasion, such as the importance of social interaction.

There have been two approaches taken in studying tax evasion. The first was to collect survey or interview data and use econometric analysis to provide a quantitative determination of the relationships. The second was to use experiments to provide an opportunity for designing the environment to permit the investigation of particular hypotheses.

When income levels ascertained from interviews were contrasted to those given on the tax returns of the same individuals, a steady decline of declared income as a proportion of reported income appeared with income rises. This finding is in agreement with the comparative statics analysis. Table 16.2 provides a sample of data to illustrate this. Interviewees were placed in income intervals according to their responses to interview questions. The information on their tax declaration was then used to determine assessed income. The percentage is found by dividing the assessed income by the midpoint of the income interval.

Econometrics and survey methods have been used to investigate the importance of attitudes and social norms in the evasion decision. The study reported in table 16.3 shows that the propensity to evade taxation is reduced by an increased probability of detection and an increase in age. An increase in income reduces the propensity to evade. With respect to the attitude and social variables, both an increase in the perceived inequity of taxation and of the number of other tax evaders known to the individual make evasion more likely. The extent of tax evasion is increased by the attitude and social variables but also by the experience of the taxpayer with previous tax audits. The social variables are clearly important in the decision to evade tax.

As far as the effect of the tax rate is concerned, data from the US Internal Revenue Services Taxpayer Compliance Measurement Program survey of 1969 shows

Table 16.3
Explanatory factors

Variable	Propensity to evade	Extent of evasion
Inequity	0.34	0.24
Number of evaders known	0.16	0.18
Probability of detection	−0.17	
Age	−0.29	
Experience of audits	0.22	0.29
Income level	−0.27	
Income from wages and salaries	0.20	

Source: Spicer and Lundstedt (1976).

that tax evasion increases as the marginal tax rates increases but is decreased when wages are a significant proportion of income. This result is supported by employing the difference between income and expenditure figures in National Accounts as a measure of evasion. In contrast, a study of Belgian data found precisely the converse conclusion, with tax increases leading to lower evasion. Therefore these studies do not resolve the ambiguity about the relation between marginal tax rates and tax evasion.

Turning now to experimental studies, tax evasion games have shown that evasion increases with the tax rate and that evasion falls as the fine is increased and the detection probability reduced. Further results have shown that women evade more often than men but evade lower amounts and that purchasers of lottery tickets, presumed to be less risk averse, are no more likely to evade than nonpurchasers but evade greater amounts when they do evade. Finally the very nature of the tax evasion decision has been tested by running two sets of experiments. One was framed as a tax evasion decision and the other as a simple gamble with the same risks and payoffs. For the tax evasion experiment some taxpayers chose not to evade even when they would under the same conditions with the gambling experiment. This suggests that tax evasion is not viewed as just a gamble.

There are two important lessons to be drawn from this brief review of the empirical and experimental results. First, the theoretical predictions are generally supported except for the effect of the tax rate. The latter remains uncertain with conflicting conclusions from the evidence. Second, it appears that tax evasion is more than the simple gamble portrayed in the basic model. In addition to the basic element of risk, there are social aspects to the evasion decision.

16.6   Effect of Honesty

The evidence discussed in the previous section has turned up a number of factors that are not explained by the basic model of tax evasion. Foremost among these are that some taxpayers choose not to evade even when they would accept an identical gamble and that there are social aspects of the evasion decision. The purpose of this section is to show how simple modifications to the model can incorporate these factors and can change the conclusions concerning the effect of the tax rate.

The feature that distinguishes tax evasion from a simple gamble is that taxpayers submitting incorrect returns feel varying degrees of anxiety and regret. To some, being caught would represent a traumatic experience that would do immense damage to their self-image. To others, it would be only a slight inconvenience. The innate belief in honesty of some taxpayers is not captured by representing tax evasion as just a gamble nor are the nonmonetary costs of detection and punishment captured by preferences defined on income alone. The first intention of this section is to incorporate these features into the analysis and to study their consequences.

A preference for honesty can be introduced by writing the utility function as

$$U = U(Y) - \chi E, \tag{16.9}$$

where χ is the measure of the taxpayers honesty and, with $E = Y - X$ the extent of evasion, χE is the utility (or psychic) cost of deviating from complete honesty. To see the consequence of introducing a psychic cost of evasion, assume that taxpayers differ in their value of χ but are identical in all other respects. Those with higher values of χ will suffer from a greater utility reduction for any given level of evasion. In order for them to evade, the utility gain from evasion must exceed this utility reduction. The population is therefore separated into two parts, with some taxpayers choosing not to evade (those with high values of χ) while others will evade (those with low χ). It is tempting to label those who do not evade as honest, but this is not really appropriate, since they will evade if the benefit is sufficiently great.

Let the value of χ that separates the evaders from the nonevaders be denoted $\hat{\chi}$. A change in any of the parameters of the model (p, F, and t) now has two effects. First, it changes the benefit from evasion, which alters the value of $\hat{\chi}$. For instance, an increase in the rate of tax raises the benefit of evasion and increases $\hat{\chi}$ with the consequence that more taxpayers evade. Second, the change in the parameter affects the evasion decision of all existing tax evaders. Putting these effects together, it becomes possible for an increase in the tax rate to lead to more evasion in aggregate. This is in contrast to the basic model where it would reduce evasion.

The discussion of the empirical evidence has drawn attention to the positive connection between the number of tax evaders known to a taxpayer and the level of that taxpayer's own evasion. This observation suggests that the evasion decision is not made in isolation by each taxpayer but is made with reference to the norms and behavior of the general society of the taxpayer. Given the empirical significance of such norms, the second part of this section focuses on their implications.

Social norms have been incorporated into the model of the evasion decision in two distinct ways. One approach is to introduce them as an additional element of the utility cost to evasion. The additional utility cost is assumed to be an increasing function of the proportion of taxpayers who do not evade. This formulation captures the fact that more utility will be lost, in terms of reputation, the more out of step the taxpayer is with the remainder of society. The consequence of this modification is to reinforce the separation of the population into evaders and nonevaders.

An alternative approach is to explicitly impose a social norm on behavior. One such social norm can be based on the concept of Kantian morality and, effectively, has individuals assessing their fair contribution in tax payments toward the provision of public goods. This calculation then provides an upper bound on the extent of tax evasion. To calculate the actual degree of tax evasion, each taxpayer performs the expected utility maximization calculation, as in (16.1), and evades whichever is the smaller out of this quantity and the previously determined upper bound. This formulation is also able to provide a positive relation between the tax rate and evaded tax for some range of taxes and to divide the population into those who evade tax and those who do not.

The introduction of psychic costs and of social norms is capable of explaining some of the empirically observed features of tax evasion that are not explained by the standard expected utility maximization hypothesis. This is achieved by modifying the form of preferences, but the basic nature of the approach is unchanged. The obvious difficulty with these changes is that there is little to suggest precisely how social norms and utility costs of dishonesty should be formalized.

16.7   Tax Compliance Game

An initial analysis of the choice of audit probability was undertaken in section 16.4. It was argued there that the practical situation involves a revenue service that chooses the probability to maximize total revenue, taking as given the tax rate and the punishment. The choice of probability in this setting requires an analysis of the interaction between the revenue service and the taxpayers. The revenue service reacts to the declarations of taxpayers, and taxpayers make declarations on the basis of the expected detection probability.

Such interaction is best analyzed by formalizing the structure of the game that is being played between the revenue service and the taxpayers. The choice of a strategy for the revenue service is the probability with which it chooses to audit any given value of declaration. This probability need not be constant for declarations of different values and is based on its perception of the behavior of taxpayers. For the taxpayers a strategy is a choice of declaration given the audit strategy of the revenue service. At a Nash equilibrium of the game the strategy choices must be mutually optimal: the audit strategy must maximize the revenue collected, net of the costs of auditing, given the declarations; the declaration must maximize utility given the audit strategy.

Even without specifying further details of the game, it is possible to make a general observation: predictability in auditing cannot be an equilibrium strategy. This can be established by the following steps: First, no auditing at all cannot be optimal because it encourages maximal tax evasion. Second, auditing of all declarations cannot be a solution either because no revenue service incurs the cost of auditing where full enforcement induces everyone to comply. Finally, prespecified limits on the range of declarations to be audited are also flawed. Taxpayers tempted to underreport income will make sure to stay just outside the audit limit, and those who cannot avoid being audited will choose to report truthfully. Exactly the wrong set of taxpayers will be audited. This establishes that the equilibrium strategy must involve randomization.

But how should the probability of audit depend on the information available on the tax return? Since the incentive of a taxpayer is to understate income to reduce their tax liabilities, it seems to require that the probability of an audit should be higher for low-income reports. More precisely, the probability of an audit should be high for an income report that is low compared to what one would expect from someone in that taxpayer's occupation or given the information on previous

Revenue service

		Audit	No audit
Taxpayer	Evasion	$Y-T-F, T+F-C$	$Y, 0$
	No evasion	$Y-T, T-C$	$Y-T, T$

Figure 16.7
Audit game

tax returns for that taxpayer. This is what theory predicts and what is done in practice.

A simple version of the strategic interaction between the revenue service and a taxpayer is depicted in figure 16.7. The taxpayer with true income Y can either evade (reporting zero income) or not (truthful income report). By reporting truthfully, the taxpayer pays tax T to the revenue service (with $T < Y$). The revenue service can either audit the income report or not audit. An audit costs C for the revenue service to conduct but provides irrefutable evidence on whether the taxpayer has misreported income. If the taxpayer is caught evading, he pays the tax due, T, plus a fine F (where the fine includes the cost of auditing and a tax surcharge so that $F > C$). If the taxpayer is not caught evading, then he pays no tax at all. The two players choose their strategies simultaneously, which reflects the fact that the revenue service does not know whether the taxpayer has chosen to evade when it decides whether to audit. To make the problem interesting we assume that $C < T$, so the cost of auditing is less than its potential gain, which is to recover the tax due.

There is no pure strategy equilibrium in this tax compliance game. If the revenue service does not audit, the agent strictly prefers evading, and therefore the revenue service is better off auditing as $T + F > C$. On the other hand, if the revenue service audits with certainty, the taxpayer prefers not to evade as $T + F > T$, which implies that the revenue service is better off not auditing. Therefore the revenue must play a mixed strategy in equilibrium, with the audit strategy being random (i.e., unpredictable). Similarly for the taxpayer the evasion strategy must also be random.

Let e be the probability that the taxpayer evades, and p the probability of audit. To obtain the equilibrium probabilities, we solve the conditions that the players must be indifferent between their two pure strategies. For the government to be indifferent between auditing and not auditing, it must be the case that the cost from auditing, C, equals the expected gain in tax and fine revenue, $e[T + F]$. For the taxpayer to be indifferent between evading and not evading, the expected gain from evading, $[1 - p]T$ equals the expected penalty pF. Hence in equilibrium the probability of evasion is

$$e^* = \frac{C}{T + F},$$ (16.10)

and the probability of audit is

$$p^* = \frac{T}{T + F},$$ (16.11)

where both e^* and p^* belong to the interval $(0, 1)$ so that both evasion and audit strategies are random.

The equilibrium probabilities are determined by the strategic interaction between the taxpayer and the revenue service. For instance, the audit probability declines with the fine, although a higher fine may be expected to make auditing more profitable. The reason is that a higher fine discourages evasion, thus making auditing less profitable. Similarly evasion is less likely with a high tax because a higher tax induces the government to audit more. Note that these results are obtained without specifying the details of the fine function, which could be either a lump-sum amount or something proportional to evaded tax. Evasion is also more likely the more costly is auditing, since the revenue service is willing to audit at a higher cost only if the taxpayer is more likely to have evaded tax.

The equilibrium payoffs of the players are

$$u^* = Y - T + e^*[T - p^*[T + F]],$$ (16.12)

for the taxpayer and

$$v^* = (1 - e^*)T + p^*[e^*[T + F] - C],$$ (16.13)

for the revenue service. Substituting into these payoffs the equilibrium probabilities of evasion and audit gives

$$u^* = Y - T,$$ (16.14)

$$v^* = T - \frac{C}{T + F}T.$$ (16.15)

Because the taxpayer is indifferent between evading and not evading, his equilibrium payoff is equal to his truthful payoff $Y - T$. This means that the unpaid taxes and the fine cancel out in expected terms. Increasing the fine does not affect the taxpayer. However, a higher fine increases the payoff of the revenue service, since it reduces the amount of evasion. Hence increasing the penalty is Pareto-improving in this model. The equilibrium payoffs also reflect the cost from evasion. Indeed, for any tax T paid by the taxpayer, the revenue service effectively receives $T - \Delta$, where $\Delta = \frac{C}{T+F} T$ is the deadweight loss from evasion. Thus evasion involves a deadweight loss that is increasing with the tax rate.

16.8   Compliance and Social Interaction

It has been assumed so far that the decision by any taxpayer to comply with the tax law is independent of what the other taxpayers are doing. This decision is based entirely on the enforcement policy (penalty and auditing) and economic opportunities (tax rates and income). In practice, however, we may expect that someone is more likely to break the law when noncompliance is already widespread than when it is confined to a small segment of the population. This observation is supported by the evidence in table 16.3, which shows that tax compliance is susceptible to social interaction.

The reasoning behind this social interaction can be motivated along the following lines: The amount of stigma or guilt I feel if I do not comply may depend on what others do and think. Whether they also underpay taxes may determine how I feel if I do not comply. As we now show, this simple interdependence between taxpayers can trigger a dynamic process that moves the economy toward either full compliance or no compliance at all.

To see this, consider a set of taxpayers. Each taxpayer has to decide whether to evade taxes or not. Fixing the enforcement parameters, the payoff from evading taxes depends on the number of noncompliers. In particular, the payoff from noncompliance is increasing with the number of noncompliers because then the chance of getting away with the act of evasion increases. On the other hand, the payoff from compliance decreases with the number of noncompliers. The reason can be that you suffer some resentment cost from abiding with the law when so many are breaking the law. Therefore individuals care about the overall compliance in the group when choosing to comply themselves.

Because of the way interactions work, the choice of tax evasion becomes more attractive when more taxpayers make the same choice of breaking the law. The

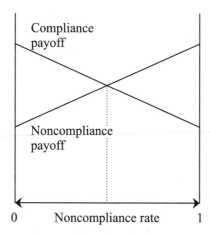

Figure 16.8
Equilibrium compliance

aggregate compliance tendency is toward one of the extremes: only the worst outcome of nobody complying or the best outcome of full compliance are possible.
This is illustrated in figure 16.8 depicting the payoff from compliance and noncompliance (vertical axis) against the noncompliance rate in the group (horizontal
axis). At the intersection of the two payoff functions taxpayers are indifferent
between compliance or noncompliance. Starting from this point, a small reduction in noncompliance will break the indifference in favor of compliance and trigger a chain reaction toward increasing compliance. Alternatively a small increase
in noncompliance triggers a chain reaction in the opposite direction making noncompliance progressively more and more attractive.

In this situation, how do we encourage taxpayers to abide by the law when the
dynamic is pushing in the opposite direction? The solution is to get a critical mass
of individuals complying to reverse the dynamic. This requires a short but intense
audit policy backed by a harsh punishment in order to change the decisions of
enough taxpayers that the dynamics switch toward full compliance. When at this
new full-compliance equilibrium, it is possible to cut down on audit costs because
compliance is self-sustained by the large numbers of taxpayers who comply. It follows from this simple argument that a moderate enforcement policy with few
audits and light penalties over a long period is ineffective. Another interesting implication of this model is that two countries with similar enforcement policies can
end up with very different compliance rates. Social interaction can be a crucial explanation for the astoundingly high variance of compliance rates across locations

and over time that are much higher than can be predicted by differences in local enforcement policies.

16.9   Conclusions

Tax evasion is an important and significant phenomenon that affects both developed and developing economies. Although there is residual uncertainty surrounding the accuracy of measurements, even the most conservative estimates suggest the hidden economy in the United Kingdom and United States to be at least 10 percent of the measured economy. There are many countries where it is very much higher. The substantial size of the hidden economy, and the tax evasion that accompanies it, require understanding so that the effects of policies that interact with it can be correctly forecast.

The predictions of the standard representation of tax evasion as a choice with risk were derived and contrasted with empirical and experimental evidence. This showed that although it is valuable as a starting point for a theory of evasion, the model did not incorporate some key aspects of the evasion decision, most notably the effects of a basic wish to avoid dishonesty and the social interaction among taxpayers. The analysis was then extended to incorporate both of these issues.

Further Reading

The literature on tax evasion is summarized in:

Cowell, F. A. 1990. *Cheating the Government*. Cambridge: MIT Press.

For a comprehensive survey of the extent of tax evasion in wide range of countries:

Schneider, F., and Enste, D. H. 2000. Shadow economies: Size, causes, and consequences. *Journal of Economic Literature* 38: 77–114.

The earliest model of tax compliance is:

Allingham, M., and Sandmo, A. 1972. Income tax evasion: A theoretical analysis. *Journal of Public Economics* 1: 323–38.

The economic approach to crime is developed in:

Becker, G. 1968. Crime and punishment: An economic approach. *Journal of Political Economy* 76: 169–217.

Empirical and experimental evidence is found in:

Baldry, J. C. 1986. Tax evasion is not a gamble. *Economics Letters* 22: 333–35.

Mork, K. A. 1975. Income tax evasion: Some empirical evidence. *Public Finance* 30: 70–76.

Spicer, M. W., and Lundstedt, S. B. 1976. Understanding tax evasion. *Public Finance* 31: 295–305.

On the effect of social interaction on law compliance:

Glaeser, E. L., Sacerdote, B., and Scheinkman, J. A. 1996. Crime and social interaction. *Quarterly Journal of Economics* 111: 506–48.

A game-theoretic model of the strategic interaction between taxpayer and enforcement agency, including honest taxpayers is in:

Graetz, M., Reinganum, J., and Wilde, L. 1986. The tax compliance game: Towards an interactive theory of law enforcement. *Journal of Law, Economics and Organization* 2: 1–32.

Scotchmer, S. 1987. Audit classes and tax enforcement policy. *American Economic Review* 77: 229–33.

On the effect of fiscal corruption and the desirability of a flat tax see:

Hindriks, J., Keen, M., and Muthoo, A. 1999. Corruption, extortion and evasion. *Journal of Public Economics* 74: 395–430.

Exercises

16.1. Economic efficiency requires that consumers exploit all opportunities to increase their welfare. Does this argument legitimize tax evasion?

16.2. Should the welfare of tax evaders be included in an assessment of social welfare? What if their inclusion implied that tax evasion should not be punished? Would you provide the same arguments for violent crimes?

16.3. Consider a consumer with utility function $U = Y^{1/2}$.

a. Defining the coefficient of absolute risk aversion by $R_A(Y) = -\frac{\partial^2 U/\partial Y^2}{\partial U/\partial Y}$, show that this is a decreasing function of Y.

   The consumer is faced with a gamble that results in a loss of 1 with probability $p = 0.5$ and a gain of 2 with probability $1 - p$.

b. Show that there is a critical value of income Y^* at which the consumer is indifferent between participating in this gamble and receiving income Y^* with certainty. Hence show that the gamble will be undertaken at any higher income but will not at any lower income.

16.4. A consumer with utility function $U = Y^{1/2}$ has to choose between a job that provides income Y_0 but no possibility of evading tax and a job that pays Y_1 but makes evasion possible. What value of Y_1 makes the consumer indifferent between these two jobs? How does a change in the tax rate affect this level of income?

16.5. Given utility function $U = -e^{-Y}$.

a. Show that the coefficient of absolute risk aversion $R_A(Y) = -\frac{U''}{U'}$ is constant (where U' and U'' denote the first and second derivative of U with respect to Y, respectively).

Show that $U' > 0$ (positive marginal utility of income) and that $U'' < 0$ (diminishing marginal utility of income).

b. Show that the undeclared income, $Y - X$, is independent of Y for a consumer with this utility function. (*Hint*: For a function $y = e^{f(x)}$, the derivative is $\frac{dy}{dx} = e^{f(x)} \frac{df(x)}{dx}$.)

16.6. For the utility function $U = \log(Y)$:

a. Show that the coefficient of relative risk aversion $R_A(Y) = -\frac{U''}{U'}$ is constant (where U' and U'' denote the first and second derivative of U with respect to Y, respectively).

b. Show that the proportion of income not declared, $\frac{X}{Y}$, is independent of Y for a consumer with this utility function.

(*Hint*: Let $X = \alpha Y$ in the first-order condition and show that Y can be eliminated.)

16.7. In a state-contingent income space, each person's indifference curves are generally bowed in toward the origin. Why does this imply that the person is risk averse?

16.8. Does it matter whether p and F are interpreted as subjective or objective quantities? If the revenue service chooses to prosecute celebrities for evasion while fining non-celebrities, does it believe in the objective interpretation?

16.9. A consumer with utility function $U = Y^{1/2}$ determines the amount of income to declare to the tax authority.

a. Denoting the probability of detection by p, the tax rate by t, and the fine by F, provide an expression for the optimal value of X.

b. For $F = \frac{1}{2}$ and $p = \frac{1}{2}$ show that the declaration X is an increasing function of t.

c. Assume that the revenue authority aims to maximize the sum of tax revenue plus fines less the cost of auditing. If the latter is given by $c(p) = p^2$, graph the income of the revenue authority as a function of p for $Y = 10$, $F = \frac{1}{2}$, and $t = \frac{1}{3}$. Hence derive the optimal value of p.

16.10. A consumer has a choice between two occupations. One occupation pays a salary of \$80,000 but gives no chance for tax evasion. The other pays \$75,000 but does permit evasion. With the probability of detection $p = 0.3$, the tax rate $t = 0.3$, and the fine rate $F = 0.5$, which occupation will be chosen if $U = Y^{1/2}$?

16.11. Use the parameter values from the previous exercise with the modification that pay in the occupation permitting evasion is given by \$90,000$[1 - n]$, where n is the proportion of the population choosing this occupation. What is the equilibrium value of n? How is this value affect by an increase in t?

16.12. Consider the simultaneous move game between a taxpayer and a tax inspector. The taxpayer chooses whether or not to underreport their taxable income. The tax inspector chooses whether or not to audit the income report. The cost of auditing is $c > 1$ and the fine (including tax payment) imposed if the taxpayer is caught cheating is F (with $F > c > 1$). With a truthful report the taxpayer has to pay a tax of 1 unit of income. The payoffs are given in the matrix where the first number in each cell denotes the tax inspector's payoff and the second number is the taxpayer's payoff. Find the Nash equilibria of this game, considering both pure and mixed strategies.

	Underreport	Truthful report
Audit	$F - c, -F$	$1 - c, -1$
No audit	$0, 0$	$0, -1$

16.13. A revenue service announces that it will only audit income declarations below a critical level Y^*. If you had an income in excess of Y^*, what level of income would you announce? Once declarations are made, will the revenue service act according to its announced auditing plans?

16.14. Consider the game between taxpayer and revenue service described in the payoff matrix below.

	Audit	No audit
Honest	$100, -10$	$100, 10$
Evade	$Y, 5$	$150, T$

a. For what value of T is (Evade, No audit) a Nash equilibrium?

b. Can (Evade, Audit) ever be a Nash equilibrium? What does this imply about the punishment structure?

c. Does a simultaneous move game capture the essence of the auditing problem?

16.15. Is tax evasion just a gamble?

16.16. "Those who follow social customs are fools." True or false?

16.17. Assume that 10 percent of the population will always evade paying taxes no matter what anyone else does. Equally 10 percent of the population will never evade paying taxes. The remaining 80 percent are more likely to evade when the proportion evading increases. Prove that there will be at least one equilibrium level of tax evasion. Show how multiple equilibria can occur. Which equilibria are stable?

16.18. Consider the optimal audit strategy of a tax authority. All taxpayers have either a low income Y_L or a high income Y_H, with $Y_L < Y_H$. They file a tax return, but the rich taxpayers may attempt to underreport. The proportions of taxpayers with high and low incomes are known, but a personal tax return can only be verified through an audit that costs c. There is a constant tax rate on income t and a fine consisting of a surcharge F on any underpaid tax. The parameters c, t, and F are not chosen by the tax authority.

a. Suppose that the tax authority can pre-commit to its audit polity. What is the optimal audit strategy for the tax authority? Is such a policy credible? Why or why not?

b. If there is a fixed fraction of high-income taxpayers who are known to report truthfully, what could be a credible audit strategy? What is the impact on the equilibrium audit strategy of an increase in the cost of auditing?

16.19. Tax evasion is sometimes described as "contagious," meaning that an increase in evasion encourages yet further evasion. In such circumstances, is the only equilibrium to have everyone evading?

16.20. An experiment is conducted in three different countries. Participants are told their income levels (in units of the local currency), the tax rate, the probability of detection, and the fine structure. These parameters are the same for all participants. It is found that the amount of income not declared is, on average, different among the countries. Discuss possible explanations for this finding.

VII MULTIPLE JURISDICTIONS

17.1   Introduction

Fiscal federalism is the division of revenue collection and expenditure responsibilities among different levels of government. Most countries have a central (or federal) government, state or county governments, town councils, and, at the lowest level, parish councils. Each level has restrictions on the tax instruments it can employ and the expenditures that it can make. Together they constitute the multi-leveled and overlapping administration that governs a typical developed country.

The central government can usually choose whatever tax instruments it pleases, and although it has freedom in its expenditure, it usually focuses on national defense, the provision of law and order, infrastructure, and transfer payments. The taxation powers of state governments are more restricted. In the United Kingdom, local governments can levy only property taxes; in the United States, both commodity and local income taxes are allowed. Their responsibilities include education, local infrastructure, and the provision of health care. Local governments provide services such as rubbish collection and maintenance of parks. The responsibility for the police and fire service can be at either the state or local level. Levels of government are connected by overlapping responsibilities and the transfer payments made between them.

The issue of fiscal federalism is not restricted to the design of government within countries. Indeed, the recent impetus for the advancement of this theory has been issues involving the design of institutional structures for the European Union. The progress made toward economic and monetary integration has begun to raise questions about subsidiarity, which is the degree of independence that individual countries will maintain in the setting of taxes. Such arguments just involve the application of fiscal federalism, albeit at a larger scale.

These observations lead to a number of interesting economic questions. First, why should there be more than one level of government? Using the logic of economic reasoning, multi-level government can only be justified if it can achieve something that a single level cannot. Explanations of what this can be must revolve around access to information and how the information can be best utilized. If this argument is accepted, and it is explored in detail below, then a second question arises. How are the functions of government best allocated among the levels? A brief sketch of how this allocation works in practice has already been given: Is this outcome efficient, or does it reflect some other factors?

The next section of the chapter considers the rationale for multi-level government, focusing on the availability of information. An overview of arguments in favor of multi-level government are then given. This is followed by a more detailed analysis of some of the key issues, and the concept of an optimal structure is investigated. The issue of accountability and decentralization is analyzed next. The essential elements of interregional risk sharing are then presented, and the distinction between insurance and redistribution is discussed. Empirical evidence is provided on the extent of decentralization by countries and functions, and the main determinants of the observed decentralization.

17.2   Arguments for Multi-level Government

The economic arguments for having government are founded on the two principles outlined in chapter 4. If there is market failure, the government can intervene in the economy to increase efficiency. It can also intervene to improve equity, regardless of whether the economy is efficient or not. These arguments justify intervention; to justify multi-level government, the case must be made that objectives of efficiency and equity are better served by a combination of local and central government.

If the correct decisions are made about the level of public good provision and about taxes, then it does not matter at which level of government they are taken. Provided that there are no resources wasted in overlapping responsibilities, the number of levels of government is a matter of indifference. A case for multi-level government must therefore be sought in differences in information and political process that allow some structures to achieve better outcomes than others.

Decisions should be taken at a national level if they involve public goods that serve the entire economy. The obvious example here would be defense, whose benefits cannot be assigned to any particular community within the economy. It is common to argue that all citizens should have the same access to the law, have the same rights under the law, and be subject to the same restrictions. An application of this equity argument supports a legal system that is organized and administered from the center. Given the central provision of these services, it is natural to support them through centrally organized taxes.

Other public goods, namely the local public goods of chapter 6, benefit only those resident within a defined geographic area. The level of supply of these goods could be determined and financed at the national level but there are three arguments to suggest a lower level decision is preferable.

First, determination at the local level can take account of more precise information available on local preferences. In this context, local ballots and knowledge of local circumstances may help in reaching a more efficient decision. Second, if a decision were to be made at the national level, political pressures may prevent there from being any differentiation of provision among communities, whereas it might be efficient to have different levels of local public good provision in different areas. Finally, the Tiebout hypothesis investigated in chapter 6 argued that if consumers have heterogeneous preferences, then efficiency requires numerous communities to form and offer different levels of public good provision. This will not be possible if decisions are taken at a national level.

If these arguments for determining and providing public goods at a local level are accepted, then it follows almost inevitably that financing should be determined at the same level. To do otherwise, and to set a tax policy that was uniform across the economy, would result in transfers among regions. Those regions choosing levels of public good provision that were high relative to their tax base would not generate sufficient tax revenue to finance their provision, while those with relatively low levels would raise excessive revenue. These deficits and surpluses result in implicit transfers among regions. Such transfers may not be efficient, equitable, or politically acceptable.

Similar arguments can be repeated for the other roles of government such as the control of externalities and some aspects of the reallocation of income. The provision of services, even if they have the nature of private goods (e.g., garbage disposal), can be subject to the same reasoning. This process suggests that different levels of government should be constructed to ensure that decisions are made at the most appropriate level. There is a limit, though, in that duplication of effort and wasted resources should be avoided. The precise design of the structure of government then emerges from the trade-off between increasing the number of levels to ensure that decisions are made at the correct point and reaping the resource benefits of having fewer levels.

The general observations made above can now be refined into more detailed arguments. We first explore the costs of imposing uniformity and then consider positive arguments for decentralization.

17.2.1   The Costs of Uniformity

Uniform provision of public goods and services by all jurisdictions will only ever exactly meet the needs of the entire population when preferences are homogeneous.

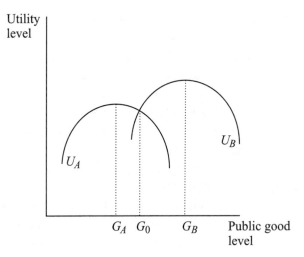

Figure 17.1
Costs of uniformity

When they are not, any form of uniform provision must be a compromise between competing levels of demand. As such, it must involve some loss in welfare relative to differentiated provision.

This argument can be illustrated by considering an economy where there are two groups of consumers who have different tastes for the economy's single public good. The public good is financed by a uniform income tax. Denote the two groups by A and B, and assume that members of group B have a relatively stronger preference for the public good than those of group A, taking into account the higher tax rate that this implies. The utility levels of the two groups can then be graphed against the quantity of public good provision as in figure 17.1. The preferred choices of public good provision are denoted as G_A and G_B (with $G_A < G_B$). Now consider the choice of a uniform level of provision, and let this level be G_0. Assume that this level lies between G_A and G_B (the argument easily extends to cases where it lies outside these limits). The loss of welfare to society is then given by $L = n_A[u_A(G_A) - u_A(G_0)] + n_B[u_B(G_B) - u_B(G_0)]$ compared to what would be achieved if each group could be supplied with its preferred quantity.

The value of the loss can be minimized by setting the location of G_0 so that the marginal benefit for group B of having more public good, $n_B u'_B(G_0) > 0$, just offsets the marginal loss of group, A, $n_A u'_A(G_0) < 0$, but the essential point is that the loss remains positive. Furthermore the loss increases the more widely dispersed are preferences and the more members there are of each group.

This analysis shows how uniformity can be costly in terms of forgone welfare. A policy of uniformity can then only be supported if the costs of differentiation exceed the benefit. Such costs could arise in the collection of information to determine the differentiation and in the administration costs of a differentiated system. These arguments will be explored further below. The next section considers, however, the limit of the benefits that can arise from differentiation.

17.2.2   The Tiebout Hypothesis

Although the costs of uniformity as illustrated above are indisputable, it is another step to show that decentralization is justified. The route to doing this is to exploit the Tiebout hypothesis that was analyzed in section 6.6 in connection with the theory of local public goods. The exact same arguments are applicable here. Each community can be treated as an independent provider of local public goods. If the consumers in the economy have heterogeneous tastes, then there will be clear advantages to jurisdictions having different levels of provision. Each can design what it offers (its tax rates, level of provision, and type of provision) to appeal to particular groups within society. By choosing the jurisdiction in which to live (i.e., by voting with their feet), the consumers reveal their tastes for public goods. In the absence of transactions costs, or other impediments to freedom of movement, an efficient equilibrium must ensue.

The limits to this argument explored in the context of local public goods are also applicable here. Transactions costs are relevant in practice, and the problem of optimally dividing a finite population into a limited number of jurisdictions will arise. The fact that the first-best allocation will not be achieved does not necessarily undermine the preference-matching argument for decentralization. There are clearly still benefits to decentralization, even when this cannot be taken to the level required by the Tiebout hypothesis. Starting from a uniform level of services that is too little for some consumers and too much for others, a move away from this uniform level by some jurisdictions must benefit some of the consumers. This way even restricted decentralization can be increasing in efficiency. This argument can be easily understood from figure 17.1.

The Tiebout hypothesis shows the benefits achievable by decentralization. Although these are not fully realizable, a limited version of the same argument suggests that even restricted decentralization will improve on uniform provision.

17.2.3   Distributive Arguments

The regions that constitute any economy are endowed with different stocks of resources. Some may be rich in natural resources, such as oil and coal, and others may have a well-educated workforce with high levels of human capital. Such differences in endowments will be reflected in disparities in living standards among regions.

The ability to differentiate public good provision among the regions then allows more accurate targeting of resources to where they are required. This is an equity argument for not having uniform provision. Decentralized decision-making allows each region to communicate its needs to the center and permits the center to make differential allocations to the regions.

This process will be designed to offset the differences in living standards caused by endowments. Typically there will be no compensation for differences in preference for public good provision such as giving more to a region wishing to spend more on public goods. This form of redistribution between regions is called an *equalization* formula and will be explored in chapter 18 when discussing intergovernmental grants.

17.3   Optimal Structure: Efficiency versus Stability

The previous arguments have explored a number of advantages of fiscal decentralization. These have involved both efficiency and equity aspects. The issue that remains is what is the optimal structure or the correct number of levels of administration. The difficulty that arises here is that the optimal division may differ from one public good to another. The examples in the introduction have discussed how fire services are organized at a very local level, education at a higher level, and defense at an even higher one. There are many other public goods provided by the federal government. If each were to be allocated at the correct level of decentralization, this would imply an equally large number of levels of government.

Each level of government brings with it additional costs. These involve all the factors that are necessary to provide administration. Buildings, staff, and equipment will all be required, as will elections to choose politicians. The politicians will also require compensation for the time devoted to political activity. These costs are replicated each time an additional level of government is introduced.

Consequently introducing further levels of government is not costless. The choice of the optimal degree of decentralization must take these costs into account and balance them against the benefits. From such a process will emerge the optimal structure. This will depend on the relative sizes of costs and benefits but is most likely to result in a level of decentralization such that some decisions are taken at a higher level than would be best if decentralization were costless.

This argument is now illustrated in a simple spatial model that trades off scale economies against diversity of preference. The point of departure is that centralized decision-making produces a "one-size-fits-all" outcome that does not reflect the heterogeneity of tastes. The uniform provision follows from political economy considerations preventing centralized majority voting from allocating different levels of public goods to different districts. It is only by decentralizing the majority voting at the district level that it is possible to differentiate public good provision, but at some cost of duplication.

Suppose that there is one public good that can be provided either at the federal level or at the regional level. We model the federation as the line segment $[0, 1]$, with points on the line representing different geographical locations. The public good can be located anywhere along the line, and individuals are characterized by their ideal location for the public good. With central provision the public good is located at $\frac{1}{2}$, the midpoint of the line segment. The farther away from this point individuals are located, the less they like the public good provided at the federal level. This is shown in figure 17.2.

Alternatively, provision can be decentralized. Each region is then represented by an interval on the line segment. Region L is the left-interval $\left[0, \frac{1}{2}\right]$ and region R the right-interval $\left[\frac{1}{2}, 1\right]$. Individuals are assumed to be uniformly distributed, so both regions are of equal size. With decentralized provision the public good is located at the midpoint of each interval, that is, $\frac{1}{4}$ in the left-region and $\frac{3}{4}$ in the right-region. There is a fixed cost C (per capita) of providing the public good at

0   Centralized   1

Region L Region R

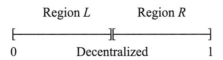

0   Decentralized   1

Figure 17.2
Centralization and decentralization

the central level, and due to duplication the cost is $2C$ with decentralized provision (i.e., the number of individuals across whom the cost of public good provision is spread is reduced by one-half).

The utility function of each individual i under centralization is

$$u_i^c = 1 - \alpha\left|\tfrac{1}{2} - i\right| - C, \tag{17.1}$$

and under decentralization,

$$u_i^d = \begin{cases} 1 - \alpha\left|\tfrac{1}{4} - i\right| - 2C & \text{for } i \in \left[0, \tfrac{1}{2}\right], \\ 1 - \alpha\left|\tfrac{3}{4} - i\right| - 2C & \text{for } i \in \left[\tfrac{1}{2}, 1\right], \end{cases} \tag{17.2}$$

where $\left|\tfrac{1}{2} - i\right|$ and $\left|\tfrac{1}{4} - i\right|$ denote the distance between the public good's location and the ideal location of individual i, respectively, under centralization and decentralization for an individual i located in the left-region ($\left|\tfrac{3}{4} - i\right|$ for one located in the right-region). The rate at which utility decreases with the distance is given by the parameter α.

We can define when decentralization is socially optimal by considering the trade-off between duplicating the cost of public good provision against taking provision closer to individual preferences. The socially optimal solution maximizes the sum of all individual utilities. Since individual utilities differ only in the distance to the public good location (because of the equal cost sharing) the sum of utilities will depend on the average distance. Under centralized provision, the average distance from $\tfrac{1}{2}$ is, due to the uniform distribution, just equal to $\tfrac{1}{4}$. Note that this distance is actually minimized by locating the public good at the midpoint $\tfrac{1}{2}$. Decentralization brings the average distance in either region down to $\tfrac{1}{8}$. This positive effect of decentralization has to be balanced against the extra cost C of providing the public good twice. Therefore decentralization is the optimal solution if and only if the extra cost C is less than the advantage of reducing the average distance by $\tfrac{1}{4} - \tfrac{1}{8}$ evaluated at the rate α at which utility falls with distance; that is, $C \leq \alpha\left[\tfrac{1}{4} - \tfrac{1}{8}\right] = \tfrac{\alpha}{8}$. In summary, decentralization is optimal if and only if $C \leq \tfrac{\alpha}{8}$.

These arguments show that the optimal amount of decentralization will be achieved when the benefits from further decentralization, in terms of matching the diversity of tastes, outweigh the cost of differentiating the public good provision. In practice, the extent of decentralization is determined through the political process. Using this basic model, we can now illustrate the tendency for majority voting to lead to excessive decentralization.

In order to look at the incentive for decentralization under majority voting, we assume that decentralized provision prevails when a majority of voters are favorable in at least one region. This assumption is innocuous given the symmetry between regions: if there is a majority in favor of decentralization in one region, there must also be an equivalent majority in the other region. We concentrate on the incentive of the left-region for decentralization.

The majority in the left-region is formed by those who are either to the left or to the right of the individual at the regional midpoint $\frac{1}{4}$. It is easily seen that if this central individual prefers decentralization, then all those to his left also have the same preferences because they are located further away from the centralized provision but share the cost equally. Therefore there will be a majority in favor of decentralization in the left-region if the decisive individual $i = \frac{1}{4}$ prefers decentralization, that is, if

$$u_i^c = 1 - \alpha\left|\tfrac{1}{2} - \tfrac{1}{4}\right| - C \le u_i^d = 1 - \alpha\left|\tfrac{1}{4} - \tfrac{1}{4}\right| - 2C. \tag{17.3}$$

It can therefore be concluded that decentralization is a majority voting equilibrium if and only if $C \le \frac{\alpha}{4}$.

This result suggests excessive decentralization under majority voting because the critical cost level under majority voting is higher than the critical cost level for optimality. In particular, for any cost C between $\frac{\alpha}{8}$ and $\frac{\alpha}{4}$ majority voting leads to decentralization $\left(C < \frac{\alpha}{4}\right)$, although it is not socially optimal $\left(C > \frac{\alpha}{8}\right)$. Therefore under majority voting there is *excessive decentralization*: voters who are located at the extremes have an incentive to support decentralized provision to get a public good closer to what they want, but the democratic process does not internalize the negative externalities imposed on voters located in the center who suffer from the extra cost and little or worse preference matching.

17.4   Accountability

Politicians may pursue a range of different objectives. At times they may be public-spirited and dedicate themselves fully to furthering public interest. But they may also pursue their own interests, even if these differ from those of their constituents. Some may want to derive private gains while in office or actively seek perks of office. Some may extend clientilistic favors to their families and friends. But the most important way in which they can act against the best interests of their constituents is by choosing policies that advance their own interests or those of special groups to which they are beholden.

A government is *accountable* if voters can discern whether it is acting in their interest and sanction them appropriately if they are not, so that incumbents anticipate that they will have to render accounts for their past actions. The problem is then to confront politicians with a trade-off between diverting rents and losing office or doing what voters want and getting re-elected. In this view, elections can be seen as an accountability mechanism for controlling and sorting good from bad incumbents. By "good incumbent," we mean someone who is honest, competent, and not easily bought off by special interests.

The standard view of how electoral accountability works is that voters set some standard of performance to evaluate governments, and they vote out the incumbent unless these criteria are fulfilled. However, elections do not work well in controlling and sorting politicians. There are severe problems in monitoring and evaluating the incumbent's behavior in order to make informed decisions about whether or not to re-elect. Voters face a formidable agency problem because they are inevitably poorly informed about politicians' behavior and type. Moreover the electoral sanction (pass or fail) is such a crude instrument that it can hardly induce the politicians to do what the public wants.

From this perspective it might be reasonable to try to organize competition among politicians in order to control them. In this respect the Brennan and Buchanan (1980) view is that decentralization is an effective mechanism to control governments' expansive tendencies. The basic argument is that *competition among different decentralized governments can exercise a disciplinary force* and break the monopoly power of a large central government. Comparing performance in office among different incumbents helps in sorting good types from bad types as well as controlling the quality of their decisions. Hence one votes against an incumbent if his performance is bad relative to others, in order to induce each incumbent to behave in the public interest.

To see the logic of the argument, consider a simple example. Suppose that the circumstances under which politicians make decisions can be good (state a) or bad (state b). Governments decide to adopt policy A, which is better for their constituents in the good state a, or policy B, which is better in the bad state b. Governments need not pursue the public interest and can rather advance their own interests by choosing policy A in state b and policy B in state a to get some private gains (e.g., a rent $r > 0$). Suppose that politicians place a value V on being re-elected and that this value satisfies $V > r$. The payoff matrix is shown in figure 17.3: the first number in each cell is the government payoff, and the second number is voters welfare. If the government is re-elected, it gets the extra value V. The government knows the prevailing conditions (i.e., whether a or b has occurred), but all that citizens observe is their current welfare.

	State *a*	State *b*
Policy *A*	0, 3	*r*, 0
Policy *B*	*r*, 1	0, 1

Figure 17.3
Political accountability and voter welfare

To induce politicians to act as well as they can under this information structure, voters must set the correct re-election rule. If voters set the standard the incumbent must meet in order to be re-elected too high (e.g., committing to vote for the incumbent if the welfare level is at least 3), then the incumbent cannot be re-elected whatever he does if conditions turn out to be bad (state *b*). Consequently the incumbent has the incentive to obtain the rent *r* and leave office. Alternatively, if the voters set the standard for re-election lower, say at 1, the incumbent will be able to divert rent when conditions happen to be good (state *a*) and be re-elected by giving voters less than what they could obtain. Then voters are in a quandary because whatever they decide to do, the politicians will sometimes escape from their control and divert rent.

Suppose now that the electorate can compare the outcome of its incumbent with other incumbents (in different constituencies) facing exactly the same circumstances. Then from the observation of outcomes elsewhere, voters can potentially infer whether the prevailing conditions are good or bad and thereby get the most they can under either condition. The information will be revealed if there is at least one government that chooses a different policy from that of the others. The voting rule then becomes: When conditions are good, vote for the incumbent if the outcome is at least 3. When conditions are bad, vote for the incumbent if the outcome is at least 1. Otherwise, vote the incumbent out. Hence a government facing good conditions *a* knows that by choosing the appropriate policy *A*, it will be re-elected for sure and get *V*, which is more than the rent *r* it can get by choosing *B* and being voted out. In turn a government facing bad conditions *b* knows that by choosing B it will be re-elected and get V, which is better than what it would get by adopting the wrong policy A to get the rent r but no chance of being re-elected. Therefore, comparing the performance of their incumbent with other incumbents facing similar circumstances, voters can gain increased control over their politicians and deduce what is attributable to circumstances as opposed to government actions.

Another argument for why decentralization should lead to greater efficiency and accountability is that a central decision-maker does not need to please all jurisdictions to get re-elected but simply a majority of them. However, this argument is usually balanced against the fact that the value of holding office is larger in a centralized arrangement and thus politicians are more eager to win election, which in a conventional political agency model may increase accountability and efficiency.

17.5   Risk Sharing

Interregional insurance is fundamentally about sharing risk among a group of regions so that no region bears an undue amount of risk. Because of this risk sharing, insurance can arise even when all parties are risk averse. What is necessary for interregional insurance to be possible is that the risks the parties bear are, to some degree, independent of each other. That is, when one region suffers a loss, there are other regions (or group of regions) that do not suffer a loss. While such independence is usually true of almost all individual risks for which standard forms of insurance exist (fires, car accidents, sicknesses, etc.), it is less obvious at the regional level.

There are some fundamental principles in mutual insurance. First, risk sharing is more effective, the broader the basis on which risks are pooled. This is a consequence of Borch's theorem on mutual insurance. Second, it is more advantageous for any region to engage in mutual insurance with other regions when risks are negatively correlated across regions. Third, there must be a degree of symmetry across regions. The reason is that with an asymmetric regional distribution of risks, some regions will systematically and persistently subsidize others. The distributional considerations will then dominate insurance aspects. Fourth, risk-sharing arrangements require reciprocal behavior: a region with a favorable shock accepts to help out other regions if it can reasonably expect that those regions will in turn help it out in bad circumstances. With voluntary insurance, participants

	State a	State b
Region a	$y_a + \Delta$	y_a
Region b	y_b	$y_b + \Delta$

Figure 17.4
Regional distribution of income

are free to opt out at any time, so there is also the possibility of a risk-sharing agreement without commitment.

17.5.1   Voluntary Risk Sharing

A model of voluntary insurance between two regions when aggregate income is constant is as follows: In each period two regions, indexed $i = \{a, b\}$, receive an income y_i, and one region is randomly selected to receive a monetary gain $\Delta > 0$. Each has the same probability $\frac{1}{2}$ of receiving this gain, and the total income is fixed at $Y = y_a + y_b + \Delta$. The regional income distribution is given in figure 17.4.

With constant aggregate income, risk aversion requires the smoothing of regional income across states of nature. Optimal risk-sharing arrangements imply full insurance, which requires that the region receiving the gain Δ transfer one-half of this gain to the other region. Denoting such a transfer by t^*, then $t^* = \frac{\Delta}{2}$. Therefore the gain is equally shared among regions, and regional income is constant.

Let $u_i(x)$ denotes the utility of region i from disposal income x. Then it is readily seen that both regions are better off with such an optimal risk-sharing arrangement, since

$$u_a\left(y_a + \frac{\Delta}{2}\right) \geq \frac{1}{2}u_a(y_a + \Delta) + \frac{1}{2}u_a(y_a), \tag{17.4}$$

$$u_b\left(y_b + \frac{\Delta}{2}\right) \geq \frac{1}{2}u_b(y_b + \Delta) + \frac{1}{2}u_b(y_b). \tag{17.5}$$

Without commitment, complete risk sharing is not guaranteed. We must take into account the possibility that the region receiving the gain may refuse to transfer some of the gain to the other region. A risk-sharing agreement without commitment must be "self-enforcing" in the sense that no region has an incentive to defect unilaterally from the agreement. To be self-enforcing, the risk-sharing arrangement must be such that the expected net benefits from participating is at any time larger than the one time gain from defection (by not making the transfer when called upon). If full insurance is not possible, it is still possible to design partial insurance by limiting transfers when the participation constraint is binding.

Let t_i be the transfer made by region i to the other region when region i receives the gain Δ. On receiving the gain Δ, region i can trade off the immediate gain of defecting by refusing to make the transfer t_i, against the cost of being excluded from any future insurance arrangement, and to bear regional income variation alone. Taking region a, the gain from defection when receiving Δ is

$$u_a(y_a + \Delta) - u_a(y_a + \Delta - t_a). \tag{17.6}$$

The cost of losing insurance in the next period (which will be discounted at rate $\delta < 1$ when compared to the gain) is

$$\left[\tfrac{1}{2}u_a(y_a + \Delta - t_a) + \tfrac{1}{2}u_a(y_a + t_b)\right] - \left[\tfrac{1}{2}u_a(y_a + \Delta) + \tfrac{1}{2}u_a(y_a)\right]. \tag{17.7}$$

The participation constraint holds if the gain from future insurance exceeds the cost of defecting. Comparing the two values and rearranging, we find that region a has no incentive to defect if

$$\left[1 + \frac{\delta}{2}\right]u_a(y_a + \Delta - t_a) + \frac{\delta}{2}u_a(y_a + t_b) \geq \left[1 + \frac{\delta}{2}\right]u_a(y_a + \Delta) + \frac{\delta}{2}u_a(y_a), \tag{17.8}$$

and similarly region b has no incentive to defect if

$$\left[1 + \frac{\delta}{2}\right]u_b(y_b + \Delta - t_b) + \frac{\delta}{2}u_b(y_b + t_a) \geq \left[1 + \frac{\delta}{2}\right]u_b(y_b + \Delta) + \frac{\delta}{2}u_b(y_b). \tag{17.9}$$

We can draw several implications from this simple model of risk sharing without commitment. First, the time horizon will influence the amount of mutual insurance that is sustainable. Indeed, the value attached to continued insurance depends on the discount rate (reflecting the time horizon). At one extreme when $\delta \to 0$ (extremely short horizon), the value of future insurance is zero and regions always defect. No insurance is possible. At the other extreme when $\delta \to 1$ (very long horizon), the value of future insurance is sufficiently high that full insurance is possible $\left(t_i = \frac{A}{2}\right)$. And by a continuity argument, for intermediate discounting values $\delta \in (\underline{\delta}, \bar{\delta})$ with $0 < \underline{\delta} < \bar{\delta} < 1$, only limited insurance is possible $\left(t_i < \frac{A}{2}\right)$. Therefore the expected time horizon limits the amount of risk sharing. For values $\delta \geq \bar{\delta}$, complete risk sharing can be achieved. For intermediate values $\underline{\delta} < \delta < \bar{\delta}$, there is partial risk sharing. And for values $\delta < \underline{\delta}$, no risk sharing is possible.

The second implication is that the level of risk sharing that regions can achieve increases with risk aversion. The reason is that regions put more weight on the gain from long-term insurance against the short-term gain from defecting. This is immediately seen from the participation constraints. Indeed, the income distribution on the left-hand side of equations (17.8) and (17.9) is less uncertain than the income distribution on the right-hand side, which makes the participation constraints more likely to be satisfied under increased risk aversion.

A third implication concerns the effect of income inequality. Intuition would suggest that mutual insurance is more likely if regions are ex ante identical and that regional inequality limits the scope for insurance. But this is not true. The reason is that risk-sharing redistributes ex post from the region with a positive shock to the other region, but it does not redistribute ex ante from the rich to the poor regions. More surprisingly the increased inequality, while maintaining constant the aggregate income, can improve insurance. To see this, start from income equality $y_a = y_b$. Using the participation constraint, we can calculate the level of risk sharing that is possible. Then we increase y_a and reduce y_b by the same amount. The participation constraints are then affected because income levels influence the demand for insurance. It is then possible to show that for some standard utility functions the amount of risk sharing has increased with inequality.

17.5.2   Insurance versus Redistribution

In practice, interregional insurance is organized in a federation through federal taxes and transfers. The effect of such a federal tax system is to redistribute income from high- to low-income regions. By pooling income risk across the regions, the federal tax system provides insurance against region-specific shocks. However, to the extent that there is ex ante income inequality among regions, federal taxes also provide ex ante regional redistribution. We ignore the stabilizing effect of federal taxation, which refers to the possibility of smoothing shocks over time (between bad years and good years). The insurance motive for the federal tax system is explicitly recognized in many countries. For instance, in the UK part of the tax system is actually called "National Insurance." To appreciate the amount of insurance federal taxes can provide, it is necessary to disentangle redistribution from insurance components. Redistribution acts on the initial income distribution, while insurance responds to income shocks (either permanent or temporary).

Assume that region i's income at time t is subject to permanent shock ψ_i^t and temporary shock η_i^t. Both shocks are assumed to be mean zero. Thus regional income at time t can be written

$$y_i^t = y_i^0 + \sum_{s=1}^{t} \psi_i^s + \eta_i^t. \tag{17.10}$$

Suppose that the federal tax system taxes all regions' incomes at the same rate τ and redistributes total tax revenue as a uniform transfer to all regions. It follows that region i at time t pays taxes τy_i^t and receives transfers from the federation based on the average tax payment

$$\tau E\left[y_i^0 + \sum_{s=1}^{t} \psi_i^s + \eta_i^t\right] = \tau E[y_i^0] = \tau \bar{y}^0. \tag{17.11}$$

The regional income after tax and transfer is

$$x_i^t = y_i^0 + \tau(\bar{y}^0 - y_i^0) + (1 - \tau)[\Sigma \psi_i^s + \eta_i^t]. \tag{17.12}$$

The income change can be decomposed into an insurance part and a redistribution part as follows:

$$x_i^t - y_i^t = \underbrace{\tau(\bar{y}^0 - y_i^0)}_{\text{Redistribution}} - \underbrace{\tau[\Sigma \psi_i^s + \eta_i^t]}_{\text{Insurance}}. \tag{17.13}$$

Using this decomposition, it is interesting to measure the extent of insurance provided by federal taxation in practice. Empirical studies for the US federal tax system clearly suggest the presence of intranational insurance. Although there is disagreement about the exact magnitude of the insurance, all studies find that the redistribution effect largely dominates the insurance effect. They also find that insurance is rather modest, in the sense that it cannot smooth more than a ten cents on a dollar change in state income caused by asymmetric shocks.

17.6   Evidence on Decentralization

17.6.1   Decentralization around the World

The degree of decentralization of government activity can be measured in several different ways. Oates (1972) distinguishes three measures of fiscal decentralization: (1) share of total public revenue collected by the central government, (2) share of the central government in all public expenditures (including income redistribution payments), and (3) share of the central government in current government consumption expenditures.

The first measure based on revenue collection raises the problem that the center may collect revenue for regions. It underestimates the degree of decentralization to the extent that regions get back substantial portions of the revenue collected at the central level. The second measure, including income redistribution payments, also underestimates the degree of decentralization because the redistribution of income is mostly the role of central governments regardless of how decentralized a country is. The same argument applies for excluding defense spending, which is the other public good that is uniformly provided by central governments. So the more appropriate measure is the concentration of total government current consumption. Such information is readily available in the rich database at Brown University, in which total government expenditures are the consolidated sum of all expenditures at different government levels. Consolidation matters to prevent double-counting of intergovernmental grants and transfers.

Table 17.1 shows the patterns of decentralization around the world and suggests some clear trends. Developed countries are generally more decentralized. Latin America countries decentralized mostly during the period 1980 to 1995.

Table 17.1
Share of central government expenditure in total expenditures

Countries	1975	1985	1995
Developed	0.57	0.49	0.46
Russia	—	0.61	0.63
Latin America	0.76	0.71	0.70
Asia	0.79	0.74	0.72
Africa	0.88	0.86	0.82
World	0.76	0.68	0.64

Source: Vernon Henderson's dataset, 1975–1995, Brown University.

However, government consumption in Latin America remains substantially more centralized, with spending at the central level close to 70 percent against central spending less than 50 percent in developed countries. African countries are the most centralized and display little decrease in centralization (with almost all government spending occurring at the central level). Developed countries exhibit the most substantial decreases among all regions in centralization. The world level average (involving up to 48 countries) also reveals a general trend toward greater decentralization, with the central spending share declining from 75 percent in 1975 to 64 percent in 1995.

17.6.2   Decentralization by Functions

Previously the degree of decentralization was shown to differ quite substantially among countries. It is instructive to measure the decentralization of public expenditures by function to see whether this is consistent with normative advice. From a normative point of view decentralization is desirable when the need to tailor spending to local preferences dominates the possible economies of scale and inter-regional spillovers.

The Government Finance Statistics of the IMF contain the data for breaking down government activities by functions and levels. All local expenditures refer to expenditures of the state, regional and provincial governments. Table 17.2 indicates the functional decentralization of government activity country by country. Housing and community amenities are the most decentralized, with an average of 71 percent, followed closely by education and health with an average of 64 percent each. The least decentralized are the expenditures for social security and welfare with an average of 18 percent. This is consistent with the normative view that income redistribution is better achieved at the central level.

17.6.3   Determinants of Decentralization

Decentralization is a complex process, and we have provided but a snapshot of the enormous normative literature on how best to allocate different responsibilities between central and local governments and the possible efficiency gains of decentralization. However, the positive issue of why and when decentralization occurs deserves also some attention.

The positive literature on decentralization suggests certain empirical regularities concerning the forces that promote decentralization. Oates (1972) finds in a

Table 17.2

Local expenditures as a percentage of total government expenditure by function, 1995 to 1999

Country	Education	Health	Social welfare	Housing	Transport	Total
Australia	72	48	10	77	85	50
Canada	94	96	31	74	90	60
Denmark	45	95	55	29	51	56
France	37	2	9	82	42	19
Germany	96	28	21	93	57	38
Ireland	22	48	6	70	43	25
Netherlands	33	5	14	79	35	26
Norway	63	78	19	87	31	38
Russia	83	90	10	96	68	39
Spain	71	63	6	93	62	36
United Kingdom	68	0	20	40	61	26
United States	95	43	31	32	75	49
Average	64	64	18	71	56	38

Source: IMF, *Government Finance Statistics Yearbook*, 2001 (Washington, DC).

cross-sectional analysis that both country size and income per capita play a crucial role in explaining decentralization. The empirical evidence suggests that for different measures of decentralization, larger and richer countries are more decentralized. To better control for interregional geographic and cultural differences, Oates and Wallis (1988) use a panel analysis of 48 US states. They find that diversity as measured by urbanization increases decentralization.

In a very interesting study, Panizza (1999) estimates a theoretical model of decentralization that allows a test for the preference sorting effect. He uses a linear country model like the one presented previously in the optimal structure section. The level of public good provision is determined at the central level by majority voting (i.e., by the median voter's preference). The central government provides a uniform public good level whose value decreases with the spatial distance between citizens and the central government. Local government provision is closer to the preferences of citizens and so more valuable. Since voters benefit more from local provision, increasing central provision reduces overall demand for the public good. Central government decides its share in provision of the public good, anticipating how that share influences overall demand for the public good. Using cross-sectional analysis and standard measures of decentralization, Panizza finds that decentralization increases with country size, income per capita, the level of democracy, and ethnolinguistic fractionalization.

A important limit of the existing empirical testing of decentralization is that it ignores a central force in the process of decentralization, namely the threat of separation. The possibility of secession has been a powerful force in limiting the ability of the central government to exploit peripheral minorities of voters for the sake of the majority of the population. The idea is that a unitary government is more willing to devolve more power and responsibility when the threat of secession is more credible. It has been a recurrent feature in Europe that the decision to decentralize is not necessarily guided by efficiency considerations but is also driven by distributional and political forces. When rich regions, which today transfer large amounts of income to poorer regions, demand more decentralization, it is to limit their net contributions. They often do that because they do not believe anymore in the mutual insurance effect that such transfers might change directions in the near future. Also the size of the regional redistribution has become so visible that it creates an insurmountable political problem. The perception is that rich regions become better off by seceding, and to prevent such countries from breaking apart, concessions in the form of larger devolution of responsibilities and resources to regions have been taking place. Italy and Belgium are two good illustrations of the sort of decentralization forced by the pressing demand of the rich regions Lombardy and Flanders, respectively. It is clear that in those cases the efficiency argument that decentralization allows policy choices that better reflect local preference was not the key force. Richer regions demand more autonomy because the regional income inequality is such that mutual insurance becomes pure redistribution. Moreover the demand for more autonomy is exacerbated, rightly or wrongly, by the perceptions in the rich regions that the regional transfers are largely influenced by opportunistic behavior of the receiving regions (i.e., some form of moral hazard problem at the regional level).

17.7   Conclusions

There is a considerable controversy as to what public activities should be decentralized or centralized. There is also empirical evidence of increasing decentralization around the world. In this chapter we considered the costs and benefits of decentralization. We saw that one important advantage of a decentralized system is the tailoring of the provision of public goods and services to local preferences. The idea is that local government is closer to the people and so more responsive to their preferences than central governments. Another advantage of decentralization is to foster intergovernmental competition making government more efficient and more accountable to the electorate.

There are also disadvantages of a decentralized system. Some of them, like fiscal competition, are covered in the next chapter. The main disadvantage of decentralization is probably its failure to exploit all the economies of scale in the provision of public goods. Another disadvantage is to limit the scope for interregional risk sharing through the federal fiscal system.

Optimal federalism results from trade-offs among the various costs and benefits due to decentralization. It provides normative conclusions about the allocation of responsibilities between central and local levels. However, from a more positive perspective, political and distributional considerations can lead to different conclusions. The best illustration is that too much decentralization will result from a democratic choice.

Further Reading

The optimal government structure with overlapping jurisdictions is analyzed in:

Casella, A., and Frey, B. 1992. Federalism and clubs: Toward an economic theory of overlapping political jurisdictions. *European Economic Review* 36: 635–46.

Hochman, O., Pines, D., and Thisse, J. 1995. On the optimal structure of local governments. *American Economic Review* 85: 1224–40.

The excessive decentralization with majority rule is in:

Alesina, A., and Spolaore, E. 1997. On the number and size of nations. *Quarterly Journal of Economics* 112: 1028–56.

Cremer, H., de Kerchove, A.-M., and Thisse, J. 1985. A economic theory of public facilities in space. *Mathematical Social Sciences* 9: 249–62.

The empirical analysis of the determinants of decentralization is in:

Oates, W. E. 1972. *Fiscal Federalism.* New York: Harcourt Brace Jovanovich.

Oates, W. E., and Wallis, J. 1988. Decentralization in the public sector: An empirical study and local government. In H. S. Rosen, ed., *Fiscal Federalism: Quantitative Studies.* Chicago: University of Chicago Press, pp. 5–32.

Panizza, U. 1999. On the determinant of fiscal centralization: Theory and evidence. *Journal of Public Economics* 74: 97–139.

The study of secession and break-up of nations is in:

Buchanan, J., and Faith, R. 1987. Secession and the limits of taxation: Toward a theory of internal exit. *American Economic Review* 77: 1023–31.

Bolton, P., and Roland, G. 1997. The break up of nations: A political economy analysis. *Quarterly Journal of Economics* 112: 1057–90.

Government accountability is in:

Brennan, G., and Buchanan, J. 1980. *The Power to Tax*. New York: Cambridge University Press.

Przeworski, A., Stokes, S., and Manin, B., eds. 1999. *Democracy, Accountability, and Representation*. Cambridge: Cambridge University Press.

Seabright, P. 1996. Accountability and decentralization in government: An incomplete contracts model. *European Economic Review* 40: 61–89.

Risk sharing is analyzed in:

Genicot, G., and Ray, D. 2003. Endogenous group formation in risk sharing arrangements. *Review of Economic Studies* 70: 87–113.

Kocherlakota, N. 1996. Implications of efficient risk sharing without commitment. *Review of Economic Studies* 63: 595–609.

Lockwood, B. 1999. Inter-regional insurance. *Journal of Public Economics* 72: 1–37.

Persson, T., and Tabellini, G. 1996. Federal fiscal constitutions: Risk sharing and moral hazard. *Econometrica* 64: 623–46.

Persson, T., and Tabellini, G. 1996. Federal fiscal constitutions: Risk sharing and redistribution. *Journal of Political Economy* 104: 979–1009.

The relation of the federal fiscal system and insurance is in:

Sorensen, B. E., and Yosha, O. 1997. Federal insurance of US states: An empirical investigation. In A. Razin and E. Sadka, eds., *The Economics of Globalization: Policy Perspectives from Public Economics*. Cambridge: Cambridge University Press, pp. 156–72.

Exercises

17.1. Two jurisdictions have preferences described by $U^A = -[\theta^A - G^A]^2$ and $U^B = -[\theta^B - G^B]^2$, where G^j is the quantity of the local publc good in jurisdction j and $\theta^j > 0$ is a parameter.

  a. What is the optimal quantity of public good for the two jurisdictions?

  b. If the public good is centrally provided so that $G^A = G^B$, find the quantity that maximizes $U^A + U^B$.

  c. Calculate the loss from enforcing uniformity of provision.

17.2. The Tiebout hypothesis has been likened to consumers "voting with their feet." In many voting situations the electors can gain by voting strategically. Why will a consumer never make a strategic choice of jurisdiction?

17.3. Is the allocation of the population between jurisdictions likely to be the efficient division in an economy where property rental is the norm or one where property ownership is the norm?

17.4.   (Preference matching 1) Consider a society with many persons who can choose freely to live in either region 1 or region 2. It is more expensive to live in region 2: it costs c_1 to live in region 1 and $c_2 = c_1 + \Delta$ to live in region 2 (with $\Delta > 0$). Individuals differ in their incomes, denoted by y. Income takes on values between 0 and 1 and is uniformly distributed. Individuals care about the income of those living in their region. The mean income of a region $j = 1, 2$ is a function of the average value of y in that region, denoted by $\bar{y}_j$. An individual with income y choosing to live in region j with mean income $\bar{y}_j$ derives utility net of cost of $U = [1 + y][1 + \bar{y}_j] - c_j$. Hence richer individuals place greater value on living together with other rich residents.

a. Suppose that all individuals simultaneously make their location choices. Show that in any equilibrium (where no one wishes to move given the location choice of everyone else) both regions must be occupied if $\frac{1}{2} < \Delta < 1$, that is the cost differential is neither too high nor too low. What would happen if $\Delta > 1$ or $\Delta < \frac{1}{2}$?

b. For $\frac{1}{2} < \Delta < 1$ show that in any equilibrium where the mean income differs across regions, every resident of region 1 must have a lower income than every resident of region 2.

c. Show that there exists a critical level of income y^* such that all individuals with higher income choose to live in region 2 and all individuals with lower income choose to live in region 1. Provide an expression for this critical income level.

d. Show that in the equilibrium with income sorting, it is possible to make everyone better off by changing slightly the residential choices. [*Hint*: Consider a small change in the critical income y^*.]

17.5.   (Preference matching 2) Consider two districts A and B with two types of residents, rich (R) and poor (P). Rich residents have an income of $Y_R = 2,000$ and poor residents have an income of $Y_P = 1,000$. Both districts provide a local public good for their residents. The rich residents value the local public good more than the poor residents. That is, the value of the local public good to each resident is $V_i = \frac{Y_i G}{10} - \frac{G^2}{2}$ for $i = R, P$, where G is the level of local public good provision. The cost of the local public good per resident is $C = 5G$.

a. What are the marginal value and the marginal cost of the local public good for each type of resident?

b. What is the willingness to pay of the rich residents for the local public good? What is the willingness to pay of the poor residents?

c. In district A there are 400 rich residents and 200 poor residents, whereas in district B the numbers are reversed. What would be the public good provision in each district if it was decided by majority voting? What type of residents would not be happy with this voting outcome?

17.6.   Consider the previous exercise and now suppose both types of residents can migrate to the other district.

a. Which residents will move?

b. What will be the equilibrium distribution of residents?

c. Are there still residents unhappy with the amount of local public good?

d. Is the provision of public good efficient (according to the Samuelson rule)? Explain why or why not.

17.7. Consider the previous exercise with the situation before migration, and suppose that the government requires the rich residents to contribute $\frac{3}{4}$ of the cost of local public good provision where they live and the poor residents to contribute $\frac{1}{4}$ of the cost.

a. How much public good will be provided under majority voting in each district?

b. Is there any resident who wants to move (and, if so, who and where)? Why or why not?

17.8. There are two regions. Both can undertake some investment in a local public good that improves the welfare of their residents. However, there are some spillovers in these investment decisions. If region 1 provides the public good, region 2 obtains some spillover benefits, and vice versa. More precisely, let g_1 and g_2 be the local public good levels in region 1 and 2 and their respective welfare levels be $W^i(g_i, g_j) = 2[a\sqrt{g_i} + b\sqrt{g_i g_j}] - cg_i$ for $i \neq j$ (with $i, j = 1, 2$), where $a > 0$ and $0 < b < c$.

a. Find the Nash equilibrium levels of g_1 and g_2 when public investment decisions are taken simultaneously. What is the equilibrium welfare level of each region?

b. Suppose that public investment decisions are centralized. What levels of g_1 and g_2 maximize the total welfare $W^1(g_1, g_2) + W^2(g_2, g_1)$? Are these levels higher or lower than in part a? Explain briefly. Is the welfare of each region higher than in part a? Why or why not?

c. Discuss a possible interregional transfer scheme based on public investment in the other region that could induce each region to choose noncooperatively in a Nash equilibrium the same public investment levels as in part b. Explain.

17.9. There are two regions $j = 1, 2$ and two goods, a private good x and a pure public good g. There are n_j identical residents in region j. Each resident is endowed with a fixed amount of private good that can be turned into a public good at a unit cost equal to one. The utility of each resident in region j is $U^j = x_j + \theta_j \log(g)$.

a. Suppose that $\theta_1 < \theta_2$ and $n_1 < n_2$. Suppose also that each region chooses its public good provision independently so that the common level of public good is the sum of regional provisions $g = \sum_j g_j$. How much public good will each region provide in the (Nash) equilibrium? (*Hint*: Beware of corner solutions.)

b. How does the equilibrium outcome change if we assume that $\theta_1 < \theta_2$ and $n_1 > n_2$?

c. Now assume that public good provision is decided jointly for the two regions by a central authority (centralized setting). Majority voting implies that public good provision is then based on the preference of the median (larger) region; that is region 2 in part a and region 1 in part b. The advantage is to spread the cost more widely, and the disadvantage is to impose the preference of one region on the other. Find the optimal public good provision and compare with spending levels in part a and part b. Is it possible for spending to fall with centralization?

d. What is the welfare effect of centralization for each region when region 1 is larger? Does your conclusion change if region 2 is larger? Why or why not?

17.10. (Caplin and Nalebuff) There are two regions $j = 1, 2$ competing for residents through their policy choice. The policy choice of each region j is represented by a point x_j on the interval $[0, 1]$. Prospective residents differ in their policy preferences. A resident of type θ who lives in region j with policy x_j has utility $U(x_j; \theta) = -[\theta - x_j]^2$. Thus type

θ's preferred policy is $x = \theta$. Assume a triangular population distribution on the interval $[0, 1]$. Given the policy choice of each region, each resident chooses the region with the policy closer to his most preferred policy. In equilibrium no region wishes to change its policy given the policy of the other region and no individual wishes to move given the policy choices.

a. If both regions are utilitarian (i.e., maximize the sum of their residents' utilities), show that in equilibrium the two regions locate at $\frac{1}{3}$ and $\frac{2}{3}$ respectively with the population equally divided between them.

b. Show that if both regions are Rawlsian (i.e., they maximize the minimum utility of their residents) they will locate at $\frac{1}{4}$ and $\frac{3}{4}$ respectively, again with the population evenly distributed. Who are the worst-off residents? Compare with your answer in part a.

c. Now assume region 1 is Rawlsian and region 2 is utilitarian. Show that the equilibrium involves region 1 locating at 0.2 and region 2 locating at 0.6 with those to the left of 0.4 living in region 1 and the larger group to the right of 0.4 living in the utilitarian region 2. Who are the worst-off residents?

d. Comparing parts a and c, show that if one region switches to a more egalitarian objective (while the other is utilitarian), then society as a whole becomes less egalitarian. (*Hint*: Compare the welfare of the worst-off residents in cases a and c.)

e. Similarly, comparing parts b and c, show that if one region switches to a more egalitarian objective (when the other is Rawlsian), then society as a whole becomes more egalitarian.

17.11. Re-do the previous exercise with an inverted triangular distribution of population. Show that if one region switches to a more egalitarian objective, the welfare of the worst-off resident always improves no matter what the objective of the other region is. (*Hint*: The population distribution is bimodal.)

17.12. What principles should govern the allocation of power across different levels of government?

17.13. Is it possible that a federal social insurance scheme oversupplies risk sharing? Explain briefly.

17.14. Discuss the following statement: "A community of a higher order should not interfere in the internal life of a community of a lower order, ... but rather should support it in case of need and help to coordinate its activity with the activities of the rest of society always with a view to the common good." (John Paul II)

17.15. Describe the argument of yardstick competition to control policy-makers. What are the main difficulties if yardstick competition is to be applied in practice to control performance of policy-makers?

17.16. Discuss the relative costs and benefits of decentralization.

18 Fiscal Competition

18.1 Introduction

What is the role of competition among governments? If competition is the fundamental force for efficient economic performance in the private sector, why should it be different for the public sector? Why cannot the same disciplining effect of competition be applied to the public sector as well? In the private sector, competition will promote efficiency because firms that best satisfy consumers' preferences will survive and prosper, while others will lose customers and fail. Extending this argument to the public sector, competition among governments and jurisdictions should induce them to best serve the will of their residents. If they fail to do so, residents will vote with their feet and leave for other jurisdictions that offer a better deal.

The purpose of this chapter is to show that if the private competition analogy has some merit, it also needs to be seriously qualified. The chapter is organized as follows: First, the efficiency aspects of fiscal competition are presented. Second, the distributional aspects of residential mobility are evaluated. The key issue is how mobility limits the possibility of redistributing income. Third, the role of intergovernmental transfers is discussed both in terms of efficiency and redistribution. Fourth, some evidence on fiscal competition and intergovernmental interactions is given. Last, the main results from fiscal competition theory are summarized and evaluated in the concluding section.

18.2 Tax Competition

Tax competition refers to the interaction among governments due to interjurisdictional mobility of the tax base. It does not include the fiscal interaction among governments resulting from public good spillovers, where residents of one jurisdiction consume the public goods provided by neighboring jurisdictions. The cause of tax competition is that independent jurisdictions finance public expenditure by placing a tax on a mobile tax base. For example, a tax on capital will cause capital to seek a better return in alternative jurisdictions, and an income tax will cause workers to move jurisdiction if they are mobile. The loss of tax base by one jurisdiction represents a gain to the others, so mobility causes an externality among jurisdictions.

In the model we consider tax competition arises because jurisdictions finance provision of a public good with a tax on locally employed capital. Capital moves across jurisdictions in response to tax differentials, while residents are typically immobile (or at least less mobile). In the competitive version of tax competition, jurisdictions are "too small" (relative to the economy) to affect the net return to capital that is determined worldwide. As a result each jurisdiction sets its tax on locally employed capital, taking as given the net-of-tax price of capital. Tax rates in other jurisdictions do not matter, and there is no strategic interaction among jurisdictions when setting their taxes. We say that jurisdictions behave competitively. When jurisdictions are "large" relative to the economy, each jurisdiction can affect the net return to capital by varying its own tax rate. In this case the tax rate chosen in one jurisdiction varies with the taxes in other jurisdictions. Jurisdictions behave strategically: they set their tax in response to the tax rates in other jurisdictions.

Both the competitive and strategic versions of the tax competition model produce the same important conclusion, namely that public goods are underprovided relative to the efficient Samuelson rule level. The reason is that each jurisdiction perceives the mobility of capital and keeps its tax low to preserve its tax base. To understand the inefficiency arising from intergovernmental competition, it is useful to consider a simple model in which we assume, in turn, that jurisdictions behave competitively and then strategically.

18.2.1   Competitive Behavior

The assumption of perfect competition means that the mobile factor of production is available to the "small" jurisdiction at a fixed price. Suppose that capital is the mobile factor of production and that the jurisdiction seeks to impose a tax on capital and to use the revenue to provide public goods and services to its residents, or to directly transfer cash to them. If capital were perfectly immobile, a local source-based tax on capital would reduce the net rate of return to capital by the exact amount of the tax. This capital tax would make the residents better off at the expense of capital owners (who are not necessarily residents).

In contrast, when capital is costlessly mobile, local capital taxation cannot affect the net return to capital. The reason is that the imposition of the local tax drives capital out of the jurisdiction until the increase in the gross rate of return is sufficient to compensate capital owners for local taxes. However, the outflow of capital from the jurisdiction reduces the remuneration of labor. The resulting loss of income to the residents will exceed the value of the tax revenue collected from capital taxation. Except for the case where public expenditures have greater value to local residents than the tax revenue used to finance them, the net effect of capital taxation is to harm immobile residents. Therefore with perfect competition and costless mobility, the taxation of capital is impossible, whereas it may be desirable without mobility. Capital taxes that help immobile residents when capital is immobile harm them when this factor is perfectly mobile.

Assume that the local production process uses mobile capital, and immobile labor. The production function is $F(K_i, L)$, where K_i is the aggregate capital and L is aggregate labor employed in jurisdiction i. Each worker is endowed with one unit of labor. Under constant returns to scale, $F(K_i, L) = LF\left(\frac{K_i}{L}, 1\right) = Lf(k_i)$ where k_i is the capital–labor ratio. The production function $f(k_i)$ gives the per capita output, which is increasing and concave $(f''(k_i) < 0 < f'(k_i))$. The concavity of the production function reflects diminishing returns to capital as it is combined with the immobile stock of labor. Let ρ denote the net return to capital outside the jurisdiction, and let t_i denote the per unit tax on the capital employed in the jurisdiction i. With costless mobility of capital, the local supply of capital equates its net return in the jurisdiction i with its net return elsewhere:

$$f'(k_i) - t_i = \rho. \tag{18.1}$$

With exogenously fixed ρ, the fact that $f'(k_i)$ is decreasing in k_i implies that a higher tax drives capital away, so $\frac{dk_i}{dt_i} < 0$. Assuming that the net revenue collected from local capital taxation accrues to workers in the form of cash transfers or public goods of the same value, the net income of workers will be

$$y_i = f(k_i) - f'(k_i)k_i + t_i k_i$$

$$= f(k_i) - \rho k_i, \tag{18.2}$$

where the second equality follows from the arbitrage condition $f'(k_i) = \rho + t_i$. Because taxation reduces the amount of capital in the jurisdiction, it is then easily seen that the welfare of the workers, as measured by their net income y_i, is maximized by setting $t_i = 0$.

18.2.2   Strategic Behavior

It is now assumed that jurisdictions behave strategically. The strategic interaction makes the equilibrium analysis more delicate, and it is useful to describe the equilibrium outcome rigorously. Consequently this section will use more calculus than usual and can be skipped with little loss of continuity by those who wish to.

Consider two countries ($i = 1, 2$) that levy a tax on the return to capital. Capital is mobile and is used together with some fixed amount of labor to produce output. The production function is $F(K_i, L)$, where K_i is the aggregate capital and L is aggregate labor employed in country i. The quantity of labor available and the production technology are the same for the two countries, and each worker is endowed with one unit of labor. Under constant returns to scale, $F(K_i, L) = LF\left(\frac{K_i}{L}, 1\right) = Lf(k_i)$, where k_i is the capital–labor ratio. The production function $f(k_i)$ gives the per capita output, which is increasing and concave ($f''(k_i) < 0 < f'(k_i)$). There is a fixed stock of capital $\bar{k}$ that allocates itself between the two countries, so $k_1 + k_2 = \bar{k}$. Each country levies a per unit tax t_i on the capital that is employed within its boundaries. The revenue raised is used to supply a level of public services of $G_i = t_i k_i$. Due to capital mobility the tax choice of one jurisdiction affects the size of the tax base available to the other country.

Given the pair of tax rates, costless mobility implies the equality of the after-tax return to capital across countries:

$$f'(k_1) - t_1 = f'(k_2) - t_2$$

$$= f'(\bar{k} - k_1) - t_2. \tag{18.3}$$

This arbitrage condition produces an allocation of capital across countries that depends on the tax rates, as illustrated in figure 18.1.

The partition of the capital stock between the two countries is represented on the horizontal axis with the capital levels measured from the two corners (from left to right for country 1). The corresponding marginal product of capital in each country is measured on the vertical axis (the left axis for country 1). Note that if the tax rates do differ (e.g., $t_1 > t_2$), then capital is inefficiently allocated because the marginal product of capital differs across countries ($f'(k_1) > f'(k_2)$). It can also be seen that an increase in the tax rate in country 1 reduces the net return to capital in that country and causes some capital to move away to country 2. The converse holds when the tax in country 2 is increased.

These observations can be demonstrated formally by taking the total differential of the arbitrage condition (18.3) with respect to t_1 and k_1 to give

$$f''(k_1) \, dk_1 - dt_1 = -f''(\bar{k} - k_1) \, dk_1. \tag{18.4}$$

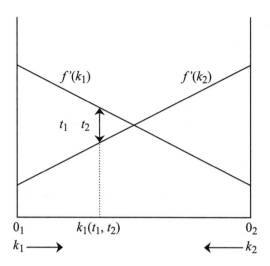

Figure 18.1
Allocation of capital

Then the variation in k_1 in response to the tax change dt_1 is

$$\frac{dk_1}{dt_1} = \frac{1}{f''(k_1) + f''(k_2)} < 0. \tag{18.5}$$

The sign of this expression follows from the assumption of a decreasing marginal product of capital, $f'' < 0$. Note that this assumption implies some regulating forces in the allocation of capital because when capital moves from 1 to 2, its marginal product decreases in country 2 at rate $-f''(k_2)$ and rises in country 1 at rate $f''(k_1)$. When setting its tax rate, country 1 will take into account how capital responds. That is, it will incorporate the movement of capital described above into its decision problem.

Assuming that the net revenue collected from local capital taxation accrues to workers in the form of cash transfers or public goods of the same value, we have the net income of workers (or residents) in country 1 as

$$y_1 = f(k_1) - f'(k_1)k_1 + t_1 k_1. \tag{18.6}$$

Each country maximizes the net income of its residents taking into account capital flows resulting from tax changes. Because the amount of capital employed in each country also depends on the other country's tax rate, there is strategic fiscal interaction among countries: neither can set its own tax rate without taking into account what the other is doing.

The optimal choice of each country is found by applying the usual Nash assumption: each takes the tax rate of the other as given when maximizing. By this reasoning, the best response of country 1 to the other country's tax t_2 is described by the following first-order condition:

$$\frac{dy_1(t_1, t_2)}{dt_1} = -k_1 f_1'' \frac{dk_1}{dt_1} + k_1 + t_1 \frac{dk_1}{dt_1}$$

$$= [k_1 f_2'' + t_1] \frac{dk_1}{dt_1} = 0, \tag{18.7}$$

where the second equality is obtained by using (18.5) to substitute for $k_1 = k_1[f_1'' + f_2''] \frac{dk_1}{dt_1}$. Therefore the best-response function for country 1 can be written as

$$t_1 = -k_1 f_2'' = r_1(t_2), \tag{18.8}$$

and similarly for country 2 as

$$t_2 = -k_2 f_1'' = r_2(t_1). \tag{18.9}$$

A Nash equilibrium is a pair (t_1^*, t_2^*) such that the tax choice of each country is a best response to the other country's tax choice, $t_1^* = r_1(t_2^*)$ and $t_2^* = r_2(t_1^*)$. The symmetry of the model implies that both countries choose the same taxes in equilibrium, so $t_1^* = t_2^*$, and consequently capital is evenly distributed between jurisdictions with $k_1 = k_2 = \frac{\bar{k}}{2}$. The Nash equilibrium in taxes is thus

$$t_1^* = t_2^* = -\frac{\bar{k}}{2} f'' \left(\frac{\bar{k}}{2} \right). \tag{18.10}$$

We can also find the slope of the best-response function $r_1(t_2)$ to evaluate the nature of strategic interdependency between the two countries. The first-order condition $\psi_1(t_1, t_2) = k_1 f_2'' + t_1 = 0$ implicitly defines t_1 as a function of t_2, and we need to know how the optimum choice of t_1 will respond to changes in t_2. Differentiating the first-order condition totally, we have

$$\frac{\partial \psi_1}{\partial t_1} dt_1 + \frac{\partial \psi_1}{\partial t_2} dt_2 = 0. \tag{18.11}$$

Recall that with a fixed stock of capital, the loss of tax base by one jurisdiction represents a gain to the others, so $\frac{dk_1}{dt_1} = -\frac{dk_2}{dt_1} = -\frac{dk_1}{dt_2}$. This gives the slope of the best response as

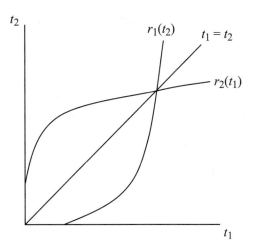

Figure 18.2
Symmetric Nash equilibrium

$$\frac{dr_1}{dt_2} = \frac{[f_2'' - k_1 f_2'''] \, dk_1/dt_1}{1 + [f_2'' - k_1 f_2'''] \, dk_1/dt_1}, \tag{18.12}$$

where $\frac{dk_1}{dt_1} < 0$, and $f''' < 0$. It follows that for $f''' \geq 0$ the slope of the best-response function satisfies $0 < \frac{dr_1}{dt_2} < 1$. Tax rates are strategic complements: a lower tax in country 2 attracts capital away from country 1, which in response cuts its own tax rate.

It is now easily seen that such a Nash equilibrium with $t_1^* = t_2^* = t^*$ involves inefficiently low taxes and that jointly increasing taxes to $t > t^*$ is beneficial to both countries. First, observe that from the perspective of the two countries together, the stock of capital is fixed at $\bar{k}$. Hence it is simply a fixed factor. Provided both countries levy the same tax rate $t = t_1 = t_2$, half of the capital, $\frac{\bar{k}}{2}$, will be located in each country regardless of the level of the taxes. The welfare of the workers in each country, as measured by their net income $y = f(k) - f'(k)k + tk$, is then improved, since $\frac{t\bar{k}}{2} > \frac{t^*\bar{k}}{2}$. In fact with the cooperative tax setting the countries can maximize the net income of their residents by fully taxing the mobile factor, whereas the noncooperative equilibrium leads to a lower tax on capital. Welfare is higher with cooperation. This loss in potential welfare is the efficiency cost of fiscal competition.

Although the model just considered leads to the extreme conclusion that the tax is pushed to its maximum with cooperation, this was not the major point of the analysis. What the model does illustrate are the forces that are at work when an attempt is made to tax a mobile factor of production. The movement of the factor generates an externality among countries that is not internalized when their governments conduct individual optimization of taxes. This externality is due to the fact that a higher tax in one country pushes some of the factor to the other country. This has the beneficial effect of increasing the other country's tax base and its tax revenue at any given tax rate. Cooperation among countries in the choice of taxes internalizes this externality and allows them to choose a mutually preferable set of tax rates.

Consequently competition for mobile factors of production results in tax rates that are lower than is optimal for the countries involved. Implicitly each country can be understood to be trying to undercut the other to attract the mobile factor of production. This undercutting puts downward pressure on tax rates to the detriment of all countries. The policy principle that emerges from this scenario is that international cooperation on the setting of tax rates is beneficial.

As already noted, although the argument has been phrased in terms of countries, the same results would apply within a federal structure in which the separate jurisdictions at any level set their own tax rates. It is possibly more relevant in such a context because the factors of production may be more mobile than they are between countries. Furthermore, for tax competition to arise, the tax base need not be a factor of production but simply needs to be mobile between jurisdictions. For example, the argument applies equally well to the taxation of commodities provided that purchases can be made mobile through cross-border shopping. The resulting equilibrium with cross-border shopping will have inefficiently low commodity taxes. The taxes will be lower, the higher the perceived elasticity of cross-border shopping. This is so as long as goods are taxed according to the *origin principle* (i.e., the goods are taxed where they are produced). If the *destination principle* is applied, the goods are taxed in the country where they are consumed and the incentive for cross-border shopping would disappear. However, the destination principle of taxation is costly to operate because it requires that all taxes levied in the country of production be rebated when the good is exported. This is only possible if border controls are maintained. The same commodity taxes must be levied on all imports into the country of final consumption, with tax revenue also accruing to this country.

As such, the tax competition argument provides some important reasons for being cautious about the benefits of fiscal federalism that were described in the previous chapter. Giving jurisdictions too much freedom in tax setting may lead to mutually damaging reductions in taxes—the so-called race to the bottom.

18.2.3   Size Matters

Difference in country size, production technologies, factor endowments, or residents' preferences can be expected to cause the countries to choose different tax rates. An interesting aspect of the ensuing asymmetric tax competition is the so-called benefit of smallness. The idea is that although fiscal competition is inefficient, it can actually benefit small countries. Of course, such a gain comes at the expense of larger countries.

This can be seen in our simple two-country model by assuming they differ in their number of residents only. Suppose that country 1 is "large" with a share $s > \frac{1}{2}$ of the total population and country 2 is "small" with population share $1 - s < \frac{1}{2}$. The capital market-clearing condition is then

$$sk_1(t_1, t_2) + [1 - s]k_2(t_1, t_2) = \bar{k}, \tag{18.13}$$

where $\bar{k}$ is the (worldwide) average capital–labor ratio. The arbitrage condition implies equality of the after-tax return on capital across countries:

$$f'(k_1) - t_1 = f'(k_2) - t_2$$

$$= f'\left(\frac{\bar{k}}{1 - s} - \frac{sk_1}{1 - s}\right) - t_2. \tag{18.14}$$

Differentiating the arbitrage condition gives the capital outflow in response to a domestic tax increase

$$\frac{dk_1}{dt_1} = \frac{1 - s}{[1 - s]f''(k_1) + sf''(k_2)} < 0, \tag{18.15}$$

and by analogy, for the small country

$$\frac{dk_2}{dt_2} = \frac{s}{[1 - s]f''(k_1) + sf''(k_2)} < 0. \tag{18.16}$$

From (18.15) and (18.16) it follows that both countries face a capital outflow after an increase in their own tax rate, but this outflow is less severe in the large country. Indeed, when $t_1 = t_2$, we have $k_1 = k_2$, $f''(k_1) = f''(k_2)$, and thus $\frac{dk_2}{dt_2} < \frac{dk_1}{dt_1} < 0$ for $s > 1 - s$. The larger country faces a less elastic tax base and thereby chooses a higher tax rate than the smaller country, so in equilibrium $t_1 > t_2$. Because the small country charges a lower tax on capital, it will employ more capital per unit of labor, $(k_2 > k_1)$ increasing per capita income and making its residents better off than the residents of the large country. It is even possible

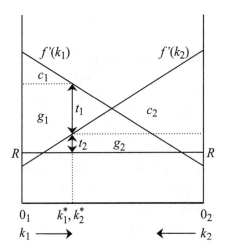

Figure 18.3
Advantage of smallness

that for a sufficiently large difference in size, the small country will be better off than it would be without tax competition.

This benefit of smallness is illustrated in figure 18.3, where for country $i = 1, 2$ per capita income is denoted $c_i = f(k_i) - f'(k_i)k_i$ and tax revenue is denoted $g_i = t_i k_i$. The net return to capital, denoted by R, is the same for both countries by arbitrage and is adjusted to tax choices in order to clear the market. It is then readily seen that the residents of the small country are better off taxing less, since $c_2 + g_2 > c_1 + G_1$.

We can obviously extend this reasoning to show that if the number of countries competing for capital increases, each country having a lower population share will perceive a greater elasticity of its tax base and choose lower taxes: the larger the number of countries, the more intense the competition and the lower the equilibrium taxes. Again, commodity taxation competition displays a close similarity to capital tax competition when countries differ in population size, with the smaller country setting the lower tax rate as it perceives a higher elasticity of its domestic tax base.

18.2.4   Tax Overlap

A common feature of fiscal federalism is that higher and lower levels of government share the same tax base. This tax base overlap gives rise to vertical fiscal

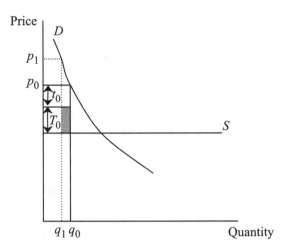

Figure 18.4
Tax overlap

externalities. With tax competition among jurisdictions, the horizontal fiscal externality on other regions is positive—an increase in tax rate by one region raises the tax base of others. In contrast, if different levels of government share the same tax base, then the tax levied by one government will reduce the tax base available to other levels of governments. This introduces a negative vertical externality. Not surprisingly such vertical externalities lead to overtaxation in equilibrium because each level of government neglects the negative effect of its taxation on the other levels of government.

The joint taxation of cigarettes by Canadian federal and provincial governments is a good example. Figure 18.4 illustrates this tax overlap problem. The supply curve, S, is assumed to be perfectly elastic, and the demand curve, D, is downward-sloping. Suppose that the initial federal excise tax rate is T_0 and the provincial tax rate is t_0. The corresponding price is p_0 and the quantity of cigarettes consumed is q_0. Tax revenue is $T_0 q_0$ for the federal government, and $t_0 q_0$ for the provincial government. If the provincial government raises its tax rate to $t_1 = t_0 + \Delta$, the consumer price increases by the amount of the tax increase $p_1 = p_0 + \Delta$, and the quantity consumed decreases to q_1. The tax revenue of the provincial government increases by $[t_1 - t_0]q_1 - t_0[q_0 - q_1]$, but due to the reduction in the consumption of cigarettes, revenue for the federal government decreases by $T_0[q_0 - q_1]$, as represented by the shaded area in figure 18.4. A similar vertical externality (but in the opposite direction) would arise if the federal government were to raise its tax rate. If both levels of government neglect the revenue losses incurred by the other government when making their tax choices, then both governments are underestimating the cost of raising tax revenue from the common tax base and will tend to choose tax rates that are inefficiently high.

When vertical and horizontal externalities are combined, the noncooperative equilibrium outcome is ambiguous: it involves excessively low taxes if the horizontal externalities dominate the vertical externalities. Canada again provides an important example because most provincial governments levy their personal income tax as a fraction of the federal income tax. On top of this each province levies a surtax on high-income residents. The bias in the perceived marginal cost of taxation caused by tax base overlap may explain why Canadian provinces have introduced high-income surtaxes when tax competition for mobile high-income taxpayers predicts the reverse.

18.2.5   Tax Exporting

In any country some of the commodities that are sold within its borders will be purchased by nonresidents (especially cross-border shoppers). This will be particularly true if the country is especially important in the context of international tourism. It will also be encouraged under fiscal federalism with a single market covering all jurisdictions. Similarly some of the productive activity carried out in a country will be undertaken by firms that repatriate their profits to another country. Whenever there is such economic activity by nonresidents, the possibility for tax exporting arises.

Tax exporting is the levying of taxes that discriminate against nonresidents. A simple example would be the imposition of a higher level of VAT on restaurants located in centers of tourism. The motive for such tax exporting is to shift some of the burden of revenue collection onto nonresidents and to lower it on residents. All else held constant, this is clearly of benefit to residents. However, all else is not constant in practice, and the same argument will apply to all countries. As for tax overlap, tax exporting provides an argument for why tax rates may be set too high when countries compete.

Another form of tax exporting is the taxation of capital employed in the country but owned by nonresidents. The simplest version of this form of tax exporting can be described with the previous model of tax competition by assuming that country 1's residents have a capital endowment $\bar{k}_1 > 0$ that differs from that of country 2, $\bar{k}_1 \neq \bar{k}_2$. Capital owners in each country are free to invest their capital in their home country or abroad. The level of social welfare in country 1 is measured by the net income of its workers, $y_1 = f(k_1) - f'(k_1)k_1 + t_1 k_1$, where k_1 is the amount of capital employed in country 1, plus the net income of its capital owners, $\rho\bar{k}_1$. The capital market-clearing condition requires that

$$\bar{k}_1 - k_1 = -[\bar{k}_2 - k_2].\tag{18.17}$$

That is, if $k_1 < \bar{k}_1$, country 1 is employing less capital than its endowment, and its net export of capital has to be equal to the net import of capital from country 2. For country 1 the problem is to set its tax t_1 on capital given the tax of country 2 so as to maximize

$$f(k_1) - f'(k_1)k_1 + t_1 k_1 + \rho\bar{k}_1,\tag{18.18}$$

where $k_1 = k_1(t_1, t_2)$ is the amount of capital employed in country 1 given tax rates t_1, t_2 and ρ is the net return to capital. Using $\rho = f'(k_1) - t_1$, the objective function can be written as follows:

$$W_1 = f(k_1) + \rho[\bar{k}_1 - k_1];\tag{18.19}$$

that is, country welfare is equal to total production $f(k_1)$ plus the net return to capital export $\rho[\bar{k}_1 - k_1]$. When deriving the first-order condition, we must differentiate W_1 with respect to t_1 taking into account the change in capital supply $\frac{dk_1}{dt_1}$ and the change in the net return to capital $\frac{d\rho}{dt_1}$. This gives

$$\frac{dW}{dt_1} = [f'(k_1) - \rho]\frac{dk_1}{dt_1} + [\bar{k}_1 - k_1]\frac{d\rho}{dt_1}$$

$$= t_1 \frac{dk_1}{dt_1} + [\bar{k}_1 - k_1]\left[f''\frac{dk_1}{dt_1} - 1\right] = 0.\tag{18.20}$$

To solve this first-order condition, we can use (18.5) to get $f_1''\frac{dk_1}{dt_1} - 1 = -f_2''\frac{dk_1}{dt_1}$, which gives

$$t_1 = f_2''(\bar{k}_1 - k_1),\tag{18.21}$$

and by analogy for country 2 using (18.17),

$$t_2 = -f_1''(\bar{k}_1 - k_1),\tag{18.22}$$

with $f_i'' < 0$. Therefore in any equilibrium, if country 1 has the larger endowment of capital so that $\bar{k}_1 > \bar{k}_2$, it will export capital ($k_1 < \bar{k}_1$) and prefer to subsidize capital $t_1 < 0$. The reason is the *terms-of-trade effect*. By subsidizing capital, the country with large endowment of capital can raise the net return to capital. Because the other country will import capital from country 1, it will tax capital $t_2 > 0$ as a means of taxing nonresidents. This is the tax-exporting effect. Next, note that the initial asymmetry in capital endowments leads countries to set different tax rates. This nonuniform tax equilibrium has important implications in terms of productive efficiency. Indeed, the efficient allocation of capital requires its marginal product to be equalized across countries. But because country 1 subsidizes capital and country 2 taxes it, the marginal product of capital is higher in country 2 than in country 1, $f_2' > f_1'$. Therefore, in equilibrium, country 1 attracts too much capital and country 2 too little, relative to what efficiency recommends.

18.2.6   Efficient Tax Competition

Tax competition has been seen as producing wasteful competition. There are circumstances, however, where tax competition may be welfare enhancing. We consider two examples.

The first example is the case where countries seek to give a competitive advantage to their own firms by offering *wasteful subsidies*. In equilibrium all countries will do this, so the effect of each country's subsidy cancels out with that of the others. Since the subsidies cancel, no country gains an advantage, and all countries will be better off giving no subsidy. This is the Prisoners' Dilemma once again. Tax competition may help overcome this inefficient outcome by allowing firms to locate wherever they choose and preventing governments from discriminating between domestic and foreign firms operating within a country. The mobility of the firms will force governments to recognize that their subsidy will not only give a competitive advantage to their domestic firms but that it will also attract firms from other countries. Because the government cannot discriminate between the domestic and foreign firms operating within its borders, it will have to pay the subsidy to both types of firms, thereby eliminating the competitive advantage. Therefore mobility eliminates the potential gains from the subsidy and raises its cost by extending its payment to foreign firms.

Tax competition can therefore improve welfare by reducing the incentive for countries to resort to wasteful subsidies to protect their own industries. Notice that the nondiscrimination requirement plays a crucial role in making tax competition welfare improving. If discrimination were possible, then governments could continue to give wasteful subsidies to their domestic firms.

The second example is the use of tax competition as a *commitment device*. In the tax competition model, governments independently announce tax rates and then the owners of capital choose where to invest. A commitment problem arises here because the governments are able to revise their tax rates after investment decisions are made. If there were a single government and investment decision were irreversible, then this government would have an incentive to tax away all profits. The capital owner would anticipate this incentive when making its initial investment decision and choose not to invest capital in such a country.

Tax competition may help to solve this commitment problem. The reason is that intergovernmental competition for capital would deter each government from taxing away profits within its borders because it would induce reallocation of capital between countries in response to differences in tax rates. Tax competition is a useful commitment device as it induces governments to forgo their incentive to tax investment in an effort to attract further investment or to maintain the existing investment level.

The original insight that tax competition leads to inefficiently low taxes and public good provision was obtained in models with benevolent decision-makers. An alternative approach is to consider public officials that seek in their decision-making to maximize their own welfare and not necessarily that of their constituencies. From this perspective, tax competition may help discipline *nonbenevolent* governments. For instance, if we view governments as "leviathans" mainly concerned with maximizing the size of the public sector, then tax competition may improve welfare by limiting taxation possibilities and thereby cutting down the size of government that would be otherwise excessive. This argument suggests that the public sector should be smaller, the greater the extent to which taxes and expenditures are decentralized. The evidence on this is, however, mixed. In fact there is not much evidence on the relationship between fiscal decentralization and the overall size of the public sector.

An analogous argument applies to governments with some degree of benevolence, possibly due to electoral concerns. When political agency problems are introduced, this inefficiency of competition among governments is no longer so clear. Intergovernmental competition makes the costs of public programs more visible, as well as their benefits, in ways that make public officials accountable for their decisions. Stated briefly, competition may induce government officials to reduce waste and thus reduce the effective price of public goods.

18.3   Income Distribution

When the powers for tax setting are devolved to individual jurisdictions, the Tiebout hypothesis asserts that the outcome will be efficient. The basis for this argument is that there are enough jurisdictions for individuals to sort themselves into optimal locations. For practical purposes it is not possible to appeal to this large-numbers assumption, and questions need to be asked about the outcome that will emerge when only a small, predetermined number of jurisdictions exist. The Tiebout hypothesis is also silent about how the policy of a jurisdiction emerges. It is possible that equilibrium results in all the residents of any jurisdiction being identical, so that there is no need to resolve different points of view. More generally, though, it is necessary to explore the consequences of political decision-making, expressed through elections, on the choice of policy.

An important set of issues revolve around income distribution and the role that this has in determining the composition of the population in jurisdictions. For instance, will it always be the case that the rich wish to detach themselves from the poor so that they can avoid being subject to redistributive taxation? Also, if they have the option, would the poor wish to live with the rich? These questions are now explored under perfect and imperfect mobility.

18.3.1   Perfect Mobility

The difficulty that mobility poses for redistribution is seen most strongly in the following example: Consider individuals who differ only in income level y and who can choose to reside in one of the two available jurisdictions. The jurisdictions independently set a constant tax rate t between 0 and 1 and pay a lump-sum transfer g subject to a budget balance constraint. Individuals care only about their income after taxes and transfers, so their preferences are given by

$$u(t, g; y) = g + [1 - t]y. \tag{18.23}$$

The tax-transfer pair (t, g) in each jurisdiction is chosen by some unspecified collective decision rule (e.g., majority voting). We are looking for an equilibrium in which the two jurisdictions differ and offer different tax and transfer schemes, thereby inducing the sorting of types across jurisdictions (as the Tiebout hypothesis would predict).

With no loss of generality, suppose that it is jurisdiction 1 that sets the higher tax rate. Then, to attract any individuals, it must also provide a higher level of transfer, that is, $(t_1, g_1) > (t_2, g_2)$. Individuals with different income levels differ in their preferences for redistribution. From (18.22), if a type y prefers the high-tax jurisdiction 1, then all those with lower income levels will also prefer this jurisdiction. And, if a type y prefers the low-tax jurisdiction 2, then all those with higher income levels will also prefer this jurisdiction. Therefore, if both jurisdictions are occupied in equilibrium, there must exist a separating type y^* who is just indifferent between the two tax schemes and all those who are poorer, with $y \leq y^*$, join jurisdiction 1 and all those who are richer, with $y > y^*$, join jurisdiction 2. That is, the jurisdiction undertaking more redistribution attracts the poorest individuals.

However, this cannot be an equilibrium because the richest individual in the poor jurisdiction loses out from intrajurisdictional redistribution and will prefer to move to the rich jurisdiction and become a net beneficiary of redistribution as its poorest resident. Therefore there cannot be an equilibrium with different tax-transfer schemes.

There remains the possibility of a symmetric equilibrium with individuals evenly divided between the two jurisdictions. In other words, perfect mobility leads to harmonization of tax-transfer schemes, even though agents differ in their preferences. Mobility does not lead to the sorting of types across jurisdictions as Tiebout predicts. The possibility for the rich to detach themselves from the poor to escape redistributive taxation induces jurisdictions either to abandon any taxation or to choose the same tax rate.

18.3.2   Imperfect Mobility

Suppose now that consumers have one of two income levels. Those with the higher income level are termed the "rich," and those with the lower income are the "poor." The two groups are imperfectly mobile but to different degrees. The rich (group 1) have income 1 and poor (group 0) have income 0. For simplicity, there is an equal number of poor and rich in the total population. The focus is placed on one of the jurisdictions (e.g., region 1) and the proportions from each group residing there are denoted x_1 and x_0, where the subscript denotes income group. The remainder, $[1 - x_1]$ and $[1 - x_0]$, are located in the other jurisdiction. Redistribution implies that the rich are subject to taxation and the poor are recipients of a transfer. Accordingly, each jurisdiction levies a head tax t on its rich residents to pay a transfer b to each of its poor residents. The feasible choices are restricted by the budget constraint $tx_1 = bx_0$.

In addition to income differences each individual is characterized by a preference for location x, with $0 \leq x \leq 1$, where a low x implies a preference for region 1 and a high x implies a preference for region 2. It is assumed that x is uniformly distributed within income groups. Individuals care only about their net income and their location. Given the pair of transfers (b, b^*) in the two regions, the payoff of a poor individual with preference x is

$$b - d_0 x \qquad \text{in region 1,}$$

$$b^* - d_0[1 - x] \qquad \text{in region 2,} \tag{18.24}$$

where $d_0 > 0$ measures the degree of attachment to location of the poor, with higher attachment equivalent to lower mobility. Given the tax pair (t, t^*), the payoff of a rich individual with preference x is

$$[1 - t] - d_1 x \qquad \text{in region 1,}$$

$$[1 - t^*] - d_1[1 - x] \qquad \text{in region 2.} \tag{18.25}$$

Given the tax policies, the population is divided between the two regions. The proportion of poor joining region 1, $x = x_0$, is defined by the type that is indifferent between the two regions, so

$$b - d_0 x_0 = b^* - d_0[1 - x_0], \tag{18.26}$$

and thus

$$x_0 = \frac{1}{2} + \mu_0 \left[\frac{b - b^*}{2} \right], \tag{18.27}$$

with $\mu_0 = \frac{1}{d_0}$ denoting the mobility of the poor. Higher mobility of the poor increases their migration in response to transfer differential. The poor are evenly distributed across regions in case of uniform transfers $b = b^*$.

Similarly the proportion of rich, $x = x_1$ joining region 1 is given by the indifference condition

$$[1 - t] - d_1 x_1 = [1 - t^*] - d_1[1 - x_1]. \tag{18.28}$$

Defining the mobility of the rich by $\mu_1 = \frac{1}{d_1}$ yields

$$x_1 = \frac{1}{2} + \mu_1 \left[\frac{t^* - t}{2} \right], \tag{18.29}$$

with equal taxes inducing equal division of the rich between the two regions, $x_1 = \frac{1}{2}$. Taxing more drives out some of the rich (i.e., x_1 decreases with t).

Budget balance implies that the transfer a region can afford to pay depends on who it attracts. The transfer paid to each poor resident is

$$
\begin{cases}
b = \dfrac{tx_1}{x_0} & \text{in region 1,} \\[4mm]
b^* = \dfrac{t^*[1 - x_1]}{1 - x_0} & \text{in region 2.}
\end{cases}
\tag{18.30}
$$

Assume that both governments follow a policy of maximal redistribution. Then region 1 sets its tax rate t taking as given the tax rate of the other, t^*, so as to maximize the transfer given to its poor residents, b, correctly anticipating the induced migration. The migration response of the rich to a small tax change is proportional to their mobility

$$
\frac{dx_1}{dt} = -\frac{\mu_1}{2} < 0.
\tag{18.31}
$$

How the poor respond to a small tax change depends on the migration response of the rich and is given by total differentiation

$$
dx_0 = \frac{\mu_0}{2}\left[\frac{d(b - b^*)}{dt}dt + \frac{d(b - b^*)}{dx_0}dx_0\right].
\tag{18.32}
$$

Evaluating this expression around $t = t^*$ (i.e., with $x_i = \frac{1}{2}$) for separate changes in t and x_0 gives

$$
\frac{d(b - b^*)}{dt} = \frac{x_1 + t[dx_1/dt]}{x_0} - \frac{t^*[d(1 - x_1)/dt]}{1 - x_0} = 1 - 2t\mu_1,
\tag{18.33}
$$

$$
\frac{d(b - b^*)}{dx_0} = \frac{-tx_1}{[x_0]^2} - \frac{t^*[1 - x_1]}{[1 - x_0]^2} = -4t.
\tag{18.34}
$$

Therefore the migration response of the poor to a domestic tax change can go either way,

$$
\frac{dx_0}{dt} = \frac{[1/2] - t\mu_1}{[1/\mu_0] + 2t} \gtrless 0.
\tag{18.35}
$$

It is worth noting that more taxation can drive out the poor: $\frac{dx_0}{dt} < 0$ if $t > \frac{1}{2\mu_1}$. The reason is that if the rich are sufficiently mobile (high μ_1), a tax increase induces so many rich to leave that the poor will find it better to follow them. In such circumstances the poor will chase the rich.

Putting these points together the (symmetric) equilibrium tax choice can be determined. Region 1 chooses its tax rate t so as to maximize the transfer to its poor residents b taking as given the tax choice of the other region and correctly anticipating the migration responses of the rich and the poor. The necessary first-order condition is

$$\frac{db}{dt} = \frac{x_1}{x_0} + \left[\frac{t}{x_0}\right]\frac{dx_1}{dt} + \frac{db}{dx_0}\left[\frac{dx_0}{dt}\right] = 0. \tag{18.36}$$

Using the migration changes as given by (18.31) and (18.35) and evaluating the condition at the symmetric outcome in which both regions pick the same tax-transfer scheme and each group divides evenly between the two regions, the first-order condition becomes

$$\frac{db}{dt} = 1 - t\mu_1 - 2t\left[\frac{[1/2] - t\mu_1}{[1/\mu_0] + 2t}\right] = 0. \tag{18.37}$$

This gives the following symmetric equilibrium

$$t = t^* = \frac{1}{\mu_1 - \mu_0}. \tag{18.38}$$

Consequently the equilibrium level of redistributive taxation is inversely proportional to the difference in the mobility of the rich and the poor. Higher mobility of the rich reduces taxation, but this is partially offset by the mobility of the poor. The reasoning behind this is that in equilibrium the poor chase the rich, so it is not possible for the rich to detach themselves from the poor.

The logic of the conclusion also applies in a model with capital and labor mobility. With this extension it implies that the possibility for taxing capital increases with the mobility of labor. So the problem of tax competition is more associated to the *relative* mobility of capital with respect to the mobility of labor.

18.3.3   Race to the Bottom

In a context where there are no legal barriers to migration, so that the forces of fiscal competition are at work, any attempt at redistribution or the provision of social insurance in a country would be impossible because it would induce emigration of those who were supposed to give (the rich) and immigration of those who were supposed to receive (the poor). The most extreme predictions of this form imply a "race to the bottom" but receive little theoretical or empirical support. This is probably due to the presence of significant costs and barriers to migration.

For example, welfare shopping has been discouraged in Europe by limiting portability between member states and requiring, for eligibility, previous employment in the country. However, underprovision of social insurance in an integrated market is an issue that cannot be ignored in the European Union. Even if it has not been a pressing issue to date, fiscal competition for capital and labor factors has already arrived. The Irish experience of the success of reduced corporation taxes is evidence of this. And with the EU enlargement, this issue will become even more pressing.

18.4   Intergovernmental Transfers

The reasons for organizing intergovernmental transfers are twofold: efficiency and redistribution. We consider the two in turn.

18.4.1   Efficiency

A critical insight from the analysis of tax competition is that increasing the tax rate in one region benefits other regions by increasing their tax bases. We now consider how transfers between regions can be employed to secure efficiency.

If we take the tax base to be the capital stock and the aggregate supply of capital to be fixed, then the tax-induced outflow of capital from the region taxing more represents an inflow of capital to the other regions. In particular, another region j benefits from increased revenue by the amount $t_j \Delta k_j$, where t_j is its tax rate and Δk_j the fiscally induced capital inflow. The problem facing each region is to choose the tax rate on capital to finance the public good level that maximizes the welfare of its residents subject to the budget constraint $G = tk(t)$. The optimal regional level of public good is given by the fact that the marginal benefit of public good MB must be high enough to not only cover its marginal cost, MC, but also to offset the negative impact of capital outflow on tax revenue, denoted by $t\Delta k < 0$. Then we obtain the following modified Samuelson rule

$$MB = MC - t\Delta k. \tag{18.39}$$

The context of identical regions provides a useful reference for isolating the fiscal-externality inefficiency from other equity and efficiency aspects that would arise when regions differ and choose different tax rates and public good levels. With identical tax rates, t, the cost of a capital outflow from one region is exactly offset by the benefits from the resulting capital inflows to other regions. It follows that if regions were to take into account such external benefits, they would no longer perceive capital outflows as a cost. The efficient provision of public good (as given by the usual Samuelson rule) would then obtain with

$$MB = MC. \tag{18.40}$$

The central authority can achieve this efficient outcome by means of *revenue-matching grants*. The idea is to correct the externality by providing a subsidy to the revenue raised by each region. The matching rate to a region is the additional revenue that accrues to other regions when this region raises its tax rate. Then regions are correctly compensated for the positive externalities generated when they raise their taxes.

Differences among regions bring about a second inefficiency from tax competition, namely that different tax rates induce a misallocation of capital across regions, such that the marginal product of capital is relatively high in high-tax regions (see figure 18.3). It follows that matching rates should be differentiated to induce all regions to choose the same tax rate and at the same time to internalize the fiscal externality. Tax harmonization requires the payment of a higher subsidy to regions with a low preference for taxation and public goods. In practice, however, the central government may not have the political authority nor the information required to impose differentiated matching grants. The information problem is rather severe because all regions can claim to be of the low-tax type in order to obtain a higher subsidy. With tax overlap, the matching rate will be negative to represent the reduction in tax revenues for other levels of government when the region raises additional revenue from the common tax base (see figure 18.4).

Expenditure externalities can also be corrected with *expenditure-matching grants*. For example, spending by a local government on education or public infrastructure improves the potential earnings of its residents by making them more productive, and this will increase the federal government's revenue from income, payroll, and sales taxes. To induce the local government to internalize this vertical expenditure externality, the federal authority can use expenditure-matching grants. Matching grant programs specify that the federal government matches on a dollar-for-dollar basis local expenditure up to some maximum. The effect is to lower the price of local public goods and thereby offset the tendency for local governments to underprovide public expenditures generating positive externalities.

An important example of vertical expenditure externalities in Canada is the substitutability between expenditures on unemployment benefits at the federal

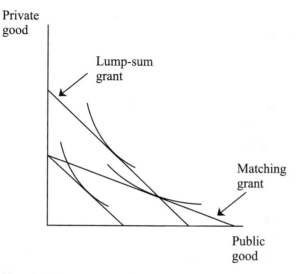

Figure 18.5
Matching versus lump-sum grant

level and welfare benefits at the provincial levels. If the federal government reduces unemployment benefits or their duration, more people will apply for welfare benefits, increasing spending at the provincial level. Conversely, employment programs by provincial government that allow welfare recipients to regain eligibility to unemployment benefits will lead to higher spending at the federal level.

In the United States, until 1996, the federal government could bear 50 to 80 percent of the cost of some welfare expenditures undertaken by states (e.g., Aid to Families with Dependent Children, Food Stamp, and Medicaid programs). In 1996 the AFDC matching system was replaced by a lump-sum grant. Interestingly, as illustrated in figure 18.5, this matching system has proved to be more effective in stimulating local public expenditures than a lump-sum subsidy of the same amount. The reason is simply that the lump-sum grant can be used in any way the recipient wishes, in contrast to the matching grant that is increasing with the amount of public spending. In that perspective matching grants are also called "conditional" grants because they place some restrictions on their use by the recipient, and the lump-sum grants are called "unconditional" grants. Figure 18.5 also indicates the distortionary effect of matching grants: higher welfare can be attained at the same cost with lump-sum grants. This is the advantage of the freedom of choice that "unconditional" grants provide.

The attraction of matching grants is to internalize expenditure externalities. However, lump-sum grants also have their own attraction, which is to maintain fiscal discipline (at the heart of the EMU). The idea here is that by creating a hard budget constraint, they impose a very useful discipline on decentralized expenditure decisions. More generally, a *hard budget* constraint implies that decentralized governments must place a basic reliance on their own sources of revenue and must not be overly dependent on transfers from the federal government. Self-financing is a powerful incentive device, and it is essential that local governments do not turn to the federal authority to bail them out of fiscal difficulties by resorting to expansible matching grants.

18.4.2   Redistribution

Intergovernmental grants are also used to channel resources from wealthy jurisdictions to poorer ones. Such transfers are based on equalization formulas that measure the fiscal need and fiscal capacity of each jurisdiction, locality or province. *Fiscal equalization* then involves higher grants to those jurisdictions with the greatest fiscal need and the least fiscal capacity. If the objective is to equalize taxable capacity, the central government can supplement the revenue base of poorer jurisdictions by matching any revenues they collect by the addition of a further percentage. This form of equalization is sometimes called "power equalization."

In practice, equalization grants play a major role in countries like Australia, Denmark, Canada, Germany, Sweden, and Switzerland and involve substantial transfers from wealthy to poor jurisdictions. In the United States such equalizing grants have never played an important role in allowing poorer states to compete effectively with fiscally stronger ones, but the equalization formula has been the basis of local school district finance in many states.

Typically an equalization system sets the transfer to each region equal to the difference between its observed tax base and the average tax base of all regions, multiplied by some standard tax rate, usually equal to the average tax among all the regions. Accordingly, if b_i is the tax base of region i with $\bar{b}$ the average tax base among regions and $\bar{t}$ the average tax rate, then the equalization transfer to region i is given by

$$T_i = \bar{t}[\bar{b} - b_i] \gtreqless 0 \qquad \text{for } b_i \lesseqgtr \bar{b}. \tag{18.41}$$

The use of the average tax rate as the standard tax rate is to accommodate a diversity of regional spending behavior. The intention is that equalization compensates for difference in fiscal capacities but not for difference in preferences for public spending. Indeed, when all regions choose the same tax rate, the formula guarantees equal revenues. The equalization formula can also correct for fiscal externalities. A tax cut by one region increases not only its tax base at the expense of other regions but also relative to the average tax base, thereby reducing the entitlement of this region to equalization grants.

Fiscal equalization is a contentious issue. In some cases, as in Canada, it may provide the cement that holds the bricks of the federation together. In other cases, like Italy or Belgium, it may become the source of division, where rich regions weary of large and durable transfers to poor regions, actually seek the break up of the federation.

18.4.3   Flypaper Effect

When considering the budgetary decisions of the recipients of intergovernmental grants, models of rational choice suggest that the response to a lump-sum grant should be roughly the same as the response to an equal increase in income resulting from a federal tax cut. But empirical studies of the response to grants have rejected this equivalence. There is instead strong evidence that local government spending is more sensitive to grants than it is to increasing income through tax cuts.

Among the best estimates of this in the United States: the marginal propensity for state and local governments to spend out of personal income in the state is about 10 percent. But the marginal propensity for state and local governments to spend out of grants from the federal level is around 80 to 90 percent. This has been known as the "flypaper effect" to say that money sticks where it hits. This is intriguing because it suggests that the same budget could give rise to different choices depending on what form the increment to the budget takes. It has been suggested that this may reflect the behavioral regularity that money on hand (from grants) has a different effect on spending than where the money must be raised (by taxation).

This can be understood with the following thought experiment: Say you have lost your ticket for the cinema and you must decide whether to buy a new one. Now suppose instead that you lose the same amount of money, would you be as willing to buy the ticket in the first place. Although in both cases you face exactly the same budget constraint, it is less likely that you will buy the new ticket after losing the original one than if you lost the equivalent amount of money.

The fly paper effect also casts serious doubt on the idea that local governments are more responsive to local demand. Indeed, taking the estimates above, one might think that if the local government were strictly responding to local demand, $100 per capita of federal grants would lead to about $90 per capita tax reduction and $10 additional spending, but it is entirely the other way around with about $90 additional spending and $10 of reduced local taxes.

18.5   Evidence

18.5.1   Race to the Bottom

The central result of the tax competition model is that increasing mobility of capital will drive down the equilibrium tax on capital. This canonical model is at the heart of concerns about capital tax competition within the European Union. In response to this growing concern, the OECD published a report (OECD 1998) comprising about twenty recommendations to counter what was perceived as "harmful" tax competition of capital income. This issue was also taken seriously by the European Union in December 1997. The EU commission agreed with a "Code of Conduct" in business taxation, as part of a "package to tackle harmful tax competition." The Code is aimed at identifying tax measures that reduce the level of tax paid below the "usual" level. In particular, a measure is considered as "harmful" if the tax advantage is restricted only to nonresidents, or if it is "ring-fenced" from the domestic market, or if the tax break is granted without any real economic activity taking place.

The central motivation for these reforms is the race to the bottom in capital taxation. To appreciate the relevance of this we must evaluate the existence and magnitude of this race to the bottom. Table 18.1 shows the statutory corporate income tax rates in 1982 and 2001 for a group of EU and G7 countries. The statutory tax rate includes local tax rates and any supplementary charges made. Except for Italy and Ireland, all countries have significantly reduced their statutory tax rate. In 1982, Ireland had the lowest rate at 10 percent and Germany the highest rate at 64 percent, while both the United States and the United Kingdom had a rate around 50 percent. In 2001, Ireland had still the lowest rate at 10 percent but both Germany and the United States had reduced their rate just below 40 percent, and the rate in the United Kingdom was down to 30 percent. Over this period Austria, Finland, and Sweden have cut their statutory rate by more than one-half.

Table 18.1
Statutory corporate income tax

	1982	2001
Austria	61	34
Belgium	45	40
Canada	45	35
Finland	60	28
France	50	35
United Kingdom	53	30
Germany	62	38
Greece	42	38
Ireland	10	10
Italy	38	40
Japan	52	41
Netherlands	48	35
Portugal	55	36
Sweden	61	28
United States	50	49

Source: Devereux et al. (2002).

Table 18.2
Statutory and effective corporate income tax rates

	1982	1984	1986	1988	1990	1992	1994	1996	1998	2001
Median statutory	50	48	46	43	39	38	37	36	37	35
Average effective	43	42	41	38	36	37	36	36	34	32

Source: Devereux et al. (2002).

Table 18.2 shows the fall in the *median* statutory corporate income tax rates over the last two decades for the same group of countries. Between 1982 and 2001, the median statutory tax rate for this group fell from 50 percent to 35 percent. The statutory tax rate is likely to be important in determining the incentive for firms to shift investment between countries. However, the tax base is also likely to be relevant. A higher tax rate does not necessarily imply higher tax payments, since effective tax payments also depend on the definition of the tax base. Governments with different tax rates can also adjust their rates of depreciation allowances for capital expenditure. The rate allowed for firms to spread the cost of capital against tax varies considerably across countries. Adjusting the statutory tax rate to take account of this effect and other difference in tax base, we obtain the "effective" average tax rate. It measures the proportion of total profit taken in tax. The evolution of the "effective" rate does not replicate the statutory rate. There is a decline from 43 percent in 1982 to 32 percent in 2001, but the fall is less pronounced than for the statutory rate. The lower fall in the effective rates indicates that the reduction in the statutory rates has been partially offset by less generous allowances for capital expenditures (broader tax base).

18.5.2   Race to the Top

It is natural for economists to think that competition among jurisdictions should stimulate public decision-makers to act more efficiently and limit their discretion to pursue objectives that are not congruent with the interest of their constituency. Tests of this hypothesis led to substantial empirical research investigating whether intergovernmental competition through fiscal decentralization affects public expenditures.

The evidence as reviewed in Oates (1999) supports strongly the conclusion that increased competition tends to restrict government spending. But the fact that spending falls with more competition does not mean that resources are more efficiently allocated as competition increases. The problem is that it is hard to come up with measures of the quality of locally provided public services. However, there is one notable exception, which is education where standardized test scores and postgraduation earnings provide performance measures that are easily comparable across districts. Following this strategy, Hoxby (2000) finds that greater competition among school districts has a significant effect both in improving educational performances and reducing expenditures per student.

Besley and Case (1995) develop and test a political model of yardstick competition in which voters are poorly informed about the true cost of public good provision. They use data on state taxes and gubernatorial election outcomes in the United States. The theoretical idea is that to see how much of a tax increase is due to the economic environment or to the quality of their local government, voters can use the performance in others jurisdictions as a "yardstick" to obtain an assessment of the relative performance of their own government. The empirical evidence supports the prediction that yardstick competition does indeed influence local tax setting. From that perspective intergovernmental competition is good for disciplining politicians and limiting wasteful public spending.

18.5.3   Tax Mimicking

A substantial body of empirical studies has emerged testing for interdependence among jurisdictions in tax and expenditure choices. An early and very influential piece of work is by Case et al. (1993) who test a model in which a state's expenditure may generate spillovers to nearby states. The novelty of this work is to allow for spatially correlated shocks as well as spillovers. Data from a group of states showed strong evidence of fiscal interdependence and the effects arising from interdependence were large. A dollar increase in spending in one state induced neighboring states to increase their own spending by seventy cents.

Brueckner and Saavedra (2001) test for the presence of strategic competition among local governments using data for seventy cities in the Boston metropolitan area. Where capital is the mobile factor and population fixed, local jurisdictions were found to choose property tax rates that take into account the mobility of capital in response to tax differentials. Property taxes are the only important source of local revenue. The authors use spatial econometric methods to relate the property tax rate in one community to its own characteristics and to the tax rates in competing communities. They found that tax rate in one locality is positively and significantly related to tax rates in contiguous localities. This means that the tax interdependence generates upward-sloping reaction functions. The same conclusion was obtained with similar methodology by Heyndels and Vuchelen (1998) in their study of property-tax mimicking among Belgian municipalities.

Turning to welfare migration, Saavedra (1998) uses spatial econometric estimates of cross-sectional welfare benefits (AFDC) for the years 1985, 1990, and 1995 for all states in the continental United States. She find strong evidence that a given state's welfare benefit choice is affected by benefit levels in nearby states for each year. Moreover the findings show significant and positive spatial interdependence, suggesting that a given state will increase its benefit level as benefits in nearby states rise.

18.6   Conclusions

The role of competition may be thought a device to secure better fiscal performance, or at least to detect fiscal inefficiency. If market competition by private firms provides households with what they want at least cost, why cannot intergovernmental competition lead to better governmental activities? Poorly performing governments will lose out and better performing ones will be rewarded. Although appealing, the analogy can be misleading, and the competitive model is not directly transferable to fiscal competition among governments. Once there is more than one jurisdiction, the possibility is opened for a range of fiscal externalities to emerge. Such externalities can be positive, as with tax competition, and lead to tax rates that are too low. Competition among governments to render high-quality services may give way to competition for undercutting tax rates to attract mobile factors from neighboring jurisdictions. Given capital mobility, any attempt by local government to impose a net tax on capital will drive out capital until its net return is raised to that available elsewhere. The revenue gain from the higher tax rate will be more than offset by an income loss to workers due to the reduction in the locally employed capital stock. Fiscal harmonization across jurisdictions would be unanimously preferred. Alternatively, the externalities can be negative, as with tax overlapping, and put upward pressure on tax rates. This is the common pool problem leading to overspending and overtaxation.

Interestingly, when there is no clear division of power, there is competition between central and local governments not only for the same tax base but also for the same local voter base. The federal government is competing with the local government for the provision of what might otherwise be local government services (child care, education, police, etc.). The implication of that is the overexpansion of public spending. To make things worse, tax bases as well as consumers of public services are mobile and need not move together. By voting with their feet to sanction inefficient government, consumers of public services can move to escape fiscal obligations rather than to obtain efficient public services. At the extreme, given household mobility, public services may be used and benefits may be received in one region, while income is derived and taxes are paid in another.

Such externalities can be corrected, and intergovernmental transfers are one means of doing so. Grants may be either conditional (matching grants and categorical grants) or unconditional (lump-sum block grants). Each type of grant involves different incentives and induces different behaviors for local governments. The final mix of increased expenditure versus lower local taxes depends on the preferences guiding local choices. Empirical studies are essential to compare the costs and benefits of intergovernmental competition. The presence of fiscal interaction between jurisdictions is not compelling evidence of harmful tax competition. Tax interactions can also be due to a political effect where electoral concern induces local governments to mimic tax-setting in neighboring jurisdictions. In such a case competition can be an effective instrument to discipline and control officials.

Recall the question raised at the beginning of this chapter on the analogy between market competition and government competition. The main lesson from the fiscal competition theory is that intergovernmental competition limits the set of actions and policies available to each government. There is no doubt that the constraints that are imposed on the authority of governments do constrain or limit actions, and this way both "good" and "bad" actions can be forestalled. Whether or not we view intergovernmental competition as harmful reflects our perception of the quality of governments. Unconstrained actions of a benevolent governments are good, but they can be very costly when governments abuse power.

Further Reading

The earliest studies on fiscal interaction due to interjurisdictional spillovers were:

Oates, W. E. 1972. *Fiscal Federalism*. New York: Harcourt Brace Jovanovich.

Pauly, M. V. 1970. Optimality, public goods and local governments: A general theoretical analysis. *Journal of Political Economy* 78: 572–85.

Williams, A. 1966. The optimal provision of public goods in a system of local governments. *Journal of Political Economy* 74: 18–33.

The competitive version of tax competition was first analyzed by:

Beck, J. H. 1983. Tax competition, uniform assessment, and the benefit principle. *Journal of Urban Economics* 13: 127–46.

Further contributions include:

Wilson, J. D. 1986. A theory of interregional tax competition. *Journal of Urban Economics* 19: 296–315.

Zodrow, G., and Mieszkowski, P. 1986. Pigou, Tiebout, property taxation and the underprovision of local public goods. *Journal of Urban Economics* 19: 356–70.

The pioneering studies of strategic tax competition are:

Mintz, J., and Tulkens, H. 1986. Commodity tax competition between member states of a federation: Equilibrium and efficiency. *Journal of Public Economics* 29: 133–72.

Wildasin, D. 1988. Nash equilibria in models of fiscal competition. *Journal of Public Economics* 35: 229–40.

Asymmetric tax competition is analyzed in:

Bucovetsky, S. 1991. Asymmetric tax competition. *Journal of Urban Economics* 30: 167–81.

DePater, J. A., and Myers, G. 1994. Strategic capital tax competition: A pecuniary externality and a corrective device. *Journal of Urban Economics* 36: 66–78.

Wilson, J. D. 1991. Tax competition with interregional differences in factor endowments. *Regional Science and Urban Economics* 21: 423–51.

Wilson, J. D. 1999. Theories of tax competition. *National Tax Journal* 52: 269–304.

Mobility and community formation is in:

Caplin, A., and Nalebuff, B. 1997. Competition among institutions. *Journal of Economic Theory* 2: 306–42.

Tiebout, C. 1956. A pure theory of local expenditures. *Journal of Political Economy* 64: 416–24.

Westhoff, F. 1977. Existence of equilibria in economies with local public good. *Journal of Economic Theory* 14: 84–112.

Mobility and redistribution are discussed in:

Epple, D., and Romer, T. 1991. Mobility and redistribution. *Journal of Political Economy* 99: 828–58.

Hindriks, J. 1999. The consequences of labor mobility for redistribution: Tax versus transfer competition. *Journal of Public Economics* 74: 215–34.

On the design of intergovernmental transfers see:

Hines, J., and Thaler, R. 1995. The flypaper effect. *Journal of Economic Perspectives* 9: 217–26.

Inman, R., and Rubinfeld, D. 1996. Designing tax policy in federalist economies: An overview. *Journal of Public Economics* 60: 307–34.

Tests of the Tiebout hypothesis are described in:

Epple, D., and Sieg, H. 1999. Estimating equilibrium models of local jurisdictions. *Journal of Political Economy* 107: 645–81.

Epple, D., and Romer, T. 2001. Interjurisdictional sorting and majority rule: An empirical analysis. *Econometrica* 69: 1437–66.

Rhode, P., and Strumpf, K. 2003. Assessing the importance of the Tiebout hypothesis: Local heterogeneity from 1850 to 1990. *American Economic Review* 93: 1058–77.

Evidence on fiscal competition is given in:

Baldwin, R., and Krugman, P. 2004. Agglomeration, interaction, and tax harmonization. *European Economic Review* 48: 1–23.

Devereux, M., Griffith, R., and Klemm, A. 2002. Corporate income tax reforms and international tax competition. *Economic Policy* 17: 450–495.

Hines, J. 1999. Lessons from behavioral responses to international taxation. *National Tax Journal* 52: 305–22.

OECD. 1998. *Harmful Tax Competition: An Emerging Global Issue*. Paris: OECD.

For evidence on efficiency-enhancing competition:

Besley, T., and Case, A. 1995. Incumbent behavior: Vote seeking, tax setting and yardstick competition. *American Economic Review* 85: 25–45.

Hoxby, C. M. 2000. Does competition among public schools benefit students and taxpayers? *American Economic Review* 90: 1209–38.

For evidence on strategic fiscal interaction:

Brueckner, J., and Saavedra, L. 2001. Do local governments engage in strategic tax competition? *National Tax Journal* 54: 203–29.

Case, A., Rosen, H., and Hines, J. 1993. Budget spillovers and fiscal policy interdependence: Evidence from the states. *Journal of Public Economics* 52: 285–307.

Heyndels, B., and Vuchelen, J. 1998. Tax mimicking among Belgian municipalities. *National Tax Journal* 51: 89–101.

Saavedra, L. 2000. A model of welfare competition with empirical evidence from AFDC. *Journal of Urban Economics* 47: 248–79.

Exercises

18.1. Why is source-based taxation of capital income likely to induce undertaxation of capital?

18.2. How does source-based taxation compare with residence-based taxation for the efficiency of cross-border investment?

18.3. What are the implications of source-based taxation for the efficiency of cross-border investment?

18.4. Consider a world economy consisting of N identical countries, each endowed with one unit of labor. Labor is immobile. The world economy also contains one unit of capital that is freely mobile across countries. All countries have identical production functions given by $F(L, K) = L^{3/4}K^{1/4}$, where L denotes labor and K denotes capital. The price of output is fixed at \$1.

a. Suppose that none of the countries tax either capital or labor. Find the equilibrium interest rate and allocation of capital across countries. What is the total income received by capitalists (the owners of the fixed factor of production) and workers? Evaluate the interest rate and income levels for $N = 2$ and $N = 20$.

b. Consider the impact of a tax at rate τ on capital income in country 1 if other countries do not tax capital income. Assume that tax revenues are used to buy output at the fixed price of \$1. What is now the after-tax return on capital invested in country 1? What is the equilibrium interest rate and allocation of capital across countries? Find the total income received by capitalists and workers and the tax revenues in country 1 as a function of N and τ.

18.5. Consider the exercise above and set the capital income tax rate in country 1 at $\tau = 0.20$.

a. Find the change in total capital income, total labor income, and the revenue raised in country 1 for $N = 2$ and $N = 100$.

b. What happens to the before-tax marginal product of capital in the countries without taxes for $N = 2$ and $N = 100$?

c. Are the workers in country 1 better off as a result of the tax? What about the impact of the tax on the welfare of the workers in nontaxing countries?

d. Discuss the tax-shifting between workers and capitalists as the number of countries increases from $N = 2$ to $N = 100$.

18.6. Consider a world economy composed of two countries, A and B. There is a fixed world population of size H that allocates between countries on the basis of the utility levels offered. Each consumer is characterized by a parameter x that measures their attachment to country A (and by $1 - x$, which is their attachment to country B). The parameter x is distributed uniformly across the population with values from 0 to 1. Let the utility level in country A of a consumer with attachment x be equal to $M - x - t^A$, where t^A is the tax rate in country A (and so utility in B is $M - [1 - x] - t^B$). Assume that there always exists a value of x that partitions the population between those who choose country A and those who choose country B.

a. For given tax levels in the two countries, determine the value of x at which the population partitions.

b. For a given partition of population, state the budget constraint for the government in each country.

c. Using the answers to parts a and b, state the decision problems of the two governments when they act as independent "leviathans" and attempt to maximize revenue. What is the equilibrium level of taxes?

d. What are the efficient taxes that maximize the sum of tax revenues?

e. What are the implications of these findings for tax policy?

18.7. Consider a world economy composed of two countries, A and B. There is a fixed stock of capital, K, that allocates between the countries on the basis of the after-tax return. Let the after-tax return in country i, $i = A, B$, be equal to $r - mK^i - t^i$, where K^i is the quantity of capital that locates in country i and t^i is the tax rate in country i.

a. Provide an interpretation of the parameter m.

b. Assuming that each country chooses its tax rate to maximize tax revenue, calculate the Nash equilibrium choice of tax rates.

c. What is the effect on the equilibrium tax rates of reducing m? Explain this result.

d. What are the efficient tax rates?

e. What are the implications of these findings for tax policy?

18.8. A car manufacturer can choose to locate a new plant in country A or country B. Your job is to determine where to locate this new plant. The only inputs used in car production are labor and capital, and the production function is Cobb-Douglas: $F(L, K) = L^{1/2}K^{1/2}$, where L is the labor input and K the capital input. In country A, labor costs $7 per unit and capital costs $7 per unit, while in country B, labor costs more ($8) but capital costs less ($6).

a. In which country should you locate the new plant so as to minimize cost per unit of output (i.e., average cost)?

b. Now assume that country A subsidizes labor so that labor costs $6 per unit in country A. Does it change the location decision of the firm?

c. Instead of subsidizing labor, suppose that country A subsidizes capital so that capital costs $6 per unit. Does it change the location decision of the firm?

d. What happens if both countries act identically in either taxing or subsidizing capital and labor? What would be the location decision of the firm? Has any country an incentive to alter its tax-subsidy choice, and if so, how?

18.9.   The federal government would like to give grants to local states to promote free medical vaccinations for children. However, because of a limited budget the federal government wishes to target its spending as efficiently as possible.

a. Define what would be a matching grant, and explain why it could be preferable to a block grant.

b. Now consider a closed-end matching grant that matches state spending dollar for dollar up to a specified amount, at which point the subsidy is phased out. Do you think a closed-end matching grant is preferable to an open-end matching grant?

18.10. Consider two countries, 1 and 2, with population shares λ_1 and λ_2 such that $\lambda_1 + \lambda_2 = 1$. There is a world stock of capital, equal to 1, to be allocated between the two countries. The production function is $f(k_i) = k_i - \frac{k_i^2}{2}$, k_i standing for per capita capital invested in country $i = 1, 2$. Production factors are paid their marginal productivity. Capital moves freely between the two countries. Denote its net price by p. The representative consumer in country $i = 1, 2$ owns $\bar{k}_i$ units of capital. Country i, $i = 1, 2$, taxes capital at rate t_i. Tax revenue is paid out as a transfer to the representative consumer. Country i chooses t_i so as to maximize the net income of its representative consumer: $y_i = f(k_i) - f'(k_i)k_i + p\bar{k}_i + t_i k_i$

a. What are the first-best tax levels t_1 and t_2 in this setting?

b. Express the demand for capital in country i as a function of p and t_i. Using the equilibrium condition of the international capital market, $\lambda_1 k_1 + \lambda_2 k_2 = 1$, solve for p as a function of tax rates and population shares. If t_1 increases, how will p react? How do you interpret this result?

c. Show that each country's objective function can also be written as $f(k_i) + p[\bar{k}_i - k_i]$.

d. Find the first-order condition for country i's choice of the tax rate, and show how the sign of the tax rate depends on the net exporting position of the country.

e. Suppose now that $\lambda_1 = \lambda_2 = \frac{1}{2}$, $\bar{k}_1 = \frac{1}{2}$ and $\bar{k}_2 = \frac{3}{2}$. Draw the tax response functions, and find the equilibrium taxes and the corresponding values of p, k_1, and k_2. Is this equilibrium outcome efficient? How can you measure the inefficiency of tax competition?

f. Express equilibrium taxes as functions of the parameters λ_1, λ_2, $\bar{k}_1$, and $\bar{k}_2$, and show that the equilibrium taxes must be of opposite signs.

18.11. Consider a linear city composed of two different jurisdictions. The two extremes of the city are $-\frac{1}{2}$ and $\frac{1}{2}$, and the city center is located at 0. Jurisdiction 1 is located to the left of the city center and jurisdiction 2 to the right. The city is inhabited by a continuum of individuals that are uniformly distributed with a total mass of 1. Each jurisdiction has a population of $\frac{1}{2}$. The median voter of jurisdiction 1 is located at $-\frac{1}{4}$, while the median voter of jurisdiction 2 is located at $\frac{1}{4}$. Each jurisdiction has a job center, located respectively at $-\frac{1}{3}$ and $\frac{1}{3}$. Wages are exogenous and equal to $\gamma > 1$ in jurisdiction 1 and 1 in jurisdiction 2. There are ad valorem taxes on wages t_1 and t_2 paid to the jurisdiction where work is undertaken. Individuals incur a commuting cost equal to $\frac{1}{2}$ per unit of distance to their workplace. Jurisdictions are run by majority-elected governments that maximize net income. Net income is the sum of the median voter's net wage plus fiscal revenue per capita, $[1 - t_i]w_i + t_j N_j w_j$ when the median voter in j works in jurisdiction i, with N_j denoting the number of people working in j.

a. Suppose that each individual works in the jurisdiction where she gets the highest after-tax wage net of commuting costs. Compute the number of workers N_1, N_2 in each jurisdiction as a function of the wage taxes t_1 and t_2.

b. Suppose that in equilibrium jurisdiction 2's median voter works in jurisdiction 1. Find the Nash equilibrium in taxes. Do the jurisdictions tax or subsidize wages? Explain briefly. Give a condition on γ under which this equilibrium exists. (*Hint:* In such an equilibrium the median voter in 2 chooses to work in jurisdiction 1.)

c. Suppose now that in equilibrium jurisdiction 2's median voter works in jurisdiction 2. Find the Nash equilibrium in taxes. Does either jurisdiction subsidize the wage? Why or why not? Give a condition on γ such that this equilibrium exists. Compare your answer to that of part b. Interpret the difference.

18.12.   The 1996 welfare reform in the United States devolved responsibility for welfare programs to the states. Does the theory suggest it was the right the policy?

18.13.   What is meant by the "race to the bottom"? Does evidence suggest that such a race is occurring?

18.14.   In many countries the capital owned by nonresidents is taxed. What are the effects of such tax exporting? Is it profitable to subsidize capital owned by nonresidents?

VIII ISSUES OF TIME

19 Intertemporal Efficiency

19.1 Introduction

Time is an essential component of economic activity. The passage of time sees the birth and death of consumers and the purchase, depreciation, and eventual obsolescence of capital. It sees new products and production processes introduced, and provides a motive for borrowing and saving. Time also brings with it new and important issues in public economics such as the benefits from the provision of social security (pensions) and the effect of government policy on economic growth. The remaining chapters of the book are devoted to exploring these issues.

The competitive economy described in chapter 2 provided a firm foundation for the discussion of economic efficiency and equity in a static setting. This economy also underpinned the analysis of efficiency failures and the policy responses to them. It also taught a number of important lessons about economic modeling. For all these reasons it has been one of the most influential and durable models in economics. Despite its usefulness the model has shortcomings when it is applied to economic issues involving time. We presented the competitive economy as being *atemporal*—having an absence of any time structure. A temporal structure can be added by interpreting commodities as being available at different times so that the commodity "bread for delivery today" is a distinct commodity from "bread available tomorrow." The list of commodities traded is then extended to include all commodities at all points in time. Since only the labeling of commodities has changed, all the results derived for the economy—the efficiency theorems in particular—remain valid.

Although analyzing time in this way has the benefit of simplicity, it also has one major shortcoming. This shortcoming is best understood by considering the implications of the equilibrium concept we applied to the model. Equilibrium was found by selecting a set of prices that equate supply and demand on all markets. Moreover it was assumed that no trade takes place until these equilibrium prices are announced. The implication of this structure is that all agreements to trade present commodities, and commodities to be consumed in the future, have to be made at the start of the economy. That is, contracts have to be negotiated and agreed, and equilibrium prices determined, before production and consumption can take place. This produces a poor representation of an intertemporal economy that misses the gradual unfolding of trade, and this is the very essence of time. It is also an untenable interpretation: the need to make trades now for all commodities into the future requires all consumers and firms to be present at the start of the economy and to know what all future products will be. Consequently, if issues of time are to be properly addressed, a better model is needed. We consider two alternative models of time: the overlapping generations economy, whose focus is on population structure, in this chapter, and an alternative set of models, focusing on growth through capital accumulation and technological innovation, in chapter 21.

The *overlapping generations economy* is one alternative to the competitive economy that introduces time in a more convincing manner. This model has the basic feature that the economy evolves over time with new consumers being born at the start of each period and old ones dying. At any point in time the population consists of a mix of old and young consumers. The lifespans of these generations of young and old overlap, which gives the model its name and provides a motive for trade between generations at different points in their life cycle. This evolution of the population allows the overlapping generations economy to address many issues of interest in public economics.

Overlapping generations economies are important, not only because they give a simple yet realistic model of the life cycle but also because of their many surprising properties. Foremost among these properties, and the one that is focus of this chapter, is that the competitive equilibrium can fail to be Pareto-efficient despite the absence of any of the sources of market failure identified in part III. The potential failure of Pareto-efficiency provides an efficiency-based justification for assessing the benefits of government intervention. Among such interventions the one with the most important policy implications is social security (or pensions). Social security can transfer wealth across points in the life cycle and between the generations. Given the impending "pensions crises" that are slowly developing in many advanced economies as the elderly population increases relative to the number of workers, social security is an issue of major policy concern.

This chapter sets out the structure of a basic overlapping generations economy with production. It presents the decision problems facing the consumers and the producers in the economy. The solutions to these problems are then used to characterize the equilibrium of the economy and to determine the steady-state equilibrium in which consumption and output per capita are constant. Both Pareto-efficient steady states and the optimal Golden Rule steady state are characterized. It is then shown that the economy can settle into an inefficient steady state that is the important result from a policy perspective. The nature of the inefficiency and the reason why it arises are discussed.

19.2   Overlapping Generations

19.2.1   Time and Generations

The two features of economic activity connected with the passage of time that we wish to capture are the accumulation of capital and the fact that the lifespan of each individual is short relative to the lifespan of the economy. The model we now develop incorporates the first aspect by allowing capital to be transferable across time periods and to depreciate steadily over time. The second aspect is introduced by letting each consumer have a finite life set within the infinite life of the economy.

In the overlapping generations economy, time is divided into discrete periods, with the length of the unit time interval being equal to the time between the birth of one generation and the birth of the next. There is no end period for the economy; instead, economic activity is expected to continue indefinitely. At the beginning of each period a new generation of young consumers is born. Each consumer lives for two periods of time. The population grows at a constant rate, so, if the rate of population growth is positive, each generation is larger than the previous one. Generation t is defined as the set of consumers who are born at the start of period t. Denoting the population growth rate by n, if generation t is of size H_t, then the size of generation $t + 1$, H_{t+1}, is given by $H_{t+1} = [1 + n]H_t$.

The population at any point in time is made up of young and old consumers; it is this overlapping of two consecutive generations that gives the model its name. This generational structure is shown in figure 19.1 where the solid lines

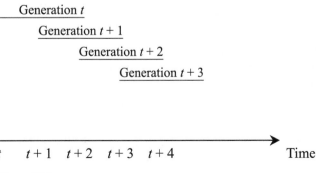

Figure 19.1
Generational structure

represent the lifespan of a generation. It is the differing motives for trade for the old and the young, due to their different lifecycle positions, that give economic content to the model.

At each point in time the economy has a single good that is produced using capital and labor. This good can either be consumed or saved to be used as the capital input in the next period. (Thinking of potatoes may be helpful. When harvested, they can be either eaten or put aside to be used for planting in the next year.) The existence of capital as a store of value allows consumers to carry purchasing power from one period to the next. To simplify, we assume that capital does not depreciate during the production process. Consumers plan their consumption to maximize lifetime utility and the level of production is chosen so as to maximize profits. All markets are competitive. An allocation of production is feasible for the economy if consumption plus saving by the two generations alive at each point in time is no greater than total output.

19.2.2 Consumers

The modeling of consumers is designed to capture a very simple form of life-cycle behavior. Each consumer works only during the first period of their life and inelastically supplies one unit of labor. This unit of labor is their entire endowment. Hence the total quantity of labor in the economy is equal to the number of young consumers. In their second period of life each consumer is retired and supplies no labor. Retired from work, old consumers live off the savings they accumulated when working. They are fully aware of their own mortality and plan their consumption profile accordingly. The income earned by a consumer during the first period of their life is divided between consumption and savings. Second-period consumption is equal to savings plus interest. With the exception of their date of birth, consumers are otherwise identical.

All consumers have identical preferences over consumption in the two periods of life. For a consumer born in period t, these preferences are represented by the utility function

$$U = U(x_t^t, x_t^{t+1}), \tag{19.1}$$

where x_t^t is consumption when young and x_t^{t+1} consumption when old. There is no explicit disutility from the supply of the single unit of labor in the first period of life.

The budget constraint of a typical consumer can be constructed by noting that labor income is equal to the sum of consumption and saving. In the first period of life, consumption, x_t^t, and saving, s_t, must satisfy the budget constraint

$$w_t = x_t^t + s_t, \tag{19.2}$$

where w_t is the wage received for the single unit of labor. Savings accrue interest at rate r_{t+1} (with interest paid in period $t+1$), so the value of second-period consumption x_t^{t+1} is given by

$$x_t^{t+1} = [1 + r_{t+1}]s_t. \tag{19.3}$$

Combining (19.2) and (19.3) gives the life-cycle budget constraint

$$w_t = x_t^t + \frac{x_t^{t+1}}{[1 + r_{t+1}]}. \tag{19.4}$$

Before proceeding to further analysis of consumer choice, it is worth emphasizing an important point: there are no financial assets in this economy. Instead, saving takes the form of investment in real capital. The interest rate is therefore equal to the return on capital, and the same interest rate guides the investment in capital by firms.

From (19.1) and (19.4) the utility-maximizing consumption plan satisfies the first-order condition

$$\frac{\partial U / \partial x_t^t}{\partial U / \partial x_t^{t+1}} = [1 + r_{t+1}]. \tag{19.5}$$

In (19.5) the left-hand side is the intertemporal marginal rate of substitution between consumption in the two periods of life. The right-hand side is the intertemporal marginal rate of transformation. The solution to this choice problem is illustrated in figure 19.2.

19.2.3   Production

The productive sector of the economy is assumed to consist of many competitive firms all producing with the same constant-returns-to-scale production technology. These assumptions allow the firms to be aggregated into one single representative firm modelled by an aggregate production function. Using a representative firm greatly simplifies the presentation.

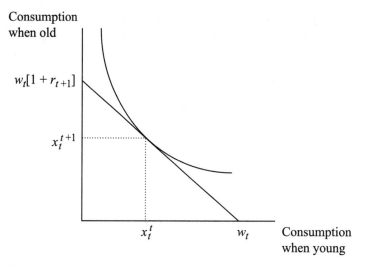

Figure 19.2
Consumer choice

It has been assumed that the capital used in production does not depreciate (this simplifies matters, but has no significant economic consequences). At the end of the production process in each period, the firm has (1) the (undepreciated) capital used in production and (2) new output. The sum of these is the total output of the economy, which is divided between saving (to be re-invested as capital) and consumption. To be consistent, the aggregate production function is defined to measure the *gross* output of the firm which is the sum of new output plus the un-depreciated capital. Denote this production function by $F(K_t, L_t)$, where K_t is the capital stock in period t and L_t is aggregate labor supply. An allocation is feasible if gross output is equal to the sum of consumption for the two generations alive at time t plus savings

$$F(K_t, L_t) = H_t x_t^t + H_{t-1} x_{t-1}^t + H_t s_t. \tag{19.6}$$

The representative firm chooses its use of capital and labor to maximize profits, π_t, where

$$\pi_t = F(K_t, L_t) - w_t L_t - r_t K_t. \tag{19.7}$$

Note that this expression for profit values net output and the undepreciated capital equally and assigns a rental rate of r_t for the use of capital. The necessary condition for choice of the level of capital is

$$F_K = r_t. \tag{19.8}$$

This is just the usual statement that capital should be employed up to the point at which its marginal product, F_K, is equal to its cost, r_t. The first-order condition for the quantity of labor input is

$$F_L = w_t, \tag{19.9}$$

so labor is employed up to the point at which its marginal product, F_L, is equal to the wage, w_t.

This development of the firm's decision problem allows the results to be related to standard results from microeconomics. However, an alternative presentation is more helpful in the context of an overlapping generations economy with a possibly variable population. In this case what matters for economic welfare is not just how much is produced but, instead, how much is produced per unit of labor. An increase in production per unit of labor (with labor equal to the number of young consumers) can allow an unambiguous increase in welfare provided that it is correctly distributed, but an increase in production, without reference to the size of population, cannot. To capture these observations, it is preferable to re-phrase the formulation of the production function.

It is now assumed that the production function satisfies constant returns to scale. This assumption makes it possible to write

$$Y_t = L_t F\left(\frac{K_t}{L_t}, 1\right) = L_t f\left(\frac{K_t}{L_t}\right), \tag{19.10}$$

where $\frac{K_t}{L_t}$ is the capital–labor ratio. Defining $y_t = \frac{Y_t}{L_t}$ and $k_t = \frac{K_t}{L_t}$, we determine net output per unit of labor by way of a function that has the capital–labor ratio as its sole argument

$$y_t = f(k_t). \tag{19.11}$$

It is assumed that this function satisfies $f(0) = 0$, $f' > 0$ and $f'' < 0$ so that no output can be produced without capital and the marginal product is positive but decreasing. From (19.10) it follows that the marginal product of capital is

$$\frac{\partial Y_t}{\partial K_t} \equiv F_K = f', \tag{19.12}$$

and the marginal product of labor

$$\frac{\partial Y_t}{\partial L_t} \equiv F_L = f - \frac{K_t}{L_t}f' = f - k_t f'. \tag{19.13}$$

These derivatives can be used to rewrite (19.8) and (19.9) as

$$f'(k_t) = r_t, \tag{19.14}$$

and

$$f(k_t) - k_t f'(k_t) = w_t. \tag{19.15}$$

Conditions (19.14) and (19.15) represent the optimal choice of capital and labor for the firm when the production function is expressed in terms of the capital–labor ratio. This pair of conditions characterize the choices arising from profit maximization by the firm.

19.3   Equilibrium

At an equilibrium for the overlapping generations economy it is necessary that consumers maximize utility, that the representative firm maximizes profit, and that all markets clear. Since there is a single good that can be used as capital or consumed, market clearing can be captured by the equality of demand and supply on the capital market.

Granted this fact, there are two ways in which equilibrium can be viewed. The first is to consider the *intertemporal equilibrium* of the economy. Here, by inter-temporal, is meant a sequence of values for the economic variables that ensure markets are in equilibrium in every time period. This intertemporal equilibrium determines the full time-path for the endogenous variables $(x_t^t, x_t^{t+1}, k_t, w_t,$ and $r_t)$ and hence their changes from one period to the next. The alternative form of equilibrium is to consider the steady state of the economy. The *steady state* is the situation where the endogenous variables remain constant over time. Such an equilibrium can be thought of as a long-run position for the economy. By defini-tion, once the economy reaches a steady state, it never leaves it.

To describe either form of equilibrium, it is first necessary to characterize equi-librium in the capital market. Equilibrium is achieved when the quantity of capital used in production is equal to the level of savings, since capital is the only store of value for saving. By definition, saving is labor income less consumption, so $s_t = w_t - x_t^t$. Hence, since there are H_t young consumers in period t, the equality of total savings in period t with capital used in period $t + 1$ requires that

$$H_t[w_t - x_t^t] = K_{t+1}. \tag{19.16}$$

Dividing through by H_t, and recalling that $H_{t+1} = [1+n]H_t$ and $H_t = L_t$, expresses this in terms of the capital–labor ratio as

$$w_t - x_t^t = k_{t+1}[1+n].   \tag{19.17}$$

When (19.17) is satisfied, there is equilibrium in the capital market.

19.3.1   Intertemporal Equilibrium

An intertemporal equilibrium is a sequence $\{x_t^t, x_t^{t+1}, k_t, w_t, r_t\}$ of the endogenous variables that attains equilibrium in every time period t. In each time period all consumers must maximize utility, the representative firm must maximize profit, and the capital market must be in equilibrium. Putting these together, we have the set of conditions that must be simultaneously satisfied for the economy to be in equilibrium:

· Utility maximization: (19.4), (19.5)

· Profit maximization: (19.14), (19.15)

· Market clearing: (19.17)

   The equilibrium determined by these conditions should be seen as one where the economy develops over time. The way that this works can be understood by following the economy from its very beginning. Let the economy have an initial capital stock, k_1, in period 1. This capital stock is endowed by nature and belongs to consumers who are already in the second period of life at the start of economic activity. The level of capital and the initial labor force determine the interest rate, r_1, and wage rate, w_1, from (19.14) and (19.15). Correspondingly (19.5), (19.4), and (19.17) simultaneously determine x_1^1, x_1^2, and k_2. Starting with k_2, the process can be repeated for the next time period. Continuing forward in this way generates the entire equilibrium path of the economy.

   Although the intertemporal behavior of the overlapping generations economy is of great analytical interest, it will not be pursued in detail here. Instead, our focus will be on the steady state from this point on.

19.3.2   Steady State

In steady state all variables are constant. Consequently consumers in all generations must have the same lifetime consumption plan. The quantity of capital per worker must also remain constant. These observations suggest an interpretation of the steady state as the long-run equilibrium in which the economy has reached the limit of its development (but note that this interpretation is only strictly true if the economy converges to the steady state).

Since all variables are constant in the steady state, the notation can be simplified by dropping the subscripts referring to time. The steady-state equations determining the wage and the interest rate are $w = f(k) - kf'(k)$ and $r = f'(k)$, where k, w, and r are the (constant) capital–labor ratio, wage rate and interest rate. Each consumer's budget constraint can then be written as

$$x^1 + \frac{x^2}{1 + f'(k)} = f(k) - kf'(k), \tag{19.18}$$

where x^1 and x^2 are the steady-state consumption levels in the first period and the second period of the consumer's life. The steady-state capital market equilibrium condition becomes

$$f(k) - kf'(k) - x^1 = [1 + n]k. \tag{19.19}$$

These equations can be used to provide a helpful means of displaying the steady-state equilibrium. Solving (19.18) and (19.19) for the consumption levels x^1 and x^2 gives

$$x^1 = f(k) - kf'(k) - [1 + n]k, \tag{19.20}$$

and

$$x^2 = [1 + n]k[1 + f'(k)]. \tag{19.21}$$

The interpretation of (19.20) and (19.21) is that each value of the steady-state capital–labor ratio k implies a steady-state level of first-period consumption from (19.20) and of second-period consumption from (19.21). As k is varied, this pair of equations generates a locus of $\{x^1, x^2\}$ pairs. This is termed the *consumption possibility frontier*. It shows the steady-state consumption plans that are possible for alternative capital–labor ratios.

There are basic economic reasons for expecting the consumption possibility frontier to describe a non-monotonic relationship between x^1 and x^2 as illustrated in figure 19.3. When $k = 0$, it can be seen immediately that x^1 and x^2 are both zero—no output can be produced without capital. This is illustrated by the frontier beginning at the origin in the figure. When k becomes positive, x^1 and x^2 also become positive. As k is increased, we move further around the frontier with both x^1 and x^2 increasing. For large values of k, x^1 may begin to fall; x^1 can even become zero since $f(k)$ increases at an ever slower rate while $[1 + n]k$ increases at a

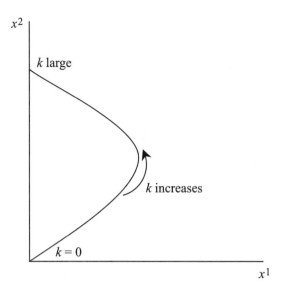

Figure 19.3
Consumption possibilities

constant rate. The actual shape of the frontier depends on how quickly the returns to capital decrease as the capital input is increased while holding labor input constant. What is underlying this is that low values of k do not allow much to be produced, so consumption must be low. As k increases, more consumption becomes possible. However, at high values of k decreasing returns to capital become important and consumption must be decreased in order to support the reproduction of a very high capital stock.

The importance of this construction is the following interpretation: All points on the frontier are potentially steady-state equilibria. Each point determines a pair $\{x^1, x^2\}$ and an implied value of the capital–labor ratio, k. The steady state that will actually arise as the competitive equilibrium of the economy is determined by the interaction of consumer preferences and the consumption possibility frontier. The question then arises as to the efficiency properties of the consumption pair $\{x^1, x^2\}$ or equivalently of the value of k. That is, are all values of k equally good or are some preferable to others? If some are preferable, will the competitive economic activity result in an optimal value of k in equilibrium? The answers to these questions are given in the following sections. Before proceeding to these discussions, we first look at how the competitive equilibrium is determined.

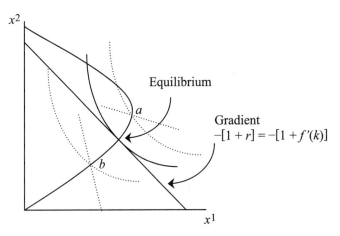

Figure 19.4
Steady-state equilibrium

The optimal choice of the consumer is a point where the highest attainable indifference curve is tangential to the budget constraint. The budget constraint has gradient $-[1 + r]$. In a steady-state equilibrium the consumption plan $\{x^1, x^2\}$ must also be on the consumption possibility frontier and tangential to the budget constraint. The equilibrium is found by moving around the frontier until a value of k is reached at which the indifference curve is tangent to the budget constraint defined by the rate of interest, $r = f'(k)$, at that level of capital. A steady-state equilibrium satisfying this condition and two nonequilibrium allocations, at a and b, are shown in figure 19.4.

19.4   Optimality and Efficiency

19.4.1   The Golden Rule

The central message of the previous section was that the competitive equilibrium will occur at some point on the consumption possibility frontier. The consumer's preferences, in conjunction with the production function, will determine precisely which point this is. Having reached this conclusion, it is now possible to determine whether any of the points on the frontier are preferable to others.

To do this, it is first necessary to clarify in what sense one point can be preferable to another. In a steady state every consumer in every generation has an identical lifetime consumption plan. Consequently there are no equity issues involved so "preferable" will have to be stronger than just raising welfare through redistribution. If one point is to be preferred to another, it must in the sense of a Pareto improvement. But if a Pareto-preferred allocation can be found, it implies that the competitive equilibrium is not efficient—a finding that would show the First Theorem of Welfare Economics does not apply to the overlapping generations economy.

The analytical strategy that we employ is to show that there is an optimal value of the capital–labor ratio. This is the content of this section. The next step is to show that there are other values that are Pareto-inferior to the optimal value. This is undertaken in the next section.

In the construction of the consumption possibility frontier it was noted that each consumption allocation was related to a unique value of the capital–labor ratio. This observation allows the study of the efficiency of alternative consumption allocations to be reinterpreted as the study of alternative capital–labor ratios. The optimum level of the capital–labor ratio can then be taken as that which maximizes total consumption in each period. The relation that this level of capital satisfies is termed the Golden Rule and the resulting capital–labor ratio is the Golden Rule level. Rules such as this are important throughout the theory of economic growth.

The total level of consumption in period t is the sum of consumption by the young and by the old. This is given by $x_t^t H_t + x_{t-1}^t H_{t-1}$. Since $H_{t-1} = \frac{H_t}{[1+n]}$, this can written alternatively in terms of consumption per capita as $x_t^t + \frac{x_{t-1}^t}{1+n}$. In the steady state the optimal capital stock that maximizes consumption per capita must solve

$$\max_{\{k\}} \; x^1 + \frac{x^2}{1+n}.$$ (19.22)

Equation (19.22) can be expressed in a more convenient way by noting that consumption in any period must be equal to total output less additions to the capital stock, or

$$x_t^t H_t + x_{t-1}^t H_{t-1} = H_t f(k_t) - H_t[k_{t+1}[1+n] - k_t].$$ (19.23)

At a steady-state equilibrium (19.23) reduces to

$$x_1 + \frac{x_2}{[1+n]} = f(k) - nk,$$ (19.24)

so that the maximization in (19.22) is equivalent to

$$\max_{\{k\}} f(k) - nk. \tag{19.25}$$

Hence the optimal capital–labor ratio, denoted k^*, satisfies the first-order condition for this optimization

$$f'(k^*) = n. \tag{19.26}$$

The condition in (19.26) is called the Golden Rule and the capital–labor ratio k^* is termed the Golden Rule capital–labor ratio. It is the optimal capital–labor ratio in the sense that it maximizes consumption per head. Its relation to Pareto-efficiency is addressed in the next section.

Returning to the competitive economy, we have a simple rule for determining whether its equilibrium achieves the Golden Rule. The choice of capital by the firm ensures that $f' = r$. Combining this equality with the Golden Rule shows that if the competitive economy reaches a steady-state equilibrium with $r = n$, this equilibrium will satisfy the Golden Rule. Since no other equilibrium will, $r = n$ must be the Golden Rule rate of interest. Hence the competitive economy achieves the Golden Rule when its interest rate is equal to the rate of population growth. If this occurs, it will have a capital–labor ratio $k = k^*$.

Some further analysis provides more insight into the structure of the Golden Rule equilibrium. From (19.20) and (19.21) total differentiation shows that $dx^1 = -[1 + n + kf''] \, dk$ and $dx^2 = [1 + n][1 + f' + kf''] \, dk$. Then

$$\frac{dx^2}{dx^1} = -\frac{[1 + n][1 + f' + kf'']}{[1 + n + kf'']}. \tag{19.27}$$

This expression is the gradient of the consumption possibility frontier at a point corresponding to a given value of k. At the Golden Rule capital–labor ratio k^*, with $f' = n$, (19.27) reduces to

$$\frac{dx^2}{dx^1} = -[1 + n]. \tag{19.28}$$

To understand what this implies, recall that with $r = n$ the gradient of the consumer's budget constraint is $-[1 + n]$. The maximal budget constraint with this gradient will thus be tangential to the consumption possibility frontier at the point corresponding to the Golden Rule capital–labor ratio. Denote the implied consumption levels at this point by x^{1*}, x^{2*}; see figure 19.5. Therefore, for the competitive equilibrium to achieve the Golden Rule, when offered this budget

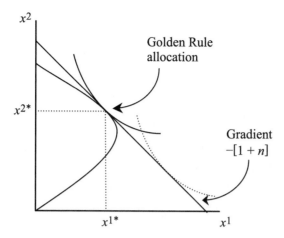

Figure 19.5
Golden Rule and competitive equilibrium

constraint, the consumer must want to choose the quantities x^{1*}, x^{2*}. The solid indifference curve in figure 19.5 illustrates such an outcome. The coincidence of the Golden Rule allocation and the consumer's choice can only happen with an unlikely combination of preferences and technology. In fact the optimal choice for the consumer with this budget constraint will almost always be somewhere other than at the Golden Rule. With the dashed indifference curve in figure 19.5 the Golden Rule will not be a competitive equilibrium.

19.4.2   Pareto-Efficiency

Having now characterized the Golden Rule capital–labor ratio and its corresponding rate of interest, it is possible to address the question of Pareto-efficiency. To do this, first note that if $k > k^*$, so that the equilibrium capital stock exceeds the Golden Rule level, then $r < n$ and the rate of interest is less than the rate of population growth. The converse is true if $k < k^*$. These relations are a simple consequence of the decision process of the firm and the concavity of the production function. In treating Pareto-efficiency, we should take the cases of $k > k^*$ and $k \leq k^*$ separately. We begin with $k > k^*$.

It the capital–labor ratio is above k^* the economy has overaccumulated along its growth path. Consequently it is in a steady state with an excessive capital–labor ratio. The analysis of the Golden Rule has shown that such a steady state fails to maximize consumption per head. We now show that it is also not

Pareto-efficient. This is achieved by describing a Pareto-improving reallocation for the economy.

The first point to note is that there is a single good available in the economy, so capital simply represents units of the good withheld from consumption. It is therefore feasible at any point in time to reduce the capital stock and to raise consumption simply by consuming some of the capital stock (i.e., eating the potatoes put aside for planting.) So, in an economy that has overaccumulated, the consumers alive in any period with an excessive capital stock ($k > k^*$) can consume some of the existing capital stock so as to reduce the stock to the level k^*. Undertaking this consumption has two consequences:

1. It raises the welfare of the existing generations because it increases their present consumption at no cost.

2. It raises the welfare of all following generations because it places the economy on the Golden Rule path and so maximizes their consumption.

Clearly, consumption of the excess of the capital stock above the Golden Rule level raises the consumption of those currently alive and of all those who follow. This is a certain Pareto improvement. Therefore any steady state with $k > k^*$ and $r < n$ is not Pareto-efficient.

When $k \leq k^*$, no such Pareto improvements can be found. In this case the economy has accumulated insufficient capital over the growth path. For the economy to move to the Golden Rule, it must accumulate additional capital. This can only be achieved if one (or more) of the generations is willing to forgo consumption. This has two effects:

1. It reduces the welfare of the generations who give up consumption to increase the capital stock.

2. It raises the welfare of all following generations because it moves the economy closer (or on to) the Golden Rule.

Consequently, since at least one generation must reduce their consumption in the transition to a Golden rule steady state, no Pareto improvement can be made from the initial position. Therefore all states with $k \leq k^*$ are Pareto-efficient.

In summary, any steady state with $k > k^*$ and $r < n$ is not Pareto-efficient. Such states are called *dynamically inefficient*. Those with $k \leq k^*$ are Pareto-efficient and are termed *dynamically efficient*. The fact that steady states that are not Pareto-efficient can exist despite the model satisfying all the standard behavioral and informational assumptions that describe a competitive economy shows that the First Theorem of Welfare Economics cannot be extended to include overlapping generations economies. Therefore these economies demonstrate that competition does not always lead to efficiency even when none of the standard causes of inefficiency (e.g., monopoly) are present. This observation is the most fundamental to emerge out of the analysis of the overlapping generations economy. As we will see, it provides the motive for studying numerous forms of policy intervention.

The discussion has concluded that a steady-state equilibrium with $r < n$ is not Pareto-efficient despite the economy satisfying all the standard competitive assumptions. However, it might still be suspected that to arrive at a steady state with $r < n$ requires some unusual structure to be placed on the economy. To show that this is not so, consider the following example: The utility function of the single consumer in each generation is given by

$$U(x^1, x^2) = \beta \log(x^1) + [1 - \beta] \log(x^2), \tag{19.29}$$

and the production function is Cobb-Douglas with $y = Ak^\alpha$. From the five equations describing a steady state the interest rate can be calculated to be (the derivation of this result is undertaken in exercise 19.7)

$$r = \frac{\alpha[1 + n]}{[1 - \beta][1 - \alpha]}. \tag{19.30}$$

This will only be equal to the Golden Rule rate when

$$n = \frac{\alpha}{[1 - \beta][1 - \alpha] - \alpha}. \tag{19.31}$$

If preferences and production do not satisfy this condition, and there is no reason why they should, the economy will not grow on the Golden Rule growth path. This example illustrates that a Golden Rule economy will be the exception rather than the norm. A dynamically inefficient steady state occurs when $r < n$. Using the solution for r in (19.30), we can write this inequality as

$$\frac{\alpha}{1 - \alpha} < \frac{n}{1 + n}[1 - \beta]. \tag{19.32}$$

From (19.32) it can been seen that this is most likely to arise when the following occurs:

1. The increase in output following a marginal increase in the capital–labor ratio is small (α low).

2. The rate of population growth is high (n large).

3. The consumer places a high weight on second-period consumption ($1 - \beta$ large).

In conclusion, the efficiency of the steady-state equilibrium is dependent on the relation of the capital stock to the Golden Rule level. The economy may reach an equilibrium at a dynamically inefficient steady state that is not Pareto-efficient. In such a case a Pareto improvement can be achieved by consuming some of the capital stock. A Cobb-Douglas example illustrated the factors that may lead to dynamic inefficiency.

Now that it has been demonstrated that the competitive equilibrium of the overlapping generations economy need not be Pareto-efficient, it remains to explain why. There is a significant difficulty in doing this: there is no agreed explanation for the inefficiency. To explore this further, consider a very simple variant of the economy. In this variant there is no production, and hence no capital. Instead, each young consumer is endowed with one unit of a consumption good while old consumers are endowed with nothing. Clearly, each consumer would like to even out consumption over the lifespan and so would trade some consumption when young for consumption when old. But such a trade is not possible. The young could give the old some consumption, but the old have nothing to trade in exchange. Therefore the only equilibrium is that no trade takes place (a position called *autarky*), whereas a Pareto-efficient allocation would have consumption in both periods of life.

It was in this setting that the inefficiency result was initially discovered. At first sight it might seem that it is just the structure of the economy—in particular, the lack of any way of transferring purchasing power across periods—that prevents the attainment of Pareto-efficiency. There are two responses to this. First, in the standard competitive economy the efficiency result holds independent of any particular details of the economy. Second, the analysis of this chapter has already shown that inefficiency can hold even if consumers are able to hold savings that transfer purchasing power across periods. Inefficiency usually arises when the market provides the wrong price signals. This is the case, for example, with monopoly and externalities. Here one might suspect the inefficiency to be due to an interest rate that provides the wrong signal for investment. But this cannot be the explanation because in a model without production there is no interest rate.

There is one point that is agreed on. Because the overlapping generations economy has no end, it can have an infinite number of consumers and, counting the good in each period as a different good, an infinite number of goods. The inefficiency only arises if there is a double infinity of consumers and goods. We have already seen that the competitive economy with a finite number of goods and consumers is Pareto-efficient. If the number of consumers is infinite, but the number of goods finite, we have the idealized competitive model with each consumer being insignificant relative to the market, and efficiency again holds. Finally, with a finite number of consumers but an infinite number of goods, the economy is again efficient.

19.5   Testing Efficiency

The Golden Rule, and the characterization of dynamic efficiency, provide conditions that are very simple to evaluate. Before this can be done credibly, there is an important issue concerning the assumptions describing the economy that needs to be addressed. The critical assumption is that of a constant growth rate in the population. The importance of constant growth lies in the fact that the Golden Rule is determined by the equality of the interest rate to the growth rate of population. If the growth rate is not constant, then this simple condition cannot be used. To provide a general means of testing efficiency, an extension must be made to the analysis.

A more general condition can be motivated as follows: In the economy we have described, the growth rate of capital is equal to the growth rate of population in the steady state. Observing this, the new investment in each period is nK. The total payments to the owners of capital are rK. The difference between these, $rK - nK$, measures the total flows out of the firm—which we can call dividend payments. The economy is dynamically efficient if $r \geq n$, which implies that dividend payments are positive so that funds are flowing out of the firm to the consumption sector. Conversely, the economy is dynamically inefficient if $r < n$, so funds are flowing to the firm. The logic of looking at the flows in or out of firms provides a more general method of testing efficiency than comparing the interest rate to the population growth rate, since it holds under much less restrictive assumptions.

The general version of the test is to look at the difference between gross profit (the generalization of rK) and investment (the generalization of nK). The value of this difference, as a proportion of GDP, for a selection of countries is presented in table 19.1. All the values in the table are positive, which is clear evidence that the countries are dynamically efficient. However, given the high values reported in the table, these countries remain at some distance from achieving the Golden Rule.

Table 19.1
Gross profit minus investment as a proportion of GDP

Year	England	France	Germany	Italy	Japan	United States
1965	9.4	13.6	8.5	22.9	15.2	6.9
1970	7.5	11.8	7.8	18.9	11.6	5.6
1975	6.0	10.9	12.4	16.6	6.8	14.4
1980	10.1	8.3	8.4	12.9	7.5	10.2
1984	13.9	12.9	13.8	17.3	9.4	6.7

Source: Abel et al. (1989).

19.6   Conclusions

The overlapping generations economy provides a very flexible representation of how an economy evolves through time. It captures the natural features that consumers' lives are short relative to the lifespan of the economy and that consumers allocate consumption in a rational way over their life cycle. The concept of the steady state also gives a description of equilibrium that is simple to apply.

The most interesting feature of the economy is that its lack of an ending means that there is a double infinity of goods and consumers. The double infinity is responsible for creating a potential inefficiency of the competitive equilibrium. Note the complete contrast to the static model. The chapter has characterized both efficient and optimal steady-state equilibria. The characterization of efficiency produces a simple test of dynamic efficiency that, as the evidence suggests, is met by a range of economies.

Further Reading

The classic paper which introduced the overlapping generations economy is:

Samuelson, P. A. 1958. An exact consumption-loan model of interest with or without the social contrivance of money. *Journal of Political Economy* 66: 467–82.

It should be noted that the focus of this paper is on providing an intertemporal model that determines the interest rate endogenously. The inefficiency result, which has generated an immense literature since, is an almost unintentional by-product of this.

The model used here was introduced in:

Diamond, P. A. 1965. National debt in a neo-classical growth model. *Journal of Political Economy* 55: 1126–50.

Two interesting discussions (but note the first is very technical) of the inefficiency result are:

Geanakoplos, J. 1987. Overlapping generations model of general equilibrium. In J. Eatwell, M. Milgate and P. Newman, eds., *The New Palgrave: A Dictionary of Economics*. London: Macmillan.

Shell, K. 1971. Notes on the economics of infinity. *Journal of Political Economy* 79: 1002–11.

For a study of the role of money in overlapping generations, see:

Hahn, F. H. 1982. *Money and inflation*. Oxford: Blackwell.

The empirical analysis of efficiency is taken from:

Abel, A. B., Mankiw, N. G., Summers, L. H., and Zeckhauser, R. J. 1989. Assessing dynamic efficiency. *Review of Economic Studies* 56: 1–19.

Exercises

19.1.   "The interest rate is just the rental price of capital. Therefore competition will ensure a price that leads to economic efficiency." True or false?

19.2.   A consumer has preferences described by $U = \log(x_1) + \delta \log(x_2)$, where x_t denotes consumption in period t and $0 < \delta < 1$. Assume that the price of consumption is 1 in both periods and that the interest rate is r. If the consumer has income $M > 0$ in period 1 and no income on period 2, find her optimal level of savings and consumption plan. How is savings affected by changes in the interest rate and the discount factor δ? Explain your results.

19.3.   If a firm's production function is $Y = K^\alpha L^{1-\alpha}$, show that it can earn at most zero profit. Use this production function to express the output–labor ratio as a function of the capital–labor ratio. Discuss the properties of the function derived.

19.4.   Why might the purchase of capital (instead of the rental of capital) affect a firm's profit-maximization decision?

19.5.   The production technology of an economy is given by $y_t = k_t^\alpha$, with $0 < \alpha < 1$.

a. Verify that the equilibrium wage rate must be $w_t = [1 - \alpha]k_t^\alpha$ and the interest rate $r_t = \alpha k_t^{\alpha-1}$.

b. Show that capital market equilibrium in a steady state requires $x_1 = [1 - \alpha]k^\alpha - [1 + n]k$.

c. Hence use the consumer's budget constraint to show that $x_2 = [1 + n]k[1 + \alpha k^{\alpha-1}]$.

d. Use these relationships to calculate the consumption possibility frontier. Sketch this frontier and locate the Golden Rule capital–labor ratio.

19.6.   If a consumer has preferences $U = x^1 x^2$ over the steady-state levels of consumption in the two periods of life, show that the utility-maximizing choices satisfy $\frac{x^2}{x^1} = 1 + r$. Use this result to calculate the capital–labor ratio in the steady-state equilibrium given the consumption possibility frontier from exercise 19.4. What is the effect on the capital–labor ratio of an increase in n and α? Explain.

19.7.   Let each consumer have preferences described by the utility function

$$U(x^1, x^2) = \beta \log(x^1) + (1 - \beta) \log(x^2),$$

and let the production function be given by

$$y = k^\alpha.$$

a. Demonstrate that utility maximization results in demands that satisfy

$$\frac{x_2}{x_1} = \frac{[1 + r][1 - \beta]}{\beta}.$$

b. Using the result in part a, the consumer's budget constraint and the capital market equilibrium condition, show that the steady-state value of k satisfies

$$[1 - \beta][1 - \alpha] = [1 + n]k^{1-\alpha}.$$

c. Employing the factor price condition $r = \alpha k^{\alpha - 1}$, show that the steady-state interest rate is

$$r = \frac{\alpha[1 + n]}{[1 - \beta][1 - \alpha]}.$$

19.8.   Governments frequently manipulate the interest rate as part of economic policy. Is this a method for ensuring that the Golden Rule is achieved?

19.9.   Economic inefficiency arises through market failure. What is the market failure in the overlapping generations economy?

19.10.   A possible explanation for the inefficiency might be the fact that the consumers are not all alive at the same time and therefore some mutually advantageous trades cannot occur. Consider an economy where consumer t receives an endowment of 1 unit of the single consumption good at time t and obtains utility only from consumption at times t and $t + 1$. All consumers meet at time 0 to trade. What is the equilibrium? Is efficiency restored?

19.11.   Consider an economy with one consumer in each generation. Each consumer has an endowment of one unit of the consumption good when young and nothing when old. There is no production and the consumption good cannot be stored.

a. What are the consumption levels in the two periods of life if there is no trade? If preferences are given by $U = \min\{x_t^t, x_t^{t+1}\}$, what level of utility is achieved?

b. At any point in time, what are the feasible consumption allocations between the young and the old consumers who are alive at that point? Given the preferences, which allocation is optimal?

c. Can the optimal allocation be reached by trade?

d. Is the inefficiency in the production model a consequence of the existence of capital?

19.12.   Assume, instead, that the economy in exercise 19.10 lasts only for two periods. In the first period, there is only a young consumer. In the second period, there is one old consumer and a new young consumer. At the end of the second period, the economy terminates.

    a. What is the equilibrium allocation for this economy?

    b. Is it efficient?

    c. What is the fundamental difference between this economy and that of exercise 19.10?

19.13. Assume that a consumer born in t has preferences represented by $U = x_t^t x_t^{t+1}$ and that the production technology is described by $y_t = k_t^\alpha$.

    a. Show that $x_t^t = \frac{w_t}{2}$ and $s_t = \frac{w_t}{2}$. Hence demonstrate that the dynamics of the capital stock are given by $\frac{[1-\alpha]}{2} k_t^\alpha = [1 + n]k_{t+1}$.

    b. Setting $\alpha = 0.5$, $n = 0.05$, and $k_0 = 0.01$, calculate the values of $k_1, \ldots, k_{20}$. How quickly is the steady state reached? How is the level of the steady state k affected by an increase in n?

19.14. Obtain data on population growth and the real interest rate. Do the data indicate dynamic efficiency or inefficiency?

19.15. Consider an economy in which there is one consumer born at the start of each time period. Each consumer lives for two periods and receives an endowment of 1 unit of the consumption good when young. At the start of the economy there is a consumer who is already old. This consumer owns one unit of money but has no endowment of the consumption good. Money has no intrinsic value.

    a. Can money be valuable in a finite economy (one that has a known end point)?

    b. Can money be valuable in an infinite economy?

    c. Can money allow efficiency to be attained?

20 Social Security

20.1 Introduction

A typical social security system provides income during periods of unemployment, ill-health or disability, and financial support, in the form of pensions, to the retired. Although the generosity of systems varies among countries, these elements are present in all developed economies. The focus of this chapter is the economic implications of financial assistance to the retired. The overlapping generations economy proves to be ideal for this purpose.

In economic terms, the analysis of the part of the social security system that provides assistance during unemployment or ill-health is concerned with issues of uncertainty and insurance. Specifically, unemployment and ill-health can be viewed as events that are fundamentally uncertain, and the provision of social security is insurance cover against bad outcomes. In contrast, retirement is an inevitable outcome, or at least an option, once the retirement age has been reached. Insurance is therefore not the main issue (except for the problem of living for longer than accumulated wealth can finance). Instead, the issues that are raised with pensions are the potential transfers of resources between generations and the effect on savings behavior in the economy. Both of these issues require a treatment that is set within an explicitly intertemporal framework.

The pensions systems in many developed economies are coming under pressure in a process that has become known as the "pensions crisis." The roots of this crisis can be found in the design of the systems and the process of change in population structure. The potential extent of this crisis provides strong ground for holding the view that reform of the pension system is currently one of the most pressing economic policy challenges.

After describing alternative forms of pension systems, the nature of the pensions crisis is described. This introduces the concept of the dependency ratio and how this ratio links pensions and pension contributions. The economic analysis of social security begins with a study of their effect on the equilibrium of the economy. Chapter 19 introduced the overlapping generations economy and showed how its competitive equilibrium may be inefficient. The potential for inefficiency opens up the possibility of efficiency-enhancing policy interventions. From this perspective we consider whether social security can be used to secure a gain in efficiency. The fact that a social security program may enhance efficiency can be understood from the effect of social security on the level of the capital stock. If a social security program has the form of forced saving, so that consumers are provided with greater second-period income than they would naturally choose, then the program will raise the capital stock through the increased savings it generates. This will be beneficial in an undercapitalized economy. Conversely, if the program simply transfers earnings from those who are working to those who are retired, savings will fall and hence the level of capital. These observations motivate the search for a social security program that can guide the economy to the Golden Rule.

The fall in the birth rate is one of the causes of the pensions crisis. It is an interesting question to consider how a change in the birth rate affects the level of welfare at the steady state of an overlapping generations economy. We pursue this issue by considering how the birth rate affects the structure of the consumption possibility frontier, both in the absence and in the presence of a social security program. Social security may be beneficial for the economy, but there are issues of political economy connected with the continuation of a program. The introduction of a program with the structure observed in practice results in a transfer of resources toward the first generation of retired (they receive but do not contribute) and away from some of the generations that follow. This raises the question of how such a program is ever sustained, since each generation has an incentive to receive but not to contribute. The final analytical issue is to review the concept of Ricardian equivalence and its implications for social security. Ricardian equivalence is the observation that by changing their behavior, consumers are able to offset the actions of the government. We show the consequences this can have for social security and address the limitations of the argument. Finally, after having completed the analytical material, we return to address some of the proposals that have been made for the reform of social security programs.

20.2   Types of System

One defining characteristic of a social security system is whether pensions are paid from an accumulated fund or from current tax contributions. This feature forms the distinction between fully funded and pay-as-you-go social security systems. The economic effects, both in terms of efficiency and distribution, between these two polar forms of system are markedly different.

In a *pay-as-you-go* social security program the current contributions through taxation of those in employment provide the pensions of those who are retired.

At any point in time the contributions to the system must match the pension payments made by the system. The social security systems presently in operation in the United States, the United Kingdom, and numerous other countries are broadly of this form. The qualifier "broadly" is used because, for example, although the US system owns some assets and could afford a short-term deficit, the assets would fund only a very short period of payments. At each point in time a pay-as-you-go system satisfies the equality

Benefits received by retired = Contributions of workers.   (20.1)

This equality can be expressed in terms of the number of workers and pensioners by

$$\beta R = \tau E,$$ (20.2)

where τ is the average social security contribution of each worker, β is the average pension received, E the number of workers in employment, and R the number of retired. If there is a constant rate of growth of population, so that the workforce is a constant multiple of the retired population, then $E = [1 + n]R$. Using this in (20.2) yields $\beta R = \tau[1 + n]R$ or

$$\beta = [1 + n]\tau.$$ (20.3)

This relationship implies that the tax paid when young earns interest at rate n before being returned as a pension when old. Hence in a pay-as-you-go pension system the return on contributions is determined by the growth rate of population.

In a *fully funded system* each worker makes contributions toward social security via the social security tax, and the contributions are invested by the social security program. The program therefore builds up a pension fund for each worker. The total pension benefits received by the worker when retired are then equal to their contribution to the program plus the return received on the investment. Such a program satisfies the equalities

Pensions = Social security tax plus interest = Investment plus return.   (20.4)

The implication of this constraint is that the fund earns interest at rate r, so the pension and the tax are related by

$$\beta = [1 + r]\tau.$$ (20.5)

A fully funded social security system forces each worker to save an amount at least equal to the tax they pay. It remains possible for workers to save more if they choose to do so. If, in the absence of social security, all workers chose to save an amount in excess of the taxed levied by the program then, holding all else constant, a fully funded system will simply replace some of the private saving by an equivalent amount of public saving. In this case a fully funded system will have no effect on the equilibrium outcome. We explore this observation further when we discuss Ricardian equivalence in section 20.8. In more general settings with a variety of investment opportunities, the possibility must be considered that the rate of return on private savings may differ from that on public savings. When it does, a fully funded system may affect the equilibrium. This point arises again in the analysis of pension reform.

Contrasting these two forms of system, it can be observed that a pay-as-you-go system leads to an intergenerational transfer of resources, from current workers to current retired, whereas a fully funded system can at most cause an intertemporal reallocation for each generation. This observation suggests that the two systems will have rather different welfare implications; these will be investigated in the following sections. In addition the pay-as-you-go system has a return of n on contributions and the fully funded system has a return of r. These returns will differ unless the economy is at the Golden Rule allocation.

Systems that fall between these two extremes are termed *non–fully funded*. Such systems make some investments, but the payments made in any given period may be greater than or less than the revenue, composed of tax payments plus return on investment, received in that period. The difference between payments and revenue will comprise investment, or disinvestment, in the pension fund.

20.3   The Pensions Crisis

Many countries face a pensions crisis that will require that their pensions systems be significantly reformed. This section identifies the nature and consequences of this crisis. Once the analysis of social security is completed, we return in section 20.9 to review a range of proposals for reform of the system in the light of this crisis.

The basis of the pensions crisis is threefold. First, the birth rate has fallen in most developed economies. Although immigration has partially offset the effect of this in some countries, there has still been a net effect of a steady reduction in the addition of new workers. The second effect is that longevity is increasing, since people are on average living longer. For any given retirement age, this is increasing the number of retired. Third, there is also a tendency for the retirement age to fall.

Table 20.1
Dependency ratio (population over 65 as a proportion of population 15–64)

	1980	1990	2000	2010	2020	2030	2040
Australia	14.7	16.7	18.2	19.9	25.9	32.3	36.1
France	21.9	21.3	24.5	25.4	32.7	39.8	45.4
Japan	13.4	17.2	25.2	34.8	46.9	51.7	63.6
United Kingdom	23.5	24.1	24.1	25.3	31.1	40.4	47.2
United States	16.9	18.9	18.6	19.0	25.0	32.9	34.6

Source: OECD (http://www.oecd.org/dataoecd/40/27/2492139.xls).

The net effect of these three factors is that the proportion of retired in the population is growing, and it is this increase that is problematic. In general terms, as the proportion of the population that is retired rises, the output of each worker must support an ever larger number of people. Output per capita must rise just to keep consumption per capita constant. If output does not rise quickly enough, then productivity gains will be diluted and output per capita will fall. Furthermore, supporting the retired at a given standard of living will impose an increasing burden on the economy.

The size of this effect can be seen by looking at forecasts for the *dependency ratio*. The dependency ratio measures the relative size of the retired population and is defined as the size of the retired population relative to the size of the working population. Table 20.1 reports the dependency ratio for a range of countries over the recent past and forecasts for its development into the future. The countries in the table are typical with the dependency ratio forecast to increase substantially—in all cases the ratio more than doubles from 1980 to 2040. This means that those working have to support an increasing proportion of retired. In some cases, for instance, Japan, the forecast increase in the dependency ratio is dramatic.

The consequence of the increase in the dependency ratio can be expressed in more precise terms by looking at the relationship between the contributions to pay for social security and the resulting level of social security. Using the identity (20.2) for a pay-as-you-go system and dividing through by E, the relationship between social security tax, pension, and dependency ratio is given by

$$\tau = \beta D, \tag{20.6}$$

where D is the dependency ratio, $\frac{R}{E}$. Hence as D rises, τ must increase if the level of the pension β is to be maintained. Alternatively, the pension decreases as D increases if the tax rate is held constant. If some combination of such changes is

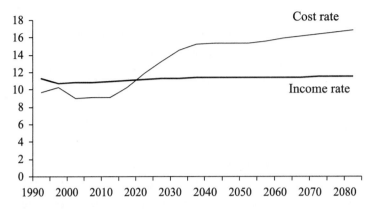

Figure 20.1
Annual income and cost forecast for OASI (Source: www.ssa.gov/OACT/TR/TR04)

not made, then the social security system will go into deficit if the dependency ratio increases. Neither a deficit, a falling pension, or an increasing tax are attractive options for governments to present to their electors.

These factors can be seen at work in forecasts for the future path of the US social security program as predicted by the Board of Trustees of the Federal Old-Age and Survivors Insurance and Disability Insurance Trust Funds (OASDI). Figure 20.1 shows the forecast deficit for the US Old-Age and Survivors Insurance Fund (but does not include the Disability Insurance Fund). The income rate is defined as the ratio of income from payroll tax contributions to the OASDI taxable payroll (effectively the average tax rate for social security contributions) and the cost rate is the ratio of the cost of the program to the taxable payroll. The projections are based on the structure of the social security program remaining much as it is today (in terms of the rate of tax and the value of benefits). As the figure shows, the fund is forecast to go into deficit in 2018 and remain in deficit unless some significant reform is undertaken.

To avoid such deficits, what these facts imply is that governments face a choice between maintaining the value of pension payments but with an ever-increasing tax rate, or they must allow the value of pensions to erode so as to keep the tax rate broadly constant. For example, the UK government has reacted to this situation by allowing the real value of the state pension to steadily erode. As shown in table 20.2 the value of the pension has fallen from almost 40 percent of average earnings in 1975 to 26 percent in 2000, and it is expected to continue to fall, especially since the pension is now indexed to prices rather than earnings. These reduc-

Table 20.2
Forecasts for UK basic state pension

Date	Rate as percentage of average earnings
1975	39.3
1980	39.4
1985	35.8
1990	29.1
1995	28.3
2000	25.7

Source: UK, Department of Work and Pensions (http://www.dwp.gov.uk/asd/asd1/abstract/Abstrat2003.pdf).

tions have taken the value of the pension well below the subsistence level of income. Consequently pensioners with no other source of income receive supplementary state benefits to take them to the subsistence level. This reduction in the state pension has been accompanied by government encouragement of the use of private pensions. We return to this in the discussion of reforms in section 20.9.

In conclusion, the basis of the pensions crisis has been identified, and it has been shown how this impacts on the state pensions that will be paid in the future. The depth of this crisis shows why social security reform is such an important policy issue. The chapter now proceeds to look at the economic effects of social security as a basis for understanding more about the arguments behind the alternative reforms that have been proposed.

20.4   The Simplest Program

Having set out the issues connected with social security programs, the focus is now placed on their economic effects. The fundamental insight into the effect of social security upon the economy can be obtained using the simple model of section 19.4.2. In this economy there is no production but only the exchange of endowments. Although simple, this economy is still capable of supporting a role for social security.

In the economy under analysis, each consumer receives an endowment of one unit of the single consumption good in the first period of their life but receives no endowment in the second period. To simplify, the population is assumed to be constant. As already noted in chapter 19, the equilibrium of this economy without any government intervention has the endowment entirely consumed when young

Consumption
when old

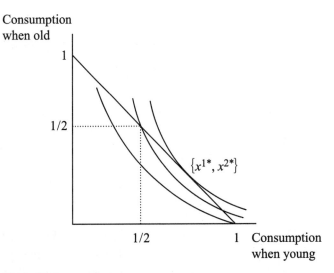

Figure 20.2
Pareto improvement and social security

so that there is no consumption when old. This has to be the equilibrium, since the old have nothing to offer the young in trade. This autarkic equilibrium is not Pareto-efficient, since all consumers would prefer a more even distribution of consumption over the two periods of life.

How can a social security program improve on the autarkic equilibrium? Consider a pay-as-you-go program that taxes each young consumer half a unit of consumption and transfers this to an old consumer. The lifetime consumption plan for every consumer then changes from the autarkic equilibrium consumption plan of $\{1, 0\}$ to the new consumption plan of $\{\frac{1}{2}, \frac{1}{2}\}$. Provided that the preferences of the consumers are convex, the new allocation is preferred to the original allocation. Since this applies to all generations, the social security system has achieved a Pareto improvement. This argument is illustrated in figure 20.2. The Pareto improvement from the social security system is represented by the move from the lowest indifference curve to the central indifference curve.

In fact a far stronger conclusion can be obtained than just the ability of social security to achieve a Pareto improvement. To see this, note that the assumption of a constant population means that the per capita consumption possibilities for the economy lie on the line joining $\{1, 0\}$ to $\{0, 1\}$. In the same way that the Golden Rule was defined for the economy with production, the Golden Rule allocation can be defined for this economy as that which maximizes utility subject to the first- and second-period consumption levels summing to 1. Denote this allocation by $\{x^{1*}, x^{2*}\}$. The Golden Rule allocation can then be achieved by a pay-as-you-go social security program that transfers x^{2*} units of the consumption good from the young consumer to the old consumer.

These arguments show how social security can achieve a Pareto improvement and, for the simple exchange economy described, even achieve the Golden Rule allocation. The social security program is effective because of the intergenerational transfer that it engineers and the consequent revision in the consumption plans. The optimality result was built upon the use of a pay-as-you-go program. In contrast, a fully funded program cannot be employed, since there is no commodity that can be used as an investment vehicle. The form in which these conclusions extend to the more general overlapping generations economy with production is now discussed.

20.5   Social Security and Production

It has already been shown how social security can obtain a Pareto improvement in an overlapping generations economy with no production. When there is production, a wider range of effects can arise, since social security affects the level of savings and hence capital accumulation. These additional features have to be accounted for in the analysis of social security.

The concept of the Golden Rule and its associated capital–labor ratio was introduced in chapter 19. This showed that the optimal capital stock is the level which equates the rate of interest to the rate of population growth. If the capital stock is larger than this, the economy is dynamically inefficient and a Pareto improvement can be made by reducing it. When it is smaller, the economy is dynamically efficient, so no Pareto improvement can be made, but the economy is not in an optimal position. These observations then raise the questions: How does social security affect capital accumulation? Can it be used to move a nonoptimal economy closer to the Golden Rule?

To answer these questions, consider a social security program that taxes each worker an amount τ and pays each retired person a pension β. The program also owns a quantity K_t^s of capital at time t. Equivalently, it can be said to own k_t^s, $k_t^s = \frac{K_t^s}{L_t}$, of capital per unit of labor. A social security program will be optimal if the combination of τ, β, and k_t^s is feasible for the program and ensures the economy achieves the Golden Rule.

A feasible social security program must satisfy the budget identity

$$\beta L_{t-1} = \tau L_t + r_t k_t^s L_t - [k_{t+1}^s L_{t+1} - k_t^s L_t], \tag{20.7}$$

which states that pension payments must be equal to tax revenue plus the return on capital holdings less investment in new capital. Since the population grows at rate n, in a steady state the identities $L_{t-1} = \frac{L_t}{1+n}$, $L_{t+1} = [1+n]L_t$ and $k_{t+1}^s = k_t^s \equiv k^s$ can be used in (20.7) to generate the steady-state budget identity

$$\frac{\beta}{1+n} = \tau + [r-n]k^s. \tag{20.8}$$

Noting that the pension, β, which is received in the second period of life, is discounted in a consumer's budget constraint (since $x^1 + s = w - \tau$ and $[1+r]s + \beta = x^2$, it follows that $s = \frac{x^2 - \beta}{1+r}$), the budget constraint under the program can be written

$$x^1 + \frac{x^2}{1+r} = w - \tau + \frac{\beta}{1+r}. \tag{20.9}$$

The condition describing consumer choice remains

$$\frac{U_1(x^1, x^2)}{U_2(x^1, x^2)} = 1 + r. \tag{20.10}$$

Equilibrium on the capital market requires that private savings are equal to total capital less the capital owned by the social security program. This condition can be expressed as

$$w - x^1 - \tau = [1+n][k - k^s]. \tag{20.11}$$

The choices of the representative firm do not change, so the conditions relating factor prices to capital still apply with

$$f'(k) = r, \tag{20.12}$$

$$f(k) - kf'(k) = w. \tag{20.13}$$

The steady-state equilibrium with the pension program is the solution to equations (20.8) to (20.13).

The aim now is to investigate the effect that the social security policy can have on the equilibrium. To see why it may be possible to design a program that can achieve the Golden Rule, it should be noted that the failure of the competitive equilibrium without intervention to achieve efficiency results from the savings behavior of individuals leading to over- or underaccumulation of capital. With the correct choice of social security program the government can effectively force-save for individuals. This alters the steady-state level of the capital stock and hence the growth path of output.

In equations (20.8) to (20.13) there are five private-sector choice variables (k, x^1, x^2, w, and r) that are treated as endogenous, plus the three variables (β, τ and k^s) that describe the social security program. Given that there are six equilibrium conditions, the pension system can choose any two of the variables describing the program with the third determined alongside the endogenous variables. To analyze the system, it is simplest to treat β as endogenous and τ and k^s as exogenous.

The method of analysis is to assume that the Golden Rule is achieved and then to work back to the implications of this assumption. Consequently let $r = n$. From the firm's choice of capital, the Golden Rule is consistent with a capital stock that solves $f'(k^*) = n$ and hence a wage rate that satisfies $w = f(k^*) - k^* f'(k^*)$. The important observation is that with $r = n$, the budget constraint for the social security program collapses to

$$\frac{\beta}{1+n} = \tau + [r - n]k^s = \tau, \tag{20.14}$$

so a program attaining the Golden Rule must have the form of a pay-as-you-go system with $\beta = [1 + n]\tau$. It is important to observe that any value of k^s is consistent with (20.14) when $r = n$, including positive values. This observation seems to conflict with the definition of a pay-as-you-go program. These comments are rationalized by the fact that we are working with the steady state of the economy. The social security program may own a stock of capital, $k^s > 0$, but in operating the pay-as-you-go-system, it does not add to or subtract from this level of capital. Instead, the return on the capital it owns is just sufficient to maintain it at a constant level. It remains true that along any growth path, including the steady state, a pay-as-you-go system cannot increase its capital holdings.

The values of the tax and capital stock of the program required to support the Golden Rule can now be found by using the fact that the program is pay-as-you-go to reduce the consumer's budget constraint to

$$x^1 + \frac{x^2}{1+r} = w. \tag{20.15}$$

Combining this constraint with the condition describing consumer choice indicates that the demand for first-period consumption must depend only on the wage rate and the interest rate, so $x^1 = x^1(w, r)$. Using the conditions for the choice of the firm, we have that the wage rate and interest rate depend on the level of capital, so demand for first-period consumption can be written as

$$x^1 = x^1(w, r) = x^1(f(k) - kf'(k), f'(k)) = x^1(k). \qquad (20.16)$$

The capital market-clearing condition can then be written as

$$w - x^1(k) - \tau = [1 + n][k - k^s]. \qquad (20.17)$$

Using the conditions for the choice of the firm and evaluating at the Golden Rule level generates

$$\tau = [f(k^*) - k^* f'(k^*) - x^1(k^*) - [1 + n]k^*] + [1 + n]k^s. \qquad (20.18)$$

Condition (20.18) determines pairs of values $\{\tau, k^s\}$ that will achieve the Golden Rule.

Any pair $\{\tau, k^s\}$ that satisfies (20.18) will generate the Golden Rule, provided that the capital stock held by the program is not negative. For instance, if the program holds no capital, so that $k^s = 0$, then the value of the social security tax will be

$$\tau = f(k^*) - k^* f'(k^*) - x^1(k^*) - [1 + n]k^*. \qquad (20.19)$$

Although the discussion to this point has implicitly been based on the tax, τ, being positive, it is possible that the optimal program may require it to be negative. If it is negative, the social security program will generate a transfer from the old to the young.

As an example, if $x^1(w, r) = \frac{w}{2}$ and $f(k) = k^\alpha$, then $k^* = \left[\frac{\alpha}{n}\right]^{1/[1-\alpha]}$ (see exercise 20.3 for the details of this derivation). Substituting these values into (20.19) gives

$$\tau = \left[\frac{\alpha}{n}\right]^{1/[1-\alpha]} \left[\frac{[1 - \alpha]n}{2\alpha} - [1 + n]\right]. \qquad (20.20)$$

If the rate of population growth is 5 percent, then the tax will be negative whenever

$$\frac{1}{43} < \alpha. \qquad (20.21)$$

For this example the tax rate is positive only for very small values of α.

The results have shown that attainment of the Golden Rule requires a pay-as-you-go social security system. By implication, a fully funded program will fail to attain the Golden Rule. In fact an even stronger result can be shown: a fully funded program will have no effect on the equilibrium. To demonstrate this result, observe that a fully funded program must satisfy the identity that the value of pension paid must equal the value of tax contributions plus interest, or

$$\beta L_{t-1} = \tau L_{t-1}[1 + r_t] = k^s L_t[1 + r_t]. \tag{20.22}$$

Evaluated at a steady state,

$$\beta = \tau[1 + r] = k^s[1 + n][1 + r]. \tag{20.23}$$

The substitution of (20.23) into the equilibrium conditions (20.8) to (20.13) shows that they reduce to the original market equilibrium conditions described in (19.18) to (19.21). The fully funded system therefore replaces private saving by public saving and does not affect the consumption choices of individual consumers. It therefore has no real effect on the equilibrium and, if the initial steady state were not at the Golden Rule, the fully funded social security program would not restore efficiency. This observation is discussed further in section 20.8.

This analysis has demonstrated how a correctly designed social security program can generate the Golden Rule equilibrium, provided that it is not of the fully funded kind. A fully funded system does not affect the growth path. In contrast, a pay-as-you-go system can affect the aggregate levels of savings and hence the steady-state capital–labor ratio. This allows it to achieve the Golden Rule.

20.6   Population Growth

The fall in the rate of population growth is an important factor in the pensions crisis. While operating a simple pay-as-you-go program, a decreasing population size makes it harder to sustain any given level of pension. Observing this fact raises the general question of how the level of welfare is related to the rate of population growth. This section addresses this issue both with and without a social security program.

Assume first that there is no social security program in operation. Recall that the consumption possibility frontier is defined by a pair of consumption levels x^1 and x^2 that satisfy the conditions

$$x^1 = f(k) - kf'(k) - [1 + n]k \tag{20.24}$$

and

$$x^2 = [1 + n]k[1 + f'(k)]. \tag{20.25}$$

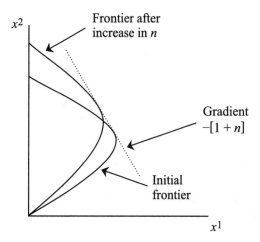

Figure 20.3
Population growth and consumption possibilities

The effect of a change in the population growth rate can be determined by calculating how it modifies this consumption possibility frontier. For a given value of k, it follows that $\frac{\partial x^1}{\partial n} = -k$ and $\frac{\partial x^2}{\partial n} = k[1 + f'(k)]$. Consequently, holding k fixed, an increase in the growth rate of population reduces the level of first-period consumption but raises the second-period level. This moves each point on the consumption possibility frontier inward and upward. Furthermore, when evaluated at the Golden Rule capital–labor ratio, these changes in the consumption levels satisfy

$$\frac{\partial x^2/\partial n}{\partial x^1/\partial n} = -[1 + f'(k^*)] = -[1 + n]. \tag{20.26}$$

Hence, for a small increase in n, the point on the frontier corresponding to the Golden Rule equilibrium must shift upward along a line with gradient $-[1 + n]$. The consequence of these calculations is that the shift of the consumption possibility must be as illustrated in figure 20.3.

How the level of welfare generated by the economy is affected by an increase in n then depends on whether the initial equilibrium level of capital is above or below the Golden Rule level. If it is below, then welfare is reduced by an increase in the population growth rate—the capital stock moves further from the Golden Rule level. The converse occurs if the initial equilibrium is above the Golden Rule. This is illustrated in figure 20.4 where the initial equilibrium is at e^0 with a

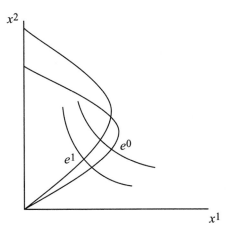

Figure 20.4
Population growth and consumption possibilities

capital–labor ratio below the Golden Rule. The equilibrium moves to e^1 following an increase in n. It can also be seen in the figure that if the initial equilibrium had been at a point on the frontier above the Golden Rule, then the upward shift in the frontier would imply that the new equilibrium moves onto a higher indifference curve.

Now introduce a social security system and assume that this is adjusted as population growth changes to ensure that the Golden Rule is satisfied for all values of n. For a small change in n, the Golden Rule allocation moves along the line with gradient $-[1+n]$, as noted above. However, for large increases in n, the gradient of this line becomes steeper. This moves the Golden Rule equilibrium as shown in figure 20.5 to a point below the original tangent line. As a consequence the increase in population growth must reduce the per capita level of consumption $x^1 + \frac{x^2}{1+n}$. Therefore, even with an optimal social security scheme in operation, an increase in population growth will reduce per capita consumption.

The effect of changes in the rate of population growth are not as clear as the simple equilibrium identity for a pay-as-you-go program suggests. As well as the mechanics of the dependency ratio, a change in population growth also affects the shape of the consumption possibility frontier. How welfare changes depends on whether a social security program is in operation and on the location of the initial equilibrium relative to the Golden Rule. If an optimal program is in operation, then an increase in population growth must necessarily reduce the level of per capita consumption.

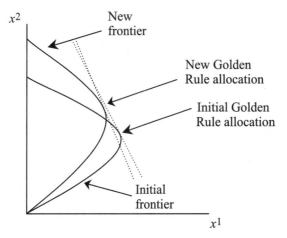

Figure 20.5
Population growth and social security

20.7   Sustaining a Program

In the simple economy without production, a social security program involving the transfer of resources between generations achieves a Pareto improvement. This raises the obvious question of why such a program will not always be introduced.

The basic nature of the pay-as-you go pension program described above is that the young make a transfer to the old without receiving anything directly from those old in return. Instead, they must wait until their own old age before receiving the compensating payment. Although these transfers do give rise to a Pareto improvement, it can be argued that it is not in the young consumer's private interest to make the transfer provided they expect to receive a transfer. (Think of the generations playing a game. Giving a transfer cannot be a Nash equilibrium strategy.) If the young consumers do not give their transfer but still expect to receive their pensions, then their consumption level will be increased. Clearly, this makes them better off, so they will not wish to make the transfer. Since the social security system is not individually rational, how can the young be persuaded to consent to the imposition of the social security program?

Two different answers to this question will be considered. The first answer is based on altruism on the part of the young—they are willing to provide the transfer because they care about the old. This rationalizes the existence of a social security program but only by making an assumption that moves outside the standard economic framework of individual self-interest. The second answer works with the standard neoclassical model of self-interest but shows how the program can be sustained by the use of "punishment strategies" in an intertemporal game. It should be stressed that the fact that participation in a social security program is mandatory is not by itself a valid explanation of the existence of the program. All programs have to have willing participants to initiate them (so they must be individually rational at their introduction) and need continuing support to sustain them.

Altruism refers to feelings of concern for others beside oneself. It is natural to think that altruism applies to close family members, but it may also apply to concern for people generally.

Although the existence of altruism takes us outside the standard perspective of behavior driven by narrow self-interest, it need not affect the tools we employ to analyze behavior. What is meant by this is that altruism alters the nature of preferences but does not affect the fact that a consumer will want to achieve the highest level of preference possible. Consequently, given a set of altruistic preferences, the consumer will still choose the action that best satisfies those preferences subject to the constraint placed on their choices. The standard tools remain valid but operate on different preferences.

There are numerous ways to represent altruism, but one of the simplest is to view it as a consumption externality. Writing the utility of a consumer in generation t in the form

$$U_t = U(x_t^t, x_t^{t+1}, x_{t-1}^t), \tag{20.27}$$

gives an interpretation of altruism as concern for the consumption level, x_{t-1}^t, achieved by a member of the earlier generation (which is usually interpreted as the parent of the consumer). A very similar alternative would be to assume that

$$U_t = U(x_t^t, x_t^{t+1}, U_{t-1}), \tag{20.28}$$

so that altruism is reflected in a concern for the utility of the member of the earlier generation.

Both of these forms of altruism provide a motive for a social security program that transfers resources from the young to the old. Consider (20.27). A consumer with this utility function can be thought of as choosing their personal consumption levels x_t^t, x_t^{t+1}, and a transfer, τ, to the old consumer. The effect of the transfer is to raise the consumption level x^t_{t-1}, since the budget constraint of the old consumer is

$$x^t_{t-1} = [1 + r_t]s_{t-1} + \tau. \qquad (20.29)$$

Provided that the marginal utility generated by an increase in x^t_{t-1} is sufficiently high, the consumer will willingly choose to make a positive transfer. In this sense the provision of social security has become individually rational because of altruism.

The second reason why transfers may be sustained is now considered. A rational explanation for participating in a social security program can be found in the fact that each young person expects a similar transfer when he is old. Young persons can then be threatened with having this removed if they do not themselves act in the appropriate manner. This punishment can sometimes (but not always) be sufficient to ensure that compliance with the social security program is maintained.

To give substance to these observations, it is best to express the argument using the language of game theory. The analysis so far has shown that the strategy to provide a transfer is not a Nash equilibrium. Recall that in the determination of a Nash equilibrium each individual holds the strategies of all others constant as they consider their own choice. So, if all others are providing transfers, it will be a better strategy not to do so but to still receive. If others are not transferring, then it is also best not to do so. Therefore not providing a transfer is a dominant strategy, and the individually rational Nash equilibrium must be for no transfers to take place.

These simple Nash strategies are not the only ones that can be played. To motivate what else can be done, it is best to think about repeated games and the more sophisticated strategies that can be played in them. A repeated game is one where the same "stage" game is played once each period for an endless number of periods by the same players. The Prisoner's Dilemma given in the matrix in figure 20.6 has the general features of the social security model. It is not exactly the same, since the social security model has many generations of consumers and not just the two given in the game.

If both players contribute to social security, then a payoff of 5 is attained. If neither contributes, the payoff is only 2. This reflects the fact that the social security equilibrium is Pareto-preferred to the equilibrium without. However, the highest payoff is obtained if a player chooses not to contribute but the other does. When played a single time, the unique Nash equilibrium is for both players to choose

Player 1

	Contribute	Don't contribute
Contribute	5, 5	0, 10
Don't contribute	10, 0	2, 2

Player 2

Figure 20.6
Social security game

Don't contribute—if the other contributes, then it pays not to. This reasoning applies to both players and hence the equilibrium. This equilibrium is inefficient and is Pareto-dominated by {Contribute, Contribute}.

The situation is completely changed if the game is repeated indefinitely. Doing so allows the efficient equilibrium {Contribute, Contribute} to be sustained. The strategy that supports this is for each player to choose Contribute until their opponent chooses Don't contribute. Once this has happened, they should continue to play Don't contribute from that point on.

To evaluate the payoffs from this strategy, assume that the discount rate between periods is δ. The payoff from always playing Contribute is then

$$5 + 5\delta + 5\delta^2 + 5\delta^3 + \cdots = 5\left[\frac{1}{1-\delta}\right]. \tag{20.30}$$

Alternatively, if Don't contribute is played unilaterally a temporary gain will be obtained but the payoff will then fall back to that at the Nash equilibrium of the single-period game once the other player switches to Don't contribute. This gives the payoff

$$10 + 2\delta + 2\delta^2 + 2\delta^3 + \cdots = 10 + 2\left[\frac{\delta}{1-\delta}\right]. \tag{20.31}$$

Contrasting these, playing Contribute in every period will give a higher payoff if

$$5\left[\frac{1}{1-\delta}\right] > 10 + 2\left[\frac{\delta}{1-\delta}\right] \tag{20.32}$$

or

$$\delta > \frac{5}{8}. \tag{20.33}$$

That is, {Contribute, Contribute} will be an equilibrium if the players are sufficiently patient. The reason behind this is that a patient player will put a high value on payoffs well into the future. Therefore the reduction to a payoff of 2 after the first period will be very painful. For a very impatient player, only the payoff of 10 will really matter and they are driven to Don't contribute.

The strategy just described is known as a "punishment strategy": the deviation from Contribute is punished by reversion to the inefficient Nash equilibrium. Although the punishment will hurt both players, the point is that it will not happen in equilibrium, since the optimal play with these strategies is always to choose Contribute when players are patient. In summary, in an infinitely repeated game, punishment strategies can be used to support efficient equilibria.

The same line of reasoning can be applied to the analysis of social security. What is different in this context is that the same players do not interact every period. Instead, it is a different pair of old and young consumers that meet in each period. However, the punishment strategy can still be employed in the following way: Each consumer when young will provide a transfer of size x to the old consumer that overlaps with them only if that old person alive at the same time provided a transfer in the previous period; otherwise no transfer is provided. If all generations of consumers play according to this strategy, then the transfers can be made self-supporting.

There remains one important limitation to this use of punishment strategies in the social security environment. To implement the strategy, each young consumer must know whether the transfer was made in the period before they were alive. This issue does not arise in the standard application of punishment strategies, since the players are alive in all periods—they need only remember what happened in the previous period. Consequently some form of verification device is necessary to support the punishment strategy. Without the verification the only equilibrium is for there to be no transfers which is a Pareto-inferior outcome.

This discussion of pay-as-you-go social security has shown how such a system can be sustained even when there is a short-run incentive for consumers not to make the required transfers. The basis for this claim is that social security in an overlapping generations economy has the nature of a repeated game so that strategies that punish the failure to provide a transfer can be employed. What this analysis shows is that an apparent act of generosity—the gift of a transfer to the older generation—can be made to be rational for each individual. So the provision of social security may occur not through altruism but through rationality.

20.8   Ricardian Equivalence

Ricardian equivalence refers to the proposition that the government can alter an economic policy and yet the equilibrium of the economy can remain unchanged. This occurs if consumers can respond to the policy by making off-setting changes in their behavior that neutralize the effect of the policy change. In terms of the present chapter, Ricardian equivalence holds when the government introduces, or changes, a social security system and yet the changes in individual behavior render the policy change ineffectual.

Such equivalence results have already featured twice in the text. On the first occasion, in the analysis of the private purchase of public goods, it was shown that by changing their purchases, the individuals could offset the effect of income redistribution. Furthermore it was also rational for the individuals to make the off-setting changes. The second case of equivalence arose in the derivation of the optimal social security program where it was noted that a fully funded system would not affect the capital–labor ratio. The explanation for this equivalence was that consumers react to a fully funded social security program by making a reduction in their private savings that ensures that total savings is unchanged.

The common feature of these examples is that the effect of the policy change and the off-setting reaction involves the same individuals. It is this that provides them with a direct incentive to modify their behavior. Clearly, this is true only of a social security system that is fully funded with a return equal to that on private savings. If social security is anything but fully funded, a change in the system will affect a number of generations, since the system must be redistributive over time. In the case of pay-as-you-go, social security involves purely intertemporal redistribution. A change in a program can therefore affect consumers in different generations who need not be alive at the time the program is changed nor even be alive at the same time. At first sight, this would seem to mean that it cannot be possible for equivalence to hold. This argument is in fact correct given the assumptions made so far.

To obtain a basis for eliminating the effect of policy, it is necessary to link the generations across time so that something that affects one generation directly somehow affects all generations indirectly. The way that this can be done is to return to the idea of altruism and intergenerational concern. Intuitively we can think of each consumer as having familial forebears and descendents (or parents and children in simple language). This time we assume that each parent is concerned with the welfare of their children, and that their children are concerned with the welfare of the grandchildren. Indirectly, although they are not alive at the same time in the model, this makes the parents concerned about the grandchildren. What effect does this have? It makes each family act as if it was a dynasty stretching through time, and its decisions at any one moment take into account all later consequences. A change in a social security program then causes a reaction right through the decision process of the dynasty.

To provide some details, let the utility of the generation born at time t be

$$U_t = U(x_t^t, x_t^{t+1}, \tilde{U}_{t+1}). \tag{20.34}$$

It is the term $\tilde{U}_{t+1}$ that represents the concern for the next generation. Here $\tilde{U}_{t+1}$ is defined as the maximum utility that will be obtained by the children, who are born at $t+1$, of the parent born in t. The fact that the family will act as a dynasty can then be seen by substituting for $\tilde{U}_{t+1}$ to give

$$U_t = U(x_t^t, x_t^{t+1}, U(x_{t+1}^{t+1}, x_{t+1}^{t+2}, \tilde{U}_{t+2})). \tag{20.35}$$

If this substitution is continually repeated, then the single parent born at t ultimately cares about consumption levels in all future time periods.

By this fact it is now possible to demonstrate that Ricardian equivalence applies to social security in these circumstances. Consider an initial position with no social security program and no population growth (so $n = 0$). The consumer at t reflects his concern for the descendent by making a bequest of value b^t. Hence the consumption level in the second period of life is

$$x_t^{t+1} = s_t[1 + r_{t+1}] - b_t, \tag{20.36}$$

and that of his descendent is

$$x_{t+1}^{t+1} = w_{t+1} + b_t - s_{t+1}. \tag{20.37}$$

Assume that a social security program is now introduced and that each consumer has one descendent. Under the terms of the program, young consumers are taxed an amount τ to pay a pension of equal value to old consumers. Then the consumption level of each parent satisfies

$$x_t^{t+1} = s_t[1 + r_{t+1}] + \tau - \hat{b}_t, \tag{20.38}$$

and that of his descendent

$$x_{t+1}^{t+1} = w_{t+1} + \hat{b}_t - \tau - s_{t+1}. \tag{20.39}$$

But note that if the bequest is changed so that $\hat{b}_t = b_t + \tau$, the same consumption levels can be achieved for both the parent and the child as for the case with no pension. Furthermore, since these consumptions levels were the optimal choice initially, they will still be the optimal choice. So the old consumer will make this change to their bequest, and the social security scheme will have no effect.

The conclusion of this analysis is that the change in the bequest can offset the intertemporal transfer caused by a social security system. Although this was only a two-period system, it can easily be seen that the same logic can be applied to any series of transfers. All that the dynasty has to do is adjust each bequest to offset the effect of the social security system between any two generations. The outcome is that the policy has no effect. This is the basic point of Ricardian equivalence.

It must be noted that there are limitations to this argument. First, it is necessary that there be active intergenerational altruism. Without this there is no dynastic structure, and the offsetting changes in bequests will not occur. In addition the argument only works if the initial bequest is sufficiently large that it can be changed to offset the policy without becoming negative. Does it apply in practice? We clearly observe bequests but many of these may be unintentional and occur due to premature death.

The concept of Ricardian equivalence can be extended into other areas of policy. Closely related to social security is the issue of government debt, which is also an intergenerational transfer (but from children to parents), and its effects on the economy. This was the initial area of application for Ricardian equivalence, with changes in bequests offsetting changes in government debt policy. Furthermore, if links are made across households, it becomes possible for changes in household choices to offset a policy that causes transfers between households. This has lead to the question of whether "everything is neutral." The answer depends on the extent of the links.

20.9   Social Security Reform

The basic nature of the pensions crisis facing a range of economies was identified in section 20.3: increasing longevity and the decline in the birth rate are combining to increase the dependency ratio. Without major reform or an unacceptably high increase in tax rates, the pension programs will either go into deficit or pay a much reduced pension. A variety of reforms have been proposed in response to this crisis. Some of these are now briefly reviewed.

Underlying the crisis is the fact that the pension systems are essentially of the pay-as-you-go form. With such a structure an increase in the dependency ratio will always put pressure on the pension system. The reform most often discussed in the United States is for the social security system to move toward a fully funded structure. Once the system reaches the point of being fully funded, pensions are paid from the pension fund accumulated by each worker. This breaks the identity relating pensions to the dependency ratio. A fully funded system can operate either as a government-run scheme or on the basis of private pensions. We comment on this choice below. For now, we note that as well as reducing the real value of the pension, the UK government has moved in the direction of a fully funded program by encouraging the use of private pensions. The difficulty with this approach is that it relies on workers making adequate provision for their retirement—and there is much evidence that this is not the case.

If an economy were to reform its pension system, it would take some time to transit from the pay-as-you-go system to the fully funded system. The reform requires that a capital fund be established that takes a period of investment. Furthermore the pay-as-you-go system cannot be terminated abruptly. Those already retired will still require the provision of their pensions, and those close to retirement will have too little time to invest in a pension fund and so will require the continuation of the pay-as-you-go element. These facts imply that those who are in work during the transition process will have to both pay the pensions of the retired and pay to finance their own pension fund. In simple terms, they are paying for two sets of pensions and fare badly during the reform process. At the very least, this suggests that there could be significant political pressure against the proposed reform.

It is interesting to consider the extent to which social security provision is determined by political considerations. Evidence on this is provided by Mulligan, Gil, and Sala-i-Martin in their analysis of social security and democracy. Their key finding is that social security has little to do with the voting process because countries without voting still supply public insurance in the same way. They even observe for Chile that most of the growth in social security spending occurred under nondemocratic regimes, and payroll taxes reached extremely high levels under General Pinochet. In fact they report on nine dynamic case studies—Greece, Portugal, Spain, Italy, Argentina, Brazil, Chile, Peru, and Uruguay—for the period

1960 to 1990. The countries were selected on the basis of their extreme political changes over this period. With the exception of Greece, it is found that formerly nondemocratic countries do not, relative to their democratic neighbors, change their social security programs after experiencing democracy (in terms of the amount of public insurance spending, and the design of tax and benefit formulas). Similarly formerly democratic countries do not change their program when they become nondemocratic. Furthermore multiple regression studies of the determinants of public insurance spending, controlling for population age and per capita income, find neither a significant partial correlation between democracy and social insurance spending (relative to GDP), nor a significant interaction between democracy and the other variables in a spending regression. These results suggest that the role of political constraints on social security may sometimes be overstated.

It is useful to stress a classical error that often accompanies discussion of switching to a fully funded system. The error arises from comparing the likely rates of return on personal accounts with those paid under the current pay-as-you-go system. The proposition that suggests switching to the fully funded system to benefit from the opportunity for higher rates of return is a fallacy. Compare first the real rate of return delivered by the existing social security over the last decades (about 2 percent per year) with the risk-free rate of return of 3 to 4 percent that personal accounts could guarantee by holding inflation-indexed US Treasury securities. The return in the existing system is only 2 percent because of the arithmetic of the pay-as-you-go system.

Suppose that all workers contribute a fixed fraction of their incomes to social security. The key point is that today's contributions cover the pension benefits of today's retirees, who were the previous generation of workers that contributed. The total return corresponds to the growth of overall wage income (population plus productivity growth rate). Thus the real rate of return in an ongoing system is 2 percent if the economy grows at that rate in the long run.

There is a fallacy to the argument that 3 to 4 percent yield on personal accounts is better. The fallacy is that the return on the existing system is low because workers start with a liability to provide for the retirees of the previous generation. If the workers could defect from their liability to the current elderly, they could earn a rate much higher than 2 percent, even if no personal accounts were introduced. But, of course, no one wants to cut the benefits of the elderly who contributed to the system throughout all their working lives. To put it differently, the opportunity of a higher rate of return with personal accounts comes from the misleading feature that they come with no obligation to raise the pensions of the current elderly. This is the feature that accounts for the differences in returns. Moreover the higher expected return is offset by at least the perception of greater risk. This is not to say that the returns in the existing system are risk-free. The major risk in the present system is probably that pension benefits paid in the future are subject to the political whims of future governments.

The distributional effects of a reform from a pay-as-you-go system to a fully funded system are illustrated by the simulation reported in table 20.3. This simulation determines the growth path of an economic model for a reference case in which the state pension is held constant. Applied to the United Kingdom, the model assumes that the value of the pension is 20 percent of average earnings. For the application to Europe, the value is taken to be 40 percent. A reform is then considered where an announcement is made in 1997 (the year the research was conducted) that the state pension will be steadily reduced from the year 2020 until being phased out in 2040. The aim of the long period between announcement and reduction is to allow for adjustment in private behavior. The removal of the state pension implies that private savings will have to increase to compensate.

The negative ages in the first column of table 20.3 refer to consumers who had not yet been born in 1997, so a consumer with age −10 in 1997 will be born in 2007. The numbers in the second and third columns shows the percentage by which the lifetime wage of that age group would need to be changed in the reference case to give the same level of welfare as in the reform case. Hence the value

Table 20.3
Gains and losses in transition

Age in 1997	United Kingdom	Europe
>57	0	0
50–57	−0.09	−0.6
40–50	−1.1	−2.3
30–40	−3.0	−5.7
20–30	−3.8	−7.2
10–20	−2.3	−4.2
0–10	0.7	1.7
−10–0	3.95	9.2
−20––10	6.5	15.7
−40––30	7.4	18.7
<−40	7.2	18.9

Source: Miles (1998).

of −1.1 for the age group 40 to 50 in the United Kingdom shows that this group is worse off with the reform—a reduction of 1.1 percent of their wage in the base case would give then the same welfare level as in the reform case.

The values in table 20.3 show that the pension reform hurts those early in life who must pay the pensions of the retired and pay into their own retirement fund. Ultimately the reform benefits consumers in the long run. The long-run gain comes from the fact that the reduction in the pension leads to an increase in private saving. Private saving has to be invested, so there is also an increase in the capital stock. The consequence of this capital stock increase depends on the initial level of capital compared to the Golden Rule level. In the simulations, capital is initially below the Golden Rule level and remains so throughout the transition. But since this is moving the economy closer to the Golden Rule, there is ultimately a gain in welfare for later generations. The structure of the gains and losses also illustrates the political problem involved in implementing the reform: those who must vote in favor of its implementation are those who lose the most. This political problem will be exacerbated by the aging of the electorate that is expected over the next 50 years. Estimates of the age of the median voter are given in table 20.4. These estimates reveal that the age of the median voter is likely to rise from the midforties to the midfifties. So the electorate will become dominated by the age group that will lose most if the pension system reform is undertaken.

Table 20.4
Age of the median voter

Country	Year	Age of median voter
France	2000	43
	2050	53
Germany	2000	46
	2050	55
Italy	1992	44
	2050	57
Spain	2000	44
	2050	57
United Kingdom	2000	45
	2050	53
United States	2000	47
	2050	53

Source: Galasso and Profeta (2004).

It has already been noted that a fully funded scheme run by the government is equivalent to a system of private pension provision. This is only strictly true in an economy, like the overlapping generations model we have studied, that has a single capital good. In a more practical setting with a range of investment assets, the equivalence will only hold if the same portfolio choices are made. Moving from a pay-as-you-go system to a fully funded system run by the government raises the issue of the portfolio of investments made by the pension fund. In the United States the assets of the fund are invested entirely in long-term Treasury debt. Such debt is very low risk, but as a consequence it also has a low return. This is not a portfolio that any private sector institution would choose, except one that is especially risk-averse. Nor is it one that many private investors would choose. Permitting the social security fund to invest in a wider portfolio opens the possibility for a higher return to be obtained but introduces questions about the degree of investment risk that the pension fund could accept. In addition changing the portfolio structure of the social security fund could have significant macroeconomic consequences because of its potential size.

A further issue in the design of a pensions system is the choice between a *defined contributions* system and a *defined benefits* system. In a defined contribution scheme, social security contributions are paid into an investment fund, and at the time of retirement the accumulated fund is annuitized. What annuitized means is that the fund purchases an annuity that is a financial instrument paying a constant income to the purchaser until his date of death. In a defined benefits scheme, contributions are made at a constant proportion of income and the benefit is a known fraction of income at retirement (or some average over income levels in years close to retirement).

The consequences of these differences are most apparent in the apportionment of risk under the two types of system. With a defined contributions system, the level of payment into the pension fund is certain for the worker. What is not certain is the maturity value of the pension fund, since this depends on the return earned on the fund, or the pension that will be received, since this depends on the rate offered on annuities at retirement. All risk therefore falls upon the worker. With a defined benefits system, the risk is placed entirely on the pension fund, since it must meet the promises that have been made. The pension fund receives contributions that it can invest, but it runs the risk that the returns on these investments may not meet pension commitments. This is currently the situation of the US fund where the forecast deficit is a consequence of the defined benefits it has promised.

Assuming that a defined contributions scheme is chosen, there is a further reform that can be made. In the discussion of the simulation it was noted that the reform involved a move from a state pension scheme to private pension schemes. In a defined contribution system there is no real distinction between state and private schemes in principal. When put into practice, distinctions will arise in the choice of investment portfolio, the returns earned on the portfolio and the transactions costs incurred in running the scheme. If moving to a fully funded system pensions, the choice between state and private become a real issue. One option is to use a public fund, either directly administered or run privately after a competitive tendering process. Alternatively, a limited range of approved private funds could be made available. Both choices would lead to a problem of monitoring the performance of the schemes given the fundamentally uncertain nature of financial markets. In addition seeking low transactions costs could prove detrimental to other areas of performance. A final option is to make use of an open selection of private investment funds. Doing so relies on investors making informed choices between the providers and between the funds on offer to ensure that the risk characteristics of the fund match their preferences. Such a scheme will not work with poorly informed investors and may run foul of high transactions costs. Both of these have been significant problems in the United Kingdom where "misselling"—the selling of pensions plans with inappropriate risk characteristics for the purchasers—and high costs have accompanied the move toward the private financing of pensions.

The reform of pensions systems is an issue with much current policy relevance. A range of reforms have been suggested to cope with the forecast change in the dependency ratio. Some of these represent adjustments to the structure of pension schemes, whereas others seek a major reorganization of pension provision.

20.10   Conclusions

Social security in the form of pensions is important both in policy relevance and for its effect on the economy. The generosity of a pension scheme has implications for individual's savings behavior and, in the aggregate, for capital accumulation. Since an economy may reach an inefficient steady state, the designs of pension schemes have an impact on economic efficiency.

Demographic changes and changes in employment behavior are currently putting existing state pension schemes under pressure because of their fundamentally pay-as-you-go nature. Reform proposals have focused on a move to a fully funded system, but such a reform can be detrimental to the welfare level of consumers living during the transition period.

Further Reading

The data on the dependency ratio is taken from:

Bos, E., Vu, M. T., Massiah, E., and Bulatao, R. A. 1994. *World Population Predictions 1994–95 Edition: Estimates and Projections with Related Demographic Statistics*. Baltimore: Johns Hopkins University Press.

A survey of policy issues in social security is:

Banks, J., and Emmerson, C. 2000. Public and private pension spending: Principles, practice and the need for reform. *Fiscal Studies* 21: 1–63.

The original analysis of an optimal program can be found in:

Samuelson, P. A. 1975a. Optimum social security in a life-cycle growth model. *International Economic Review* 16: 539–44.

Policy neutrality is analyzed in:

Bernheim, B. D., and Bagwell, K. 1988. Is everything neutral? *Journal of Political Economy* 96: 308–38.

The analysis of social security and democracy is conducted in:

Mulligan, C. B., Gil, R., and Sala-i-Martin, X. 2002. Social security and democracy. NBER Working Paper 8958.

Mulligan, C. B., Gil, R., and Sala-i-Martin, X. 2004. Do democracies have different public policies than nondemocracies? *Journal of Economic Persperctives* 18: 51–74.

The forecasts on the effect of pension reform are taken from:

Miles, D. 1998. The implications of switching from unfunded to funded pension systems. *National Institute Economic Review* (165): 71–86.

The forecasts of the age of the median voter are from:

Galasso, V., and Profeta, P. 2004. Lessons for an aging society: The political sustainability of social security systems. *Economic Policy* 38: 63–115.

Extensive discussion of reform proposals are in:

Diamond, P. A. 1997. Macroeconomic aspects of social security reform. *Brookings Papers on Economic Activity* (2): 1–87.

Diamond, P. A. 2001. Issues in Social Security Reform. In S. Friedman and D. Jacobs, eds., *The Future of the Safety Net: Social Insurance and Employee Benefits*. Ithaca: Cornell University Press.

Exercises

20.1.   Some economists argue that immigration will overwhelm the welfare system, others that immigration will avert a pensions crisis. Which view do you support, and why?

20.2.   If you work for 30 years and wish to retire for 15 years on 50 percent of your working income, how much of your income must be saved when working? (Assume that the interest rate and income when working are constant, and that there are no taxes.)

20.3.   Assume that all consumers have preferences represented by $U = x_t^t x_t^{t+1}$. If the budget constraint is $x_t^t + \frac{x_t^{t+1}}{[1+r_{t+1}]} = w_t - \tau + \frac{\beta}{[1+r_{t+1}]}$, determine the relationship between the level of savings and the parameters τ and β of the social security program. Assuming that $y_t = k_t^\alpha$, find the steady-state level of the capital–labor ratio. Solve for the social security programs that lead to the Golden Rule. Show that none of these programs is fully funded. What is the form of the pay-as-you-go system that achieves the Golden Rule?

20.4.   For the economy described in exercise 20.3, relate the structure of social security programs achieving the Golden Rule to dynamic efficiency and inefficiency.

20.5.   A common policy is to make pension contributions tax deductible and to insist that the pension fund be annuitized on retirement. Explain the logic behind this policy.

20.6.   To avoid a pensions crisis, the UK government is reducing the real value of the guaranteed state pension. Assuming that much of the population is unaware of this, is the policy credible?

20.7.   Consider an economy with a single consumer. The government gives the consumer a bond with a face value of $1,000. Has the wealth of the consumer increased? Alternatively, the government levies a tax of $1,000 on the consumer and promises to pay a pension. Has the wealth of the consumer decreased?

20.8.   "The operation of a pay-as-you-go pension system is like a hotel with an infinite number of rooms: the hotel can never be full, since a vacancy can be obtained by making all occupants move along one room. Both are theoretical constructs, and neither has practical value." Discuss.

20.9.   Consider a consumer with true preferences $U = [x_t^t]^\alpha [x_t^{t+1}]^{1-\alpha}$. Rather than acting on the basis of these preferences, the consumer is myopic and does not realize the true value of second-period consumption. The myopic preferences are given by $U = [x_t^t]^\alpha [\rho x_t^{t+1}]^{1-\alpha}$, $\rho < 1$.

   a. Determine how the level of saving depends on ρ.

   b. How does the level of welfare measured by true preferences depend on ρ?

   c. Assume that there is a population of H consumers who act according to these myopic preferences and that the equilibrium interest rate is $r_{t+1} = a - bs_t$, where s_t is the total level of savings in the economy. Can myopia ever increase the consumers' true utilities?

   d. Does this form of myopia provide a justification for social security?

20.10. For the myopia model, assume a pay-as-you-go pension system. The consumers over-estimate the generosity of the pension scheme and believe that the pension, β, and the social security tax, τ, are related by $\beta = (1 + \phi)\tau$, where $\phi > 0$. There is no population growth, so the true value of the pension is $\beta = \tau$. What effect does an increase in ϕ have on savings? Does welfare increase or decrease in ϕ? Should we have the social security program when consumers have this from of myopia?

20.11. Consider an economy where individuals live for two periods only. Their utility function over consumption in periods 1 and 2 is given by $U = 2\log(C_1) + 2\log(C_2)$, where C_1 and C_2 are period 1 and period 2 consumption levels respectively. They have labor income of \$100 in period 1 and labor income of \$50 in period 2. They can save as much of their income in period 1 as they like in bank accounts, earning interest rate of 5 percent per period. They have no bequest motive, so they spend all their income before the end of period 2.

a. What is each individual's lifetime budget constraint? If they choose consumption in each period so as to maximize their lifetime utility subject to their lifetime budget constraint, what is the optimal consumption in each period? How much do the consumers save in the first period?

b. Suppose that the government introduces a social security system that will take \$10 from each individual in period 1, put it in a bank account, and transfer it back to them with interest in period 2. What is the new lifetime budget constraint? What is the effect of this social security system on private savings? How does the system affect total savings in society?

20.12. Consider the previous exercise and suppose that the introduction of social security induces the individuals to retire in period 2. So they receive no labor income in period 2.

a. What is the new optimal consumption in each period? How much do the consumers save? How does it compare with previous exercise? Explain.

b. Now building on this example, should the actual social security system lead to early retirement? Why or why not? What is the evidence on the impact of social security on the retirement decision in the United States and elsewhere?

20.13. Consider an individual who lives for two periods and has utility of lifetime consumption $U = \log(C_1) + \frac{1}{1+\delta}\log(C_2)$, where C_1 and C_2 are the consumption levels in the first and second period respectively, and δ, $0 < \delta < 1$, denotes the per period discount rate. Suppose that the individual has an income of $Y_1 > 0$ in the first period and no income in the second period, so $Y_2 = 0$. He can transfer some income to the second period at a before-tax rate of return of r, so saving \$$S$ in the first period gives \$$[1 + r]S$ in the second period. The government levies a capital tax at rate τ on capital income received in the second period. The tax proceeds are paid as a lump-sum transfer to the following generation. The present generation does not care about the next one.

a. What is the lifetime consumption profile of this individual? What is his lifetime indirect utility function expressed as a function of Y_1 and $[1 - \tau]r$?

b. Evaluate the change in initial income Y_1 that is required to compensate the individual for the welfare loss due to the capital income tax τ.

c. What is the impact of a tax rate change on consumption level in the first period? And in the second period? What conclusion about the welfare cost of capital income taxation can you draw from your analysis?

20.14. Consider an economy where individuals live for two periods only. They have the utility function over consumption in period 1 (C_1) and period 2 (C_2) given by $U = 2\log(C_1) + 2\log(C_2)$. The labor income of each individual in period 1 is fixed at \$10, and there is no labor income in period 2. They can save as much of their income in period 1 as they like in bank accounts, earning interest rates of 200 percent per period (recall, a period is the entire active life). The income tax rate is 50 percent, which is used to pay back the public debt inherited from the past generation.

a. Derive the optimal lifetime consumption profile of this consumer. What would be the consumption profile without income tax?

b. Suppose that a "retirement saving program" is introduced allowing each consumer to save up to 20 percent in the first period in a tax-free account. Compare the lifetime budget constraints with and without the retirement savings program.

c. Derive the optimal lifetime consumption profile with the retirement savings program. Explain the impact of this program on private savings.

d. Now suppose that the retirement savings program in part b is replaced by a new savings program taxing investment income on the first 50 percent of savings and exempting any savings in excess of 50 percent from taxation. Draw the budget set associated with this program, and find the optimal lifetime consumption profile. Explain the difference with the program in part b.

e. If the threshold for tax-exempt savings in part b is increased from 50 to 51 percent, how would this affect private savings? How does this affect total savings in society?

20.15. A sixty-year-old widow is considering claiming her social security widow benefit now. The primary insurance amount (PIA) from her deceased spouse is \$15,000. If she claims them now, she will receive only 72 percent of her PIA for the rest of her life. If she claims her benefits at age 65, she will receive 100 percent of her PIA for the rest of her life. Suppose that her life expectancy is 80.

a. What is the present discounted value of her benefits when claiming at either age 60 or age 65? At what age should she claim her benefits?

b. Suppose now that her life expectancy is longer. How would it change your recommendation in part a?

c. If she expected to get remarried at age 60, how might your answer change? Will her remarriage affect her benefits anyway?

20.16. "Social security reduces private savings, since individuals who retire earlier have fewer earnings to save." True or false?

20.17. Suppose that the government seeks to raise savings and is considering expanding the Individual Retirement Accounts (IRAs) to do this. US evidence suggests that IRA holders save more than non-IRA holders.

a. How can the theory explain that IRAs increase savings? What are the income effects and the substitution effects? What about the replacement effect of substituting IRAs for savings already done outside the program?

b. Is the evidence-based prediction that IRAs increase savings necessarily correct? Why or why not? How might the distinction between private and national savings affect the analysis?

20.18. What are the advantages and problems related to a reform of social security that consists of switching to individual annuitized accounts?

20.19. Social security requires mandatory participation in most countries. Milton Friedman (1999) states that "The fraction of a person's income that is reasonable for him or her to set aside for retirement depends on that person's circumstances and values. It makes no more sense to specify a minimum fraction of income that must be spent on housing or transportation." Discuss the possible implications of making participation in social security voluntary. You can also use arguments of adverse selection and moral hazard covered in chapter 9.

21 Economic Growth

21.1 Introduction

Economic growth is the basis of increased prosperity. Growth comes from the accumulation of capital (both human and physical) and from innovation that leads to technical progress. These advances raise the productivity of labor and increase the potential for consumption. The rate of growth can be affected by policy through the effect that taxation has on the return to investments. Taxation can also finance public expenditures that enhance productivity. In most developed countries the level of taxes has risen steadily over the course of the last century: an increase from about 5 to 10 percent of gross domestic product at the turn of the twentieth century to between 30 and 40 percent at present is typical. Such significant increases raise serious questions about the effect taxation has on economic growth.

Until recently economic models that could offer convincing insights into this question were lacking. Much of the growth literature focused on the long-run equilibrium where output per head was constant or modeled growth through exogenous technical progress. By definition, when technical progress is exogenous, it cannot be affected by policy. The development of endogenous growth theory has overcome these limitations by explicitly modeling the process through which growth is generated. This allows the effects of taxation to be traced through the economy and predictions made about its effects on growth.

The chapter begins with a review of exogenous growth models. The concept of the steady state is introduced, and it is shown why growth is limited unless there is some external process of technical progress. The exogenous growth model is employed to prove the important result that the optimal long-run tax rate on capital income should be zero. Actual tax systems are some way from this ideal position, so the welfare cost of the nonoptimality is also addressed.

Endogenous growth models are then considered. A brief survey is given of the various ways in which endogenous growth has been modeled. The focus is then placed on endogenous growth arising from the provision of a public input for private firms. It is shown that there is an optimal level of public expenditure that maximizes the growth rate of consumption. This model provides a positive role for government in the growth process. The optimality of a zero tax on capital extends to endogenous growth models with human capital as an input. With this result in mind, a range of simulation experiments has assessed the effect on the growth rate of changes in the tax structure in this setting. The differences in structure and parameter values between the experiments provides for some divergent conclusions.

The analytical results and the simulations reveal that economic theory provides no definitive prediction about how taxation affects economic growth. The limitations of the theory places an increased reliance on empirical evidence to provide clarification. We look at a range of studies that have estimated the effect of taxation on economic growth. Some of these studies find a significant effect, and others do not. We discuss the many issues involved in interpreting these results.

21.2   Exogenous Growth

The exogenous growth theory that developed in the 1950s and 1960s viewed growth as being achieved by the accumulation of capital and increases in productivity via technical progress. The theory generally placed its emphasis on capital accumulation, so the source of the technical progress was not investigated by the theory. It was assumed instead to arise from some outside or exogenous factors.

The standard form of these growth models was based on a production function that had capital and labor (with labor measured in man-hours) as the inputs into production. Constant returns to scale were assumed, as was diminishing marginal productivity of both inputs. Given that the emphasis was on the level and growth of economic variables rather than their distribution, the consumption side was modeled by either a representative consumer or a steadily growing population of identical consumers.

Our analysis begins with the simplest of these growth models, which assumes that both the rate of saving and the supply of labor are constant. This model is a special case of the general *Solow growth model*. Although the assumption of a constant saving rate eliminates issues of consumer choice, the model is still able to teach important lessons about the limits to growth and the potential for efficiency of the long-run equilibrium. The key finding is that if growth occurs only through the accumulation of capital, there has to be a limit to the growth process if there is no technical progress.

21.2.1   Constant Savings Rate

The fact that there are limits to growth in an economy when there is no technical progress can be most easily demonstrated in a setting in which consumer optimization plays no role. Instead, it is assumed that a constant fraction of output is invested in new capital goods. This assumption may seem restrictive, but it allows a precise derivation of the growth path of the economy. In addition the main conclusions relating to limits on growth are little modified even when an optimizing consumer is introduced.

Consider an economy with a population that is growing at a constant rate. Each person works a fixed number of hours and capital depreciates partially when used. There is a single good in the economy that can be consumed or saved. The only source of savings is investment in capital. Under these assumptions the output that is produced at time t, Y_t, must be divided between consumption, C_t, and investment, I_t. In equilibrium, the level of investment must be equal to the level of saving.

With inputs of capital K_t and labor L_t employed in production, the level of output is

$$Y_t = F(K_t, L_t). \tag{21.1}$$

It is assumed that there are constant returns to scale in production. Output can be either consumed or saved. The fundamental assumption of the model is that the level of savings is a fixed proportion s, $0 < s < 1$, of output. As savings must equal investment in equilibrium, at time t investment in new capital is given by

$$I_t = sF(K_t, L_t). \tag{21.2}$$

The use of capital in production results in its partial depreciation. We assume that this depreciation is a constant fraction δ, so the capital available in period $t + 1$ is given by new investment plus the undepreciated capital, or

$$
\begin{aligned}
K_{t+1} &= I_t + [1 - \delta]K_t \\
&= sF(K_t, L_t) + [1 - \delta]K_t.
\end{aligned}
\tag{21.3}
$$

This equation is the basic capital accumulation relationship that determines how the capital stock evolves through time.

The fact that the population is growing makes it preferable to express variables in per capita terms. This can be done by exploiting the assumption of constant returns to scale in the production function to write $Y_t = L_t F\left(\frac{K_t}{L_t}, 1\right) = L_t f(k_t)$ where $k_t = \frac{K_t}{L_t}$. Dividing (21.3) through by L_t, the capital accumulation relation becomes

$$\frac{K_{t+1}}{L_t} = sf(k_t) + \frac{[1 - \delta]K_t}{L_t}. \tag{21.4}$$

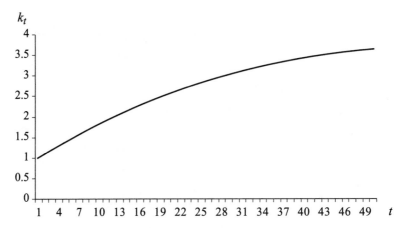

Figure 21.1
Dynamics of the capital stock

Denoting the constant population growth rate by n, labor supply grows according to $L_{t+1} = [1 + n]L_t$. Using this growth relationship, the capital accumulation relation shows that the dynamics of the capital–labor ratio are governed by

$$[1 + n]k_{t+1} = sf(k_t) + [1 - \delta]k_t. \tag{21.5}$$

The relation in (21.5) will trace the development of the capital stock over time from an initial stock $k_0 = \frac{K_0}{L_0}$. To see what this implies, consider an example where the production function has the form $f(k_t) = k_t^\alpha$. The capital–labor ratio must then satisfy

$$k_{t+1} = \frac{sk_t^\alpha + [1 - \delta]k_t}{1 + n}. \tag{21.6}$$

For $k_0 = 1$, $n = 0.05$, $\delta = 0.05$, $s = 0.2$, and $\alpha = 0.5$. Figure 21.1 plots the first 50 values of the capital stock. It can be seen that starting from the initial value of $k_0 = 1$, the capital stock doubles in 13 years. After this the rate of growth slows noticeably, and even after by the fiftieth year it has not yet doubled again. The figure also shows that the capital stock is tending to a long-run equilibrium level that is called the *steady state*. For the parameters chosen, the steady-state level is $k = 4$, which is achieved at $t = 328$, though the economy does reach a capital stock of 3.9 at $t = 77$. It is the final part of the adjustment that takes a long time.

The steady state is achieved when the capital stock is constant with $k_{t+1} = k_t$. Denoting the steady-state value of the capital–labor ratio by k, we have from the capital accumulation condition that k must satisfy

Output

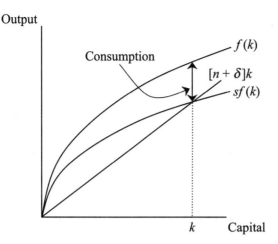

Figure 21.2
The steady state

$$[1 + n]k = sf(k) + [1 - \delta]k \tag{21.7}$$

or

$$sf(k) - [n + \delta]k = 0. \tag{21.8}$$

The solution to this equation is called the steady-state capital–labor ratio, and it can be interpreted as the economy's long-run equilibrium value of k.

The solution of this equation is illustrated in figure 21.2. The steady state occurs where the curves $sf(k)$ and $[n + \delta]k$ intersect. If this point is achieved by the economy, the capital–labor ratio will remain constant. Since k is constant, it follows from the production function that $\frac{Y_t}{L_t}$ will remain constant as will $\frac{C_t}{L_t}$. (However, it should be noted that as L is growing at rate n, then Y, K, and C will also grow at rate n in the steady state.) It is the constancy of these variables that shows there is a limit to the growth achievable by this economy. Once $\frac{C_t}{L_t}$ is constant, the level of consumption per capita will remain constant over time. In this sense a limit is placed on the growth in living standards that can be achieved. The explanation for this limit is that capital suffers from decreasing returns when added to the exogenous supply of labor. If excessive capital is employed, the return will fall so low that the capital stock is unable to reproduce itself.

Although we have not yet included any policy variables, this analysis of the steady state can be used to reflect on the potential for economic policy to affect the equilibrium. Studying figure 21.2 reveals that the equilibrium level of k can be raised by any policy that engineers an increase in the savings rate, s, or an upward shift in the production function, $f(k)$. However, any policy that leads only to a one-off change in s or $f(k)$ cannot affect the long-run growth rate of consumption or output. By definition, once the new steady state is achieved after the policy change, the per capita growth rates of the variables will return to zero. Furthermore any policy that only increases s cannot sustain growth, since s has an upper limit of 1 that must eventually be reached. If policy intervention is to result in sustained growth, it has to produce a continuous upward movement in the production function. A mechanism through which policy can achieve this is studied in section 21.3.2.

A means for growth to be sustained without policy intervention is to assume that output increases over time for any given level of the inputs. This can be achieved by labor or capital (or both) becoming more productive over time for exogenous reasons summarized as "technical progress." A way to incorporate this in the model is to write the production function as $f(k, t)$, where the dependence on t captures the technical progress that allows increased output. Technical progress results in the curve $f(k, t)$ in figure 21.2 continuously shifting upward over time, thus raising the steady-state levels of capital and output. The drawback of this approach is that the mechanism for growth, the "growth engine," is exogenous, so preventing the models from explaining the most fundamental factor of what determines the rate of growth. This deficiency is addressed by the endogenous growth models of the next section, where we explore the mechanisms that can drive technical progress.

Returning to the basic model without technical progress, we have by condition (21.8) that the steady-state capital–labor ratio is dependent on the savings rate s. This raises the question as to whether some saving rates are better than others. To address this question, it is noted first that for each value of s there is a corresponding steady-state capital–labor ratio at the intersection of $sf(k)$ and $[n + \delta]k$. It is clear from figure 21.2 that for low values of s, the curve $sf(k)$ will intersect the curve $[n + \delta]k$ at low values of k. As s is increased, $sf(k)$ shifts upward and the steady-state level of k will rise. The relationship between the capital–labor ratio and the savings rate implied by this construction is denoted by $k = k(s)$. We have observed that $k(s)$ is an increasing function of s up until the maximum value of $s = 1$.

Employing the link between s and k allows the level of consumption per capita to be written as

$$c(s) = [1 - s]f(k(s)) = f(k(s)) - [n + \delta]k(s), \tag{21.9}$$

where the second equality follows from definition (21.8) of a steady state. What is of interest are the properties of the savings rate that maximizes consumption. The first-order condition for defining this savings rate can be found by differentiating $c(s)$ with respect to s. Doing so gives

$$\frac{dc(s)}{ds} = [f'(k(s)) - [n+\delta]]k'(s) = 0. \tag{21.10}$$

Since $k'(s)$ is positive, the savings rate, s^*, that maximizes consumption is defined by

$$f'(k(s^*)) = n + \delta. \tag{21.11}$$

The savings rate s^* determines a level of capital $k^* = k(s^*)$, which is called the *Golden Rule* capital–labor ratio. If the economy achieves this capital–labor ratio at its steady state, it is maximizing consumption per capita. The same logic applies here as it did in the derivation of the steady state in chapter 19 (though δ was assumed to be zero in the overlapping generations economy).

The nature of the Golden Rule is illustrated in figure 21.3. For any level of the capital–labor ratio, the steady-state level of consumption per capita is given by the vertical distance between the curve $[n+\delta]k$ and the curve $f(k)$. This distance is maximized when the gradient of the production function is equal to $[n+\delta]$, which gives the Golden Rule condition. The figure also shows that consumption will fall if the capital–labor ratio is either raised or lowered from the Golden Rule

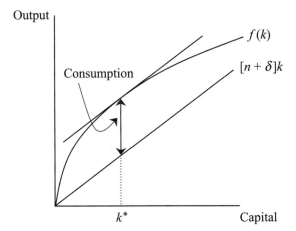

Figure 21.3
The Golden Rule

level. In line with the definitions of chapter 19, an economy with a steady-state capital stock below the Golden Rule level, k^*, is dynamically efficient—it requires a sacrifice of consumption now in order to raise k—so a Pareto improvement cannot be found. An economy with a capital stock in excess of k^* is dynamically inefficient, since immediate consumption of the excess would raise current welfare and place the economy on a path with higher consumption.

For an example of these calculations, let the production function be given by $y = k^\alpha$, with $\alpha < 1$. For a given savings rate s the steady state is defined by the solution to

$$sk^\alpha = [n+\delta]k. \tag{21.12}$$

Solving this equation determines the steady state capital–labor ratio as $k = \left[\frac{s}{n+\delta}\right]^{1/(1-\alpha)}$. From this solution the per capita level of consumption follows as

$$c(s) = k^\alpha - (n+\delta)k = \left[\frac{s}{n+\delta}\right]^{\alpha/[1-\alpha]} - [n+\delta]\left[\frac{s}{n+\delta}\right]^{1/[1-\alpha]}. \tag{21.13}$$

We adopt the parameter values $n = 0.025$, $\delta = 0.025$, and $\alpha = 0.75$, and plot in figure 21.4 the level of consumption as a function of s. In the figure note that consumption rises with s until the optimal saving rate is reached, at which point the equilibrium capital stock is equal to the Golden Rule level, and then falls again for higher values.

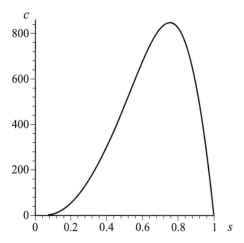

Figure 21.4
Consumption and the saving rate

Formally, the fact that the savings rate is fixed leaves little scope for policy analysis. However, studying the effect of changes in the savings rate reveals the factors that would be at work in a more general model in which the level of savings is a choice variable that can be affected by policy variables. By definition, the per capita level of the variables is constant once the steady state has been achieved. The living standards in the economy reach a limit and then cannot grow any further unless the production function is continually raised. Changes in the savings rate affect the level of consumption but not its growth rate.

21.2.2 Optimal Taxation

The analysis of the fixed savings model has touched on some of the potential consequences of policy intervention. As a tool for policy analysis, the model is very limited given the lack of choice variables that can be affected by policy. This shortcoming is now overcome by studying a variant of the *Ramsey growth model* in which a representative consumer chooses an intertemporal consumption plan to maximize lifetime utility. Using this model, we analyze the optimal taxes on labor and capital income.

The Ramsey model has a single representative consumer who chooses the paths of consumption, labor, and capital over time. The single consumer assumption is adopted to eliminate issues concerning distribution among consumers of differing abilities and tastes, and to place the focus entirely on efficiency. For simplicity, it is also assumed that the growth rate of labor, n, is zero. There is a representative firm that chooses its use of capital and labor to maximize profits. Given that the market must be in equilibrium, the choices of the consumer drive the rest of the economy through the level of savings, and hence capital, that they imply. The supply of labor and capital from the consumer combine with the factor demands of the firm to determine the equilibrium factor rewards.

The aim is to characterize the optimal tax structure in this economy. We assume there is a government that requires revenue of amount g_t at time t. It raises this revenue through taxes on capital and labor, which are denoted by τ_t^K and τ_t^L respectively. The government chooses these tax rates in the most efficient manner.

The choices of the consumer are made to maximize the discounted sum of the flow of utility. Letting $0 < \beta < 1$ be the discount factor on future utility, the consumer's preferences are described by

$$U = \sum_{t=0}^{\infty} \beta^t U(C_t, L_t). \tag{21.14}$$

The specification of the utility function implies that the consumer has an infinite life. This can be justified by treating the consumer as a dynasty with concern for descendents. Further discussion of this assumption can be found in section 20.8.

As there is a single consumer, the capital stock is equal to the savings of this consumer. This observation allows the budget constraint for the consumer to be written as

$$C_t + K_{t+1} = [1 - \tau_t^L]w_t L_t + [1 - \delta + [1 - \tau_t^K]r_t]K_t. \tag{21.15}$$

The utility maximization decision for the consumer involves choosing the time paths of consumption, labor supply and capital for the entire lifespan of the economy. The formal decision problem is

$$\max_{\{C_t, L_t, K_t\}} \sum_{t=0}^{\infty} [\beta^t U(C_t, L_t) + \beta^t \lambda_t [(1 - \tau_t^L)w_t L_t$$

$$+ [1 - \delta + [1 - \tau_t^K]r_t]K_t - C_t - K_{t+1}]], \tag{21.16}$$

where λ_t is the multiplier on the budget constraint at time t.

In solving this optimization, it is assumed that the representative consumer takes the factor rewards w_t and r_t as given. This captures the representative consumer as a competitive price-taker. (It is helpful to note that when we consider the government optimization below, the dependence of the factor rewards on the choice of capital and labor is taken into account by the government. This is what distinguishes the consumer who *reacts* to the factor rewards and the government that *manipulates* the factor rewards.) With fixed factor rewards the necessary conditions for the choices of C_t, L_t, and K_{t+1} are

$$U_{C_t} - \lambda_t = 0, \tag{21.17}$$

$$U_{L_t} + \lambda_t [1 - \tau_t^L]w_t = 0, \tag{21.18}$$

and

$$\beta \lambda_{t+1} [1 - \delta + [1 - \tau_{t+1}^K]r_{t+1}] - \lambda_t = 0. \tag{21.19}$$

Using the first condition to substitute for λ_t in the second condition gives

$$U_{L_t} + U_{C_t}[1 - \tau_t^L]w_t = 0. \tag{21.20}$$

Stepping the first condition one period ahead and then substituting for λ_{t+1} in the third gives

$$\beta U_{C_{t+1}}[1 - \delta + [1 - \tau_{t+1}^K]r_{t+1}] - U_{C_t} = 0. \tag{21.21}$$

Conditions (21.20) and (21.21) describe utility maximization by the consumer. To interpret these, it should be observed that there are two aspects to the consumer's decision. First, within each period the consumer needs to optimize over the levels of consumption and labor supply. The efficient solution to this within-period decision is described by (21.20), which ensures that the marginal utilities are proportional to the relative prices. Second, the consumer has to allocate their resources efficiently across time. Condition (21.21) describes efficiency in this process by linking the marginal utility of consumption in two adjacent periods to the rate at which consumption can be transferred through time via investments in capital. Taken together for every time period t, these necessary conditions describe the optimal paths of consumption, labor supply, and capital investment for the consumer.

The representative firm is assumed to maximize profit by choosing its use of capital and labor. Since the firm rents capital from the consumer, it makes no irreversible decisions, so it need do no more than maximize profit in each period. The standard efficiency conditions for factor use then apply and equate marginal products to factor rewards. Hence the interest rate and the wage rate satisfy

$$F_{K_t} = r_t \tag{21.22}$$

and

$$F_{L_t} = w_t. \tag{21.23}$$

Following these preliminaries, it is possible to state the government optimization problem. The sequence of government expenditures $\{g_t\}$ is taken as given. It is assumed that these expenditures are used for a purpose that does not directly affect utility. Formally, the government chooses the tax rates and the levels of consumption, labor supply, and capital to maximize the level of utility. The values of these variables must be chosen for each point in time, so government decisions form a sequence $\{\tau_t^K, \tau_t^L, C_t, L_t, K_t\}$. The choices of C_t, L_t, and K_t must be identical to what would be chosen by the consumer given the tax rates τ_t^K and τ_t^L. This can be achieved by imposing conditions (21.20) and (21.21) as constraints on the optimization. When these constraints are satisfied, it is as if the consumer were making the choice. As already noted, the government explicitly takes into account the endogenous determination of the factor rewards.

The optimization also has to be constrained by the budget constraints of the consumer and government, and by aggregate production feasibility. However, if any two of these constraints hold, the third must also hold. Therefore one of them need not be included as a separate constraint for the optimization. In this case it is the consumer's budget constraint that is dropped. The government budget constraint that taxes must equal expenditure is given by

$$\tau_t^K r_t K_t + \tau_t^L w_t L_t = g_t. \tag{21.24}$$

In addition the aggregate production condition for the economy is that

$$C_t + g_t + I_t = F(K_t, L_t). \tag{21.25}$$

By the definition of investment, this becomes

$$C_t + g_t + K_{t+1} = F(K_t, L_t) + [1 - \delta]K_t. \tag{21.26}$$

From the determination of the factor prices (21.22) and (21.23) the government optimization problem that determines the efficient taxes is

$$\max_{\{\tau_t^K, \tau_t^L, C_t, L_t, K_t\}} \sum_{t=0}^{\infty} \beta^t [U + \psi_t[\tau_t^K F_{K_t} K_t + \tau_t^L F_{L_t} L_t - g_t]$$

$$+ \theta_t[F + [1 - \delta]K_t - C_t - g_t - K_{t+1}] + \mu_{1t}[U_{L_t} + U_{C_t}[1 - \tau_t^L]F_{L_t}]$$

$$+ \mu_{2t}[\beta U_{C_{t+1}}[1 - \delta + [1 - \tau_{t+1}^K]F_{K_{t+1}}] - U_{C_t}]]. \tag{21.27}$$

The complete set of first-order necessary conditions for this optimization involves the derivatives of the Lagrangian with respect to all the choice variables at every point in time plus the derivatives with respect to the multipliers at every point in time. However, to demonstrate the key result concerning the value of the optimal capital tax, only the necessary conditions for the tax rates and for capital are required. The other first-order conditions will add further information to the solution but do not bear on the determination of the capital tax.

The necessary condition for the choice of τ_t^K is

$$\psi_t F_{K_t} K_t - \mu_{2t-1} U_{C_t} F_{K_t} = 0, \tag{21.28}$$

for τ_t^L the necessary condition is

$$\psi_t F_{L_t} L_t - \mu_{1t} U_{C_t} F_{L_t} = 0, \tag{21.29}$$

and for K_t it is

$$\psi_t[\tau_t^K[F_{K_t} + K_t F_{K_t K_t}] + \tau_t^L F_{L_t K_t} L_t] + \theta_t[F_{K_t} + 1 - \delta] - \frac{1}{\beta}\theta_{t-1}$$

$$+ \mu_{1t} U_{C_t}[1 - \tau_t^L]F_{L_t K_t} + \mu_{2t-1} U_{C_t}[1 - \tau_t^K]F_{K_t K_t} = 0. \tag{21.30}$$

The two conditions for τ_t^K and τ_t^L can be used to substitute for μ_{1t} and μ_{2t-1} in the condition for K_t. Canceling terms and using the fact that constant returns to scale implies $K_t F_{K_t K_t} + L_t F_{L_t K_t} = 0$, condition (21.30) reduces to

$$\psi_t \tau_t^K F_{K_t} + \theta_t [F_{K_t} + 1 - \delta] - \frac{1}{\beta} \theta_{t-1} = 0. \qquad (21.31)$$

Along the growth path of the economy this equation is only one part of the complete description of the outcome induced by the optimal policy. However, by focusing on the steady state in which all the variables are constant, it becomes possible to use the information contained in this condition to determine the optimal tax on capital.

Consequently the analysis now moves to consider the steady state that is reached under the optimal policy. To be in a steady state, it must be the case that the tax rates and the level of government expenditure remain constant over time. In addition the levels of capital, consumption, and labor supply will be constant. Moreover being in a steady state also implies that $\theta_t = \theta_{t-1}$. Using these facts, we have in the steady state the necessary condition for the choice of the capital stock as

$$\psi \tau^K F_K + \theta [F_K + 1 - \delta] - \frac{1}{\beta} \theta = 0. \qquad (21.32)$$

This can be simplified further by observing that in the steady state the choice condition for the consumer (21.21) reduces to

$$\beta [1 - \delta + [1 - \tau^K] F_K] - 1 = 0. \qquad (21.33)$$

We use (21.33) to substitute for β, and the final condition for the choice of the capital stock is

$$[\psi + \theta] \tau^K F_K = 0. \qquad (21.34)$$

Given that the resource constraints are binding, implying that ψ and θ are positive, and that the marginal product of capital, F_K, is positive, the solution to (21.34) has to be $\tau^K = 0$. This is the well-known result (due originally to Chamley and Judd) that the long-run value of the optimal capital tax has to be zero.

The analysis has concluded that in the steady state, which we can interpret as the long-run equilibrium, income from interest on capital should not be taxed. This result is easily interpreted. First, note that the result does not say that the tax should be zero when we are on the growth path to the steady state—it was derived

Table 21.1
Welfare cost of taxation

Initial tax rate (%)	Increase in consumption (%)	Welfare cost (% of tax revenue)
30	3.30	11
50	8.38	26

Source: Chamley (1981).

for the steady state and so applies only to that situation. This does not prevent the tax being positive (or negative) along the growth path. Second, the zero tax on capital income implies that all taxation must fall upon labor income. If labor were a fixed factor, this conclusion would not be a surprise, but here labor is a variable factor. Finally, the reason for avoiding the taxation of capital is that the return on capital is fundamental to the intertemporal allocation of resources by the consumer. The result shows that it is optimal to leave this allocation un-distorted to focus distortions on the choice between consumption and labor within periods.

Since the optimal tax rate is zero, any other value of the tax rate must lead to a reduction in welfare compared to what is achievable. An insight into the extent of the welfare cost of deviating from the optimal solution is given in table 21.1. These results are derived from a model with a Cobb-Douglas production function and a utility function with a constant elasticity of intertemporal substitution (see equation 21.45 below). The policy experiment calculates what would happen if a tax on capital is replaced by a lump-sum tax. The increases in consumption and the welfare cost are measured by comparing the steady state with the tax to the steady state without. When a tax rate of 30 percent on capital income is replaced by a lump-sum tax, consumption increases by 3.3 percent and the welfare cost of the distortionary tax is measured at 11 percent of tax revenue. The increases in consumption and the welfare cost are both higher for an initial 50 percent tax rate.

In summary, the optimal tax policy is to set the long-run tax on capital to zero. This outcome is explained by the wish to avoid intertemporal distortions. As a consequence all revenue must be raised by taxation of labor income. This will cause a distortion of choice within periods but does not affect the intertemporal allocation. The conclusion is very general and does not depend on any restrictive assumptions. Simulations of the welfare cost of nonoptimal policies show that these can be a significant percentage of the revenue raised.

21.3   Endogenous Growth

Decreasing returns to capital have already been identified as the source of the limit on growth in the exogenous growth model. The removal of this limit requires the decreasing marginal product of capital to be circumvented in a way that is, ideally, determined by choices made by the agents in the economy. Models that allow both sustained growth and explain its source are said to generate "endogenous growth." There have emerged in the literature four basic methods by which endogenous growth can be achieved. All of these approaches achieve the same end—that of sustained growth—but by different routes. We briefly review these four approaches and then focus attention on government expenditure as the source of endogenous growth.

21.3.1   Models of Endogenous Growth

The first, and simplest, approach to modeling endogenous growth, the *AK model*, assumes that capital is the only input into production and that there are constant returns to scale. This may seem at first sight to simply remove the problem of decreasing returns by assumption, but we will later show that the *AK* model can be given a broader interpretation. Under these assumptions the production function is given by $Y_t = AK_t$, hence the model's name. Constant returns to scale ensures that output grows at the same rate as the capital stock.

To show that this model can generate continuous growth, it is simplest to return to the assumption of a constant saving rate. With a saving rate s the level of investment in time period t is $I_t = sAK_t$. Since there is no labor, the capital accumulation condition is just

$$K_{t+1} = sAK_t + [1 - \delta]K_t = [1 + sA - \delta]K_t. \tag{21.35}$$

Provided that $sA > \delta$, the level of capital will grow linearly over time at rate $sA - \delta$. Output will grow at the same rate, as will consumption. The model is therefore able to generate continuous growth.

The second approach is to match increases in capital with equal growth in other inputs. One way to do this is to consider *human capital* as an input rather than just raw labor time. The level of the human capital input is then the product of the quality of labor and labor time. Doing so allows labor time to be made more productive by investment in education and training, which raise human capital.

Technical progress is then embodied in the quality of labor. The model requires two investment processes: one for investment in physical capital and another for investment in human capital. There can either be one sector, with human capital produced by the same technology as physical capital, or two sectors with a separate production process for human capital. The standard form of production function for such a model would be

$$Y_t = F(K_t, H_t), \tag{21.36}$$

where H_t is the level of human capital. If the production function has constant returns to scale in human capital and physical capital jointly, then investment in both can raise output without limit even if the quantity of labor time is fixed.

The one-sector model with human capital actually reduces to the AK model—this is the broader interpretation of the AK model referred to above. To see this, note that under the one-sector assumption output can be used for consumption, or invested in physical capital, or invested in human capital. This means that the two capital goods are perfect substitutes for the consumer in the sense that a unit of output can become one unit of either. The perfect substitutability implies that in equilibrium the two factors must have the same rate of return. Combining this with the constant returns to scale in the production function results in the two factors always being employed in the same proportions. Therefore the ratio $\frac{H_t}{K_t}$ is constant for all t. Denoting this constant value by $\frac{H}{K}$, we write the production function as

$$Y_t = K_t f\left(\frac{H}{K}\right) = AK_t, \tag{21.37}$$

where $A \equiv f\left(\frac{H}{K}\right)$. This returns us to the AK form.

A two-sector model can have different production functions for the creation of the two types of capital good. This eliminates the restriction that they are perfect substitutes and moves away from the AK setting. In a two-sector model different human and physical capital intensities can be incorporated in the production of the two types of capital. This can make it consistent with the observation that human capital production tends to be more intensive in human capital—through the requirement for skilled teaching staff, and so forth.

The next two approaches focus on inputs other than labor. If output depends on labor use and a range of other inputs, technological progress can take the form of the introduction of *new inputs* into the production function without any of the old inputs being dropped. The additional inputs allow production to increase, since the expansion of the input range prevents the level of use of any one of the inputs becoming too large relative to the labor input. An alternative view of technological progress is that it takes the form of an increase in the *quality of inputs*. Expenditure on research and development results in better quality inputs that are more productive. Over time old inputs are replaced by new inputs, and total productivity increases. Firms are driven to innovate in order to exploit the position of monopoly that goes with ownership of the latest innovation. This is the process of "creative destruction" that was seen by Schumpeter as a fundamental component of technological progress.

A special case of this approach, and the one on which we will focus, is to use a *public good* as the additional input in the production function. This can allow for constant returns in the private inputs to production and also constant returns to private capital, provided that the level of the public good is raised to match. The analytical details of this model are described below because it is a useful vehicle for thinking about the channels through which public expenditure can have an impact on growth.

A final approach to endogenous growth is to assume that there are *externalities* among firms that operate through learning-by-doing. Investment by a firm leads to parallel improvements in the productivity of labor as new knowledge and techniques are acquired. Moreover this increased knowledge is a public good so the learning spills over into other firms. Spillovers make the level of knowledge, and hence labor productivity, dependent on the aggregate capital stock of the economy. Decreasing returns to capital for a single firm (for a given use of labor) then translate into constant returns for the economy.

The common property of these models of endogenous growth is that there are growth-related choices that can be influenced by policy. The government can encourage (or discourage) investment in human capital through subsidies to training or the tax treatment of the returns. Subsidies to research and development can encourage innovation, as can the details of patent law. From among these many possibilities, for the remainder of the chapter we focus on the interaction of taxation and economic growth.

21.3.2 Government Expenditure

Endogenous growth can arise when capital and labor are augmented by additional inputs in the production function. One case of particular interest for understanding the link between government policy and growth is when the additional input is a public good financed by taxation. The existence of a public input provides a positive role for public expenditure and a direct mechanism through which policy can affect growth. This opens a path to an analysis of whether there is a sense in which an optimal level of public expenditure can be derived in a growth model.

A public input can be introduced by assuming that the production function for the representative firm at time t takes the form

$$Y_t = AL_t^{1-\alpha}K_t^{\alpha}G_t^{1-\alpha}, \tag{21.38}$$

where A is a positive constant and G_t is the quantity of the public input. The structure of this production function ensures that there are constant returns to scale in L_t and K_t for the firm given a fixed level of the public input. Although returns are decreasing to private capital as the level of capital is increased for fixed levels of labor and public input, there are constant returns to scale in public input and private capital together. For a fixed level of L_t, this property of constant returns to scale in the other two inputs permits endogenous growth to occur.

It is assumed that the public input is financed by a tax on output. Assuming that capital does not depreciate in order to simplify the derivation, the profit level of the firm is

$$\pi_t = [1 - \tau]AL_t^{1-\alpha}K_t^{\alpha}G_t^{1-\alpha} - r_tK_t - w_tL_t, \tag{21.39}$$

where r_t is the interest rate, w_t the wage rate, and τ the tax rate. From this specification of profit, the choice of capital and labor by the firm satisfy

$$[1 - \tau]\alpha AL_t^{1-\alpha}K_t^{\alpha-1}G_t^{1-\alpha} = r_t \tag{21.40}$$

and

$$[1 - \tau][1 - \alpha]AL_t^{-\alpha}K_t^{\alpha}G_t^{1-\alpha} = w_t. \tag{21.41}$$

The government budget constraint requires that tax revenue equal the cost of the public good provided, so

$$G_t = \tau Y_t. \tag{21.42}$$

Now assume that labor supply is constant at $L_t = L$ for all t. Without the public input, it would not be possible given this assumption to sustain growth because the marginal product of capital would decrease as the capital stock increases. With the public input, growth can now be driven by a joint increase in private and public capital, even though labor supply is fixed. From (21.38) and (21.42) the level of public input can be written as

$$G_t = [\tau A]^{1/\alpha} L^{[1-\alpha]/\alpha} K_t. \tag{21.43}$$

This result can be substituted into (21.40) to obtain an expression for the interest rate as a function of the tax rate:

$$r_t = [1 - \tau]\alpha A^{1/\alpha}[L\tau]^{[1-\alpha]/\alpha}. \tag{21.44}$$

The economy's representative consumer is assumed to have preferences described by the utility function

$$U = \sum_{t=1}^{\infty} \beta^t \frac{C_t^{1-\sigma} - 1}{1 - \sigma}. \tag{21.45}$$

This specific form of utility is adopted to permit an explicit solution for the steady state. The consumer chooses the path $\{C_t\}$ over time to maximize utility. The standard condition for intertemporal choice must hold for the optimization, so the ratio of the marginal utilities of consuming at t and at $t+1$ must equal the gross interest rate. Hence

$$\frac{\partial U/\partial C_t}{\partial U/\partial C_{t+1}} \equiv \frac{C_t^{-\sigma}}{\beta C_{t+1}^{-\sigma}} = 1 + r_{t+1}. \tag{21.46}$$

By solving for $\frac{C_{t+1}}{C_t}$ and then subtracting $\frac{C_t}{C_t}$ from both sides of the resulting equation, this optimality condition can be written in terms of the growth rate of consumption as

$$\frac{C_{t+1} - C_t}{C_t} = [\beta[1 + r_{t+1}]]^{1/\sigma} - 1. \tag{21.47}$$

Finally, substituting the solution (21.44) for the interest rate allows the growth rate of consumption to be related to the tax rate by

$$\frac{C_{t+1} - C_t}{C_t} = \beta^{1/\sigma}[1 + [1 - \tau]\alpha A^{1/\alpha}[L\tau]^{[1-\alpha]/\alpha}]^{1/\sigma} - 1. \tag{21.48}$$

The result in (21.48) demonstrates the two channels through which the tax rate affects consumption growth. First, taxation reduces the growth rate of consumption through the term $[1 - \tau]$, which represents the effect on the marginal return of capital reducing the amount of capital used. Second, the tax rate increases growth through the term $\tau^{[1-\alpha]/\alpha}$, which represents the gains through the provision of the public input.

Further insight into these effects can be obtained by plotting the relationship between the tax rate and consumption growth. This is shown in figure 21.5 under

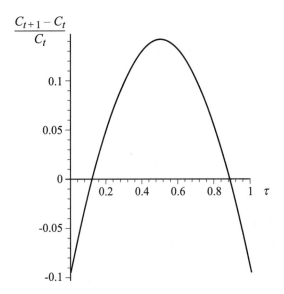

Figure 21.5
Tax rate and consumption growth

the assumption that $A = 1$, $L = 1$, $\alpha = 0.5$, $\beta = 0.95$, and $\sigma = 0.5$. The figure displays several notable features. First, for low levels of the public input, growth is negative, so a positive tax rate is required for there to be consumption growth. Second, the relationship between growth and the tax rate is nonmonotonic: growth initially increases with the tax rate, reaches a maximum, and then decreases. Finally, there is a tax rate that maximizes the growth rate of consumption. Differentiating (21.48) with respect to τ gives the tax rate that maximizes consumption growth as

$$\tau = 1 - \alpha. \tag{21.49}$$

For the values in the figure, this optimal tax rate is $\tau = 0.5$. To see what this tax rate implies, observe that

$$\frac{\partial Y_t}{\partial G_t} = [1 - \alpha]\frac{Y_t}{G_t} = 1, \tag{21.50}$$

using $G_t = \tau Y_t$ and $\tau = 1 - \alpha$. Hence the tax rate that maximizes consumption growth ensures that the marginal product of the public input is equal to 1, which is also its marginal cost.

   This model reveals a positive role for government in enhancing growth through the provision of a public input. It illustrates a sense in which there can be an optimal level of government. Also, if the size of government becomes excessive, it reduces the rate of growth because of the distortions imposed by the tax used to finance expenditure. Although simple, this model does make it a legitimate question to consider what the effect of increased government spending may be on economic growth.

21.4   Policy Reform

The analysis of section 21.2.2 has demonstrated the surprising and strong result that the long-run tax rate on capital should be zero. Although the derivation was undertaken for an exogenous growth model, the result also applies when growth is endogenous. The basic intuition that the intertemporal allocation should not be distorted applies equally in both cases. This is an important conclusion, since it contrasts markedly with observed tax structures. For example, in 2002 the top corporate tax rate was 40 percent in the United States, 30 percent in the United Kingdom and 38.4 percent in Germany. Although Ireland was much lower at 16 percent, the OECD average was 31.4 percent.

This divergence of the observed tax rates from the theoretically optimal rate raises the possibility that a reform of the actual system can raise the rate of economic growth and the level of welfare. This question has been tested by simulating the response of model economies to policy reforms involving changes in the tax rates on capital and labor. Such studies have provided an interesting range of conclusions that are worth close scrutiny.

Before discussing these results, it is helpful to clarify the distinction between the effect of a change in taxation on the *level* of output and its effect on the rate of *growth* of output. This distinction is illustrated in figure 21.6, which shows three different growth paths for the economy. Paths 1 and 2 have the same rate of growth—the rate of growth is equal to the gradient of the growth path. Path 3, which has a steeper gradient, displays a faster rate of growth.

Assume that at time t_0 the economy is located at point a and, in the absence of any policy change, will grow along path 1. Following this path, it will arrive at point b at time t_1. The distinction between level and growth effects can now be described. Consider a policy change at time t_0 that moves the economy to point c with consequent growth along path 2 up to point d at time t_1. This policy has a *level effect*: it changes the level of output but not its rate of growth. Alternatively, consider a different policy that causes the economy to switch from path 1 to path 3 at t_0, so at time t_1 it arrives at point e. This change in policy has affected the rate

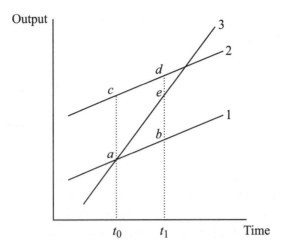

Figure 21.6
Level and growth effects

of growth but not (at least initially) its level. Of course, output eventually achieves a higher level because of the higher growth rate. This second policy has a *growth effect* but no level effect. Most policy changes will have some combination of level and growth effects.

The basic setting for the simulation analysis is an endogenous growth model with both physical and human capital entering the production function. The consumption side is modeled by a single, infinitely lived representative consumer who has preferences represented by the utility function

$$U = \frac{1}{1-\sigma}\sum_{t=0}^{\infty}\beta^t[C_t L_t^{\alpha}]^{1-\sigma}, \tag{21.51}$$

where C_t is consumption and L_t is leisure. Alternative studies adopt different values for the parameters α and σ. The second area of differentiation between studies is the range of inputs into the production process for human capital, in particular, whether it requires only human capital and time or whether it also needs physical capital. The analytical process is to specify the initial tax rates, which usually take values close to the actual position in the United States, and then calculate the initial growth path. The tax rates are changed and the new steady-state growth path calculated. The two steady states are then contrasted with a focus placed on the change in growth rate and in levels of the variables.

Author	Features	Utility parameters	Initial tax rates and growth rate	Final position	Additional observations
Lucas (1990)	Production of human capital does not require physical capital	$\sigma = 2$ $\alpha = 0.5$	Capital 36% Labor 40% Growth 1.50%	Capital 0% Labor 46% Growth 1.47%	33% increase in capital stock 6% increase in consumption
King and Rebelo (1990)	Production of human capital requires physical capital (proportion = 1/3)	$\sigma = 2$ $\alpha = 0$	Capital 20% Labor 20% Growth 1.02%	Capital 30% Labor 20% Growth 0.50%	Labor supply is inelastic
Jones, Manuelli, and Rossi (1993)	Time and physical capital produce human capital	$\sigma = 2$ $\alpha = 4.99$ α calibrated given σ	Capital 21% Labor 31% Growth 2.00%	Capital 0% Labor 0% Growth 4.00%	10% increase in capital stock 29% increase in consumption
Pecorino (1993)	Production of human capital requires physical capital	$\sigma = 2$ $\alpha = 0.5$	Capital 42% Labor 20% Growth 1.51%	Capital 0% Labor 0% Growth 2.74%	Capital and consumption different goods, consumption tax replaces income taxes

Figure 21.7
Growth effects of tax reform

Figure 21.7 summarizes some of the policy experiments and their consequences. The experiment of Lucas involves elimination of the capital tax with an increase in the labor tax to balance the government budget. This policy change has virtually no growth effect (it is negative but very small) but a significant level effect. In contrast, King and Rebelo and Jones et al. find very strong growth and level effects. King and Rebelo consider the effect of an increase in the capital tax by 10 percent, whereas Jones et al. mirror Lucas by eliminating the capital tax. What distinguishes the King and Rebelo analysis is that they have physical capital entering into the production of human capital. Jones et al. employ a higher value for the elasticity of labor supply than other studies. The model of Pecorino has the feature that capital is a separate commodity to the consumption good. This permits different factor intensities in the production of human capital, physical capital, and the consumption good. Complete elimination of the capital tax raises the growth rate, in contrast to the finding of Lucas.

The importance of each of the elements in explaining the divergence between the results is studied in Stokey and Rebelo (1995). Using a model that encompasses the previous three, they show that the elasticity of substitution in production matters little for the growth effect but does have implications for the level effect—with a high elasticity of substitution, a tax system that treats inputs asymmetrically will be more distortionary. The elimination of the distortion then leads to a significant welfare increase. The important features are the factor shares in production of human capital and physical capital, the intertemporal elasticity of substitution in utility and the elasticity of labor supply. Stokey and Rebelo conclude that the empirical evidence provides support for values of these parameters that justify Lucas's claim that the growth effect is small.

A range of estimates have been given for the effects of taxation on growth involving several different policy experiments. Some of the models predict that the growth effect is insignificant; others predict it could be very significant. What distinguishes the models are a number of key parameters, particularly, the share of physical capital in human capital production, the elasticities in the utility function, and the depreciation rates. In principal, these could be isolated empirically and a firm statement of the size of the growth effect given. To do so, and thus claim an "answer," would be to overlook several important issues about the restrictiveness of the model. Moreover it would not be justifiable to provide an answer without consulting the empirical evidence. Tax rates have grown steadily over the last century in most countries, so there should be ample evidence for determining the actual effect. Consequently the next section considers empirical evidence on the effect of taxation.

21.5 Empirical Evidence

We have presented two theoretical perspectives upon the link between taxation and growth. The endogenous growth model with a public good as an input provided a positive channel through which taxation could raise growth. The relationship was not monotonic because increases in the tax rate above the optimum would reduce the growth rate. In practice, economies could be located on either side of the optimum. Similarly the evidence from the simulations provides a wide range of estimates for the effect of taxation on economic growth from negligible to significant. Since the theory is so inconclusive, it is natural to turn to the empirical evidence.

At first glance a very clear picture emerges from this: tax revenue as a proportion of gross domestic product has risen significantly in all developed countries over the course of the last century, but the level of growth has remained relatively

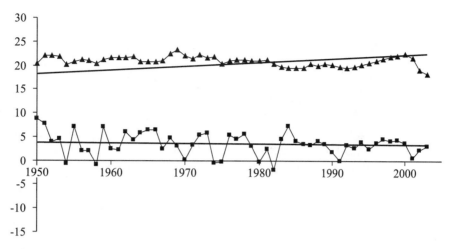

Figure 21.8
US tax and growth rates (Source: US Department of Commerce: www.bea.doc.gov/)

stable. This suggests the immediate conclusion that in practice, taxation does not affect the rate of growth. Data to support this claim is displayed in figures 21.8 and 21.9. Figure 21.8 plots the growth rate of US gross domestic product and federal government tax revenue as a percentage of gross domestic product since 1930. Trend lines have been fitted to the data series using ordinary least squares regression to show the trend over time. The two trend lines show a steady rise in taxation (the upper line) and a very slight decline in the growth rate (the lower line). Although the variance of the growth process reduces after 1940, statistical tests on US data have found no statistical difference between the average rate of growth prior to 1942 and after 1942. The data for the United Kingdom in figure 21.9 tell a very similar story. The trend lines show an increase in taxation but, in contrast to the United States, an increase in the rate of growth.

The message from these figures appears compelling but must be considered carefully. There are two reasons for this. First, a contrast between tax rates and growth across time cannot answer the counterfactual question: If taxes had been lower, would growth have been higher? To do so requires a study involving countries with different regimes. Second, there are substantive issues that have to be resolved about the definition of the tax rate that should be used in any such comparison.

To understand the problem of definition, consider figure 21.10 which illustrates a typical progressive income tax. There is an initial tax exemption up to income

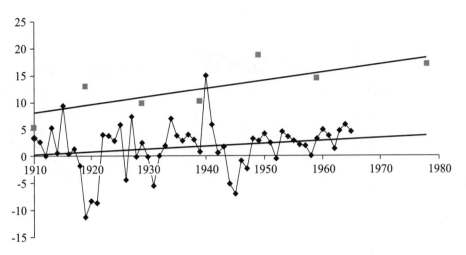

Figure 21.9
UK tax and growth rates (Sources: Feinstein 1972; *UK Revenue Statistics, Economic Trends*)

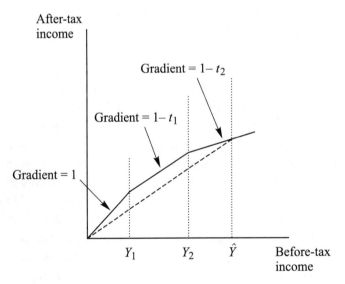

Figure 21.10
Average and marginal tax rates

level Y_1, then a band at tax rate t_1, and a final band at rate t_2, $t_2 > t_1$. What is important about the figure is that it shows how the marginal rate of tax differs from the average rate of tax. For instance, at income $\hat{Y}$ the marginal rate is one minus the gradient of the graph while the average rate is one minus the gradient of the ray to the graph (shown by the dashed line). With a progressive tax system, the marginal rate is always greater than the average rate.

The data displayed in figures 21.8 and 21.9 uses tax revenue as a fraction of gross domestic product to measure the tax rate. This measure captures the average rate of tax. However, what matters for economic behavior is the marginal tax rate—the decision on whether or not to earn additional income depends on how much of that income can be retained. This suggests that the link between growth and taxation should focus more on how the marginal rate of tax affects growth.

The difficulty with undertaking the analysis comes in determining what the marginal tax rate actually is. Figure 21.10 illustrates this problem: the marginal tax rate is 0, t_1, or t_2 depending on the income level of the consumer. In practice, income tax systems typically have several different levels of exemption (e.g., married and single persons allowances), several marginal rates, and interact with social security taxes and with the benefit system. All this makes it difficult to assign any unique value to the marginal rate of tax. The same comments apply equally to corporation tax, which has exemptions, credits, and depreciation allowances, and to Value Added Taxation, which has exemptions, zero-rated goods, and lower-rated goods. In brief, the rate of growth should be related to the marginal rate of tax, but the latter is an ill-defined concept.

Given these preliminaries, it is now possible to review the empirical evidence. The strongest empirical link between taxation and growth was reported in Plosser (1993). Plosser regressed the rate of growth of per capita gross domestic product on the ratio of income taxes to gross domestic product for the OECD countries and found a significant negative relationship. The limitation of this finding is that the OECD countries differ in their income levels and income has been found to be one of the most significant determinants of growth. Taking account of this, Easterly and Rebelo (1993) showed that the negative relationship all but disappears when the effect of initial income is accounted for.

Easterly and Rebelo extend this analysis by using several different measures of the marginal tax rate in regressions involving other determinants of growth, notably initial income, school enrollments, assassinations, revolutions, and war casualties. In response to some of the difficulties already noted, four different measures of the marginal tax rate are used: statutory taxes, revenue as a fraction of gross domestic product, income weighted marginal income tax rates, and marginal rates from a regression of tax revenue on tax base. From a number of regressions involving these variable, Easterly and Rebelo conclude: "The evidence that tax rates matter for economic growth is disturbingly fragile."

A very similar exercise is undertaken in Mendoza, Milesi-Ferretti, and Asea (1997). The clear finding is that when initial GDP is included in the regressions, the tax variable is insignificant. Evidence contrary to this is presented in Leibfritz, Thornton, and Bibbee (1997). Their regression of average growth rates for OECD countries over the period 1980 to 1995 against three measures of the tax rate (average tax rate, marginal tax rate and average direct tax rate) showed that a 10 percent increase in tax rates would be accompanied by a 0.5 percent reduction in the rate of growth, with direct taxation reducing growth marginally more than indirect taxation.

One possible route out of the difficulties of defining the appropriate tax rate is to adopt a different method of determining the effect of fiscal policy. Engen and Skinner (1996) label the regressions described above as "top-down," since they work with aggregate measures of taxation. Instead of doing this, they propose a "bottom-up" method that involves calculating the effect of taxation on labor supply, investment, and productivity, and then summing these to obtain a total measure. Doing this suggests that a cut of 5 percent in all marginal rates of tax and 2.5 percent in average rates would raise the growth rate by 0.22 percent.

An alternative line of literature—Barro (1991), Dowrick (1993), and de la Fuente (1997)—has considered the more general issue of how fiscal policy has affected growth. In particular, the relationship of growth to the composition and level of public sector spending is investigated. The results of de la Fuente show that if public spending (measured as the share of total government expenditure in gross domestic product) increases, growth is reduced (an increase in government spending of 5 percent of gross domestic product reduces growth by 0.66 percent), whereas an increase in public investment will raise growth. There are four significant points to be made about these findings. First, government spending may just be a proxy for the entire set of government non–price interventions—including, for example, employment legislation, health and safety rules, and product standards—and that it may be these, not expenditure, that actually reduce growth. Second, since the share of public spending in gross domestic product is very closely correlated to the average tax rate, it is not clear which hypothesis is being tested.

The final points are more significant. Levine and Renelt (1992) have shown that the finding of a negative relationship is not robust to the choice of conditioning variables. Finally, as noted by Slemrod (1995), the method of the regressions is to use national income, Y, as the left-hand-side variable and government expenditure, G, as the right-hand-side variable. In contrast, economic theory usually views the causality as running in the opposite direction: government expenditure is seen as being determined by the preferences of the population as expressed through the political system. An extreme version of this view is captured in Wagner's law, which relates government expenditure to national income via the income elasticity of demand for government-provided goods and services. If Y (or the growth of Y) and G are related via an equilibrium relationship, then a simple regression of Y on G will not identify this.

This review of the empirical evidence leads to the following observations. A visual inspection of tax rates and growth rates suggests that there is little relationship between the two. This is weak evidence, but it does find support in some more detailed investigations in which regression equations that include previously identified determinants of growth, especially initial income, reveal that tax rates are insignificant as an explanatory variable. Other regressions find a small but significant tax effect. All these results are hampered by the difficulties in actually defining marginal rates of tax and in their lack of an equilibrium relationship.

21.6   Conclusions

Growth is important, since without it living standards will stagnate, if not decline. The effect of even small changes in the growth rate can be dramatic. With a growth rate of 2 percent it takes 35 years to double the level of income but at a rate of 5 percent it takes just 14 years. Even if economic policy only succeeds in increasing the growth rate from 2 to 3 percent, it will reduce the time taken to double income by 12 years. The cumulative effect of a policy that affects the growth rate will eventually dominate anything achieved by a policy that affects only the level of economic variables.

In an exogenous growth model the economy must eventually reach a limit to its growth unless there is technical progress. The effects of policy are limited in this form of model because in the long run they cannot affect the growth rate. Nevertheless, these models provide some insight into what policy must achieve in order for it to have a lasting effect on economic growth. In particular, the exogenous growth model provides a simple setting for demonstrating the important result that efficiency requires that the tax rate on capital income must be zero in the long run.

The limitations of the exogenous growth model lead to the development of theories of endogenous growth. The literature on endogenous growth has provided a range of mechanisms by which taxation can affect economic growth. This chapter has described the range of models and has discussed the results that have been obtained. In quantitative terms, a wide range of theoretical predictions arise for the size of the tax effect, from the insignificant to considerable. The size of the growth rate effect depends just about equally on the structure of the model and on the parameter values within the model. The production process for human capital is also critical, as are the elasticities in the utility function and the rates of depreciation. A fair summary is that the theoretical models introduce a range of issues that must be considered but do not provide any convincing or definitive answers.

The conclusions of the empirical evidence are not quite as diverse as for the theory. Although there are some disagreements, the picture that emerges is that the effect of taxation, if there is any at all, is relatively minor. However, the estimates have to be judged by taking account of the difficulty of defining the appropriate measure of the tax rate and the choice of appropriate regressors. The problems of growth may prove to be significant but that is unlikely. As far as policy is concerned, this is a reassuring conclusion because it removes the need to be overly concerned about growth effects when tax reforms are planned.

Further Reading

The classic summary of exogenous growth theory can be found in:

Solow, R. M. 1970. *Growth Theory: An Exposition*. Oxford: Oxford University Press.

The data in table 21.1 are taken from:

Chamley, C. 1981. The welfare cost of capital income taxation in a growing economy. *Journal of Political Economy* 89: 468–96.

Three detailed surveys of growth theory which differ in their emphasis are:

Aghion, P., and Howitt, P. 1998. *Endogenous Growth Theory*. Cambridge: MIT Press.

Barro, R. J., and Sala-I-Martin, X. 1995. *Economic Growth*. New York: McGraw-Hill.

De La Croix, D., and Michel, P. 2002. *A Theory of Economic Growth*. Cambridge: Cambridge University Press.

The proof that the optimal capital tax rate is zero can be found in:

Chamley, C. 1986. Optimal taxation of capital income in general equilibrium with infinite lives. *Econometrica* 54: 607–22.

Judd, K. 1985. Redistributive taxation in a simple perfect foresight model. *Journal of Public Economics* 28: 59–83.

The model of endogenous growth with a public input was first proposed by:

Barro, R. J. 1990. Government spending in a simple model of endogenous growth. *Journal of Political Economy* 98: S103–25.

The simulations of the effect upon growth of changes in the tax rate are taken from:

Jones, L. E., Manuelli, R. E., and Rossi, P. E. 1993. Optimal taxation in models of endogenous growth. *Journal of Political Economy* 101: 485–517.

King, R. G., and Rebelo, S. 1990. Public policy and endogenous growth: Developing neoclassical implications. *Journal of Political Economy* 98: S126–50.

Lucas, R. E. 1990. Supply-side economics: An analytical review. *Oxford Economic Papers* 42: 293–316.

Pecorino, P. 1993. Tax structure and growth in a model with human capital. *Journal of Public Economics* 52: 251–71.

Stokey, N. L., and Rebelo, S. 1995. Growth effects of flat-rate taxes. *Journal of Political Economy* 103: 519–50.

Some of the data in figure 21.9 are from:

Feinstein, C. H. 1972. *National Income, Expenditure and Output of the United Kingdom*, 1855–1965. Cambridge: Cambridge University Press.

For empirical evidence on the effect of taxation on economic growth:

Barro, R. J. 1991. Economic growth in a cross section of countries. *Quarterly Journal of Economics* 106: 407–44.

Dowrick, S. 1993. Government consumption: Its effects on productivity growth and investment. In N. Gemmel, ed., *The Growth of the Public Sector: Theories and Evidence*. Aldershot: Edward Elgar.

Easterly, W. 1993. How much do distortions affect growth? *Journal of Monetary Economics* 32: 187–212.

Easterly, W., and Rebelo, S. 1993. Fiscal policy and economic growth. *Journal of Monetary Economics* 32: 417–58.

Engen, E. M., and Skinner, J. 1996. Taxation and economic growth. *NBER Working Paper* 5826.

de la Fuente, A. 1997. Fiscal policy and growth in the OECD. *CEPR Discussion Paper* 1755.

Leibfritz, W., Thornton, J., and Bibbee, A. 1997. Taxation and economic performance. *OECD Working Paper* 176.

Levine, R., and Renelt, D. 1992. A sensitivity analysis of cross-country growth models. *American Economic Review* 82: 942–63.

Mendoza, E., Milesi-Ferretti, G. M., and Asea, P. 1997. On the ineffectiveness of tax policy in altering long-run growth: Harberger's superneutrality conjecture. *Journal of Public Economics* 66: 99–126.

Plosser, C. 1993. The search for growth. In Federal Reserve Bank of Kansas City symposium series. *Policies for Long Run Growth*, 57–86. Federal Reserve Bank of Kansas City: Kansas City.

Slemrod, J. 1995. What do cross-country studies teach about government involvement, prosperity, and economic growth. *Brookings Papers on Economic Activity* 2: 373–431.

Exercises

21.1.　What is the difference between exogenous growth and endogenous growth? Why does the latter give a larger role for public policy?

21.2.　What are the main features of a steady state in the exogenous growth model?

21.3.　In the exogenous growth model what are the effects on the steady-state consumption and capital–labor ratio of an increase in the savings rate and of an increase in the population growth rate? Give a graphical illustration of each effect on the steady state.

21.4.　What are the determinants of the Golden Rule capital–labor ratio in the exogenous growth model?

21.5.　What are the three determinants of growth in the exogenous growth model?

21.6.　In the long-run steady state of the (Solow) exogenous growth model, growth in aggregate output, consumption, and investment is determined by exogenous growth in the labor force. True or false?

21.7.　Explain how in the (Solow) exogenous growth model, output and consumption per worker converge in the long run to steady-state levels. Show that output per worker increases in the long run when the savings rate increases or when the population growth rate decreases. Check if these two predictions are consistent with the data.

21.8.　In the Solow growth model, assume that the aggregate production function is $Y = zF(K, L)$, where Y is total output, z is total productivity, K is the total capital input, and L is the total labor input. Suppose that the Cobb-Douglas form for the production function $F(K, L) = K^\alpha L^{1-\alpha}$, where $0 < \alpha < 1$.

　　a. Find an expression for the output per worker as a function of the capital–labor ratio.

　　b. Suppose that the marginal product of capital increases for each level of capital, given the labor input level. What is the effect of this capital productivity increase on the aggregate production function? Show graphically the impact of this productivity increase on the steady-state capital–labor ratio and output per worker. Explain briefly.

21.9.　Consider the Solow growth model with Cobb-Douglas production function $Y = z[K^\alpha L^{1-\alpha}]$, where Y is total output, z is total productivity, K is the total capital input, and L is the total labor input.

a. Show that in the competitive equilibrium, α is the fraction of national income that goes to the remuneration of capital and $1 - \alpha$ is the fraction that goes to the remuneration of labor.

b. Use the (average) labor share in national income from your own country for the period 1990 to 2000 to find the value of α.

c. Use your answer to part b to calculate the "Solow residual" z using the aggregate output, capital, and labor $(Y, K, \text{ and } L)$ from your country for each year in the period 1990 to 2000. How has this measure of total productivity evolved over time in your country? Is there a productivity slowdown? Explain the possible reasons of this evolution (inventions, government regulations, price of energy, etc.).

21.10. Assume that output per unit of labor is related to the capital–labor ratio by

$$y_t = \rho \log(k_t),$$

and that saving is a fixed proportion, s, of output.

a. What is the capital accumulation condition?

b. Derive the equation characterizing the steady-state capital–labor ratio.

c. For the parameter values $k_0 = 0.5$, $s = 0.1$, $\delta = 0.05$, $n = 0$, and $\rho = 2$, plot the capital–labor ratio and the consumption–labor ratio as functions of time.

d. What is the effect of an increase in ρ on the capital–labor ratio?

e. Repeat part c, starting the economy above the steady-state capital–labor ratio. Explain the observed growth path.

21.11. If the production function is given by $y_t = \log(k_t)$, $n = 0.05$, and $\delta = 0.1$, and savings is a fixed fraction of output, calculate the steady-state level of consumption per unit of labor. Plot the steady-state level of consumption per unit of labor as a function of s. Show that it is maximized when $\frac{1}{k} = 0.15$.

21.12. Consider the Solow growth model as described in the preceding exercise and include government spending. The government purchases $G = Lg$ units of consumption good in the current period with g a positive constant. The government finances its public purchases with a lump-sum tax on consumers, where $T = G$ denotes the balanced budget total taxes. Suppose that consumers spend a fraction $1 - s$ of their disposable income (where $0 < s < 1$ is the savings rate) so that $C = [1 - s][Y - T]$.

a. Show in a diagram how the capital–labor ratio is determined and what its value is in a steady state.

b. How many steady states are possible?

c. Concentrate on the steady state with the highest capital–labor ratio. What is the impact of an increase in public spending per worker g on the capital–labor ratio and output per worker in the steady state? What are the effects on aggregate output, consumption, and investment? What is the effect on the growth rate? Explain briefly.

21.13. Can the Solow growth model account for the persistence in income inequality across countries due to persistent difference in population growth rates? Explain and discuss.

21.14. Consider the Ramsey growth model with utility function

$$U = \sum_{t=0}^{\infty} \beta^t [\log(C_t) + \log(1 - L_t)]$$

and production function

$$Y_t = K_t^\alpha L_t^{1-\alpha}.$$

Assume there are no taxes.

   a. Derive the conditions describing a steady state.

   b. Solve these conditions to obtain the steady-state values of C, K, and L.

   c. What is the effect on the steady state of an increase in β?

21.15. Repeat the previous exercise but include a tax on interest income. Graph the steady-state capital–labor ratio against the tax rate. Comment on the results.

21.16. Consider the endogenous growth model with a public input as described in the text with the parameter values $A = 1$, $L = 1$, $\beta = 0.95$, and $\sigma = 1$. Solve for the growth rate of consumption as a function of α and graph for various values of α. What is the effect of increasing α? Comment on your findings.

21.17. What are the determinants of growth in production and consumption in the endogenous growth model?

21.18. "If the government can increase the efficiency of human capital accumulation, it could persistently raise the rate of economic growth in the endogenous growth model." True or false? Explain your answer.

21.19. "Profit is the incentive to innovate. Government intervention can only reduce it, and therefore stifle the innovation process." Discuss the expected relation between taxation and growth in the light of this statement.

21.20. Consider a tax system where the first $5,000 of income is tax free, the next $10,000 is taxed at 25 percent, and all income above $15,000 is taxed at 50 percent. There is a population of consumers with who earn wages between $2 and $32 per hour. Wages are uniformly distributed in the population. All consumers have preferences described by $U = \log(C) - L/1,000$:

   a. Find the mean average tax rate for the population.

   b. Find the mean marginal tax rate for the population.

   How do these mean rates differ from the actual rates?

21.21. Using the results of the previous exercise, find the mean labor-supply response to an increase in the 25 percent rate to 26 percent. Now consider a consumer of mean wage rate facing the mean tax rate found in part b above. What increase in this mean rate of tax has the same effect as the 1 percent increase in the 25 percent rate? Does the use of the mean marginal rate provide a good indication of the labor supply response?

21.22. In the endogenous growth model explain why per capita income levels do not necessarily converge across countries, even when countries are initially identical except for human capital levels.

Index